Conciliation and Mediation in India

Global Trends in Dispute Resolution

VOLUME 11

Series Editor

Nadja Alexander is Director of the Singapore International Dispute Resolution Academy and Professor of Law at Singapore Management University. Professor Alexander is an award-winning author and educator in the field of negotiation and dispute resolution. She is known for the passion, energy and creativity she brings to her various roles as scholar, policy adviser, mediation practitioner and trainer. She has been identified by *Who's Who Legal* as a global thought leader in mediation.

Introduction

Global Trends in Dispute Resolution offers readers a garden rich in ideas and insights into contemporary dispute resolution principles, processes, and practices. The series leads the way in first-class debate and analysis of dispute resolution trends across our rapidly globalising world. More particularly, its volumes analyse dispute resolution developments in various geographical regions around the world and in relation to diverse transnational practice areas. These practice areas include not only well-established legal categories such as intellectual property, construction, and resources law, but also emerging dispute resolution trends ranging from dispute systems design to cross-border mediation in private and public law.

Objective

With a particular focus on new initiatives and dispute resolution practices, the *Global Trends in Dispute Resolution* series aims to provide practitioners, scholars, policymakers, and 'pracademics' (that elusive yet rapidly emerging category of practical academics and academically-oriented practitioners – you know who you are) with the resources both to cultivate the dispute resolution gardens of the world and to explore new paths within and beyond them.

Frequency of Publication

A volume is published whenever an interesting topic presents itself.

The titles published in this series are listed at the end of this volume.

Conciliation and Mediation in India

Gracious Timothy Dunna

Wolters Kluwer

Published by:
Kluwer Law International B.V.
PO Box 316
2400 AH Alphen aan den Rijn
The Netherlands
E-mail: international-sales@wolterskluwer.com
Website: www.wolterskluwer.com/en/solutions/kluwerlawinternational

Sold and distributed by:
Wolters Kluwer Legal & Regulatory U.S.
7201 McKinney Circle
Frederick, MD 21704
United States of America
E-mail: customer.service@wolterskluwer.com

ISBN 978-94-035-2015-5

e-Book: ISBN 978-94-035-1985-2
web-PDF: ISBN 978-94-035-2002-5

To the Alpha and the Omega.

Commit your work to the Lord, and your plans will be established.

—Proverbs 16:3

Editor

Gracious Timothy Dunna is an arbitration and mediation counsel. His practice areas have primarily revolved around domestic and international commercial arbitrations (ad hoc and institutional arbitrations of various rules, including SIAC, CIETAC, JCAA, ICADR, DIAC, and ICA). He has acted as counsel and cocounsel in high-stakes, complex, and large arbitration matters relating to building, franchise, sales, joint ventures, license and distribution, power purchase, partnerships, and more, besides various arbitration-related court proceedings.

Construction and engineering disputes form a significant part of Gracious' practice, covering projects like roads and highways, tunnels, thermal power plants, refineries, and marine works. He is the sole legal advisor to India's Ministry of Defense (Navy) for two of the largest naval infrastructure projects on the eastern and western coasts, together valuing over INR 33,500 crores, covering over 13,000 acres, involving dockyards, fleet buildings, covered dry berths, roads, townships, marine works, air station, armaments depots, etc.

Besides contentious work, Gracious is trained and experienced in consensual dispute settlement. As a mediation practitioner, his practice has predominantly been in commercial and family-business disputes. As an accredited and impaneled mediator, he has relevant experience in cross-border mediations.

Gracious has a robust academic background. He obtained an L.L.M. from the Straus Institute for Dispute Resolution, Pepperdine University Caruso School of Law. He is a recipient of two prestigious awards—the JAMS scholarship (JAMS is a leading ADR service provider in the USA) and The Hague Academy of International Law scholarship.

Gracious has published extensively, including law review articles published in some of the most respected and renowned journals. He is often cited as a source in legal academics and has also contributed various chapters in books. Gracious is a Board Member of the Society of Construction Law—India (a leading body creating standards in construction law and practice) and a member of the International Task Force on Mixed-Mode Dispute Resolution, which is a combined effort of the College of Commercial Arbitrators, the International Mediation, and the Straus Institute for Dispute Resolution.

Contributors

Sandeep Bhalothia is an in-house lawyer currently working as Head of Legal Affairs with Augmented Era, Dubai, focusing on technology and privacy law, ADR, and contract drafting. He is an SCMA Accredited Mediation Advocate and a Certified Islamic Arbitrator and Expert by IICRA. Sandeep is a graduate of Jindal Global Law School (India) and recipient of the Distinguished Alumni Award.

Shraddha Bhosale is an Indian-qualified lawyer having 10 years of experience in dispute resolution. She is currently General Counsel with the Weikfield Group, an Indian multinational conglomerate headquartered in Pune. She is also Cofounder of her independent law practice, Squarely Legal. Shraddha underwent mediation training from the Cologne Academy on Business Negotiation and Mediation, University of Cologne. She is the former Deputy Manager of the ICC International Centre for ADR in Paris and has administered international mediation cases under the ICC Rules. As a cocurricular pursuit, Shraddha enjoys teaching mediation topics at law schools in India.

Kudrat Dev is the Founder of YCM, India's first youth conflict management, and mediation initiative. She believes youth is the R&D force of our species with untapped potential to lead change in preventing and resolving disputes. She has diverse work experience in London and India as a commercial dispute resolution lawyer, a conflict coach, and a civil and commercial mediator accredited by the Civil Mediation Council, UK. Kudrat is a Chevening Scholar and holds an L.L.M. in Law and Linguistics from SOAS, London. She has conducted pioneer training workshops for experienced mediators at the Delhi government's mediation centers, Art of Living teachers, college students, and underprivileged youth on conflict management skills. The Ministry of Corporate Affairs has invited Kudrat as a trainer on mediation and negotiation skills. Creating value in challenging times, particularly in conflicts, is her passion.

Dr. Kabir Duggal is an attorney in Arnold & Porter's New York office focusing on international arbitration and Lecturer-in Law at Columbia Law School, teaching International Investment Law and Arbitration. Dr. Duggal acts as a consultant for the

United Nations Office of the High Representative for Least Developed Countries on the creation of a novel Investment Support Program and conducted training and capacity-building sessions for several Governments, including Colombia, Saudi Arabia, Myanmar, India, and the Philippines on public international law and dispute resolution. He serves on the Federal Republic of Somalia's New York Convention Task Force and the WTO Negotiating Team (International Board). Dr. Duggal is the Cofounder of REAL (Racial Equality for Arbitration Lawyers), a nonprofit advocating greater representation in international arbitration.

Shashank Garg is an arbitrator and seasoned dispute resolution practitioner skilled in international commercial arbitration, sports arbitration, construction arbitration, mediation, and litigation, representing clients in ad hoc and institutional arbitrations under leading institutional rules. Previously, he was a partner at Advani & Co., and in-charge of its Delhi office. He is the cochair of SCL India's Young Leaders Group, a nominated member (India) of ICC Commission on Arbitration and ADR, and a member of the Arbitration Committee of the Delhi International Arbitration Centre. Shashank was the ICC YAF's Regional Chapter Coordinator (India), 2017–2019. Shashank, a widely published author, is the editor of *Alternative Dispute Resolution: The Indian Perspective* (OUP).

Judith B. Ittig is a practicing attorney and commercial arbitrator, and mediator. She is a Fellow of the American College of Construction Lawyers, Fellow of the College of Commercial Arbitrators, Fellow/Chartered Arbitrator of CIArb, Member of The National Academy of Distinguished Neutrals, Founding Fellow of the Asian Institute of Alternative Dispute Resolution, and Certified Mediator, IMI. She has mediated hundreds of construction and commercial disputes on private and public sector projects in the United States and internationally. She serves on the AAA's Master Mediator Panel and its Neutrals' Training Faculty and CPR's mediator panel. She is listed in *SuperLawyers* (Construction Litigation), *The Best Lawyers in America* (Alternative Dispute Resolution and Construction Law), and the *International Who's Who of Commercial Mediation*.

A. J. Jawad has been a mediator since 2007 and has extensive experience in commercial, contractual, matrimonial, and child custody cases. He is a trainer with the MCPC, Supreme Court of India, where he has trained lawyers and judges across India and conducted Training of Trainers (ToT) workshops for the MCPC. Jawad is impaneled with the SIMC as an India-specialist mediator. He is accredited by SIMI (Level-3 Mediator) and impaneled with the Bombay Chamber of Commerce. He is also impaneled as an arbitrator with the Madras High Court. Jawad is a mediator and global faculty member at ADR-ODR International, UK, where he has been involved with mediation training programs at universities in the UK and India. He is the Partner and Head of ADR Services at KDLex Chambers. Jawad also teaches at MNLU Mumbai as a specialist guest faculty.

Sahil Kanuga coheads the International Dispute Resolution & Investigations Practice at a research and strategy-driven international law firm, Nishith Desai Associates. Sahil has worked on an array of complex matters, including Indian and international arbitrations. A focused problem-solver, he understands that business goals shape legal strategies. Sahil is impaneled as an India-Specialist Mediator by the SIMC Singapore. He is also on the Mediate India Advisory Board. Sahil has been recognized as Future Leader—*Who's Who Legal Guide: Arbitration 2021*, while *Legal 500* also commends Sahil's strength in civil and constitutional law. *The RSG India Report 2017* identified Sahil as "client focused" and "solution-orientated."

Manisha T. Karia (Deshmukh) is practicing as an advocate-on-record in the Supreme Court of India with more than 20 years of practice. She routinely appears and argues complex matters before the Supreme Court, High Court of Delhi, National Company Law Appellate Tribunal, National Consumer Disputes Redressal Commission. Manisha regularly represents multinational and Indian companies, public sector undertakings, statutory bodies, state governments, and private individuals. She is on the panel of amicus curiae of the Supreme Court since 2014 and appointed as amicus in several matters. Manisha is a trained and practicing mediator and serves as the ambassador of the Bangladesh International Mediation Society in India.

Tejas Karia is Partner and Head—Arbitration at Shardul Amarchand Mangaldas. He specializes in international and domestic commercial arbitrations and commercial mediations. He has represented multinational and Indian corporations as counsel in ad hoc and institutional arbitrations and sits as an arbitrator. Tejas contributed to the drafting of 2015 amendments to the Indian Arbitration Act. He is recognized as "Global Leader" by *Who's Who Legal*, "Leading Lawyer in Dispute Resolution" by *Asialaw Leading Lawyers*, "Leading Individual" by *Legal 500*, ranked for Arbitration by *Chambers & Partners*, and "Litigation Star" by *Benchmark Litigation*. Tejas is a member of the SIAC Court of Arbitration, the Governing Council of Indian Law Society and ICC Commission on Arbitration and ADR, and the Vice-Chairman of SCL India. He is a Fellow of CIArb, Director of CIArb-India, and the IAF-India.

Nisshant Laroia is a graduate of GNLU, Gandhinagar, an advocate, a mediation-enthusiast, and the Founder of The PACT, a niche platform dedicated to promoting mediation among young practitioners. Nisshant has trained more than five thousand participants in mediation, negotiation, and conciliation in his professional journey. He provides bespoke training programs. Nisshant acts as a coach and mentor to aspiring practitioners. He has mediated matters at government-run mediation centers, apart from his private mediation practice. He is an accredited mediator at IICA and the Indian Institute of Arbitration and Mediation; an accredited mediation advocate, SCMA, London; and a certified cross-border mediator and scholar of PSMA, Charles University, Prague. Nisshant is also an associate member of CIArb, London.

Joel Lee is a professor at NUS, Singapore. He co-pioneered the teaching of negotiation and mediation in Singapore universities and has played a significant role in developing mediation in Singapore in education and practice. A graduate of Victoria University of Wellington and Harvard Law School, Joel is a partner with CMP-Cambridge (USA) and a principal mediator at the Singapore Mediation Centre. Joel was a member of the IMI's

Independent Standards Commission and Intercultural Taskforce and a key member of the Ministry of Law's Working Group on International Commercial Mediation. Joel is presently the founding chair of the SIMI Board and a certified trainer of neurolinguistic programming. He coedited *An Asian Perspective on Mediation* and coauthored *Singapore Mediation Handbook*. Joel is the General Editor of *The Asian Journal on Mediation*.

Anant Merathia is an advocate practicing litigation and ADR, with over 16 years of experience in India and Singapore. After L.L.M. at NUS, Singapore, in 2006, he worked with Singapore law firms as a registered foreign lawyer in the corporate and arbitration practice groups. Anant moved back to India in 2009 and has built a formidable practice in corporate insolvency and restructuring of companies under IBC, 2016, apart from corporate and commercial advisory, shareholder litigations, and arbitrations. He advises financial institutions, investors, companies, promoters, insolvency professionals before NCLT and NCLAT under the Insolvency Code. Anant also acts as a mediator in commercial disputes.

Arjun Natarajan is an advocate practicing civil and commercial laws and arbitration law—as a counsel and arbitrator. He regularly represents the Delhi Metro Rail Corporation Ltd. in arbitrations and allied litigation. He is a certified mediator and one of the first persons in India impaneled with the Ministry of Corporate Affairs—Govt. of India, in his capacity as an expert in mediation and conciliation who has successfully undergone the requisite training. In his arbitration practice, besides private appointments, he has been appointed as a sole arbitrator by the Hon'ble High Court of Delhi in an arbitration under the aegis of Delhi International Arbitration Centre.

Laila Ollapally is a full-time mediator and founder of the Centre of Advanced Mediation Practice (CAMP), a pioneering private mediation initiative in Bangalore, India. Established in 2015, CAMP seeks to promote mediation as a form of Alternate Dispute Resolution. Ms. Ollapally has been a lawyer for over three decades, practicing in the Supreme Court of India and the High Court and Consumer Courts of Karnataka. She has mediated several hundred cases, including complex commercial disputes referred by the Supreme Court and State High Courts. She has been nominated to the *International Who's Who Legal of Commercial Mediation* and serves as a panel member of Singapore International Mediation Centre, Kyoto International Mediation Centre & ADR Centre, Italy. Laila is a Weinstein Fellow with JAMS Foundation. She extensively trains judges, lawyers, and advocates on mediation and negotiation.

Raj Panchamatia is Partner with Khaitan & Co. in its dispute resolution practice and has rich experience in commercial dispute resolution. He has advised clients on various claims in arbitration under most major arbitration rules. Raj is a member of SIAC's India Users Counsel and, as a SIMI Accredited Mediator, he is on the Panel of SIMC as an India-Specialist Mediator. Raj is also a member of the ICC India Arbitration Group and the co-convener of the IAF Western Region. Raj also played a key role in the drafting of the MCIA Arbitration Rules. Raj has been recognized as Future Leader in

Arbitration by *Who's Who Legal* in their Global Guide for Arbitration in 2021 and also by *Chambers and Partners* in the field of Arbitration in their 2021 Ranking.

Dr. Ajay Kumar Pandey is Professor and the Executive Director of Clinical Programmes at Jindal Global Law School. He holds an L.L.M. in Clinical Legal Education from Vanderbilt University Law School, USA, as a Fulbright Scholar and M.Phil. in International Law from the Center for Jawaharlal Nehru University, New Delhi. He is a member of the Global Alliance for Justice Education steering committee and the board, representing South and Central Asia and the Middle East. Ajay has served as a member of the editorial board of *Kali's Yug* (a journal on women and law, published by Women's Action Research and Legal Action for Women). He has edited India's well-established monthly legal magazine, *Legal News and Views*, published by the Indian Social Institute, New Delhi. Ajay has also worked as an international consultant with the UNDP in Vietnam and Afghanistan.

Pratyush Panjwani is an associate at Hanotiau & van den Berg. He focuses his practice on international commercial and investor-State dispute resolution, both ad hoc and under a wide variety of institutional rules, spanning various industry sectors. Before moving to Hanotiau & van den Berg, Pratyush worked in a leading dispute resolution law firm in New Delhi. Across his career, Pratyush has advised and represented several clients (including sovereign States) in complex civil litigations and arbitrations. He has also acted as tribunal secretary in several international arbitrations. In 2016, Pratyush obtained his L.L.M. in International Dispute Settlement (MIDS) from Geneva. He completed his Bachelor of Arts and Laws at the National Law University Delhi in 2014.

Harshad Pathak is an Indian-qualified lawyer with commercial arbitration, investor-state dispute settlement, and public international law as his core practice areas. An alumnus of the Geneva L.L.M. in International Dispute Settlement and the National Law University, Delhi, he is currently pursuing a Ph.D. in International Investment Law and Arbitration at the University of Geneva. He also acts as a consultant to Mayer Brown and assists with the firm's international arbitration and public international law practice.

Jatan Rodrigues is an associate at Shardul Amarchand Mangaldas' Mumbai practice. His primary area of practice is international arbitration. Jatan has also acted for parties in arbitration-related litigation before Indian courts, and advised Indian parties on private and public international law issues. He holds an L.L.M. in International Dispute Resolution from the Queen Mary University of London and a B.A.L.L.B. from Goa University.

Jonathan Rodrigues is a certified mediator with an academic background in psychology and law from Goa University. He leads the Online Mediation vertical at CAMP, Bangalore. Jonathan holds an L.L.M. (distinction) in Mediation and Conflict Resolution from the University of Strathclyde, UK. He is a visiting faculty at MNLU Mumbai, which hosts India's only postgraduate course in mediation. Jonathan founded The PACT, a firm dedicated to mediation awareness and training. He blogs regularly at Mediate.com and the IMI. Jonathan is also a peripatetic lecturer and spoke at TEDx (Panjim) on the multi-door dispute resolution system, highlighting mediation advocacy in India.

Badrinath Srinivasan, L.L.M., FIII, MCIArb, is Senior Manager (Legal) in an organization of the Government of India. Badrinath frequently writes on contract law and arbitration at various forums, including at the Practical Academic Blog.

Ishana Tripathi teaches at Jindal Global Law School. Over the past decade, she has worked with leading Indian law firms such as AZB & Partners and J. Sagar Associates in the areas of commercial dispute resolution and M&A. She has also worked as a consultant with various European multinationals. In mediation and ODR, she has consulted for and worked on policy papers and drafted governing rules with Indian policy organizations such as Vidhi Centre for Legal Policy and Agami.

Anil Xavier is the President of the Indian Institute of Arbitration & Mediation and Chairman of the Asia Pacific Centre for Arbitration & Mediation (APCAM). He is a practicing advocate since 1991, APCAM International Certified Arbitrator, APCAM International Certified Mediator, and IMI Certified Mediator. He is impaneled as an international mediator with SIMC, Singapore; FIMC, Italy; MHKJMC, China; JIMC, Japan; and IDRRMI, Hong Kong. Xavier was a member of the ISC of IMI and Senior Fellow of DRI, Hamline University, USA. He has been continually nominated as the world's leading practitioner in ADR by *Who's Who Legal*, London, since 2016.

Summary of Contents

Table of Contents

Foreword by Michael Mcilwrath

This is a book of hope, a serious framework for optimism for India's ability to embrace and even pioneer modern methods of dispute resolution. It could not have arrived in a moment more primed for change, during a historical period of momentous transition when the world has been forced to adapt to new and often better ways of doing things.

To say that this book offers a structure for a brighter future rests on the assumption that the present is not ideal. Indeed, it is far from it. It would be naïve not to acknowledge that India has a problem when it comes to providing access to civil justice for a large portion of the population or efficient civil justice for those who have access.

It would also be naïve—and arrogant—for a foreign lawyer such as myself to suggest that there exists one giant solution to the complex and far-ranging problems that India faces in administering civil justice. What I can do, however, is to note that this book offers a framework for optimism.

I first visited India 22 years ago. In 1999, I was a newly hired litigation counsel for a large Italian company. The purpose of my trip was to try to settle a dispute over equipment delivered to a refinery. Despite a positive relationship between our companies, we were unable to agree on any settlement, and I was unable to convince the counterparty of the value of attempting mediation, especially given the positive commercial relationship between our companies.

The result was a decade in which I would travel to Kolkata once or twice per year for an arbitration conducted under the Arbitration & Conciliation Act of 1996 before three esteemed Indian jurists. It was over a dispute that we did not want to have. During this lengthy arbitration, one of our outside counsel decided to retire from law practice to raise her family. Our Senior Counsel was elected to a government position and resigned. His replacement, sadly, passed away after only a year on the case. Two of the arbitrators, having reached a certain age, resigned on orders from their doctors before an award could be delivered.

Of course, this case was far from my only responsibility. And between my trips to Kolkata, I handled a variety of other major matters around the world. The company for which I worked was growing at a rapid pace and merging with other companies in the

Americas, Europe, Asia, and the Middle East. Claims were filed and were often adjudicated. As time passed, I discovered that the use of mediation was growing in many countries, and a higher percentage of disputes would settle early.

Legal systems around the world were discovering that mediation was an effective tool to put control of the disputes in the hands of the parties, to give them back the power to decide their own destinies. And, at the same time, it substantially lightened the financial burden of disputes while also reducing the court dockets.

Meanwhile, back in our arbitration in India, support personnel continued to come and go in the case. A key witness died. A new hotel was built where we moved our hearings. But rarely did our case seem to advance any closer to a resolution.

At a hearing late in the arbitration, I meekly asked the arbitral tribunal—all retired judges—if they saw any end in sight. They scolded me for my ignorance. If we had been in court, I was told, it would have taken many years longer to reach the stage that we had in our arbitration. The arbitration was actually proceeding at a good pace by their standards. This was no solace to my company or me. And I also received no answer to my question about a possible end date.

The arbitration eventually did end with an award that was, as is often the case, disappointing for both sides. It ended up costing more than either side expected, but the result was less than what two commercial parties could have agreed in a settlement.

This is only an anecdote; one person's experience in one case can hardly represent the entirety of how disputes are conducted in a country. But I suspect my anecdote would not present any surprises to other international in-house counsels who have experienced dispute resolution in India.

I could have ended here on a note of bitter pessimism and despair over civil justice in India, but I gave away in the first sentence that I am instead optimistic.

In the years 2016 and 2017, I had the honor of chairing the Global Pound Conference (the GPC), a series of conferences held in 28 cities across 22 countries. It began in Singapore and finished in London, bringing together numerous dispute resolution stakeholders.

The GPC provoked debates on dispute resolution tools and techniques, stimulated new ideas, and generated actionable data on what corporate and individual dispute resolution users actually need and want, both locally and globally. The objective was to help shape the future of civil justice in a way that is fair and accessible.

Of all the countries that participated in the GPC, by far the most enthusiastic was India. So great was the desire to participate that we—the organizers—felt obligated to extend the conference from in-person gatherings to online voting over the questions the GPC posed to stakeholders. This happened only in India, where we could not ignore the tremendous interest in finding better ways of resolving conflict. The value of mediation loomed large in the results of the voting, both in India and globally.

Also, in recent years, international mediation competitions have been organized in places like Paris and Vienna, where the presence of Indian law schools, and students from those schools, is so great and so successful that winning rounds are often marked by Indian students competing against those from other Indian law schools.

There are, in no uncertain terms, clear signs of a desire to create an environment for access to civil justice that can be achieved without subjecting every dispute to formalistic legal court or arbitration procedures.

The global pandemic that is still raging at the time of this writing is driving radical change in how we do things, including how we resolve disputes. What is needed is the structure, the framework, to help guide the changes.

Hence this book.

As Gracious Timothy Dunna points out in his introductory chapter, negotiation may be about "what to do," but mediation is about "how to do it."

The chapters are not idealistic speculations but the work of formidable thought-leaders in dispute resolution with global reputations. They know their subject matter. The contributors describe all the relevant elements of how mediation is used and can be used to resolve different types of disputes in India and in international cases. And they address the involvement of each of the stakeholders in this process.

It is a book that I wish had been available when I first traveled to India in 1999 in the forlorn hope of resolving a dispute with a commercial partner. But it is now 22 years later, and there is no time to waste. We can revisit in another 22 years—in 2043—the impact this book will have had on access to civil justice in India. I believe history will record it as substantial and valuable.

Michael Mcilwrath
Chair, ICC Governing Body for Dispute Resolution Services
Former Vice President-Litigation, Baker Hughes Company

Foreword by Ratan K. Singh

Although mediation-like procedures have been informally practiced in India from time immemorial, its focused push is a relatively recent phenomenon. The modern idea of mediation rests on statutes (including rules and regulations) and case law, which has profited from the institutional support of the judiciary and court-annexed mediation programs, given that a large majority of mediations in India are court-mandated (rather than party choice). As a dispute resolution process, while mediation has witnessed an upscale in the recent past, it has not attained the desired visibility, even in the commercial world, which is particularly becoming more mindful about the ever-increasing cost and time spent in adversarial forms.

Thus, mediation's promulgation must persevere and, in that, literature is vital. Over the last decade, though mediation has attained immense popularity in India, not much has been written about it. This is why I was delighted to hear about the publication of this book.

Conciliation and Mediation in India results from the relentless pursuit of a young scholar and lawyer to supply practitioners, academics, neutrals, and students of law, with the academic literature on the many facets of mediation in India, providing a comprehensive treatment of the legal framework, principles, and procedure of mediation. In these pages, the contributors have narrated their research and experience in an intellectually stimulating manner for all interested in studying and reflecting upon this field of law and practice. Suffice to say, this book addresses the dearth and need for significant work on mediation and conciliation in India.

In the simplest of terms, mediation is finding a positive side of conflicts and making use of them to commence an educational process through the mediator, reconstructing broken relationships, and bridging communication to arrive at an outcome that is beneficial in the long run. It is a free and fair negotiation between the parties, in which the mediator acts as a facilitator of the process. Its larger picture carries the potential of promoting the rule of law, wherein users can participate in the self-reliant determination of their conflicts. A legal framework, respect for rights, satisfaction of the outcome, confidentiality, choice of neutral, etc., are just part of the package that really make a difference when mediation is compared with its competitors.

I have always found mediation's self-reliance or self-determination the most profound of its attributes—the participants decide what is best for themselves. They know how their industry works better than anyone else and, therefore, have the potential to reach outcomes that simply cannot be achieved through adversarial processes. It also promulgates better relationships, repairs them, breaks misunderstanding, creates a communication channel, and serves interests over rights or liabilities. There lies the attractiveness of this process.

Advocates play a crucial role in the process and in building mediation in India generally. They must, therefore, understand that they cannot simply assume the role of a mediation advocate (or a mediator even) unless they make a determined effort, put down their swords and shields, and commit themselves to the process and the interest of their clients. They must sincerely be amicable, collaborative, and perceptive if mediation is to work.

Mediation is not a case disposal system, yet some conceive it thus. It is a manner of handling relationships; tricks and traps do not constitute consensual dispute resolution. Effectively guiding a client through the mediation process requires a certain open-mindedness and a fair bit of honesty to listen to and understand your clients' interests and that of their counterparts. Hence, there is some delicateness to the process involving the service of various skills and strategies by the mediator and the mediation advocate. The contributors have done exceedingly well in explaining this in their narrative.

Unlike adversarial processes, there is no dichotomy of a victor or a vanquished; it is a win-win. Hence, users are increasingly attracted to mediation and settlement advocacy, which offers positive outcomes that may well go beyond the apparent controversy. For decades, users have looked only to courts and arbitral tribunals when they need assistance with their conflicts. However, the problem has been that the advocate's only tool is often a hammer, and the nail is mistaken for a problem. Soaring costs, delay, unpredictability, and sourness are usually the unwarranted bonuses that come along with adversarial approaches.

Mediation, of course, expects much from its users as well, primarily, empathy, patience, and understanding. Only then can a conflict drown, and can consensus emerge as a natural result of the conciliatory interaction between the parties and the supportive intervention of the mediator. Through a mediator, a user can have greater information, which causes the maximization of choice in decision-making, raising the chances for a solution that will be acceptable to parties at either end of the spectrum of a conflict. Hence, a mediated settlement is reasonably more enduring and positive as compared to a negotiated one.

While mediation has many positives, it cannot receive serious consideration from users without a robust legal framework to support it. That, in particular, is an under-theorized area in the Indian context. This book offers an extensive overview of the laws applicable to mediation and conciliation in India by venturing into subject-specific/topical treatments of commercial, government, family, investor-State, insolvency, community, and other fields. Hence, through the publication of this book, the editor and contributors have done their duty to inform the legal community and stakeholders about the law, principles, and procedures of mediation and its immense potentialities. There is, now, simply no excuse for not trying mediation as the first and appropriate step to resolving conflicts.

Universities, too, will find immense value in adopting this as part of their teaching programs since mediation is now a mandatory course for any law student. Mediation and negotiation are essential skills for lawyers of the present and future generations.

Hence, to all those curious about mediation principles and procedures and committed to a serious mediation practice—this is a must-read. I find the writing to be instructive and provocative. I earnestly hope that this book (along with its future editions) will inform the people and generate a movement or culture for participatory justice in the years to come.

Ratan K. Singh FCIArb, FIACL
Senior Advocate & Arbitrator
International Member, Keating Chambers

Preface

This book was conceptualized in September 2018, after India's historical unity with 45 other signatories to the UN Convention on International Settlement Agreements Resulting from Mediation (also called the "Singapore Convention"). From 2018 to 2021, the book took shape under the editorship of Gracious Timothy Dunna and distinct voices from the mediation world in India. Together with the authors, and based on the editor's view, this book expresses (with much clarity) India's mediation and conciliation law and procedure. The motif is that much has been written about mediation and conciliation, but there is very little searching about the law and procedure applicable to it, which itself is so diverse that this book limits itself to some core themes.

There is no doubt that mediation is "the" dispute resolution choice of the next generation lawyer. The change in the landscape is indeed significant, offering a new (and perhaps a more appropriate) door for dispute resolution advocates. Be that as it may, the "present" is riper than it has ever been for India to truly embrace mediation. It is not as if there have not been attempts in the past. But the "now" is admittedly different—there is a minimum sufficiency of awareness, forums, and support to witness a steady development of a mediation culture in India.

Despite the reasonably widespread awareness about its potential advantages, fostering a mediation culture takes time and effort. Equally, it takes time and effort to build trust among the lawyers and users. On the one hand, we have known that mediation is a means of avoiding the pitfalls of adversarial modes of dispute resolution, but, on the other hand, the status of mediation and conciliation law in India leaves much to be desired. Unfortunately, mediation is not yet ingrained in the present-day Indian psyche. It is like a new graft, like a new heart or a new kidney. And as with the human body, it looks for an opening to reject it despite its potential to revitalize. While the body takes its time to accept the change, the discourse must continue, and the momentum must keep rising.

Present-day lawyers, judges, and users are becoming more and more convinced that early conflict resolution through facilitated negotiations is more efficient, especially in terms of user satisfaction. Mediation, hence, merits further exploration in

India, along with the development of the stakeholder's understanding since mediation has suffered from misperceptions for many years. Therefore, bringing clarity to the concept, law, and procedure is indispensable, and this book provides a firm base for precisely that purpose.

Take, for instance, the possibility that the underutilization of mediation has much to do with past experiences. Let us say it was because the process would not have made proper sense because it was not managed well; there would have been far too many adjournments and/or gaps between sessions; the users would not have been educated about the process, empowered, and encouraged; or the lawyers would have given a false impression about mediation as a mere formality to comply. Such a "mediation" (if you can call it that) is a complete failure as an "alternative."

There is little doubt that this book will have continued success, given that it is one of a kind without any specific competing publication that addresses the themes and subthemes discussed here. It takes into account all the major and fundamental areas that require literature and discussions to further mediation and conciliation in India's dispute resolution landscape. The foreign authors have especially been kind to support this academic work—the belief is that mediation will not develop if only country-X is doing it, but when all the countries are together doing it. In fact, that has been a significant reason for the success of international arbitration under the New York Convention and the adoption of UNCITRAL Model Law on International Commercial Arbitration, a path that international mediation must now follow.

Overall, this book takes into account where India stands at present, the Singapore Convention, important statutes, court decisions, academic works, and the 2018 Model Law on Mediation that bequeath a broad understanding of the subject for legal practitioners, judges, neutrals (arbitrators, mediators, and conciliators), users, and technical experts, who wish to understand it at all levels. It is, thus, hoped that the response to this book would be enthusiastic and welcoming.

Acknowledgments

This book would have never seen the light of day without the sincere and faithful support of the people who caused this book to happen. I am thankful to the generosity of Kluwer International for adopting this book project. Kiran Gore, especially, lent her support from start to finish.

I thank the authors who reposed their trust and faith in me as the editor. I consider their contributions to this book as my honor and privilege, and I take pleasure in the interactions and discussions we had (especially for the chapters I have coauthored with). The gravity of this book is its authors, most of whom I have met in my journey and pursuit of good learning and practice of ADR. This is why this book is special to me, besides its uniqueness. The harmony of so many voices truly expresses what can only be called a symphony.

My heartfelt gratitude also goes to my peers and colleagues, who spent their valuable time supporting me with the review process and offering me their frank opinion and perspectives. Thank you, Juhi Gupta, Bhavya Mahajan, Parul Khanna, and Yashraj Samant, for being a source of support and academic checks and balances. Jatan Rodrigues has my special thanks for the value he added to the chapters in the reviews. I also express my gratitude to the research assistants (students): Ridhima Sharma, Parth Sharma, Syamantak Sen, and Vatsala Walia. They supplied me with clear research (summarizing a number of court decisions), proofread the chapters, organized the footnotes as per Bluebook standards.

Many more have been thanked by the authors in their respective chapters. Although their names have not been reproduced here, my sincere appreciation goes without saying.

Last but not least, I am indebted to my parents, Cdr Dunna Rajarao (Retd.) and Dunna Rajaratnamu, for their love and support like the Rock of Gibraltar. From sunrise to sunset, I was reminded to follow through and summit my ambitions. If not for this, the book would not have come to reality.

Introduction

Gracious Timothy Dunna

But you never knew—did you?—a lawsuit, if it was prosecuted vigorously enough and lasted long enough, where at the end there was anything left for the parties to quarrel over.

—Joseph H. Choate

This *tour d'horizon* of mediation and conciliation showcases a broad and comprehensive canvassing of a range of themes, providing a solid foundation about the law and procedure of mediation and conciliation in India (with relevant hints on practice). It adopts a lucid approach by first dwelling on the essential topics or concepts that set the stage for discussing the specialized areas.

Accordingly, the book is artificially partitioned into four segments. Its first segment pitches tent in introductory themes like a primer on mediation and conciliation in India, the role of a mediator, the approach to disputes in mediation, and ethics. With these foundations laid, the book transposes to its second segment, onto some specialized themes, which have been handpicked for their relevance to India. These include themes like court-connected mediations, commercial disputes, institutional mediation, government disputes, family disputes, insolvency and bankruptcy disputes, and so on. Keeping in mind that the Indian audience is relatively new to mediation, the book is aware of the need for establishing a solid understanding of these specialized themes to promulgate a widespread practice in these areas. At the same time, these chapters should not be understood to be a comprehensive discourse on the substantive aspects of the selected themes.

The book then migrates to its third segment, to the UN Convention on International Settlement Agreement on Mediation ("Singapore Convention") and Part III of the Arbitration and Conciliation Act 1996, setting out a commentary on the most important texts on mediation and conciliation (the cornerstone of facilitated negotiations in India). The authors have attempted a treatise-like discussion of the texts—the whole shebang.

For the sake of completeness, the book culminates with the twin chapters "Ready, Set, Mediate" for advocates and mediators. From soup to nuts, these chapters synthesize the process, techniques, and approaches that experienced mediators and mediation advocates have found to be most valuable in their preparation for a mediation. Readers will particularly value these contributions, given the lack of attention to preparatory issues in literature. Likewise, the twin chapters set a roadmap for fresh and seasoned mediators and mediation advocates.

This edition of the book has received exceptional contributions from a diverse group of legal practitioners, academicians, in-house counsel, as well as foreign lawyers. There is a generous amount of research and writing dispensed by the authors, who took on this challenge (and the burden) to provide comprehensive coverage and literature on the themes included here. Building on this foundation, the editor has ensured that the chapters provide a solid discussion of the law and procedure (as well as practice), offering prescriptive guidance to assist anyone who wishes to dive into mediation and conciliation in India. The nature and scope of this book should appeal most to practitioners, neutrals, and academics (including students), providing them with a profitable read on mediation and conciliation in India.

While a Mediation Bill was introduced in the Parliament's winter session in 2021, the tell-tale signs are rather gloomy. The Mediation Bill was immediately sent to a Parliamentary Standing Committee of Law and Justice. An ideal mediation legislation would need to contemplate amendments to a substantial number of other statutes on civil procedure, contract, arbitration, legal services authority, companies, micro small & medium enterprises, and so on. This would require a detailed analysis of the consequences a mediation legislation will have. Besides that, the legislature's task is fairly easy—to simply adopt the UNCITRAL Model Law on Mediation 2018. The Model Law is designed to assist nation States in reforming and modernizing their laws on mediation procedure; most importantly, it provides uniform rules in respect of the mediation process and aims at encouraging the use of mediation and ensuring greater predictability and certainty in its use. These goals cannot be achieved if India deviates from the Model Law, thus, making India unattractive for international mediations. The adoption does not inhibit the legislature from adding additional value features like the pre-institution mediation, time limits, online and community mediations, Mediation Council of India, and others. However, the Model Law must be the backbone (like in the case of the Arbitration & Conciliation Act 1996, which was also based on UNCITRAL's model text). Thankfully, UNCITRAL has provided a draft Guide to Enactment and Use of the Model Law (dated April 1, 2020), which should be the premise on which to prepare the Mediation Bill—the legislature is urged to consider the use of the UNCITRAL texts. It is hoped that this edition stands up to scrutiny and meets the expectations of many who have longed for a book of this kind. Most importantly, it is also hoped that, in a few years, readers will (excitedly) ask for a second edition.

CHAPTER 1

Introduction to Mediation and Conciliation in India

Gracious Timothy Dunna

§1.01 PRELIMINARIES

Mediation is the new arbitration; it is the "new black." Elbowing its way in the dispute resolution scene in India, its significance is exquisitely highlighted in *M. R. Krishna Murthi v. New India Assurance Co. Ltd.*, where the Supreme Court said that:[1]

> [Mediation] as a concept of dispute resolution, even before dispute becomes part of adversarial adjudicatory process, would be of great significance. Advantages of mediation are manifold. This stands recognized by the legislature as well as policy-makers and needs no elaboration. Mediation is here to stay. It is here to evolve. It is because of the advantages of mediation as a method here to find new grounds. It is here to prosper, as its time has come. ... In fact, the way mediation movement is catching up in this country, there is a dire need to enact Indian Mediation Act as well.

The statement sums up mediation's advance toward widespread use and practice in India, offering disputing parties a radical approach to resolving disputes—a system by which disputes can be resolved by reconciling interests (rather than determining the rights and liabilities).

Mediation is a form of dispute resolution generally found outside the adjudicative forums of the court of law or an arbitral tribunal, where disputing parties take the assistance of a neutral third party in their attempt to settle their dispute consensually. This may be considered a simple definition of mediation, with a caveat that an overarching meaning and understanding may not be as straightforward to discover. For instance, mediations can (and do) frequently take place in and out of adjudicative

1. (2020) 15 SCC 493.

forums at various stages. This is why the big picture of mediation fits well with all forms of alternative dispute resolution (ADR) (adjudicatory and conciliatory).

At this juncture of this chapter (and this book), the terms "mediation" and "conciliation" are being used univocally and, wherever appropriate, an emphasis on its distinction will be made plain. Virtually, however, both processes comprehend various tools and techniques devised to allow parties to settle their disputes expeditiously, economically, and without prejudice to their continuing relationship (if any). In both processes, this is done in a manner that is not necessarily premised on the parties' legal rights or duties.

Mediation is among the residents of alternative dispute resolution methods (sometimes "appropriate" or "amicable" dispute resolution) or ADR methods. While ADR may be categorized into *families* of settlement-based (or conciliatory) and adjudicatory forms—which have further layers of *genus* and *species*—its quintessence is party autonomy.[2] Here, settlement-based mechanisms (also called consensual dispute resolution or CDR) are negotiation, mediation, and conciliation. The adjudicatory forms are further divisible into binding and non-binding alternatives. Arbitration is one such adjudicatory form of ADR, which is final, binding, and enforceable. Another adjudicatory form of ADR may be Dispute Boards, usually found in construction contracts under different nomenclatures; they are binding but not final and often incorporated as a pre-arbitral step.

Thus, the Indian perspective considers ADR to be a range of procedures between two extremes of a spectrum—a continuum of dispute resolution. On the one end, it is incredibly facilitative, and parties have the highest ownership of the outcome; on the other end, it is exceptionally evaluative, and parties have no ownership of the outcome. The motif behind "ownership of result" is that an adjudicative process results in a binding decision on the merits or substance of the case, but in a settlement-based process, the result is driven by the parties and self-determined through negotiation (with or without the facilitation of a third-party neutral). Hence, depending on where one puts his finger on the spectrum or continuum of dispute resolution, it may or may not involve the intercession or assistance of a neutral third party, whom we generally refer to as arbitrator, mediator, conciliator, or expert, as the case may be.

§1.02 SALIENT FEATURES OF MEDIATION

The motivation to choose mediation (over arbitration or litigation) may be for a variety of reasons. These motivations that gravitate parties to mediation are generally enumerated: finality, privacy, informality, speed, low cost, and neutral expertise.

2. Calling it "out-of-court" may be inadequate and faulty since modern ADR is well intertwined with the court system, or the public judicial setup, in India. Thus, "out-of-court" may be an appropriate description if the intent is to exclude adjudication by court as part of the justice dispensation system.

However, the most appealing feature about mediation as a problem-solving process comes from its traditional selling points of self-determination and voluntariness.[3] This is an ability to craft individualized justice, one that is based on parties' terms, interests, and values. This is indispensable and must never be underrated—mediation gives each party a voice and the opportunity for personal expression and participation.[4] With such open communication, mediation offers cooperation and creative problem-solving possibilities and an ambiance for parties to orient themselves collaboratively in search of mutually agreeable solutions.

This problem-solving potential of mediation is more pronounced when considering the "conflict ladder," which usually escalates from a difference to disagreements, polarization, loss of communication, threats, conflicts, and finally to disputes. While any adjudicatory mechanism can only be invoked when an apparent dispute has arisen, mediation (or mediation-like procedures, including structured/principled negotiation) may be applied right when a difference or disagreement has emerged. Hence, mediation can also be conceived as a dispute prevention (or avoidance) tool by which parties can encourage alignment of interests, improve cooperation, prevent or minimize the adverse impact of problems, and curb adversarial attitudes. CDR tools are precisely designed to deal promptly and realistically with problems, differences of opinion, or disagreements when they arise, de-escalate tensions, resolve problems, or achieve instant resolution of disputes.

Speedy resolution and relative economy in avoiding costs and delays in contentious proceedings are also well known about mediation. Much has been written on this, and there is enough evidence to suggest it. Although, depending on the complexity of issues, the nature of the agreed procedures, the number of parties involved, and the process management skills of the mediator, the average timeline and economy of a mediation process may fluctuate. In one such instance, parties took nearly a year to reach a mediated settlement, while arbitration proceedings ran laterally for efficiency and safeguarding interests.

Privacy and the avoidance of precedents are rarely discussed vis-à-vis mediation. Mediation involves not being open to the public, protecting sensitive and personal exchanges, including financial information. Confidentiality is a sacred canon of the mediation process. Such confidentiality extends not only to the proceedings but also to the settlement itself and any subsequent contentious proceedings, binding all the participants, including the mediator. An extension of this privacy and confidentiality is that mediation settlements do not establish a precedent. Unlike judgments delivered by

3. *See generally*, Model Standards of Conduct for Mediators (Am. Arbitration Ass'n, 2005) (besides regulating the conduct of mediator, it defines mediation as a voluntary process grounded in party self-determination); Robert A. Baruch Bush & Joseph P. Folger, The Promise Of Mediation: The Transformative Approach To Conflict (2005) (generally asserting that the central ideology and distinguishing feature of mediation is its voluntariness, as reflected in mediation rhetoric that focuses on empowerment and recognition).
4. *See generally*, James R. Maxeiner, Philip K. Howard, Gyooho Lee & Armin Weber, Failures of American Civil Justice in International Perspective Ch. 6 (2011) (describing how little opportunity litigants have to be heard by judge or by jury in the American civil justice system, which reflects the Indian system, in principle).

a court, settlements in one dispute cannot be used as a precedent in similar situations. Thus, mediation (and ADR, generally)[5] is desirable if parties wish to avoid a precedent.

Mediation allows parties to select their mediator and gives the freedom to choose an expert in pertinent fields, including law, business, finance, accounting, engineering, technology, and others. Thus, a panel of mediators brings to the table extensive complementary knowledge, skill, and experience. Take the example of a construction dispute. A panel of mediators may consist of an advocate familiar with construction law and contracts, an architect or engineer familiar with the project type, and a construction manager familiar with project management issues. This, however, is different in the case of court-annexed mediations, where a mediator is appointed by way of a roster system and must be one of the following:[6] retired judges of the Supreme Court, High Courts, or District and Sessions Court; or retired officers of Delhi Higher Judicial Service; or legal practitioners with at least 10 years standing at the India Bar at the level of Supreme Court, High Court, or District Court; or an expert or other professional with at least 15 years standing; or an expert in mediation or conciliation.

Another trademark of mediation is its informality and flexibility in comparison to arbitration or court proceeding. Mediations are free from the clutches of rules of evidence or procedures (as under the Code of Civil Procedure 1908 or the Indian Evidence Act 1872). The freedom from technical constraints and to assemble various process choices make mediation highly conducive to potential settlements. This again describes a core value of this process.

Thus, in arriving at settlements, parties enjoy voluntarism and broad flexibility, making mediated settlements more ironclad than regular agreements negotiated between the parties. This qualitative character of a mediated settlement (in comparison to a regular negotiated agreement) is significant, which is why (for example) a conciliated settlement is given the effect and status of an arbitral award on agreed terms, and a mediated settlement in court-annexed mediation is given the effect and status of a decree on agreed terms. Such finality may be one of the significant advantages of mediated settlements for many parties who want to get disputes behind them and move on. However, where serious fairness concerns stem from unconscionability, fraud, or corruption and the like, parties may take recourse of available remedies under the applicable statutory provisions to challenge such mediated settlements.

An essential dimension of mediation has been its ability to integrate with other ADR processes, like arbitration. This blending or integration of mediation and arbitration procedures offers a myriad advantages that ensure a final resolution. A few

5. Since arbitral awards do not function as a strict form of precedent.
6. Delhi High Court Mediation Rules, 2004, Samadhan, http://dhcmediation.nic.in/the-rules, Rule 4 (on qualifications of persons to be impaneled under Rule 3).

examples of these hybrid processes are generally called: Med-Arb, Arb-Med, Arb-Med-Arb, and so on. Each of these is pragmatic and profitable in its way. For more, *see* Chapter on Mixed-Mode Dispute Resolution.[7]

With these salient features, one may consider or assess the suitability of mediation in the context of their dispute by asking some basic questions:

- Is the ability to control the outcome a vital objective?
- Will the dispute require facilitation by a third party capable of understanding complex or technical factual issues?
- Is the preservation of cost, time, face, and relationship a desirable objective?
- Is there a vital interest that will require complete protection of confidentiality?

Positive answers to these questions will support the choice of mediation, while negative answers will support the use of traditional litigation or arbitration. Anecdotally, parties almost always answer "Yes" to all of the above questions.

[A] Mediation's Application: "Mediatability"

The term "mediatability" is not a legal term but is used here to bring out two aspects:

(i) Mediatability, as in disputes or issues that parties have agreed to mediate or, in which regard, the parties have arrived on a mediated settlement. This is purely a matter of the parties' agreement.
(ii) Mediatability, as in the subject matter of dispute that can or cannot be settled by mediation or a mediated settlement. This is primarily an issue of public policy of India and mandatory exclusions (by statute or judicial law) on the application of mediation.

Here, mediatability (as in the subject matter of dispute) forms the central theme of discussion since it is complex and scattered under Indian law.

Under Part III of the Arbitration and Conciliation Act 1996 ("Arbitration Act"), section 61(1) provides that Part III (on conciliation) only extends to disputes arising out of a legal relationship, whether contractual or not, and to all proceedings relating to it. Regarding "international commercial conciliation," the dispute must be considered "commercial" under the law in force in India.[8] Further, section 61(2) provides that Part III shall not apply where certain disputes may not be submitted to conciliation under any law for the time being into force.

7. The first use of the term "mixed modes" in the context of dispute resolution was in an unpublished draft working paper by Thomas J. Stipanowich and Stephanie B. Blondell (Pepperdine University). *See* Thomas J. Stipanowich & Stephanie Bell Blondell, *Mixing Modes: Complexity and Paradox in Dispute Resolution* (unpublished draft, Sept. 16, 2012) [on file with the author]. The first public use of the term was a presentation by the author at the October 2015 annual meeting of the College of Commercial Arbitrators. *See* Thomas J. Stipanowich, *Arbitration and Settlement: Can We Develop Principled Approaches to Mixed Mode Dispute Processes?*, College of Commercial Arbitrators Annual Meeting (New York, N.Y., Oct. 23, 2015) [on file with the author].
8. Arbitration & Conciliation Act, 1996, §1(2) Explanation and §2(1)(f).

Concerning court-connected mediations, in *Afcons Infrastructure Ltd. v. Cherian Varkey Construction Co. Pvt. Ltd.*[9] ("*Afcons Infrastructure*"), the Supreme Court categorized the subject matter of disputes that may be considered suitable or unsuitable for reference to mediation. The enumeration in *Afcons Infrastructure* is indicative of the subject matters that are mediatable. Accordingly, cases that are considered "not suitable" are the following:[10]

- Representative suits under Order I, Rule 8 of the Civil Procedure Code (CPC), which involve public interest or interest of numerous persons who are not parties before the court.
- Disputes relating to election to public offices.
- Cases involving grant of authority by the section after inquiry, such as suits or grant of probate or letters of administration.
- Cases involving serious and specific allegations of fraud, fabrication of documents, forgery, impersonation, coercion, etc.
- Cases requiring protection of sections, such as claims against minors, deities, and mentally challenged and suits for declaration of title against the government.
- Cases involving prosecution for criminal offenses.

Similarly, cases categorized "suitable" for mediation are classified under five broad headings:

(1) All cases relating to trade, commerce, and contracts.
(2) All cases arising from strained relationships, such as matrimonial cases.
(3) All cases where there is a need to continue the preexisting relationship, such as disputes between neighbors and members of societies.
(4) All cases relating to tortious liability, including motor accident claims.
(5) All consumer disputes.

Despite the Supreme Court's exposition on mediatability, there are nevertheless a few aberrations in case law. However, these should not be considered good law. For instance, a criminal case for rape (punishable under the Indian Penal Code 1860) suffered a controversy when the Madras High Court agreed to grant bail on the condition that the accused tried "mediation" with the victim.[11] The court failed to consider that the prosecution is by the State under criminal jurisprudence and not by

9. (2010) 8 SCC 24, ¶¶ 27–28.
10. *See* Mediation Scheme (for District and Taluka Courts and other Courts), Guidelines for Effective Implementation of ADR Mechanism, Bombay High Court, http://northgoacourts.nic.in/download/BHCMediationScheme.pdf.
11. V. Mohan v. State, 2015 SCC Online Mad 3578 (the matter was forwarded to the mediation center, and it was directed that a compromise should be made in the form of an MOU).

the victim. Further, by section 376 of the Indian Penal Code 1860, rape is a non-compoundable criminal offense and, therefore, it just could not have been compromised by the parties.[12] The bail was canceled after a strong criticism and Supreme Court's observations that a liberal approach in rape cases was nothing short of a spectacular error:[13]

> 19. We are compelled to say so as such an attitude reflects lack of sensibility towards the dignity, the *élan vital*, of a woman. Any kind of liberal approach or thought of mediation in this regard is thoroughly and completely sans legal permissibility.
>
> (emphasis supplied)

With mediation, change is the only constant. In recent years, the scope of mediatability has swelled and stretched into newer fields of law by way of specific statutory provisions and rules. For example, the Companies (Mediation and Conciliation) Rules 2016 were introduced by way of section 442 of the Companies Act 2013, providing for referral of disputes to mediation by the National Company Law Tribunal (NCLT) and National Company Law Appellate Tribunal (NCLAT). Similarly, by way of section 32(g) of the Real Estate (Regulation and Development) Act 2016, the Real Estate Regulatory Authority can make recommendations to the government on measures to facilitate amicable conciliation of disputes between the promoters and the allottees through dispute settlement forums set up by the consumer or promoter associations. The government has most recently considered options such as mediation for the resolution of specific tax disputes.

[B] Distinguishing Mediation from Other ADR Forms

As a segue, mediation must be distinguished from other forms of ADR, given that mediation may notoriously sound both distinct and similar to arbitration and negotiation. Arbitration is a method of dispute resolution involving one or more neutral third parties whose decision—called an arbitral award—is binding on the parties to the dispute. Such neutral third parties who resolve the dispute are called arbitrators.

This entire process is governed by Parts I and II of the Arbitration and Conciliation Act 1996 ("Arbitration Act"), which provides for the agreement to arbitrate, submission of disputes to arbitration, the composition of the arbitral tribunal, conduct

---

12. Victim-offender mediation derived from the concept of restorative justice, however, is a different philosophy of criminal justice that focuses on repairing the harm done to people and relationships, rather than only punishing the offenders. This should not be confused with a typical mediation. Because crime hurts, justice should heal—this put restorative justice in a nutshell. *See generally*, DAVID MIERS, AN INTERNATIONAL REVIEW OF RESTORATIVE JUSTICE (CRIME REDUCTION RESEARCH SERIES PAPER 10) (2001); Carmel Benjamin, *Why Is Victim/Offender Mediation Called Restorative Justice?*, Paper presented at the Restoration for Victims of Crime Conference, Australian Institute of Criminology and Victims Referral and Assistance Service, Melbourne (1999); John Braithwaite, *Principles of Restorative Justice*, available at http://johnbraithwaite.com/wp-content/uploads/2016/03/Principles%20of%20Restorative%20Justice.pdf.
13. State of M.P. v. Madanlal (2015) 7 SCC 681, 688.

of the arbitration proceedings, making of the arbitral award, termination of proceedings, recourse against the arbitral award, enforcement of the arbitral award, as well as the recognition and enforcement of foreign arbitral awards. The Arbitration Act lays down the entire framework that governs the arbitration process, including post-award circumstances.

Fundamentally, the arbitral tribunal and the arbitration procedures are creatures of the parties. However, parties control neither the arbitral tribunal nor the binding arbitral award, which gives this process its integrity and credence.[14] *Au contraire*, courts, and civil procedures codes are created under the judicial and legislative systems. But, like arbitration, parties have no control over the court or the judgment. There is an inherent rigidity in the procedures and a minimal degree of participation from the parties.

On the other hand, negotiation is a process where two or more parties work through their dispute to settle.[15] Negotiation forms a fundamental component of mediation, but it is also essentially independent in nature. It is primarily about reconciling the parties' interests, which yields more satisfactory results than determining who is correct (as in adjudication), which in turn costs less and satisfies more than an adjudication.

While the negotiation model is about "what to do,"[16] the mediation model is about "how to do it." Negotiation is the "substance," whereas mediation is the "form." Beyond this simplistic differentiation, the benefits of third-party involvement are significant. Some of which are:[17] the use of separate private sessions; to have communication rules enforced by a neutral party; for balancing any disparities between the parties; for reviving communications that have reached an impasse;[18] and, throughout the process, enabling a greater scope for sharing interest, option generation, and use of objective criteria.

[C] Mediation's Approach to Disputes

Being a party-centric process, mediation is potent with a variety of applications. That being so, the glass ceiling lies only at the end of creativity—of the parties and the

14. *See* Richard C. Reuben, *Democracy and Dispute Resolution: Systems Design and the New Workplace*, 10 HARV. NEGOT. L. REV. 11, 44–45 (2005).
15. *See generally*, ROGER FISHER ET AL., GETTING TO YES: NEGOTIATING AGREEMENT WITHOUT GIVING IN (2012) (hereinafter "FISHER"); WILLIAM URY, GETTING PAST NO: NEGOTIATING IN DIFFICULT SITUATIONS (2017). *See also*, ANUROOP OMKAR, THE ART OF NEGOTIATION AND MEDIATION: A WISHBONE, FUNNY-BONE, AND A BACKBONE (2015).
16. Principled negotiation is based on four fundamental components: separating people from the problem, focusing on interest and not positions, inventing options for mutual gain, and insisting on the use of objective criteria. *See generally*, FISHER, *supra* note 15.
17. *See generally*, DAVID SPENCER, ESSENTIAL DISPUTE RESOLUTION 41 et seq. (2005) (explaining the connection between mediation and negotiation, and how mediations are negotiated).
18. *See generally*, Marjorie Corman Aaron, *The Value of Decision Analysis in Mediation Practice*, NEG. J. 123 (April 1995) (that when parties in legal dispute are at a negotiation impasse caused by widely divergent assessments of the trial, at least one of them is unrealistic. To break the impasse, the mediator must attempt to influence one or both assessments through decision analysis, which should lead to a movement in settlement options).

mediator. Whatever the initial want of a party, a well-executed mediation process is often known to shift the goalpost, sometimes more than once. This means that a party may start with having a set of demands, move on to unearthing or discovering particular needs to be met, and realizing his real interests, which he then seeks to secure. And even being faced with some concerns, the process of mediation allows those to be addressed in some satisfactory manner. Though this may not all happen in any given mediation, the process is robust and flexible enough to stand by the parties and the mediator, whatever be their quest.

A mediation usually proceeds as follows.[19] The parties start the day in their own rooms. The mediator visits each party briefly to introduce themselves, sign the mediation agreement (if this has not already been done), and deal with any immediate queries and concerns. The mediator then brings the parties together for a joint introductory session. At this meeting, everyone introduces themselves, and each party is allowed to make an opening statement. This statement is often based on their mediation statement and can be made by the parties or, if they wish or feel unable to speak at that time, by their advisor (a mediation advocate or even a non-lawyer representative). Mediators often implement ground rules, like not interrupting while the other person is speaking. After the joint session comes to an end, the parties return to their rooms. Thereafter, the mediator then visits each party, where he further explores the issues and scope for settlement. It is possible that this may lead to further joint sessions or meetings between individuals or representatives. If a settlement is reached due to these meetings and discussions, the focus will turn to agree on the wording of a settlement agreement to finalize matters. If a settlement is not reached on the day, the mediator may request a second session. The mediation process takes typically more than a day. And, in many cases, the negotiations are spread out over several mediation meetings. And (if asked), the mediator may give a settlement proposal on the terms which he thinks the parties are likely to settle. But if the parties cannot reach an agreement and the mediator considers that a settlement is not possible, the mediation is terminated. As a process, mediation has a structure, but it is inherently flexible and informal, unlike conventional litigation (and arbitration, to some extent).

That being the process, the approach to disputes in mediation is unique in that it is interest oriented. In negotiation parlance, "positions" are what people say they want in a conflict, but "interests" refer to what people need and what motivates them. In any mediation, the approach is not about the conflicting positions (or the legal right and duties), but it is conflicting interests (their needs, desires, concerns, and fears). This is significant since mediation allows parties to create broad-based remedies. For instance, a party's interest may lie in mending the past and future relationship, rather than only damages. Mediation gives parties the window to look beyond the formal confines of a

19. Most High Courts in India have adopted their own set of rules for mediation and conciliation; these rules apply to the district courts established under the High Courts. Generally, the mediation rules prescribe that the parties to a dispute may agree on the mediation procedure. However, the essence of a mediation process is the same, including the mandatory pre-institution mediation under Pre-Mediation and Conciliation Rules 2018.

legal dispute and see using practical lenses to lead the parties to a mutually beneficial solution.

CDR (whether mediation, conciliation, or negotiation) is generally interest-oriented and not rights-oriented—it is generally referred to as "principled negotiation." In any form of negotiation, whether assisted or not, parties tend to take a position and haggle with the other side to drive a hard bargain. Such "positional bargaining" tends to make the parties lock themselves to their position, leading to either an impasse or an undesirable outcome. And when parties do budge from such a position, it may leave them with a loss of face. This is sometimes also called distributive bargaining. The alternative to this is "principled negotiation," which has four key elements.[20]

[1] Separate the People from the Problem

Emotions and egos of parties become entwined with the issues surrounding the dispute leading to complications. This becomes a barrier to settlement. It is essential to see the problem as an issue to be tackled by the parties together. So, it is not one side versus another but rather all sides versus the problem.

[2] Focus on Interests, Not Positions

Positional bargaining is not an effective method to negotiate. If parties stop focusing on their positions and seek to identify each other's interests, it can result in a win-win situation where each party's needs and interests are satisfied.

[3] Invent Options for Mutual Gain

Parties need to brainstorm a range of possible options and choices to resolve the issues at hand. Even if parties have found a solution, it is worth exploring all available options to ensure that the outcome satisfies the needs of all parties in the best possible way.

[4] Insist on Using Objective Criteria

Instead of arguing on the facts or other aspects of the matter, it is better to rely on objective criteria to settle differences. Objective criteria refer to an impartial, independent standard such as market value, law, industry protocol, or expert opinion.

The above approach is supplemented by other tools and techniques, like the Best Alternative to a Negotiated Agreement (BATNA), which refers to the best alternative available to a party if the mediation fails, and no settlement is reached. A party can arrive at its BATNA only when he goes to mediation knowing what he wants to achieve from it, in terms of both financial and non-financial settlement and what is likely to be asked of him by the other party. For example, a party may determine that its

20. *See* FISHER, *supra* note 15, at pp. 17–96.

BATNA is to litigate. In case mediation fails, such a party will want to proceed to litigate the dispute at hand. Parties in mediation often apply this as it helps a party understand and evaluate any proposals before it. So, if the proposal before a party is better than its BATNA, a party will likely accept the proposal resulting in the dispute settlement. In mediation, parties often also attempt to predict the other side's BATNA to understand their bottom line or fallback option.

When considering what might amount to a reasonable settlement offer, a party should consider what he is realistically likely to recover if he succeeds in his claim in arbitration or court; how long it is likely to take to get to a full hearing and then for the court or the tribunal to deliver its decision; the prospects of him succeeding in his claim after understanding the strengths and weaknesses of his claim, and those of the other party; and the "litigation risk" or the risk of losing his claim.

"Reality testing" is one such other technique. Parties use this technique to educate the other side of the consequences of no agreement. A party can question the other side what the consequences of failing to settle are. This will force both sides to think of the options before them if they already have not done so. If a party has underestimated the consequences of not settling, this might aid that party to appreciate any proposals on the table. If this dose of reality is not enough, a party can consider indicating their opponent the consequences of a failed negotiation, what will happen if negotiations fail, their BATNA. A party may also consider asking what the other party intends to do if the negotiation fails, which would mean the other side's BATNA.

Mediators also use this technique to challenge the case or assertions of a party and get them to do a reality check of their expectations, risks, or even proposals. This is typically done by way of a series of questions that the mediator asks the concerned party. However, a mediator can also either give a gestalt evaluation (the mediator's overall sense of reasonable settlement value) or provide detailed feedback on the strengths and weaknesses of the parties' positions on each issue. A powerful technique, it has the potential to make a party empathize with the other. Reality testing goes hand in hand with the Worst Alternative to a Negotiated Agreement (WATNA). It is the opposite of BATNA and indicates the worst alternative in case parties fail to settle. As important as working out the BATNA, a party should also work out its counterpart—WATNA. The weaker the WATNA, the weaker the negotiating position.

[D] Diagnostics of Deciding to Mediate

The decision to mediate is usually based on many parameters that become apparent based on the facts and circumstances of the case at hand. There are, nevertheless, many generalized/standard reasons for an advocate and/or user to consider before accepting or requesting mediation to settle. The following five are substantial factors:

(i) A settlement gives finality, certainty, and closure through an agreed outcome that is acceptable to the parties in dispute.

(ii) A settlement avoids enormous direct costs (such as fees and expenses paid to lawyers, consultants, and experts), indirect costs (such as overheads and resources spent toward assembling the facts, serving as witnesses, and otherwise process the dispute), and other hidden costs to the extent they can be measured (such as the inefficiencies, delays, loss of quality that disputes cause to the construction process itself, and the costs of strained relationships with other parties).

(iii) A settlement avoids exposure to the public about the case's commercial and/or personal sensitivities, minimizing the risk of negative publicity. Parties can take cover under the protection of a confidentiality clause.

(iv) A settlement avoids disruptions in the relationship between disputing parties or at least maintaining some ongoing relationship, which is generally in the parties' long-term interests. In personal matters, preservation of relationship usually takes primacy, demanding that an attempt at mediation be made at the earliest.

(v) A settlement has the potential for a wide variety of remedies, which are only limited by the parties' creativity and are unexpectable from adversarial forums.

Interestingly, these decision factors more-or-less match the national survey results of the Global Pound Conference held at Chandigarh on May 12–13, 2017. When asked "what is achieved by participating in a non-adjudicative process," the voting results revealed the following hierarchically: improving or restoring relationships; reduced costs and expenses; better knowledge of the strengths/weaknesses of the cases or likelihood of settlement; retaining control over the outcome; compliance (e.g., avoiding cost sanctions, meeting contractual obligations); and tactical/strategic advantage.

A timely mediation, in such circumstances, can help tie things together. There is an appropriate time and stage when the abovementioned considerations are most positive and constructive for the parties. An early recourse to mediation is almost always a worthwhile consideration when considering mediation. It is more pragmatic but becomes far more complex with time and anchored positions. Take, for instance, construction disputes. The Pre-action Protocol for Construction and Engineering Dispute (Protocol)[21] inspires the use of "without prejudice" meetings before the commencement of court proceedings.[22] At these meetings, parties are required to consider how to resolve the dispute without recourse to litigation, which may involve agreeing to mediation.[23] Parties are, therefore, expected by UK courts to consider if mediation might enable settlement without commencing court proceedings and to continue to consider the possibility of settling even after the court proceedings have started.[24] In this regard, Lord Justice Mummery pointed to the potential benefits of attempting ADR proceedings at an early stage, making the point that "litigation hardens

21. Pre-action Protocol for Construction and Engineering Disputes 2nd Edition, UK Justice, https://www.justice.gov.uk/courts/procedure-rules/civil/protocol/prot_ced.
22. *Id.*, at ¶ 9.1.
23. *Id.*, at ¶ 9.3.
24. *See* Practice Direction on Pre-action Conduct and Protocols, UK Justice, https://www.justice.gov.uk/courts/procedure-rules/civil/rules/pd_pre-action_conduct.

attitudes" and that costs become an "additional aggravating issue" that can make it harder to settle as proceedings advance.[25]

Still, why mediation? Why not simply negotiate if the motivation is to ultimately compromise.[26] Take, for instance, that prior negotiations have taken place, and possible settlements were discussed. However, parties lose their momentum due to loss of trust or a sudden imbalance between parties. Mediation can be an appropriate process to employ when negotiations have failed for such reasons. In such cases, mediation may be able to achieve the results which negotiations could not. When negotiations fail, dispute resolution efforts may scatter, leaving gaps and unexplored areas, further escalating the situation with the passage of time. Even otherwise, mediation is somewhat superior, given the facilitative assistance of a neutral third party and structured process with one focus—resolution. Thus, where relationships especially matter, negotiations may be insufficient as a process, potentially creating a rift (or widening it). But, almost always, it leads to a chain reaction of rising conflict.

It is not to say that mediation will always be successful (i.e., result in a settlement). Despite best efforts in mediation, it sometimes happens that parties are thwarted. That, however, gives a reason for parties to take stock of things. Even though preliminary discussions hit a stumbling block, there are always potential opportunities in the future to revive them. It is worth recognizing that mediations often narrow the issues in dispute, bring more clarity in future proceedings, saving both time and costs for the parties. At the very least, parties are pushed to the wall, making them reevaluate the strengths and weakness of their respective cases, which can potentially spark renegotiations and open up possibilities to consider other tools and forms of ADR, like binding expert determination on (at least) some of the issues.

§1.03 MEDIATION IN INDIA

Settlement of disputes in an amicable way has been the hallmark of the Indian civilization. History tells that a mediation-like order has been prevalent in India in one form or another. In ancient India, disputes were often resolved (by bodies not established by monarchs) through village councils known as *Kulani* and other village assemblies known as *Gorth* or *Puga* that decided disputes.[27] These institutions had representation from all groups and communities. Pre-British rule, India had a village governance system called the *panchayat*, which was essentially a body constituted by respected village elders who assisted in resolving community disputes. Among the businessmen, in pre-British rule, *Mahajans* (for instance) were considered to be these impartial and respected businessmen of the villages, who were requested to resolve disputes by using an informal procedure and trying to come to an amicable solution.

25. Bradford v. James, [2008] EWCA Civ 837.
26. *See* Allison M. Malkin & Gracious Timothy Dunna, *Commercial Mediation: An Evolving Frontier of Alternative Dispute Resolution in India*, *in* ALTERNATIVE DISPUTE RESOLUTION: THE INDIAN PERSPECTIVE (Shashank Garg ed. 2018).
27. *See* Ankur Khandelwal, *Assessing the Scope of Mediation in India: Upholding the Principles of Justice*, 12(2) ASIAN DISP. REV. 52, 52 (2010).

Many of these traditional settings continue to be so in the villages, preserved in their customary forms, going as back as the *Vedic* period.[28]

But the so-called modern mediation in India may be traced back to three crucial statutory regimes: Arbitration and Conciliation Act 1996, Legal Services Authorities Act 1987 (LSA), and Code of Civil Procedure 1908, which will be primarily engaged in the course of the other chapters. Most recently (and a critical juncture of modern mediation in India) is Chapter IIIA on pre-institution mediation and settlement, introduced in 2018 by an amendment to the Commercial Courts, Commercial Division, and Commercial Appellate Division of High Courts Act 2015 ("Commercial Courts Act"). Section 12A of the Commercial Courts Act requires parties to attempt mandatory mediation to resolve a dispute before filing a claim with the court.[29] The government has also enacted the Commercial Courts (Pre-Institution Mediation and Settlement) Rules 2018 (PIMS Rules) for mediations under section 12A.

There are, of course, other statutes that incorporate a specific mediation or conciliation mechanism in the context of disputes that may arise concerning said statutes. For instance, the Industrial Disputes Act 1947 (IDA) embodies a comprehensive conciliation framework for the settlement of industrial disputes,[30] involving a third party, a Conciliation Officer, who is required to investigate the dispute create a settlement plan.[31] The IDA is now superseded by the Industrial Relations Code 2020 (IRC), which retains the Conciliation Officer. IRC was introduced with the object to "minimize the friction between the employers and workers and provide provisions for investigation and settlement of industrial disputes."[32] Accordingly, the Conciliation Officer's role comes into play where an "industrial dispute" and a strike or lockout notices have been received. After which, the Conciliation Officer has a stipulated period from the date of commencement of conciliation to send reports to the parties and the appropriate government.[33]

Similarly, some other statutes and forums have incorporated mediation (or mediation-like procedures). Section 442 of the Companies Act 2013 introduced a provision that authorizes the Central Government to maintain a Mediation and

28. *See* Anil Xavier, *Mediation: Its Origin and Growth in India*, 27 Hamline J. Pub. L. & Pol'y 297 (2006) (discussing *panchayat* and *pancha* which were a system of conflict settlement in villages and tribes, and the Mahajans, who were respected businessmen helping resolve mercantile conflicts); Supreme Court of India, Mediation Training Manual of India, https://main.sci.gov.in/pdf/mediation/MT%20MANUAL%20OF%20INDIA.pdf, pp. 1–4 (tracing mediation in a very elementary form back to ancient times in the post-Vedic period in India).
29. *See generally*, Chitra Narayan, *Legislation Seeks to Boost Mediation Use for Commercial Matters in India*, 36(9) Alternatives 131 (2018).
30. Industrial Disputes Act, 1947, §4 (duty of mediating in and promoting the settlement of disputes) and §5.
31. *See* P. M. Bakshi, *"Conciliation" under the Industrial Disputes Act 1947: Should It Necessarily Remain: A Fifth Wheel to the Coach*, 29(2) J. Ind. L. Inst. 236 (1987). *See generally*, William H. Simkin, Mediation and the Dynamics of Collective Bargaining 25–26 (1971) (defining conciliator, in a collective bargaining scenario as a "mild form of intervention limited primarily to scheduling conferences, trying to keep the disputants talking, facilitating other procedural niceties, carrying messages back and forth between the parties, and generally being a 'good fellow' who tries to keep things calm and forward-looking in a tense situation").
32. Industrial Relations Code, 2020 (No. 35 of 2020).
33. Industrial Relations Code, 2020, §53(5).

Conciliation Panel that provides mediation between parties during any pending proceedings before the Central Government, NCLT. After that, the Central Government introduced the Companies Mediation and Conciliation Rules 2016, which provide provisions for conducting mediation or conciliations. Likewise, Lok Adalats are used in disputes where monetary compensation is claimed, including insurance disputes and automobile accident proceedings. A public evaluation process is presided over by a judge or panel of neutrals who propose a monetary settlement after briefly hearing the factual background and claims involved in a dispute. In the form of offers and counteroffers, negotiation may take place on a limited basis during the Lok Adalat process, after which the Lok Adalat judge proposes a specific settlement.

Experientially, there is a gradual shift in dispute resolution using consensual dispute settlement mechanisms like mediation.[34] Courts have especially been active in promoting mediation in recent times. In *M. R. Krishna Murthi v. New India Assurance Co. Ltd.*, the Supreme Court asked the government to consider the feasibility of setting up a Motor Accidents Mediation Authority (MAMA) by making necessary amendments in the Motor Vehicles Act. In the interregnum, the Supreme Court directed the National Legal Services Authority (NALSA) to set up Motor Accident Mediation Cells, which could either function independently under the aegis of NALSA or be handed over to Supreme Court's Mediation and Conciliation Project Committee (MCPC).

Time and again, the Supreme Court has accentuated the need for settling disputes between parties, particularly in commercial matters. In the words of V. R. Krishna Iyer:[35]

> Commercial causes, we may observe prolegomenary fashion, should, as far as possible, be adjusted by non-litigative mechanisms of dispute-resolution, since forensic processes, dilatory and contentious, hamper the flow of trade and harm both sides, whoever wins or loses the *lis*. That is why arbitration is often prudently resorted to when controversies erupt in the course of business dealings. But when basic differences spring up as to which is the arbitration clause that governs, in a plurality of contracts or several steps in evolving a final contract but containing divergent arbitral provisions, the Court comes into the picture, willy nilly. Even so, having regard to the larger interests of justice, an exercise in pre-trial settlement, consistent with judicial non-alignment, is desiderable, and so we had suggested to counsel, at an earlier hearing, to bring the parties together on the limited question of the arbitral locus and law, but notwithstanding genuine efforts by Counsel, and perhaps due to substantial factors weighing with the parties, the effort proved fruitless. A legal adjudication may be flawless but heartless, but a negotiated settlement will be satisfying, even if it departs from strict law. The respondent's Counsel stated that his client—a foreign State Trading Organization—was rather keen—and this may well be true—on getting the law declared by this Court for future guidance and so we proceed to narrate the litigative story and cut the legal knot for the benefit of both sides. Since the subject-matter relates to the sensitive

34. *See* M. R. Krishna Murthi v. New India Assurance Co. Ltd. and Ors. (2020) 15 SCC 493 ("the way mediation movement is catching up in this country"). *See also*, Anil Xavier, *Mediation Is Here to Stay!*, IND. Y.B. INT'L L. POL'Y 363 (2009) (that the expectations of parties of legal services are changing—the new requirement is "resolution" and not "litigation").
35. Agarwal Engineering Co. v. Technoimpex Hungarian Machine Industries Foreign Trade Co. (1977) 4 SCC 367, 367.

> area of foreign trade we still hope the dispute, even after our pronouncement, will be dissolved and goodwill and business dealings revived between the parties to their mutual benefit.

Long before the present-day outcry for the use of mediation, the Supreme Court has made some perceptive observations about the need for adopting consensual dispute resolution means. A few important motifs that have put mediation in the spotlight have been issues like swelling litigation costs, court's overworked dockets, dilatory tactics that parties adopt which contribute to undue delays in the courts of the first instance, as well as appellate courts—problems in the court system that the use of mediation may ameliorate.[36] Moreover, in many instances, ad hoc arbitrations in India have seemingly become a glorified form of litigation, hung on the same peg as litigation. It may also be protracted, extravagant, belligerent, and frustrating. In that background, mediation in India (as spoken by the Supreme Court) has gained much recognition and importance.[37] The Law Commission of India has, time and again, echoed the Supreme Court's view.[38]

In exchange for protracted and costly adjudication, mediation offers parties the possibility of preserving time, relationships, and face, and it offers the potential to generate progressive and creative settlement options. The benefits of mediation are appealing and far outweigh the plus points of arbitration and litigation. While many problems plunge over existing litigation and arbitration structures, mediation comes as a savior, serving expeditious and inexpensive justice while being flexible enough to meet the interests of disputing parties and giving a platform for remedies that may not be available in traditional adversarial forums.

Sure, the problem of arrears in courts has assumed severe proportions, necessitating a search for alternates and supplements to the traditional forums, and while that may be a great motivation to bring our attention to mediation, it should not be the

36. *See generally*, Anirudh R. *Adversarial Process Problems: The Need for Mediation as an Alternative Disputes Resolution Mechanism*, 3 RGNUL Stud. Res. Rev. 55 (2016).
37. *See generally*, Anil Kumar Singh, *ADR Mechanism in India: Achievements and Challenges*, 5(8) Ind. J. Res. (August 2016) (that ADR may not be a replacement of litigation, but that it may be used to make our traditional court systems work more efficiently and effectively).
38. *See* Law Commission of India, Report No. 184 (2002), https://lawcommissionofindia.nic.in/reports/184threport-PartI.pdf (on the Legal Education & Professional Training and Proposals for Amendments to the Advocates Act 1961 and the University Grants Commission Act 1956, recommending ADR training for students and lawyers); Law Commission of India, Report No. 186 (2003), https://lawcommissionofindia.nic.in/reports/186th%20report.pdf (on Proposal to Constitute Environmental Courts, recommending that the proposed environmental courts should encourage conciliation and mediation at any stage of the proceeding—be it in appeal or an original petition); Law Commission of India, Report No. 222 (2009), https://lawcommissionofindia.nic.in/reports/report222.pdf (need for justice-dispensation through ADR, etc.); Law Commission of India, Report No. 237 (2011), https://lawcommissionofindia.nic.in/reports/report237.pdf (reporting a view that the first recourse should be to effect conciliation and mediation between the warring spouses and the recourse to filing of a charge sheet under section 498A of the Indian Penal Code should be had only in cases where such efforts fail and there appears to be a prima facie case, further, that counseling of parties should be done by professionally qualified counsellors and not by the Police); Law Commission of India, Report No. 238 (2011), http://lawcommissionofindia.nic.in/reports/report238.pdf (Amendment of section 89 of the Code of Civil Procedure, 1908 and Allied Provisions).

rationale for choosing mediation. Consider the danger of such a rationale for mediation in India. Mediation would be perceived only in terms of reducing court arrears. Mediation advocacy would be motivated by the inability of our courts to handle the existing load of cases. Yes, easing the burden of courts is undoubtedly an important objective, but it needs to be emphasized that it is not the conception. Mediation is not for docket management.

Mediation fulfills its instrumental and intrinsic functions, which are equal, if not greater value, like litigation or arbitration.[39] In other words, mediation is not to be regarded as a mere tool to manage the burden of courts or cope with the lengthy and expensive adjudicatory processes. Mediation is a unique alternative process in itself; it is an independent means of providing access to justice, which comes with a myriad of remedies to a dispute and, most importantly, the opportunity for parties to articulate their case, be fully heard, and self-determine. Hence, developing the ethics, probity, and integrity of an alternative framework like mediation is absolutely necessary.

Currently, there is no comprehensive standard and holistic statutory framework for consensual dispute resolution in India. In practice, mediation and conciliation are admittedly not distinct, and if a legal distinction does exist, the Indian laws governing these processes must be streamlined for more certainty and clarity for judges, practitioners, neutrals, and users. Therefore, whichever be the school of thought on the mediation-conciliation divide, the general perspective is still that a legislative unscrambling of the use of terms "mediation" and "conciliation" is long due. There is a need for certainty and a consistent approach concerning both processes and the law governing them, which would be a big step in developing a mediation culture in India.

To bring uniformity and harmony between different legislations relating to mediation is the absolute need of the hour. A clear law will enable legal practitioners, users, and proponents to be comfortable using mediation. A powerful mediation enactment in India will change the approach of consensual dispute resolution in India, making mediation a more viable option for dispute resolution, so also a viable profession or practice area. For India to gradually morph into an advanced mediation culture, a comprehensive legal framework is vital, which will also be the source of developing specific species of legislation on mediation to further implant consensual dispute resolution practice covering a diversity of areas with deeper market penetrations.[40]

Mediation advocates and mediators are increasingly becoming visible, and the boundaries between traditional contentious practice and ADR practice are gradually blurring. But there is a disconnect between theory and practice in mediation and mediation advocacy, in the sense that mediation in India is still largely in its primitive stages compared to international standards or other (more sophisticated) jurisdictions.

39. *See* Justice Dhananjaya Y. Chandrachud, *Mediation—Realizing the Potential and Designing Implementation Strategies*, https://lawcommissionofindia.nic.in/adr_conf/chandrachud3.pdf.
40. For example, sports mediation. *See generally*, IAN S. BLACKSHAW, SPORT, MEDIATION AND ARBITRATION (2009).

One may speculate this to be a cultural issue (legal and societal) and that we have generally become a litigating society for mixing ego with economic reasoning. Whatever the reason, mediation is not yet fully ingrained in the present-day Indian psyche of advocates and disputing parties. It is like a new graft, like a new heart or a new kidney. And as with the human body, it looks for an opening to reject it. While the body takes its time to accept the change, the present-day discourse on mediation has come a long way. It needs a focus shift and a change from any stereotypical ideology that mediation is generally branded with. It needs emerging literature, continuing training and education programs, corporate in-house training programs, law school courses, and more domestic and international student competitions—fixating on mediation and development of mediator practice and advocacy.[41]

[A] Global Pound Conference, Chandigarh (2017)

In 2017, India hosted the world's most extensive ADR event series called the Global Pound Conference (GPC) in Chandigarh on May 12–14. The conference was titled "Shaping the Future of Dispute Resolution and Improving Access to Justice." GPC was a series of conferences in 22 countries at which delegates were asked the same series of questions to obtain data to contribute to the debate on how current dispute resolution processes can evolve to serve the needs of their users better. The questions aimed to find out what parties want from commercial dispute resolution processes, how current systems can be improved, and identifying obstacles to change and how these can be overcome. The GPC data was split into answers given by users of dispute resolution processes (4/57%); advisors (17.77%, such as lawyers or other consultants); providers of adjudicative processes (15.74%, such as judges or arbitrators); providers of non-adjudicative processes (54.31%, such as mediators and conciliators); influencers (7.61%, such as researchers and educators).

The core questions of the survey were split into four categories: (i) what do users want, need, and expect; (ii) how is the market currently addressing parties' wants, needs, and expectations; (iii) how can dispute resolution be improved; (iv) what action items should be considered and by whom? The voting results at GPC Chandigarh are perhaps the most important empirical data on India concerning ADR, including mediation:[42]

41. *See generally*, Jacquelin Nolan-Haley, *Mediation: The "New Arbitration,"* 17 HARV. NEG. L. REV. 61, 79–83 (2012) (on inconsistent messages in advocacy, persistence of bad faith practice, negative conduct in mediation and abuse of confidentiality, and "legal" mediation practice that is no different any contentious proceeding).
42. *GPC Series Data and Report*, INTERNATIONAL MEDIATION INSTITUTE, https://imimediation.org/research/gpc/series-data-and-reports/.

Selected Questions	*Top Responses (in Hierarchical Order)*
In commercial disputes, what is achieved by participating in non-adjudicative processes (mediation or conciliation) (whether voluntary or involuntary—e.g., court ordered)?	- Improving or restoring relationships. - Reduced costs and expenses. - Better knowledge of the strengths/weaknesses of the case or likelihood of settlement.
Currently, the most effective commercial dispute resolution processes usually involve which of the following?	- Combining adjudicative and non-adjudicative processes (e.g., arbitration/litigation with mediation/conciliation). - Non-adjudicative dispute resolution methods (mediation or conciliation).
To improve the future of commercial dispute resolution, which of the following processes and tools should be prioritized?	- Non-adjudicative dispute resolution method (mediation or conciliation). - Combining adjudicative and non-adjudicative processes (e.g., arbitration/ litigation with mediation/ conciliation).
Which of the following would most improve commercial dispute resolution?	Legislation or conventions that promote recognition and enforcement of settlements, including those reached in mediation. - Accreditation or certification systems for dispute resolution providers. - Cost sanctions against parties for failing to try non-adjudicative processes (e.g., mediation or conciliation) before litigation/arbitration.
What is the most effective way to improve parties' understanding of their options for resolving commercial disputes?	- Education in business and/ or law schools and the broader business community about adjudicative and non-adjudicative dispute resolution options. - Requiring parties to attempt non-adjudicative options (i.e., mediation or conciliation) before initiating litigation or arbitration.

Selected Questions	*Top Responses (in Hierarchical Order)*
To promote better access to justice for those involved in commercial disputes, where should policy makers, governments and administrators focus their attention?	- Legislation or conventions promoting recognition and enforcement of settlements including those reached in mediation. - Making non-adjudicative processes (mediation or conciliation) compulsory and/or a process where parties can "opt-out." - Pre-dispute or early-stage case evaluation or assessment systems. - Use of protocols promoting non-adjudicative processes (mediation or conciliation) before adjudicative processes.

GPC also published a report on the global trends and regional differences apparent in the global voting results.[43] The Asian continent showed much desire for increased regulation. Stakeholders in Asian jurisdictions voted consistently to highlight the role of legislation or international conventions to promote the enforcement and recognition of settlements. Since practical experience rarely reveals difficulties with enforcement, this regional trend may indicate that a more developed regulatory framework would assist acceptance and use of non-adjudicative dispute resolution processes like mediation and conciliation. On another aspect, when regions segmented the global data, it was clear that efficiency was the key priority in all regions except Asia, where the key priority was the certainty and enforceability of outcomes. This may indicate an important underlying difference about how stakeholders in Asia (including India) perceive non-adjudicative dispute resolution processes.

[B] Mediation Initiatives in India

The MCPC was set up in 2005 for encouraging amicable resolution of disputes pending in the courts per section 89 of the CPC.[44] The MCPC initiated a court integrated mediation process, which has proved to be very successful. MCPC has conducted and disseminated the 40-hour mediation training program for mediator accreditation, trainers, referral judges training program, and other such awareness programs.

43. *Id.*
44. Abhishek M. Singhvi, *Beating the Backlog: Less Talk, More Action* (2007) 2 SCC J-9, J-16 ("Alternative or consensual dispute resolution—ADR or CDR—outside the traditional justice system, by mediation, conciliation, and other methods, have also received considerable impetus and dynamism by the setting up of an Apex Court committee to create modules of implementation at different High Courts, in addition to the already successful Lok Adalats").

The foremost effort of the MCPC has been the 40-hour mediation training. The training and 10 actual mediations form the essential qualification required for a mediator to be able to be entrusted with the task of mediating disputes. The MCPC also formulated the Mediation Training Manual of India to streamline mediation training and functioning in India. The manual was a product of various experts drawn from different mediation centers in the country.

MCPC has given a boost to court-annexed mediation and helped mediation grow not only as an "alternative" but also as another effective mechanism of dispute resolution. The Supreme Court and almost all 24 High Courts and the district courts have court-annexed mediation centers, and these are the most prominent mediation institutions in India. The courts have taken the lead in institutionalizing mediation, providing training, certification, and referrals. These court-annexed mediation centers have led to the emergence and growth of private mediation institutes across India.

However, further attention is required in the expansion of infrastructure and resources relating to court-connected mediations. From the websites of several High Courts, it can be ascertained that most High Courts have their separate set of rules governing mediation. But barring a few High Courts, there is simply no data available to show the status of mediation cases referred, successes/failure of matters, and the number of settlements arrived at and effectively implemented.

There is also a need for framing policies, including a national policy, to promote and support its effective implementation. The 2018 Land Pooling Policy of Delhi Development Authority (DDA) sets a simple example.[45] Land Pooling was introduced as a new paradigm for urban development of Delhi, whereby the private sector would play an active role in assembling land and developing physical and social infrastructure. Under this concept, owners (or groups of owners) pool land parcels for development per prescribed norms and guidelines, making them partners in the development process.[46] The Land Pooling Policy is open to all landowners who own land in the areas notified by DDA/Government under the Policy. As per clause 12(ii) of the Regulations for Operationalization of Land Policy 2018, the grievances among the landowners, developer entities, or the service-providing agency must be resolved by way of a multitier dispute resolution mechanism.[47] It provides that there should be an inbuilt provision in the agreement entered between a consortium and developer entities and in

45. *See also*, the IBBI (Model Bye-Laws and Governing Board of Insolvency Professional Agencies) Regulations 2016 (an Insolvency Professional Agency shall submit to IBBI its bylaws, which are to be consistent with the Model Bye-Laws and that under clauses 21 and 22 of the Regulations, the grievance redressal policy is required to provide for mediation); National Intellectual Property Rights Policy 2016 (promoting ADRs in the resolution of IP cases by strengthening mediation and conciliation centers, and developing ADR capabilities and skills in the field of IP); National Water Policy 2012 (that a permanent Water Disputes Tribunal at the Center should be established to resolve the disputes expeditiously in an equitable manner using mechanism like arbitration and mediation).
46. This was brought as an alternative to the Land Acquisition, Development and Disposal Policy of Delhi approved in 1961, which could not keep pace with the increasing demand of urbanization. The process of acquisition was increasingly challenged by landowners due to low compensation as compared to the market value.
47. The Regulations were enacted in exercise of the powers conferred by subsection (1) of section 57 of the Delhi Development Act, 1957, with the previous approval of Central Government.

the agreement between consortium/developer entities with the service-providing agencies. This inbuilt mechanism commences with conciliation or mediation. And only if the process of mediation fails, the parties can resort to arbitration under the provisions of the Arbitration and Conciliation Act 1996.

[C] Institutional Mediation and Conciliation

The overall development of ADR has also led to the growth of organizations or institutions devoted to conciliation and mediation services. In particular, two institutions in India have taken giant leaps in bringing international standards of institutional mediation to India—the Indian Institute of Arbitration and Mediation (IIAM) located in Cochin and New Delhi and the CAMP Arbitration and Mediation Practice (CAMP) based in Bangalore.

Both IIAM and CAMP have international affiliations with some of the top institutions worldwide, cooperating and encouraging a mutual development of conciliation and mediation. IIAM is one of the pioneering institutions in India, providing ADR services since 2001. CAMP is also well known for providing high-quality mediation and conciliation services in Bangalore and Online Dispute Resolution services.[48]

A key initiative of IIAM to inculcate mediation in India has been the "Pledge to Mediate," whereby a signatory pledges that, in the event of a dispute, he would be prepared to explore mediation before pursuing full-scale litigation. A signatory, therefore, pledges to consider mediation as a first resort to resolve disputes and insert a mediation clause in its agreements and forms, whenever appropriate. Not only is the pledge cost-free and not legally binding but also a signatory (especially an organization) stands to benefit from an expression of good corporate governance and goodwill.

Besides IIAM and CAMP, there is the International Centre for Alternate Dispute Resolution (ICADR), an autonomous organization headquartered in New Delhi and working under the Ministry of Law and Justice (Central Government). Its regional centers are located in Hyderabad and Bangalore, fully funded and supported by the respective State Governments. ICADR was set up to oversee the development of ADR in India, and its object included teaching and training ADR personnel, developing infrastructure, providing institutional services for various ADR mechanisms, and so on. ICADR also provided mediation and conciliation services.

However, ICADR is now superseded by the New Delhi International Arbitration Center (NDIAC), established under the NDIAC Act 2019. NDIAC will be an autonomous and independent institution to conduct arbitration, mediation, and conciliation proceedings. The NDIAC Act seeks to transfer the existing ICADR to the Central Government. Upon notification by the Central Government, all the rights, title, and interest in the ICADR will be transferred to the NDIAC.

48. *See generally*, Abhishek Rathore & Ankit Bhandari, *Mechanism of Online Dispute Resolution*, 6 GNLU J. L. Dev. Pol. 94 (2016).

These institutions in the Indian landscape have given parties the option to refer their disputes to be settled through mediation or conciliation under the rules of the selected institution. Once the dispute is referred, these institutions conduct professional case management under a competitive and transparent fee structure. It arranges all the logistics, facilities, and services required to conduct conciliation proceedings smoothly. If parties are unable to agree on a mediator or a conciliator jointly, the institution helps the parties choose the neutral from a panel of domestic and international neutrals.

§1.04 MEDIATION-CONCILIATION DIVIDE

As an emerging mediation culture, India has many challenges. One, in particular, concerns the mediation-conciliation divide in both private and court-annexed realms. Practitioners, including many commentators, take divergent views on the difference between mediation and conciliation in practice and the law governing the processes.

Hence, there is no uniformity, though there may be a tendency to use these terms interchangeably, given their shared boundaries. As a result, this issue has practical and legal relevance, such that the dichotomy is damaging to a growing practice. There are two denominations, which either reject or advocate the difference between mediation and conciliation: one takes the "pragmatic approach," while the other takes a "formalistic approach."

[A] Pragmatic Approach

Those advocating the "pragmatic approach" suggest that mediation and conciliation are terms essentially referring to the same process and that any difference is only superficial. The premise (before delving further with their propositions) assumes that private mediation is governed by Part III of the Arbitration Act, as opposed to those which are court-referred under governed by the framework of CPC and LSA 1987.

Second, since there are no statutory definitions of mediation and conciliation, proponents of the pragmatic approach refer to the functions of a "conciliator" scripted under sections 67 and 73 of the Arbitration Act to define the processes indirectly.[49] Section 73, specifically, adds to the role of a conciliator in stating that "[w]hen it appears to the conciliator that there exist elements of a settlement which may be acceptable to the parties, he shall formulate the terms of a possible settlement and submit them to the parties for their observations." At the same time, formalists suggest

49. *See generally*, SRIRAM PANCHU, MEDIATION PRACTICE & LAW THE PATH TO SUCCESSFUL DISPUTE RESOLUTION 321 (2015) ("In the arena of private mediation there is no provision in Arbitration and Conciliation Act providing the mediator immunity for things done or omitted to be done bona fide during the course of mediation. Nor is there a provision protecting a mediator from being compelled to testify regarding the mediation proceedings. The Model Civil Procedure Mediation Rules (which are the basis for the Rules adopted by the High Courts) provide in Rule 22 that a mediator is protected from civil and criminal liability and from having to be summoned by the court to testify as regards the mediation proceedings. Similar protection is required under the ACA").

that role of the "conciliator" is contemplated to be proactive and interventionist (as opposed to the role of a "mediator" which is restricted to that of a mere facilitator);[50] the pragmatists argue that (by definition) mediation is much broader than mere facilitation. Mediation is a process that has several models based on the mediator's interaction and intervention (the dimensions). Combining these dimensions presents distinct models of mediation to be identified which is logical in theory and relevant in practice.[51]

Pragmatists view that a mediator's approach or conduct is never a constant dynamic during mediation. It fluctuates over the scales of "interaction" and "intervention," depending on the dynamics of the mediation session. For instance, an "advisory mediation" or a "counsel mediation" involves a high level of mediator intervention in the problem, like advising or providing reasonable settlement terms.[52] Thus, a mediator in these cases assumes the parties' responsibility when it appears that there exist elements of a settlement that may be acceptable to the parties. Mediation, therefore, notably includes that necessary feature wherein a mediator might assume a more proactive and interventionist role.

The bottom line of the pragmatic view is that conciliation is nothing but a proactive or interventionist form of mediation. A conciliation that never witnesses section 73 in operation (in terms of a settlement option from the conciliator) would still be called "conciliation." In other words, a conciliator's formulation and reformulation of possible terms of settlement is not a necessary part of the conciliation process—section 73 is not an attribute that is a *sine qua non* to conciliation.

Pragmatists also respond with reliance on the United Nations Commission on International Trade Law (UNCITRAL) Model Law on International Commercial Conciliation 2002 (amended in 2018) complemented by the UNCITRAL Conciliation Rules 1980, which Rules were foundational in the enactment of Part III on conciliation under the Arbitration Act. The UNCITRAL had in mind a broad notion of conciliation, which was also referred to as "mediation." The Model Law defined conciliation as "a process,

50. *See generally*, HENRY J. BROWN & ARTHUR L. MARIOT, ADR PRINCIPLES AND PRACTICE 127 (1997) ("Mediation is a facilitative process in which disputing parties engage the assistance of an impartial third party, the mediator, who helps them to try to arrive at an agreed resolution of their dispute. The mediator has no authority to make any decisions that are binding on them, but uses certain procedures, techniques and skills to help them to negotiate an agreed resolution of their dispute without adjudication"); STEPHEN B. GOLDBERG ET. AL, DISPUTE RESOLUTION: NEGOTIATION, MEDIATION, AND OTHER PROCESSES 123 (1999) (mediation is negotiation carried out with the assistance of a third party. The mediator, in contrast to the arbitrator or judge, has no power to impose an outcome on disputing parties. Despite the lack of "teeth" in the mediation process, the involvement of a mediator alters the dynamics of negotiations. Depending on what seems to be impeding (an) agreement, the mediator may attempt to encourage exchange of information, provide new information, help the parties to understand each other's views, let them know that their concerns are understood; promote a productive level of emotional expression; deal with differences in perceptions and interest between negotiations and constituents (including lawyers and client); help negotiators realistically, assess alternatives to settlement, learn (often in separate sessions with each party) about those interest the parties are reluctant to disclose to each other and invent solutions that meet the fundamental interests of all parties).
51. *See* Nadja Alexander, *The Mediation Metamodel: Understanding Practice*, 26(1) CONFLICT RES. Q. (2008).
52. *Id.*

whether referred to by the expression conciliation, mediation or an expression of similar import, whereby parties request a third person or persons ('the conciliator') to assist them in their attempt to reach an amicable settlement of their dispute arising out of or relating to a contractual or other legal relationship. The conciliator does not have the authority to impose upon the parties a solution to the dispute."[53] The UNCITRAL, which was using the term "conciliation," has now shifted to using the term "mediation" in the amendments of 2018 for a wider acceptance.

The pragmatic approach also considers the test of reconciling the use of "mediation" and "conciliation" separately under the Arbitration & Conciliation Act 1996 and the CPC 1908. Arguably, pragmatists consider it to be a drafting error since the scales showing the equivalence of the terms "mediation" and "conciliation" are overwhelmingly precise and sound, leaving no scope for a distinction between the terms. Typically, where the words used in the statutory provision are vague and ambiguous, or where the plain and ordinary meaning of its words or grammatical construction thereof would lead to confusion, absurdity, repugnancy with other provisions, the courts may, instead of adopting a plain and grammatical construction, use the interpretive tools to set right the situation, by adding or omitting or substituting words in the statute.[54] When faced with a defective provision in a statute, courts prefer to assume that the draftsman had committed a mistake rather than concluding that the legislature has deliberately introduced an absurd or irrational statutory provision.[55]

A departure from the literal rule of plain and straight reading can be only in exceptional cases, where the anomalies make the literal compliance of a provision impossible or absurd or impractical to defeat the very object of the provision. However, pragmatists submit that when the terms "mediation" and "conciliation" are reasonably understood in one particular sense and are assigned a particular meaning in common parlance, the manner of placement of these words in the Arbitration Act and CPC lead to an absurd result, rendering mediations without legal status. Therefore, pragmatists justify that it must be regarded as a clerical or typographical error in drafting, resulting in two words being used separately, which mean the same thing.

Assuming "mediation" and "conciliation" to be legally synonymous may indeed help draw some coherent conclusions, keeping in mind that the main effort of the pragmatic approach is about legal harmonization of mediation and conciliation and promoting a standardized framework.[56]

---

53. Model Law on Conciliation, 2002, Art. 1(3).
54. *See* Afcons Infrastructure Limited & Anr. v. Cherian Varkey Construction Co. Pvt. Ltd. (2010) 8 SCC 24 (the principles of statutory interpretation are well settled. Where the words of the statute are clear and unambiguous, the provision should be given its plain and normal meaning, without adding or rejecting any words. There is, however, an exception to this general rule).
55. *Id.*
56. *See* SRIRAM PANCHU, MEDIATION PRACTICE & LAW THE PATH TO SUCCESSFUL DISPUTE RESOLUTION 321 (2015) ("While court-annexed mediation has received quite a fillip in the last decade, the field of private mediation is yet to take off and it will be some time before its potential is realized and achieved. However, the legislative framework must be put in place to ensure its success when that time comes. Having established mediation centers in the Supreme Court, all High Courts and some district courts, there is a need to ensure that the process continues to move forward").

First, whether parties mediate or conciliate, it would be doing so under the framework of the Arbitration Act, giving mediations sanctity and not leave it unhinged without any legal framework.

Second, although "mediation" and "conciliation" are separated under section 89 of CPC 1908, it does not evidence a diversity in concept but merely a diversity in the forums where the process of mediation may be undertaken under a different legal regime—either the Arbitration Act or the LSA 1987—depending on whether parties have consented. Thus, where section 89(2)(a) is in operation, where the parties consent to conciliate, parties would be referred to conciliation under the Arbitration Act, whereby a successful settlement has the effect of an arbitral award on agreed terms under sections 74 and 30 of the Act, and the settlement is placed before the court for disposal of the *lis*. On the other hand, where section 89(2)(c) is in operation, where the parties do not consent, the parties are referred to mediation under the LSA 1987, whereby a successful settlement has the effect of Lok Adalat award, which is deemed to be a decree of the civil court under section 21 of the LSA 1987, and the settlement is placed before the court for disposal of the *lis*. In either case, the pragmatists proffer that section 89 is not a divider between the two concepts. Instead, it provides two different forums with two different governing laws—one that takes the parties to the arbitration (when there is consent) and the other that takes the parties to LSA 1987 (when consent is absent).

[B] Formalistic Approach

The proponents of the formalistic approach state that private mediations are without any legislative support or legal recognition, sort of hanging in midair without legal status, though the two processes may be essentially the same as involving a third-party neutral who facilitates the negotiation between the parties to bring parties to an amicable solution (in conciliation, the third-party neutral being more "interventionist" by providing settlement propositions).[57] This may also be the majority view.

A mediator facilitates discussion between the parties directly or by communicating with each other through the mediator, by assisting the parties in identifying issues, reducing misunderstandings, clarifying priorities, exploring areas of compromise, generating options in an attempt to solve the dispute, and emphasizing that it is the parties' responsibility for making decisions which affect them. On the other hand, a conciliator in the exercise of his powers under sections 67 and 73 of the Arbitration Act makes proposals for a settlement of the dispute by formulating or reformulating the terms of a possible settlement. In a way, a mediator's role is lesser than that of a conciliator, or a conciliator's role is greater than that of a mediator.

57. *See* SRIRAM PANCHU, MEDIATION PRACTICE & LAW THE PATH TO SUCCESSFUL DISPUTE RESOLUTION 321 (2015) ("Currently, the law does not protect the title 'mediator'. Mediators operating under the court mediation scheme are regulated by rules framed under the CPC but there is no regulation of mediators outside of the court mediation scheme. There is no requirement for training or certification, code of conduct or regulation of behavior. These aspects are essential for the success of mediation").

Formalists often rely on the Delhi High Court's decision in *Shri Ravi Aggarwal v. Shri Anil Jagota*,[58] where the court took the view that a mediated settlement agreement partakes the character of a private agreement which is sought to be enforced by one of the parties alleging a breach while the other party is alleging due compliance. The court held that the remedy of execution of such mediated settlements was not available under the provisions of the Arbitration Act and that its enforcement had to be in the manner of enforcing a private agreement. The decision demonstrates that settlement agreements in private mediations would not be enforceable under sections 73 and 74 of the Arbitration Act.[59]

Some formalists, nevertheless, concede that the "practice" of mediation and conciliation may not be distinct—that an evaluative form of mediation would tantamount to an interventionist conciliation. But legal separation takes precedence in the formalists' view, particularly since the enforcement regimes for mediation and conciliation are unequivocally distinct. The statutory construct that governs conciliation—i.e., the Arbitration Act—does not govern private mediation, and the statutory constructs that govern court-referred mediations and conciliations are also substantially different. Formalists, thus, emphasize these distinctions to posit the reason for the differential treatment of conciliation and mediation in section 30 of the Arbitration Act and section 89 of the CPC 1908, given that these statutory provisions separate "mediation" and "conciliation" terms with a punctuation mark (comma). Thus, applying the rules of statutory interpretation, the formalists argue that the legislature makes a clear distinction between conciliation and mediation.

Further, formalists refer to section 62 of the Arbitration Act to show that conciliation is only possible with the parties' consent. This includes scenarios for referring parties to conciliation under section 89 of the CPC—Part III of the Arbitration Act governs the court-referred conciliation proceedings.[60] When a settlement is reached in a court-referred conciliation, it is enforceable like a decree of the court having regard to section 74 (read with section 30) of the Arbitration Act. Since the court continues to retain control and jurisdiction over the cases which it refers to conciliations, such conciliated settlements are placed before the court for its record and disposal of the *lis*. With respect to the settlement of issues that were not the subject matter of the suit (and parties may go beyond), such settlements are also governed by section 74 (read with section 30) of the Arbitration Act.

In case of court-referred mediations under the auspices of section 89 and Rule 1A Order X of the CPC 1908, the court may refer parties to mediation without their consent, after which the mediation proceedings are governed under the LSA 1987, as well as the Mediation Rules of the respective High Court (which Rules are generally based on the Civil Procedure Mediation Rules of the Civil Procedure Alternative Dispute Resolution

58. (2009) SCC Online Del 1475.
59. Cf. SRIRAM PANCHU, MEDIATION PRACTICE & LAW THE PATH TO SUCCESSFUL DISPUTE RESOLUTION 321 (2015) (that the matter should have been considered with a broader view and a settlement agreement reached by consent should have been given effect to).
60. *See* Afcons Infrastructure Ltd. v. Cherian Varkey Construction Co. (P) Ltd. & Ors (2010) 8 SCC 24.

and Mediation Rules 2003). But first, the court would refer parties to a suitable institution or person, who is deemed to be a Lok Adalat and, as a result, the LSA 1987 is applied as if the dispute were referred to a Lok Adalat under the provisions of LSA 1987. In a way, court-referred mediations are deemed to be a reference to Lok Adalat. However, as the court retains its control and jurisdiction over the matter, the mediated settlement will have to be placed before the court for recording the settlement and disposal of the *lis*. Whenever such a settlement is placed before the court, it shall apply the principles of Rules 3 and 3A of Order XXIII of CPC 1908 (on the compromise of suit) and then render a decree in accordance with the settlement.

However, if the mediated settlement includes issues that were not the subject matter of the suit, the same will be governed by section 21 of the LSA 1987, by which the mediated settlement shall be deemed to be a decree of a civil court. The legal circumstances governing court-referred mediations are entirely unlike court-referred conciliations.

Thus, there is a discord in the present position of law governing mediation and conciliation. It is generally agreed that there is no law governing mediation in India. But even if we go by the view that the Arbitration Act may also govern private mediation, such position becomes inconsistent with the clear difference between mediation and conciliation in court-referred processes. Any which way, India is in a situation where mediations (private, including institutional mediation) lack the requisite legislative support and legal recognition, or that it lacks clarity, at the least.

On a related note, pre-litigation mediation laws are also generally critiqued for being restrictive in their outworking. For instance, while the Commercial Court Act 2015 (or CCA 2015) mandates pre-litigation mediation—that parties must mandatorily (irrespective of any consent) mediate before instituting a suit in a court—it gives no opportunity to parties to mediate in private settings before a mutually appointed mediator, or by appointing a mediation institution. Rather, the CCA 2015 redirects parties to a court-referred-like system primarily governed by the LSA 1987, whereby parties may only mediate before an authority specified or recognized under the CCA 1987. This is generally considered a constrained approach, and perhaps such an approach may have been necessary for the lack of any statutory framework governing mediation in private settings and the unsuitability of the Arbitration Act, which necessitates consent between parties.

[C] The Mediation Bill

On December 20, 2021, a Bill on mediation was introduced in the winter session of the Parliament.[61] However, the Mediation Bill was referred to a Parliamentary Standing Committee on Law and Justice. While the Bill is a welcomed and is expected to be

61. Areeb Uddin Ahmed, *Centre Will Introduce New Law on Mediation: Law Minister Kiren Rijiju*, Bar & Bench (2021), https://www.barandbench.com/news/law-policy/centre-will-introduce-new-law-on-mediation-law-minister-kiren-rijiju.

serious game changer in the landscape of laws covering dispute resolution in India, the Bill was riddled by numerous issues, some of which are covered hereinbelow.

[1] Conformity with the Model Law on Mediation 2018

The Bill does not conform with the UNCITRAL Model Law on Mediation 2018, which provides all aspects of the mediation law, including the ratification of the 2018 UN Convention on International Settlement Agreements Resulting from Mediation (the "Singapore Convention")—something that is expected to be uniform among the Convention parties (as far as possible).

The Model Law is designed to assist countries in reforming and modernizing their laws on mediation procedure; most importantly, it provides uniform rules in respect of the mediation process and aims to encourage the use of mediation and ensure greater predictability and certainty in its use.

These goals cannot be achieved if India deviates from the Model Law, thus, making India unattractive for international mediations. The adoption does not inhibit the legislature from adding additional value features like pre-litigation mediation, time limits, online and community mediations, Mediation Council of India, etc. However, the Model Law must be the backbone (like in the case of the Arbitration & Conciliation Act 1996, which is also based on a UNCITRAL Model Law).

UNCITRAL has also provided a draft Guide to Enactment and Use of the Model Law (April 1, 2020), which may be relied upon in the preparation of the Mediation Bill 2021.

[2] Providing a Universal Coverage of Other Statutes

The Bill covers a number of amendments to other statutes like the Indian Contract Act 1872 (section 28), the Arbitration & Conciliation Act 1996 (Part III), and the Code of Civil Procedure 1908 (section 89 and relevant Rules under various Orders). In addition, any other statute providing for resolution of dispute through conciliation in accordance with the Arbitration & Conciliation Act 1996 is also construed as reference to mediation under the Bill. This ensures a universal consistency among various relevant/related statutory provisions.

Similarly, the Bill will need to contemplate that in case of court or tribunal-annexed mediations, it is the respective rules that will govern the court or tribunal-annexed mediations, and that mediation by a Lok Adalat will be governed by the relevant provisions (or rules) under the Legal Services Authorities Act 1987.

Furthermore, since the Bill will be a stand-alone Act on mediation, it is important this is the primary legislation for mediation in India. Hence, the Bill should have an overriding effect, except where the Bill is contemplated to not apply (like in case of court or tribunal-annexed mediations). Similarly, the Bill's application is doubtful in scenarios where an arbitral tribunal attempts to facilitate the settlement of a dispute on its own (instead of referring the same to a mediator) under section 30 of the Arbitration & Conciliation Act 1996. In such cases, the provisions of Part I of the said Act will apply and the settlement will have the status of an arbitral award on agreed terms under section 30 of the said Act.

[3] *Reference to a "Place of Mediation" for the Application of Mediation Bill in International Scenarios*

The inclusion of "place of mediation" as a concept to govern the application of the Mediation Bill would be incompatible in the case of international mediations. For example, where foreign law governs the mediation proceedings, but the mediation takes place in India, the Bill would also end up applying to the mediation. As a consequence, a challenge against the mediated settlement would then lie both in India and abroad. Hence, "place of mediation" only creates confusion and would never work in the context of international mediations, which do not operate based on the concept of "place" or "seat" as per the Singapore Convention.

If at all, the only relevance of a place of mediation would be to determine the competent court (i.e., where a set-aside action will lie) if the Mediation Bill applies to the mediation either by express choice or where both parties' place of business/ habitual residence is in India. The following matrix, in the form of a table, comments on the different criteria available for the application of the Mediation Bill in international mediations. In that, columns 2 and 3 are preferable for their legal coherence:

(1) Place of Mediation	*(2) Place of Business*	*(3) Choice of Law*	*(4) Choice of Court*
Not to be considered a determining factor for considering the application of Part I of the Bill since international mediations (as per the Singapore Convention) do not operate on "place."	Unless parties agree otherwise, the parties' place of business/ habitual residence in India should determine the application of the Bill.	Where parties have expressly agreed on the application of the Bill, the Bill should apply to such mediations.	Where the Bill applies, and unless otherwise agreed by the parties, the court within whose territorial limits the mediation takes place should have jurisdiction.

[4] *Inclusion of an Express Coverage of Investor-State Disputes*

The Singapore Convention is crucial since its signatories/parties will recognize the use of mediation as a legitimate and credible tool for resolving cross-border disputes. While it is clear that the commercial disputes/commercial mediation will most likely be contemplated in the Mediation Bill, the Bill should spell out or expressly include investor-State disputes.

Mediation, aided by the Singapore Convention, is now a credible addition to the investor-State disputes settlement (ISDS) processes. Arbitration will not always be a solution for ISDS involving India or Indian investors, given the increasing costs, general dissatisfaction over the award, loss of time and resources, etc.

[5] *Inclusion of an Express Coverage of Investor-State Disputes*

The Singapore Convention is crucial since its signatories/parties will recognize the use of mediation as a legitimate and credible tool for resolving cross-border disputes. While it is clear that the commercial disputes/commercial mediation will most likely be contemplated in the Mediation Bill, the Bill should spell out or expressly include investor-State disputes.

[6] *Pre-institution or Pre-litigation Mediation*

In a revolutionary way, the Mediation Bill captures pre-institution/pre-litigation mediation, setting the general law that parties must take steps to settle their disputes, irrespective of the existence of a mediation agreement, and before the filing of any suit or proceeding in any court/tribunal or commencing any substantive proceedings before an arbitral tribunal. The Bill contemplates that such pre-institution mediation may be conducted before any mediation institution/service provider or a mediator of the parties' choice.

This necessitates a corresponding amendment in section 12A of the Commercial Courts Act 2015, whereby pre-institution mediation is not restricted to only those conducted by the authorities constituted/authorized under the Legal Services Authorities Act 1987.

§1.05 MEDIATION FRAMEWORK

There are many accepted approaches to explaining the notion of mediation, such as categorizing mediation as an "alternative" to litigation before a judicial body or by taking a more holistic approach of a multifaceted dispute resolution framework. The subsequent chapters have been thoughtfully inserted to expound on mediation and its allied themes in an overarching manner.

For starters, however, taking the definitional route, the book follows the grounding provided by the UNCITRAL Model Law on International Commercial Mediation and International Settlement Agreements Resulting from Mediation 2018 (Model Law on Mediation). The Model Law on Mediation defines mediation as "a process, whether referred to by the expression mediation, conciliation or an expression of similar import, whereby parties request a third person or persons ('the mediator') to assist them in their attempt to reach an amicable settlement of their dispute arising out of or relating to a contractual or other legal relationship."[62] While the explanation may seem pretty

62. Model Law on International Commercial Mediation and International Settlement Agreements Resulting from Mediation, 2018, Art. 1, para. 3.

elementary, there are several undergirding aspects that hold this explanation together. Indeed, these aspects may be as complex as the legal framework governing arbitration or litigation (if not more).

There is a hexagonal approach to describing the legal framework that would govern a mediation. *One*, there is the agreement to mediate, which lays down the contractual foundations. *Two*, the procedure, or in the case of institutional mediation, a set of curial or procedural rules that enable a streamlined procedure. *Three*, a choice of substantive law that would govern the resulting mediated settlement agreement. *Four*, an ethical code,[63] generally available as soft law, would govern the mediator and the participants. *Five*, a mediation statute that forms the backbone of the process and gives it legal status. Finally, *six*, an international convention for cross-border enforcement of the settlement agreements resulting from mediation.

This hexagonal interplay makes the process of mediation a legally robust mechanism for dispute settlement and integrate-able with other forms of dispute settlement—the Convention is the cornerstone of international mediation. In the subsequent chapters, the authors will refer to this hexagonal relationship to emphasize mediation's robustness for dispute resolution.

§1.06 CONCLUDING REMARKS

Mediation as a viable alternative is still in an amorphous state. This is not only from the standpoint of mediation as an isolated (self-contained) dispute settlement mechanism but also in combination with other (more established) modes like arbitration and litigation. Carefully implemented strategies are necessary for achieving a high degree of acceptability, including developing awareness, inculcating mediation advocacy, building capacities, creating institutional frameworks and legal standards (including ethics).

Resistance to change is quite natural, including from the stakeholders (all boiling down to the lack of awareness and capacity).[64] But imagine, for example, trying to slide a heavy crate across a concrete floor—you may push harder and harder on the crate and not move it at all. This is because the static friction responds to what you do—it increases to be equal to and in the opposite direction of your push. But if you finally push hard enough, the crate seems to slip suddenly and starts to move.[65] And once in motion, it is easier to keep it in motion than it is to get it started. Mediation, too, will experience the same.

There is a significant responsibility on the shoulders of advocates, followed by users. Advocates have an overriding duty to assisting the courts in furthering the use of ADR, including mediation and facilitating the speedy, effective, and efficient resolution

63. *See generally*, MODEL STANDARDS OF CONDUCT FOR MEDIATORS (Am. Arbitration Ass'n 2005). *See also*, Omer Shapira, *A Critical Assessment of the Model Standards of Conduct for Mediators (2005): Call for Reform*, 100 MARQ. L. REV. 81 (2016).

64. *See* Justice Dhananjaya Y. Chandrachud, *Mediation—Realizing the Potential and Designing Implementation Strategies*, https://lawcommissionofindia.nic.in/adr_conf/chandrachud3.pdf.

65. *See Chapter 5 Further Applications of Newton's Laws: Friction, Drag and Elasticity*, UNIVERSITY OF CENTRAL FLORIDA, https://pressbooks.online.ucf.edu/phy2053bc/chapter/friction/.

of disputes. Hence, advocates (along with their clients, the users) must evaluate their dispute resolution options meticulously and avoid a remedy that is worse than the damage/injury. Else, one might just end up like the pigeons who were terrified by the appearance of a kite and called upon the Hawk to defend them. When the pigeons admitted the Hawk into the cote, they found that he made more havoc in one day than the Kite could pounce upon pigeons in a whole year. In the form of allegories, these concluding remarks best express the issues concerning the use of mediation.

CHAPTER 2
Role and Approach of the Mediator

Jonathan Rodrigues & Joel Lee

§2.01 INTRODUCTION

Anecdotally, 70% of all disputes that get referred to mediation internationally are settled. Detractors of mediation will want to focus on the 30% that do not get settled and use that as a reason for not referring a matter to mediation, citing the waste of time or resources, or how mediation does not guarantee an outcome. We do not propose to argue these points here, except to note the immortal words of the internet meme philosophers, "Haters Gonna Hate." Putting the haters aside, 70% by any measure is an impressive figure. It is even more impressive when you consider that 70% that are settled have already seen attempts to resolve them, by either the parties or their advocates. And chances are, those parties and their advocates are probably convinced, going into mediation, that there is no way mediation will succeed where they have failed. Regardless, there is a 70% settlement rate.

Something about the mediation process almost "magically" brings parties together and helps them identify and explore solutions to their dispute that they could not do otherwise. Of course, the mediation process itself has no life on its own, and what magic happens occurs through the expert guidance of a skilled mediator.

It is important at this point to highlight that mediators are not homogenous. Every mediator has their style and modus operandi, which can be affected by their, *inter alia*, background, profession, training, personality, and culture. A mediator also evolves at different points in their career, and their thinking and behaviors at mediation can change from age to age. And while one might be tempted to think that, at the very least, mediators need to go through some form of uniform basic training, even this would not be accurate. Some jurisdictions do not require training, assessment, or accreditation before someone can hang their shingle out as a mediator. Of course, in a situation like this, the Latin maxim "caveat emptor"[1] springs to mind. Other jurisdictions have more stringent requirements. For example, in India, mediators may be required (by institutions or court-annexed centers) to participate in a standard 40-hour training before they can advertise their professional services as a "mediator."

The authors submit that for one to represent themselves as a mediator, that person must have the requisite knowledge, technique, and mediation skills. This chapter will explore the approach that a mediator might take to resolve the parties' dispute. We will next look at the various techniques a mediator might deploy at various points in the mediation process. We will be looking at both these areas fairly generally. This chapter will then turn its attention to a perennial debate about whether the role of a mediator should be facilitative or evaluative before looking at some of the techniques that a mediator can use to deal with barriers to settlement in mediation.

Before moving on, we would like to highlight that the rest of this chapter assumes that a mediator understands the basic definition and concept of mediation. Put simply, it is a process facilitated by a third-party neutral to assist parties in resolving their dispute. Parties enter into this process voluntarily and are empowered as the decision-makers to their outcome. The mediator, therefore, has no power to impose an outcome on the parties, and any settlement agreement the parties come to is, subject to the requirements of contract law, a binding contract which can then be enforced in the domestic courts. In cross-border disputes, the settlement agreement may be enforced internationally either by suing overseas or having a domestic judgment recognized overseas or by the mechanisms of the Singapore Convention on Mediation.

§2.02 FUNDAMENTALS OF THE APPROACH

[A] Three Approaches: Interest, Rights, and Power

How does a mediator approach resolving a dispute between the parties? Ury, Brett, and Goldberg suggest three basic approaches to resolving disputes: interests, rights, and power.[2] The difference in these three approaches is perhaps best understood through an illustration.

Consider a dispute occurs where a miner claims the loss of his boots against the mining company. The miner expects the mining company to take responsibility for his loss because he feels that they should have provided adequate security. This claim gets rejected by the shift boss, citing some company workplace rules. The miner then escalates the matter and is joined by other miners in union solidarity resulting in a protest. The matter comes to the superintendent's attention, who, once made aware of the situation, replaces the stolen boots for the miner.

The resolution to this situation could have been any of the following scenarios: a binding decision of a third party, a decision by the miner to drop his claim or by the

---

1. "Let the buyer beware."
2. *See* WILLIAM L. URY, JEANNE M. BRETT & STEPHEN B. GOLDBERG, GETTING DISPUTES RESOLVED 3–19 (1988) (hereinafter "URY").

organization to grant it, or a negotiated agreement. In each of these scenarios, the parties could have focused their attention on determining who is right, determining who is powerful/dominant, or reconciling their underlying interests, respectively.

When the miner pressed his claim that the organization should do something about his stolen boots, the miner focused on rights (blaming the company for failing to provide adequate security). When the shift boss responded by referring to the rules, he followed the miner's lead and continued the confrontation based on the rights narrative. The frustrated miner then provokes a walkout with other miners, displaying his (or their) power and the organization's dependency on the workforce in the mine's production. Of course, the organization could have equally threatened their jobs or salaries.

What the superintendent chose to do was to focus on reconciling interests. Interests are essentially what one is truly concerned about and encompass our needs and concerns. The miner was interested in having boots and a shift's pay, and the company was interested in the miner working his assigned shift. So, although rights and power were involved, the superintendent approached the stolen boots situation as a joint problem, one that the company could help solve and focus on for its benefit (e.g., improved security for the miners and equipment belonging to the organization leading to happier and more productive miners).

There is an interrelationship between interests, rights, and power. Represented as concentric circles, interests represent the innermost circle. Rights would be the middle circle, and the outermost circle would be power. This suggests that interests are often embedded in the language of rights and liabilities and power dynamics. Therefore, reconciliation of interests must also take place in those contexts (Figure 2.1).

Figure 2.1 Relationship Between Interest, Rights, and Power

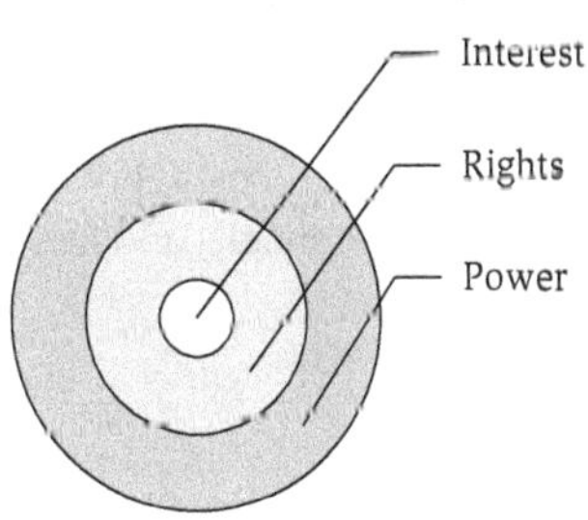

This explains why attempts to resolving disputes do not always focus on interests. Some mediations may focus on determining who is right (e.g., when advocates argue about the merits of the case or the position at law), while others may focus on who is more powerful (e.g., when parties are exchanging threats).

A mediator, therefore, seeks to resolve a dispute by navigating through these three circles. Many mediated settlements need to be a good mix of all the three: satisfaction of parties' interests, a discussion of rights and liabilities, and addressing relative power and dominance.

[B] Criteria of the Approach

How does one decide what approach to use? Ury, Brett, and Goldberg[3] suggest that all three approaches generate costs and benefits. Therefore, when considering the most appropriate approach for the dispute at hand, one may focus on four criteria:

(i) transaction costs;
(ii) satisfaction with outcomes;
(iii) effect on the relationship; and
(iv) recurrence of disputes.

These criteria provide a basis for assessing one's dispute resolution approach, noting the possible effects (and side effects) of focusing on interests, rights, or power. In determining which approach is more appropriate, one is likely to encounter the interrelationship of the criteria. In the words of Ury, Brett, and Goldberg:[4]

> These four different criteria are interrelated. Dissatisfaction with outcomes may produce strain on the relationship, which contributes to the recurrence of disputes, which in turn increases transaction costs. Because the different costs typically increase and decrease together, it is convenient to refer to all four together as the costs of disputing. When we refer to a particular approach as high cost or low-cost, we mean not just transaction costs but also dissatisfaction with outcomes, strain on the relationship, and recurrence of disputes.
>
> Sometimes one cost can be reduced only by increasing another, particularly in the short term. If father and son sit down to discuss their conflicting interests concerning curfew, the short-term transaction costs in terms of time and energy may be high. Still, these costs may be more than offset by the benefits of a successful negotiation—an improved relationship and the cessation of curfew violations.

We suggest that in most situations, it is the reconciliation of interests, rather than the determination of who is right or who is more powerful/dominant, that is the most effective. This is not to suggest that an interests-based focus is always appropriate, but it does tend to result in lower transaction costs, greater satisfaction with outcomes, better relationships (professional and personal), and less likely recurrence of disputes.[5]

§2.03 MEDIATION STAGES

We now turn to look through the lens of the various techniques a mediator might deploy at various points in the mediation process.

One of the key roles of the mediator is as a process manager, and this process is often expressed through the stages of mediation. The mediator guides parties through the stages of mediation that helps them move from problem to solution. There are

3. *Id.*
4. *Id.*
5. *Id.*

many models of the stages of mediation. Some represent it visually as a diamond, and some have more stages than others.

Regardless of the model, the mediation process can be distilled into broadly four stages: (i) opening; (ii) exploration; (iii) negotiation (joint and private sessions); and (iv) closing. To be clear, these four stages occur during the mediation itself.

It is useful here to point out that there are sometimes two other stages that might precede depending on the mediator's preferences, the institution providing mediation services, the number of parties, the complexity and nature of the case, the existence of ongoing arbitration/litigation proceedings, etc.

These are the stages of convening and pre-mediation. The former involves preliminary case management, including bringing parties to the table, getting an agreement to mediate, and setting up logistical matters. The latter can involve getting parties and their advocates to think through their interests, encourage them to do research, and develop a plan or strategy for the mediation session. It can also cover some matters typically covered in the opening stage, like setting guidelines for the mediation and confirming authority to settle.

Figure 2.2 provides a visual representation of the stages of mediation. We will now go on to look at the four stages that occur within a mediation.

Figure 2.2 Stages of Mediation

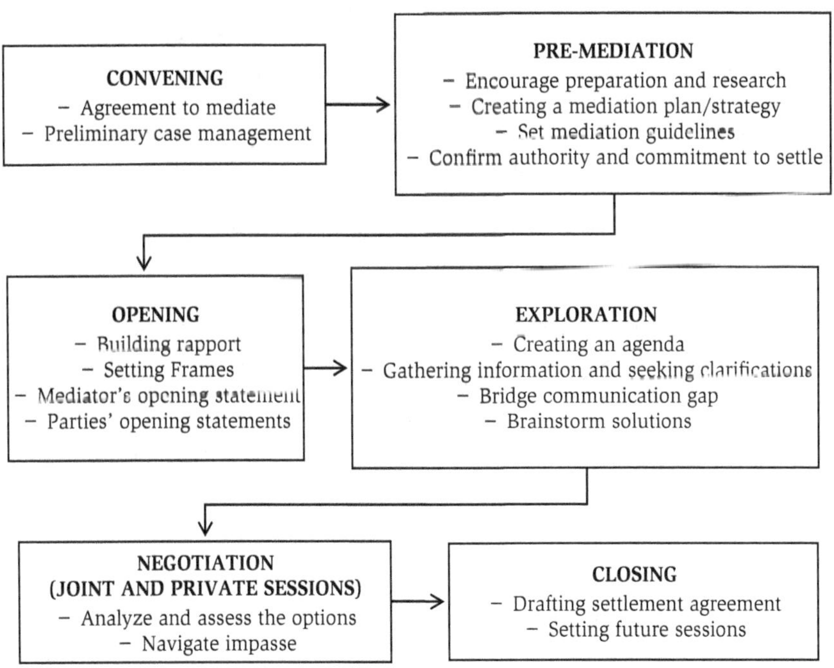

[A] Opening

As mentioned, the stages of convening and pre-mediation sometimes precede the opening stage. The opening is the first time when all parties, their advocates (if any), and the mediator convene, and this is a key and important part in ensuring that the mediation gets off to a good start. There are two main parts to the opening: the mediator's opening statement and the parties' opening statements.

Turning first to the mediator's opening statement, we paraphrase a familiar adage, "An ounce of framing is worth a pound of reframing." The opening is where the mediator sets all the frames needed to ensure that the mediation goes as smoothly as possible.

Through the mediator's opening statement, the mediator seeks to achieve several things:

(1) *Introductions*: The mediator introduces himself and establishes his credentials. This seeks to give parties and their advocates confidence in the expertise of the mediator and establishes credibility. As part of these introductions, the mediation may also want to confirm parties and advocates' schedules for the mediation and reassure parties that choosing to come to mediation was the correct thing to do. Parties and advocates are also asked to introduce themselves. While this may be a seemingly small gesture, it can serve as an important step in personalizing parties to one another, smoothen the way for an eventual agreement. Essentially, rapport building begins here.

(2) *Purpose and principles of mediation*: The mediator uses this opportunity to check and clarify with the party what their purpose is and what they expect from the mediation process. It is trite to say that while many people (advocates and laypeople alike) think they know what mediation is, they often have misconceptions, which, if not corrected, can impede what mediation is trying to achieve. Some of the things that may be clarified are as follows:

- *Voluntariness*: Mediation is largely a voluntary process in two ways. First, in engaging in the process of mediation (this may not apply if parties are at the table because of some requirement making mediation mandatory). Second, in entering into any kind of agreement. This second aspect of voluntariness is more important. It reflects the principle in mediation that parties are empowered to solve their problems and, in appropriate circumstances, terminate the mediation.
- *Confidentiality*: A key aspect of mediation is that "what happens in mediation stays in mediation." This manifests in two ways. First, anything that is said in mediation is confidential. Second, anything that is said in a private session exists within a more specific bubble of confidentiality. Confidentiality is important in mediation because parties need to be comfortable with sharing information with the mediator. Without

quality information, the mediator is unable to help parties define the problem and explore solutions.

- *Role of the mediator*: The mediator uses this opportunity to set and clarify expectations about their role. Many parties and advocates come to mediation expecting the mediator to play a pseudo-adjudicative role and simply "tell them what to do." The mediator must clarify that their role is to help parties share their perspectives about the dispute, define the problem, and guide them to explore solutions. In other words, the mediator does not have the power to impose a decision on the parties, and any outcome reached will be because the parties agreed to it. The mediator is also likely to clarify at this stage that they are neutral and impartial vis-à-vis the parties and that there are no conflicts of interest.
- *Role of the parties and advocates*: It is also important for the mediator to set and clarify expectations about the role of parties and advocates. Many people come into mediation with an adversarial, win-lose mindset. This should not be surprising as most people's reference experience for dispute resolution is litigation. The adversarial mindset is, of course, anathema to mediation, and it is at this early point where the mediator has the opportunity to influence how parties and advocates should act and respond in mediation. Parties should be open about their interests and concerns, be prepared to consider possible solutions presented by the other party, and be prepared to present possible solutions for the other party's consideration. Advocates should not play a passive, or aggressive, or passive-aggressive role. Advocates need to understand that they are there to help the mediator and the parties find a workable solution to their problem and protect their interests (and not necessarily the legal position) of their clients. To this end, the mediator sees advocates as partners in that collaborative endeavor.
- *Outcome*: As mentioned, many parties come to mediation seeking a win-lose victory. Mediation seems to achieve some form of a mutually beneficial outcome for the parties. This requires a cooperative and collaborative mindset that searches for solutions rather than victory. It is also useful at this point for parties and advocates to be reminded that any settlement agreements reached are binding.

(3) *Process of mediation*: The mediator should familiarize the parties and advocates with the process of mediation. This includes the stages of mediation, the taking of breaks, joint and private sessions, etc. It serves the important purpose of reducing uncertainty and, thereby, cognitive dissonance on the part of parties and advocates, making them more open and comfortable to what occurs during the mediation.

(4) *Establish guidelines for communication and interaction:* For mediation to succeed, open and constructive communication is vital. This is sometimes difficult to achieve because parties in dispute may have had acrimonious

interactions. As such, the mediator needs to establish certain guidelines for communication and interaction. These can include the following:

- Parties taking turns to speak.
- Keeping interruptions to a minimum.
- Ensuring that all communication and interaction are respectful and constructive.
- No abusive language.

(5) *Authority to settle*: The mediator needs to confirm with parties that they have the authority to decide for themselves or the person/organization they represent. This is crucial to ensuring a productive session, where commitments made will be respected.

Now that the mediator has delivered the opening statement, the parties are invited to deliver their opening statements. These statements might be scripted or spontaneous, and are intended for parties to share their perspectives on the matter, how it has affected them, and what they hope to achieve in mediation. The expression of emotions is welcome, although it is expected that these be expressed civilly and constructively to invite empathy and not attract hostility.

While it may vary from mediator to mediator, many mediators prefer the parties to make the opening statement, as it is, after all, their problem. Advocates are usually invited to speak after the parties, highlighting certain points or raising points that their clients may not have raised. Advocates must not hijack the mediation by speaking on their client's behalf and steer the discussion toward legal positions and rights. Again, it is understandable that advocates are much more familiar with litigation and arbitration and are more used to speaking on behalf of their clients on matters of law. But it is important to remember that this is not mediation's purpose and the mediator has to manage the process carefully so that this purpose is not railroaded.

Once parties and advocates have spoken, the mediator follows up with clarifying questions and some form of summary. The summary serves three purposes. First, it is to check in with parties and advocates whether the mediator has understood what they have said correctly. Second, it provides an opportunity for corrections to be made. Finally, it allows the mediator to neutralize and reframe the parties' narratives to pave the way for discussing solutions.

[B] Exploration

The second stage is exploration. This is usually done in a joint session, although it may be done in a private session in certain circumstances. At this point, the mediator has heard the parties' respective sides to the story. The next step is for the mediator to help parties identify the issues they need to discuss to find a solution to their problem. This is done by setting an agenda, which helps keep the conversation focused on the goals and objectives that the parties seek to achieve. It is not within our scope to do a deep dive into agenda setting here, save to make two points. First, agenda items should be inclusive of what any party wants to talk about related to the dispute. Second, agenda items should be phrased neutrally and should not have any sense of priority assigned to it. Put another way, the mediation process is party-centric, and parties should sense that they are key to determining in which direction the mediation proceeds.

Once an agenda has been set, the mediator guides the parties and advocates in gathering more information about the issues. Good options cannot be generated and explored without quality information about parties' interests, perspectives, and constraints. Hence experienced mediators know the value of gathering information and seek to do so in both joint and private sessions. Good mediators make an effort to thoroughly understand the parties and their backgrounds. Of course, the process of information gathering can be catastrophic if mistaken for an inquisition, an interrogation, or a cross-examination. As such, the mediator needs to build and maintain trust and rapport with the parties during this process. At this point, the mediator may deploy various communication skills, including listening, summarizing, reflecting, acknowledging, encouraging, reframing, questioning, just to name a few.

Once enough information has come out, the mediator can then guide parties in exploring the parameters of each issue and begin to brainstorm solutions and generate options.

[C] Negotiation

There is usually not a clear line between the stages of exploration and negotiation. It is more useful to think of these two stages as systemically linked and that the mediator may move from exploration to negotiation and back again as more information surfaces and more options are identified.

This stage seeks to encourage negotiations between the parties. The purpose is to get parties to consider, analyze, and assess the options created and find ways to navigate the impasses that occur. Again, it is important to remember that one seeks an integrative outcome from these negotiations and where parties are looking for opportunities to create practical solutions that are mutually acceptable to both parties.

This can be done by bridging the gap between the parties sufficiently such that they negotiate directly in joint sessions or where the gap is not ready to be closed in private sessions.

At this point, it is appropriate to note that it is at this stage that the use of private sessions may feature quite significantly. The exploration stage typically sees parties in joint sessions. However, some mediators prefer using private sessions in the exploration stage and may move to a joint session only when the parties seem to find common ground or settle on some issues on the agenda. Other mediators prefer to keep the dialogue flowing between parties, build an ongoing relationship of trust, and only go to private sessions when necessary. Much ink has been spilled about whether joint or private sessions are better. The authors take the position that both can be useful, and a mediator must always have a strategic purpose in choosing one over another. Put another way, one or the other should not be used by default or just because the mediator would feel more comfortable. The choice must serve the parties.

In terms of negotiation, while there are many negotiation tools and frameworks that can apply, the authors would like to focus briefly on shuttle negotiation, which is used a fair bit when parties are not in a position to negotiate directly. Shuttle negotiation, by definition, occurs in private session and can be an effective tool in the following circumstances:

- When parties are at loggerheads, the mediator cannot keep the language civil, thus derailing the conversations.
- When parties do not seek to continue the working relationship and simply want to get the matter done and dusted.
- When offers made by either party are anchored in the insult zone, and parties refuse to budge from their positions.
- When parties begin doubting each other based on the offers made at the table and have serious allegations about unrelated matters, not relevant at the mediation.
- When a mediator notices one side is overwhelmed by the language, personality, or the number of stakeholders and representatives on the other side.

[D] Closing

The goal of mediation is to settle the dispute and bring peace and closure to everyone involved, and as anecdotally indicated earlier, 70% of all matters referred to mediation will be settled. In these circumstances, and before asking the parties or their advocates to draft a settlement agreement, the mediator will generally perform a few functions:

- *Loose ends*: Sometimes, in the haste to reach an agreement, parties and advocates may have overlooked certain issues or points which, while ancillary, still need to be resolved. These may have been issues parked for further discussion during the earlier stages of the mediation. The mediator should draw these loose ends for parties and advocates to tie down. For example: in an employment dispute, the mediator will casually check with both parties if they have their expectations clear on the timelines of this renewed contract—when would the salary slip be modified, when would the office space be provided, who gets to choose the personal assistant, how will the promotion be communicated, what happens to the legal notice sent by Party A to Party B for damages?
- *Contextual considerations*: Sometimes, the settlement agreement will be carried out in a location or jurisdiction where norms and customs might differ. This is especially so in cross-border deal mediations. The mediator should ensure that the agreement must be in tune with commonly accepted industry practices and business ethics and not illegally disrupt the status quo of the land, where the impact of the dispute can have diverse consequences on the innumerable stakeholders. If these conditions are not factored in, there are chances that the deal will not be honored and consequently lead to further disputes and loss of hard-earned goodwill.

- *Stress-testing and contingency planning*: Sometimes, the euphoria of agreement may cause parties to take on an overly rosy view of the deal. The mediator should guide the parties and advocates into considering likely hypothetical situations that may occur and consider how they might deal with those situations, and where necessary, set up contingency arrangements.
- *Legal and ethical practices*: The mediator should make sure the settlement achieved has met the criteria of both legal and ethical best practices. The settlement agreement must, of course, be legitimate and enforceable in the court of law. This means that the requirements for a valid contract must be met and that there are no vitiating factors that might affect its validity. For example, the settlement agreement must be entered voluntarily, free from any coercion or threat or misrepresentation. To be fair, it is also the responsibility of parties' advocates to also ensure that these requirements are met. After all, it is in their client's best interests for their settlement agreement to be enforceable and sustainable.

Once these are done, an advocate then moves to the task of drafting the settlement agreement. It is important to note that there are likely to be many iterations of the draft, and there may be matters upon which negotiations have to be made, or in some cases, remade. During this process, the mediator can, of course, assist. They may also invite parties to:

- clarify any doubts, misunderstandings, misinterpretations, or misconceptions about anything that was said or done. These moments often produce free-flowing apologies and compliments;
- express mutual expectations regarding honoring the deal and taking responsibility to realize it is executing within the deadline;
- renovate outdated communication channels between parties—setting new guidelines for meetings, exchange of emails, etc.;
- confirm if the entire deal must remain private and confidential or if parties wish to explore media and public relation exercises.

Of course, this assumes that mediation results in settlement. In a minority of cases, settlement is not immediately reached. The mediator does not hang their head in failure as how they handle this lack of settlement may nonetheless pave the way for future settlement. At this point, the mediator may:

- thank the parties and advocates for their good faith efforts. It is important that parties and advocates do not feel like the time they have spent in mediation was a waste of time, and that at the very least, it was a worthy attempt. This can influence their future attitude toward the present dispute or in future disputes;
- highlight the progress they have made and the possible points of agreements that have already been reached. This can serve two functions. First, it is common for parties to leave the mediation without a settlement and subsequently build on the work done in mediation and reach a settlement. Second,

even if the matter does not get settled outside court, advocates have found that the discussions at mediation have helped focus their case theory on the real issues in dispute, resulting in both time and costs savings for the parties;
- plant the seed for parties to come back to mediation after some time has passed so that they can consider the matter with fresh eyes.

§2.04 MEDIATOR APPROACHES: FACILITATIVE AND EVALUATIVE

There is a perennial debate among mediators about what is sometimes referred to as the facilitative and evaluative divide. Put simply, some believe that a mediator's role should only facilitate a negotiation between the parties, whereas others feel that a mediator's role extends to being evaluative about the substantive matters therein. Leonard Riskin is believed to have begun the trend of labeling neutrals for their styles of mediating.[6] This section seeks to look at both approaches before briefly concluding.

[A] Facilitative Approach

The facilitative approach is often labeled as the "true form,"[7] or the purest form of mediation, whereby a facilitative neutral is simply expected to assist participants in arriving at their solution[8] without playing any kind of a role related to decision-making. As a facilitator, the neutral is not concerned about appraising the agreement arising out of the negotiation between the participants but is rather focused on assisting participants voluntarily reach that self-determined agreement—keeping their "own view regarding the conflict hidden."[9]

This is not to say that the neutral's role here is being apathetic or ignorant of the participants' grievances and interests related to the dispute. On the contrary, this approach is based on the belief that "people involved in the situation have the best understanding of what they need for themselves and from each other."[10] Almost like a tailor who stitches according to the client's desired measurements, a facilitative neutral offers the participants the space to decide their best fit. Entrusted with the power and responsibility of making their own decisions, the results produced by the participants through a facilitative approach are fit better and are more durable.

---

6. *See generally*, Leonard L. Riskin, *Understanding Mediators' Orientations, Strategies, and Techniques: A Grid for the Perplexed*, 1(7) Harv. Neg. L. Rev. 7, 24 (1999) (hereinafter "Riskin").
7. *See generally*, Kimberlee K. Kovach & Lela P. Love, *"Evaluative" Mediation Is an Oxymoron*, 14(2) Alternatives to High-Cost Litigation 31 (1996).
8. *See generally*, Carrie Menkel-Meadow, *The Many Ways of Mediation: The Transformation of Traditions, Ideologies, Paradigms, Practices*, 11 Negotiation J. 217 (2012).
9. *See* Katie Shonk, *Types of Mediation: Choose the Type Best Suited to you Conflict*, Program on Negotiation—Daily Blog (Harvard Law School) (Apr. 12, 2021), https://www.pon.harvard.edu/daily/mediation/types-mediation-choose-type-best-suited-conflict/.
10. *See Models of Mediation*, Steve Hindmarsh, https://www.stevehindmarsh.co.uk/help-and-advice/models-of-mediation/.

On this, Leonard Riskin writes:[11]

> The mediator who facilitates assumes that the parties are intelligent, able to work with their counterparts, and capable of understanding their situations better than the mediator and, perhaps, better than their lawyers. Accordingly, the parties can create better solutions than any mediator might create. Thus, the facilitative mediator assumes that his principal mission is to clarify and to enhance communication between the parties in order to help them decide what to do.

From a literature perspective, it would be safe to state that nearly every mediation practitioner and academic agrees that a facilitative approach leaves no room for an advisory role for a mediator. Facilitative mediation is often seen as a "dialogue process designed to capture the parties' insights, imagination, and ideas that help them to participate in identifying and shaping their preferred outcomes."[12] Therefore, facilitative mediators are expected to enable smooth conversations, promote understanding of issues, guide the participants to focus on interests, encourage creative brainstorming of solutions to problems,[13] including innovative and unorthodox fixes from outside the normative legal box,[14] and conclusively assisting participants to resolve the dispute through a mutually agreed settlement, drafted by themselves, or their advocates.

For a facilitative mediator, parties must understand the mediator's role, especially if parties expect that the mediator will either make the decision or, at the very least, provide an evaluation of the outcome. This should be done fairly early on in mediation, and the authors have suggested that this be explicitly addressed in the mediator's opening statement.

The facilitative role limits the mediator's involvement in the process, restricting any participation in the settlement. Thus, many commentators express it: a facilitative mediator is called to oversee the process, while the participants oversee the outcome.[15] This means that a facilitative mediator prioritizes the means over the end. Being in charge of the process while allowing parties to focus on the resolution, facilitative mediators still have the responsibility to ensure that participants make calculative decisions based on proper knowledge of relevant information and comprehension of the issues.[16] Greenebaum draws a parallel between purposeful involvement of a facilitative neutral and a referee in sports. "They apply the rules and affect the flow, but they do nothing to help the contestants play the game."[17]

Despite not having the legal authority to impose settlements or pass definite orders, the mediator still plays a significant role in helping parties reach a mutually

11. *See generally*, Riskin, *supra* note 6.
12. *See* Joseph P. Stulberg, *Facilitative Versus Evaluative Mediator Orientations: Piercing the "Grid" Lock*, 24(4) Florida State Univ. L. Rev. 985, 1001 (1997) (hereinafter "Stulberg").
13. *See* Lela P. Love, *The Top Ten Reasons Why Mediators Should Not Evaluate*, 24(4) Florida State Univ. L. Rev. 937, 939 (1997).
14. *See generally*, Carole J. Brown, *Facilitative Mediation: The Classic Approach Retains Its Appeal*, Mediate.com (December 2002), https://www.mediate.com/articles/brownc.cfm.
15. *See generally*, Zena Zumeta, *Facilitative Mediator Responds, A*, 2000(2) J. of Disp. Resol. 335 (2000).
16. *See* Tanya M Marcum, Charles R Stoner & Sandra J Perry, *Reframing the Mediation Lens: The Call for a Situational Style of Mediation*, 36 Southern Illinois Univ. L.J. 317, 319 (2012).
17. *See* Edwin H Greenebaum, *On Teaching Mediation*, 1999(1) J. of Dispute Resol. 116, 130 (1999).

satisfactory conclusion. What does a facilitative mediator do then? It is trite that when parties are in dispute, a clear barrier to dispute resolution is a failure to communicate effectively. Therefore, the mediator's skill in restoring communication channels is crucial. As a communication facilitator, the functions a facilitative mediator serves include the following:

- Creating a neutral, safe, and supportive environment for parties to share their perspectives on the dispute, explore their needs and concerns, and constructively work together[18] to find solutions.
- Asking questions to draw out information about interests[19] that lie beneath the parties' extreme initial positions and clarify perspectives, concerns, and constraints. Sometimes, the mediator may receive unhelpful, even irrational responses. The facilitative mediator does not evaluate those responses and understands that it is part of guiding the communication. The onus is on the participants to listen and consider what surfaces in that process.
- Summarize things that have been said to facilitate understanding, as well as to neutralize and reframe appropriately to pave the way for an agreement
- Eliciting responses from parties to developments in the mediation to increase understanding. For example, the mediator may ask one party to respond to what has just been shared by the other party or invite parties to focus on identifying potential overlaps in their respective interests to construct "the common ground on which settlement options start to build."[20]

The idea is to move parties from their polar positions and past orientation and move them toward a mindset focused on the future and problem-solving.[21] This may involve starting on easy to resolve matters and discouraging those that might generate further friction between parties. It should not be taken that by discouraging discussions about the troublesome past, the mediator avoids the difficult issues. The difficult issues must be tackled, and discussion about the past must be sufficient to resolve issues. The mediator, however, may discourage conversations that lead to allegations and counter-allegations that go counter to the purpose of the mediation.

At this point, the authors would like to also focus on several things that are particularly important to a facilitative mediation.

---

18. *See* Murray S. Levin, *The Propriety of Evaluative Mediation: Concerns about the Nature and Quality of an Evaluative Opinion*, 16(2) Ohio State J. on Disp. Resol., 267, 268 (2000) (hereinafter "Levin").
19. *See* Susan Nauss Exon, *The Effects That Mediator Styles Impose on Neutrality and Impartiality Requirements of Mediation*, 42 Univ. of San Francisco L. Rev. 577, 591 (2008) (hereinafter "Exon").
20. *See* Genevieve A Chornenki & Christine E Hart, Bypass Court: A Dispute Resolution Handbook 77 (2nd ed., 2001).
21. *See id.*

[1] Empathy

Much is made of the importance of empathy in interpersonal interactions. Empathy is often considered the "soul of mediation."[22] And while the image of an empathetic and counselor-like mediator attempting to repair a broken relationship is commonly mistaken for a classical mediator,[23] it is important to realize that the mediator does not seek to counsel or aim for reconciliation between the parties. The mediator must, however, work sufficiently with the parties' emotions such that they can move from the past and look to solutions to their problem. This may involve talking about their emotions in a contained and constructive manner.

[2] Active Listening

A key part of being a communication facilitator is the ability to listen actively. It is not surprising that a large part of "creating an optimal environment for negotiation and coaching the parties through a negotiation process"[24] involves active listening. A facilitative mediator is expected to be more than just an attentive listener. They need to be on the empathic end of the "listening scale" (*see* Figure 2.3), as they unearth the sources of parties' emotions and work with the parties in expressing these constructively. The mediator's attitude toward conversation reflects poise, inclusivity, and care, and their impact is weighed by their ability to drive conversations via silence, creating environments for self-reflection that inspires parties to innovate their creative solutions.

Figure 2.3 Listening Scale

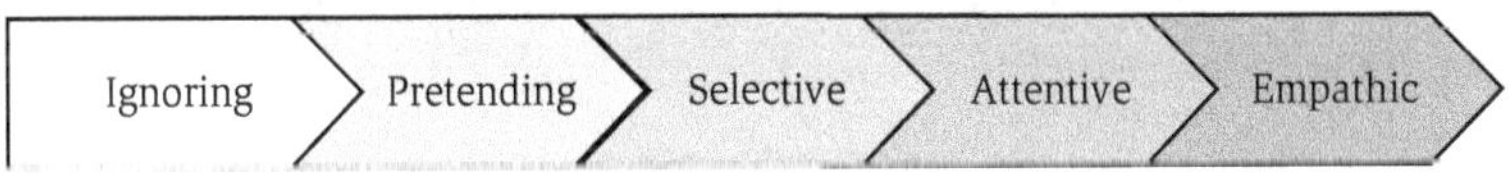

[3] Process Interventions

Facilitative mediators tend to focus more on the process rather than content. Joseph B. Stulberg emphasizes the rationale behind having a "know-nothing" neutral in a facilitative mediation setting:[25]

22. *See generally,* Sarathi Susheela, *Empathy in Mediation,* MEDIATE.COM (May 2000), https://www.mediate.com/articles/susheela-empathy-mediation.cfm.
23. *See generally,* Sarathi Susheela, *Empathy in Mediation,* MEDIATE.COM (May 2000), https://www.mediate.com/articles/susheela-empathy-mediation.cfm. *See also,* Kenneth M. Roberts, *Mediating the Evaluative-Facilitative Debate: Why Both Parties Are Wrong and a Proposal for Settlement,* 39 LOY. U. CHI. L. J. 187, 193 (2007) (hereinafter "Roberts").
24. *See* Nadja Alexander, *The Mediation Meta-Model: Understanding Practice,* 26(1) CONFLICT RESOL. QUARTERLY, 97, 111 (2008).
25. Stulberg, *supra* note 12.

> for the process to work, the mediator need not have expertise in the subject matter of the dispute ... it is rare for a facilitative mediator to have subject matter expertise. In most cases, those who choose pure facilitative mediation prefer that the mediator not have subject matter experience in the disputed area at all. A lack of experience eliminates the danger that the mediator will interject evaluative information. When additional information is necessary, the facilitative approach requires the mediator to recommend that parties look to outside authorities for professional or legal advice.

Therefore, a mediator will make process interventions from time to time. Since the parties are responsible for arriving at a resolution, a facilitative neutral will only intervene to straighten up the process if at all it is going astray. This can be to ensure equal speaking opportunities for parties or to prevent the process from being derailed.

While doing so, a facilitative neutral must be vigilant and respectful of the power balance between advocates and their clients. Although advocates have indirect influence over their parties through their advice, the parties must hold power and influence over decision-making. The mediator must also ensure that the process does not get hijacked by advocates.

A facilitative mediator encourages participants to explore numerous possible outcomes and keeps the discussion ongoing until participants decide whatever outcome is relevant to their interests. In the process of keeping this communication window open, the neutral "validates and normalizes parties' points of view"[26] when necessary and reminds participants to analyze the diverse options on the table before agreeing to settle. Introducing confirmatory documentation or corroborative material facts (evidence in civil court terminology) is a welcome practice in facilitative mediation, as long as it is employed to further decision-making discussions and not trespass into the problematic past.

A facilitative neutral encourages participants to prioritize their underlying interests over the legal rights at stake. Endorsing flexibility and freedom to discuss creative solutions, Jane Kidner writes:[27]

> once the parties are unencumbered by the strict rules, procedures, and remedies of the civil justice system, and underlying interests are open to being discussed, the focus of the mediation can turn to more creative problem-solving, and include an unlimited number of permutations and combinations of possible resolutions.

[4] Faith in Mediation

Facilitative mediation takes time and requires patience on the part of parties and advocates. And, of course, in the midst of a dispute, patience is often in short supply. As such, the mediator is often required to demonstrate faith in the process, display calm and confidence in the parties' abilities and encourage them when things are not

26. *See* Jaime Abraham, *Divorce Mediation—Limiting the Profession to Family/ Matrimonial Lawyers*, 10 Cardozo J. Conflict Resol. 241, 246 (2008).
27. *See* Jane Kidner, *The Limits of Mediator Labels: False Debate Between Facilitative Versus Evaluative Mediator Styles*, 30 Windsor Rev. Legal & Soc. Issues 167, 173 (2011) (hereinafter "Kidner").

going as smoothly or as quickly as they might like. Instructing a simple balance between temperament and time, John W. Allen writes:[28]

> Participants need time to vent their frustrations and strong feelings and to find their own routes to what each individual recognises as a reasonable result. Facilitation also requires perseverance. Although no one should ever be required to reach an agreement, it is reasonable that the parties and their counsel be strongly encouraged to stay the course until the methods of facilitation are given reasonable chance to work. The participants must be encouraged to not depart without giving the mediator adequate notice and an opportunity to persuade them to stay.

Having said this, sometimes, despite the mediator's best efforts, parties may choose to walk away from the mediation. This is fine and is part of the parties' empowerment. A facilitative mediator does not measure success by settlement and is therefore not concerned about participants choosing not to settle at the end of the session. Instead, a facilitative mediator characterizes success by the ability to provide decision-makers with the information they can use to reevaluate their positions, make informed business decisions, and engage in a systematic modification of their initial positions, or an "organized retreat." The goal is to guarantee that the participants' settlement or nonsettlement is based on sufficient information and understanding, for the settlement to be legitimately executed.[29]

[B] Evaluative Approach

With mediation gaining considerable recognition, the evaluative style of mediating evolved to focus on legal rights and merits of claims rather than interests only. Similar to the courtroom, the parties consider themselves adversaries and, therefore, unlike the facilitative approach, the evaluative mediator focuses on "what" the parties want and how much they are willing to compromise in order to achieve the bigger picture.

This kind of mediation is often adversarial throughout, with the evaluative mediator pressing the disputants to make new demands and offers more in line with his or her evaluations.[30] An evaluative mediator's approach stems from the assumption that parties want and need guidance regarding the appropriate grounds for settlement.[31]

Proponents of the evaluative style assert that disputants often seek out the opinion of a mediator and this opinion is of more help than a hindrance to the

28. John W Allen, *Let the Dodge Brother Drive You Home—Using the Dodge Act and Facilitative Mediation to Resolve Probate and Trust Litigation*, 22 Michigan Prob & Est Plan J. 6, 7 (2002–2003).
29. *See* Greta Baksa, Different Mediation Styles and Their Use in Family Mediation 249, 252 (Polgári Jogi Tanszék, 2012), http://epa.oszk.hu/02600/02687/00005/pdf/EPA02687_jogi_tanulmanyok_2012_02_249-259.pdf.
30. *See* Levin, *supra* note 18, at p. 269.
31. *See generally*, Riskin, *supra* note 6.

constructions of settlements.[32] Despite the legal focus, an evaluative mediator is not expected to embrace traditional adversarial methods—dictate resolutions or order a ruling.[33]

Contrary to popular criticism, an evaluative mediator does not ignore the interests of the participants and rather focuses practically on the core legal issue at hand[34] during the mediation discussions in both joint and private conferences.[35] Besides having a legal background, Kenneth Roberts outlines further expectations of an evaluative mediator:[36]

> it is essential for an evaluative mediator to have at least some substantive experience with the subject matter in dispute. Such knowledge is necessary in order to ask appropriate questions, guide the parties in a reasonable direction, and help the parties realistically re-evaluate their claims.

The role of an evaluative mediator is not restricted to simply guiding the parties' conversations. It is expected that the evaluative mediator "makes recommendations, points out case flaws and strengths, predicts court outcomes, and evaluates case components."[37] A mediator playing an evaluative role would benefit from having "training, experience, and objectivity"[38] as subject matter expertise is often prioritized over other skills in disputes categorized as highly complicated or unique.

An evaluative mediator focuses on the underlying substance and cause of a dispute,[39] not to address what went wrong and how it could have been prevented but to analyze the consequences of the situation and how it affects the reparation. Adherents to the evaluative approach believe that "the barrier to resolution is rooted in the parties' unrealistic opinions about the value of their claims."[40] Therefore, assessing the dispute and weighing up options and alternatives to fix the situation define an evaluative mediator's role.

In a typical evaluative mediation setting, there is an unspoken expectation for the mediator to be an "agent of reality." An evaluative mediator is commissioned to help disputants reevaluate their positions more realistically before presenting them on the table. Further, beyond that stage, they are also expected to help participants appraise

---

32. *See* John Bickerman, *Evaluative Mediator Responds*, 14(6) ALTERNATIVES TO THE HIGH COST OF LITIGATION 70, 70 (1996) ("[Parties] often want-and expect-a mediator to explore strengths and weaknesses of the case [...] Without sacrificing neutrality, a mediator's neutral assessment can provide participants with a much-needed reality check") (hereinafter "Bickerman").
33. *See* Roberts, *supra* note 23, at p. 195.
34. *See id.*
35. A joint conference or a general conference or a joint meeting is when the mediator meets both sides to the dispute together. A private conference, or a caucus, or a private meeting is when the mediator meets either of the parties for a confidential discussion.
36. *See* Roberts, *supra* note 23, at p. 195.
37. *See id.*
38. *See* J. Brad Reich, *Attorney v. Client: Creating a Mechanism to Address Competing Process Interests in Lawyer-Driven Mediation*, 26(2) SOUTHERN ILLINOIS UNIV. L.J. 183, 187 (2002).
39. *See* Richard Birke, *Evaluation and Facilitation: Moving Past Either! Or*, J. OF DISP. RESOL. 309, 315 (2000) (hereinafter "Birke").
40. *See* Roberts, *supra* note 23, at p. 196.

the settlement on the table before they sign the settlement agreement.[41] In this evaluative role, the mediator provides new information, helps parties realize the costs and risks of litigation, and points out weaknesses and strengths of each side, either in private caucuses or with both parties present.[42]

Robert A. Baruch Bush further distinguishes the evaluative role as directive and nondirective, clarifying that the directive mediator provides evaluations and exerts pressure on the parties to agree with them.[43] Alternatively, the nondirective role concerns assessing the issues, but the information assimilated may be only used to dissect the decision-making, with the evaluative mediator staying away from influencing discussions.[44]

Roberts writes about the four tasks that Riskin assigned to both the directive and nondirective evaluative roles. The directive approach would constitute the evaluative mediator engaging in:

- assessing the strengths and weaknesses of each side's case;
- predicting outcomes;
- proposing position-based resolutions; and
- urging parties to accept a particular proposal.[45]

The evaluative mediator, in a nondirective approach, would be:

- educating oneself about the parties' interests;
- predicting the impact of failing to settle;
- developing and suggesting broad-interest-based proposals; and
- urging parties to accept a proposal.[46]

The evaluative approach is most appreciated in crunch cases, where a looming deadline can either make or break a relationship—business, professional or personal. Participants seeking a focused discussion on a prioritized issue on the agenda prefer an evaluative mediator, despite the limited scope of creative solutions. Though it narrows the options and alternatives, an evaluative mediator can channel the energy onto one issue and keep away all other forms of distraction. Being a domain expert, an evaluative mediator uses their own experience to help the parties focus on prioritizing the issues, determining how much time to spend on each issue, and leading the parties toward a reasonable solution.[47]

It must be clear that an "evaluative mediator does not explicitly judge or try a case, or even advocate for a particular side," but at the same time, participants do not want to be a part of mediation with the neutral behaving like a referee, forcing them to

41. *See* Birke, *supra* note 39, at p. 315.
42. *See* Roberts, *supra* note 23, at p. 196.
43. Robert A. Baruch Bush, *Substituting Mediation for Arbitration: The Growing Market for Evaluative Mediation, and What It Means for the ADR Field*, 3(1) PEPP. DISP. RESOL. L.J. 111, 114 (2002) (hereinafter "Bush").
44. Roberts, *supra* note 23, at p. 196.
45. Riskin, *supra* note 6, at pp. 27–28.
46. *Id.*, at pp. 30–31.
47. *See* Roberts, *supra* note 23, at p. 200.

play nice.[48] Participants often seek out a neutral who is willing and able to provide an opinion on their issue. An evaluative neutral has her or his task cut out in terms of getting involved in the mediation. Roberts explains:[49]

> The advantage of a neutral third-party mediator is the value he adds by providing information, organizing the discussion, and assisting the parties in the re-evaluation of their positions. Suggesting possible outcomes and consequences, settlement possibilities, and appropriate bargaining ranges are all designed to help align the parties and bring them closer to settlement.

Murray S. Levin suggests that the evaluative approach is modeled on settlement conferences held by judges.[50] Scaling the dispute based on legal concepts of fairness and merits of the facts of the case, an evaluative mediator might also make formal or informal recommendations as to a fair settlement of the dispute. Evaluative mediators may prefer meeting in separate private sessions with participants (and/or with their advocates)—a practice often termed "shuttle diplomacy"[51]—before convening for a joint conference. These private sessions help participants evaluate their legal position, the costs, and the benefits of pursuing a legal resolution rather than settling in mediation. This is essential in preparing participants for dealing with hostile bargaining and adversarial language that might be used at the table upon joint conferencing.

Some evaluative mediators also use these early private sessions as an opportunity for fine-tuning the parties' offers before they can be shared at the table, especially if the mediator feels the offers lie in the insult zone or negative bargaining zone. Thus, in a directive role, the evaluative mediator would also impact the structure of the conversations beyond the role of influencing the outcome of the mediation.[52] The proactive role of the evaluative mediator is obvious and helps trace its motivation and emergence from court-mandated or court-referred cases[53]—where the chances of winning the case in court were analyzed by gambling on the most likely outcome.[54]

Evaluative mediation is based on the fundamental belief that participants can benefit when a knowledgeable and objective mediator mentors and counsels them on the merits of their demands.[55] Providing expert case evaluation, substantive settlement recommendations, and persuasive skills is not some bonus but elements belonging to the essential toolbox for any evaluative mediator, in addition to scrutinizing the

48. *See id.*
49. *See* Roberts, *supra* note 23, at pp. 195–196, 200.
50. Levin, *supra* note 18, at p. 268.
51. Shuttle diplomacy could be illustrated as a practice where the participants are seated in two separate rooms and the mediator keeps moving from one room to the other with ideas, offers and concerns, relaying information between participants, without them communicating with each other directly.
52. *See* Robert A. Baruch Bush, *Staying in Orbit, or Breaking Free: The Relationship of Mediation to the Courts over Four Decades*, 84 North Dakota L. Rev. 705, 735 (2008).
53. *See* Exon, *supra* note 19, at p. 593.
54. *See* Maureen E. Laflin, *Preserving the Integrity of Mediation Through the Adoption of Ethical Rules for Lawyer-Mediators*, 14 Notre Dame J.L. Ethics & Pub. Policy 479, 485 (2000).
55. *See* Stulberg, *supra* note 12, at p. 995 (summarizing an assertion made by Riskin, *supra* note 6, at p. 24).

conversation.[56] Batting for a clear impression of the evaluative style over a decade ago, Dorothy Noce asserted that with the advocate's presence, an evaluative mediator is free to discuss the law and simulate what the judge would decide on the merits of the facts of the case, as presented during the mediation. She also highlights a typical practice of an evaluative mediator to use suggestive questioning or hypothetical questioning regarding their chances in court and reminds advocates to refrain from asking such questions in joint conversations with both participants.[57]

An evaluative mediator often helps disputants understand the law and the legal implications of their positions, consciously or unintentionally, corroborating the advice received by the participants from their advocates. This advice makes participants more accommodating to revised settlement figures, which seemed like a huge compromise during prior conversations with their advocates.[58] An evaluative mediator focuses on one of the core elements of successful negotiation—an alternative to the courtroom. Since the mediation process occurs within the context of an impending litigation or arbitration battle, an evaluative mediator must be comfortable discussing alternative outcomes if offers at the table are not accepted, and the dispute is not settled. This enduring attitude to drive participants to an agreement by projecting and evaluating their chances in court is relevant and valuable to the role of an evaluative mediator, but persistence cannot be misunderstood for coercion and intimidation.

On a lighter note, some concerned critics, quite understandably so, in a fit of anxiety and animation, have assassinated the character of evaluative mediators, labeling them as a "Muscle Mediator" who "knocks some sense" into disputants by "banging their heads together" or "twisting their arms." Brushing aside such a vivid misinterpretation of an evaluative mediator role, it is important to confirm that the mediator's strategy is classified as evaluative "if the mediators analyzed the case in a balanced fashion, pointing out each side's strengths and weaknesses. In such a strategy, the mediators made suggestions, discussed the merits of both cases, and gave opinions or advised the parties on steps they should take."[59]

We began discussing the evaluative role in the first paragraph by mentioning that the mediator continuously explores how much the participants are willing to give to meet their demands. Directing the participants toward settlement requires the evaluative mediator to apply overt pressure tactics to obtain incremental concessions from each side until a settlement was reached.[60] An evaluative mediator seeks to engage participants in distributive, positional-bargaining rather than the integrative approach of interest-based negotiation. The evaluative mediator is not a passive spectator but a

---

56. *See* Bush, *supra* note 43, p. 113.
57. *See* Dorothy J. Della Noce, *Evaluative Mediation: In Search of Practice Competencies*, 27(2) CONFLICT RESOL. QUARTERLY 193, 198 (2009) (hereinafter "Noce").
58. *See* James H. Stark, *Preliminary Reflections on the Establishment of a Mediation Clinic*, 2 CLINICAL L. REV. 457, 487 (1996). On a related note, sometimes advocates welcome mediator evaluations as an aid in addressing what may be referred to as a "client control problem." The advocate anticipates that the mediator's evaluation will confirm the advocate's own assessment of the case, and this will encourage an unrealistic client to adjust expectations.
59. James A. Wall, Timothy C. Dunne & Suzanne Chan-Serafin, *The Effects of Neutral, Evaluative, and Pressing Mediator Strategies*, 29(2) CONFLICT RESOL. QUARTERLY 127, 136 (2011).
60. *See* Noce, *supra* note 57, at p. 202.

dynamic force, widely encouraged and expected to be influential, argumentative, and persuasive in their conversations with the participants. An evaluative mediator constantly generates concessions from the participants, encouraging them to compromise on nonnegotiable demands and lead them toward an agreement. To be convincing in this pursuit, an evaluative mediator is expected to have both qualification and experience, but beyond these two key features, the element of preparation is also vital. An apathetic neutral who does not consider prior research and analysis important will be poorly positioned to render an evaluation, despite being an industry expert.[61]

[C] Evaluation Versus Facilitation: A False Dichotomy?

At first blush, evaluation and facilitation seem to be polar opposites. An evaluative mediator takes a view as to what the outcome should be and reels the parties toward that agreement. They are not interested in the polarized position taken by the party and do not pay the participant a visit at the pole. Instead, the evaluative mediator positions himself at a neutral meeting point and expects the parties to get to that consensus. Some evaluative mediators contribute their views of the case's merits, the consequences of a failure to settle, and the benefits of particular settlement proposals. They might even present a proposal for adoption by the participants by presenting them gently for consideration or aggressively advocating their adoption.

On the other hand, the facilitative mediator gently nudges the participants to a common ground. They visit the parties at the polar ends of their dispute, understand their perspective, view the dispute from their angle, and encourage them to move from those poles to a common ground.

But is this a false dichotomy? The writers suggest that dichotomy is a false one and that it is not helpful to suggest that mediation is just one thing or another.

Suppose we accept that mediation revolves around the principles of parties' self-determination, the mediator's neutrality, and providing parties with the opportunity of exploring solutions to their problem outside of their strict legal rights. In that case, regardless of one's approach, these principles must be adhered to. And both evaluation and facilitation are valid ways of assisting parties to manifest their goals in mediation.[62]

Yeo suggests that part of the problem is through an overly narrow definition of what evaluation means.[63] Facilitation purists have equated the evaluative approach with an exclusive focus on resolving disputes via their legal rights. Put this way, even evaluative mediators should take issue with this definition. In his later article, Riskin acutely observed that these critics had confused what his grid had represented and did

61. *See* Scott H. Hughes, *Facilitative or Evaluative Mediation: May Your Choice Be a Wise One*, 59 The Alabama Lawyer 246, 247 (1998).
62. *See* Javier Yeo, *The Facilitative-Evaluative Divide: Have We Lost Sight of What Is Important?* 1 Contemp. Issues in Mediation 35, 35 (2016).
63. *Id.*

not fully consider what evaluative conduct entails.[64] The reality is that facilitative mediators engage in evaluative behaviors all the time. Even Kovach & Love, as proponents of a facilitative model of mediation, concede that "evaluation inheres in every aspect of human conduct, as well as many mediator techniques."[65] These include "challenging proposals that might derail the negotiation or that seem unrealistic or suboptimal" and "making suggestions about possibilities for resolution in order to stimulate the parties to generate options."[66] Kovach and Love include these evaluative activities as "essential parts of a mediator's facilitative role."[67]

Another part of the problem is that evaluation and facilitation were represented, in Riskin's Grid, as being on different continuum ends. Mediators and scholars were presented with an Aristotelian conundrum, one that forced an "either-or" choice and which excluded the possibility of an approach that embraced both facilitative and evaluative conduct in a complementary way. Even Riskin acknowledges that his continuum misrepresented the facilitative-evaluative orientation as a dichotomy when "evaluative and facilitative often travel in tandem."[68]

It should be emphasized that accepting that facilitation and evaluation are complementary does not mean that every evaluative behavior is appropriate. Evaluative conduct should be used to aid the mediator in their facilitative orientation.

§2.05 DEALING WITH IMPASSE

Commentators sometimes speak of impasse as if it were something that only happens from time to time during the mediation. The reality is that impasses are part and parcel of mediation. Technically, when parties come for mediation, they are at an impasse. Mediation then is the process within which the mediator assists the parties in unraveling the knots of impasse.

Typically, several things cause an impasse. The next section looks at two common barriers to settlement: psychological traps and difficult negotiating tactics.

[A] Barriers to Settlement

[1] Psychological Traps

John Wade speaks about psychological traps or cognitive biases as hampering decision-making.[69] His work on systematic risk analysis on litigators and negotiators

64. *See* Leonard L Riskin, *Replacing the Mediator Orientation Grids, again: Proposing a New New Grid System*, 23(8) ALTERNATIVE HIGH COST LITIG. 1, 25 (2005) (hereinafter "Leonard Riskin").
65. *See* Riskin, *supra* note 6, at p. 74 (on Riskin's grid).
66. *See* Riskin, *supra* note 6, at pp. 79–80 (on the risks of Riskin's grid).
67. *See* Kimberlee K. Kovach & Lela P. Love, *Mapping Mediation; The Risks of Riskin's Grid*, 3(71) HARV NEGOTIATION L REV 71 at 89 (1998).
68. *See* Leonard Riskin, *supra* note 64, at p. 15 (on the "New New Grid").
69. John Wade, *Systematic Risk Analysis for Negotiators and Litigators: How to Help Clients Make Better Decisions*, SSRN, https://ssrn.com/abstract=2405727 (An earlier version of this paper appears in 13 BOND L. REV. 462–485 (2002)).

highlights the role a mediator can play in assisting parties in entangling themselves from mental blocks in finding solutions to their problems. The mediator can engage in different means, or the same means in different ways, to assist parties in looking at the issue from a fresh perspective. Inspired by Wade's work, here are a few traps or biases analyzed from a mediator's view.

[i] Anchoring Trap

In conflict resolution, the first offer that gets made by one or both parties determines how far apart the parties are and the range that must be closed for parties to agree. Hence, parties may ask for a higher (or lower) amount than what they would be content with so that they have more negotiating room. This is known as anchoring.

Mediators often coach parties to present their anchors in a credible zone so that the mediation begins on the front foot. Sometimes, one party may anchor their offer so high (or so low) that it loses credibility and is considered an insulting offer. Often, this will then only provoke an equally insulting counteroffer.

This trap has similar consequences to the "sunken-cost trap" (standing by earlier wrong choices) and the "framing trap" (triggering a premature answer with a wrong question or statement) that Wade mentions in his writing.

[ii] Fixed-Pie Trap

Parties often try to base their arguments on what others have achieved in similar situations and want the same outcome. Further, disputing parties often view a negotiated transaction as zero-sum, meaning that a gain for the counterpart is a loss of themselves. This traps them firmly in a fixed-pie mentality, making them blind to possible creative and value-added deals they have not explored before. This can, in turn, lead to unwise and un-retractable decisions.

This psychological trap is much like the "status quo trap" or the "easily available information trap." In the thick of disputes, parties only see or hear what they wish to perceive and filter out anything presented or said by the other side that does not align with their preconceived expectations and understandings. This "ignoring trap" is also known as confirmation bias.

[iii] Winner's Curse

This refers to the worry that a party experiences when their counterpart agrees to their offer, perhaps a bit faster or more readily than they had expected. It leads to doubt about whether they have been taken advantage of and if they should have asked for more. This is similar to what is referred to in sales as "buyer's remorse" and can cause many parties to renege their commitment to what has been agreed.

[iv] Overconfidence Trap

Mediators find many parties entering a session wearing metaphorical armor or carrying a metaphorical shield. They are not open to the possibility that they may not have received the best advice—financially, legally, or personally, or that there may be possible solutions that they have not considered. Put another way, parties are often unrealistically confident in what they think they know. This trap is related to the "confirming evidence trap" wherein parties who are convinced of a particular narrative of their dispute only search for facts and figures that prove themselves right. You will often find them delusional about their case, relying on fictional or hearsay information, which is detrimental to decision-making.

[2] Navigating Difficult Negotiating Tactics

Apart from psychological traps, impasses can also result from parties engaging in difficult negotiating tactics. Needless to say, one reason why parties choose to engage in these tactics is precisely because they have fallen into these psychological traps!

The Program on Negotiation Blog has listed a few hard-bargaining techniques employed by negotiators, and it would be helpful for mediators to keep a lookout for these so that they can steer the parties back toward a collaborative approach.[70]

[i] Manipulative Tactics

Such tactics are employed by parties who excessively use humor, flattery, or intelligence to charm the mediator. Some parties use emotions to manipulate the mediator into taking a side, while others engage their advocate for a tag team exercise of "good cop, bad cop." The mediator needs to be aware of these situations and maintain neutrality, politely reminding them that the decision-making responsibility lies with the parties and the mediator is not invested in the outcome.

Manipulation can also be used to inflate one side's egos or annoy the counterpart so that no deal is possible. Parties may intentionally change their schedules, send in substitutes or additional representatives, sometimes with limited authority to settle. Further, junior advocates might be used to and frustrate senior advocates on the other side. Walking in late, constantly attending to "urgent" phone calls, name-dropping, inquiring about unpleasant personal and professional memories, boasting about recent exploits, unnecessarily complaining about conditions, etc., are some of the myriad theatrical strategies that can be employed. A good mediator is aware of these and does not let them derail the mediation process.

70. *See* PON Staff, *10 Hard-Bargaining Tactics to Watch Out for in a Negotiation: The Best Hard-Bargaining Tactics Can Catch You off Guard*, PROGRAM ON NEGOTIATION—DAILY BLOG (HARVARD LAW SCHOOL) (Sept. 28, 2020), https://www.pon.harvard.edu/daily/batna/10-hard ball-tactics in negotiation/.

[ii] Pressure and Delay Tactics by Parties

Time pressure is sometimes used to either force or stall a settlement. In the first scenario, parties instigate each other to make decisions in haste, laying down unreasonable deadlines and timelines for the other side to make decisions on settlements or keep up commitments after reaching an agreement. These impractical offers or demands by the dominating party sometimes put the other side on the back foot, often building a metaphorical shield between the parties. Alternatively, mediators can come across as bench-warming parties who employ delay tactics with no real intention to settle. These delay tactics can include the following:

- Prematurely rejecting offers without any rational reason.
- Nonparticipation in modifying or supplementing offers on the table.
- Mocking offers by discrediting the other side's research and intentions.
- Introducing unheard hierarchical decision-making models on their side.
- Anchoring offers or counteroffers in the insult zone and demonstrating no intent to settle.
- Ignoring offers being made or invitations to counteroffers by deviating to other related or unrelated issues.

[iii] Power and Rights Tactics

Many parties come into mediation with an inflexible "right versus wrong" mentality and conduct themselves as if they were in a courtroom. They are unapologetically adversarial by citing precedents, spewing courtroom jargon, analyzing cases, promoting bureaucracy, insisting on documentation, and raising industry inquiry.

Power imbalances inevitably exist in mediation. However, powerful parties sometimes employ "blanketing" as a strategy to disempower the other side and pressure them to accept unjust deals. Meaning, these parties prefer attending mediation with either large teams consisting of various experts or small teams consisting of one or two big personalities in the industry. They will predominantly refer to their vast victories in litigation or arbitration, their accessibility to resources, and their connections in the business and political world. Sometimes, even a weaker party will try to play the power game by putting up a show in an attempt to mislead their counterpart into thinking that they are stronger than they actually are!

These tactics are not conducive to collaboration and run counter to what mediation is seeking to achieve.

[B] Mediator Interventions

Now that we have considered two of the things that might cause an impasse, this section will turn to look at some mediator interventions to move parties past the impasse. As we consider these interventions, the authors may label some interventions as evaluative or facilitative. These labels should be read in the context of our conclusion drawn in section §2.04 on the facilitative-evaluative divide.

[1] Reality Testing

As mentioned earlier, parties can come into mediation with unrealistic expectations and beliefs. Reality testing is a very useful intervention for the mediator as it can right these expectations and beliefs and guide the parties toward more productive discussions. This can involve questioning the strength of the parties' case or pointing out to the parties things that they might not have otherwise considered. For example, the mediator could, either by directly raising it or asking questions, point the costs involved in the trial, the timelines involved, the stresses that occur, and the unpredictable nature of the court proceedings.[71] This is typically done in a private session so as not to put parties on the defensive.

[2] Provide Input

A mediator might seek to change the dynamic by providing some form of input:

- The most obvious form would be in terms of process. They could direct parties to consider another agenda item, perhaps one that is easier to resolve. Or to get them to refocus on their core interests and concerns. Or to get them to brainstorm creative solutions. On the latter, a mediator could use "What if" questions to help parties explore their zone of possible agreement.
- Another type of input would be in terms of facilitating communication. The impasse might result from parties talking past one another, being mired in their perceptions and biases, or simply not understanding one another. Through active listening, paraphrasing, summarizing, and reframing, a skillful mediator can help parties bridge this communication gap.
- Sometimes, the input may be content-based. For example, parties might be hard-pressed to think of creative solutions to their problems. It is not that they do not want to, just that it is sometimes difficult to when one is overly focused on the problem. In these cases, the mediator may have to prime the well and suggest some possible options for them to consider. It is important to emphasize that in this situation, it is not about deciding that parties should adopt a particular deal and pushing them toward it. Instead, it gives the parties two or three examples of what a collaborative agreement might look like to begin thinking on that track.
- Sometimes parties are at their wit's ends. Try as they may, they do not seem to be making progress and would like the mediator to evaluate what the mediator thinks they should do. To the authors' minds, this should really be a last resort and should not involve the mediator making any kind of pronouncement on

71. *See* Levin, *supra* note 18, at p. 269.

what would happen in court. In other words, the mediator does not step into the shoes of an adjudicator.

[3] Influencing Behaviors

One of the key things a mediator can do is to influence behaviors. This, they already do by guiding parties through the process and their questions and other linguistic interventions. However, a mediator can also influence behaviors in three other ways. During the course of a mediation, parties will engage in various behaviors, some of which will be helpful to the mediation, others less so:

- Where parties engage in positive or constructive behaviors, the mediator can point these out and reinforce them. This can be in the form of direct praise, express hope and optimism for the outcome, or indicate that parties are on the right track and making the right choices.
- Conversely, where parties engage in negative or nonconstructive behaviors, the mediator should discourage them. While some might suggest that a mediator could reprimand the parties, we would suggest caution unless the mediator has a great rapport with the parties, and the parties will take the reprimand in the spirit it is intended. Otherwise, we would suggest more indirect ways of discouragement. For example, a mediator might question what the behavior is trying to achieve relative to the goals of the mediator and what was being discussed at that point in time. The mediator could also point out the behavior, explain the impact and consequences of the behavior.
- It is useful to point out that the mediator serves as a model for the behaviors they want parties to engage in. So, a mediator can influence how parties behave and communicate by manifesting those behaviors.

[4] Coaching the Parties

Drawing from the previous point about modeling behaviors, the mediator can help parties move beyond impasse by coaching them in constructive negotiating behaviors. Sometimes, despite their best intentions, parties simply do not know how to communicate or negotiate in a way that does not rub the other party wrongly. A mediator could coach parties on the content of constructing their offers (so that the offers made are credible and within the zone of possible agreement) or how they deliver their offers.

[5] Humor, Metaphors and Props to Lighten the Atmosphere

Sometimes, what is needed is a good distraction. When parties are in an impasse, they often fixate on the conflict and the unpleasant effects of that conflict. Distracting them can allow them to "reset" psychologically. This could be by calling for a break or using humor, telling a metaphor, or even using props. Of course, this must be done sparingly;

otherwise, parties and advocates might lose confidence in the mediator and the mediation process.

[6] Riding Shotgun with the Decision-Makers

In some intractable cases, parties may not seem willing to move toward settlement despite using every tool from the toolbox. The mediator could meet privately with advocates for an honest conversation that involves reality testing and getting advocates to drive sense into their clients. As the parties' closest ally and who is being paid to help them resolve the dispute, the influence of advocates can be very helpful in moving parties and assuring them that making a deal is viable.

§2.06 CONCLUSION

Readers may be familiar with the story of the four blind men and the elephant. Stated simply, four blind men, each felt a part of the elephant and thinking that what they had felt represented the entirety of what an elephant was, began arguing with one another about the nature of an elephant.

Examining mediation and the role of a mediator is like that. Many of the arguments revolving around mediation are often about mistaking certain parts of mediation and the mediator's role to represent the entirety of what it is. It would be an understatement to say that mediation is a complex creature.

This chapter has sought to give readers a sense of the complexity of mediation and the roles that a mediator can play. With the different opinions, models, approaches, roles, and variations that can exist, there is a real risk that we will miss the forest for the trees. Despite all these differences, keeping one's eye on the forest means that there are things that must hold true in order for anything to be considered mediation. At the root of mediation reside certain core values: empowerment, self-determination, collaboration, neutrality. These must never be compromised.

CHAPTER 3

Mediation and Ethics

Sandeep Bhalothia & Anil Xavier[*]

§3.01 INTRODUCTION

With mediation's widespread awareness and increased use, the question of ethics or professional responsibility arises naturally. And if there are none, to begin with, it is quite the predicament and, thus, imperative to develop a binding ethical code for mediators that would not only inform and guide mediators in making ethical choices and holding them accountable but also help users to have confidence in the process and the mediator. At the outset, this chapter does not provide coverage on negotiator ethics (for advocates and advisors representing clients)—that deserves its own chapter.[1]

This chapter discusses India's existing framework on mediator ethics (or the lack of it), its effective (or ineffective) application, and its general importance to the practice of mediation in both court-annexed and private settings. After going through that discourse, the authors highlight the need for a proper, comprehensive, and effective, ethical code, without which mediation is exposed to doubt, distrust, and cynicism. The present need is felt greater when considering the recent legal and technological developments, such as the UN Convention on International Settlement Agreements Resulting from Mediation (the Singapore Convention) and e-mediation/online dispute resolution (ODR). In particular, the Singapore Convention stipulates that a mediated settlement agreement may be refused enforcement if "[t]here was a serious breach by

* The able assistance of Farhan Zia is gratefully acknowledged.

1. *See generally*, AMERICAN BAR ASSOCIATION—SECTION OF LITIGATION, ETHICAL GUIDELINES FOR SETTLEMENT NEGOTIATIONS (August 2002), https://www.americanbar.org/content/dam/aba/administrative/dispute_resolution/dispute_resolution/settlementnegotiations.pdf.

the mediator of standards applicable to the mediator or the mediation without which breach that party would not have entered into the settlement agreement."[2]

The statement that mediations in India often manifest a dilution of parties' right to self-determination holds water. This is particularly so in the context of court-annexed mediations, which, although can only be supported anecdotally, advocates will admit that there is a ring of truth to it (at least). Court-annexed mediations often witness "muscle" mediation, i.e., an aggressive mediator excessively pushing parties to settle. Given the dearth of Indian case laws, we recurrently ride on the coattails of foreign case law to draw two things that: (i) ethical violations are frequent even in some of the more advanced mediation cultures; and (ii) those instances may well inform (sometimes mirror) the ethical issues faced in India's mediation practice.

Jacobs v. New York Financial Center Hotel[3] is one such instance of muscle mediation. A district court refused to dismiss a complaint filed, even though a pre-litigation settlement had been signed. The plaintiff's basis was that "the mediator told him that defendants' offer was open only during the mediation session,"[4] even though an applicable statute provided at least seven days to consider a waiver agreement. The plaintiff was given only five hours, in which he hassled to settle and received no benefits. The court held that the settlement was voidable and did not bar a subsequent suit. It observed: "[t]he short, intense time was insufficient to allow full consideration of the terms of the agreement."[5]

There are often instances where mediators "threaten" extreme consequences if the parties fail to settle. This goes farther from coercion by a muscle mediator. For example, in *Vitakis-Valchine v. Valchine*,[6] a wife alleged that the mediator (in divorce mediation) pressed her to allow the husband to dispose of the frozen embryos that she wanted to retain. She alleged that the mediator told her that the embryos were not "lives in being," that the judge would "never give her custody of the embryos," and that the court would not require the husband to pay child support "if she were impregnated with the embryos after the divorce." On the district court's set aside of the agreement, the Court of Appeal held that the alleged misconduct by the mediator was invalid. The mediator acted as an agent of the court in court-ordered mediation, and the mediator abused his position. The wife had testified that the mediator threatened to report her to the judge for failing to agree to a reasonable settlement offer and that even if she signed the agreement that she did not like, she could protest those provisions at the final hearing. The mediator has substantially violated the ethical rules.

The above two introductory instances drive us to consider how the mediator should ensure self-determination. The question is justified, and mediators will find it difficult to pinpoint a source of direction or guidance that governs their

2. UN Convention on International Settlement Agreements Resulting from Mediation, 2018, Art. 5(1)(e).
3. 1997 WL 375737 (S.D.N.Y. July 7, 1997).
4. *Id.*, at 2.
5. *Id.*, at *2.
6. 793 So. 2d 1094 (Fla. Dist. Ct. App. 2001).

actions/conduct in mediation vis-à-vis the principle of parties' self-determination.[7] Self-determination is, after all, linked with neutrality, impartiality, conflict of interest, and mediator evaluation/advice.[8] In particular, mediation intervention needs an appropriate balancing, which (in turn) necessitates clear ethical standards for mediators to follow.

In this chapter, contemporary laws and guidelines enacted in various States are also generally considered to understand ethical frameworks and possible counts on which they can ameliorate (seeing its valuable utility for India) to further the practice and popularity of mediation alternative mode of dispute resolution. The chapter also explores through the existing national and international ethical guidelines and academic recommendations to propose a general framework that can be employed for mediation in India.

§3.02 LEGAL ETHICS

[A] Ethics in Practice of Law

"Ethics," in simple terms, means an acceptable mode of conduct. The *Black's Law Dictionary* defines "ethical" and "legal ethics" as follows:

> *ethical, adj.* (16c) 1. Of or relating to moral obligations that one person owes another; esp., in law, of or relating to legal ethics ... .[9]
>
> *legal ethics.* (1882) 1. Standards of professional conduct applicable to members of the legal profession. [...] 2. The study of such standards. 3. A lawyer's practical observance of or conformity to established standards of professional conduct.[10]
>
> (internal citation omitted)

Legal ethics may also be broadly understood as a branch of moral science as per which the advocate owes ethical duties toward the society, court, client, opponent, profession, and himself. And, more specifically, these are standards of professional conduct that advocates are bound to adhere to. For this reason, the Bar Council of India (BCI) was established under section 4 of the Advocates Act 1961 (Advocates Act). The BCI has the mandate (under section 7(1)(b)) to set the standards of professional

7. Cf. Kristine Paranica, *The Implications of Intimate Partner Violence on Ethical Mediation Practice*, 88 North Dakota L. Rev. 907, 914 (2012) (in cases of intimate partner violence, the abused person's self-confidence and ability to stand up for herself is often compromised due to the abuse. This makes mediation, a process that relies on the self-determination of all parties, questionable. It requires that during the entire process, mediators be able to "judge" a party's capacity to exercise self-determination. Asking appropriate questions, for example, can help the mediator understand this). *See also*, Domestic Violence Screening Protocol For Mediators of Domestic Relations Conflicts, Office of Dispute Resolution State Court Administrative Office Michigan Supreme Court, https://courts.michigan.gov/Administration/SCAO/Resources/Documents/standards/odr/Domestic%20Violence%20Screening%20Protocol%20for%20Mediators.pdf.
8. *See* Suzanne McCorkle, *The Murky World of Mediation Ethics: Neutrality, Impartiality and Conflict of Interest in State Codes of Conduct*, 23(2) Conflict Resol. Quarterly 177 (2005).
9. Bryan A. Garner, Black's Law Dictionary 632 (9th ed., 2009).
10. *Id.*, at p. 976.

conduct and etiquette for advocates and, in this regard, section 49(1)(c) empowers the BCI to make rules governing the conduct of advocates. Accordingly, the BCI has framed the 'Rules on Professional Standard for Advocates' (Professional Rules).[11]

The rudimental precept of the Advocates Act and the Professional Rules is that the advocate has a dual responsibility: to uphold the client's interest fearlessly and to conduct himself as an officer of the court. Thus, an advocate is expected to adhere to the highest standards of probity and honor, reflecting a privileged position in society that derives from the nobility of the profession. His service to the common man should be compassionate, moral, and lawful. And if there is a breach of legal ethics (i.e., in a case of professional misconduct against an advocate), he can be brought before the disciplinary committee.[12] For instance, in *Sambhu Ram Yadav v. Hanuman Das Khatry*,[13] the Supreme Court observed that offering a bribe by any advocate is misconduct of the highest degree as it not only obstructs the administration of justice but also erodes the reputation of the profession in the opinion of the public.

In summary, one gets the sense of legal ethics in both narrow and broad terms. Narrowly, it points to the system of professional rules and regulations that govern the conduct of advocates.[14] But broadly speaking, it is simply a moral obligation (as understood central to traditions, custom, philosophy, and religion). And in many ways, the broader sense of legal ethics cuts more deeply as it concerns the people's moral lives as advocates.[15]

To inculcate ethics as part of a law student's education and training, the BCI mandates two professional ethics and professional accounting courses.[16] Hence, law schools that the BCI recognizes are required to teach these courses. The objective of this is quite apparent: to develop among law students a crucial understanding of ethical issues inherent in the practice of law, the common scenarios in which they typically arise, and the application of ethical standards. But beyond that, it informs law students about the broader role of lawyers in the community.

Despite the above, ethical standards may be rendered otiose if an enforcement mechanism does not support them. Thus, in speaking of ethics, it is not enough to merely speak of the ethical obligations but also the consequences of breaching such obligations. Under BCI's Professional Rules, if an advocate is found in breach of these

11. *Standards of Professional Conduct and Etiquette*, http://www.barcouncilofindia.org/wp-content/uploads/2010/05/BCIRulesPartVonwards.pdf (Chapter II, Part VI) (hereinafter "Professional Rules").
12. *See* Advocates Act, 1961, §§35, 36, and 36B (complaints and inquiry against an advocate). *See also*, Advocates Act, 1961, §49(1)(f) (on the rule for complaints against advocates and procedure to be followed by disciplinary committees of the State Bar Council and the Bar Council of India); Rules on Professional Standard for Advocates (Part VII on disciplinary proceedings and review).
13. AIR 2001 SC 2509.
14. For example, advocates must not communicate with a judge to discuss any matter pending before the judge or any other judge; advocates must make full and frank disclosures to their clients relating to his connections with the parties; advocates must not in any way communicate, negotiate, or call for settlement upon with any party who is represented by another advocate except through that advocate representing the parties.
15. *See* Deborah L. Rhode & David Luban, Legal Ethics 3 (1992).
16. *See* Rules of Legal Education, 2008, http://www.barcouncilofindia.org/wp-content/uploads/2010/05/BCIRulesPartIV.pdf (Paper No. 22, schedule II, Part II(B)).

Professional Rules or any other rules or regulations promulgated by the BCI, the BCI can initiate disciplinary proceedings and review against that advocate under Part VII of the Professional Rules.

We refer to the Advocates Act and the Professional Rules to generally inform us when we consider the precincts of mediator ethics. But separately, we must consider if mediation is the practice of law. And if so, is there an issue of unauthorized practice of law?

[B] Mediation and Practice of Law

Mediation boasts of its interdisciplinary nature (and in many ways, more than arbitration). Hence, it is not uncommon for mediators to come from a variety of professions besides legal. But this poses a challenge, expounded in the following two scenarios.

One, since (for the longest time) advocates have dominated mediator practice, practitioners and academics have shown curiosity if mediation can be considered the practice of law. *Two*, if mediation were the practice of law, would not nonadvocates be subject to unauthorized practice of law. After all, most mediations have many elements of law and legal drafting involved. And in evaluative mediation (or in conciliations), there may even be assessments of a party legal case. But if mediation were not the practice of law, what ethical standards govern mediators (advocates and nonadvocates) and which regulatory authority should be concerned. Thus, it would need to be clarified why mediation by nonadvocates would not qualify as unauthorized practice of law.

Much has been discussed on the above-posed challenge in foreign jurisdictions, particularly the United States (US).[17] The most prominent work on this has been the American Bar Association's (ABA's) 'Resolution on Mediation and the Unauthorized Practice of Law' (Resolution) adopted by the ABA's "Section of Dispute Resolution" in 2002. The authors consider this to be the most authoritative work on this issue, which should also apply to India's discourse on whether mediation is the practice of law. The ABA concluded that both the public interest and the practice of mediation would benefit from greater clarity concerning this issue if they were introduced in the statutes governing the practice of law and that such provision of the statutes should be interpreted and applied in such a manner as to permit all individuals to serve as mediators, regardless of whether they are attorneys. Lastly, the ABA resolved that the following principles should inform the enforcement of such statutory provisions:

> *Mediation is not the practice of law*. Mediation is a process in which an impartial individual assists the parties in reaching a voluntary settlement. Such assistance does not constitute the practice of law. The parties to the mediation are not represented by the mediator.

---

17. *See generally*, Carrie Menkel-Meadow, *Is Mediation the Practice of Law?* 14(5) ALTERNATIVES 60 (May 1996); Bruce E. Meyerson, *Mediation Should Not Be Considered the Practice of Law*, 18 ALTERNATIVES 122-123 (June 1996); Andrew S. Morrison, *Is Divorce Mediation the Practice of Law? A Matter of Perspective*, 75 CALIFORNIA L. REV. 1093 (1987).

Mediators' discussion of legal issues. In disputes where the parties' legal rights or obligations are at issue, the mediator's discussions with the parties may involve legal issues. Such discussions do not create an attorney-client relationship, and do not constitute legal advice, whether or not the mediator is an attorney.

Drafting settlement agreements. When an agreement is reached in a mediation, the parties often request assistance from the mediator in memorializing their agreement. The preparation of a memorandum of understanding or settlement agreement by a mediator, incorporating the terms of settlement specified by the parties, does not constitute the practice of law.[18] If the mediator drafts an agreement that goes beyond the terms specified by the parties, he or she may be engaged in the practice of law. However, in such a case, a mediator shall not be engaged in the practice of law if (a) all parties are represented by counsel and (b) the mediator discloses that any proposal that he or she makes with respect to the terms of settlement is informational as opposed to the practice of law, and that the parties should not view or rely upon such proposals as advice of counsel, but merely consider them in consultation with their own attorneys.

Mediators' responsibilities. Mediators have a responsibility to inform the parties in a mediation about the nature of the mediator's role in the process and the limits of that role. Mediators should inform the parties: (a) that the mediator's role is not to provide them with legal representation, but rather to assist them in reaching a voluntary agreement; (b) that a settlement agreement may affect the parties' legal rights; and (c) that each of the parties has the right to seek the advice of independent legal counsel throughout the mediation process and should seek such counsel before signing a settlement agreement.

(footnotes/citations are external)

What is most essential to the definition of "practice of law" is creating an attorney-client relationship, which brings along a set of duties toward the client.[19] For example, uphold the client's interest, not disclose communication between the client and himself, not act on the instructions of any person other than his client, not charge depending on the success of matters, not appear for opposite parties, and so on. This is absent in mediation; mediators, when providing mediation services, do not create such attorney-client relationships and assume such duties toward the parties.

But if asked to what extent ethical standards apply to advocates acting as mediators, the parties still cannot be considered clients. As a caveat, an advocate serving as a mediator should inform parties (not represented by advocates) about his role—that he does not represent them. The advocate, too, should be considered to have

18. *See* Department of Dispute Resolution Services of the Supreme Court of Virginia, Guidelines on Mediation and the Unauthorized Practice of Law 27–28 (Fall 1998), http://www.courts.state.va.us/courtadmin/aoc/djs/programs/drs/mediation/resources/upl_guidelines.pdf ("Mediators who prepare written agreements for disputing parties should strive to use the parties' own words whenever possible and in all cases should write agreements in a manner that comports with the wishes of the disputants … Unless required by law, a mediator should not add provisions to an agreement beyond those specified by the disputants"). *See also*, Massachusetts Bar Association, *Ethics Opinion No. 85-3* (March 1985) (attorney acting as mediator may draft a marital settlement agreement "but must advise the parties of the advantages of having independent legal counsel review any such agreement, and must obtain the informed consent of the parties to such joint representation").

19. *See* Professional Rule, *supra* note 11 (Part VI, Chapter II, section II, on duty to the client).

a corresponding duty to explain the mediator's role (and the difference between him and the mediator) to his client.

Admittedly, when considering an evaluative style of mediation (or conciliation under Part III of the Arbitration & Conciliation 1996), we stub our toe. As confirmed by the ABA's resolution, evaluative mediators or conciliators do not run into the unauthorized practice of law. Parties and advocates often want such service from the mediator that he provides expert feedback or settlement options after he has considered/evaluated the merits and demerits of the parties' case. Yet, this is not the practice of law because the parties have no reasonable basis for believing that the mediator will advise solely on behalf of any individual party. *Au contraire*, this is true in the case of the advocate, as stated in the BCI's Professional Rules:[20]

> 15. It shall be the duty of an advocate fearlessly to uphold the interests of his client by all fair and honorable means. An advocate shall do so without regard to any unpleasant consequences to himself or any other. He shall defend a person accused of a crime regardless of his personal opinion as to the guilt of the accused. An advocate should always remember that his loyalty is to the law, which requires that no man should be punished without adequate evidence.
>
> [...]
>
> 19. An advocate shall not act on the instructions of any person other than his client or his authorized agent.
>
> 33. An advocate who has advised a party in connection with the institution of a suit, appeal or other matter or has drawn pleadings, or acted for a party, shall not act, appear or plead for the opposite party in the same matter.

This again sets an important distinction between the role of an advocate versus a mediator. A party expects his advocate to represent his interests solely and provide advice and counsel only to him. But a mediator, on the other hand, is neutral, with no duty toward any individual party. Thus, when a mediator implicitly/explicitly suggests that something will affect the arbitrator's award of damages, he is doing so from a neutral perspective, probing the parties' assumptions about their cases, etc.

§3.03 NEED FOR MEDIATOR ETHICS

To not put the cart before the horse, before we ask what its content should be, we ask if mediation calls for an ethical standard/regulation in the first place. "Whether to regulate or not to regulate" is a household debate in the mediation community—one that has resulted in the *diversity versus consistency* dilemma.[21]

Conventionally, the proponents of regulation argue that mediation is a new field. It is often the case that participants are unacquainted with the concept (or the process) of mediation or the mediator's position and role (such as neutrality, competency, and

---

20. *Id.*
21. *See generally*, Nadja Alexander, *The Art of Regulation*, 8(1) QUT L. Rev. 1 (2008) (hereinafter "Alexander"); Kimberlee K. Kovach, *The Evolution of Mediation in the United States: Issues Ripe for Regulation May Shape the Future of Practice*, *in* Global Trends in Mediation 425 (Nadja Alexander ed., 2006) (hereinafter "Kovach").

conflict of interests).[22] Without an overarching regulation on ethics, it is serious for parties to bring a challenge, say, against coerced settlements and hold the mediator accountable (depending on whether the mediator enjoys an immunity). Hence, even though self-determination is the essence of mediation, court-annexed mediations (a system incentivized by the number of settlements achieved) regularly provide anecdotal evidence of coercive tactics by mediators.[23] Occasionally, mediators also repress the parties to keep going on, downplaying several factors on which parties would rather end the mediation.[24] But in the absence of any regulatory framework governing ethics, parties are usually at the end of the stick with no legal recourse in misconduct cases by the mediator.

On the other hand, the opponents to a regulation emphasize the voluntariness of mediation and argue that the introduction of regulations would negate its intended purpose, i.e., party autonomy. Justice P. B. Majmudar (Retd.) is reported saying, "I feel the rules governing ethics of lawyers should never have had to be codified, but there are black sheep in every profession."[25] That same statement also makes a case for regulating mediation—to avoid or (at least) significantly decrease the chances of ethical violations. The scandal of a bad example on the part of the mediator is such that it can tear down users' trust/confidence in mediation.

Regulation, as such, can come in different forms. These are mainly market regulation (soft laws, guidelines, etc.), self-regulation (contractual), and formal/legal regulations (statutes, rules, regulations, and case law). These forms of mediation regulation do not appear in exclusivity in the Indian mediation regime. There is often a mixture of these forms of regulation when considering the entire spectrum of issues that can be subject to regulation. This is relevant since the modern approach (beyond the *diversity versus dilemma*) is that regulation is inevitable; the crux of the debate has now shifted to what aspects of mediation need formal/legal regulation and what should be let free to the market and self-regulation.[26]

As far as standard-setting is concerned, a regulation (whichever it may be) would need to address qualifications, competency standards, certification or registration mediators, and ethics. These standard-setting issues have a sort of filtering character, determining who may be called a mediator and what he must live up to. In positing the form of regulation for standard-setting, one must also ascertain the type of mediation in question—private, court-annexed, or statutory mediation? On this basis, it would be reasonable to deduce that standard-setting in court-annexed and statutory mediations should be covered by formal/legal regulation (living up to market standards), and

22. *See generally*, Kovach, *supra* note 21.
23. *See* Nancy A. Welsh, *The Thinning Vision of Self-determination in Court-Connected Mediation: The Inevitable Price of Institutionalization?* 6 HARVARD NEGOTIATION L. REV. 1 (2001).
24. *See* Timothy Hedeen, *Coercion and Self-determination in Court-Connected Mediation: All Mediations Are Voluntary, But Some Are More Voluntary Than Others*, 26(3) THE JUSTICE SYSTEM JOURNAL 273–291 (2005).
25. *See* Kartikeya, *HC Judge Gives Tips on Ethics in Law*, THE TIMES OF INDIA (Sept. 8, 2008, 8:00 AM), https://m.timesofindia.com/city/mumbai/hc-judge-gives-tips-on-ethics-in-law/articleshow/3457189.cms.
26. *See* Alexander, *supra* note 21.

private mediation should be left to the market and self-regulation. But as the authors have also mentioned in their concluding remarks to this chapter, an overarching is conceivable to promulgate sustainable and uniform policies and guidelines on mediator ethics, balancing it with party autonomy and market regulation. Having considered the possibility of multiple sources of ethical standards, the authors have tried to graphically represent a matrix of ethical standards or rules that can (and do) subject a mediation or the mediator:

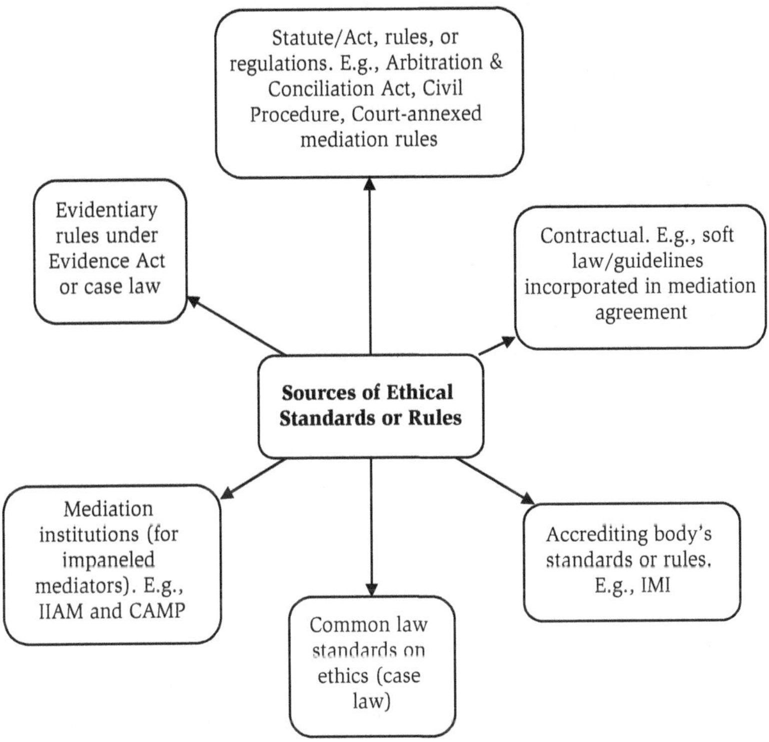

[A] New Developments and Current Scenarios

[1] Article 5(1)(e) of Singapore Convention

As India prepares to ratify the Singapore Convention (or adopt the 2018 Model Law on Mediation), the legislature will need to introduce statutory provisions, and courts will need to develop some jurisprudence around mediator ethics. Under Article 5(1)(e) of the Singapore Convention, where relief is sought to enforce an international mediated settlement, Indian courts may refuse to grant such relief if there is proof that "[t]here was a serious breach by the mediator of standards applicable to the mediator or the mediation without which breach that party would not have entered into the settlement agreement."

It would, hence, be up to Indian courts to determine the applicable standards, whether they be sourced from the applicable law or an applicable code of conduct.[27] Several questions would need to be appropriately determined; for example, on what basis a breach would be considered "serious,"[28] or which standards apply if multiple standards are applying simultaneously (a conflict of ethical standards),[29] or what kind of evidence would be necessary to show "proof" of a serious breach of applicable standards? These issues, among other things, need:[30]

> the development of a substantial body of case-law or other pronouncements by enforcing authorities before it can be said with any certainty what types of conduct would cross the line, the words used in the defences are sufficient to establish that the threshold should be high. Whether or not the misconduct of the mediator was such that a party would not have entered into the settlement agreement without it would be a finding of fact that courts and other enforcing authorities are in a position to make based on available evidence.

Not deviating too much from the point, the above discourse concerns the treatment of ethical violations vis-à-vis the enforceability of the settlement agreements that require a body of case laws that can only come to exist if there is an "effective" implementation of mediator ethics in the national law, by way of rules, regulations, and statutory provisions. Beyond that, industry standards would need to develop hand in hand. Mediators in India do (commonly) subscribe to some code of conduct or code of ethics (from either their accrediting body or an institution), which is likely identified in the mediation agreement, under which the parties and the mediator have agreed to operate.

[2] COVID-19 and E-Mediation

In the postcrisis age of the COVID-19 pandemic, practitioners, professionals/neutrals, and users find themselves compelled to shift to online platforms for conducting proceedings. But along come issues of confidentiality and neutrality in varied forms.

---

27. *See generally*, UNCITRAL, *Report of Working Group II (Dispute Settlement) on the Work of its Sixty-Sixth Session (New York, 6–10 February 2017)* (A/CN.9/901, Feb. 16, 2017), pp. 14–17.
28. *See* Timothy Schnabel, *The Singapore Convention on Mediation: A Framework for the Cross-Border Recognition and Enforcement of Mediated Settlements*, 19 PEPPERDINE DISP. RESOL. L.J. 1, 51–52 (2019) (highlighting, among other things, that alleged breaches of standards must be serious, "not just questionable conduct or a minor breach," and the authority considering refusal cannot "apply standards on a post hoc basis (e.g., . . . cannot deny relief based on an argument that the mediator should have followed certain best practices or other jurisdictions' requirements")).
29. *Id.*, at ¶ 87 ("[T]he standards applicable were not only those applicable to the conciliator but those applicable to the process. It was mentioned that such standards took different forms such as the law governing conciliation and codes of conduct, including those developed by professional associations").
30. *See* Eunice Chua, *The Singapore Convention on Mediation—A Brighter Future for Asian Dispute Resolution*, ASIAN J. INT'L L. 1, 5–6 (2019).

Confidentiality can be easily compromised as the mediation can be recorded using various technological tools if conducted online. Some well-known video calling applications like Zoom (widely used for conducting e-mediation) have faced backlash for lack of security and privacy.[31] Thus, ethical norms have suffered from potential dilutions under rapidly changing conditions, be it domestic or international. Demand for unique software applications that specially cater to the needs of e-mediation has now emerged.

With the pandemic, some form of information communication technology (ICT) has become an integral part of the mediation process.[32] And recognizing the importance of ethics in ODR, the National Centre for Technology & Dispute Resolution (a US-based center) has developed a guidance note on the Ethical Principles for Online Dispute Resolution (Ethical Principles for ODR). A relevant extract from the preamble states that:[33]

> It is intended that the Ethical Principles for Online Dispute Resolution will find a wide audience, *instilling further confidence in the integration of ODR into systems and institutions* as the stakeholders in systems of ODR become more expansive and inclusive. They are designed to *guide and foster ethical ODR systems and practice in both the public and private spheres*. It is likely that *more specific or additional principles may be articulated in the future from within particular sectors and jurisdictions*.
>
> (emphasis supplied)

Also relevant for Indian practice, these Ethical Principles for ODR focus on several technology-related ethical issues like accessibility, accountability, competence, confidentiality, empowerment, equality, fairness, honesty, impartiality, informed participation, innovation, integration, legal obligation, neutrality, protection from harm, security, and transparency. On confidentiality, the document states that the "development and implementation of ODR systems, processes and practitioners [must] maintain confidentiality following all legal obligations and in a manner that is consistent, in particular, with the principles of Legal Obligation, Informed Participation, Security, and Transparency." The International Council has promulgated other similar standards for Online Dispute Resolution (ICODR), which also features a comprehensive study by the National Institution for Transforming India (NITI) Aayog on Designing the Future of Dispute Resolution: The ODR Policy Plan for India.[34]

---

31. *See, e.g.*, Tom Warren, Zoom Faces a Privacy and Security Backlash as It Surges in Popularity, THE VERGE (Apr. 1, 2020), https://www.theverge.com/2020/4/1/21202584/zoom-security-privacy-issues-video-conferencing-software-coronavirus-demand-response.
32. *See generally*, SUSAN NAUSS EXON, ADVANCED GUIDE FOR MEDIATORS Ch. 7 (2015) (Chapter 7 addresses advanced ethical issues, including the use of technology. Other subthemes include mediator manipulation, informed consent, and good faith participation by mediation participants).
33. Leah Wing, *Ethical Principles for Online Dispute Resolution*, THE NATIONAL CENTER FOR TECHNOLOGY AND DISPUTE RESOLUTION, http://odr.info/ethics-and-odr/. *See also*, Leah Wing, *Ethical Principles for Online Dispute Resolution: A GPS Device for the Field*, 3(1) INT'L J. ODR 12–29 (2016).
34. NITI AAYOG, DESIGNING THE FUTURE OF DISPUTE RESOLUTION: THE ODR POLICY PLAN FOR INDIA 65–69, 85–103 (October 2020), https://niti.gov.in/sites/default/files/2020-10/Draft-ODR-Report-NITI-Aayog-Committee.pdf.

§3.04 EXISTING ETHICAL STANDARDS

Mediations, whether court-annexed or private, need the trust of the users and accountability to raise the professional status of mediators or the credibility/integrity of mediation. This is possible with a code of ethics for mediators, specialized and continuous training, and a regulator supervising and holding mediators accountable to ethical standards. Since mediation is a specialized domain and the skills required of a mediator are much different from those needed for a judge or a bureaucrat, a periodic review mechanism (of the standards and their implementation) is profitable in advancing mediation practice.

However, a survey of existing ethical standards applicable to mediators in court-annexed mediation (which subsumes a large majority of mediation practice in India) reveals that ethical standards are either nonexistent or ineffective for their lack of enforcement. Even statutes with self-contained mediation or conciliation mechanisms, such as the Industrial Relations Code 2020, the Hindu Marriage Act 1955, and the Micro, Small and Medium Enterprises Development Act 2006, do not address ethical issues, except perhaps a general provision on confidentiality. Such a state of things widens the already existing vacuum in mediation practice in India.

[A] Model Rules for Court-Annexed Mediation

[1] Mediator Ethics

Section 89 of the Code of Civil Procedure 1908 (CPC) and the mediation rules of various High Courts primarily govern court-annexed mediations. The mediation rules promulgated by the High Courts are virtually the same as the Draft Alternative Dispute Resolution and Mediation Rules 2003 (Model ADR Rules and Model Mediation Rules, respectively), prepared by a committee appointed by the Supreme Court, as per the direction given in *Salem Bar Association v. Union of India.*[35] We examine some of such High Court mediation rules.

The Model Mediation Rules are quite extensive, in the sense that they contain a wide coverage of training and preparation of manual, appointment of a mediator, panel of mediators, qualification of empanelment, disqualification of persons, duty of disclosure, the procedure for mediation, role, representation, parties' good faith obligation, confidentiality, privacy, immunity of the mediator, etc. Besides, the Model Mediation Rules extensively defines the ethics that a mediator must follow; Rule 27 provides the following:

> The mediator shall:
> (1) follow and observe these Rules strictly and with due diligence;
> (2) not carry on any activity or conduct which could reasonably be considered as conduct unbecoming of a mediator;
> (3) uphold the integrity and fairness of the mediation process;

35. (2003) 1 SCC 49.

(4) ensure that the parties involved in the mediation and fairly informed and have an adequate understanding of the procedural aspects of the process;
(5) satisfy himself/herself that he/she is qualified to undertake and complete the assignment in a professional manner;
(6) disclose any interest or relationship likely to affect impartiality or which might seek an appearance of partiality or bias;
(7) avoid, while communicating with the parties, any impropriety or appearance of impropriety;
(8) be faithful to the relationship of trust and confidentiality imposed in the office of mediator;
(9) conduct all proceedings related to the resolutions of a dispute, in accordance with the applicable law;
(10) recognize that mediation is based on principles of self-determination by the parties and that mediation process relies upon the ability of parties to reach a voluntary, undisclosed agreement;
(11) maintain the reasonable expectations of the parties as to confidentiality;
(12) refrain from promises or guarantees of results.

The buck does not stop with setting out ethical standards applicable to a mediator. The Model Mediation Rules also provide for the consequence of a breach of ethical standards. Accordingly, under Rule 8, a mediator's appointment may be canceled "[u]pon information furnished by the mediator [...] or upon any other information received from the parties or other persons, if the court, in which the suit is filed, is satisfied, after conducting such inquiry as it deems fit, and after giving a hearing to the mediator, that the said information has raised a justifiable doubt as to the mediator's independence or impartiality [...]." Likewise, under Rule 9, a member of the panel of mediators (referred to in Rule 3) may be removed from the said panel by the court which impaneled him, if:

(iii) he *exhibits or displays conduct*, during the continuance of the mediation proceedings, *which is unbecoming of a mediator*;
(iv) the Court which empaneled, *upon receipt of information, if it is satisfied, after conducting such inquiry as it deem fit, is of the view, that it is not possible or desirable to continue the name of that person in the panel*,

provided that, before removing or deleting his name, under clause (iii) and (iv), the Court shall hear the mediator whose name is proposed to be removed or deleted from the panel and shall pass a reasoned order.

(emphasis supplied)

And as a result of any proceedings against the mediator under Rules 8 and 9, the Model Mediation Rules (under Rule 5) disqualify such person from being impaneled, i.e., "any person against whom disciplinary proceedings have been initiated by the appropriate disciplinary authority which are pending or have resulted in a punishment."

As seen above, the Model Mediation Rules sufficiently address the ethical standards, not only the contents of such code of ethics but also its consequences against the mediator, thus, contributing to the credibility of the mediation process by inculcating best practices among mediators. Accordingly, if there is a breach of these ethical standards, the Model Mediation Rules provide a grievance redressal mechanism against the mediator, though the punishments (besides disqualification and removal from the panel) have not been set out. Thus, a mediator is held accountable for his conduct that violates ethical standards.

[2] Duty of the Court

Under section 89 of the CPC, courts may refer parties to mediation without obtaining their consent.[36] In this regard, the Model ADR Rules (under Rule 5(f)) provide the procedure for reference by the court to mediation; in that, if one party applies to the court for mediation, the court, after hearing all the parties, can refer the matter for mediation.

The exercise of such power of "non-consensual reference" raises the question of whether courts (exercising such power of reference) have increased responsibility toward the mediation process; "with great power, there must also come great responsibility."[37] This power of mandatory reference is not ordinary, to say the least; it is extraordinary as it can even be exercised in domestic violence-related cases.[38] Hence, courts can take parties away from the traditional dispute resolution forum and place them in mediation. And while the former is highly regulated (with a robust code of ethics applying to judges and advocates), the latter is lacking any proactive implementation/enforcement of ethical standards.

Thus, if a court can refer parties to mandatory mediation, then the court must also oversee the propriety of the mediation process, shielding it from any unethical practices. This principle/modus operandi predominantly features in the Model Mediation Rules (such as Rules 8 and 9), where the court may be moved with information on the conduct of the mediation or about the mediator for action against the mediator. These actions can be the cancelation of appointment under Rule 8, removing the panel under Rule 9, or the disqualification from being impaneled under Rule 5(ii). Even on the policy, it is highly likely that if parties were to experience a mediation fuming ethical violations, the process is sure to lose its integrity and value in the public's eyes.

In instances where the High Court mediation rules do not specifically provide effective implementation/enforcement of mediation rules, courts may apply this principle at the stage when considering the conversion of the settlement into a decree on agreed terms. Order XXIII Rule 3 of the CPC provides (subject to the satisfaction of the court) that if a suit has been adjusted wholly or in part by any lawful agreement or compromise, then the court shall order such agreement, compromise, or satisfaction to

---

36. *See* Afcons Infrastructure Ltd. & Anr. v. Cherian Varkey Construction Co. Pvt. Ltd. & Ors. (2010) 8 SCC 24, ¶ 26 (if the parties are not agreeable for either arbitration or conciliation, both of which requires consent of all parties, the court has to consider which of the other three ADR processes (Lok Adalat, Mediation and Judicial Settlement) which do not require the consent of parties for reference is suitable and appropriate and refer the parties to such ADR process).
37. In 1817, British Member of Parliament, William Lamb, is recorded saying this.
38. Sandeep Bhalothia, Mediation in Domestic Violence Case: Whether to Use or Not to Use?—An Indian Perspective, Mediate.com (September 2017), https://www.mediate.com/articles/bhalothias2indian.cfm.

be recorded, and shall pass a decree. On this, the Allahabad High Court (for example) has observed that:[39]

> In our opinion the word "lawful" in Order XXIII, Rule 3, does not merely mean binding or enforceable. *A contract which is brought about either by undue influence, misrepresentation or fraud is, ... avoidable* [...]. Section 23 of the Act indicates when the consideration or object of an agreement is unlawful. These are cases where it is forbidden by law or is of such a nature that, if permitted, it would defeat the provisions of any law, or is fraudulent, or involves or implies injury to any person or property, or where the court regards it as immoral or opposed to public policy. *We think that the word "lawful" in Order XXIII, Rule 3, refers to agreements which in their very terms or nature are not "unlawful," and may therefore include agreements which are avoidable at the option of one of the parties thereto because they have been brought about by undue influence, coercion or fraud.*
>
> (emphasis supplied)

On a similar note, the Allahabad High Court has also observed that:[40]

> The *parties cannot be rushed into a compromise.* The *essence of a compromise is in a voluntary agreement*, between the parties, to settle the matter by mutual consent. The procedure prescribed under *Order XXIII Rule 3 CPC, rules out all elements of fraud, misrepresentation, coercion and anything which makes a compromise non voluntary.*
>
> (emphasis supplied)

Thus, the CPC does give the court some teeth to examine the voluntariness of a settlement agreement before converting it into a consent decree. This should necessarily include mediated settlements, in that whether the precincts of ethical standards in mediation suffered from any violation. In doing so, the court would be applying the principles emanating from the High Court mediation rules (as discussed above) that governed the entire mediation process, including its ethical considerations.

[B] Standards and Accrediting Bodies

The private world of mediation has different nuts and bolts, unlike court-annexed mediation. In private mediations, ethical standards can hail from different sources, such as the mediator's accrediting body, the institutional rules (*see* next segment), or contractual incorporation of ad hoc standards.

The International Mediation Institute (IMI), which seeks to develop global professional standards for mediators and mediation advocates, has developed the IMI Code of Conduct (IMI Code), which provides mediation users with a concise statement of ethical standards that they can expect from IMI Certified Mediators. And if ever a user believes that the standards were not met or violated, a user can initiate the

39. Quadri Jahen Begum v. Fazal Ahmad, AIR 1928 All 494.
40. Jageshwar Dayal & Ors. v. Rajjan Lal, 2019 (11) ADJ 207.

Professional Conduct Assessment Process requesting that a mediator's conduct be independently assessed for any violation of the IMI Code.[41]

The IMI Code of Conduct puts numerous ethical responsibilities on the mediator, such as conflict of interest, diligence, impartiality, informing users of the process, fairness and integrity of the process, confidentiality, etc. Like the IMI, the Singapore International Mediation Institute (SIMI) provides the SIMI Code of Professional Conduct (SIMI Code). The SIMI Code specifically obligates the mediator to accept an assignment only if he feels reasonably competent and is required to share his relevant background and experience to better understand the users.

SIMI mediators are not permitted to accept the mediation assignment if it will materially affect their independence, neutrality or impartiality, or there is a conflict of interest. The SIMI mediators are also required to ensure the confidentiality of the entire mediation process, and for a period of up to 12 months following the end of a mediation, SIMI mediators will not represent any party from that mediation in an advisory capacity.[42] Furthermore, if a mediation user believes that the concerned mediator has not complied with the SIMI Code, then the user can initiate the assessment process by loading a complaint.[43]

[C] Institutional Mediation

Mediation institutions also provide for their code of professional conduct that it applies to its impaneled mediators. Institutional mediation greatly aids in overcoming the absence of any statutory framework or legislative provision governing mediator ethics. Institutions, therefore, provide a complete paradigm for users to have not only the convenience of a centralized set of rules, fee schedule, service, etc., but also a process and panel of mediators who are bound by a code of professional conduct. Trust, in these circumstances, comes more easily.

The Asia Pacific Centre for Arbitration & Mediation (APCAM) has its presence in more than 10 countries in the Asia-Pacific region (including India). It provides the APCAM Mediators' Code of Professional Conduct (APCAM Code). Accordingly, *inter alia*, mediators under the APCAM Panel:

(i) must not accept an appointment without first disclosing anything within their knowledge that may materially affect their independence, neutrality, or impartiality; and
(ii) must not represent in an advisory capacity of any party within 12 months following the end of mediation; and

41. Available at—https://www.imimediation.org/practitioners/professional-conduct-assessment-process/.
42. Available at—http://www.simi.org.sg/Portals/0/Code%20of%20Conduct/SIMI%20Code%20Of%20Professional%20Conduct%20%5BJAN%202017%5D.pdf.
43. Available at—http://www.simi.org.sg/Portals/0/Code%20of%20Conduct/SIMI%20Assessment%20Of%20Professional%20Conduct%20%5BJAN%202017%5D.pdf.

(iii) make sure and be satisfied that the parties are attending the mediation voluntarily and they have reached an agreement of their own volition and knowingly consent to any resolution.

But if a party to a mediation believes there has been a lack of compliance with the APCAM Code, they can submit a complaint to this effect to APCAM through the Mediators' Conduct Assessment process.

Indian mediation institutions like the Indian Institute of Arbitration and Mediation (IIAM) and CAMP Arbitration & Mediation Practice (CAMP), providing institutional mediation services, have also implemented their code of conduct to govern mediators. These are extensive and adhere to international standards promulgated by the APCAM or IMI. Similarly, the International Chamber of Commerce (ICC) Mediation Rules 2014 (administered by the ICC International Centre for ADR) require that before an appointment, the mediator shall sign a statement of acceptance, availability, impartiality, and independence, and disclose in writing to the Center any facts or circumstances which might be of such a nature as to call into question the mediator's independence in the eyes of the parties, as well as any circumstances that could give rise to reasonable doubts as to the mediator's impartiality. As in many institution rules, ICC Mediation Rules mandate a mediator to inform the parties how the mediation will be conducted and that the proceedings shall be confidential.

§3.05 CANNONS OF MEDIATOR ETHICS

The tractate of standards forms the cannons of mediator ethics. This core content of a mediator's ethical obligations may be similarly found in any source of mediator ethics, be it institutional, court-annexed, or contractual incorporation of an ad hoc code. The following segments expound on these ethical cannons. Readers are also advised to pay a visit to the tabular comparison of three codes of conduct in the Appendix, which impresses a better sense of ethical considerations.

[A] Confidentiality

Confidentiality is the substructure of mediation. It proffers integrity to the process and confidence in the mediator, furthers parties' self-determination, and is maintained by the mediator during and after the process is completed or terminated. This is because a mediator can better perform his role if he can understand (to the best extent possible) the "motives and possibly even bona fides of the conduct of each party."[44] For this to happen, parties need to be frank with the mediator.[45] That, however, is not quite possible without the assurance of a mediator who can keep things confidential.

44. International Association of Machinists and Aerospaceworkers, Afl-cio, Appellee, v. National Mediation Board et al., National Airlines, Inc., Appellants, 425 F.2d 527 (D.C. Cir. 1969).
45. *See* The Harvard Law Review Association, *Protecting Confidentiality in Mediation*, 98(2) HARVARD L. REV. 441–459 (1984).

Concerning the communication within a mediation, confidentiality is found in two tiers: between the mediator and the party and between the parties. None can be disclosed outside the mediation when governed by a confidentiality requirement. The communication between the mediator and a party in a private session or caucus cannot also be disclosed to the other party unless the party expressly allows the mediator.

Confidentiality also concerns the neutrality of a mediator.[46] A lack of trust in the mediator's assurance of confidentiality can raise doubts in the mind of the parties about the mediator's precepts or his neutrality. That is sure to deter a party from being open and unreserved to the mediator. Thus, the lack of confidentiality greatly undermines the role of the mediator among users. Without it, mediation can be highly prejudicial, used as a tool for discovering sensitive information. Such situations are not unlikely, especially if the parties (or advocates) are differently situated in their knowledge and awareness about the mediation process or its governing framework.

But absolute confidentiality is still a matter of debate as far as Indian law is concerned. A mediator may often confront dilemmatic situations wherein his duty of confidentiality may tussle with a different obligation, say, arising out of public interest. Take, for instance, "if the mediator learns from one party in a confidential session of information affecting [...] the ability to provide support for spouse or children, the mediator's obligation to promote disclosure may conflict with the obligation to protect confidentiality."[47] In the circumstances like these, absolute confidentiality may turn unethical.[48]

In the recommendations given by Justice M. N. Venkatachaliah Committee on India's draft ADR Act,[49] it was suggested that confidentiality should not be made applicable if the disclosure is necessary to prevent any physical or psychological injury to a party, or if it is necessary for the interests of preventing or revealing the commission of a crime (including an attempt to commit a crime), or the concealment of a crime, or a threat to a party. This suggestion was accepted and incorporated in the APCAM Mediators' Code of Professional Conduct (Article 4e). Thus, a clear ethical standard is warranted, which is well exposited, enumerating the norms and exceptions.

[B] Impartiality

Simply put, impartiality means freedom from favoritism, bias, or freedom. It concerns the state of mind and is the ability of the mediator to screen out biases and opinions of either party so that neither is favored.

46. *See id.*, at pp. 445–446; Lawrence R. Freedman & Michael L. Prigoff, *Confidentiality in Mediation: The Need for Protection*, 2(1) J. Disp. Resol. 27–46, 38 (1986).
47. Brad Honoroff & Susan Opotow, *Mediation Ethics: A Grounded Approach*, 23(2) Negotiation J. 155–172, 159 (2007).
48. *Id.*, at p. 161.
49. Draft Indian ADR Act (Recommendations submitted by Justice M. N. Venkatachaliah Committee to the Supreme Court of India) (on file with the authors).

Bias being psychological in characteristic, any intervention by the mediator can potentially be seen as an act favoring one party. Moreover, a mediator cannot regulate his internal biases, which he might not even be aware of (subconscious bias). Nevertheless, the mediator can practice the appearance of unbiasedness. It is a mediator's ethical obligation to conduct the mediation impartially and avoid such conduct that would give the appearance of partiality toward, for example, a party's personality, sex/gender, religion/background, views/beliefs, etc. His action must be as neutral as possible, and that is why neutrality (concerning impartiality) is often considered the other side of the coin (even though the term does not frequently appear in ethical codes).

The word "neutral" comes from the Latin word *neuter*, which means "neither of them," indicating lack of partiality, favoritism, the taking of sides.[50] Hence, often the terminologies "mediator" and "neutral" are used interchangeably.[51] The term "neutral" occasionally appears in definitions that define mediation as a voluntary, nonbinding process in which a neutral third party helps the disputants reach a mutually beneficial resolution. Mediators also occasionally inform the parties about their role as that of "neutral" intermediary.

But it goes without saying that a mediator will cast on neutrality when confronting an ethical dilemma.[52] In this regard, Cobb and Rifkin also explain neutrality as "equidistance" (different from neutrality vis-à-vis "impartiality").[53] Neutrality as "equidistance" means that a mediator acts neutrally when he intervenes to favor a side to maintain the power balance between two parties. Here, the bias is positive, as long as it brings symmetry to the negotiations.[54] Such positive reinforcement can help the mediator to refrain from the bias of favoring any outcome based on his personal beliefs of merit, the bias of culture, gender, religion, and so on.

[C] Conflict of Interest

A conflict of interest can arise from a mediator's involvement with either the subject matter of the dispute or his relationship with a party (past or present, personal or professional) that raises justifiable doubts about the mediator's independence and impartiality. A mediator is obligated to avoid such a situation since any perceived, actual, and potential conflicts of interest can be detrimental to the process of mediation. And before taking a mediation, he must make necessary inquiries whether his involvement in the dispute will lead to a potential or actual conflict of interests—an obligation that continuously runs throughout the mediation process.

---

50. *See* Douglas Yarn, Dictionary of Conflict Resolution 322 (1999). *See also* Christopher Moore, The Mediation Process: Practical Strategies for Resolving Conflict 32 (2014).
51. *See* Kevin Gibson, Leigh Thompson & Max H. Bazerman, *Shortcomings of Neutrality in Mediation: Solutions Based on Rationality*, 12(1) Negotiation J. 69 (1996).
52. *See id.*, at p. 70.
53. Sara Cobb & Janet Rifkin, *Practice and Paradox: Deconstructing Neutrality in Mediation*, 16(1) Law & Social Inquiry 41–46 (1991).
54. *Id.*, at p. 44.

The Arbitration & Conciliation Act 1996 (ACA), for instance, provides that the conciliator who is appointed shall be independent and impartial.[55] The 2018 UNCITRAL Model Law on Mediation states similarly.[56] The Model Law requires that the mediator discloses any actual or potential conflict that can question his impartiality. Potential conflicts of interest include the mediator's current or potential relationships with any parties or their counsels. If that be the case, the parties' consent should be necessary to proceed with the mediation thereafter. As commented concerning the Uniform Mediation Act (prepared by the Uniform Law Commission of the US), such requirement protects the core of the legislation, i.e., a party's self-determination, by providing parties with such information necessary for them to decide whether the mediator should be retained.[57]

About court-annexed mediation, Rule 7(a) of the Model Mediation Rules provides for the duty of the mediator to disclose certain facts: "(a) When a person is approached in connection with his possible appointment ..., he shall disclose in writing to the parties, any circumstances likely to give rise to a justifiable doubt as to his independence or impartiality." Rule 7(b) further states that the mediator shall "throughout the continuance of the mediation proceedings, without delay, disclose to the parties in writing, about the existence of any of the circumstances" that are likely to give rise to "justifiable doubt as to his independence or impartiality."

In practice, conflicts are most commonly encountered when the mediator is also a practicing advocate, i.e., if the mediator has also represented one of the parties as an advocate. This raises a challenge to the mediator's impartiality.[58] But in such cases, if the parties have consented to the appointment of such a mediator, should a mediator weigh his impartiality over self-determination? Commentators have argued that even if there is consent from both parties, best practices demand that a mediator withdraws if he believes that a conflict of interests exists.[59]

Furthermore, a question arises if impartiality should be maintained even after the mediation has been terminated. There is no clear answer to this under Indian law. In the US, for instance, there is a considerable divide on this issue. The State of Michigan, for example, prohibits post-mediation relationships without parties' consent, and the State of North Carolina puts a blanket prohibition.[60] However, the State of Alabama, for example, allows it for unrelated matters with the permission of all parties.[61]

---

55. Indian Arbitration & Conciliation Act, 1996, §§64, 67.
56. UNCITRAL Model Law on International Commercial Mediation and International Settlement Agreements Resulting from Mediation, 2018, Art. 9.
57. Uniform Mediation Act, §9(a)(1) (*see* comments on section 9).
58. *See* Michelle D Gaines, *A Proposed Conflict of Interest Rule for Attorney-Mediators*, 73 Wash L. Rev. 699, 704 (1998).
59. Diane K. Vescovo, Allen S. Blair & Hayden D. Lait, *Essay—Ethical Dilemmas in Mediation*, 31 U. Mem. L. Rev. 59 (2000).
60. *See* Suzanne McCorkle, *The Murky World of Mediation Ethics: Neutrality, Impartiality and Conflict of Interest in State Codes of Conduct*, 23(2) Conflict Resol. Quarterly (2005).
61. *Id.*

[D] Role of Mediator

Mixing the role of a mediator with that of another profession may be quite problematic. The role of a mediator is to facilitate the parties' voluntary agreement, which substantially differs from other professional-client relationships like that with an advocate, a doctor, or an accountant.[62] An advocate, for example, renders advice in the interest of his client alone, whereas a mediator is there to facilitate the negotiation between the parties and not offer any professional advice in any one parties' interest. A slippage (in this regard) on the part of the mediator can cause a loss to his neutrality.[63]

The degree of a mediator's role from a simple facilitator to a more proactive/evaluative facilitator often boils down to what the parties want/expect of their mediator. But it must not cross over into another attorney-client-like relationship, which would undermine his impartiality and parties' self-determination. Similarly, mixing a mediator's role with any another profession can be problematic—a mediator must not fuse his role with, say, a chartered accountant, a doctor, etc., and create a different professional-client relationship, though he may well use his knowledge, experience, or qualifications in order to facilitate the parties to a settlement (say, for "reality testing"[64]).

By their rules and/or code of conduct for mediators, many mediation institutions disallow mediators from giving legal or professional advice.[65] Some mediation institutes also provide parties the option to choose between facilitative and evaluative mediation methods, though "evaluative" here does not mean that the mediator assumes any attorney-client relationship when providing his assessment (legal or technical) on the merits of the case. For instance, JAMS Mediation Rules provide that "[i]f a mediator offers an evaluation of a party's position or the likely outcome in court or arbitration, or offers a recommendation with regard to settlement, the mediator should ensure that the parties understand that the mediator is not acting as an attorney for any party and is not providing legal advice."[66]

62. American Bar Association, *Model Standards of Conduct for Mediators*, ABA (standard VI, A5).
63. *See* NANCY H. ROGERS & CRAIG A. MCEWEN, MEDIATION LAW, POLICY & PRACTICE §10 (1994).
64. Reality testing is the technique employed by a mediator that invites a party to adjust his perceptions of the claim by testing them. The mediator invites the party to reassess and articulate his claims and positions, helping the party discover the potential drawbacks or falls out in their position or merits of the case. The mediator employs this technique through a series of hard, pinpointed questions, often by relying on his personal knowledge, experience, or qualifications.
65. *See, e.g.*, HKIAC Mediation Rules, 1999, Rule 4(a); VIAC Rules of Arbitration and Mediation, 2018, Art. 12(5); ADR Institute of Canada, National Mediation Rules & Code Conduct for Mediators, 2012, Rule 6.2.
66. JAMS, Mediators Ethics Guidelines, Guideline VI.

[E] Self-Determination of Parties

Self-determination is fundamental to mediation, wherein the mediator's role is in ensuring that parties arrive at a voluntary and uncoerced resolution to their dispute.[67] Self-determination requires that parties be able to exercise free will without any fear of their safety.[68] Self-determination in mediation helps parties understand their independent ability for negotiation and decision-making in disputes. This boosts their "strength of self," such as self-respect, self-reliance, and self-confidence.[69] The ABA Model Standards of Conduct for Mediators, for example, emphasizes this element by directing mediators to uphold self-determination and balancing it with the obligation to facilitate a quality process.[70] As such, several international institutions also refer to it in varied ways,[71] including Indian mediation institutions and the Model Mediation Rules for court-annexed mediations.[72]

§3.06 CONCLUDING REMARKS

Putting everything in perspective, there is ultimately no national-level regulatory system in place to either promulgate or enforce ethical standards for mediators. An occupation that is not regulated in any way and does not have an overseeing authority cannot be considered a "profession" in any sense because, without proper regulations, such a person cannot serve the public fully and ethically.[73] Thus, for mediation to be considered a profession and to ensure the public's trust in the process, a governing or regulatory body must be set up to ensure adherence to the highest ethical standards.

India must closely consider the recommendations of Justice M. N. Venkatachaliah Committee on the draft ADR Act. There is merit in the Committee's recommendation to form an ADR Council of India (ADR Council) that will frame the policies and guidelines for uniform professional standards regarding all matters relating to arbitration and mediation (private, court-annexed, or statutory mediations). This is needed not because everyone will behave unethically in their absence but because he may be held accountable when a person deviates from the ethical standards. In the long run, this is what will improve the mediation experience for

67. *See* John D. Feerick, *Standards of Conduct for Mediators*, 79(6) JUDICATURE 316 (1995).
68. *See* Kristine Paranica, *The Implications of Intimate Partner Violence on Ethical Mediation Practice*, 88 N.D. L. REV. 907, 910 (2012).
69. *See* ROBERT A. BARUCH BUSH & JOSEPH P. FOLGER, THE PROMISE OF MEDIATION: THE TRANSFORMATIVE APPROACH TO CONFLICT 13 (2004).
70. American Bar Association, *Model Standards of Conduct for Mediators*, ABA (standard I, A1).
71. IIAM Mediation Rules, 2020, Rule 1(D); ICADR International Mediation Rules, Rule 3; ADR Institute of Canada, National Mediation Rules & Code Conduct for Mediators, 2012, Rule 7(1); IMI Model Mediation Rules, 2016, Art. 5.
72. Model Mediation Rules for Court-Annexed Mediation, 2003, Rule 27(10) (recognize that mediation is based on principles of self-determination by the parties and that mediation process relies upon the ability of parties to reach a voluntary, undisclosed agreement).
73. Jack Goetz & Jennifer Kalfsbeek, *Serving the Public: The Case For Formally Professionalizing Court-Connected and Litigated-Case Mediation*, AMERICAN INSTITUTE OF MEDIATION (April 2014), http://www.americaninstituteofmediation.com/pg1036.cfm.

parties, motivating prospective litigants to opt for mediation. However, in creating these policies and guidelines, the Council would need to overcome the challenge of striking a delicate balance between uniformity and accountability in mediation, on the one hand, and flexibility and party autonomy, on the other hand.

For court-annexed mediations, in particular, the Committee recommended the formation of a National Court-Annexed ADR Supervision Committee for overseeing the court-annexed ADR programs and for making policy, rules, and regulations with respect to training modules of mediators and accreditation, impanelment, code of conduct, and disciplinary processes of mediators and arbitrators impaneled with court-annexed ADR centers. The Mediation and Conciliation Project Committee (MCPC) of the Supreme Court of India (the existing body prescribing mediator training and court-annexed programs) would need to be eclipsed.

APPENDIX: COMPARISON OF ETHICAL CANNONS UNDER THREE IMPORTANT INSTRUMENTS

Ethical Cannons	APCAM Mediators' Code of Professional Conduct (Asia Pacific Centre for Arbitration & Mediation)	Model Standards of Conduct for Mediators (American Bar Association)	JAMS Mediators Ethics Guidelines (Private Mediation Service Provider)
1. Self-Determination	[3] Process (a) Mediators shall satisfy themselves that the parties to the mediation and their advisers understand the characteristics of the mediation process, their roles as parties and advisers, and the role of a mediator. The Mediator shall ensure that before the mediation begins, the parties have understood and agreed the terms and conditions which will govern the mediation including those relating to obligations of confidentiality on the Mediator and on the parties. It is best practice for those terms to be contained in a written Agreement to Mediate unless the parties or the circumstances dictate otherwise. (b) (ii) Mediators shall conduct the process with fairness to all parties and shall take particular care to ensure that all parties have adequate opportunities to be heard, to be involved in the process and to have the opportunity to seek and obtain legal or other counsel before finalizing any resolution.	[A] A mediator shall conduct a mediation based on the principle of party self-determination. Self-determination is the act of coming to a voluntary, uncoerced decision in which each party makes free and informed choices as to process and outcome. Parties may exercise self-determination at any stage of a mediation, including mediator selection, process design, participation in or withdrawal from the process, and outcomes. [1] Although party self-determination for process design is a fundamental principle of mediation practice, a mediator may need to balance such party self-determination with a mediator's duty to conduct a quality process in accordance with these Standards. [2] A mediator cannot personally ensure that each party has made free and informed choices to reach particular decisions, but, where appropriate, a mediator	[I] The right of the parties to reach a voluntary agreement is central to the mediation process. Consequently, a mediator should act and conduct the process in ways that maximize its voluntariness. In most cases that are not court-ordered, parties to the mediation process arrive willing and able to engage in assisted negotiation. On infrequent occasions, however, a mediator may perceive that a party is being forced into and/or through the process, for example, by a family member or representative. In that event, a mediator should explore carefully with that party and the other parties, within the bounds of discretion and confidentiality, whether the mediation process should proceed, and, in any case, strive to ensure that the concerns of the reluctant party regarding the process are fully addressed.

	(iii) Mediators shall take reasonable steps to prevent any misconduct that might invalidate an agreement reached at mediation or create or aggravate a hostile environment. Mediators will also be satisfied that the parties have reached agreement of their own volition and knowingly consent to any resolution.	should make the parties aware of the importance of consulting other professionals to help them make informed choices. [B] A mediator shall not undermine party self-determination by any party for reasons such as higher settlement rates, egos, increased fees, or outside pressures from court personnel, program administrators, provider organizations, the media or others.	Court-ordered mediation often carries an aspect of involuntariness into the process. A mediator should be sensitive to this dynamic and assure the parties that although they have been ordered to attend the mediation, a settlement can be reached only if it is to their mutual satisfaction.
2. Impartiality	2(b) Independence, Neutrality & Impartiality (i) Mediators shall not accept an appointment without first disclosing anything within their knowledge that may, or may be seen to, materially affect their independence neutrality or impartiality. This duty to disclose is a continuing obligation throughout the mediation process. (ii) The existence of circumstances potentially affecting, or appearing to affect, a Mediator's independence, neutrality or impartiality will not	[A] A mediator shall decline a mediation if the mediator cannot conduct it in an impartial manner. Impartiality means freedom from favoritism, bias or prejudice. [B] A mediator shall conduct a mediation in an impartial manner and avoid conduct that gives the appearance of partiality. [1] A mediator should not act with partiality or prejudice based on any participant's personal characteristics, background, values and beliefs, or performance at a mediation, or any other reason. [2] A mediator should neither give nor accept a gift, favor, loan or other item of value that raises a question as to the mediator's actual or perceived impartiality.	[V] A mediator should remain impartial throughout the course of the mediation. A mediator should be aware of and avoid the potential for bias based on the parties' backgrounds, personal attributes, or conduct during the session, or based on any pre-existing knowledge of or opinion about the merits of the dispute being mediated. A mediator should endeavor to provide a procedurally fair process in which each party is given an adequate opportunity to participate. If a mediator becomes incapable of maintaining impartiality, the mediator should withdraw promptly.

Ethical Cannons	APCAM Mediators' Code of Professional Conduct (Asia Pacific Centre for Arbitration & Mediation)	Model Standards of Conduct for Mediators (American Bar Association)	JAMS Mediators Ethics Guidelines (Private Mediation Service Provider)
	automatically imply unfitness to act as a mediator provided these circumstances have been fully disclosed and addressed to the satisfaction of the parties and the Mediator. (iii) Mediators shall always act in an independent, neutral and impartial way. They shall act in an unbiased manner, treating all parties with fairness, quality and respect. If at any time a Mediator feels unable to conduct the process in an independent, neutral and impartial manner, (s)he shall express that concern and shall offer to withdraw from the mediation. Such circumstances include — Financial or personal interests in the outcome of the mediation. Existing past or future financial, business or professional relationship with any of	[3] A mediator may accept or give de minimis gifts or incidental items or services that are provided to facilitate a mediation or respect cultural norms so long as such practices do not raise questions as to a mediator's actual or perceived impartiality. [C] If at any time a mediator is unable to conduct a mediation in an impartial manner, the mediator shall withdraw.	A mediator should disclose any information that reasonably could lead a party to question the mediator's impartiality. A mediator may proceed with the process unless a party objects to continuing service. A mediator should withdraw if a conflict of interest exists that casts serious doubt on the integrity of the process. After a mediation is completed, a mediator should refrain from any conduct involving a party, insurer or counsel to the mediation that reasonably would cast doubt on the integrity of the mediation process, absent disclosure to and consent by all parties to the mediation. This does not preclude the mediator from serving as a mediator or in another dispute resolution capacity with a party, insurer or counsel involved in the prior mediation. A mediator should exercise caution in accepting items of value, including gifts or payments for meals, from a party, insurer or counsel to a

	the parties or their representatives about which the Mediator is aware. Other potential source of bias or prejudice concerning a person or institution which may affect that Mediator's independence, neutrality or impartiality or reasonably create an appearance of partiality or bias.		mediation during or after a mediation, particularly if the items are accepted at such a time and in such a manner as to cast doubt on the integrity of the mediation process. A mediator should also avoid conflicts of interest in recommending the services of other professionals. If a mediator is unable to make a personal recommendation without creating a potential or actual conflict of interest, the mediator should so advise the parties and refer them to a professional referral service or association. The JAMS Conflict of Interest Policy provides additional information regarding restricted conduct and should be adhered to by a JAMS mediator.
3. Conflict of Interest	[2c] Conflict of Interest (i) Mediators shall conduct reasonable inquiries to determine if any interests, conflicts of interests or potential biases may exist. They shall have a continuing duty to disclose any interests, conflicts of interests or potential	[A.] A mediator shall avoid a conflict of interest or the appearance of a conflict of interest during and after a mediation. A conflict of interest can arise from involvement by a mediator with the subject matter of the dispute or from any relationship between a mediator and any mediation participant, whether past or present, personal or professional,	[V.] A mediator should remain impartial throughout the course of the mediation. A mediator should be aware of and avoid the potential for bias based on the parties' backgrounds, personal attributes, or conduct during the session, or based on any pre-existing knowledge of or opinion about the

Ethical Cannons	APCAM Mediators' Code of Professional Conduct (Asia Pacific Centre for Arbitration & Mediation)	Model Standards of Conduct for Mediators (American Bar Association)	JAMS Mediators Ethics Guidelines (Private Mediation Service Provider)
	biases that may become apparent during the mediation process. (ii) Following any such disclosures, a Mediator shall decline to participate as a mediator in a particular case if any of the parties raises an objection, unless a contract or applicable law or Court order nevertheless requires the Mediator's participation. Even then, if a Mediator personally believes that the matters disclosed would inhibit their actual impartiality, the Mediator should withdraw as the mediator. (iii) After accepting appointment, and until the mediation process ends, Mediators shall not enter into financial, business, professional, family or social relationships or acquire financial or personal interests that are likely to affect or might reasonably	that reasonably raises a question of a mediator's impartiality. [B.] A mediator shall make a reasonable inquiry to determine whether there are any facts that a reasonable individual would consider likely to create a potential or actual conflict of interest for a mediator. A mediator's actions necessary to accomplish a reasonable inquiry into potential conflicts of interest may vary based on practice context. [C.] A mediator shall disclose, as soon as practicable, all actual and potential conflicts of interest that are reasonably known to the mediator and could reasonably be seen as raising a question about the mediator's impartiality. After disclosure, if all parties agree, the mediator may proceed with the mediation. [D.] If a mediator learns any fact after accepting a mediation that raises a question with respect to that mediator's service creating a potential or actual conflict of interest, the mediator shall disclose it as quickly as practicable. After disclosure, if all parties agree, the mediator may proceed with the mediation. [E.] If a mediator's conflict of interest might reasonably be viewed as	merits of the dispute being mediated. A mediator should endeavor to provide a procedurally fair process in which each party is given an adequate opportunity to participate. If a mediator becomes incapable of maintaining impartiality, the mediator should withdraw promptly. A mediator should disclose any information that reasonably could lead a party to question the mediator's impartiality. A mediator may proceed with the process unless a party objects to continuing service. A mediator should withdraw if a conflict of interest exists that casts serious doubt on the integrity of the process. After a mediation is completed, a mediator should refrain from any conduct involving a party, insurer or counsel to the mediation that reasonably would cast doubt on the integrity of the mediation process, absent disclosure to and consent by all parties to the mediation. This does not preclude the mediator from serving

	create the appearance of conflict of interest, partiality or bias, without making a prior disclosure to all the parties and gaining their consent. (iv) Within 12 months following the end of a mediation, Mediators shall not represent in an advisory capacity, either formally or informally, any party to a mediation in the same or a substantially related matter, unless all parties to the mediation expressly consent to that representation after full disclosure. Acting as a neutral in other dispute resolution proceedings (eg. as a mediator or arbitrator) that may involve some or all of the parties will not be considered a representation in an advisory capacity for the purposes of this clause. (v) At no time following the end of a mediation shall Mediators adduce evidence or testify on behalf of one of the parties in making or defending a claim	undermining the integrity of the mediation, a mediator shall withdraw from or decline to proceed with the mediation regardless of the expressed desire or agreement of the parties to the contrary. [F.] Subsequent to a mediation, a mediator shall not establish another relationship with any of the participants in any matter that would raise questions about the integrity of the mediation. When a mediator develops personal or professional relationships with parties, other individuals or organizations following a mediation in which they were involved, the mediator should consider factors such as time elapsed following the mediation, the nature of the relationships established, and services offered when determining whether the relationships might create a perceived or actual conflict of interest.	as a mediator or in another dispute resolution capacity with a party, insurer or counsel involved in the prior mediation. A mediator should exercise caution in accepting items of value, including gifts or payments for meals, from a party, insurer or counsel to a mediation during or after a mediation, particularly if the items are accepted at such a time and in such a manner as to cast doubt on the integrity of the mediation process. A mediator should also avoid conflicts of interest in recommending the services of other professionals. If a mediator is unable to make a personal recommendation without creating a potential or actual conflict of interest, the mediator should so advise the parties and refer them to a professional referral service or association. The JAMS Conflict of Interest Policy provides additional information regarding restricted conduct and should be adhered to by a JAMS mediator.

Ethical Cannons	APCAM Mediators' Code of Professional Conduct (Asia Pacific Centre for Arbitration & Mediation)	Model Standards of Conduct for Mediators (American Bar Association)	JAMS Mediators Ethics Guidelines (Private Mediation Service Provider)
	against another party to the same mediation where they have acquired confidential information from the other party, unless all that information is no longer confidential or unless the party protected by the confidentiality gives consent.		[VII] A mediator should withdraw from the process if the mediation is being used to further illegal conduct, or for any of the reasons set forth above: lack of informed consent, a conflict of interest that has not or cannot be waived, a mediator's inability to remain impartial, or a mediator's physical or mental disability. In addition, a mediator should be aware of the potential need to withdraw from the case if procedural or substantive unfairness appears to have undermined the integrity of the mediation process.
4. Confidentiality	[4] Confidentiality (a) Mediators shall keep confidential all information acquired in the course of serving as a mediator in a mediation unless — (i) Compelled to make a disclosure by law, by a Court of Law or by some governmental agency having appropriate authority and jurisdiction; or (ii) Required under paragraph 4(b), in which event the	[A.] A mediator shall maintain the confidentiality of all information obtained by the mediator in mediation, unless otherwise agreed to by the parties or required by applicable law. [1.] If the parties to a mediation agree that the mediator may disclose information obtained during the mediation, the mediator may do so. [2.] A mediator should not communicate to any non-participant	[IV.] It is crucial that the mediator and all parties have a clear understanding as to confidentiality before the mediation begins. Before a mediation session begins, a mediator should explain to all parties (a) any applicable laws, rules or agreements prohibiting disclosure in subsequent legal proceedings of offers and statements made and documents produced during the session, and

	recipients of the confidential information shall themselves be bound to maintain the confidentiality; or (iii) The specific information comes into the public domain (otherwise than as a result of a disclosure by the Mediator); or (iv) The parties release the Mediator from the confidentiality restriction; or (v) Necessary to defend the Mediator from any proceedings or charges for which (s)he risks incurring any liability. (b) Provided that information which has been disclosed as confidential in clause (a)relates to such information, revealing or relating to — (i) the attempt to commit any physical or psychological threat or injury to a party; or (ii) the commission of a crime, including an attempt to commit a crime, the mediator may inform the party giving such information that (s)he is not bound by confidentiality and ascertain whether	information about how the parties acted in the mediation. A mediator may report, if required, whether parties appeared at a scheduled mediation and whether or not the parties reached a resolution. [3.] If a mediator participates in teaching, research or evaluation of mediation, the mediator should protect the anonymity of the parties and abide by their reasonable expectations regarding confidentiality. [B.] A mediator who meets with any persons in private session during a mediation shall not convey directly or indirectly to any other person, any information that was obtained during that private session without the consent of the disclosing person. [C.] A mediator shall promote understanding among the parties of the extent to which the parties will maintain confidentiality of information they obtain in a mediation. [D.] Depending on the circumstance of a mediation, the parties may have varying expectations regarding confidentiality that a mediator should address. The parties may make their own rules with respect to confidentiality, or the accepted practice	(b) the mediator's role in maintaining confidences within the mediation and as to third parties. A mediator should not disclose confidential information without permission of all parties or unless required by law, court rule or other legal authority. A mediator must not use confidential information acquired during the mediation to gain personal advantage or advantage for others, or to affect adversely the interests of others. If the mediation is being conducted under rules or laws that require disclosure of certain information, a mediator should so notify the parties prior to beginning the mediation session. In addition, a mediator's notes, the parties' submissions and other documents containing confidential or otherwise sensitive information should be stored in a reasonably secure location and may be destroyed 90 days after the mediation has been completed or sooner if all parties so request or consent.

Ethical Cannons	APCAM Mediators' Code of Professional Conduct (Asia Pacific Centre for Arbitration & Mediation)	Model Standards of Conduct for Mediators (American Bar Association)	JAMS Mediators Ethics Guidelines (Private Mediation Service Provider)
	such information is genuine. The mediator may weigh the gravity of such information and decide whether (s)he needs to disclose the information to the opposite side or not, or whether (s)he need to withdraw from mediation. (c) The Mediator may, however, disclose having previously served as a mediator in a mediation involving one or more of the parties, provided none of the details of that case are disclosed. (d) Mediators shall discuss confidentiality with the parties before or at the beginning of the mediation and obtain their consent to any communication or practice by the Mediator that involves the disclosure of confidential information. (e) Mediators may use or disclose confidential information obtained during a mediation when, and to the extent that, they believe it to be necessary	of an individual mediator or institution may dictate a particular set of expectations.	

	to prevent physical or psychological injury to a party, the commission of a crime (including an attempt to commit a crime), the concealment of a crime, or threat to a party. Before using or disclosing such information, if not otherwise required to be disclosed by law, Mediators must, if they consider it appropriate, make a good faith effort to persuade the party and/or the party's counsel or other advisers, to act in such a way that would remedy the situation.		
5. Diligence and Process	[2a] DiligenceMediators may accept an assignment to act as Mediator in any situation where they feel competent to serve in that capacity. [3a] ProcedureMediators shall satisfy themselves that the parties to the mediation and their advisers understand the characteristics of the mediation process, their roles as parties and advisers, and the role of a mediator. The Mediator shall ensure that before the mediation begins, the parties have understood and agreed the terms and conditions which will govern the mediation including those relating to obligations of	[A.] A mediator shall conduct a mediation in accordance with these Standards and in a manner that promotes diligence, timeliness, safety, presence of the appropriate participants, party participation, procedural fairness, party competency and mutual respect among all participants. [1.] A mediator should agree to mediate only when the mediator is prepared to commit the attention essential to an effective mediation. [2.] A mediator should only accept cases when the mediator can satisfy the reasonable	[III.] A mediator should have sufficient knowledge of relevant procedural and substantive issues to be effective. It is the mediator's responsibility to prepare before the mediation session by reviewing any statements or documents submitted by the parties. A mediator should refuse to serve or withdraw from the mediation if the mediator becomes physically or mentally unable to meet the reasonable expectations of the parties. [I.] A mediator should ensure that all parties understand and agree to mediation as a process, the mediator's

Ethical Cannons	APCAM Mediators' Code of Professional Conduct (Asia Pacific Centre for Arbitration & Mediation)	Model Standards of Conduct for Mediators (American Bar Association)	JAMS Mediators Ethics Guidelines (Private Mediation Service Provider)
	confidentiality on the Mediator and on the parties. It is best practice for those terms to be contained in a written Agreement to Mediate unless the parties or the circumstances dictate otherwise. (b)(i) Fairness and Integrity of the processMediators shall explain the mediation process to the parties and their advisers, and be satisfied that that they consent to the process being used and to the Mediator selected (unless applicable law, court rules or contract require use of a particular process and/or mediator). Mediators shall ensure that, if there are to be any pre-mediation private communications with the Mediator, all parties are aware they will have equal opportunity to raise issues. [3c] Termination of the Process (i) The Mediator shall ensure the parties understand that they may withdraw from the mediation at any time by informing the Mediator and all other parties without being required to give any justification for doing so.	expectation of the parties concerning the timing of a mediation. [3.] The presence or absence of persons at a mediation depends on the agreement of the parties and the mediator. The parties and mediator may agree that others may be excluded from particular sessions or from all sessions. [4.] A mediator should promote honesty and candor between and among all participants, and a mediator shall not knowingly misrepresent any material fact or circumstance in the course of a mediation. [5.] The role of a mediator differs substantially from other professional roles. Mixing the role of a mediator and the role of another profession is problematic and thus, a mediator should distinguish between the roles. A mediator may provide information that the mediator is qualified by training or experience to provide, only if the	[III.] A mediator should have sufficient knowledge of relevant procedural and substantive issues to be effective. It is the mediator's responsibility to prepare before the mediation session by reviewing any statements or documents submitted by the parties. A mediator should refuse to serve or withdraw from the mediation if the mediator becomes physically or mentally unable to meet the reasonable expectations of the parties. role in that process and all parties' relationship to the mediator. The parties should also understand the particular procedures the mediator intends to employ, including whether and in what manner the mediator may help the parties evaluate the likely outcome of the dispute in court or arbitration if they cannot reach settlement through mediation. In addition, a mediator should be satisfied that the parties have considered and understood the terms of any

	(ii) Mediators may withdraw from a mediation if a negotiation among the parties assumes a character that to the Mediator appears unconscionable or illegal. [3d] Feedback Unless inappropriate in the circumstances, Mediators shall, at the conclusion of a mediation, invite the parties and advisers and any co-mediators or assistant mediators, to complete a Feedback Form and send the same to the Reviewer or APCAM. The feedback shall remain confidential and shall be used for preparing the Feedback Digest by the Reviewer as per guidelines given by APCAM, to be used in the Mediator's profile.	mediator can do so consistent with these Standards. [6.] A mediator shall not conduct a dispute resolution procedure other than mediation but label it mediation in an effort to gain the protection of rules, statutes, or other governing authorities pertaining to mediation. [7.] A mediator may recommend, when appropriate, that parties consider resolving their dispute through arbitration, counseling, neutral evaluation or other processes. [8.] A mediator shall not undertake an additional dispute resolution role in the same matter without the consent of the parties. Before providing such service, a mediator shall inform the parties of the implications of the change in process and obtain their consent to the change. A mediator who undertakes such role assumes different duties and responsibilities that may be governed by other standards. [9.] If a mediation is being used to further criminal conduct, a mediator should take appropriate steps including, if necessary,	settlement, and should, if appropriate, advise the parties to seek legal or other specialized advice. If the mediator perceives that a party is unable to give informed consent to participation in the process or to the terms of settlement due to, for example, the impact of a physical or mental impairment, the process should not continue until the mediator is satisfied that such informed consent has been obtained from the party or the party's duly authorized representative. In the event that, prior to or during a mediation session, it becomes appropriate to discuss the possibility of combining mediation with binding arbitration, the mediator should explain how a mediator's role and relationship to the parties may be altered, as well as the impact such a shift may have on the disclosure of information to the mediator. The parties should be given the opportunity to select another neutral to conduct the arbitration procedure. [VI] A mediator should ensure that the parties understand that the

Ethical Cannons	APCAM Mediators' Code of Professional Conduct (Asia Pacific Centre for Arbitration & Mediation)	Model Standards of Conduct for Mediators (American Bar Association)	JAMS Mediators Ethics Guidelines (Private Mediation Service Provider)
		postponing, withdrawing from or terminating the mediation. [10.] If a party appears to have difficulty comprehending the process, issues, or settlement options, or difficulty participating in a mediation, the mediator should explore the circumstances and potential accommodations, modifications or adjustments that would make possible the party's capacity to comprehend, participate and exercise self-determination. [B.] If a mediator is made aware of domestic abuse or violence among the parties, the mediator shall take appropriate steps including, if necessary, postponing, withdrawing from or terminating the mediation. [C.] If a mediator believes that participant conduct, including that of the mediator, jeopardizes conducting a mediation consistent with these Standards, a mediator shall take appropriate steps including, if necessary, postponing, withdrawing from or terminating the mediation.	mediator's role is that of neutral intermediary, not that of representative of or advocate for any party. A mediator should not offer legal advice to a party. If a mediator offers an evaluation of a party's position or of the likely outcome in court or arbitration, or offers a recommendation with regard to settlement, the mediator should ensure that the parties understand that the mediator is not acting as an attorney for any party and is not providing legal advice. A mediator should be particularly sensitive to role differences if any party is unrepresented by counsel at the mediation, and should explain carefully the limitations of the mediator's role and obtain a written waiver of representation from each unrepresented party. If a mediator assists in the preparation of a settlement agreement and if counsel for any party is not present, the mediator should advise each unrepresented party to have the agreement

			independently reviewed by counsel prior to executing it. A mediator should make an effort to keep abreast of developments within the mediator's jurisdiction concerning what constitutes the practice of law. Different bar associations have issued conflicting opinions about whether and when a mediator engages in the practice of law, and certain states or courts have rules regarding how and in what manner a mediator may evaluate the merits of a dispute.
6. Fees	[3e] (i) Mediators shall, before accepting appointment, agree with the parties how their fees and expenses will be calculated, and how they will be paid by the parties (and if shared between the parties, in what proportions). Mediators who withdraw from a case shall return to the parties any fees already paid relating to the period following withdrawal. (ii) Mediators shall not suggest to the parties that their remuneration should be based on or related to the outcome of the mediation.	[A.] A mediator shall provide each party or each party's representative true and complete information about mediation fees, expenses and any other actual or potential charges that may be incurred in connection with a mediation. [1.] If a mediator charges fees, the mediator should develop them in light of all relevant factors, including the type and complexity of the matter, the qualifications of the mediator, the time required and the rates customary for such mediation services.	Nil.

Ethical Cannons	APCAM Mediators' Code of Professional Conduct (Asia Pacific Centre for Arbitration & Mediation)	Model Standards of Conduct for Mediators (American Bar Association)	JAMS Mediators Ethics Guidelines (Private Mediation Service Provider)
		[2.] A mediator's fee arrangement should be in writing unless the parties request otherwise. [B.] A mediator shall not charge fees in a manner that impairs a mediator's impartiality. [1.] A mediator should not enter into a fee agreement which is contingent upon the result of the mediation or amount of the settlement. [2.] While a mediator may accept unequal fee payments from the parties, a mediator should not allow such a fee arrangement to adversely impact the mediator's ability to conduct a mediation in an impartial manner	
Solicitation & Advertisement	[1a] Promotion of Mediators' Services Subject to applicable laws and to regulations governing professional practice, Mediators shall present and promote their practice in a truthful way. They may quote freely from, and link to, their Profile on the APCAM website and they are free to replicate that Profile, or extracts from it, for their own professional purposes.	[A.] A mediator shall be truthful and not misleading when advertising, soliciting or otherwise communicating the mediator's qualifications, experience, services and fees. [1.] A mediator should not include any promises as to outcome in communications, including business cards, stationery, or computer-based communications.	[VII] A mediator should ensure that any advertising or other marketing conducted on the mediator's behalf is truthful. A mediator should not guarantee results, especially if such guarantee could be perceived as favoring one type of disputant or industry over another.

		[2.] A mediator should only claim to meet the mediator qualifications of a governmental entity or private organization if that entity or organization has a recognized procedure for qualifying mediators and it grants such status to the mediator. [B.] A mediator shall not solicit in a manner that gives an appearance of partiality for or against a party or otherwise undermines the integrity of the process. [C.] A mediator shall not communicate to others, in promotional materials or through other forms of communication, the names of persons served without their permission.	
Advancement of Mediation Practice	Nil.	[A.] A mediator should act in a manner that advances the practice of mediation. A mediator promotes this Standard by engaging in some or all of the following: [1.] Fostering diversity within the field of mediation. [2.] Striving to make mediation accessible to those who elect to use it, including providing services at a reduced rate or on a pro bono basis as appropriate.	Nil.

Ethical Cannons	APCAM Mediators' Code of Professional Conduct (Asia Pacific Centre for Arbitration & Mediation)	Model Standards of Conduct for Mediators (American Bar Association)	JAMS Mediators Ethics Guidelines (Private Mediation Service Provider)
		[3.] Participating in research when given the opportunity, including obtaining participant feedback when appropriate. [4.] Participating in outreach and education efforts to assist the public in developing an improved understanding of, and appreciation for, mediation. [5.] Assisting newer mediators through training, mentoring and networking. [B.] A mediator should demonstrate respect for differing points of view within the field, seek to learn from other mediators and work together with other mediators to improve the profession and better serve people in conflict.	

CHAPTER 4

Court-Annexed Mediation

Raj Panchamatia & Laila Ollapally[*]

§4.01 OVERVIEW

For several years, courts and the judicial system as a whole have been enduring the strain of growing backlogs of cases. Overburdened courts, delays, and costs are preeminent concerns. For India, mediation has been an important motivator for reducing the load on the justice system and encouraging litigants (including prospective ones), who are daunted by lengthy court proceedings, to pursue alternative and appropriate options. The judiciary and the legislature have been prompt in taking steps to promote alternate modes of dispute resolution; however, the adequacy and efficiency of these steps have often been questioned by various stakeholders.

The court-annexed mediation system is one such step that responds to the unsettling circumstances: a "system" less formal, more effective, speedy, with minimum procedural claptrap, and a "process" that gives exclusive and intensive consideration to the dispute as well as the parties involved. Nonetheless, that is not to say that alternative dispute resolution (ADR) methods find their central reasoning in the challenges and inefficiency of the courts' system. Rather, the manner of introducing ADR methods in the Indian legal system exhibits ADR as a stand-alone path for resolving disputes (using its adjudicatory or nonadjudicatory options) wherever considered suitable or appropriate for the dispute in question. Against this backdrop, it has been noted that parties are more and more receptive to consensual mechanisms that impose minimal costs, consume less time, and are more satisfactory. In a well-organized court-annexed mediation system, the rewards of successful mediation are myriad.

* The able assistance of Kushagra Agarwal is gratefully acknowledged.

[A] Judicial System

India is a common law country. Its dispute resolution and justice dispensation system comprises a three-tier structure with the Supreme Court at the apex level, High Courts in the states (provincial units in India), followed by numerous other subordinate courts (e.g., the District Courts, City Civil Courts, etc.). The decisions of the subordinate courts are appealable in the respective High Courts. A High Court functions autonomously in the area of its jurisdiction, and its decisions can be challenged before the Supreme Court. The final word on a matter rests with the Supreme Court, which is also the ultimate authority of interpretation of laws. Over the years, various specialized tribunals have also been established to deal exclusively with disputes pertaining to company law, debt recovery by banks, electricity law, etc.

Like other common law countries, Indian laws can also be broadly classified as substantive and procedural laws. Substantially, substantive laws deal with our rights, while procedural laws are concerned with legal processes involving actions and remedies. In other words, substantive law is what we enforce, while procedural law deals with the rules by which we enforce it.[1] The basic statutes governing the court's civil and criminal justice system in India are the Code of Civil Procedure 1908 (CPC), the Code of Criminal Procedure, 1973, the Indian Evidence Act 1872, and the Arbitration and Conciliation Act 1996. These statutes have been laid down by the legislature and are further supplemented by the interpretations and guidelines given by the courts.

[B] Legal and Regulatory Framework of Mediation

In 1988, the Law Commission of India published its 129th Report on Urban Litigation and Mediation as Alternative to Adjudication.[2] Considering the backlog of cases, the report recommended that courts be obligated to refer a dispute for settlement by any of the ADR mechanisms after the issues are framed and proceed with the trial only when the parties fail to resolve their disputes amicably settled.

The recommendations in this report paved the way for a legislative change which came in 1999, through the CPC (Amendment) Act 1999 ("Amendment Act of 1999"), whereby section 89 of the CPC was amended to deal with the settlement of disputes outside the court. The legislative intent behind the amendment was to encourage the settlement of disputes through the various tools of ADR.[3]

In *Afcons Infrastructure Ltd. v. Cherian Varkey Construction Co. Pvt. Ltd.* ("Afcons"),[4] the Supreme Court observed many drafting errors in section 89 and provided

---

1. *See* Bharat Barrel & Drum Manufacturing Co. Pvt. Ltd. v. Employees State Insurance Corp., AIR 1972 SC 1935, ¶¶ 6–7.
2. Law Commission of India, Report No. 129 (1988), https://lawcommissionofindia.nic.in/101-169/Report129.pdf.
3. Surinder Kaur & Ors. v. Pritam Singh & Ors. (2008) 154 DLT 598, ¶ 8.
4. Afcons Infrastructure Ltd. v. Cherian Varkey Construction Co. Pvt. Ltd. (2010) 8 SCC 24, ¶13 (hereinafter "Afcons").

a coherent interpretation. The court took up the definition of "judicial settlement" and "mediation" under sections 89(2)(c) and 89(2)(d). The court pointed that "it makes no sense to call a compromise effected by the court as mediation," and "it makes no sense to describe a reference made by the court to an institution or person as judicial settlement." The *Afcons* court concluded that definitions of judicial settlement and mediation were mixed up. In other words, what is described as judicial settlement is mediation, and what is described is, in fact, judicial settlement. The court observed that "if the word 'mediation' in clause (d) and the words 'judicial settlement' in clause (c) are interchanged, we find that the said clause makes perfect sense."[5] The *Afcons* court went on to say that this mix-up was "apparently due to a clerical or typographical error in drafting." It is submitted that the court has been kind to the parliamentary draughtsman.

The amended section 89 allows the courts to refer disputes where there exist elements of settlement that may be acceptable to the parties to ADR mechanisms, including arbitration, conciliation, judicial settlement, and mediation. The related provisions incorporated by the said Amendment Act of 1999 were provided under Rules 1A–1C of Order X of the CPC. Rules 1A–1C of Order X do not specifically refer to how the powers of the court under section 89 are to be exercised, but it can generally be stated that section 89 is the substantive law, and the rules are procedural directing the court to opt for any one mode of ADR. In addition, Rules 3[6] and 3A[7] of Order XXIII of CPC provide that where the parties have adjusted a suit by any lawful agreement or compromise, or where the defendant has satisfied the plaintiff in respect of the whole or any part of the dispute, and the court is satisfied in this regard, then it shall order such agreement, compromise, or satisfaction to be recorded, and pass a consent decree accordingly.

Whenever settlements reached in mediation are placed before the court, the court applies the principles under Rule 3 of Order XXIII and then renders a decree in accordance with the settlement.[8] It is a provision for making a decree on any lawful agreement or compromise between the parties, even in cases where the agreement or compromise results from independent mediation proceedings undertaken by the parties. Ultimately, such decrees (or "consent decrees") are binding on the parties like any other court decree.[9]

As for the rules that govern mediation proceedings, the court-annexed scheme imbibes Part II titled Civil Procedure Mediation Rules ("Mediation Rules") of Civil Procedure Alternative Dispute Resolution and Mediation Rules, 2003. A special

5. *Id.*, at ¶ 15.
6. On compromise of suit.
7. That no suit shall lie to set aside a decree on the ground that the compromise on which the decree is based was not lawful.
8. *See* Afcons, *supra* note 4, ¶ 40. Moreover, if the mediated settlement includes disputes which are not subject matter of the suit, the court may direct that the same will be governed by section 21 of the Legal Services Authority Act, 1987, by virtue of which the mediated settlement shall be deemed to be a decree of a civil court.
9. *See* Raja Sri Sailendra Narayan Bhanja Deo v. State of Orissa, AIR 1956 SC 346, ¶ 8 (the consent order is as effective as an order passed on contest), following Kinch v. Walcott, LR 1929 AC 182, 493 (an order by consent is as effective as an order of the court made otherwise than by consent).

committee prescribed these constituted under the directions of the Supreme Court in *Salem Advocate Bar Association (I) v. Union of India* ("*Salem Bar (I)*").[10] After the amendment to section 89, the Supreme Court, in *Salem Bar (I)*, had directed certain modalities to be formulated for how the methods under section 89 would have to be operated. After that, in *Salem Advocate Bar Association (II) v. Union of India* ("*Salem Bar II*"),[11] the Supreme Court directed the adoption of the Mediation Rules to give effect to section 89(2)(d).[12]

The Mediation Rules have now been adopted by all the courts to implement a relatively uniform court-annexed mediation scheme across the country. The Supreme Court and the High Courts (and its subordinate courts) have adopted rules relating to mediation (based broadly on the Mediation Rules with necessary modifications according to the requirements of the State concerned).[13]

All these provisions in the form of various legislative enactments and rules concerning mediation converge at a point to develop a system that avoids multiplicity of litigation and permits parties to come to a settlement amicably.

In 2015, the legal framework concerning civil and commercial disputes in India underwent a paradigm shift with the Commercial Courts, Commercial Division, and Commercial Appellate Division of High Courts Act, 2015 ("Commercial Courts Act"). Through this legislation, the Parliament amended the CPC. It constituted separate and distinct commercial courts and commercial appellate courts at the district level and commercial division and commercial appellate division in the High Courts to deal with commercial suits that fall beyond one crore rupees' pecuniary threshold.[14] These courts were primarily set up to expedite the resolution of commercial disputes to improve the ease of doing business in India.

The Commercial Courts Act defines "commercial disputes" in an elaborate fashion to include a variety of transactions such as ordinary transactions of merchants, bankers, financiers, and traders; export or import of merchandise and services; construction and infrastructure contracts; distribution and licensing agreements; management and consultancy agreements; joint venture agreements; shareholders agreements; and insurance and reinsurance.[15]

After that, in August 2018, the legislature passed the Commercial Courts, Commercial Division and Commercial Appellate Division of High Courts (Amendment)

10. Salem Advocate Bar Association (I) v. Union of India (2003) 1 SCC 49.
11. Salem Advocate Bar Association (II) v. Union of India (2005) 6 SCC 344 (hereinafter "Salem Bar (II)").
12. Prior to finalization, the rules were circulated to the High Courts, subordinate courts, the Bar Council of India, State Bar Councils and the Bar Associations, seeking their responses. It was later forwarded to the respective High Courts to take appropriate steps for making rules in exercise of the rulemaking power subject to modifications, if any, which may be considered relevant.
13. *See* Civil Procedure Alternative Dispute Resolution and Mediation Rules, 2006 (High Court of Bombay); Mediation and Conciliation Rules, 2004 (High Court of Delhi); Alternative Dispute Resolution and Mediation Rules, 2017 (High Court of Hyderabad for Telangana and Andhra Pradesh); Tamil Nadu Mediation Rules, 2010 (High Court of Madras).
14. Commercial Courts Act, 2015, §3.
15. Commercial Courts Act, 2015, §2(1)(c).

Act, 2018 ("Commercial Courts Amendment Act") and along with reducing the pecuniary threshold for commercial disputes to INR 3 lakhs, introduced a potentially significant provision, section 12A. Section 12A provides for mandatory pre-institution mediation, i.e., if a suit does not contemplate any urgent relief, then it shall not be instituted unless the plaintiff exhausts the remedy of pre-institution mediation. The idea behind this provision was to push the litigating parties to at least attempt to resolve their differences out of court.

However, the susceptibility of this provision lies within the provision itself. Subsection (1) of section 12A provides a route to circumvent the mandatory reference to mediation. If the plaintiff, along with his plaint, moves an application for urgent interim relief, the courts can waive the mandatory reference to mediation and institute the suit. In commercial dispute resolution, parties tend to move a separate application for urgent interim reliefs along with their suit, thereby seemingly defeating the purpose of section 12A. Courts, too, have been relatively liberal in recognizing the urgency and waiving off the requirement of mandatory pre-institution mediation.[16]

After enacting section 12A of the Commercial Court Amendment Act, the Indian government also issued the Commercial Courts (Pre-Institution Mediation and Settlement) Rules 2018 (PIMS Rules) and laid down detailed procedure and manner for the pre-institution mediation as envisaged under the Commercial Courts Amendment Act. The PIMS Rules assigned specific duties to the authority (i.e., the body constituted under the Legal Services Authority Act 1987 or LSA) and the mediator. The rules also provide for processing certain forms before the institution of proceedings, issuing notice to parties, dealing with a "non-starter" situation, and preparing a failure report in case of a deadlock between the parties.

[C] What Is Meant by Mediation in India and Mediator's Role?

Mediation is considered a negotiation process in which a neutral third party, a mediator, assists the disputing parties in resolving their disputes.[17] A mediator does not decide what is fair or right; does not apportion blame or impose any terms of settlement on the parties; does not give assurance about the outcome of mediation, and does not render any opinion on the merits or chances of success the case is litigated.[18] Throughout the process, a mediator acts as a catalyst. The mediator attempts to facilitate a voluntary resolution of the dispute by empowering the parties and enabling them to communicate their views to the other, assisting them in identifying issues, reducing misunderstandings, clarifying priorities, exploring areas of compromise, and

16. *See* Sathyam Wood Industries v. Adoniss (P) Ltd. & Ors., MANU/TN/2654/2019; GSD Constructions Pvt. Ltd. v. Balaji Febtech Engineering Pvt. Ltd., MANU/MP/0451/2019; M/s M. K. Food Products v. M/s S.H. Food Products, LAWS(TLNG)-2019-2-109 (Telangana High Court, Feb. 21, 2019).
17. *See* Salem Bar (II), *supra* note 11, ¶ 65.
18. Sriram Panchu, Mediation Practice & Law: The Path to Successful Dispute Resolution 132–134 (1st ed., 2011) (hereinafter "Panchu").

encouraging them to generate options in an attempt to solve the dispute.[19] At every stage of a mediation, it is emphasized that it is the responsibility of the parties to make decisions that affect them and be self-determinant.

There may arise some conundrum as to the distinction between "mediation" and "conciliation." This is largely debated between two schools of thought that either divides the two terms or equate them to be the same. As far as legal positions are concerned, the legislative enactments use these terms as distinct. But the confusion is real. And though it is said that "mediation" and "conciliation" are fundamentally the same in their process (supposedly different only in the degree of the neutral third party's intervention),[20] there are different legal outworking.[21] *See* Chapter 1 for a detailed discussion on the divide between "mediation" and "conciliation" in India.

§4.02 FACTORS TO BE CONSIDERED BEFORE REFERRAL

The objective of section 89 is that courts endeavor to encourage out-of-court settlements through the ADR processes. But before taking any step to transfer parties to mediation, a court needs to consider the existing elements of a settlement that may be acceptable to parties. Therefore, after completing pleadings or after seeking admissions and denials, or before framing of issues, the court may have recourse to section 89. Such recourse would require it to consider and record the nature of the dispute (in a sentence or two),[22] inform the parties about the five available options (arbitration, conciliation, Lok Adalat,[23] mediation, and judicial settlement), take note of their preferences, and refer them to mediation if appropriate (with or without the parties' consent).[24] Much has been written about the inherently voluntary nature of mandatory

19. Alternative Dispute Resolution Rules, 2003, Rule 4 (which is party of the Draft Alternative Dispute Resolution and Mediation Rules, 2003). *See also*, Afcons, *supra* note 4, ¶¶ 22–23.
20. *See* Law Commission of India, Report No. 238 (Amendment to section 89 of the Code of Civil Procedure, 1908 and Allied Provision, December 2011), https://lawcommissionofindia.nic.in/reports/report238.pdf, p. 8. *See also*, Afcons, *supra* note 4, ¶ 12 (Supreme Court went ahead to define "Mediation" as a method of nonbinding dispute resolution with the assistance of a neutral third party who tries to help the disputing parties to arrive at a negotiated settlement and stated in passing that "mediation" is synonymous to "conciliation").
21. *See* Shri Ravi Aggarwal v. Shri Anil Jagota, 2009 SCC OnLine Del 1475 ("The legislature in its wisdom has not considered it appropriate to provide for a mediation settlement privately arrived at to be enforced as a decree *de hors* Part III of the said Act … [T]hough there is a valid settlement arrived at between the parties in mediation proceedings, … the question is of implementation of that settlement, and thus it partakes the character of a private agreement which is sought to be enforced by one of the parties alleging a breach while the other party is alleging due compliance … [T]he remedy of execution is not available to the appellant. The appellant … will have to initiate appropriate legal proceedings in accordance with law for seeking enforcement of the settlement in the form of a private agreement").
22. *See* Afcons, *supra* note 4, ¶ 25.
23. Lok Adalat is one of the alternative dispute redressal mechanisms special to India. It is a forum where disputes pending in the court or at pre-litigation stage are settled or compromised amicably. Lok Adalats have been given statutory status under the Legal Services Authorities Act, 1987. Under the said Act, the award (decision) made by the Lok Adalats is deemed to be a decree of a civil court and is final and binding on all parties.
24. *See* Afcons, *supra* note 4, ¶36 (mediation does not require the consent of parties for reference).

court referrals to mediation, in that it only mandates that the parties come to the table and not settle.

A party may also approach the court through an application, at any point, requesting the court's direction to refer parties to mediation.[25] Although it may be mandatory for the court to consider recourse to ADR under section 89, the actual reference is not mandatory (especially where the case falls under the category of cases that are not suitable for mediation).[26] However, in case of commercial disputes falling within the ambit of the Commercial Courts Act, it is mandatory for the plaintiff to first try mediation unless the plaintiff is seeking an urgent interim relief and the court is satisfied with the urgency.

[A] What Would Be Appropriate for Mediation?

Section 89 of the CPC begins with the words "where it appears to the court that there exist elements of a settlement." Thus, the court must form an opinion that a case can be referred to and settled through mediation. On the other hand, although Rule 1-A of Order X of the CPC may require that a court invariably refers cases to ADR, it may choose not to do so by briefly recording the reasons for not resorting to any of the settlement procedures prescribed under section 89. The Supreme Court's categorization of cases as "suitable" or "not suitable," having regard to their nature, is apposite.[27] They are only illustrative and intended to be general guidelines. Those cases that are considered "not suitable" are as follows:[28]

(i) Representative suits which involve public interest or interest of numerous persons who are not parties before the court.
(ii) Disputes relating to election to public offices.
(iii) Cases involving grant of authority by the section after inquiry, as, for example, suits or grant of probate or letters of administration.
(iv) Cases involving serious and specific allegations of fraud, fabrication of documents, forgery, impersonation, coercion, etc.
(v) Cases requiring protection of sections, as, for example, claims against minors, deities and mentally challenged and suits for declaration of title against the government.
(vi) Cases involving prosecution for criminal offenses.

Those cases (whether pending in civil courts or special tribunals) categorized "suitable" for mediation are classified under five broad headings:

(i) All cases relating to trade, commerce and contracts.

25. Although there is no specific rule under which a party can make such an application before the court to request a referral, the usual practice is to simply make an oral representation or, if need be, submit an application under section 151 of the Code of Civil Procedure, 1908 (Inherent Powers of Court).
26. *See* Afcons, *supra* note 4, ¶ 27.
27. *Id.*, at ¶¶ 27–28.
28. *Id.*, ¶ 36.

(ii) All cases arising from strained relationship, such as matrimonial cases.
(iii) All cases where there is a need for continuation of the preexisting relationship, such as disputes between neighbors and members of societies.
(iv) All cases relating to tortious liability, including motor accident claims.
(v) All consumer disputes.

[B] Consent of Parties

The issue of consent is essential for court referrals. In the case of arbitration and conciliation, a reference is only possible if the court has the parties' consent.[29] Where consent is absent, the court cannot on its own refer the parties to arbitration or conciliation. Although there is practically no difference between mediation and conciliation as processes, there are obvious differences in their legal outworking and operation under the CPC. In that, mediation does not require the consent of parties for reference. A mutual consent to mediate is not necessary, therefore, attributing some sort of a mandatory obligation on the parties.[30]

[C] Is There a Pre-litigation Obligation to Mediate?

After enacting the Commercial Courts Amendment Act and introducing section 12A, pre-institution mediation has been made a norm for commercial disputes, barring the exception where a party seeks urgent relief. Further, though section 12A imposes a mandatory obligation upon the plaintiff to initiate mediation, the PIMS Rules give the opposite party the option to refuse to participate in the mediation proceedings. If the opposite party does not respond to the authority's notice or does not appear in the mediation proceedings, it is deemed to be a "non-starter," and the authority duly records the same in its report.[31]

Notably, the pre-institution mediation regime gives no option to parties to consider private mediation instead of going before an authority or body constituted under LSA to mediate. In many ways, LSA is restrictive: it prescribed limited fees for the mediator professionals and only considered such mediators that LSA impanels. This raises serious doubts about the appropriateness of authorities constituted under the LSA for "commercial" dispute resolution, at least in respect of such disputes where the stakes are high or when the parties involved are sophisticated. Such a one-size-fits-all approach is seldom the right approach in commercial disputes, but it seems to be systemic in the pre-institution mediation scheme.

29. *Id.*
30. *See generally*, Laila T. Ollapally, *Mandatory Court Referral for Mediation—Parties Retain the Right to Voluntary Decision*, 4 SCC J-27 (2011).
31. *See* Commercial Courts (Pre-Institution Mediation and Settlement) Rules, 2018, Rules 3(3), 3(4) and 3(6) (hereinafter "PIMS Rules").

Even before introducing the Commercial Courts Act 2015, the idea of a pre-litigation mediation had been trending in a nonobligatory sense.[32] After wide publicities, some mediation centers set up "Help Desks" and "Facilitation Centres" at prominent places within the court complex to conduct pre-litigation mediations. Courts have also been taking a pro mediation approach to try and encourage parties to mediate in as many cases as possible.

For disputes which are not commercial, no regime within the Indian legal framework compels parties to try mediation in the pre-litigation phase. Therefore, a party to a civil dispute or civil proceedings is under no duty to first mediate before litigating or to take amicable steps to resolve (or narrow) the issues before taking any litigation action.

§4.03 AT WHAT STAGE CAN REFERRALS BE MADE?

Section 89 of the CPC provides for settlement of the dispute at any stage of proceedings:[33] from filing the suit papers to the stage of appellate proceedings. However, there are some statutory prescriptions (as per section 89 and Rules 1A–1C of Order X of the CPC) for considering a reference to mediation, after completing pleadings, after seeking admissions and denials or before framing of issues. So also, in the case of pending suits (in the list of long causes) that take several years to come before trial, courts may refer such matters to mediation.[34]

Generally, a good time to refer cases to mediation is when the pleadings are complete so that there is sufficient information on record about the dispute and parties have outlined their claims and positions. The appropriate time varies with each case and each set of parties. But there can be several attempts at mediation, and it is up to the parties (and their advocates) to consider the optimal circumstance to request the court referral.

[A] Referrals in Appellate Proceedings

Courts can also make referrals to try mediation in the appellate stage (or file an application made by parties to the dispute). Thus, an appellate court can pass a consent decree regarding the settlement if it is satisfied that the settlement is lawful.[35] Even at the apex court, the Supreme Court can dispose of an appeal in terms of a settlement

32. *See* K. Srinivas Rao v. D. A. Deepa (2013) 5 SCC 226.
33. *See* Moti Lal Banker v. Maharaj Kumar Mahmood Hasan Khan, AIR 1968 SC 1087, ¶ 3 (although Rule 3 of Order XXIII of the Civil Procedure Code would not apply in "execution proceedings," the provisions of Rule 2 of Order 21 and section 47 of the Civil Procedure Code enable the executing court to record and enforce a compromise in execution proceedings).
34. *See* PANCHU, *supra* note 18, p. 256.
35. *See* K. Y. Mylarasetty & Ors. v. K. S. Basappa & Ors., 2010 (1) Kar LJ 262, 263 (DB), ¶¶ 2–4 (during the pendency of the appeal, some of the original parties died and the remaining parties amicably settled the dispute. They filed a compromise petition duly signed by the parties and the respective counsels).

between the parties.[36] In all settings, after a case is transferred to mediation or referred to a court-annexed mediation center, the suit proceedings are pended until the case is referred back to the court (when there is a settlement, or when there is none).

Anecdotal evidence shows that mediation at the appellate stage may be more challenging since at least one party enjoys a favorable order. This is also why mediation at the first instance court is more susceptible to an agreement between the parties.

[B] Role of Referral Judges

The role of a referral judge in referring cases for settlement through mediation has much significance in gauging the appropriateness of mediation on a case-to-case basis. To summarize the general procedure adopted by a court, after the completion of pleadings or before framing issues,[37] the referral judge holds a preliminary hearing for the parties to appear (acquainting himself of the facts and the nature of the dispute). He then considers whether the case falls under any of the categories of cases required to be tried by courts and is not fit to be referred to any ADR processes. If the judge finds that it falls in any of the excluded categories, he records a brief order stating the inappropriateness of ADR and proceeds with the framing of issues and the impending trial. In other cases, he explains the five different alternatives (arbitration, conciliation, Lok Adalat, mediation, and judicial settlement) to enable the parties to make an informed choice. Thus, the judge plays a vital role in encouraging the parties to consider amicably settling the dispute.

At this point, the judge is to ascertain whether the parties are willing to arbitrate (informing the parties about its adjudicatory nature, cost involved, etc.). If parties are not agreeable to arbitrate, the judge ascertains whether the parties would be agreeable to conciliate (under provisions of the Arbitration and Conciliation, Act, 1996). Suppose parties are unwilling to arbitrate and conciliate (which is most likely to happen for consensus between the parties). In that case, the judge then, keeping in view the parties' preferences, refers the matter to any of the other three ADR processes, which include mediation by a neutral third-party facilitator or mediator. This time, the judge's reference may be either with or without the parties' consent. The judge explains the concept and process of mediation, its advantages in addressing the underlying interest, and its ultimate reward of a consent decree. Generally, if the case is simple or relates to matters where legal principles are settled, and there is no personal animosity between

36. *See* Cheriyan Joseph Poppallil & Ors v. Geevarghese Philip (Dead) By His Legal Representative & Ors. (1973) 3 SCC 612 (the parties came to a settlement and requested the court that the appeal may be disposed of); Bhola & Anr. v. Murthi Mandir Shri Jai Narayanji & Anr. (1978) 1 SCC 66 (the appellant's gesture of paying compensation to the respondent was acceptable and its modalities were mutually agreed).
37. Nothing prevents the judge from considering reference at a later stage. However, considering the possibility of allegations and counter-allegations vitiating the atmosphere and causing further strain on the relationship of the parties, the ideal stage for mediation is immediately after service of notice on the respondent or before the filing of objections by the respondent or after the submission of the pleadings or after recording the admission and denials (depending on the facts and circumstances, and the nature of the case).

the parties, the judge refers to a Lok Adalat. If the questions involved are complicated or may require several rounds of negotiations, the judge may then refer the matter to mediation by rendering a "referral order."[38]

There is generally a time limit that the mediation proceedings are subject to,[39] after which if the reference to mediation fails in yielding a settlement, on receiving the mediator's report, the judge proceeds with the hearing of the suit. But if there is a settlement, the judge examines the settlement (whether it is lawful and enforceable) and makes a decree in accordance with the terms of the settlement. If the judge finds that the agreement is unlawful or unenforceable (wholly or partly), the judge will desist from acting upon such an agreement and bring the same to the parties' notice. Besides, to avoid any technical or procedural difficulties in the implementation or execution of the agreement, the judge may modify or amend the terms of the settlement with the parties' consent before rendering a consent decree.

The judge may not interfere with the terms of the settlement, say when the terms seem unfair or one-sided from his point of view. He may, of course, ascertain with the parties if the terms are mutually agreeable.

§4.04 APPOINTMENT OF THE MEDIATOR

In court-annexed mediation matters, parties do not have an option or the first preference to choose a mediator. This should have rather been encouraged as the mediator would then hold a position of mutual faith and trust. In complex cases involving technical issues, a mediator of choice (selected by the parties themselves or by an institution) may improve the outcome of the mediation proceedings. If the Mediation Rules were to allow such party autonomy in the selection of mediators, a mediator of choice could then be subject to any basic disqualifiers under the rules, like Rule 5 of the Mediation Rules (any person who has been adjudged as insolvent; against whom disciplinary proceedings have been initiated; any person who is interested or connected with the subject matter of the dispute; and others).

The Mediation Rules do, however, treat institutions and their members to be qualified for enlistment in the court's panel of mediators.[40] Such mediation institutions, however, need to be recognized and its member approved by the High Court.

38. *See* Mediation and Conciliation Project Committee, Mediation Training Manual of India 68 (An ideal 'referral order' should contain among other things details like name of the referral judge, case number, name of the parties, date and year of institution of the case, stage of trial, nature of the dispute, the statutory provision under which the reference is made, next date of hearing before the referral court, whether the parties have consented for mediation, name of the institution/mediator to whom the case is referred for mediation, the date and time for the parties to report before the institution/ mediator, the time limit for completing the mediation, quantum of fee/remuneration if payable and contact address and telephone numbers of the parties and their advocates).

39. *See, e.g.*, Delhi High Court Mediation and Conciliation Rules, 2005, Samadhan, http://dhcmediation.nic.in/the-rules, Rule 18 ("Time limit for completion of mediation") (hereinafter "DHC Mediation Rules").

40. *See id.*, Rule 4 (Qualifications of persons to be empaneled under Rule 3).

Generally, a court either names/appoints a mediator or refers the case to the court-annexed mediation cell. Once referred to a court-annexed mediation cell, the cell appoints the mediator, usually by the roster or based on the requirement of the case at hand. When a court names/appoints any person, it considers his suitability for resolving the dispute and gives preference to those who have a proven record of successful mediation or who have special qualifications or experience in mediation suitable for the case at hand. Intending to provide parties with a conducive setup to mediate disputes, the District Courts and High Courts (including the Supreme Court) maintain a panel of trained mediators, which provides the necessary human resource to support consensual dispute resolution infrastructure.

Under the Commercial Courts Act, the position is different. Here, when a party approaches the authority (either the State LSA or the District LSA), the authority then appoints a mediator from its panel of mediators.[41]

[A] Can Judges Mediate? What About Retired Judges?

There is no existing practice where sitting judges mediate cases referred to mediation by themselves.[42] This is generally considered injurious to the process of mediation and the judicial office held by the judge—affecting the voluntariness and openness of the process of mediation and distressing the nature of the judicial office and the role of a judge.[43] On the other hand, retired judges can qualify for impanelment as per the Mediation Rules. Retired judges bring immense respect, experience, and status (attached from their former position), which rings apparent fairness, temperance, confidence, and understanding to their position as mediators. Nonetheless, their lifelong career as judges may pose a barrier in changing their hats from "decision makers" to "facilitators" of decision-making.

[B] Mediator Standards and Qualifications

Although the impaneled mediators do not need to have any prior mediation training or experience, mediators under the court-annexed systems are generally trained post-impanelment through training and workshops organized under the purview of the respective court or mediation cell. The Mediation and Conciliation Project Committee (an initiative of the Supreme Court of India) is the body that brought a 40-hours mediation training manual (including a code of ethics and conduct for mediators) which all other court-annexed mediation centers now adopt across India, thus,

---

41. *See* PIMS Rules, *supra* note 31, at Rule 3(7).
42. Code Civ. Proc., §89. The CPC also provides for "judicial settlement" where the court shall effect a compromise between the parties. Thus, there is a distinct process where the sitting judge can play an active role in effecting a compromise. For example, if the court feels that a suggestion or guidance by a judge would be appropriate, it can refer to another judge for a judicial settlement.
43. *See* Panchu, *supra* note 18, p. 261.

streamlining the rules and practices. In addition to the practice and procedure, the Mediation Rules also impose a code of ethics upon the mediators.[44]

There are no specific "qualifications" that mediators must have if it is the parties that mutually appoint a mediator. The appointee, however, must not be disqualified under the Mediation Rules.[45] In the case of the mediators impaneled at the court-annexed mediation center, the Mediation Rules prescribe that the following persons shall be considered qualified and eligible for being enlisted in the panel of mediators:[46]

(i) Retired judges:
  - Retired judges of the Supreme Court of India.
  - Retired judges of the High Court.
  - Retired District and Sessions Judges or retired judges of the City Civil Court or courts of equivalent status.

(ii) Legal practitioners with at least 15 years standing at the Bar at the level of the Supreme Court or the High Court or the District Courts of equivalent status.

(iii) Experts or other professionals with at least 15 years standing; or retired senior bureaucrats or retired senior executives.

(iv) Institutions that are themselves experts in mediation and have been recognized as such by the High Court, provided the members' names are approved by the High Court initially or whenever there is a change in membership.

In all cases, when a person is approached in connection with his proposed appointment as a mediator, he is obligated to disclose any circumstance likely to give rise to a reasonable doubt as to his independence or impartiality. And this is expected of him in continuance throughout the proceedings.[47]

[C] Mediator's Fee and Costs

Most court-annexed mediation systems provide free of cost service to litigants who are referred to mediation. Court-connected mediation programs are financed and funded by the government to ensure that services are free of costs. In such cases, there is neither any fee for mediators nor any cost relating to administrative services. It is probably so since the funding for court-annexed mediation projects is minimal and since it is considered important to incentivize parties to mediate. Then again, such an approach is not practical across the board. Mediation projects must focus on choice by offering free, partly paid, and fully paid services, leaving it to the parties to choose what fits their circumstances and needs.

Court-annexed mediation centers afford free services even though the Mediation Rules provide for fixing mediator's fee and sharing costs relating to administrative

44. *See, e.g.*, DHC Mediation Rules, *supra* note 39, Rule 27 (Ethics to be followed by mediator).
45. *See id.*, at Rule 5 (Disqualification of persons).
46. *See id.*, at Rule 4 (Qualification of persons).
47. *See id.*, at Rule 8 (Duty of mediator to disclose certain facts).

assistance.[48] Going by the Mediation Rules, the court may fix the mediator's fee, which is then shared equally between the parties, and the cost of administrative assistance and other ancillary expenses are again borne equally (or as otherwise directed by the court). In any case, each party bears its costs for the production of witnesses (including experts) and documents.

Under the Commercial Courts Act, the PIMS Rules prescribe a fee of INR 1,000 when a party to a commercial dispute makes an application to the authority for mediation.[49] There is also a one-time fee (quantified ad valorem basis)[50] that is to be paid to the authority before the commencement of the mediation.

§4.05 MEDIATION PROCEEDINGS

In case of a referral under section 89 of the CPC, the court has no involvement in the actual mediation proceedings, except when the court needs to pass a decree in accordance with the terms of settlement accepted by parties or when a party willfully absents himself from mediation session where the court is required to make appropriate directions, etc. It is common practice that the judge halts the court proceedings while the matter is pending before the mediator. Here again, parties are given complete autonomy to agree on the procedure. And throughout the proceedings, the parties may be present either personally or through their legal representatives. If the parties have not agreed to any procedure, the mediator follows the procedure prescribed by the Mediation Rules:

(i) He shall fix, in consultation with the parties, a schedule, the dates and the time of each mediation session, where all parties have to be present.
(ii) He shall hold the mediation at the place prescribed by the High Court or the District & Sessions Judge or the place where the parties and the mediator jointly agree.
(iii) He may conduct joint or separate meetings with the parties.
(iv) He may request each party to submit a brief memorandum setting forth the issues, which need to be resolved, and its position in respect to those issues and all information reasonably required for the mediator to understand the issue.

In conducting the proceedings, a mediator is not bound by CPC or the Indian Evidence Act, 1872, but is rather guided by the principles of fairness and justice, having regard to the rights and obligations of the parties, usages of trade, if any, and the circumstances of the dispute.[51] Under the Commercial Courts Act, the PIMS Rules also

48. *See id.*, at Rule 26 (Fee of mediator and costs).
49. *See* PIMS Rules, *supra* note 31, at Rule 3(1).
50. *See id.*, at Rule 11 read with Schedule II. For example, for a claim of INR 3,00,000 to INR 10,00,000, the mediation fee is INR 15,000, for a claim of INR 10,00,000 to INR 50,00,000, the mediation fee is INR 30,000 and so on.
51. *See, e.g.*, DHC Mediation Rules, *supra* note 39, at Rule 11 (Mediator not bound by Indian Evidence Act, 1872 or Code of Civil Procedure, 1908).

prescribe a similar course of action, the major difference is that a mediator is bound to follow the prescribed procedure, and the parties are not free to adopt any procedure they like.[52]

Such provision under the PIMS Rules, curtailing party autonomy, is manifestly antithetic to the concept of mediation. Moreover, guidelines like "principles of fairness and justice," or "rights and obligations of the parties," or the "usages of trade," are odd principles to guide a mediator. Rather, the parties' needs, concerns, goals, and priorities (their underlying interests) must guide the mediator. Of course, parties certainly consider their rights and obligations as a matter of their negotiation plan (to devise concessions, predict lawsuit outcomes, etc.), but this does not inform a mediator of his role.

[A] Timelines for Completing Mediation Proceedings

In case of a reference under section 89 of the CPC, the Mediation Rules set a time limit for completing mediation proceedings.[53] This is generally 60 days (or 90, depending on the High Court) from the first day fixed for the parties to convene before the mediator. On the expiry of the term, the mediation stands terminated unless the court, either *suo moto* or upon hearing any of the party's request, believes that an extension of time may be useful or necessary in the interest of a resolution. This is not the case in private mediations, which depends on the parties and the mediator.

Under the Commercial Courts Act, the PIMS Rules also provide for a time limit of three months from the date of application made by the plaintiff for completion of the mediation proceedings. The rules further allow a two-month extension with the consent of the parties.[54] A time-bound process promotes efficiency and also reduces the costs incurred by the parties.

[B] Confidentiality of the Process

Privacy and confined space are essential to a mediation session, and, thus, confidentiality is the cornerstone of a conciliatory process like mediation. In court-annexed systems, mediation is confidential, unlike court proceedings which are open to the public. There are, in total, three layers of protection afforded by the law: first, protection against the admissibility of evidence or statements (which include proposals) made in mediation in other proceedings; second, the duty of the mediator, the parties, and the participants to keep confidential from third parties what is said and done in mediation; third, the obligation of the mediator not to disclose information provided by a party to the mediator in confidence. In private mediation (unlike a

52. *See* PIMS Rules, *supra* note 31, at Rule 7.
53. *See, e.g.*, DHC Mediation Rules, *supra* note 39, at Rule 18 (Time limit for completion of mediation).
54. *See* PIMS Rules, *supra* note 31, at Rule 3(8).

conciliation governed by Part III of the Arbitration & Conciliation Act 1996), parties must specifically agree to these issues in their agreement to mediate.

The salient features of confidentiality in court-annexed mediations are as follows:

(i) The parties cannot rely on or introduce as evidence in arbitral or judicial proceedings, whether or not such proceedings relate to the dispute that is the subject of the mediation proceedings:[55]
   (a) views expressed or suggestions made by the other party in respect of a possible settlement of the dispute;
   (b) admissions made by the other party in the course of the mediation proceedings;
   (c) proposals made or view expressed by the mediator;
   (d) the fact that the other party had indicated to accept a proposal for settlement.

(ii) The mediator, parties, and all other participants keep confidential all matters about the mediation proceedings.[56]

(iii) When the mediator receives any factual information concerning the dispute (for instance, in a private session or caucus) from a party subject to a specific condition that it is kept confidential, the mediator cannot disclose it to the other party.[57]

(iv) There cannot be any audio, video, or stenographic recording of the mediation proceedings, and the mediator cannot record any statements made by the parties or any other participants.[58]

(v) The authority or the mediator, as the case may be, cannot retain the hard or soft copies of documents exchanged between the parties or submitted to the mediator or notes prepared by the mediator beyond a period of six months other than the application for mediation, the notice, the settlement agreement, and the failure report, if any.[59]

(vi) The mediation sessions are required to be conducted in a private environment to supplement the sanctity of confidentiality. Other persons may attend only with the permission of the parties and the consent of the mediator (and the norms of confidentiality equally bind them).

(vii) No mediator can be summoned by any party to the suit or proceeding to appear in a court of law to testify regarding information received by him or action taken by him or in respect of drafts or records prepared by him or shown to him during the mediation proceedings.[60]

Thus, the protection of confidentiality spreads across every nook and corner of the process, giving it the fullest protection where the efforts do and do not result in

55. *See also*, Arbitration & Conciliation Act, 1996, §81 (similar provision applicable to conciliations).
56. *See id.*, at §75. *See also*, PIMS Rules, *supra* note 31, at Rule 9 (Confidentiality of mediation).
57. *See* Arbitration & Conciliation Act, 1996, §70.
58. *See*, PIMS Rules, *supra* note 31, at Rule 9 (Confidentiality of mediation).
59. *See*, PIMS Rules, *supra* note 31, at Rule 7(2) (Procedure of mediation).
60. *See*, PIMS Rules, *supra* note 31, at Rule 22 (Immunity).

agreed terms. If the mediation results in a settlement, the mediator sends the agreement signed by both the parties to the court or the authority,[61] as the case may be, without mentioning what transpired during the mediation proceedings. Suppose the mediation does not yield a settlement or where the mediator is of the opinion that a settlement is not possible. In that case, the mediator is only expected to merely state one sentence in his report and send it to the court stating that the "mediation has been unsuccessful," beyond which the mediator is not to disclose anything that was discussed, proposed, or done in the mediation proceedings.[62] The protection grants the assurance that the proposed terms cannot be used against any party if there is no settlement.

Under the PIMS Rules, the mediator is expected to prepare a report recording reasons for the failure of the process and submit the same to the authority.[63] This is paradoxical to the concept of mediation, diluting the trust and integrity of the process. There is no administrative or other reason why the authority should maintain such reports/records.

[C] Does the Court or the Judge Have Any Involvement?

It is evident from section 89 of the CPC that mediation is meant to be managed by persons or institutions outside the court (and not before the court). To preserve parties' confidence, the court is not at all involved in the actual mediation proceedings. To this effect, the Mediation Rules provide that there should be no communication between the mediator and the court.[64] The court's involvement appears in cases where mediation results in a settlement in the end[65] or when it does not and is referred back to the court to continue with the remainder of the suit proceedings. And though the court which refers considers the question as to whether there are reasonable grounds to expect a settlement, the respective judge is not treated to be disqualified from trying the suit afterward if no settlement is arrived at between the parties,[66] since the court continues to retain jurisdiction over the case.[67]

If any communication between the mediator and the court is necessary, the Mediation Rules prescribe that it shall be in writing, and copies of the same shall be

61. *See,* PIMS Rules, *supra* note 31, at Rule 7(1)(viii).
62. *See* Moti Ram v. Ashok Kumar (2011) 1 SCC 466, ¶ 2 (mediation proceedings are totally confidential. If the happenings of the mediation proceedings are disclosed, it will destroy the confidentiality of the mediation process).
63. *See,* PIMS Rules, *supra* note 31, at Rule 7(1)(ix).
64. *See, e.g.*, DHC Mediation Rules, *supra* note 39, at Rule 23 (Communication between mediator and the court).
65. *See* Salem Bar (II), *supra* note 11, ¶ 57 (the mediator reports to the court and the court, after giving notice and hearing to the parties, brings the compromise into effect by passing a decree in accordance with the terms of settlement).
66. *Id.*
67. Once a civil dispute is referred to arbitration, the case goes outside the stream of the court permanently. In contrast, a dispute referred to mediation (which is a nonadjudicatory process) goes out of the domain of the court only temporarily. Even though the dispute was transferred to a court-annexed mediation center, the court retains its control and jurisdiction over the matter and the result of mediation would have to be placed before the court for passing consequential orders.

given to the parties.[68] Communication between the mediator and the court is limited under the following heads: mediator communicating with the court:

(i) about the failure of the party to attend;
(ii) about the consent of the parties;
(iii) regarding his assessment that the case is not suited for settlement through the mediation/conciliation;
(iv) that the parties have settled the dispute(s).

[D] Do Courts Order Costs Against Parties?

If a party fails to be present in the sessions notified by the mediator on account of a deliberate or willful act, the other party or the mediator may apply to the court, and in that case, the court may issue appropriate directions having regard to the facts and circumstances of the case.[69] In such cases, courts have the power to levy costs against parties unreasonably refusing to mediate or for not mediating in "good faith."[70] If the court finds that a party is absenting himself before the mediator without sufficient reason, the court may impose costs against the party.[71]

§4.06 MEDIATED SETTLEMENT AGREEMENTS

Where an agreement is reached between the parties regarding all the issues in the suit (or some of the issues[72]), the parties must sign the same.[73] After that, the signed agreement is submitted to the mediator, who then, with a covering letter signed by him, forwards the same (via the mediation center) to the court where the suit is pending.

When the mediation causes a settlement between the parties, the mediator or mediation center will report to the court, and the court, after giving notice and hearing the parties,[74] affects the compromise by passing a "consent decree"[75] in accordance

68. *See, e.g.*, DHC Mediation Rules, *supra* note 39, at Rule 23 (Communication between mediator and the court).
69. *See, e.g.*, DHC Mediation Rules, *supra* note 39, at Rule 13 (Consequences of non-attendance of parties at sessions or meetings on due dates).
70. *See, e.g.*, DHC Mediation Rules, *supra* note 39, at Rule 19 (Parties to act in good faith).
71. *See* Rudraaradya & Ors. v. Nanjundaswamy & Anr., ILR 2011 KAR 221, ¶ 8.
72. If the settlement partly covers the issues arising in the suit, the court shall render a consent decree to that extent and proceed further with the suit to decide the remaining issues. *See, e.g.*, DHC Mediation Rules, *supra* note 39, at Rule 25 of the Mediation Rules ("Court to fix a date for recording settlement and passing decree").
73. *See* Y. Sleebachen & Ors. v. State of Tamil Nadu (2015) 5 SCC 747, ¶¶ 16–20 (the counsel appearing for a party is fully competent to put his signature to the terms of any compromise upon which a decree can be passed in proper compliance with the provisions of Rule 3 and Order XXIII and such decree is perfectly valid, depending on the authority conferred on the counsel in terms of the Vakalatnama).
74. On receipt of the settlement, the court fixes a date of hearing. On such date of hearing if the court is satisfied that the parties have settled their disputes, it renders a decree in accordance with the terms of settlement. *See, e.g.*, DHC Mediation Rules, *supra* note 39, at Rule 25 (Court to fix a date for recording settlement and passing decree).

with the terms of the settlement. In this process, the court only satisfies itself that the parties have mutually agreed and that the terms are legal. What is unique is that a consent decree need not be confined only to the reliefs prayed for but relate to the subject matter of the suit.[76] Hence, the consent decree can include settlements on any related issue outside the pleadings. This way, mediation offers a more satisfying and panoramic outcome. As far as the execution is concerned, a consent decree is executable like any other decree and in the same manner in which other decrees are executed.[77]

[A] When Will the Court Reject a Settlement?

The court must satisfy itself with a lawful agreement adjusting the suit and whether the agreement is vitiated by grounds such as illegality, fraud, and misrepresentation. If the settlement, for instance, was arrived at fraudulently, the court which entertained the compromise petition may refuse to pass a consent decree in terms of the settlement.[78]

In other words, according to the principles entailing Rule 3 of Order XXIII of the CPC, a mediated settlement that is void or voidable under the Indian Contract Act, 1872, shall not be deemed as lawful. The mediated settlement would have to be the court's satisfaction that the suit has been adjusted wholly or in part by a lawful agreement. What is more, before making a mediated settlement agreement a decree, the court would have to ascertain the terms of the compromise with precision and state the rights of the parties in the operative portion of the decree with clarity to leave no room for doubt concerning the exact scope of those rights.[79]

Thus, Rule 3 of Order XXIII of the CPC does not only require a seal of approval from the court but requires the court to be satisfied that the agreement or compromise which has been entered into between the parties is lawful before accepting the same. The court is expected to apply its judicial mind while examining the terms of settlement for its legality (not its fairness) before the suit is disposed of in terms of the agreement arrived at between the parties.[80]

75. The principle under Rule 3 of Order XXIII of the Code of Civil Procedure, 1908, suggests that a decree passed on the basis of a compromise by and between the parties is essentially a contract which derives sanctity by the court superimposing its seal on the contract. *See* Jacob David Sopher v. Baldev Pathak, 1975 Mah LJ 764 (consent decree is a contract which is superadded by the command of a judge).
76. *See* Tulsan v. Pyare Lal & Ors. (2006) 10 SCC 782, ¶ 13.
77. *See* Jacob David Sopher v. Baldev Pathak, 1975 Mah LJ 764 (a consent decree can be enforced by execution).
78. *See* Banwari Lal v. Chando Devi & Anr. (1993) 1 SCC 581, ¶¶ 7, 14 (hereinafter "Banwari Lal").
79. *See* Nizam Uddin v. Ikramul Haq & Ors., AIR 1947 All 143, ¶¶ 5–8 (this case illustrates how failure on the part of the civil courts to observe the rules of procedure in framing decrees results in unnecessary litigation and waste of money).
80. *See* Banwari Lal, *supra* note 78.

[B] Can a Consent Decree Be Challenged?

Rule 3A of Order XXIII of the CPC sets out the general rule that no suit would lie to set aside a decree on the ground that the compromise on which the decree is based was "not lawful." Here, the Bombay High Court's view that Rule 3A does not bar a substantive suit in all imaginable cases but only in cases where the compromise was "not lawful." For example, in passing the consent decree, the court, on the face of it, had no jurisdiction to do so; where fraud or misrepresentation was perpetrated on the court (as distinct from fraud, coercion or misrepresentation said to have been perpetrated by one party on the other); where, on the face of it, the consent decree suffers from some palpable defect or error (like containing a term or clause opposed to the law, morality or public policy); or where the court was misled into passing the consent decree (say, because of lack of authority or limited authority of the consenting advocate or advocates not brought to the court's notice at the time). The court held that in such context, the words "not lawful" must be construed about a compromise envisaged by Rule 3A, and not in each case where a party seeks to set aside a compromise on the ground of fraud, coercion or misrepresentation practiced upon him by the other party as alleged in the present case.[81] Going by the view of the Bombay High Court, for a party seeking to set aside a compromise (or a consent decree as it were) on the ground of fraud, coercion, or misrepresentation (perpetrated by one party on another), Rule 3A would not create any bar.[82]

Besides, suppose a party to a suit who enters into a compromise, in terms of which a consent decree is made, wants to challenge a consent decree on the ground that it is not lawful. In that case, the remedy available to him is either to file an Application in the same suit to recall the consent decree on the ground that the compromise is not lawful, or that it is vitiated by fraud,[83] or to file an appeal under Rule 1A of Order XLIII[84] of CPC contending that the decree should not have been recorded. Ultimately, a consent decree is a creature of the agreement on which it is founded and is, therefore, liable to be set aside on any of the grounds that invalidate an agreement.[85]

81. *See* Jethalal C. Thakkar v. Lalbhai Hiralal Shah, 1985 Mah LJ 299, ¶ 5. *See also*, Rajwanti & Anr. v. Kishan Chand Shehrawat & Ors., 2009 (113) DRJ 166 (Rule 3A of Order XXIII of the CPC does not permit any distinction to be made between suits where challenge to consent decree is on the plea of fraud played on the court as distinct from cases where plea is of fraud having been played by one party on the other).
82. Self-determination nature of the settlement being the most likely justification for creating the bar under Rule 3A of Order XXIII of the Code of Civil Procedure.
83. *See* Kamakhaya N. Singh v. Haribansh Singh, 2008 (1) Pat LJR 410, 411; Khalil Haji Bholumiya Salar & Anr. v. Parveen w/o Sayyeduddin Razak, 2013 (3) Mah LJ 182, ¶ 17. *See also*, CODE CIV. PROC., proviso to Rule 3.
84. Right to challenge nonappealable orders in appeal against decrees: In an appeal against a decree passed in a suit after recording a compromise or refusing to record a compromise, it shall be open to the appellant to contest the decree on the ground that the compromise should, or should not, have been recorded.
85. *See* Ruby Sales & Services (P) Ltd. & Anr. v. State of Maharashtra & Ors. (1994) 1 SCC 531, ¶15.

§4.07 SHIFTING SANDS OF MEDIATION

The last decade saw some sort of an outbreak in the use and discussion about ADR, with a keen eye on mediation. The Law Commission's 238th Report on the Amendment of section 89 of the CPC, 1908, and Allied Provisions (December 2011) has further suggested amendments to section 89 of the CPC to remove the deficiencies of court-annexed mediation schemes, which is a pivotal provision for facilitating dispute resolution in civil matters. The need to keep developing court-annexed programs in mediation has been immensely felt by the community of practitioners, judges, and users.

In recent years, courts have adopted the philosophy of encouraging the amicable resolution of disputes. This philosophy has crystallized in the court practice through Rule 2A of Order XXXIV-A of the CPC, which empowers the court, at a pretrial conference, to consider any matter, including the possibility of a settlement of any or all of the issues in the proceedings and give all such directions as may appear to be necessary or desirable for securing the just, expeditious and economical disposal of the proceedings. Mediation is now built into the adjudicatory process of the courts and is one of the steps that parties are almost customarily expected to take en route to the conclusion of their dispute.

Off late, it is generally seen that court referrals (Supreme Court and High Courts) to mediation institutions have increased phenomenally. Such referrals are trending in proceedings under section 11 of the Arbitration & Conciliation Act 1996 for the arbitrator's appointment. This has encouraged private mediation and furthered its legitimacy.

Further, various legislative enactments have also expanded the reach of court-annexed mediations manifold. Various specialized tribunals and regulatory bodies have been directed to adopt ADR practices to resolve as many disputes as possible. For instance, section 442 of Companies Act 2013 and the Companies (Mediation and Conciliation) Rules 2016 provide that the central government shall maintain a panel of mediation experts to conduct mediation between parties during the pendency of any proceedings before the National Company Law Tribunal or the National Company Law Appellate Tribunal.[86] Similarly, section 32 of the Real Estate (Regulation and Development) Act 2016 provides for the Real Estate Regulatory Authority functions. One such function of the authority (for facilitating growth and promotion of healthy, transparent, efficient, and competitive real estate sector) is to recommend the government to introduce amicable conciliation of disputes between the promoters and allottees of real estate projects through available dispute settlement forums.[87]

Under the recently promulgated Consumer Protection Act 2019 (CPA), the central government has created a full-fledged system to mediate consumer disputes.[88] It obligates the state governments and the central government to establish a consumer mediation cell at each District Commission and State Commission of the particular

86. Companies (Mediation and Conciliation) Rules, 2016, Rule 3.
87. Real Estate (Regulation and Development) Act, 2016, §32(g).
88. Consumer Protection Act, 2019, Ch. V.

State and a consumer mediation cell attached with the National Commission and its regional benches.[89] It further mandates the District, State, and National Commissions to maintain a panel of mediators.[90] Section 37 of the CPA provides that at the first hearing of a complaint after its admission or a later stage, if it appears to the relevant authority that there exist elements of a settlement that may be acceptable to the parties, then it may direct the parties to give their consent, within five days, if they wish to get their dispute settled by mediation. Where the parties agree to mediate, the relevant authority shall refer the matter for mediation in accordance with the provisions of Chapter V of the CPA.

In July 2020, the government also notified the Consumer Protection (Mediation) Rules 2020, which provide for the types of consumer disputes that cannot be referred to mediation.[91] The National Consumer Disputes Redressal Commission then notified the Consumer Protection (Mediation) Regulations 2020, which set out the requirements and procedure for impanelment, the manner of training of impaneled mediators, the code of conduct governing the process for appointment of a mediator, the procedure for removal of a mediator, the role of a mediator and the procedure for conducting mediation proceedings.

[A] Infrastructure Developed by the State to Support Court-Annexed Mediations

A court-annexed mediation setup may not replicate the modernity of a private mediation institution; however, most mediation centers sufficiently provide for all the basics in logistics that create a conducive environment for parties to resolve their conflict with the assistance of a trained mediator. The facilities and support cum administrative staff are provided by the mediation center backed by its respective court. Nonetheless, there is an issue of the inefficiency of court-annexed mediation programs due to insufficient infrastructure and the number of resources. Such is the case, especially in subordinate courts and a handful of High Courts that are yet to develop the infrastructure for court-annexed mediations fully.

Moreover, referrals are encouraged by incentivizing the litigants to refund the court fees paid where a compromise or settlement has arrived.[92] The mediator and the administration's services are generally rendered free of cost to encourage parties to try the process.

[B] Increasing Use and Impact of Court-Annexed Mediation

The success of mediation centers across the country is a testimony to the increasing use and impact of court-annexed mediation programs. The numbers from Delhi,

89. *Id.*, at §74.
90. *Id.*, at §75.
91. Consumer Protection (Mediation) Rules, 2020, Rule 4.
92. Court-fees Act, 1870, §16 (as per the language, the court fee is refundable merely on a reference by court to any ADR process).

Bangalore, and Tamil Nadu Mediation Centres present a robust mediation practice across different factors like the number of referrals, the number of cases mediated, and settlement rates.[93]

The court-annexed mediation centers attached to the Delhi Mediation Centre have settled around 55,718 cases between August 22, 2015, and February 29, 2020, constituting approximately 60% of the referred case.[94] The Bangalore Mediation Centre, which began operations two years later, has settled 28,685 cases until March 6, 2017, with a settlement rate of 65%. It has just 4% of pending cases that are yet to be mediated.[95] These statistics at two of the country's better administered court-annexed schemes is an indication that mediation as a tool of dispute resolution has an appeal among litigants, especially for the benefits that entail.

§4.08 CONCLUDING REMARKS

Revisiting the purpose of section 89, it was inserted to try and see that the court itself need not necessarily decide all cases which are filed in court. Keeping in mind the law's delays and the limited number of judges, it is now imperative that the resort should be had to ADR mechanisms to bring an end to litigation between parties at an early stage. This purpose, in recent years, has been substantially achieved, although there is much distance to cover. Nevertheless, there is optimism in the upcoming developments relating to mediation in India.

At the global stage, mediation is set to start a new journey with the United Nations adopting the United Nations Convention on International Settlement Agreements Resulting from Mediation which 53 countries have signed to date. This convention, popularly known as the Singapore Mediation Convention, provides for enforcing settlement agreements that meet the prescribed conditions, just like the Convention on the Recognition and Enforcement of Foreign Arbitral Awards or the New York Convention. As a result, settlement agreements across the world can be enforced directly by a court instead of being treated only as a contract that required a civil suit to be filed for their enforcement.

On July 31, 2019, the Union Cabinet of India approved the signing of the Singapore Mediation Convention,[96] paving the way for independent legislation on mediation in India. While currently, India does not have independent legislation on mediation, the need for the same can be felt from the importance given to it by the

93. *See generally*, Alok Prasanna Kumar et al., Strengthening Mediation in India: Report on Court-Connected Mediation (Vidhi Centre for Legal Policy, December 2016), https://vidhilegalpolicy.in/wp-content/uploads/2020/06/26122016_StrengtheningMediationinIndia_FinalReport.pdf.

94. *General Statistics Report (Aug. 22, 2005 to Mar. 31, 2021)*, Delhi Mediation Centre, https://delhicourts.nic.in/dmc/statistical.htm.

95. *General Detail Statistical Report (Jan. 1, 2017 to Dec. 31, 2020)*, Bangalore Mediation Centre, https://nyayadegula.kar.nic.in/statistics_detail.html; *Pre-Litigation Cases Report (2014 to Dec. 2020)*, Bangalore Mediation Centre, https://nyayadegula.kar.nic.in/pre_litigant.html.

96. *Cabinet Approves Signing of the UN Convention on International Settlement Agreements Resulting from Mediation by India*, Press Information Bureau (July 31, 2019, 3:37 PM), https://pib.gov.in/PressReleaseIframePage.aspx?PRID=1580824.

Supreme Court also. For instance, on March 5, 2019, the Supreme Court directed the government to explore the possibility of setting up a Motor Accident Mediation Authority in every district, considering the number of road accidents in India is very high, and Indian courts witness several claims. Further, in the extremely sensitive Ayodhya dispute, a five-judge constitution bench of the Supreme Court ordered a court-monitored mediation, thus, bringing mediation to the attention of the masses in India.

Despite the fairly widespread awareness of "mediation" or "conciliation" and its potential advantages, fostering a mediation culture takes time. Equally, it takes time to build trust in mediation users, practitioners, and organizations. The litigation culture in India is dominant, and, therefore, resistance to change might come from not only people unwilling to try their disputes through an unacquainted process, or from corporations or mediation users where business practices or dispute resolution policies might just be simply adversarial and combative, but also legal practitioners who may not have experienced, equipped, or been made aware of the advantages of mediation.

CHAPTER 5

Institutional Mediation

*Shashank Garg & Tejas Karia**

§5.01 INTRODUCTION

Modern commercial mediation is a culmination of Alternative Dispute Resolution (ADR) practices from across the world. It is becoming an increasingly popular choice of dispute settlement in India, thereby creating opportunities for various mediation centers to provide their services. While mediation is a viable option for dispute resolution (and perhaps even more promising than arbitration), it remains largely unstructured (in law and practice). Institutional mediation is recognized to have immense potential in India's dispute resolution landscape, mainly since India is now a signatory to the 2018 UN Convention on International Settlement Agreements Resulting from Mediation (the "Singapore Mediation Convention").[1]

Institutional mediations are run by service providers (the institutions) who administer the entire mediation process. Every institution has its own set of rules, which provides a framework for the mediation process, and its manner or form of administration to assist the parties and the mediator in the process. Some of the leading mediation institutions are the International Chamber of Commerce (ICC), the Singapore International Mediation Center (SIMC), JAMS, Center for Effective Dispute Resolution (CEDR), and International Center for Dispute Resolution (ICDR), and so on. Indian Institute of Arbitration & Mediation (IIAM) and CAMP Arbitration and Mediation Practice (CAMP) are two of India's well-known homegrown institutions.

In a nutshell, mediation in India may be categorized into court-annexed mediation and private mediation. While court-annexed mediations are procedurally separate, they are institutionally linked with court proceedings. And even though the mediation rules and procedures followed in court annexed mediations (which are conducted

* The able assistance of Avlokita Rajvi is greatly appreciated.

1. *See* Chapter on Singapore Mediation Convention.

under the aegis of a court-annexed mediation center) are akin to private institutional mediation discussed in this chapter, there are fundamental differences that occur on legal and practice planes.[2] For starters, private mediations are entirely independent of court proceedings and may be conducted *institutionally* or ad hoc.

Generally, the contract between two parties will contain a mediation clause (as part of dispute resolution clause) which will designate a particular institution or its rules—that is how mediations are referred to a particular institution which after that proceeds to administer the case under its rules vis the appointment of the mediator, the commencement of mediation, and so on.

The chapter is given a lucid structure that deals with various elements that stem from any typical institutional mediation. As for ad hoc mediations, parties simply agree to a bespoke mediation process, where procedures are not predetermined and agreed either at the commencement stage or as the mediation progresses. From this, one may derive the salient features of ad hoc mediation, which are: flexibility, enabling the parties to determine a process that best suits them; cost-effectiveness as compared to institutionalized mediation; freedom to appoint a mediator, rather than depending on an institutional choice.

The cost and time efficiency of ad hoc mediation is often dependent on "ideal circumstances," where the process is driven by the desired level of cooperation, experience, and procedures. Without these "ideal circumstances," however, an ad hoc setup cannot be cost-effective or timely, and it may be vulnerable to procedural challenges and obstructive tactics.

Au contraire, institutional mediation, administered under the rules of that institution, brings tangible benefits to the overall process. This primarily comes from the comprehensive case management, which continues throughout the process, even after the mediator's appointment. Altogether, institutional mediation shapes essential areas like the mediator's appointment from a pool of trained and experienced mediators, the process and procedural design that is tried and tested, mediator's role and privileges, mediator's proposals, confidentiality, cost, and so on. Those benefits outweigh any "perception" of high cost.

One may even argue that institutional benefits add much value to the substantive outcome to facilitate a better agreement. Nevertheless, institutional benefits manifest significantly in the context of international commercial disputes, which generally involve high stakes, require expedited resolution, desire finality rather than multi-jurisdictional court and arbitral actions, and engage with vast cultural differences.

§5.02 AGREEMENT TO MEDIATE

Of course, the genesis of mediation is with an agreement to mediate (or mediation agreement). Institutions usually provide/recommend a range of model clauses.

For instance, the SIMC Rules recommend three different model mediation clauses: pre-dispute scenario, post-dispute scenario, and Arb-Med-Arb clause for

2. *See* Chapter on Court-Annexed Mediation.

cross-border enforceability of the settlement. Meaning that an agreement to mediate under the rules of an institution may be concluded at the time of entering into the main contract, i.e., before any dispute has arisen; alternatively, parties may decide to enter into a mediation agreement after a dispute has arisen. Similarly, ICC Rules suggest mediation clauses that provide an option to use the ICC Rules; an obligation to consider the ICC Rules; an obligation to refer the dispute to the ICC Rules while permitting parallel arbitration proceedings, if required; an obligation to refer the dispute to the ICC Rules, followed by arbitration, if required.

Mediation agreements may have various forms but may be generally understood as stand-alone mediation agreements versus those that are multistep/multitiered, hybrid, or parallel. A typical stand-alone mediation agreement may read as: "In the event of any dispute arising out of or in connection with the present contract, the parties agree in the first instance to discuss and consider referring the dispute to the ICC Mediation Rules."[3] Besides being stand-alone, mediation agreements often appear in permutations and combinations (hybrids) of Neg-Med, Med-Arb, Arb-Med, Arb-Med-Arb, etc. These formats are typically understood in the context of a single neutral for all stages (and its acceptable boundaries may be subject to debate). Having said that, these procedures may also be drafted in with a different neutral at each stage.

There is a great advantage in the coalescence of two or more dispute resolution methods that includes mediation. Mediation is inherently a conciliatory-collaborative process, whereas arbitration is an adjudicatory process—their combination gives parties the best of both worlds while ensuring all the hallmarks of ADR.

Alternatively, parties may agree to escalation clauses (also called multitier/multistep clauses) whereby parties engage in a series of steps such as structured negotiation, mediation, adjudication, neutral or expert determination before resorting to the final stop of litigation or arbitration. These clauses often stipulate a specific time frame for each step as the process moves progressively upon the dissatisfaction or disagreement of either party. For more on hybrid modes of dispute resolution, *see* the Chapter on Mixed-Mode Dispute Resolution.

§5.03 COMMENCEMENT OF MEDIATION

[A] Filing Request for Mediation

Any party (or parties) wishing to commence mediation pursuant to any institutional rules is required to file a written request for mediation (Request) with the concerned institution or the designated authority of the said institution, such as the Registrar of the institution. Typically, the requirement is also that a copy of the Request is simultaneously sent to all other parties (unless, of course, if the Request has been filed jointly).

3. *See* International Chamber of Commerce Mediation Rules, 2014 (mediation clauses, clause B) (hereinafter "ICC Mediation Rules, 2014").

Additionally, some institutional rules also contemplate that where an agreement to mediate does not exist, the party wishing to invite the other to mediation may send the Request to the institution containing the information specified under the Rules. Thereupon, the institution will inform all other parties of the proposal and assist the parties in considering the proposal.[4]

The information that needs to form part of the Request must include some basic information, such as the name(s) and address(es) of the parties and their counsels, a description of the nature of the dispute along with the claim value, the language in which the mediation is to be conducted and the location of the meetings. In instances of joint nomination by the parties, the Request should have information regarding the same and the attributes of the mediator as agreed upon by the parties. Additionally, when parties submit to an institution to mediate, the agreement allowing for the same should be furnished in the Request.

Besides following the above basic checklist, parties may consider including additional information to form part of the Request, which are often found in some institutional rules,[5] such as an agreement which allows for availing resolution mechanisms other than mediation,[6] along with information on other legal proceedings on the same matter,[7] and the relief sought by the party(ies).[8] *See* Chapter on Mediation Advocacy.

[B] Payment of Fee

Together with the Request, the party or parties filing the Request are required to pay a filing fee or registration fee, as quantified by the institution's rules that are based on a predetermined schedule. The filing fee is important, without which institutions may refuse to process the Request.

Following the processing of the Request and the commencement of the Proceedings, parties will be required to pay one or more deposits to cover the institution's remaining administrative cost and the fees and expenses of the mediator. This is also based on a predetermined schedule. In the end, after the total cost is fixed, parties are reimbursed with any excess or balance.

Interestingly, unlike arbitration rules, where cost is often an issue of determination by the arbitral tribunal, mediation rules prescribe that all deposits and costs shall be borne by the parties equally. Parties can, of course, agree otherwise; however, this

---

4. *See* ICC Mediation Rules, 2014, rule 3.1. CAMP Arbitration and Mediation Practice Private Ltd. Rules of Mediation, 2016, rule 2(ii) (hereinafter "CAMP Mediation Rules, 2016").
5. *See* ICC Mediation Rules, 2014, rules 2 and 3; Singapore International Mediation Center Mediation Rules, 2020 (Appendix A of the rules) (hereinafter "SIMC Mediation Rules, 2020"); London Court of Arbitration Rules, 2020, rules 1 and 2 (hereinafter "LCIA Arbitration Rules, 2020"); International Mediation Institution, Model Mediation Rules, 2016, rule 2 (hereinafter "IMI Model Mediation Rules, 2016, rule 2"); Indian Institute of Arbitration and Mediation, Mediation Rules, 2020, rule 2 (hereinafter "IIAM Mediation Rules, 2020").
6. ICC Mediation Rules, 2014, rule 2.1(c).
7. SIMC Mediation Rules, 2020 (Appendix A, section V).
8. IIAM Mediation Rules, 2020, rule 3(a).

is an enormous difference from arbitration rules to instill a collaborative approach throughout.

[C] Date of Commencement of Mediation

The date of commencement of mediation is a variable that depends on whether or not the parties have already agreed to refer their dispute to mediation under the auspices of a mediation institution. Its importance lies with local limitation law issues or determining the trigger in a multistep dispute resolution process.

For instance, where there is an agreement to refer disputes under the ICC Mediation Rules, the date on which the institution receives the Request is deemed the date of the commencement of the proceedings.[9] Under SIMC Mediation Rules, it is the date on which SIMC acknowledges such receipt that is considered the date of commencement of mediation.[10] As for the London Court of International Arbitration (LCIA) Mediation, the commencement date is considered to be the date of receipt of the Request and the registration fee.[11]

On the other hand, in cases wherein parties subsequently reach an agreement to refer their dispute, the ICC and SIMC Mediation Rules, for instance, provide that the proceedings shall commence on the date on which the institution sends written confirmation to the parties that such an agreement has been reached.[12] Whereas, the LCIA Rules state that the date of commencement of the mediation shall, subject to payment of the registration fee, be the date that agreement to mediate is reached.[13]

[D] Place and Language of Mediation

The place and language of mediation are provided under institutional rules by default. Given the flexibility, the institution (in consultation with the parties and the mediator) determines the location of the mediation unless there is already an agreement to that effect. The same applies to the language of the proceeding; unless parties have agreed on the language, the institution will determine the language(s) of the mediation in consultation with the parties and the mediator. One should note that the expression "place" is not the equivalent of a "seat" as in the case of arbitration. Consequently, the place of mediation does not produce the same legal effects (or the like).

9. ICC Mediation Rules, 2014, rule 2.5.
10. SIMC Mediation Rules, 2020, rule 3.2.
11. LCIA Arbitration Rules, 2020, rule 1.4.
12. ICC Mediation Rules, 2014, rule 3.3; SIMC Mediation Rules, rule 3.3.
13. LCIA Arbitration Rules, 2020, rule 2.5.

§5.04 APPOINTMENT OF THE MEDIATOR

[A] Nominations

Parties are typically given the preference to jointly nominate a mediator, either from the institution's panel or beyond the panel.[14] Some mediation centers, like the SIMC, have a panel of mediators to choose from, wherein the mediators are categorized into Ambassador, Industry Expert, International Mediator, and Specialist Mediator. Such categorization helps parties choose a mediator who can cater to specific needs of the dispute if the situation calls for it or should the need arise. But when going beyond the institutional panel of mediators (let us say, external mediator), the institutions generally reserve some right before confirming the selection of an external mediator. For instance, under the ICC Mediation Rules, the joint nomination must receive a confirmation from the institution. Similarly, under the LCIA Mediation Rules, parties have the autonomy to choose a mediator outside the pool of mediators at LCIA, provided the proposed mediator is impartial, has the necessary experience in mediation, and can devote time to the entire process.

It is usually the case that such external mediator, upon acceptance, would have to abide by the institution's code of conduct (if any).[15] After all, trust underpins the mediation process. If the parties (or the institution) cannot trust a mediator's integrity in terms of competence, diligence, neutrality, independence, impartiality, fairness, and the ability to respect confidences, mediation is unlikely to succeed.

Suppose parties are unable to agree on a mediator within a stipulated time. In that case, it is the institution that takes up the mantle to appoint the mediator either from its panel of mediators or outside its panel (e.g., from the panel of one of its partner organizations) if a suitable mediator is not found in the panel.[16] The institution may also consult with the parties in this regard.[17]

Before a mediator accepts the appointment, he furnishes his resume and provides his declaration that there are no circumstances known to him that are likely to give rise to any justifiable doubts as to his or her impartiality or independence, other than the circumstances disclosed. A copy of this is provided to the parties.[18] Importantly, this is a continuous obligation that rests upon the mediator, and an institution can replace the mediator in the course of the mediation if a conflict arises and other exceptional circumstances.[19]

As far as the number of mediators is concerned, institutional rules generally provide for a single mediator. However, parties may agree to have more than one mediator by requesting the institution to do so under its rules. In appropriate circumstances, the institution may also propose to the parties that there be more than

14. SIMC Mediation Rules, 2020, rule 4.1.
15. CAMP Mediation Rules, 2016, rule 3(iii).
16. SIMC Mediation Rules, 2020, rule 4.2.
17. ICC Mediation Rules, 2014, rule 5.2.
18. LCIA Arbitration Rules, 2020, rule 3.1; SIMC Mediation Rules, 2020, rule 4.5; CAMP Mediation Rules, 2016, rule 4; ICC Mediation Rules, 2014, rule 5; IIAM Mediation Rules, 2020, rule 3(f).
19. SIMC Mediation Rules, 2020, rule 4.8.

one mediator, such as ICC Mediation Rules.[20] IIAM Mediation Rules, for instance, take a different approach by either providing for one or three mediators. Where three mediators are to be appointed, each party shall appoint one mediator, and the parties may mutually agree upon the third mediator, who shall act as the presiding mediator. If the parties fail to agree on the third mediator, the institution will appoint the third mediator.

In considering single versus multiple (two or three) mediators, a single mediator would, of course, result in a lower cost (a trite proposition). Multiple mediators, however, could bring a substantial advantage, for instance, in the combination of a facilitator and an evaluator. This is of particular use in technical disputes (like in construction and engineering disputes), where one mediator is exceptionally skilled in the process. At the same time, the other is a technical expert who has a particular advantage for option generation and reality testing. Multiple mediators may even be preferred in multiparty mediation or where there are multiple claims involving diverse technical or legal issues, requiring diverse expertise and qualifications. There is also the advantage of balancing the cultural perspective of the parties in international conflicts.

[B] Selection Criteria

Behind the curtains, an institution may consider several factors when selecting a mediator.[21] For example, to what extent do the parties need the mediator to be skilled in one or more practice areas? This needs attention since mediators are not empowered to judge the merits of a dispute—they are not "judges" or "arbitrators." Their role is to help the parties agree, usually by getting to the roots of their problems. Not every mediator necessarily has substantive experience in all the practice areas. Hence, one may need to weigh the mediator's process skills against his legal and substantive experience. Let us say the matter involves intellectual property, patent litigation, or an arcane subject matter; parties may want a specialist as well as a skilled mediator. To balance process skills versus legal and substantive background, parties may explore the idea of co-mediation.

Co-mediation would entail additional costs, but it may significantly streamline the negotiation. For instance, one of the mediators could be tasked with analytics (take more extensive notes on interests, state of mind, impediments, possible options), whereas the other could engage more with parties in communication and manage the process. This opens up the possibility of engaging a neutral expert with competency in a specific technical area, even if he is not exceptionally skilled in the process. In this regard, the ICC Mediation Guidance Notes provide that it may be appropriate, with the agreement of the parties, for the mediator to be assisted by an independent expert who can advise the mediator on technical issues, which is vital for the mediator to

20. ICC Mediation Rules, 2014, rule 5.6.
21. ICC Mediation Rules, 2014, rule 5.

understand in assisting the parties to resolve their dispute.[22] Accordingly, experts could be appointed for their specialization in accounting, finance, engineering, information technology, construction, energy, law, and so on.

What about the mediator's style?[23] While there are quite a few styles of mediation, each depending on the nature and substance of the dispute, a facilitative style is commonly regarded as the most mainstream form of mediation. However, it is not unusual in mediation to incorporate styles other than the facilitative approach, vis evaluative and/or transformative competencies. The mediator applies these styles at different moments and in differing measures.

A facilitative mediator will be an appropriate choice if the mediation is mainly about overcoming communication barriers, identifying hidden obstacles, developing options for mutual gain, helping the parties think creatively, and enabling an agreement. On the other hand, if the parties perceive that there will be a need for the mediator to break deadlocks by giving nonbinding opinions, asking hard questions, making comments about the facts and the law of the case, guiding the parties in other more directive ways, or helping set guidelines for a settlement based on objective norms, an evaluative mediator may be a better choice. In cases where the goal is not to resolve a specific dispute but rather to improve the parties' relationship, and if that relationship is important for the future, then a transformative approach will focus more on helping the parties communicate and work together with a long-term perspective.

To what extent are the mediator's language and/or cultural skills significant? And to what extent is his location important? Where there is a diversity of cultural backgrounds among the parties, a mediator who shares only one party's cultural values and credentials may not be trusted or accepted by the other party. Hence, it is important to ensure that the mediator is sensitive to cultural diversity and can understand the differences involved and implied by cultural dynamics. The mediator's location is normally a secondary issue since travel costs are often small concerning the amount in dispute and the sums spent if there is no settlement. A neutral venue, however, can be an important consideration to reflect the neutrality of the process. All in all, selecting an "outside" mediator and holding mediations at a neutral venue can be particularly helpful where parties are from different regions, where there is a high level of hostility or an obvious power imbalance. However, location becomes less relevant if the mediation will be held virtually, but other considerations may become more acute, such as time zones and relevant technology-related skill sets.

In the special case where an institution goes beyond its panel of mediators, accreditation is a valid criterion for selecting an external mediator. It reflects the specific training undergone by the mediator under consideration. Certifications, such as those offered by the International Mediation Institution (or IMI, an independent standard-setter), provide party feedback about the mediator that displays their practice skills and competency—rendering a certain level of transparency to the mediator

22. International Chamber of Commerce, Mediation Guidance Notes 16 (2014), https://cms.iccwbo.org/content/uploads/sites/3/2014/12/icc-mediation-guidance-notes-english.pdf.
23. *See* Chapter on the Role and Approach of the Mediator.

market. Accreditations also carry with them the responsibility to uphold and advance the standards set by organizations like the IMI.[24]

§5.05 CONDUCT OF MEDIATION

[A] Mediation Procedure

At this stage, after filing the Request and the appointment of the mediator (after the mediator has submitted his declarations and disclosures, as required), the mediation needs a procedure that charts the course of conduct of the proceedings. Commonly, the mediator and the parties discuss how the mediation will be conducted.[25]

Institution rules have a variety of versions when stating this. Under the ICC Mediation Rules, a mediator is required to promptly provide the parties with a written note informing them of how the mediation shall be conducted.[26] Under the SIMC Mediation Rules, in determining the manner and procedure for the conduct of the mediation, the mediator must give due respect to the wishes of the parties and be fair and impartial.[27] The mediator may communicate this to the parties orally, in writing, in person, electronically, or otherwise, and may do so jointly or separately.[28] Under LCIA Mediation Rules, the mediator may conduct the mediation in such a manner as he or she sees fit, having in mind the circumstances of the case and the parties' wishes.[29] The mediator may communicate with the parties orally or in writing, together or individually, and may convene a meeting at a venue to be determined by the mediator after consultation with the parties.[30] Quite differently, under the IIAM Mediation Rules, IIAM will work with the parties to establish the time and location of each mediation session.[31] In cases where the parties are unable to agree on any particular procedure to be followed by the mediator, the mediator: (i) shall fix, in consultation with the parties, a schedule, the dates and the time of each mediation session; and (ii) may conduct joint or separate meetings with the parties.[32]

[B] Pre-mediation Conference

Proactive case management utilizing procedural tools dramatically helps to optimize the mediation process. A pre-mediation conference, in a way, is the genesis of the mediation proceedings and is usually organized by the institution rather than the mediator, which follows the constitution of the tribunal and is mainly driven consensually.

24. *See* Chapter on Mediator Ethics.
25. ICC Mediation Rules, 2014, rule 7.1.
26. ICC Mediation Rules, 2014, rule 7.2.
27. SIMC Mediation Rules, 2020, rule 6.6.
28. SIMC Mediation Rules, 2020, rule 6.7.
29. LCIA Arbitration Rules, 2020, rule 5.1.
30. LCIA Arbitration Rules, 2020, rule 5.2.
31. IIAM Mediation Rules, 2020, rule 4(a).
32. IIAM Mediation Rules, 2020, rule 5(c).

Take, for instance, under SIMC Mediation Rules, SIMC may arrange for a pre-mediation conference to discuss the manner and procedure for the conduct of the mediation, including setting relevant timelines.[33] A chief attribute of mediation that cannot be compromised is that mediation is premised on the parties' voluntary participation. This means that a party and the mediator may put an end to the mediation at any time.

At this point, the parties are to inform the institution, mediator, and the other party of the names of their representatives and advisors who will be attending the mediation. Accompanying this, each party is also required to identify a representative of that party authorized to settle the dispute on behalf of that party, which would have to be confirmed in writing.[34]

To ensure an effective and efficient process, parties will also need to exchange their respective statements and relevant documents. These are also called position statements or briefing papers; each party summarizes its case, the background to the dispute, and the issue to be resolved, along with the supporting documents so that that mediator can get a grip over the entire dispute at hand.[35] This, of course, needs to be mutually exchanged between the parties so that each party can also appreciate the other's understanding of the case, the priority of the issues, etc.

§5.06 ROLES OF THE PLAYERS

[A] Role of the Institution

At various stages of the mediation process, an institution can extend a helping hand, often as a matter of procedure under the institution's rules. The objective is to facilitate the achievement of a full and final settlement. Take, for instance, under the SIMC Mediation Rules, the institution can engage in: (i) appointing a suitable mediator; (ii) assisting the parties with executing an agreement to mediate; (iii) organizing the exchange of any pertinent information and documents; (iv) arranging a suitable venue and date for mediation; (v) providing administrative and logistical support; and (vi) providing case-management services.[36]

In all matters not expressly provided for in the institutional rules, the institution and the mediator shall act in the spirit of the applicable rules.[37]

[B] Role of the Mediator

With the institution providing a variety of services, a mediator is more focused on the conduct of the mediation in such a manner as he considers appropriate, considering the circumstances of the case, the requests of the parties, and the need for expediency in

33. SIMC Mediation Rules, 2020, rule 6.5.
34. LCIA Arbitration Rules, 2020, rule 5.5.
35. LCIA Arbitration Rules, 2020, rules 4.1, 4.2, and 4.3.
36. SIMC Mediation Rules, 2020, rule 6.1.
37. ICC Mediation Rules, 2014, rules 10.6; IMI Model Mediation Rules, 2016, rule 13.

settlement of the dispute.[38] Under CAMP Rules, the mediator and CAMP do not serve as agents of any of the parties at any time. The mediator is also not an agent of CAMP, nor CAMP an agent of the mediator.[39]

While a mediator's role generally pertains to the mediation sessions, it may also comprise other roles, such as reporting, keeping contact with the parties, studying, and reviewing position statement and related documents, contacting third parties where necessary, as well as drafting the settlement agreements with the consultation of the lawyers.[40]

As a matter of technique, a mediator often discloses the substance of all the information (except confidential information) he receives from one party to the other party so that the other party may be given the opportunity to explain and clarify.[41] Nothing which is communicated to the mediator in private during the course of the mediation shall be repeated to the other party or parties without the express consent of the party making the communication.[42]

A mediator attempts to facilitate the voluntary resolution of the dispute by the parties, and communicates the view of each party to the other, assists them in identifying issues, reducing misunderstandings, clarifying priorities, exploring areas of compromise, and generating options in an attempt to solve the dispute, emphasizing that it is the responsibility of the parties to take a decision which affects them.[43]

A mediator has a duty to ensure that the mediation proceeds expeditiously.[44] Under the IIAM Mediation Rules, for instance, a mediator must use his best endeavors to conclude the mediation within 60 days of his appointment, and his appointment is set to expire after three months unless there is a written consent from all the parties to extend his mandate.[45]

While a mediator is not bound by the Code of Civil Procedure 1908 or the Indian Evidence Act 1872,[46] a mediator should be guided by the principles of fairness and justice, have regard to the rights and obligations of the parties, usage of trade, if any, and the circumstances of the dispute.[47] He is normally also bound by the Code of Conduct that is subscribed by the institution, such as that promulgated by the IMI. Under the IIAM Mediation Rules, the mediator is bound by the IIAM Mediators' Professional Code of Conduct.[48]

The mediator shall not impose any decision or terms of settlement on the parties.[49] The mediator may obtain expert advice or assistance in technical matters

38. IIAM Mediation Rules, 2020, rule 5(a).
39. CAMP Mediation Rules, 2016, rule 5(ii).
40. IMI Model Mediation Rules, 2016, rule 4.1.
41. IIAM Mediation Rules, 2020, rule 5(d).
42. LCIA Arbitration Rules, 2020, rule 5.3.
43. IIAM Mediation Rules, 2020, rule 5(e).
44. IMI Model Mediation Rules, 2016, rule 4.4.
45. IIAM Mediation Rules, 2020, rule 4(e).
46. IIAM Mediation Rules, 2020, rule 4(f).
47. ICC Mediation Rules, 2014, rule 7.3.
48. IIAM Mediation Rules, 2020, rule 5(b).
49. IIAM Mediation Rules, 2020, rules 5(e) and 6(c).

with the parties' consent, and the parties shall bear any expenses incurred in this regard.[50]

Unless all the parties agree otherwise in writing, a mediator shall not act nor shall have acted in any judicial, arbitral, or similar proceedings relating to the dispute which is or was the subject of the proceedings, whether as a judge, an arbitrator, an expert or a representative or advisor of a party.[51] Under IMI Model Rules, if the mediator wishes, he/she may cause himself to be assisted clerically at the mediation by a person designated by him for that purpose. In such an event, the mediator shall ensure that such person signs a declaration of confidentially.[52]

[C] Role of Parties and Their Representatives

Under the mediation rules, all parties to the mediation must act in good faith in preparing for the mediation and during the mediation.[53] Parties are to do their best to ensure that the mediation proceeds expeditiously,[54] in that they should cooperate with the mediator and give full assistance to enable the mediation to proceed and be concluded within the time stipulated.[55]

Parties may be represented by a counsel at any stage of the mediation process and are encouraged to consult legal counsel concerning the proceedings or any proposed settlement agreements.[56] If either party is represented by any other during the mediation, such representative must be authorized to perform all (legal) acts necessary for the mediation.[57]

At its initiative or at the invitation of the mediator, each party may give suggestions for the settlement of the dispute.[58] The parties must understand that the mediator only facilitates deciding to resolve disputes and that he will not and cannot impose any settlement, nor does the mediator give any warranty that the mediation will result in a settlement.[59]

The IIAM Rules go a step further to mandate that all parties recognize that neither IIAM nor the mediator: (i) will be acting as a legal adviser or legal representative for any of the parties; (ii) has a duty to assert, analyze or protect any party's legal rights or obligations; (iii) has a duty to make an independent expert analysis of the situation, raise issues not raised by the parties or determine that other necessary parties should

50. SIMC Mediation Rules, 2020, rule 6.8; IIAM Mediation Rules, 2020, rule 5(b).
51. ICC Mediation Rules, 2014, rule 10.3.
52. IMI Model Mediation Rules, 2016, rule 6.2.
53. ICC Mediation Rules, 2014, rule 7.4; SIMC Mediation Rules, 2020, rule 6.9; IIAM Mediation Rules, 2020, rule 6(d).
54. IMI Model Mediation Rules, 2016, rule 4.4.
55. IIAM Mediation Rules, 2020, rule 6(a).
56. IIAM Mediation Rules, 2020, rule 15(b).
57. IMI Model Mediation Rules, 2016, rule 6.3.
58. IIAM Mediation Rules, 2020, rule 6(b).
59. IIAM Mediation Rules, 2020, rule 6(c).

participate in the mediation; (iv) can guarantee that a mediation session will result in a settlement.[60]

It is often the case that parties, to safeguard their rights, institute parallel legal proceedings relating to the issues in mediation. The IMI Rules make it mandatory for the parties to notify the mediator and the other party(ies) within 24 hours after taking such steps or having instituted such proceedings.[61] The intent seems to introduce transparency among the parties while giving parties the freedom to act to preserve or safeguard their rights.

§5.07 CONFIDENTIALITY

[A] Rationale Behind Mediation Confidentiality

For a successful mediation, confidentiality is a critical aspect. This is because the fundamental motivating factors behind a dispute are often legally extraneous but are still imperative for either party to disclose their true motivations. Confidentiality is also a hallmark of mediation as it makes the process completely private. The protection of confidentiality extends further, such that any disclosures made during the mediation are not admissible before any court or tribunal without the parties' prior consent.

[B] Extent of Mediation Confidentiality

There is a distinction between mediator confidentiality and confidentiality between the parties. Such distinction is imperative to recognize as it explicates who can assert privilege and who can waive it. Privilege between the parties ensures free discussion whereas, privilege between the party and the mediator ensures neutrality. Mediator confidentiality could be equated to attorney-client privilege. Without the trust that the mediator would not reveal any information shared between them in private caucus to the other party, parties are less likely to be forthcoming and honest. Further, mediation confidentiality recognizes the mediator's privilege to not testify in court, which encourages mediator neutrality as it diminishes the likelihood of the mediator being called to stand in litigation later. This, of course, is subject to any limitations imposed under other statutes and laws governing the nature of dispute at the time of mediation, as the Indian Evidence Act.[62]

In the absence of state legislation, the courts may apply the Wigmore test of confidentiality, as propounded by the Supreme Court of Canada in *R v. Gruenke*.[63] Courts in India have often alluded to the Wigmore test of confidentiality while dealing with attorney-client privilege. The test calls for implicit and explicit assurance of the attorney that the communication between them and the client shall not be disclosed. In

60. IIAM Mediation Rules, 2020, rule 15.
61. IMI Model Mediation Rules, 2016, rule 9.
62. Indian Evidence Act, 1860, §§126–129.
63. (1991) 3 SCR. 263 (Can.).

furtherance of the agenda of invoking the client's confidence, confidentiality is also encouraged to foster a complete and satisfactory relationship between the parties. The injury that may result from the disclosure of confidential information must be greater than the benefit thereby gained from the correct disposal of litigation.

Institutional rules provide for extensive confidentiality clauses which stipulate almost absolute confidentiality. A strong case for "almost absolute confidentiality" instead of "absolute confidentiality" is made to neutralize the pressing risk of abuse by a party using a mediation proceeding to sterilize incriminating or damaging evidence by introducing it in the proceedings. With an agreement for institutional mediation, the parties also bind themselves with this confidentiality clause. Institutions that manage mediations, such as the ICC, have clauses to ensure that the mediation process is strictly confidential even after the mediation has ended.[64]

§5.08 SETTLEMENT AGREEMENT

If terms are agreed upon during settlement of the dispute, the parties, with the mediator's assistance (if the parties so request), draw up and sign a settlement agreement setting out such terms.[65] By signing the settlement agreement, the parties (and persons claiming under them)[66] agree to be bound by its terms.[67] The settlement agreement is required to be in writing.[68] Once the settlement agreement is signed, the mediator normally notifies the said agreement's institution and forwards the duplicate copy.[69] Across the institutional rules, the mediation automatically comes to an end when the parties sign a settlement agreement.[70]

The settlement agreement may also be in the form of an electronic record with digital signatures. Any such electronic documentation should require an undertaking of authenticity signed by the parties or their authorized representatives.[71] In order to meet the demands of changing times, digital signatures are now seen in the same light as pen and paper signatures and are equally legally valid as the latter. The authenticity of digital signatures is tested on the anvil of public-key cryptography, which makes the duplication of digital signatures replete with uncertainties, hence ensuring authenticity.

IIAM goes further to expressly state that the settlement agreement shall have the same status as that of an arbitral award and can be executed and enforced as a court decree.[72] In this context, the guidelines and practice of the IIAM draw its legitimacy

64. ICC Mediation Rules, 2014, rules 7.1–7.6 and Appendix-III.
65. LCIA Arbitration Rules, 2020, rule 7.1; IIAM Mediation Rules, 2020, rule 10(b).
66. IIAM Mediation Rules, 2020, rule 10(c).
67. LCIA Arbitration Rules, 2020, rule 7.2; CAMP Mediation Rules, 2016, rule 8(i).
68. SIMC Mediation Rules, 2020, rule 8.1; CAMP Mediation Rules, 2016, rule 8(i).
69. ICC Mediation Rules, 2014, rule 8(2); SIMC Mediation Rules, 2020, rule 8.3.
70. LCIA Arbitration Rules, 2020, rule 6 (a); IIAM Mediation Rules, 2020, rule 11(a); SIMC Mediation Rules, 2020, rule 7.1(a); ICC Mediation Rules, 2014, rule 8; CAMP Mediation Rules, 2016, rule 7.
71. CAMP Mediation Rules, 2016, rule 8(ii); SIMC Mediation Rules, 2020, rule 8.2.
72. IIAM Mediation Rules, 2020, rule 10(c).

from section 74 of Part III of the Arbitration and Conciliation Act, 1996, which expressly mandates a settlement agreement reached upon by mediation to be viewed as a court decree.

One interesting thought is the introduction of scrutiny by the mediation institutions—a formal examination of the draft settlement agreement before the parties and the mediator signs it. As in the case of the ICC Arbitration Rules and arbitral awards,[73] the idea is to maximize the legal effectiveness of the settlement by identifying any defects that could be used in an attempt to have it set aside or resist its enforcement elsewhere.[74] This may be of particular importance to parties since the Singapore Mediation Convention includes a ground for refusal where the obligations in the settlement are not clear and comprehensible. Although such settlement will likely undergo the examination of the lawyers (and the mediator), institutions could consider offering this added service to their users. However, the counterview suggests that since the settlements are a product of parties' free will (not adjudication), then the settlements arrived between parties should not be thought of requiring scrutiny by institutions, unlike the scrutiny of arbitral awards that a tribunal renders.

§5.09 TERMINATION OF MEDIATION

Upon initiation of the mediation, institutional rules generally provide that a mediation terminates on the occurrence of any of the following circumstances: (i) if the parties settle; (ii) if the mediator concludes that the parties cannot resolve the issue through mediation or the dispute is not fit for mediation; or (iii) a refusal of one of the parties or both to continue with the mediation. The termination of the mediation leaves the confidentiality and payment obligations under the mediation agreement intact.

Upon such termination, the administering institute may invite the participants to complete a feedback form. This feedback is processed by a reviewer and later used by future potential users eliminating guesswork associated with appointing a mediator. It helps the administering institutes and panel organizers determine the mediator's suitability for specific types of disputes and allows the mediators to assess their performance from a third party's view, helping them build on their strengths and work on their weaknesses.

[A] Fees and Costs

The party or parties filing a request are generally required to include with the Request the nonrefundable filing fee.[75] No request is processed unless accompanied by the

73. ICC Arbitration Rules, 2021, Art. 34 (after the closing of the proceedings, the arbitral tribunal will draw up a draft "Award" that is submitted to the ICC Court of Arbitration for scrutiny. The Court will scrutinize all awards. In doing so, it may lay down modifications as to form and, without affecting the Arbitral Tribunal's liberty of decision, draw its attention to points of substance. In scrutinizing draft awards, the Court considers, to the extent practicable, the requirements of mandatory law at the place of arbitration).
74. *See* Jason Fry, Simon Greenberg & Francesca Mazza, The Secretariat's Guide to ICC Arbitration 327 (2012).
75. ICC Mediation Rules, 2014, rule 6.1; LCIA Arbitration Rules, 2020, rule 5.1.

filing fee.[76] Following the receipt of a request, the institution may request that the party filing the Request pay a deposit to cover the administrative expenses of the institution.[77] These are illustrated in detail on the websites and brochures of the respective institutions.

Following the commencement of the proceedings, the institution requests the parties to pay one or more deposits to cover the administrative expenses of the institution and the fees and expenses of the mediator, as set out in the rules.[78]

If any requested deposit is not paid, the institution may stay the proceedings, not appoint a mediator,[79] or even terminate the proceedings, where the institutional rules so provide.[80] Upon termination of the proceedings, the institutions fix the total costs of the proceedings and, as the case may be, reimburse the parties for any excess payment or bill the parties for payment of any balance required pursuant to the respective rules.[81] The other scenario is where the parties themselves agree in writing.[82]

Concerning proceedings that have commenced under the rules of an institution, all deposits requested and costs fixed are to be borne in equal shares by the parties,[83] unless they agree otherwise in writing. However, any party shall be free to pay the unpaid balance of such deposits and costs should another party fail to pay its share.[84] A party's other expenditure shall remain the responsibility of that party unless otherwise agreed by the parties.[85]

[B] Mediator's Role in Subsequent Proceedings

An examination of the various institutional mediation rules indicates that the mediator is obligated not to testify in any judicial or arbitral proceedings regarding any facet of the mediation. Of course, such rules in and of itself cannot create an absolute restriction and are excepted where there is an obligation by statute or by a judicial order to testify. Different rules have stated this issue differently, both wide and narrow.

Under ICC Rules, unless required by applicable law or unless all parties and the mediator agree otherwise in writing, the mediator shall not give testimony in any judicial, arbitral, or similar proceedings concerning any aspect of the mediation proceedings.[86]

76. ICC Mediation Rules, 2014, rule 6.1; LCIA Arbitration Rules, 2020, rule 3 (and *see* schedule of mediation costs).
77. ICC Mediation Rules, 2014, rule 6.2.
78. ICC Mediation Rules, 2014, rule 6.3; SIMC Mediation Rules, 2020, rule 5.2; LCIA Arbitration Rules, 2020, rule 8.2.
79. LCIA Arbitration Rules, 2020, rule 8.4.
80. ICC Mediation Rules, 2014, rule 6.4; LCIA Arbitration Rules, 2020, rule 5.3.
81. ICC Mediation Rules, 2014, rule 6.5; SIMC Mediation Rules, 2020, rule 5.4.
82. LCIA Arbitration Rules, 2020, rule 8.5.
83. ICC Mediation Rules, 2014, rule 6.6; SIMC Mediation Rules, 2020, rule 5.5; LCIA Arbitration Rules, 2020, rule 6 (*see* schedule of mediation costs).
84. ICC Mediation Rules, 2014, rule 6.6.
85. ICC Mediation Rules, 2014, rule 6.7; SIMC Mediation Rules, 2020, rule 5.7.
86. ICC Mediation Rules, 2014, rule 10.4.

Under SIMC Rules, the mediator shall not give testimony in any judicial, arbitration, or similar proceedings concerning any aspect of the mediation under the Rules, unless required by applicable law or unless all parties and the mediator agree otherwise in writing.[87]

Under IIAM Rules, the parties undertake that the mediator shall not be appointed as an adjudicator, arbitrator or representative, counsel or expert witness of any party in any subsequent adjudication, arbitration, or judicial proceedings whether arising out of the mediation of any other dispute in connection with the same contract. No party shall be entitled to call the mediator as a witness in any subsequent adjudication, arbitration, or judicial proceedings arising out of the same contract.[88]

Under the IMI Model Rules, parties waive the right (at law or otherwise) to use anything that has transpired during the mediation in evidence against each other and/or against the mediator or other persons involved in the mediation. This includes any information supplied and/or recorded during or in connection with the mediation, or regarding the contents of the agreement.[89]

Under CAMP Rules, parties shall not attempt to call upon or compel the mediator to give evidence or testify or reveal any information received, documentation, or communication made during the mediation in any legal, arbitral, or judicial proceeding.[90]

§5.10 IMMUNITY TO INSTITUTION AND MEDIATOR

Immunity to the mediation center and mediator is vital to insulate them from most, if not all, civil liability for any wrongdoing during the mediation. However, the rules of different mediation institutions provide different standards of immunity, as is discussed below.

Under the ICC Rules, the mediator, center, ICC and its employees, and the ICC National Committees and Groups (their employees and representatives) are not liable to any person for any act or omission in connection with the proceedings, except to the extent such limitation of liability is prohibited by applicable law.[91]

Under SIMC Rules, the mediator, SIMC, and its employees are not liable to any person for any act or omission in connection with the mediation unless there is fraudulent or willful misconduct.[92]

Under LCIA Rules, none of the LCIA (including its officers and employees), the LCIA Court (including its President, Vice Presidents and individual members), the Registrar, any deputy Registrar, and any mediator are liable to any party, howsoever, for any act or omission in connection with any mediation conducted by reference to the LCIA Rules, save: (i) where the act or omission is shown by that party to constitute

87. SIMC Mediation Rules, 2020, rule 9.3.
88. IIAM Mediation Rules, 2020, rule 16.
89. IMI Model Mediation Rules, 2016, rule 7.4.
90. CAMP Mediation Rules, 2016, rule 6(ii).
91. ICC Mediation Rules, 2014, rule 10.5.
92. SIMC Mediation Rules, 2020, rule 10.1.

conscious and deliberate wrongdoing committed by the body or person alleged to be liable to that party; and (ii) the extent to which any applicable law prohibits any part of this provision.[93]

Under IIAM Rules, the parties jointly and severally release, discharge, and indemnify the mediator and IIAM in respect of all liability whatsoever, whether involving negligence or not, from any act or omission in connection with or arising out of or relating in any way to any mediation conducted under these Rules, save for the consequences of fraud, dishonesty or violation of IIAM Mediators' Professional Code of Conduct.[94] If any of the parties feel that the mediator is guilty of a violation of the IIAM Mediators' Professional Code of Conduct, they are required, within one month, to initiate the IIAM Mediators' Conduct Assessment Process.[95]

Under CAMP Rules, neither CAMP nor its officers or employees nor any mediator(s) at CAMP are liable to any party(ies), counsel, or participant(s) for any alleged act or omission in connection with any mediation conducted under CAMP Rules. The CAMP Rules further specify that parties, counsel, and participants shall not make any claim against the mediator and/or CAMP, its officers, and employees for any matter in connection with or in relation to: (a) the mediation; or (b) the services provided by the mediator and/or CAMP, its officers, and employees; or (c) the dispute between the parties.[96]

Under the IMI Model Rules have a different tone and tenor. According to it, any liability of the mediator in case of damage caused by any act or omission of the mediator in the mediation shall be limited to at most the amount of any proceeds paid out by his/her professional liability insurer. Except for intentional act or gross negligence on the part of the mediator, the parties undertake to hold the mediator harmless and indemnify him/her in respect of all claims that a third party may institute as against the mediator at any time and which are related to acts or omissions of the mediator during the mediation.[97] Unless the mediation agreement indicates a different set of rules, the mediator would be bound by the Rules of Conduct for IMI Certified Mediators and subject to the IMI Complaints Scheme and disciplinary rules. A party may complain with the IMI within 12 months from the termination of the mediation following the IMI Complaints Scheme at that time in force.[98]

§5.11 CONCLUDING REMARKS

Even though each mediation institution has its own set of rules for administering the mediation, the overarching principles are essentially the same. Institutional mediation brings necessary clarity, which is generally absent in ad hoc mediations but is essential for instilling parties' trust and faith in the process. Additionally, mediation institutions

93. LCIA Arbitration Rules, 2020, rule 11.1.
94. IIAM Mediation Rules, 2020, rule 16.1.
95. IIAM Mediation Rules, 2020, rule 17.
96. CAMP Mediation Rules, 2016, rule 9.
97. IMI Model Mediation Rules, 2016, rule 11.
98. IMI Model Mediation Rules, 2016, rule 12.

have, in no small way, contributed—and have the potential to further contribute—to legitimizing and promoting mediation as a form of dispute resolution. Among many things, institutions routinely hold capacity-building events for users, practitioners, and mediators, promoting best practices; institutions also impose and insist accreditation standards upon their impaneled mediators.

Lately, institutions have shown immense potential to intervene in court proceedings and promote the legitimacy of ADR processes by assisting courts as *amici* in clarifying the application of institutional rules.[99] The Supreme Court of India had recognized the importance of institutional mediation when it observed (though in the context of court-annexed mediation) that it can instill better outcomes.[100] Adopting institutional rules involves implementing tried and tested process, comprehensive case management, selection of a suitably qualified mediator, administrative support, streamlined procedural rules, and world-class infrastructure. And there is little doubt that the time and opportunity are ripe for institutional mediation to be a front-runner in dispute resolution methods.

99. *See, e.g.*, Halliburton Company v. Chubb Bermuda Insurance Ltd (formerly known as Ace Bermuda Insurance Ltd) (2020) UKSC 48 (an example of participation of an institution before the UK Supreme Court). *See also*, International Chamber of Commerce, *ICC Court Defined as the Global Benchmark for Arbitral Institutions*, ICC WBO NEWS (Nov. 23, 2019), https://iccwbo.org/media-wall/news-speeches/icc-court-defined-as-the-global-benchmark-for-arbitral-institutions/.

100. *See generally*, K. Srinivas Rao v. D. A. Deepa (2013) 5 SCC 226.

CHAPTER 6

Mediating Commercial Disputes

Shraddha Bhosale & Sahil Kanuga

§6.01 INTRODUCTION

India has one of the fastest-growing economies globally: nearly 60% of its Gross Domestic Product comes from domestic private consumption,[1] in addition to a healthy amount of cross-border trade. Trade and commerce are significant contributors to its flourishing economy. With increasing commercial transactions, it is only reasonable to deduct the potential for disputes originating from these transactions, whether domestic or cross-border.

Commercial disputes are essentially disputes arising from business transactions, mostly contractual in nature and usually pertaining to monetary issues. Thus, one can say (with some caution) that the foundation of most commercial disputes involves money, which is of course surrounded by an array of circumstances and factors, including human emotions (after all, businesses are run by people and mediations are ultimately between persons).

A helpful frame of reference for what constitutes a "commercial dispute" is found in the Commercial Courts Act, 2015. It is defined as being a dispute arising out of: (i) ordinary transactions of merchants, bankers, financiers and traders such as those relating to mercantile documents, including enforcement and interpretation of such documents; (ii) export or import of merchandise or services; (iii) issues relating to admiralty and maritime law; (iv) transactions relating to aircraft, aircraft engines, aircraft equipment and helicopters, including sales, leasing and financing of the same; (v) carriage of goods; (vi) construction and infrastructure contracts, including tenders; (vii) agreements relating to immovable property used exclusively in trade or commerce; (viii) franchising agreements; (ix) distribution and licensing agreements; (x)

1. *See* WORLD ECONOMIC FORUM, FUTURE OF CONSUMPTION IN FAST-GROWTH CONSUMER MARKETS: INDIA 8 (January 2019).

management and consultancy agreements; (xi) joint venture agreements; (xii) shareholders agreements; (xiii) subscription and investment agreements pertaining to the services industry including outsourcing services and financial services; (xiv) mercantile agency and mercantile usage; (xv) partnership agreements; (xvi) technology development agreements; (xvii) intellectual property rights relating to registered and unregistered trademarks, copyright, patent, design, domain names, geographical indications and semiconductor integrated circuits; (xviii) agreements for sale of goods or provision of services; (xix) exploitation of oil and gas reserves or other natural resources including electromagnetic spectrum; (xx) insurance and reinsurance; (xxi) contracts of agency relating to any of the above; and (xxii) such other commercial disputes as may be notified by the Central Government.

The extensive definition is virtually all-encompassing, covering a wide array of industries and sectors; meaning, the possibilities for mediating disputes arising out of such transactions are quite limitless. Most civil disputes are largely commercial in nature. However, civil disputes such as those relating to tax, transfer of property, succession, labor and industrial relations, etc., are excluded from the purview of "commercial" disputes for the purposes of the Commercial Courts Act 2015. This does not mean that strands of such disputes cannot be mediated; mediation is equally efficacious, though in limited ways, in respect of these fields of law. For instance, mediation is currently in consideration for ascertaining tax liabilities and assessment orders, which can be mutually arrived at between the tax departments and taxpayers. Similarly, there is much scope (existing and potential) for mediation in industrial relations (for collective labor conflicts),[2] consumer disputes (which share a commercial nature),[3] and others that have some commercial angle or are monetary in nature.

Just as commercial disputes come in many forms, commercial mediation also comes in many avatars. While the dispute is commercial and the process is mediation, the legal framework, under which the mediation proceeds, has a substantial determinant effect on the institution involved, the procedural rules that apply, and the settlement's enforceability. The type of commercial mediation will therefore depend on whether it is court-referred under section 89 of the Civil Procedure Code 1908; privately conducted (ad hoc or institutional); pre-institution mediation under the Commercial Courts Act 2015; Micro, Small and Medium Enterprises Development Act 2006 (MSMED Act); Real Estate (Regulation and Development) Act 2016 (RERA); or other similar statutes concerning commercial issues. There is also mediation under the Mediation and Conciliation Rules 2016, enacted pursuant to section 469 of the Companies Act 2013, which, even though substantially commercial in nature, is

---

2. *See generally*, Ernesto Noronha & Premilla D'Cruz, *Mediation and Conciliation in Collective Labor Conflicts in India*, *in* Mediation in Collective Labor Conflicts. Industrial Relations & Conflict Management (Martin Euwema et al., eds., 2019). *See also*, Industrial Relations Code, 2020 (which repeals the Industrial Disputes Act, 1947).
3. The new Consumer Protection Act, 2019, under sections 37–38 and Chapter V provide for disputes to be first referred to mediation and the procedure to be followed as per section 74(3) of the Act read with section 101(2)(zf) and section 102(2)(p) of the Act. The Central Government and the State Government, respectively, have been empowered to make rules for providing for the persons in the consumer mediation cell.

distinguished and discussed in a separate chapter along with the Insolvency and Bankruptcy Code 2016.

Besides the subject matter typology, commercial "mediation" or "conciliation"[4] may also be domestic or international. What constitutes international commercial mediation may again depend on the specific statute in consideration. For instance, the Arbitration and Conciliation Act, 1996 defines "international commercial conciliation" in the same way as "international commercial arbitration," i.e., when the conciliation relating to disputes arising out of legal relationships, whether contractual or not, considered as commercial under the law in force in India and where at least one of the parties is foreign.[5]

In recent years, mediation has attained ranks among commercial arbitration as a preferred mode for commercial dispute resolution or, at least, has become an important step to take in the event a dispute arises between parties (before or during any contentious proceedings in arbitration or litigation). Clauses for multitier dispute resolution and mixed-mode dispute resolution are increasingly incorporated into contracts, institutional rules, and practice notes.[6] Overall, the opportunity for early dispute resolution, particularly in times like the COVID-19 pandemic,[7] has given parties the ambit to squeeze their dispute resolution budgets and opt for progressive solutions in the interest of their commercial work.

§6.02 FEATURES OF MECHANISMS FOR RESOLVING COMMERCIAL DISPUTES

[A] Attributes of Adjudicatory Processes and Their Downsides

Adjudicatory processes are typically litigation and arbitration where a neutral third party, being the judge or arbitrator (respectively), adjudicates the dispute between parties and renders a binding decision in the form of a judgment/ decree or an arbitral award, enforceable under respective statutory provisions. Such processes determine legal rights between the parties, which colloquially results in a win-lose situation for parties. The relationship between parties, or their interests, has no place in adjudicatory processes, which tend to be contentious and sometimes give rise to multiple legal actions. Compared to amicable methods, the time and cost injected in contentious proceedings are manifold and often dissatisfactory.

4. The terms "mediation" and "conciliation" are generally used in this chapter interchangeably, for the sake of convenience. A detailed discussion on the schools of thought is available in Chapter 1 on the introduction to mediation and conciliation in India. Hence, wherever the context demands a precise usage, the terms have been used in their specific senses.
5. Arbitration and Conciliation Act, 1996, §1(2).
6. *See* Chapter on mixed-mode dispute resolution.
7. *See* generally, Society of Construction Law—India, *Survey 2020-21: On the Impact of Coronavirus Pandemic on the Construction and Infrastructure Industry*, SCL INDIA (January 2021), http://dx.doi.org/10.2139/ssrn.3850832.

Adjudication is involuntary,[8] and when sued, a party has no option but to defend or suffer the consequences of nonparticipation such as ex parte proceedings.[9] These processes are nonparticipatory for parties, except as a testifying witness. And though there are limited exceptions in which a party may represent itself, it is almost always advisable to have legal representation to comprehend the legal web of complex substantive and procedural rules. The procedures and outcomes of such processes that suffer from inflexibility are governed, restricted, and controlled by statutes like the Code of Civil Procedure, 1908, and the Indian Evidence Act, 1872. In the end, after going through an intensive trial, parties have no control over the outcome and are bound by the decision. If a party is dissatisfied, the options are either to appeal the judgment in litigation or to challenge the arbitral award to set it aside (on limited grounds). Either way, the cumbersomeness and technicality increase with each appellate stage.

Adjudicatory processes are also inflexible, open to the public (at least, in case of litigation), with no opportunity for parties to communicate within the adjudication framework. The rigidness comes with the need to follow procedural and substantive law, applying it to the evidence brought by the parties before the court or the arbitral tribunal. In a way, the fact-finding done by a court or a tribunal to arrive at its decision on the rights and liabilities is always with a tunnel vision into the past rather than the future (as in mediation, which takes an interest in the effect of the dispute on the future of the parties' commercial relationship).

[B] Attributes of Mediation That Trump Adjudicatory Processes

Commercial mediation is amicable, voluntary, flexible, and party-driven. The process is facilitated by a neutral and impartial mediator whom the parties appoint. The parties are in complete control of the procedure, duration, and outcome of the process. It can be initiated at any time, even when a dispute is pending adjudication before a court or an arbitral tribunal (though it is preferable to commence dispute resolution with mediation to keep the contentiousness at bay). Its potential goes beyond the proverbial border in that mediation gives parties the opportunity to resolve and settle even the peripheral controversies that have branched out from the main dispute(s), whether as a whole or part.

In mediations, the procedure and settlement process are not controlled, governed, or restricted by statutory provisions, allowing freedom and flexibility. Moreover, its voluntary nature grants a party the prerogative to unilaterally terminate the proceedings at any stage. Thus, a binding settlement is reached only if parties arrive at a mutually acceptable agreement, which morphs into a consent decree, consent award, or merely a contract, depending on the forum or legal framework under which the

8. Although, submitting disputes to commercial arbitration is founded on consent, once it has been invoked, a party is compelled to participate or bear consequences of nonparticipation.
9. Civ. Proc. Code, order IX Rule 6.

mediation is conducted (whether a private mediation, or pre-institutional mediation, or court-referred, or others).

Mediation is relatively more rapid and less costly than adjudicatory processes. Proceedings and outcomes of a mediation can be kept private and confidential, subject to subsequent execution proceedings in courts that would require a disclosure. Since it is interest-based (unlike a rights-based adjudication), one of its keys possibilities is the preservation of the commercial relationship between the parties, giving it the potential to create new business relationships. Beyond preservation of relationship, its particulars (e.g., risk allocation in construction contracts) may also be of interest to the parties and better dealt with in mediation. In other words, it is collaborative in nature as the focus is on the present and the future, with a focus on mutual satisfaction of parties' interests, irrespective of rights and liabilities. Hence, mediation can produce creative and durable outcomes, which result in a "higher level of satisfaction" for parties because of its participatory character.[10]

Personal appearance and active participation of the parties are the cornerstones of the process. Hence, there is an optimal opportunity for parties to communicate directly with each other in the presence of the mediator, that too, a mediator of their choice or selected by the agreed procedure for appointment. Moreover, this autonomy in choosing a mediator is far-reaching since parties can choose one specializing in the subject matter of the dispute, say specialists in construction, shipping and maritime, etc.

A settlement arrived in mediation is only in respect of the dispute being settled. However, a court decree in a case adjudicated on merit may set a binding precedent for similar disputes in the future. Parties may specifically want to avoid setting a precedent in disputes revolving around new and uncertain areas of the law.[11] Parties opting for mediation can thus be insulated from a settlement's impact on future disputes. But in case of decrees or awards by consent, there is no binding precedent on future disputes.

§6.03 MEDIATING COMMERCIAL DISPUTES

[A] Mediation's Suitability for Commercial Disputes

Mediating commercial disputes has the benefit of some essential qualitative features like active participation by parties who own the process, preservation of future relationships, informality and flexibility in the resolution process, creativity and scope for option generation, bespoke nature of procedures, and the potential to highlight areas of commonality between parties. Essentially, commercial parties understand their industry best (their product, service, technicality, risk, etc.), and mediation provides a forum where parties can self-determine.

10. *See* STEPHEN B. GOLDBERG, FRANK E.A. SANDER, ET AL., DISPUTE RESOLUTION: NEGOTIATION MEDIATION AND OTHER PROCESSES 151 (1992).
11. *See* Kenneth R. Feinberg, *Mediation—A Preferred Method of Dispute Resolution*, 16(5) PEPPERDINE L. REV. S6 (1989).

Then there are some quantitative characteristics of mediation that also suit commercial disputes, like the confidential nature of the disputes, efficiency and structure, identification of underlying interests from a neutral perspective, cost-effectiveness, and expediency.

These factors are really what make up for why mediation in commercial disputes is opportune and advantageous. Nor is there any restriction on the stage or issue in which mediation can be promising. Meaning that mediation can be invoked right when parties start experiencing symptoms of a difference having arisen in relation to the contract between parties, rather than being ambushed by the consequences of such difference such as loss of time and additional costs. Confidentiality ensures that the parties' contentions are not reported by the media, as such reporting typically leads to speculation on how the dispute may be adjudged and affect the stock prices of listed companies.

Mediation is particularly suitable where parties are eager to settle rather than participate in an adversarial process which could lead to hostility. While mediating a commercial dispute, parties can give precedence to their commercial interests over their legal rights. Mediation is also suitable where businesses are not comfortable with the unpredictable nature of outcomes in adversarial methods and where parties may be looking to keep avenues for future business with each other open.

[B] Factors Causing Aversion among Commercial Parties

Despite these advantages, commercial parties are apprehensive about engaging in mediation for one or more reasons. Some of these are genuine under the given circumstances, while some are unfounded.

Commonly, there is a general lack of awareness among parties (which justly extends to Advocates) about the process of mediation and its advantages. Such a lack of knowledge deters them from choosing mediation. Hence, there is a strong misconception among parties inviting the other to mediate a sign of weakness or the lack of a meritorious claim or defense. On the other hand, for the party receiving an invitation to mediate, there is a suspicion that the process is nothing but a tool for phishing compromising information for an impending suit or arbitral action (or while such proceedings are ongoing).

Once the apprehensions are evaluated and addressed, the decision to mediate will also rely on several other factors that need consideration. For starters, it could be a simple cost-benefit analysis, i.e., for commercial parties to analyze the costs involved in the process and identify the potential benefits. If the benefits outweigh the cost by a desirable margin, then the choice to mediate may be sound on this aspect.

Enforceability too interlinks with understanding the benefits of commercial mediation—that, of course, needs to be considered under the provisions of the specific legislation governing such proceedings. Having said that, since settlements arrive with mutual consent, it is reasonable to consider that parties would comply with the terms of the settlement, thereby obviating the need for enforcement.

In deciding to mediate, several complexities may also be involved, like the nature of the commercials, a party's need for urgent interim reliefs (such as injunctions/restraining orders),[12] potential limitation/time-bars setting in, or the need for a legal precedent. While these are more legalistic considerations, some subjective concerns also bear upon the decision to mediate, such as the relationship between the parties, the commercial transaction in question (e.g., the stage of the construction project), and the power imbalance between the parties. Among these subjective concerns, one often comes across the decisional dilemma—executives or in-house counsel participating in the mediation may have an apprehension that the settlement they enter into may not be seen favorably by the rest of the organization and the owners/management. That is why it always seems easier/simpler to wake up the beast (arbitration/litigation). A practical solution to this problem could be maintaining a shared document on the company's platform and invite organization-wide comments on key aspects of the mediation process such as options and alternatives.[13]

[C] Agreement to Mediate in Commercial Contracts

Mediation is a voluntary process and requires parties to agree to mediate their disputes. This agreement to mediate (or mediation agreement) is not to be confused with an agreement to settle. A mediation agreement only casts an obligation to undergo the process of mediation without any obligation to settle on the dispute. So, an agreement to mediate may be mandated by way of a statute, as is elaborated later, but there can never be an obligation on parties to settle in mediation.

Parties may agree to a pre-dispute mediation agreement by including an appropriate clause when entering into a contract. Indian courts have upheld enforceability of pre-arbitral procedure such as mediation in multitier dispute resolution clauses.[14] However, given that mediation is fundamentally voluntary in nature and enforcing an agreement to mediate does not entirely serve its purpose in spirit, it rather contradicts an integral trait of voluntary participation. Nevertheless, the inclusion of pre-dispute mediation clauses is still reasonable and necessary since its presence may persuade parties to go through an agreed procedure for resolving disputes and exhaust what was considered important when the contract was executed. Given the potential benefits, parties may be prompted to undergo mediation to safeguard their commercial interests.

It is equally possible to enter into an agreement to mediate after a dispute has arisen. Whether pre-dispute or post-dispute, a discussion on the agreement to mediate

12. For example, major commercial transactions require some form of bank guarantees to be executed. A great many disputes arise out of premature encashment and untimely release of these guarantees. Such controversy would necessitate approaching a court for urgent interim relief, especially if one commercial party is foreign and has no other assets within the country. But even in such circumstances, parties could well pursue mediation in connection with the main dispute or transaction while seeking targeted interim relief for time-sensitive issues.
13. *See* Michael Leathes, Negotiation: Things Corporate Counsel Need to Know but Were Not Taught 21 (2017).
14. *See* Rajiv Vyas v. Johnwin Manavalan, MANU/MH/1125/2010; Haldiram Manufacturing Company Pvt. Ltd. v. DLF Commercial Complexes Ltd., 193 (2012) DLT 410.

is only possible with the assumption that both parties have agreed to mediate and, through a written agreement, both parties agree further on the terms and conditions under which the mediation will proceed. Enforceability of stand-alone mediation agreements may be viewed in the same way as mediation clauses in a multitier scheme.

In brief, however, this is largely dependent on: (a) language of the clause; (b) conduct of the parties; and (c) waiver, if any. Language-wise, the chances of enforceability are better in case of a detailed mediation agreement (preferably, institutional mediation) which contains a stipulation on good faith, time period, notice requirements, named mediator, or appointment procedure.

It is most prevalent for mediation agreements to feature multitier dispute resolution clauses (also known as multistep or escalation clauses) and less likely as a stand-alone agreement. Where parties have agreed to a multitier scheme, the tiers normally escalate from negotiation or amicable discussion to mediation, failing which parties can initiate arbitration as a binding method to resolve their disputes with finality.

Nonetheless, if the contract does not contain any agreement to mediate disputes, parties are always free to agree on mediating their dispute after it has arisen or even during any other ongoing proceeding. In such a case, a separate mediation agreement may be drawn up and executed before the commencement of the process. Some salient features of an agreement to mediate are as follows.

Scope of dispute/case summary

It is always advisable to outline the scope of the dispute being referred to mediation. This usually contains references to agreement/s under which disputes have arisen, any specific transaction/s or invoice/s or order/s placed under such agreement/s, broad contentions of the parties, and reference, where applicable, to any ongoing adversarial proceedings (litigation/arbitration) between the parties pertaining to the disputes and/or any order/s passed in such proceedings. Parties may also choose to include peripheral disputes in the scope.

Mediator's attributes and fees

Parties may agree on specific attributes that the mediator ought to have in terms of languages spoken, qualifications, country/city of residence, nationality, subject matter expertise, experience in mediating disputes, etc. Parties may choose to cap or specify a range of the mediator's fees acceptable to the parties. Parties may also spell out the number of mediators appointed in case parties are keen on co-mediation. Parties should avoid being over-specific or elaborate with the attributes and fees lest it may result in an exceedingly small pool of mediators for parties to choose from. However, where the dispute is complex and technical, the parties may choose to have a mediator with the needed technical background/industry experience (or even choose co-mediators with complementing backgrounds). In cases where parties agree to a Med-Arb model, the parties may also specify additional attributes for the mediator who, on the failure of mediation, will become the arbitrator and adjudicate the dispute.

Submission to rules of any institution for administered mediation

If parties wish to submit their dispute to the administered rules of any institution, they may incorporate such reference to the rules and the institution in their agreement. Model clauses of most institutions such as the International Chamber of Commerce (ICC) are readily available on their websites. Parties/their counsel can borrow the language to ensure accuracy of reference to the correct institution and the intended set of rules to be made applicable.

Confidentiality

In most cases, parties will want to keep the proceedings confidential. Unless prohibited by applicable law, parties have the flexibility to decide the extent of confidentiality. For example, parties may choose to keep the proceedings confidential but not the fact that mediation is ongoing or has concluded between the parties. Another example is that parties may choose whether or not to keep any settlement agreement arising from mediation confidential. They may also choose to keep the settlement agreement confidential but retain the right to disclose it for purposes of enforcement.

Procedural aspects such as time frame, language, and venue

These are important for parties to agree on to avoid procedural hurdles, especially in ad hoc mediations. It is not uncommon for parties to specify a time frame within which mediation should be concluded before proceeding to the next dispute resolution avenue in case parties do not settle in mediation. The time frame is really the parties' discretion. Complex disputes having a wider scope usually require more time because parties tend to deliberate these at length. It is, however, astonishing to note that parties have known to settle disputes even within a time frame as short as 24 hours. The language and venue are equally important for parties to specify. In case parties have not specified any of these aspects in their agreement, the mediator usually irons out these aspects with the parties or institutional rules provide for these eventualities.

Authority of parties' representatives to settle

It is essential that parties' representatives at mediation are duly authorized to negotiate and settle the dispute and sign the settlement agreement in order to bind the parties effectively. Parties may specify their representatives or may agree to place any limitation on the authority of such representatives.

Legal representation

Parties are usually assisted by lawyers at mediation. Their role is especially important when parties reach a settlement that needs to be recorded in the form of a settlement agreement. The lawyers of the parties usually work together to draft such an agreement. However, parties are free to opt out of any legal representation.

Appointment of independent experts

Where the dispute is complex and technical, the parties may choose to mutually appoint an independent expert to assist the mediator in understanding the technical aspects. Parties may choose to have a mediator with technical background co-mediate the dispute with a mediator having a law background.

Having a mediation agreement in place resolves many aspects of the mediation milieu for parties, particularly in respect of international commercial disputes. Parties in cross-border cases usually speak different languages, come from varied business and legal cultures, and have different time zones. By deciding on the language of the proceedings and choosing a suitable venue, parties can easily overcome these procedural hurdles through their mediation agreement. In many instances, parties opt for a venue in a neutral country that is equidistant from the parties' locations. Should mediation be successful, typical threshold and/or ancillary issues faced by disputing parties such as issues pertaining to applicable law, issues surrounding enforcement, and issues on matters such as forum non conveniens are bypassed.

[D] Enforceability of a Mediated Settlement Agreement

Enforceability of a settlement reached in mediation is a fundamental factor on which the decision to mediate rests. Depending on the applicable statute under which mediation is either invoked or conducted, the question of the settlement's enforceability is answered. Hence, it depends on whether it is a court-referred mediation,[15] or conciliation under Part III of the Arbitration & Conciliation Act 1996,[16] or mediation within an arbitration proceeding under section 30 of the Arbitration & Conciliation Act 1996,[17] and others. The following segments discuss mediation under three specific statutes concerning commercial disputes, which include statutory mediation or conciliation in varied forms. These are the MSMED Act, the Commercial Courts Act 2015, and the Real Estate (Regulation & Development) Act, 2016.

§6.04 CONCILIATION UNDER THE MICRO, SMALL AND MEDIUM ENTERPRISES DEVELOPMENT ACT, 2006

The MSMED Act was enacted with a view to facilitating the promotion, development, and competitiveness of enterprises classified as micro, small, and medium under the MSMED Act.

As part of the measures formulated for recovery of delayed payments to micro and small enterprises (MSEs), the provisions under Chapter V of the MSMED Act allow for a reference to be made by either party to the MSE Facilitation Council ("Facilitation Council") for resolution of payment issues between a buyer and a seller with respect to amounts due under Chapter V (particularly, sections 15–24). In case the buyer does not make payment to the supplier for his supplies of goods or services within 45 days of the acceptance of the goods or service rendered, under sections 16 and 17 of the MSMED

15. *See* Chapter on court-annexed mediation.
16. *See* Chapter on the law of conciliation.
17. *See* Chapter on mixed-mode dispute resolution.

Act, the buyer is liable to pay compound interest at a rate which is three times the bank rate notified by the Reserve Bank of India.

In this regard, section 18 provides that any party to a dispute may, with regard to any amount due under section 17, make a reference to the Facilitation Council. The Council, after examining the case filed by the MSE, issues directions to the buyer for payment of due amount along with interest as per the provisions under the MSMED Act. Every reference to the Facilitation Council under section 18 is required to be decided within a period of 90 days from the date of such reference.

The Act further provides that on receipt of such a reference, the Facilitation Council shall either itself conduct conciliation in the matter or seek the assistance of any institution or center providing alternate dispute resolution services by making a reference to such an institution for conducting the conciliation. The provisions of sections 65–81 of the Arbitration and Conciliation Act 1996 ("Arbitration Act") shall apply to such a dispute as if the conciliation were initiated under Part III of the Arbitration Act (discussed elsewhere).[18]

In the event such conciliation proceedings are unsuccessful, and no settlement is reached between the parties, section 18 empowers the Facilitation Council to either take up the dispute for arbitration or refer it to any institution or center providing such services. In such a case, the provisions of the Arbitration Act then apply to the disputes as if the arbitration was in pursuance of an arbitration agreement under subsection (1) of section 7 of the Arbitration Act.

In the event a settlement is reached during the conciliation proceedings, the Facilitation Council delivers it as an award by mutual consent in accordance with section 74 of the Arbitration Act (which is made applicable to conciliation proceedings). Hence, a settlement agreement has the same status and effect as an arbitral award under the Arbitration Acts. However, if an appellant (not being the supplier) wants to file an appeal against the award (whether a consent award or otherwise), no application for setting aside the award shall be entertained by any court unless the appellant (not being supplier) has deposited 75% of the award amount along with the application to set aside the award under section 34 of the Arbitration Act.

To boost India's enterprises, the Ministry of Micro, Small, and Medium Enterprises has also established an online portal—a delayed payment monitoring system called the MSME SAMADHAAN. MSE having Udyog Aadhaar Memorandum (UAM) number can file online applications in respect of delayed payment by buyers. Once an application is filed, it is forwarded to the concerned Facilitation Council in the state or union territory, which exercises jurisdiction over the matter, for further course of action.

Various state governments and union territories have also framed rules under subsection (3) of section 21 of the MSMED Act, which governs the functioning of a Facilitation Council within the jurisdiction. The Maharashtra Micro and Small Enterprises Facilitation Council Rules, 2007 (MSEFC Rules) provide for the composition, manner of appointment, and term of office of members of the Facilitation Council. They

18. *See* Chapter on the law of conciliation.

also stipulate the manner in which the Facilitation Council shall discharge its functions empowering it to appoint or engage the services of one or more experts as provided in section 26 of the Arbitration and Conciliation Act, 1996, and empowering it to apply to the court under section 27 of the said Act for assistance in taking evidence, among other things. The Rules permit parties to appear either personally or through legal representation before the Facilitation Council.

Mandatory conciliation or mediation under the MSMED Act provides an expedient and effective mechanism for MSEs to resolve their payment disputes amicably, taking the sting out of disputes and their impact on MSEs' commercial operations. Nevertheless, a few downsides persist, such as the lack of party autonomy, in that parties do not have a choice in the appointment of the conciliator.

Similarly, the Med-Arb model under the MSMED Act is also a departure from the more widely accepted model in which the third-party mediator and arbitrator are not the same (to avoid bias or apprehension). This is reflected in section 80 of the Arbitration Act that (unless otherwise agreed) a conciliator shall not act as an arbitrator or as a representative or counsel of a party in any arbitral or judicial proceeding in respect of a dispute that is the subject of the conciliation proceedings. However, since the MSMED Act accommodates the possibility of conciliating and arbitrating itself, parties are likely to be hesitant during the conciliation proceedings, knowing well that the conciliator will later assume the role of an arbitrator should the conciliation fail (whose decision will be binding and reasonably apprehended to be biased).

Despite these potential drawbacks of statutorily imposing a Med-Arb model upon parties, the Bombay High Court held in *Delton Electricals v. Maharashtra State Electricity Distribution Co. Ltd. & Ors.*[19] that there was no impropriety on the part of the Facilitation Council. The court opined that when the conciliation failed, reference to arbitration became necessary, and the Facilitation Council did not lack the authority to adjudicate upon the claim on merits as there was no evidence of the Facilitation Council having prejudged the issues in any manner during conciliation proceeding where both parties were involved and attempted to reach a settlement.

The 2020 report available on the online portal "MSME SAMADHAAN" shows that out of the 13,844 applications converted into cases by the MSEFC, about 4,937 cases were mutually settled.[20] It would therefore appear that the MSEFC is able to successfully conciliate and settle roughly 35% of the cases admitted before it. Overall, the MSMED Act is a propitious move to encourage the amicable settlement of disputes between buyers and sellers belonging to the micro and small industries.

§6.05 MEDIATION UNDER THE COMMERCIAL COURTS ACT, 2015

The Commercial Courts Act 2015 was enacted to constitute commercial courts for adjudicating commercial disputes. Subsequently, an amendment was passed by the

---

19. (2017) SCC Online Bom 9000.
20. Ministry of Micro Small and Medium Enterprises, *Ministry CPSEs Group Report, MSME Samadhan—Delayed Payment Monitoring System*, https://samadhaan.msme.gov.in/MyMsme/MSEFC/MSEFC_ReportWelcome.aspx?InnerRpt=1.

parliament in 2018,[21] which inserted section 12A introducing pre-institution mediation and settlement. Besides the introduction of pre-institution mediation, the specified value under section 2(1)(i) of the Commercial Courts Act stood reduced from INR 1 crore to INR 3 lakhs by the amendment in 2018, significantly increasing the disputes covered within the scope of the Act.

With the amendment in place, the Commercial Courts Act now mandates that a plaintiff or applicant seeking to institute a suit for adjudication of a commercial dispute under the Act shall first be required to initiate pre-institution mediation for the said dispute unless the plaintiff intends to seek an urgent interim relief (like an injunctive order to restrain a party).

All disputes covered under the definition of the term "commercial" under section 2(1)(c) of the said Act are triable by the Commercial Courts. While most disputes of civil nature would also be commercial, dispute relating to tax, transfer of property, succession, labor, industrial issues, etc., appear to be specifically excluded from the purview of "commercial" disputes under the said Act.

The Commercial Courts (Pre-Institution Mediation and Settlement) Rules, 2018 (PIMS Rules) stipulate the process of mediation to be followed in respect of commercial disputes under the Act.

A party to a commercial dispute may make an application to the concerned Authority (as notified by the Central Government under section 12A(2) of the Act) for initiation of the mediation process along with a fee of INR 1,000. On making an application to the said Authority for initiating pre-institution mediation, the said Authority issues a notice to the respondent party to appear and give consent to participate in the mediation on a date that does not exceed 10 days from the date of issuance of such notice. Should there be no response from such respondent to the said notice, a final notice may be issued by the Authority, or if the respondent refuses to participate in the mediation, the Authority treats the mediation to be a nonstarter and prepares a report to that effect. Such a report briefly states the reason for a nonstarter. The responding party may seek time for appearance, which is left to the Authority's discretion to grant. If on the scheduled date, the responding party does not appear, the mediation is treated as a nonstarted, and a report to that effect is issued.

But should the respondent agree to participate in the mediation, the Authority assigns the dispute to a mediator and fixes a date for a meeting. The Authority ensures that the process of mediation is completed within three months from the date of application by the applicant to initiate a mediation. With the parties' consent, the said period may be extended by two more months.

The mediation is conducted at the premises of the said Authority, and parties are permitted to appear in person or through legal representation or both. The mediator is required to explain the process of mediation to the parties at the outset of the proceedings and schedule all mediation sittings in consultation with parties. The mediator can hold meetings privately with each or either of the parties, and parties can

21. Commercial Courts, Commercial Division and Commercial Appellate Division of High Courts (Amendment) Act, 2018.

confidentially share settlement proposals with the mediator. Parties can also share settlement proposals with each other directly.

Any settlement between the parties is to be reduced to writing, bearing the signature of all the parties as well as the mediator. According to section 12A(5) of the Act, the settlement of the Act shall have the same status and effect as if it is an arbitral award on agreed terms under subsection (4) of section 30 of the Arbitration Act.

Where no settlement is reached between the parties in the stipulated time frame or where the mediator is of the opinion that no settlement is possible, the mediator can conclude the mediation by issuing a report in writing. Such a report requires the mediator to mention the reasons for the failure of parties to settle, among other particulars.

The proceedings are confidential, and parties are required to act in good faith during the process. The mediator is also required to follow certain ethics laid down under Rule 12 and act in an impartial and independent manner.

The Act also provides that the period during which the parties remain occupied with the pre-institution mediation shall not be computed for the purpose of limitation under the Limitation Act 1963. This provides parties the necessary preservation of its rights against time-bars on their claims or the invocation of arbitration/ institution of the suit. Otherwise, the general rule is that the benefit under section 14 of the Limitation Act (for exclusion of time of proceeding bona fide in court without jurisdiction) is inapplicable with respect to parties engaging in consensual dispute resolution process before invoking arbitration or instituting a suit.[22] Section 77 of the Arbitration Act also echoes the general rule.

As in the case of conciliations under the MSMED Act, pre-institution mediations are also essentially voluntary in nature, but their initiation is mandatory before the institution of a suit, and the choice is left to the parties about the extent of their participation. Though seemingly a procedural formality, the provision is a well-intended nudge and offers an expedient, cost-effective dispute resolution mechanism to parties (keeping in mind that disputes can be as low as INR 3 lakhs, for which an application or suit proceedings can be disproportionate). Similarly, another potential pitfall and compromise to party autonomy is the lack of the parties' ability to choose their mediator. Nor does section 12A give any option to parties to choose their own institution and mediation rules under which to comply with the pre-institution requirement, given the fact that sophisticated parties may prefer international institutions and certified mediators to administer or conduct the proceedings.

This severely compromises the use and effectiveness of pre-institution mediation, much of which is indicated in the available statistical data. In Maharashtra, between

22. *See* Union of India v. M/s Baga Brother & Anr., 2017 SCC Online Del 8989, ¶¶ 8–11. Cf. Geo Miller v. Rajasthan Vidyut Utpadan Nigam Ltd., 2019 SCC Online SC 1137, ¶ 27 (Supreme Court held that the time spent in "good faith" settlement discussions/negotiations might be excluded to compute the limitation period for reference of the dispute to arbitration. However, this Supreme Court seems to have been only in the context of family disputes and only in respect of negotiations (not conciliation or other ADR processes like mediation or Dispute Resolution Boards, etc.)).

July 2018 and March 2019,[23] 1,168 applications were received initiating pre-institution mediation, out of which the opposite party refused to participate or never responded in 104 cases ("non-starter"). Only 28 cases underwent the process of mediation, out of which only 2 were settled. There is simply no data in respect of the balance cases. The data of the first quarter of 2020 shows that:[24] 1,259 applications were received initiating pre-institution mediation, out of which 970 cases were nonstarters, 44 cases underwent the process of mediation, among which only 4 cases were settled. Again, there is no data in respect of the balance cases. The data of the second quarter of 2020 shows that:[25] 158 applications were received initiating pre-institution mediation, out of which only 1 case underwent the process of mediation and did not appear to have been settled. There is no information available on the outcome of the balance cases. It is likely that the sudden drop of caseload may be attributable to the outbreak of COVID-19. Similarly, in Karnataka, from July 2018 to March 2021,[26] among the 2,827 applications received initiating pre-institution mediation, 2,302 cases were nonstarters, 110 cases underwent mediation, and only 43 cases were settled.

The rather grim statistics are telling that perhaps voluntary mediation and the lack of autonomy in some fundamental issues are not preferable. There is a serious need to not merely treat the external symptom but fix the pre-institution mediation system inherently. One way to do this would be to make it optional for the parties to either undergo mediation under the aegis of an Authority constituted under the Legal Services Authorities Act 1987 or any private institution or mutually appointed mediator.

Another important aspect would be to bridge the gap between mandatory and voluntary mediation by implementing a mandatorily required initial mediation session.[27] Under this model, following the initiation of pre-institution mediation, the parties would be mandatorily required to attend an initial mediation session where the process is explained contextually for the dispute at hand. If parties, after understanding the process and weighing its pros and cons, choose to mediate, such mediation would have to be concluded within 90 days from initiation. But if after such the session, a party chooses not to move forward, then the requirement of the initial mediation session will stand fulfilled, and the applicant will not be barred from instituting the suit. And if a party remains absent during the initial mediation session, then, it will look at the peril sanctions from the concerned court.

---

23. Maharashtra State Legal Services Authority, *Statistical Data*, https://legalservices.maharashtra.gov.in/1122/Statistical-Data.
24. *Id.*
25. *Id.*
26. *See* Karnataka State Legal Services Authority, Bengaluru, *Pre-Institution Mediation Data for the Period from July 2018 to March 2021*, https://kslsa.kar.nic.in/pdfs/PIMS_data.pdf.
27. *See* Leonardo D Urso, *Italy's "Required Initial Mediation Session": Bridging The Gap between Mandatory and Voluntary Mediation*, 36(4) ALTERNATIVES TO THE HIGH COST OF LITIGATION (April 2018).

§6.06 CONCILIATION UNDER THE REAL ESTATE (REGULATION AND DEVELOPMENT) ACT, 2016

The construction and infrastructure industry are one of the largest in India, within which the real estate sector (housing, retail, hospitality, and commercial) shares a large market size which is exponentially increasing. In order to empower real estate buyers against construction delays and erring developers, the RERA was enacted. It establishes the Real Estate Regulatory Authority ("Authority"), which regulates and promotes the real estate sector, primarily by ensuring the sale of plot, apartment, or building in a project takes place in an efficient and transparent manner, by protecting the interest of consumers, and by establishing a mechanism for the speedy redressal of disputes.

With the introduction of RERA, all new projects have to be registered with the Authority, bringing greater transparency on the project for the customers, and all projects are now to be sold on carpet area basis, ensuring that the customers are clear on their expectations for the price sought. Promoters have to ensure that all the facts advertised are true, and they are liable for up to five years to repair any defects (inducing fair play and quality of construction).

Under section 31 of RERA, an aggrieved person can file a complaint with the concerned Authority for any violation of the provisions of RERA or the rules and regulations made thereunder against any promoter, allottee, or real estate agent, as the case may be. The Authority can also *suo moto* initiate proceedings under RERA.

While deciding a complaint, the Authority has the same powers as vested in the civil court under the Code of Civil Procedure, 1908, while trying a suit. The Authority is empowered to issue interim orders and directions, impose penalties and interest.

Typically, disputes under the Act mostly pertain to delay in handover of possession of unit allotted, defects in the construction thereof, mismatch in area, lack of amenities promised in the project, etc.

A complaint filed under section 31 of RERA is adjudicated by the Authority in accordance with the applicable rules and regulations. It is required to be disposed of expeditiously and in any case within 60 days from filing. Section 43 of RERA mandates the establishment of the Real Estate Appellate Tribunal having one or more benches with each bench comprising of at least one judicial member. Any person aggrieved by order of the Authority can appeal such an order before the Appellate Tribunal. Every such appeal shall be endeavored to be disposed of within a period of 60 days from its filing. An appeal from any order of the Appellate Tribunal will lie before the High Court.

Under provisions of RERA, the Government of Maharashtra established the Maharashtra Real Estate Regulatory Authority (MahaRERA) in 2017.[28] Since it was observed that several complaints filed before MahaRERA were eventually withdrawn owing to a settlement between the disputants, the MahaRERA Conciliation and Dispute Resolution Forum ("said Forum") was set up under section 32(g) of RERA. The said

28. *See* Maharashtra State Legal Services Authority, *Guidelines for Functioning of MahaRERA Conciliation and Dispute Resolution Forum* (No. MahaRERA/Secyi File No. 27148/2021, May 18, 2021), https://maharera.mahaonline.gov.in/Upload/PDF/Circular%20No%2031.pdf.

Forum was the first of its kind to be established in India and aimed to facilitate an amicable resolution of disputes between promoters and allottees, which fall under the purview of RERA.

The Forum comprises representatives from a well-known consumer body—the Mumbai Grahak Panchayat and from leading promoter associations such as CREDAI (Confederation of Real Estate Developers' Associations of India), MCHI (Maharashtra Chamber of Housing Industry), CREDAI Pune Metro, and NAREDCO (National Real Estate Development Council). Conciliation benches consisting of two conciliators, each representing either the consumer body or the promoter body, were established at various locations in Maharashtra. The conciliators undergo requisite training and certification by the said Forum. As of October 2019, there were 28 conciliation benches across Maharashtra.

The procedure followed by the said Forum is simple and efficient. A party wanting to initiate conciliation can file an online application with the said Forum, which is automatically sent to the opposing party. The opposing party can consent to such a request in seven days. On receipt of consent, the initiating party has to make a payment of INR 1,000 plus GST to the said Forum. Subsequently, the matter will be referred to the appropriate conciliation bench. If the parties settle their dispute in conciliation, a settlement agreement will be drawn up, which is binding on the parties. If any party breaches the settlement agreement, the MahaRERA will take cognizance of such breach in any subsequent proceedings that may be initiated before it. In case the parties fail to settle their dispute in conciliation, either party initiates a complaint before MahaRERA for adjudication under section 31 of RERA.

On the first day of conciliation meetings of the first 10 cases assigned by the Forum, 6 cases were amicably resolved. By October 2019, the said Forum received 512 applications, of which 442 stood disposed. The success rate of conciliation cases stood at 90% in Pune and 85% in Mumbai.[29]

As of May 2021, the statistics displayed on the MahaRERA website denote that 717 cases were received by the said Forum for conciliation with the consent of both parties. Of these, 671 cases stood disposed, and 47 cases are in progress.[30]

Such fora have also been established by the regulatory authorities of other states such as Uttar Pradesh, Kerala, and Karnataka under section 32 of RERA.

Conciliation introduced by certain Indian states under section 32(g) of RERA is a welcome step in the resolution of disputes under RERA. As these disputes mostly relate to homebuyers, the issues are rarely severely contentious where parties cannot find common ground. Thus, these disputes are apt for conciliation.

29. MahaRERA, Compendium of Best Practices (October 2019).
30. MahaRERA, *Statistics of MahaRERA Conciliation Forum* (May 29, 2021) https://maharerait.mahaonline.gov.in/searchlist/PublicViewDashboard.

§6.07 CONCLUSION

So far as legal provisions are concerned, India boasts of a robust legal framework for reference to mediation and conciliation, especially in case of commercial disputes. This is only likely to improve considering India has now signed the recent Singapore Convention in relation to mediation, particularly mediation in international commercial disputes. In addition to making pre-institution mediation mandatory in all relevant statutes concerning commercial subjects, the creation of mediation institutions and widespread awareness about the benefits of mediation should form part of the next few steps. This will likely be enhanced by the introduction of mediation-specific legislation, as is anticipated to happen.

CHAPTER 7

Mediating Company, Insolvency, and Bankruptcy Disputes

Anant Merathia[*]

§7.01 INTRODUCTION

A corporate dispute conventionally relates to any form of disagreement between two or more stakeholders on terms agreed upon either between a company and its members, persons, employees, investors and would thereby be broadly categorized as internal disputes or with external stakeholders such as vendors and consumers, third parties and government entities. The former (internal) is usually governed by the Companies Act 2013 ("Companies Act"), and the latter (external) is generally governed by other laws, among which the most prominent is the Insolvency & Bankruptcy Code 2016 (IBC), concerning issues relating to debts and defaults of the company in question. Besides IBC, disputes may also concern other laws, such as taxation, statutory compliances, and environmental issues.

In particular, when considering a commercial relationship, contracts often contain a run-of-the-mill dispute resolution clause, sometimes in the form of a multi-dispute resolution or a stand-alone arbitration. In the absence of such specific dispute resolution clauses, civil courts are normally the forum for seeking legal relief. Nevertheless, the exercise of jurisdiction under the Companies Act 2013, or the Insolvency & Bankruptcy Code 2016, is not affected by the mere presence of such dispute resolution clauses. The National Company Law Tribunal (NCLT) (or the civil courts), depending on the subject matter, adjudicates the above-described disputes either beyond or in tandem with the arbitral jurisdiction.

The Companies Act also provides for the resolution of corporate disputes through mediation. Accordingly, the Companies (Mediation and Conciliation) Rules 2016 were

* The able assistance of Dhanisha Giri and Poornima Devi is greatly appreciated.

made by the Central Government in the exercise of the powers conferred under section 442 read with section 469 of the Companies Act. The NCLT is, therefore, empowered to refer cases for resolution through mediation, either at the request of the parties or on the tribunal's *sua sponte* action where it feels there is a possibility of settlement. In light of this, the chapter highlights the importance of mediation concerning the company and corporate disputes under the Companies Act and disputes emanating from IBC.

§7.02 DISPUTES IN DIFFERENT TYPES OF COMPANIES

[A] Family-Owned Businesses

[1] Cause and Effect of Disputes

India is a country embedded with rich values and traditions. It is only likely that these values seep into the business sector as well. Hence, many businesses in India are actually owned by families or by close relatives and friends ("family-owned companies").[1] To date, family-run companies continue to exist from the pre-independence era, which have a set of values rooted that shape their operations, performance, and reputation. This is passed on from generation to generation.

In a majority of family-owned companies, the company is often loosely managed. The primary work is conducted based on mutual trust and goodwill. The business transactions are conducted through kinship and word-of-mouth,[2] creating a closely-knit network. It takes years, and in some cases decades, to create and nourish the kind of reputation and goodwill these companies generate. This is why such companies' brand reputation is often more valuable to its owners and members than any other asset owned by the company, and in many ways, it is also intertwined with the family's values and reputation.[3]

The changing economy and generational shift often lead to various transformations in ideas, opinions, composition, and functions. In that, the very foundational structure of the company often gives rise to disputes. Usually, when a dispute arises within the company, they are dealt with internally, behind closed doors.[4] The idea that disputes within the family should be resolved with internal efforts also spills into

1. *See* PwC India, India Family Business Survey 32 (2019), PWC India, https://www.pwc.in/assets/pdfs/research-insights/fbs/2019/pwc-india-family-business-survey-2019.pdf (92% of family businesses allow family members to work in their business).
2. *See* Stand Up India, *International Conference on Entrepreneurship and Women Empowerment*, The National Institute of Entrepreneurship and Small Business Development (Nov. 19, 2016), http://niesbudro.org/pdf/conference-proceedings-of-stand-up-india-international-conference-on-entrepreneurship-and-women-wmpowerment.pdf.
3. *See* Claudia B. Astrachan & Joseph H. Astrachan, *Family Business Branding: Leverage Stakeholder Trust*, Institute for Family Business (March 2015), https://blog.hslu.ch/familienunternehmen/files/2016/09/IFBRF-Branding-Report-Final-Web-Version-1.pdf [hereinafter "Astrachan & Astrachan"].
4. *See* Neil Mason, *What Goes on Behind Closed Doors*, Lexology (July 31, 2018), https://www.lexology.com/library/detail.aspx?g=76659ad6-0fe5-4c1b-9eab-671a40487e21.

company affairs and, thus, in most cases, the company ensures that disputes are resolved within the trusted circle of family, friends, and well-wishers.

However, disputes cannot always be contained and can escalate beyond the inner circle, adversely impacting the stakeholders (including the directors, shareholders, investors, and so on) as it has a direct brunt on the company's brand reputation. Recovery from such a state of affairs requires immense time, energy, and resources, to fix the perception of the business associates, employees, competitors, and others. When the news comes into the public spotlight, it is often like washing dirty laundry in public. It inevitably strains relationships between the family members, irrespective of whether they have (or had) a direct involvement.

[2] Problems Associated with Disputes

The way family-owned companies run it makes them vulnerable to various problems in the wake of these disputes. Take, for instance, the issue of documentation. Documents like the minutes of board meetings are maintained haphazardly and produced erratically, only when there are regulatory compliances to be made, which means that often there are no formal board or general body meetings (or that they are held informally) and the filings are done only to maintain statutory compliances, all in good faith. This is quite prevalent in midsized and small-sized businesses organized as corporate structures.

In such circumstances, when disputes arise, it raises several technical and procedural issues which can be blown out of proportion to make it appear as major mismanagement and violation of the statutory rules and regulations. Thus, there is often an erosion of trust; things are seen through the lens of suspicion, even though the actual facts are yet to be determined or that the ground realities are different. Some common issues raked up in such disputes are as follows:

- Dilution of shareholding.
- Change in directorship and induction of directors by one family or shareholder group, without the knowledge of the other.
- Nonissuance of notices of the board and/or general body meetings.
- Change of registered office of the company, without intimation to the aggrieved group of shareholders.
- Lack of record-keeping and allegation of tampering of documents, such as minutes of meetings or attendance registers.
- Nontransparent decision-making by sidelining a particular group.
- Siphoning of company funds.

Invariably, family-owned businesses have a varying degree of lacunae in paperwork, but when parties are at loggerheads, issues are amplified to an extent to project a strong case before the tribunals and courts. This lack of proper corporate record-keeping, the emotional involvement of parties, personal attachment to business and underlying wealth, and procedural discrepancies (among others) are some of the chief reasons for the institution of court actions and/or the prolongation of dispute resolution before courts or tribunals.

A typical company dispute may spend 5 to 10 years in the courts, by which time it would have developed a mountain of frustration. In many cases, as litigation procrastinates, parties either quit/call off the litigation or sell their shareholding to another group at rock-bottom rates or buy the other group's stake at prices that cost them an arm and a leg. Amidst these eventualities, the business and the company's intrinsic value gradually erodes, bringing great harm to the reputation, from which it is not easy to recover. The brand reputation of a family-owned company (in many ways) is its backbone.[5] Once that is tarnished, it exerts added pressure on the company to invest more effort and time to regain the trust of their clients, business associates, and well-wishers.

[3] Appropriate Modes of Dispute Resolution

Generally, adversarial modes are not appropriate for the resolution of disputes relating to family-owned companies. The stakes involved are sensitive and personal in nature, involving the hard-earned luster of the company and its members. Apart from the fact that adversarial modes of resolution can be at odds with such underlying interests, these modes are also time-intensive, lengthy, and procedurally cumbersome, such that they have the potential to widen the chasm between people involved (sometimes to the point of no return). Adversarial modes also fail to preserve family relationships, reputation, and goodwill. But besides affecting the people, such disputes have the wherewithal to:

- affect the business to the extent that it erodes the value of the assets, relationship with clients, prospects of the business, etc.; or
- cause a stalemate in the management of the company affairs;[6] or
- create opportunities for competing businesses and brands to capitalize on the company's unfortunate circumstances.

In several conflict scenarios, parties can simply agree to the buying (or even selling) of the respective shareholding, with the intent to end the conflict, at a valuation determined by a court-appointed valuer.[7] But even in such cases, parties eventually object to the valuation and continue litigating on issues not central to the dispute. Thus, the appropriateness of litigation is questionable in many such situations (even if family and friends are promoting it).

5. *See* Astrachan & Astrachan, *supra* note 3.
6. *See* Janmejaya Sinha & Varun Govindaraj, *Great Family Businesses Need Good Governance*, BCG HENDERSON INSTITUTE (Jan. 9, 2020), https://www.bcg.com/en-in/publications/2020/great-family-businesses-need-good-governance.aspx.
7. *See* Mini Raman, *Valuation in the New Regime under the Companies Act, 2013*, MONDAQ (Apr. 3, 2013), https://www.mondaq.com/india/securities/795536/valuation-in-the-new-regime-under-the-companies-act-2013.

Mediation, however, is practical. It enables parties to set aside their personal biases and differences in the pursuit to reconcile their interests (over positions) and safeguard the interest of the company. A mediator's involvement would help facilitate the communication between the parties that leads to an understanding of the real issues and narrow them down to commonly acceptable terms.

In a family-owned business, conflicts are handled mainly internally, wherein an elder of the family intervenes to somewhat act as a mediator. This is well received, considering its basis is in the values and culture of the family or families. While this model is often successful, there is great value in appointing a trained mediator, who has a set of techniques and tools that he puts to use in the designed process, which has a clear structure that can help focus on the real issues (without the baggage that an elder of the family may have to bear).

A few case studies from the author's personal experience discussed below demonstrate the proposition that mediation is appropriate for disputes within family-owned businesses.

Case study 1

A company in the hospitality business was in dispute. It ran two Vedic resorts in south India. The dispute was between the father-in-law (the patriarch) and the son-in-law. The father-in-law had set up the business, and the son-in-law was involved in the day-to-day operations. The dispute was chiefly about the difference in principles between the two generations. The father-in-law made allegations about changing the company's core ethics and business policies, financial mismanagement, and illegitimate use of the resorts (that even led to raids by the police, causing great harm to the reputation of the business). There was also a challenge to the change in the shareholding, in that the son-in-law was illegally made a majority shareholder. Accordingly, interim injunctions were sought to stay the board and general body meetings before any more damage could be done. As a result, the business was gravely hampered by the ongoing litigation.

The unexpected demise of the father-in-law made things worse. However, the son (with the advice of his advocates) reached out to his brother-in-law for settlement talks. The talks were challenging, given the demands laid out by the brother-in-law. The son addressed these demands positively only to end the contentious proceedings, which had gravely affected the family and the business—financially and reputationally. Ultimately, a settlement was reached after multiple rounds of mediations. And though it may seem that the settlement was lopsided, the son's objective was clear—to save the face of his family and the business.

Case study 2

A family owned some businesses relating to livestock farming, breeding farms, and hospitality in Karnataka and Andhra Pradesh. Family members ran these businesses as the key stakeholders. The dispute was primarily about management and control of the businesses. The businesses were doing well, generating heavy revenue, which led to differences among the family members on usage of surplus funds, including allegations of misuse and siphoning. The dispute initially started in one of the group companies but had a cascading effect on the other companies, leading to multiple court actions, which continued for nearly four years. It took that much time till some of the family members decided to settle by giving the other shareholders the option to exit, thus, buying out their shares for a mutually agreed price. This involved an elder of the family acting as a mediator, who primarily drove the negotiation in a direction that intended to safeguard the interest of the businesses.

Case study 3

A family-run company was an industry leader in the manufacturing of ferroalloys and ferrosilicon in the State of Andhra Pradesh. The disputing shareholders were two brothers, one based in Andhra and the other based in Delhi. The primary dispute was about the increase of the shareholding of the brother, who was running the manufacturing unit in Andhra and infusing funds by way of rights issue whenever the company needed funds. He defended this, stating that banking credit lines had become necessary for the company as business transactions increased. However, one of the prerequisites set out by banks was a certain ratio in the equity versus debt.

The dispute was whether notices of such rights were provided to other shareholders, including the brother in Delhi. The rise in shareholding (of the brother running the manufacturing unit in Andhra) was substantial; it rose from 30% minority to nearly 80% majority. The litigation turned bitter, climbing appellate forums. At this stage, the brothers were brought to the table by their family auditor's efforts and the advocates. The brothers could arrive at an understanding whereby it was agreed that there would be a reversal of excess shareholding to some extent, paving the way for the active participation of the brother in Delhi in the business. A key reason for why the settlement was attempted sincerely was the daunting circumstances that had damaged the company's financial health. At this point, it was perhaps apprehended that the protraction of personal feuds could lead to the business being taken over by outsiders and/or the liquidation of the company's assets by the banks.

The above case studies illustrate that mediation not only saved time, money, and other resources (which are some apparent benefits) but also preserved the business by maintaining/salvaging the foundational structure of the business—the family. While most of these mediations have been informal, the principles applied yielded positive results in protecting the dignity and reputation of the company and the people involved. There are other examples of some infamous family-business disputes resolved with the aid of mediation and reported, such as *Bela Kapoor & Ors. v. Vandana Kapoor & Ors.*,[8] *Godrej & Boyce Manufacturing Co. Ltd. v. Secur Industries Ltd. & Anr.* (the Godrej family dispute),[9] and *Reliance Natural Resources Ltd. v. Reliance Industries Ltd.* (ownership dispute concerning the Reliance Group).[10]

8. Bela Kapoor and Ors. v. Vandana Kapoor and Ors (136) DRJ 625 (2013).
9. Godrej & Boyce Manufacturing Company Limited v. Secur Industries Limited & Anr. (2013) SCC OnLine All 13621.
10. Reliance Natural Resources Ltd v. Reliance Industries Ltd (2010) 7 SCC 1.

It is a recent trend that family values are enunciated through a medium of written documents, popularly called the "family constitution," which enumerates the long-term goals, vision, principles, and strategies for a secure future of family-owned businesses. By nature, it informally imposes a kind of duty upon the family members, irrespective of their generation gap. Ideally, sacrosanct documents like the family constitution should imbibe the principles of conflict resolution, including the mechanism, to prevent family feuds that smear relationships.

[B] Small Businesses

Being a developing country and a growing economy, small businesses have flourished in India, considering the high employability ratio, nature of such businesses, and low investment needs. But they are often the starting point to building large-scale industries, including expanding outreach into foreign markets.[11] The recent trends in the Indian economy have shown a significant rise in the micro, small, and medium enterprises (MSMEs) sector and start-ups. Generally, these may be attributed to various technological advancements, globalization, sustainability, and innovation. These companies are commonly constituted to serve a local community or a select target group as a starting point. These include partnership firms and sole proprietorships, controlled investments and a fixed area of business or trade.

There is a broad but unique stratum of disputes that commonly concern small businesses, such as disputes regarding employment issues, vendors, and business partners.[12] The structure of these entities is small scale, which often does not accommodate separate HR and legal departments. Legal support is often sourced from outside as a last resort; however, resolving disputes through the formal legal channels means high legal costs and consumption of time and energy in nonbusiness activities, which are heavily detrimental to such businesses. Mediation is, thus, a viable and commercially feasible form of dispute resolution for most small businesses.

The foremost challenge with disputes involving small businesses is the interpersonal issues, including creeping hostility among the stakeholders. This is because of the reliance of small businesses on closely-knit groups and local factions that are hinged on personal relationships. Hence, mediation offers a suitable platform for dispute resolution, primarily given the lack of sophistication on the part of small businesses.[13] Mediation can help small businesses avoid financial burdens and hold their respective positions in competitive markets.[14]

---

11. *See generally*, OECD, *Small Businesses, Job Creation and Growth: Facts, Obstacles and Best Practices*, https://www.oecd.org/cfe/smes/2090740.pdf.
12. *See generally*, *Local Strength, Global Reach*, OECD OBSERVER (June 2000), http://www.oecd.org/cfe/leed/1918307.pdf.
13. RESERVE BANK OF INDIA, REPORT OF THE EXPERT COMMITTEE ON MICRO, SMALL AND MEDIUM ENTERPRISES (June 25, 2019), https://rbidocs.rbi.org.in/rdocs/PublicationReport/Pdfs/MSMES24062019465CF8CB30594AC29A7A010E8A2A034C.PDF.
14. *See Applications & Cases Status of Micro and Small Units (MSEs)*, MSME SAMADHAN—DELAYED PAYMENT MONITORING SYSTEM, https://samadhaan.msme.gov.in/MyMsme/MSEFC/MSEFC_

[C] Joint Venture Businesses

A joint venture (JV) connotes a legal entity that is somewhat in the nature of a partnership.[15] It is generally a business undertaken by two or more persons engaged in a single defined project or commercial enterprise.[16] The JV partners bring various assets and resources, pooling it all together to make the JV functional.

JVs in India are generally based on a contract. The venture lasts for as long as the JV partners have an agreement existing between them, usually renewable, and as long as they are in tune with each other. These terms also define the shareholding pattern between JV partners, the control and management powers, roles and responsibilities, warranties, and other related terms, which depend on a variety of factors like the specific industry in question.

Many JVs include foreign partners, which is a popular option for foreign direct investment,[17] of which India is an attractive place of investment. This way, local firms can collaborate with foreign investors, bringing two or more different stakeholders intending to come together and bring their specific expertise and/or strengths for a common purpose.

It is typically seen that the initial years of JV go smooth since much of the time and energy is spent toward setting up and scaling the business before it starts generating returns. While a JV may be vulnerable to disputes in any of these stages, it is pretty likely for disputes to arise when the businesses either start producing large turnovers or fail to do so after few years of effort. These disputes typically manifest in disagreements over shareholding, royalty, profit sharing, or differences in the management of the JV's affairs, incongruities in responsibility and expectations from the other partner, and so on. In particular, in cases where JVs are either time-bound or have a specific goal, there are often disagreements on whether to swerve from the original goals and directions. Disputes concerning the introduction of new players (say, through indirect assignments, change in control, etc.) can spark a fire among the partners. While the quantum of these disputes has substantially risen over the years, their lifespan in traditional dispute resolution forums leads a JV business to perilous circumstances.

Mediation, however, ensures that the loss of time in resolving a JV dispute is mitigated. It enables a status quo in relationships during the process and assures compliance from parties where a settlement is reached mutually. A JV agreement is likely to have a dispute resolution clause, and it is advisable that a mediation clause is

---

Welcome.aspx (more than 77,000 applications filed by MSME for recoveries of defaulted amounts and about 6,900 been mutually settled, as on May 20, 2021).

15. *See generally*, Nishith Desai Associates, Joint Ventures in India (2013), http://www.nishithdesai.com/fileadmin/user_upload/pdfs/Research%20Papers/Joint%20Ventures%20in%20India.pdf.
16. New Horizons Ltd v. Union of India (1995) 1 SCC 478.
17. Mihir A. Desai et al., *International Joint Ventures and the Boundaries of the Firm* (National Bureau of Economics Research Working Paper No. 9115—2002), https://www.nber.org/system/files/working_papers/w9115/w9115.pdf.

inserted, given the advantages it brings to sustaining an ongoing business. This is well illustrated in *Ashish Seth v. Sumit Mittal*[18] and *Vikram Bakshi. v. Sonia Khosla.*[19]

Case study

A Special Purpose Vehicle (SPV) was constituted as a JV between a group of Indian promoters and a foreign fund, having a ratio of 26:74, respectively. There were shareholder agreements between the JV partners, which included an arbitration clause. A dispute arose with rising allegations of oppression and mismanagement by one party against the other: the foreign partner led accusations of financial irregularities and mismanagement; the Indian partner alleged unwarranted interference by the foreign partner. It all led to a stalemate in the operations. The litigation spanned for about three years, at the end of which the advocates could encourage and direct the parties toward considering settlement. Several rounds of negotiations were held that ultimately resulted in a buyout of the Indian promoters' shareholding by the foreign counterparts, based on mutually agreed valuation. It kept the JV alive and brought closure to the litigation.

§7.03 SCOPE FOR MEDIATION IN INSOLVENCY AND BANKRUPTCY DISPUTES

[A] Introduction to IBC

The Insolvency and Bankruptcy Code 2016 (IBC) was enacted to consolidate all laws relating to reorganization and insolvency resolution of corporates, partnership firms, and individuals, in a time-bound manner, to maximize the value of assets, promote entrepreneurship, create credit availability, and balance the interests of all stakeholders (including the government).

Before IBC, the Sick Industrial Companies Act 1985 governed the reorganization and restructuring of companies with financial issues. Concerning recovery of bank dues and enforcement of security, two statutes operated hand in hand: The Recovery of Debts Due to Banks and Financial Institutions Act 1993 and the Securitization and Reconstruction of Financial Assets and Enforcement of Security Interest Act 2002. These statutes, however, were plagued with numerous issues, which included insufficient judicial infrastructure, prolonged proceedings, critical delays, and various challenges concerning the forum. This severely impacted the banking and finance sectors, increasing nonperforming assets cited to be around INR 6 lac crores in 2016 and around INR 3.6 lac crores in 2015.[20,21]

Another legal remedy (before the introduction of the IBC) was to initiate winding up proceedings under the Companies Act on various grounds (most common being

18. Ashish Seth & Ors. v. Sumit Mittal & Ors., Apr. 24, 2020, Supreme Court, MANU/SC/0397/2020.
19. Vikram Bakshi and Ors. v. Sonia Khosla (Dead) rep. by LRs., MANU/SC/0430/2014.
20. *See* Roshni Sinha, *Context to the Supreme Court Order on Stressed Assets of Banks*, PRS India (Mar. 4, 2019), https://prsindia.org/theprsblog/context-to-the-supreme-court-order-on-stressed-assets-of-banks.

failure to repay a debt), but that gave almost no opportunity to the party in liquidation to recuperate from its financial downturn. While this was relatively better in terms of its jurisdiction before the High Courts and appointments of official liquidators, the liquidation process itself took more than half a decade, at least, in any moderately sized liquidation.[22]

With the National Company Law Tribunal (NCLT) and the National Company Law Appellate Tribunal (NCLAT) having exclusive jurisdiction to adjudicate these matters, there has been a resounding success in the regime change, despite its frequent amendments.[23] IBC improved the recovery rate of stressed assets from 26.5% in 2018 to 71.6% in 2019.[24] For example, in *Swiss Ribbons Pvt. Ltd. v. Union of India*,[25] large sums of money were reportedly settled between parties during preadmission proceedings, based mainly on negotiation and likely to have been much lower than the actual quantum of claims.

However, everything is not this positive. Reports suggest that as of December 31, 2020, out of the 4,139 corporate entities admitted into the corporate insolvency resolution process (CIRP), only 317 were closed by resolution, and 1,126 were closed by liquidation. Thus, for every resolution, there are four liquidations. Though it is possible that these gloomy statistics reflect an actuality, that a majority of these companies in liquidation under IBC did not have any revival prospects and that perhaps such companies continued in business (for however long they did) only due to the emotional attachment that the promoters had with the company.

Under IBC, though the dispute settlement rate has steadily increased, there has been a proportional increase in backlogs, as well as fresh filings. Reports as of December 31, 2020, showed that among the meager 378 CIRPs withdrawn under section 12A of IBC, 269 were based on a settlement.[26] Moreover, the periods prescribed under IBC have also not been strictly followed. For instance, as of December 31, 2020, 1,481 cases (of the 1,717 ongoing cases) have gone beyond the statutory period (initially 270 days, but later amended to 330 days).[27]

---

21. *See* Reserve Bank of India, Report on Trend and Progress of Banking in India 9 (2016), https://rbidocs.rbi.org.in/rdocs/Publications/PDFs/0FRTP16A120A29D260148E58B484D4A60E381BB.PDF.
22. *See generally*, Rajeswari Sengupta & Anjali Sharma, *Corporate Insolvency Resolution in India: Lessons from a Cross-Country Comparison* (Indira Gandhi Institute of Development Research WP-2015-029—2015), http://www.igidr.ac.in/pdf/publication/WP-2015-029.pdf.
23. *See* M. S. Sahoo, *Moving up in "Ease of Resolving Insolvency,"* The Hindu Business Line (Mar. 5, 2020), https://www.thehindubusinessline.com/opinion/moving-up-in-ease-of-resolving-insolvency/article30992998.ece.
24. *See* Ministry of Corporate Affairs, Year End Review—2019 of Ministry of Corporate Affairs (2019), https://www.ibbi.gov.in/uploads/whatsnew/0610123bdd4ffc191a3ea05a847e1307.pdf.
25. Swiss Ribbons Pvt. Ltd. v. Union of India, 2019 SCC Online SC 73.
26. *See, e.g.*, Lokhandwala Kataria Construction Pvt. Ltd. v. Nisus Finance and Investment Manager LLP (2018) 15 SCC 589; Mother Pride Dairy India Pvt. Ltd. v. Portrait Advertising and Marketing Pvt. Ltd. (2017) SCC OnLine NCLAT 411; Uttara Foods and Feeds Pvt. Ltd. v. Mona Pharmachem (2018) 15 SCC 587; Vijender Kumar Singla v. Oriental Bank of Commerce & Anr. (2018) SCC OnLine NCLAT 371.
27. *See* The Quarterly Newsletter of the Insolvency and Bankruptcy Board of India (Volume 17, October–December 2020).

[B] Avenues for Mediation

Having criticized the existing regime under IBC, there are several broad avenues where infusing mediation would render much assistance in resolving differences between stakeholders, enabling them to reach acceptable resolution plans. Some of these avenues may be any of the following:

- Mediated discussions for settlement with creditors can help the stakeholders put together a resolution plan by focusing on the underlying interests and needs of the stakeholders.
- Whether there are multiple stakeholders (including those outside the IBC regime), mediation help bringing together lateral or interconnected issues emanating from other statutes, such as allottees under the Real Estate Regulatory Authority Act 2016, or workers and employees under the Employees Provident Fund and Miscellaneous Provisions Act 1952, or start-ups under Micro, Small & Medium Enterprises Development Act 2006, and so on.
- Mediation can help achieve settlements for companies in financial distress through mutually agreed repayment structure/scheme against the dues owed to stakeholders or creditors and, thus, instill the company's rehabilitation.
- Preadmission mediated settlements can be highly effective in terms of compliance since the repayment terms agreed between the parties are consensual and binding. The settlement agreement is typically filed before the NCLT and a default, after that, gives rise to a fresh cause of action.
- Since there are numerous differences among the committee of creditors and differences with the promoters, mediation can broadly help bring a neutral element into CIRP, which encourages discussions around the underlying interests of all the stakeholders and potential investors, if any.
- Mediation can significantly assist stakeholders with conflicting interests who would come under different levels of the waterfall mechanism for repayments. Using mediation to put together a resolution plan is likely to be more acceptable among the stakeholders, given that unsatisfied stakeholders are usually entangled in subsequent litigious actions over the same issues, further delaying a conclusive resolution vis-à-vis a stressed company.

Ultimately, financial creditors in any corporate insolvency resolution process know of their susceptibility to haircuts and accordingly exercise their commercial wisdom while taking any decisions. In all of this, the continuity of the corporate debtor may not necessarily be of interest or any concern. As a platform, mediation furthers the policy goal of the IBC regime, besides bringing satisfactory outcomes through self-determination.

Amidst the COVID-19 pandemic, the Government of India thought it best to suspend the institution of any fresh filing for CIRP for defaults arising from March 25, 2020,[28] resulting from government-imposed measures. The suspension was

28. Insolvency and Bankruptcy Code (Amendment) Ordinance, 2020 (No. 9 of 2020, June 5, 2020).

implemented for six months, extendable to one year from the said date. The objective was to protect companies from facing insolvencies when the entire industrial sector and the economy at large were on a weak footing. This opens up an avenue for mediated solutions. And while defaults committed before March 25, 2020, can still be instituted through a fresh filing for CIRP, even such cases would greatly benefit from mediation, given the erratic nature in which the tribunal has functioned during and postcrisis scenarios.

Another significant change amidst the pandemic crisis was the increase in the pecuniary threshold for instituting fresh filings for CIRP from INR 1 lac to INR 1 crore.[29] It would, thus, be practical for many financial and operational creditors to consider mediation rather than pursuing commercial and civil suits against the defaulters. For instance, in *India Asset Growth Fund and Ors. v. CMRS Projects Pvt. Ltd.*,[30] the NCLT encouraged the parties to consider settlement before proceeding with the contentious proceedings, considering the economic impact due to the pandemic.

§7.04 PRACTICALITIES OF MEDIATION FOR INSOLVENCY AND BANKRUPTCY DISPUTES

The foremost of mediation's advantages in resolving IBC disputes is the democratization of the process, providing party inclusivity, trust-building, and preserving relationships. This is a huge factor in bringing various stakeholders (with diverse interests) together. The Supreme Court set an important example in *Lokhandwala Kataria Construction Private Limited v. Nisus Finance and Investment Manager LLP*,[31] where the court exercised its powers under Article 142 of the Constitution (to do complete justice) and allowed a settlement between the parties in a CIRP, by taking the agreed terms on record.

Often, the difference and diversity of interests among stakeholders do not allow for an acceptable resolution plan, which must reach a benchmark of 66% of the voting share set by IBC.[32] Once a CIRP is initiated against a corporate debtor, its financial creditors form a committee of creditors (CoC). The CoC works in tandem with the insolvency resolution professional (RP) to arrive at a resolution plan after the RP (who is the face of the corporate debtors) calls for an expression of interest. If these stakeholders fail to arrive at a resolution plan, the corporate debtor must undergo a liquidation process. Here, since operational creditors (who have supplied goods or services to the corporate debtor) do not constitute a part of the CoC to contribute to

29. Ministry of Corporate Affairs, *Notification* (CG-DL-E-24032020-218898, Mar. 24, 2020), https://www.ibbi.gov.in/uploads/legalframwork/48bf32150f5d6b30477b74f652964edc.pdf. See also, M/s. Foseco India Ltd. v. M/s. Om Boseco Rail Products Ltd., MANU/NC/6038/2020 (notification to apply prospectively); M/s. Arrowline Organic Products (P) Ltd. v. M/s Rockwell Industries Ltd., MANU/NC/6868/2020 (notification to apply prospectively).
30. India Asset Growth Fund & Ors. v. CMRS Projects Pvt Ltd, MANU/NC/7132/2020.
31. Lokhandwala Kataria Construction Private Limited v. Nisus Finance and Investment Manager LLP (2018) 15 SCC 589.
32. Insolvency and Bankruptcy Code, 2016, §30.

making the resolution plan, there is a perpetual tug of war between the financial and operational creditors.

Anecdotally speaking, the percentage of recovery by financial creditors is usually much more than operational creditors. This is because typically, the liquidation value for operational creditors is lower, and, thus, they have lower priority in the waterfall mechanism of distribution in the liquidation process.[33] As a result of this marginalized treatment of operational creditors (as well as the unsecured financial creditors), there is often a loss of confidence among operational creditors and employees of the corporate debtor, who are central to the continuity of business. If mediation can be introduced to make the resolution plan, a more credible and acceptable outcome can be expected. CIRP under IBC goes through several stages, and most of these stages present an avenue for introducing mediation.

[A] Mediation upon the Initiation of a Creditor

In this scenario, the corporate debtor may opt to mediate with the creditor who has initiated the CIRP. In such scenarios, it is often seen that while the parties agree in principle, arriving on the specific terms can be time-intensive, which ultimately increases the burden vested in tribunals. These specific terms usually relate to the quantum of repayment and time allowance to make such repayment.

Usually, in the case of IBC applications about operational creditors, corporate debtors (in a bid to evade the stigma around insolvency proceedings) look to quickly resolve the issue upon issuance of a statutory demand notice (not mandated for financial creditors). Corporate debtors may want to settle the issue at this stage before proceeding further to the filing of an application before the NCLT, where the corporate debtor would be cornered and subject to immense pressure. Mediation, at this point, brings great value with the mediator navigating the parties to a junction of agreeable stances. However, a corporate debtor may be less inclined to resort to mediation if multiple proceedings are pending against it in various judicial forums.

Given that IBC disputes are commercial, with minimal emotional background, mediation (with the help of a trained and experienced mediator) is more expedient than direct negotiations. In the case of operational creditors, who have less priority for repayments and suffer a considerable haircut, mediation can be used to shorten the gap between operational and financial creditors, providing a win-win situation for both. For instance, in *Trans Oilfield Chemicals (P) Ltd v. Oren Hydrocarbons (P) Ltd*,[34] after hearing the final submissions from the advocates for the operational creditor and corporate debtor, the NCLT referred the matter to mediation, having considered it to be fit for consensual settlement. The referral did lead to a settlement, and the case was withdrawn with leeway to the creditor (granted by the NCLT) to approach the NCLT in case of any noncompliance by the corporate debtor. Similar efforts were encouraged by

33. *Id.*, at §53.
34. Trans Oilfield Chemicals (P) Ltd v. Oren Hydrocarbons (P) Ltd, MANU/NC/9268/2019.

the NCLT in *Paharpur Cooling Towers v. Dhanalakshmi Srinivasan* and *Arun Kumar Tiwari v. Rajesh Pandey.*[35]

[B] Mediation During Pre-admission Stage

In a scenario where the corporate debtor is under crisis and debt, much energy is spent in dissuading the admission of any insolvency proceeding against it. Typically, a corporate debtor will make out a case of preexisting dispute between the parties.[36] That involves getting into the merits of the case, like the quality of goods and services, breach of representation or warranty, and so on. Other times, corporate debtors raise limitations as an affirmative defense. Here too, mediation presents opportunities.

If mediation is opted at this stage, the creditor and the corporate debtor may be informed and explained the entire consequence of admission of the case and the detriments to both the parties. The author goes on to suggest that mediation should rather be mandatory at this stage.

On admission of a corporate debtor into CIRP, the chances of coming out of the insolvency resolution unscathed are relatively tricky as it requires a 90% mandate of the CoC members, which is usually unrealistic.[37] This is unless, of course, a settlement is arrived immediately by the corporate debtor, preferably before the public announcement is published by the interim RP, or before the constitution of the CoC (wherein, on a case-to-case basis, the NCLT can exercise its "inherent powers"[38] to allow withdrawal).

Interestingly, the ground reality is that operational creditors who have initiated CIRP for anything less than INR 30–40 lacs[39] found it difficult to even fund the insolvency resolution process, which they are mandated to as per regulation 33 of the Insolvency and Bankruptcy Board of India (Insolvency Resolution Process for Corporate Persons) Regulations 2016 (IBBI CIRP Regulation). Under regulation 33, the applicant initiating the process must bear the expenses; if the applicant does not fix the expenses, the NCLT fixes the expenses.

Practically, these expenses may be estimated to be anywhere between INR 1.5 to 3.5 lacs or more, which is often a predicament for some creditors who confront this only when the matter is admitted. This extra expense is perceived as throwing good money after bad. Thus, in such cases, it is prudent for the creditor (and the corporate debtor) to explore settlement options via mediation before admission of the corporate entity into CIRP. Not only is it cost-effective for the creditor, but it is also far less threatening for the corporate debtor, as it would be in a better position to resuscitate

35. Arun Kumar Tiwari and Another v. Rajesh Pandey And Ors. SPECIAL APPEAL No. 181 of 2015 (Allahabad High Court).
36. *See, e.g.*, Mobilox Innovations Private Limited v. Kirusa Software Private Limited, AIR 2017 SC 4532.
37. Insolvency and Bankruptcy Code, 2016, §12A.
38. *See* Swiss Ribbons Pvt. Ltd. v. Union of India, 2019 SCC Online SC 73.
39. *See* Ministry of Corporate Affairs, *Notification* (CG-DL-E-24032020-218898, Mar. 24, 2020), https://www.ibbi.gov.in/uploads/legalframwork/48bf32150f5d6b30477b74f652964edc.pdf (minimum threshold of default amended to INR 1 crores).

than when the company is made to undergo insolvency. Mediation would help parties to understand their best and worst-case scenarios vis-à-vis the core dispute and underlying interests.

Case study 1

A liquor manufacturing company based out of western India filed a case as an operational creditor against its collaborator and manufacturing partner on default of INR 3 crores. After a few rounds of mediation, the case was settled, wherein the parties arrived at a settlement after waiving some parts of the claim. The corporate debtor made a single payment of INR 3 crores and settled the matter within three months before the NCLT in the preadmission stage.

Case study 2

A leading Belgium-based rubber company approached the NCLT as an operational creditor against a default by its Indian client regarding USD 450,000 for the supply of raw material. The advocate for the operational creditor was given the mandate to settle the matter with the Indian company. The settlement took place successfully with a revised payment schedule, whereby 50% of the amount due was paid immediately, and the remaining was agreed to be paid over three months. The settlement was to the satisfaction of both the companies, without any collateral damage to either party, and helpful in reviving the business dealings between them.

Case study 3

A leading international trading group based out of the UAE approached the NCLT as an operational creditor against its client, a leading Indian sugar company, regarding the supply of thermal coal. Winding up proceedings were initiated for a sum of INR 15 crores. Since this process took a considerable amount of time, the advocates of the parties made settlement efforts. After multiple rounds of mediation, wherein a combination of claims was set off, the matter was settled for INR 12 crores, which was agreed to be paid per a payment schedule.

[C] Mediation in the Post-admission Stage

Once a corporate debtor is admitted into insolvency, several issues surface, and mediation holds potential in the resolution process. It must be recognized that insolvency and liquidation proceedings have multiple stakeholders: creditor instituting the CIRP, corporate debtor, promoters, RP, liquidator, the CoC, the consultation committee, financial and operational creditors, employees, workmen, government authorities, and others. With so many stakeholders and their respective multifarious thought processes, there are bound to be differences between them on multiple issues.

An ideal window for mediation is available immediately upon admission, before the newspaper publication that takes place within three days of the commencement of the CIRP, or before the constitution of the CoC. Time is of the essence in such cases. And if the mediation is successful, parties would need to make an urgent application before the NCLT to consider the settlement under its inherent powers. Since things need to move swiftly in arriving at a mutual solution, past conduct and lack of trust can potentially create a divide that tends to cause a failure even from insignificant differences. This is true, be it the preadmission or post-admission stage; parties carry a lot of baggage from their history. But an effective mediation led by a skilled mediator can play a significant role in helping parties refocus on the core issues of their commercial relationship.

In the post-admission stage, where a corporate debtor is willing to settle, the quantum and payment schedules are usually the inhibitors. Such finer details, including trust and communication, can be best bridged through mediation. With a skilled mediator at the helm of the process, a corporate debtor may also expect a level playing field during negotiations (since corporate debtors may feel vulnerable in the post-admission stage). During this stage, a mediator is also better positioned to convey (neutrally) the challenges the parties are likely to experience in the CIRP. For example, the creditor is likely to get a lesser amount at the end of the CIRP when the corporate debtor becomes vulnerable to several other claims and audits (versus what the corporate debtor is ready and willing to pay to settle).

Keeping these nuances in mind, certain cases exemplify the support offered by courts and tribunals in aid of settlements. For instance, in *Phoenix Global DMCC v. A&A International Trading Pvt. Ltd.*,[40] the NCLT exercised its inherent powers under Rule 11 of NCLT Rules 2016, allowing the withdrawal of the application based on the settlement made before the public announcement. In *Swiss Ribbons Pvt. Ltd. & Anr. v. Union of India & Ors.*,[41] the Supreme Court clarified that at any point before the constitution of the CoC, a party could approach the NCLT for withdrawal of the application, giving parties a window of opportunity to settle consensually.

Case study 1

A corporate debtor was admitted into CIRP by the NCLT on applying an operational creditor for default of INR 2.8 crores. A mutually trusted person mediated the dispute, and a settlement arrived overnight. Payment of INR 2 crores was made the next day, before the appointment of the RP. As the RP had not yet been appointed (nor any paper publication made), the parties approached the NCLT to consider the settlement terms under its inherent powers and allow the withdrawal of the creditor's application. The NCLT, accordingly, permitted the withdrawal.

Case study 2

An operational creditor filed an application against its customer (belonging to the steel sector) for dues about INR 30 lacs. The corporate debtor took the preadmission proceedings lightly, failing to appear before the NCLT despite several notices. Only after the matter entered into the CIRP did the debtor concede to the consequences and arrive at a settlement with the creditor. However, the NCLT refused to entertain a

40. Phoenix Global DMCC v. A&A International Trading Pvt Ltd, MANU/NC/3916/2017.
41. Swiss Ribbons Pvt. Ltd. v. Union of India, 2019 SCC Online SC 73.

withdrawal (given the appointment of the RP and the delays in processes). In the appeal to the NCLAT, the matter was allowed to be withdrawn. The corporate debtor paid a heavy price for its casual attitude, as it impacted its business operations, affecting the agreed payouts to the operational creditor. And so, while the aspect of mediation was successful, its implementation became immensely challenging due to the uncertainty (and the protracted proceedings before the NCLT and NCLAT, which spanned over six months).

[D] Mediation for Effecting or Approval of a Resolution Plan

It is often the case that deliberations and decisions around the resolution plan are confronted by diverse perspectives, which need to converge on acceptable grounds, in what is a negotiation between the resolution applicant and the CoC (including the member of CoC *inter se*), who are not necessarily interested in reviving the corporate debtor.

Furthermore, the resolution plan is the restructuring and reorganization plan of the corporate debtor in financial distress that is proposed by a resolution applicant who is typically a third party and, in some cases, the promoter, if permitted under section 240A of the IBC where the corporate debtor is an MSME.

Once the resolution process starts and various interested parties have put forth their expression of interests,[42] the process of shortlisting and elimination is commenced by the members of the CoC (who are primarily financial creditors) based on an evaluation matrix (and other parameters) that the CoC sets down following the laws.[43]

The submission of the resolution plans is followed by the evaluation of resolution plans on a commercial and legal basis,[44] which includes negotiations with the resolution applicants about a feasible plan for the resolution of the present financial distress of the corporate debtor.[45] Several practical parameters are considered in the negotiations between the CoC and the resolution applicant. For example, higher down payment, balance payouts and timelines, the interest of creditors in the payment structure, and (more importantly) the interest of financial creditors in the CoC who are also approving the plan.

Once the CoC approves a resolution plan,[46] the RP submits the resolution plan as approved by the CoC to the NCLT for its seal of approval.[47] However, many a time, the resolution applicant may or may not be in a position to improvise the resolution plan provided initially. Ultimately, there could be a deadlock on the plan, leaving no other option but moving the company into liquidation. Here, various legal and practical aspects play out, such as the securities held by the financial creditors, which said

42. Insolvency and Bankruptcy Board of India (Insolvency Resolution Process for Corporate Persons) Regulations, 2016, regulation 36A [hereinafter "IBBI CIRP Regulations 2016"].
43. *Id.*, at regulation 37.
44. Insolvency and Bankruptcy Code, 2016, §30.
45. IBBI CIRP Regulations 2016, regulation 38.
46. *Id.*, regulation 39.
47. Insolvency and Bankruptcy Code, 2016, §31.

creditors can enforce under section 52 of the IBC (if they chose to opt out of the resolution process).

Given the statistics in the public domain, one can infer that, in a large number of cases, financial creditors fail to look at the very objective of this law—to maximize the value of assets of a company, promote entrepreneurship, provide availability of credit to companies in the financial distress as part of its restructuring vis-à-vis the recoveries that they can make through a resolution plan before them. But if the resolution plan is not to the ideal satisfaction of the financial creditors, it is often the case that said creditors do not hesitate to reject the plan and put the company into liquidation.

On a case-to-case basis, if the financial creditor is in a position to enforce the security to recover reasonably more than if it were to go with the resolution plan, it is likely to tread on this path since it too is ultimately answerable to its stakeholders (more so, if public money is involved).

At the same time, to push a company (a going concern) off the edge into liquidation only because of a lack of adequate consensus over the resolution plan is seemingly against the intent (objective, spirit) of the law, which was meant to give companies a second chance (even if it means a change in the management). There is only a narrow stretch of water between resolution and liquidation, and, hence, mediation can be highly beneficial to the IBC ecosystem in ensuring that resolutions are reached. A trained mediator who is well versed in this field of law can help facilitate a constructive dialogue between the CoC, resolution applicant, and other concerned parties (including the dialogue among the CoC members) to arrive at a more acceptable resolution plan.

By section 31(1) of the IBC, the approved resolution plan is binding on all the stakeholders. Thus, a successfully approved resolution plan can affect different stakeholders in varied ways. This often leads to several interlocutory applications and legal contentions on equity, raised by various stakeholders but, mainly, by operational creditors and those who are either left out in the resolution plan or paid meagerly/insignificantly (often because the law mandates that a resolution applicant only pays as per whatever the liquidation value is).

Moreover, several government dues and liabilities are extinguished as per the resolution plan. This can also be the case for any ongoing litigation. It is often a matter of concern because third-party stakeholders and statutory authorities end up with extinguished claims, sometimes without any notice. At the same time, disallowing such extinguishment would discourage prospective resolution applicants from coming out of their ongoing predicament, thus, making the entire insolvency process (and the IBC's ethos) a failure.

To avoid such clashes, mediation can prove compelling and can (at least) work toward improving the position of the stakeholders placed at the lower pedestal, even though they may not get as much as those placed in the higher positions of interest. Nevertheless, the author posits that it may be sufficient enough to avoid litigations at the stage where the NCLT has to approve the resolution plan, thus, reducing enormous litigation time and resources that are often spent before the approval/finalization of the resolution plan.

Case study

In a CIRP, there was severe resistance from the promoters in the initial phase of the resolution process. The interim RP, within the contours of the IBC, made sincere efforts to run the company as a going concern, but the erstwhile management would not cooperate. Applications were moved before the NCLT, and the interim RP pleaded before the tribunal to direct the erstwhile management to cooperate; the tribunal ordered accordingly. This set a base for positive and constructive discussions between the interim RP and the erstwhile management, wherein they were explained that this legal process did not injure the company's interest but to help it come out of its present financial distress. After two months of severe challenges and ongoing discussions, the promoters and the erstwhile management gradually began to cooperate with the RP, and, eventually, the CoC members successfully passed a resolution plan. If not for the constructive dialogue at the initial stages, the window of opportunity would have been lost, leaving the company muddled in adversities and, ultimately, liquidation.

[E] Mediation for Differences Within the Committee of Creditors

CoCs tend to have their internal issues as diverse parties constitute them. If a typical residential builder was to be the corporate debtor, the CoC would normally constitute public financial institutions, banks, nonbanking financial companies, private lenders, home buyers, etc. Thus, it is bound to be the case that differences will exist between CoC members on various counts, such as interim RP's continuance (with each one's preference conflicting with the other), voting share, the inclusion of certain financial creditors, operations of the corporate debtor, involvement of the erstwhile management for technical/operational support, the appointment of external professionals such as valuers, auditors, and counsels, and so on. Conflicts among the CoC members also arise on the sharing of CIRP costs, which are initially paid by the applicant and then reimbursed by the CoC members, as ratified by the CoC.[48] The CIRP costs are after that borne by the CoC and later adjusted from operations of the corporate debtor. Some of the CoC members are unable to participate in such cost-sharing, which too leads to a different kind of conflict.

There is a near-perpetual tension between some CoC members staking a higher claim and, consequently, a higher voting percentage in the CoC than the voting share that the RP would have initially assigned based on the documents provided by the creditors. A related conflict arises when a financial creditor tries to establish itself as a nonrelated party to continue and exercise its voting rights in the CoC, which it would otherwise not be able to if it is declared as a related party by the NCLT. While this is a matter of decision by the NCLT, it is nevertheless a cause of conflict within the CoC as

48. *See* Insolvency and Bankruptcy Board of India, *Fee and Other Expenses Incurred for Corporate Insolvency Resolution Process* (Circular No. IBBI/IP/013/2018, June 6, 2018), https://ibbi.gov.in/webadmin/pdf/whatsnew/2018/Jun/Circular%20on%20Fee%20and%20other%20Expenses%20incurred%20for%20CIRP%20[June%202018]_2018-06-18%2014:06:58.pdf.

it could substantially affect the voting rights of each member and, consequently, the decision-making on all issues, including the resolution plan.

Furthermore, interim financing and funding the corporate debtor are the immense struggles. Often, conflicts arise in the conduct of forensic/transaction audit of the corporate debtor, the period for which it should be conducted, and the related costs. Cost is seemingly a repetitive concern that meets the CoC and its members at nearly every turn. This can be a predicament, particularly when the debtor has uncertain prospects as a going concern or where it is not a going concern and only has some limited assets for recovery through liquidation.

The more significant conflicts, of course, concern the resolution plan. Often, there is a disparity between members of the CoC wielding majority voting percentage and the rest of the CoC members,[49] who have lesser voting percentage based on their debt and are relatively dissatisfied on most occasions as their interests are not met. This is quite understandable since the minority have no other option but to accept the majoritarian view of the CoC. For example, many a time, homebuyers and unsecured financial creditors are at the short end of the stick.

The issues discussed here are not exhaustive but give a clear sense of the various instances in which CoC members come into conflict and are potentially in a stalemate. Trained mediators can add much value to getting the CoC members on the same page by mitigating minor differences, policy concerns, and disadvantages of a conventional bureaucratic style of decision-making of the CoC. With that, a mediator can move the member of the CoC toward a more proactive discourse, expediting the process, changing perspectives, and helping focus on the core issues that can preferably yield a resolution over recovery.

While a change in the thought process of a CoC (including its members) may take time, it has to start somewhere. It is here that a trained mediator, with no strings attached, can suitably fit in the insolvency process. While it may not be strictly mediation, RPs can potentially imbibe and apply mediation principles, tools, and techniques, to resolve any internal differences in the CoC, such as interim funding of the corporate debtor or even the approval of a resolution plan.

[F] Mediation for Differences Between Resolution Professional and Corporate Debtor

Generally, there is a lack of trust and discomfort between the RP and the management and promoters of the corporate debtor. India is a promoter-driven economy, and most companies are governed by promoter dominance, which means that most midsized and small-sized companies are built and run by promoters (likely from one generation to the other). With that comes a lot of emotional baggage, making it harder for the management and the promoters to lose both the control and the management rights to an RP (or liquidator, as the case may be). This makes for a breeding ground of trust

49. Insolvency and Bankruptcy Code, 2016, §28 (66% of the CoC's vote is required to make the decisions).

issues and resistance from the erstwhile management, who are (by law) required to cooperate with the RP,[50] especially with information gathering for the preparation of the Information Memorandum,[51] which sets out the grounds for opening an expression of interest,[52] so that third parties may show interest in uplifting the corporate debtor and work on a resolution plan for its revival/restructuring.

The RP, who generally spends a substantial amount of time litigating before the NCLT/NCLAT with the erstwhile management in trying to procure necessary information, is faced with several challenges. On the other hand, the erstwhile management has issues with the RP's lack of understanding of the practical difficulties that have arisen with the downfall. The erstwhile management usually finds it challenging to procure the heap of information that RPs generally seek as soon as they are appointed. RPs have an obligation, under section 66 of the IBC, to look into any illegal or fraudulent transactions which would need to be opined, determined, and requisite applications filed in 135 days from the initiation of the CIRP.[53] RPs are under a good amount of pressure to adhere to the timelines when facing unwarranted resistance from the erstwhile management.

The above discourse shows the common issues of conflict between RPs and the erstwhile management and promoters. Mediation offers a firm ground for trust-build, empathy, collaboration, and cooperation by bringing each one to understand the other's perspective and convincing them that they hold the same underlying interest—a suitable resolution plan for the revival of the corporate debtor.

[G] Mediation Between Resolution Professional and Third Parties

Section 14 of the IBC mandates a moratorium, during which period of the CIRP the supply of essential goods and services to the corporate debtor is not to be terminated, suspended, or interrupted.[54] This was further enhanced by an amendment on December 28, 2019,[55] which provides that where the RP considers the supply of certain goods and services critical to protect and preserve the value of the corporate debtor and manage the operations of such company as a going concern, then the supply of such goods and services shall not be terminated, suspended, or interrupted during the

50. *Id.*, §19.
51. *Id.*, §29. *See also*, IBBI CIRP Regulation 2016, regulation 36.
52. IBBI CIRP Regulation 2016, regulation 36A.
53. Insolvency and Bankruptcy Code, 2016, §43 (preferential transactions and relevant time) §45 (avoidance of undervalued transactions), §49 (transactions defrauding creditors), §50 (extortionate credit transactions), and §66. *See also*, IBBI CIRP Regulation 2016, regulation 40A.
54. Insolvency and Bankruptcy Code, 2016, §§14(2) and 14(2A) (section 14(2): "The supply of essential goods or services to the corporate debtor as may be specified shall not be terminated or suspended or interrupted during moratorium period." Section 14(2A): "Where the interim resolution professional or resolution professional, as the case may be, considers the supply of goods or services critical to protect and preserve the value of the corporate debtor and manage the operations of such corporate debtor as a going concern, then the supply of such goods or services shall not be terminated, suspended or interrupted during the period of moratorium, except where such corporate debtor has not paid dues arising from such supply during the moratorium period or in such circumstances as may be specified").
55. Insolvency and Bankruptcy Code (Amendment) Ordinance, 2020 (No. 6 of 2019, Dec. 12, 2019).

moratorium. This is except, of course, where the corporate debtor has not paid such dues arising from such supply during the moratorium. Further, the definition of essential services under section 32 of the IBC includes electricity, water, telecommunication, and IT.[56]

If a corporate debtor is not in a good position but has chances of revival, they most certainly require these essential services. But these commodities are only essential to the extent that they are not a direct input to the output produced or supplied by the corporate debtor.[57] But such essential services are vital when the RP's entire effort is in restarting/continuing the operations of the corporate debtor. While the government departments have their fair point of view in withholding these services and cannot continue to provide such services endlessly, the RP's efforts and the chances of a resolution are noticeably affected.

Further, an Ordinance in December 2019 expanded the scope of supply and service of goods to third-party vendors and suppliers.[58] The Ordinance empowers the RP to require third-party suppliers to continue providing goods and services. However, it will not apply if the corporate debtor has unpaid dues arising from such supplies during the moratorium period.[59] Thus, it would be prudent to take opportunity of the initial negotiations that take place between the RP and third-party goods and service providers to ensure a clear understanding is reached for situations of defaults, so that a stream of essentials can be maintained.

Mediation could play a significant role in such scenarios. For instance, in *Union Bank of India v. M/s. Star Agro Marine Exports Pvt. Ltd.*,[60] the resolution plan had waived off the statutory dues when presented and approved by the CoC. It is often the case that resolution plans seek waivers of statutory dues of all kinds, which CoC ultimately approves. NCLTs have taken contrary views on this issue: some have allowed the waivers, and others have rejected it. The difficulty creeps in when many of these government authorities have not been given an opportunity to be heard concerning their claims. While section 31 of the IBC clarifies that a resolution plan is binding on the Central and State government authorities, it has been a practical challenge for both the resolution applicants (who acquire companies) and the government authorities to come to a common understanding on this issue.

These concerns between RPs and third-party goods and service providers may be alleviated to a large extent if parties come to mediation to achieve common grounds and overcome any impasse. As often flagged, trained mediators can play an immense role in the relationship between an RP and third parties. Mediation must be seriously

56. IBBI CIRP Regulations 2016, regulation 32.
57. *Id.*
58. Insolvency and Bankruptcy Code (Amendment) Ordinance, 2020 (No. 16 of 2019, Dec. 28, 2019).
59. Insolvency and Bankruptcy Code, 2016, §14(2A).
60. Union Bank of India v. M/s. Star Agro Marine Exports Pvt. Ltd. (2017) SCC OnLine NCLT 20726.

explored or even made mandatory through subsequent legislative amendments on various stages of the CIRP, including liquidation.[61]

§7.05 CONCLUDING REMARKS

Mediation has proven to be effective in various forms of company disputes and other regimes of commercial dispute resolution. Section 442 of the Companies Act 2013, read with the Companies (Mediation and Conciliation) Rules 2016, confers the power to refer matters to mediation. There is, however, no express provision in the Insolvency and Bankruptcy Code 2016 that expressly provides the scope for mediation referrals by the NCTL/NCLAT. But one of the underlying themes of the Insolvency and Bankruptcy Code is speedier disposal of cases and ensure effective corporate restructuring. This chapter expands the horizons of those considerations by citing the avenues where mediation and IBC disputes make great partners.

61. The Insolvency and Bankruptcy Board of India (Liquidation Process) (Amendment) Regulations, 2018 (published vide notification No. IBBI/2017-18/GN/REG028, dated Mar. 27, 2018 in the Gazette of India, Extraordinary, Part III, section 4, No. 122 on Mar. 28, 2018).

CHAPTER 8
Mediating Government Disputes

Badrinath Srinivasan & Arjun Natarajan

§8.01 INTRODUCTION

The cliché that the government is the largest litigator is reductionist. The term "government" is used in various contexts to denote the State machinery in India. "Government" could connote the Central Government, State Government, or the local government. It could mean a Public Sector Undertaking (PSU), a local body, or even a Public-Private Partnership, depending on the government stakeholder's nature and extent of control. The term could also refer to the sectoral regulatory bodies in telecom, electricity, taxation, and so on. In general terms, each of these entities (or government entities) has various applicable rules and regulations and means of resolving disputes, both internal and external (i.e., with third parties). The spotlight of this chapter is on government disputes of the latter sense (hereinafter "government disputes"). Mediation[1] between government entities is beyond the scope of this chapter. Other preliminary considerations for this chapter are along the following lines.

Alternative dispute resolution (ADR) processes are generally available in respect of government disputes. But they are sometimes barred, expressly or impliedly, in certain situations. For instance, the issue as to whether the Registrar of Trademarks should register a trademark under the Trademarks Act 1999 is not subject to ADR, but IPR-related *inter se* issues arising under a contract are considered arbitrable (therefore,

1. The terms "mediation" and "conciliation" are at times used in this chapter interchangeably, for the sake of convenience. Both processes are legally different (though practically similar) and, hence, wherever the context demands a precise usage, the terms have been used in their specific senses. *See* §8.04[B] of this chapter referring to the difference between conciliation and mediation.

mediate-able as well).[2] Prospecting such limitations is necessary in respect of government entities.

ADR processes that may be adopted to resolve disputes might vary depending upon the nature of those entities. For instance, a PSU facing disputes with its factory workers could be asked to compulsorily go for conciliation under the erstwhile Industrial Disputes Act 1947 (now under the Industrial Relation Code 2020), while a licensee under the Oil Fields (Regulation and Development) Act 1948 who has entered a production sharing contract (PSC) with the government could refuse nonadjudicatory ADR processes and straightaway invoke arbitration (if provided for under the contract). A one-size-fits-all approach is never a workable solution concerning government entities and their disputes, given the regulatory and administrative distinctions.

Mediation involves a decision by government entities on the terms of the settlement, which involves subjective considerations. Further, decision-making in the government or government entities is generally diffusive: although there may be one official making the decision (as the competent authority), the approval for such decision may itself be based on a proposal, recommendation, and financial concurrence of officials at various levels. Unless officials at all these levels of decision-making are in sync with the strategies, or terms of the proposed settlement, or the decision in question, it is virtually impossible that a government entity will indulge in a conciliatory process effectively.

The situation is exacerbated by the number of agencies reviewing decision-making in the government, such as internal audits, government audits, vigilance inquiries, Right to Information applications, and Lok Adalat. In the current context, subjectivity in decision-making is easy to question but difficult to defend, especially since there could be many alternative approaches to a certain situation in question.

All these issues create a chilling effect on the efficacy of conciliatory processes in government disputes. At the same time, it is not as if government disputes are not settled through negotiation, mediation, or conciliation; they are routinely adopted to resolve government disputes. Hence, it is important to devise strategies, from both the policy and disputes perspective, to secure an effective mechanism for resolving government disputes. This is also why this chapter will endeavor to explore the problems of government entities in adopting any conciliatory processes and make suggestive remarks.

With that backdrop, the chapter first sets out the framework of law relating to mediation and conciliation. It then focuses on how disputes are resolved by government entities with private players (using some selected examples). We then dive into issues surrounding mediation of government disputes. Lastly, this chapter concludes with the authors' suggestive notes regarding the mediation of government disputes.

---

2. *See* Eros International Media Ltd. v. Telemax Links India Pvt. Ltd., 2016 SCC Online Bom 2179 (when there are two claimants to a copyright or a trademark in either infringement or passing off action, "that action and that remedy can only ever be an action *in personam* and it is never an action *in rem*"); Vidya Dolia & Ors. v. Durga Trading Corp. (2021) 2 SCC 1 (rights in rem and rights in personam may not be correct for determining nonarbitrability because of the interplay between the two).

§8.02 SECTORAL MEDIATION AND CONCILIATION

[A] National Highways and Roads

Recognizing liquidity constraints in the construction sector, the National Institution for Transforming India, also known as NITI Aayog, issued an Office Memorandum in 2016,[3] instructing all PSUs and government departments, dealing with public contracts, to consider setting up conciliation committees "to ensure speedy disposal of pending or new cases."[4]

Accordingly, in 2017, the National Highways Authority of India (NHAI) had constituted Conciliation Committees of Independent Experts (CCIE) to resolve issues arising out of NHAI-related contracts through conciliation.[5] In 2019, considering the well-established procedure of CCIE, it was also decided to refer disputes arising out of projects of the Ministry of Road Transport and Highways (MORTH) to CCIE on a consensual basis;[6] such projects included those executed through the regional offices of the Ministry or the State Public Works Department. The salient features of NHAI's CCIE are as follows:[7]

- Disputes are referred to CCIE by consensus; the conciliation proceedings are conducted under the Arbitration and Conciliation Act 1996 (ACA), which necessitates consent of the parties.
- Conciliation proceedings of dispute referred to CCIE must be completed within a maximum of five sittings and within six months.
- Conciliation proceedings by CCIE are not to be considered an alternative to arbitration proceedings but a forum for conciliated settlements.
- Parties are not allowed to bring Advocates to the conciliation proceedings.
- Where technical experts assist the CCIE, or where the CCIE has secretarial assistance, NHAI is to make such arrangements for the same, reimbursed by MORTH on a half-yearly basis.

3. NITI Aayog, *Initiatives to Revive the Construction Sector: Implementation of CCEA Decision dated 31 August 2016* (OM No. N-14070/1412016-PPPAU, Sept. 5, 2016), https://niti.gov.in/sites/default/files/2019-12/OM_CCEA_approval_28_Nov_2019.pdf.
4. Ministry of Road Transport & Highways, Conciliation & Settlement Mechanism for Contractual Disputes in Contract Agreements with the Contractors/Concessionaires/Consultants in *Respect* of Ministry's Projects—Panel of Independent Experts and *Constitution* of *Conciliation Committee* (No. RW/NH-33044/35/2019, Dec. 18, 2019), https://morth.nic.in/sites/default/files/circulars_document/Conciliation%20&%20settelment%20Machanism%20for%20disputs%20Panel%20of%20Independant%20Experts%20conciliation%20committee%20reg_compressed.pdf (hereinafter "MORTH Conciliation *Circular* 2019").
5. National Highways Authority of India, *NHAI Policy Guidelines Conciliation & Settlement of Contractual Disputes 2017* (No. 2.1.22/2017, June 2, 2017), https://nhai.gov.in/nhai/sites/default/files/legal_document/policy_Guidelines_Conciliation_Settlement_Mechanism.pdf. *See also*, National Highways Authority of India, *Amendment-1 dated 19.06.2017 to Policy Guidelines dated 02.06.2017 of NHAI* (June 19, 2017), https://nhai.gov.in/nhai/sites/default/files/legal_document/amendments_to_Policy_Guidelines_Conciliation.pdf.
6. *See* MORTH Conciliation *Circular* 2019, *supra* note 4.
7. *Id.*

- NHAI is to incur the costs toward the CCIE, at the first instance, which would be reimbursed on a half-monthly basis by MORTH. At the end of the conciliation proceedings, the CCIE decides the apportionment of costs between the parties.
- On receiving a settlement proposal from the CCIE, the settlement agreement is to be signed within 30 days of the proposal's receipt.
- On signing the settlement agreement, payment and other contractual obligations are to be complied with within 30 days of the signing.

As of June 2020, about 108 cases have been referred to the CCIE, involving 13,349 claims amounting to a total settlement value of nearly INR 3,743 crores.[8]

[B] Oil and Gas

On February 28, 2019, the Ministry of Petroleum and Natural Gas (MPNG) passed a Resolution to increase exploration and production of petroleum, attracting investments in an unexplored and unallocated sedimentary basin, enhancing domestic production of petroleum, and promoting ease of doing business in the petroleum exploration and production sector ("Resolution").[9]

Clause 6 of the Resolution contemplates a dispute resolution mechanism (DRM) in addition to those specified in the contracts with the government: it states that a Committee of External/Eminent Persons/Experts will be constituted for dispute resolution. Further, it states that such provisions would be incorporated in all future contracts.[10]

After that, vide notification dated December 16, 2019, the MPNG came up with some detailed guidelines governing this DRM contemplated under Clause 6 of the Resolution dated February 28, 2019.[11] Some aspects of this DRM are as follows:

- The Notification constituted a three-member committee consisting of a former bureaucrat, a former senior official of a PSU, and a senior serving official from the private sector.

8. Ministry of Road Transport & Highways, NHAI Expedites Settlement of Claims Through Conciliation, Press Information Bureau (June 17, 2020, 5:15 PM), https://pib.gov.in/PressReleseDetailm.aspx?PRID=1632105.
9. Ministry of Petroleum & Natural Gas, Resolution No. O-12015(11)/1/2019-ONG-II dated Feb. 28, 2009 (Extraordinary Gazette of India, Mar. 6, 2019), http://petroleum.nic.in/sites/default/files/Policyreforms.pdf.
10. *Id.*, Clause 6 ("6. Dispute Resolution Mechanism: *A Committee of external eminent persons/experts will be constituted for dispute resolution. For existing contracts, disputes or differences between the Contracting parties can be referred to the Committee if both the parties to the contract agree in writing for such conciliation or mediation and further agree to not invoke arbitration proceedings thereafter. This provision will also be incorporated in all future contracts*").
11. Ministry of Petroleum & Natural Gas, Notification No. Expl-15022(13)/6/2017-ONGD-V dated Dec. 16, 2019 (Extraordinary Gazette of India, Dec. 16, 2019), http://petroleum.nic.in/sites/default/files/Notification16dec19.pdf.

- The Committee has a three-year tenure, subject to an extension by the government.
- The Committee is mandated to resolve disputes referred to it by either conciliation or mediation.
- The conciliation proceedings are to be conducted as per the ACA.
- Such conciliation proceedings are to be completed within three months from the date of the first sitting of the Committee, subject to extension by the parties in writing.
- The Committee is empowered to take the service of an expert/third party to aid and assist it in discharging the Committee's functions.
- The proceedings are confidential and cannot be relied upon as evidence in arbitration/court proceedings.
- Costs and expenses of the Committee are to be borne equally by the parties.
- Parties are not to initiate or take any step to initiate any arbitral or judicial proceeding regarding a dispute that is the subject of mediation or conciliation proceedings before the Committee.

PSCs or Revenue Sharing Contracts (RSCs) signed by the government contain provisions for conciliation and arbitration. A recent Model RSC of the Open Acreage Licensing Policy—Bid Round V (August 2019) contains a dispute resolution clause that provides conciliation by the aforesaid Committee of Experts/Eminent Persons.

Article 31 of the said Model RSC mandates reference of any dispute to a Committee of Experts/Eminent Persons.[12] If parties are unable to resolve the dispute through the Committee, parties are empowered to invoke arbitration.[13] Thus, conciliation through the Committee is the first-tier mechanism through which disputes could be resolved. Given the mandatory nature of the provision referring the dispute at the first instance to the Committee for conciliation, it appears that conciliation is mandatory for the parties under the Model RSC.

Even before the aforesaid Model RSC, the PSCs and RSCs provided conciliation as one of the resolution methods.

[C] Telecom

The Telecom Regulatory Authority of India Act 1997 (TRAI Act) was enacted to provide for the establishment of the Telecom Regulatory Authority of India (TRAI), and Telecom Disputes Settlement and Appellate Tribunal (TDSAT) to regulate the telecommunication services, adjudicate disputes, dispose of appeals; to protect the interests of service providers and consumers of the telecom sector; to promote and ensure orderly growth of the telecom sector, and for matters connected in addition to that or incidental

12. *Id.*, Art. 31.2.
13. *Id.*, Art. 31.5.

to it. Pertinently, vide a notification dated January 9, 2014, the Ministry of Communication and Information Technology (Department of Telecommunications) notified the broadcasting services and cable services to be telecommunication.

Under the TRAI Act, TRAI is the regulator, whereas TDSAT is the adjudicator (original and appellate jurisdiction). In 2013, TDSAT's mediation center was established to facilitate parties to arrive at a mutually agreed resolution of their differences with the help of trained mediators.[14] In 2014, TDSAT introduced TDSAT Mediation Procedures as a chapter in TDSAT Procedures 2005.

This chapter applies to all mediations connected with any petition or other proceeding pending before TDSAT. It also applies to pre-litigation matters that come up for mediation before TDSAT's Mediation Center. The said chapter provides that mediation regarding any petition or other proceeding pending before TDSAT may be referred to TDSAT's Mediation Center and upon such a reference being made, and the chapter will govern the said reference on Mediation Procedures.

The broadcasting and cable industry sees various kinds of issues that fit mediation, including deals between various stakeholders in the industry. Such issues include routine issues like nonpayment of invoiced amounts, sector-specific issues like the threat of disconnection of signals, and actual disconnection of signals. Issues compatible with resolution through mediation encompass disputes about the execution of subscription agreements and renewal of subscription agreements.

The following statistics of TDSAT's Mediation Center indicate its performance and situation in the past years (Tables 8.1–8.4).[15]

Table 8.1 Period from July 29, 2013, to December 31, 2017

Ser.	*Year*	*Number of Cases Referred to Mediation Center*	*Number of Cases Settled by Mediation Center*	*Number of Cases Referred Back to TDSAT*	*Pending Cases*
1.	2013–2014	233	102	131	NIL
2.	2015	97	36	61	NIL
3.	2016	42	10	32	NIL
4.	2017	52	06	28	18
		424	**154**	**252**	**18**

14. *See generally*, Medha Srivastava et al., *The TDSAT Revisited*, VIDHI CENTRE FOR LEGAL POLICY 27–29 (June 2016), https://tdsat.gov.in/admin/notice/uploads/TDSAT%20Vidhi%206%20june%20 2016.pdf (hereinafter "Vidhi Report").
15. TDSAT, *Statistics of Mediation*, TELECOM DISPUTES SETTLEMENT AND APPELLATE TRIBUNAL, https:// tdsat.gov.in/writereaddata/Delhi/docs/introduction.php?y=7.

Table 8.2 *Pre-litigation Mediation*

Ser.	*Year*	*Number of Cases Referred to Mediation Center*	*Number of Cases Settled by Mediation Center*	*Number of Cases Referred Back to TDSAT*	*Pending Cases*
1.	2016	01*	00	01	00

* This case was referred to for pre-litigation mediation in 2015, but it remained unresolved and was finally closed as "unsettled" on October 7, 2016.

Table 8.3 *Period from July 29, 2013, to December 31, 2018*

Ser.	*Year*	*Number of Cases Referred to Mediation Center*	*Number of Cases Settled by Mediation Center*	*Number of Cases Referred Back to TDSAT*	*Pending Cases*
1.	2013–2014	233	102	131	NIL
2.	2015	97	36	61	NIL
3.	2016	42	10	32	NIL
4.	2017	52	12	40	NIL
5.	2018	52	18	31	3
		476	**178**	**295**	**3**

Table 8.4 *Period from July 29, 2013, to June 30, 2019*

Ser.	*Year*	*Number of Cases Referred to Mediation Center*	*Number of Cases Settled by Mediation Center*	*Number of Cases Referred Back to TDSAT*	*Pending Cases*
1	2013–2014	233	102	131	NIL
2.	2015	97	36	61	NIL
3.	2016	42	10	32	NIL
4.	2017	52	12	40	NIL
5.	2018	52	18	31	3
6.	2019	6	1	1	4
		482	**179**	**296**	**7**

In June 2016, the Vidhi Centre for Legal Policy (an independent legal think tank) released a report (an independent and noncommissioned study) called "The TDSAT

Revisited."[16] It reported that the introduction of the conciliatory mechanism established by TDSAT had indeed had a positive impact on litigation patterns before TDSAT.[17] This bears much truth since not every petition filed before TDSAT involves complicated technology and its facets. Thus, encouraging dispute resolution of telecom disputes through mediation has gone (and will go) a long way in reducing the burden on TDSAT, particularly from smaller and/or simpler matters (like those not involving complex technological issues).

[D] Renewable Energy Projects

The Ministry of New and Renewable Energy (MNRE) set up a DRM to consider the unforeseen disputes between solar and wind power developers and Solar Energy Corporation of India Ltd. (SECI) and/or National Thermal Power Corporation Ltd. (NTPC), as well as disputes relating to the extension of time requests.[18]

The disputes are resolved through a Dispute Resolution Committee (DRC), which applies to those schemes, programs, and projects implemented through/by the SECI, NTPC, and the National Hydroelectric Power Corporation Ltd. (NHPC).[19] In this regard, the detailed procedural guidelines were published by the MNRE in September 2019.[20] Although DRM has been amended on various occasions,[21] the salient features of this DRM are as follows:

(1) A three-member DRC is be set up with the approval of the MNRE.
(2) The members of the Committee must be eminent persons chosen from within the National Capital Region.[22]

---

16. *See* Vidhi Report, *supra* note 14.
17. *Id.*, p. 27.
18. Ministry of New & Renewable Energy, *Setting-up of a Dispute Resolution Mechanism to Consider the Unforeseen Disputes Between Solar/Wind Power Developers and SECI/NTPC, Beyond Contractual Agreements* (No. 283/124/2018-GRID SOLAR, June 18, 2019), http://164.100.94.214/sites/default/files/webform/notices/Order%20Dispute%20Resolution%20Mechanism-compressed.pdf.
19. *Dispute Resolution Committee (DRC) to Consider the Unforeseen Disputes Between Solar/ Wind Power Developers and SECI/ NTPC, Beyond Contractual Agreements* (No. 283/124/2018-GRID SOLAR, July 29, 2020), https://mnre.gov.in/img/documents/uploads/file_f-1596009914709.PDF (hereinafter "Order No. 283/124/2018-GRID SOLAR").
20. *Procedural Guidelines for Dispute Resolution Mechanism to Consider the Unforeseen Disputes Between Solar/Wind Power Developers and SECI/ NTPC, Beyond Contractual Agreements* (No. 283/124/2018-GRID SOLAR, Sept. 20, 2019), https://mnre.gov.in/img/documents/uploads/7dc32f804c2f4d1aaac36687aea8bc19.pdf.
21. Order No. 283/124/2018-GRID SOLAR (Dec. 9, 2019), https://mnre.gov.in/img/documents/uploads/file_f-1580894478108.pdf; Order No. 283/124/2018-GRID SOLAR (Sept. 20, 2019), https://mnre.gov.in/img/documents/uploads/109b943b78414990a5da78abfc13cda1.pdf; *Clarification on Quorum* (No. 283/124/2018-GRID SOLAR, July 10, 2020), https://mnre.gov.in/img/documents/uploads/file_f-1594390598268.PDF; Order No. 283/124/2018-GRID SOLAR (July 29, 2020), https://mnre.gov.in/img/documents/uploads/file_f-1596009914709.PDF; *Amendment* (No. 2831124/2018-GRID SOLAR-Part(1), Sept 25, 2020), https://mnre.gov.in/img/documents/uploads/file_f-1601032125515.PDF; Clarification (No. 283/124/2018-GRID SOLAR, Dec. 8, 2020), https://mnre.gov.in/img/documents/uploads/file_f-1607425546003.PDF.
22. *Members* (No. 283/124/2018-GRID SOLAR, July 23, 2020), https://mnre.gov.in/img/documents/uploads/file_f-1595503509589.pdf.

(3) The selection of the members must be such that there is no conflict of interest.
(4) The DRC is given the authority to deal with appeals on decisions of SECI, NTPC, and NHPC on:[23]
- requests for extension of time due to recognized force majeure events;
- requests for extension of time for reasons not covered under the terms of the contract; and
- disputes other than those about the extension of time between SECI, NTPC, or NHPC on the one hand and developers on the other hand.

(5) The recommendations of the DRC, along with the observations of the MNRE, would be placed before the MNRE for a final decision.
(6) The DRC is empowered to interact with the parties involved in the dispute, but no lawyers are permitted for case presentation before the DRC.
(7) DRC's fee is prescribed under Order No. 283/124/2018-GRID SOLAR dated September 20, 2019.[24]
(8) The DRC is required to record its views in writing.

[E] Ombudsman in Insurance and Banking Sectors

Government entities dominate the insurance and banking sectors.[25] The following segment summarizes how disputes in these sectors are resolved through conciliation and/or mediation.

[1] Insurance Ombudsman

The institution of Insurance Ombudsman was established by the Central Government under section 114(1) of the Insurance Act 1938, bypassing the Redressal of Public Grievances Rules 1998.[26] The said Rules were superseded by the Insurance Ombudsman Rules 2017 ("Ombudsman Rules") in the exercise of the powers conferred to the Central Government under section 24 of the Insurance Regulatory and Development Authority Act 1999 (IRDA Act).[27] Under the IRDA Act and the Ombudsman Rules, a total of 17 Ombudsman centers have been established all over India to resolve disputes

23. *Amendment* (No. 283/124/2018-GRID SOLAR, Sept. 20, 2019), https://mnre.gov.in/img/documents/uploads/109b943b78414990a5da78abfc13cda1.pdf.
24. *Id.*
25. *See*, e.g., Indian Insurance Industry Overview & Market Development Analysis, INDIAN BRAND EQUITY FOUNDATION (Mar. 22, 2021), https://www.ibef.org/industry/insurance-sector-india.aspx; Vivek Kaul, *How Private Banks Are Taking over Indian Banking*, MINT (June 17, 2019, 1:06 AM), https://www.livemint.com/industry/banking/how-private-banks-are-taking-over-indian-banking-1560706195840.html.
26. Department of Economic Affairs—Insurance Division, *Redressal of Public Grievance Rules, 1998* (Notification GSR 670(E), Nov. 11, 1998), http://ecoi.co.in/notification/Redressal%20of%20Public%20Grievances%20Rules,%201998%20-%20copy.pdf.
27. Department of Economic Affairs, *Insurance Ombudsman Rules, 2017* (Apr. 25, 2017), https://www.policyholder.gov.in/uploads/CEDocuments/Insurance%20Ombudsman%20Rules%202017.pdf.

between insurers and the insured. The following set out some key features of the Insurance Ombudsman system:

- The Insurance Ombudsman receives complaints relating to the repudiation of claims by the life insurer, health insurer, or the general insurer, premium-related issues, misrepresentation of policy terms, and other matters.[28]
- Where parties consent in writing, the Ombudsman is to act as a "counselor" and mediator regarding disputes that it can entertain.
- The complaint ordinarily lies within one year from the date on which the decision complained against was received.[29]
- Within one month of the written consent to mediate, the Ombudsman is to communicate what he deems to be a fair recommendation given the facts of the case to the complainant and the insurer.[30]
- If the complainant accepts the recommendation within 15 days of its receipt, the Ombudsman sends the recommendation and the acceptance letter to the insurer to comply.[31]
- If the complaint is not settled based on the Ombudsman's recommendations, it passes an award based on the pleadings and evidence available.

[2] Banking Ombudsman

Section 35A of the Banking Regulation Act 1949 empowers the Reserve Bank of India (RBI) to give general or specific directions to bind banking companies. In exercise of the power conferred under the said section, the RBI created a Banking Ombudsman Scheme 1995.[32] The purpose of the scheme is "to enable resolution of complaints relating to the provision of banking services and to facilitate the satisfaction, or settlement of such complaints."[33]

However, it was felt that the scope of the 1995 Scheme was too narrow; hence, the scope of authority and functions of the banking ombudsman were considered for expansion to include deficiency in banking services concerning loans and advances and other matters.[34] Further, a need was felt for empowering the banking ombudsman to act as arbitrators for certain disputes. Therefore, the RBI passed a revised scheme known as the Banking Ombudsman Scheme 2002.[35]

The 2002 Scheme was reviewed in 2005, after which the RBI considered the need to further revise the scheme owing to its narrow scope, streamlining the processes, and

---

28. *Id.*, at rule 13(1).
29. *Id.*, at rule 14.
30. *Id.*, at rule 16.
31. *Id.*
32. *Banking Ombudsman Scheme, 1995*, Reserve Bank of India, https://rbidocs.rbi.org.in/rdocs/Publications/PDFs/13038.pdf.
33. *Id.*, at Clause 2.
34. *Banking Ombudsman Scheme, 2002*, Reserve Bank of India (Ref. RPCD.BOS.No. 750/13.01.01/2001-02, June 14, 2002), https://rbidocs.rbi.org.in/rdocs/Publications/PDFs/29807.pdf.
35. *Id.*

have further control over the scheme's functioning.[36] With those goals, the RBI notified the Banking Ombudsman Scheme 2006.[37] The 2006 Scheme has been revised on three occasions in 2007, 2009, and 2017.[38] Some key features of the Banking Ombudsman Scheme 2006, as amended up to 2017,[39] are given below:

- The 2006 Scheme consists of four chapters—the first deals with certain preliminary aspects such as short title, commencement, and definitions; the second chapter pertains to the establishment of the Ombudsman; the third chapter concerns with jurisdiction, powers, and duties of the Ombudsman; and the last chapter deals with the procedure for grievance redressal. In total, there are 17 clauses in the 2006 Scheme.
- Banks covered under the said scheme include a banking company, a regional rural bank, a subsidiary bank, or a cooperative bank, having its place in India. It covers even foreign banks with a place of business in India, although they might be incorporated outside India.
- The RBI appoints one or more of its officers at the rank of Chief General Manager, or General Manager, as Ombudsman.[40] The tenure of the Ombudsman is for a maximum of three years at a time.[41]
- There are 20 ombudsmen appointed (mostly in State capital cities)[42] with a defined jurisdiction.[43] RBI deploys the staff to the office of the Ombudsman on deputation.[44] The Ombudsman exercises control and superintendence over his office, including the staff working thereunder.[45]
- The Ombudsman jurisdiction relates to considering complaints on deficiencies of banking or other services by the entities subject to the scheme.[46] These are elaborated in detail in clauses 8(1) and (2) of the 2006 Scheme. There is no pecuniary limit under the said scheme.[47]

36. *The Banking Ombudsman Scheme: Annual Report, 2005–2006*, Reserve Bank of India (May 9, 2007), ¶2.5, https://www.rbi.org.in/scripts/PublicationsView.aspx?id=9232.
37. *The Banking Ombudsman Scheme, 2006*, Reserve Bank of India, https://rbidocs.rbi.org.in/rdocs/Content/PDFs/67933.pdf.
38. *The Banking Ombudsman Scheme, 2006, & The Ombudsman Scheme for Non-Banking Financial Companies: 2018 Annual Report*, Reserve Bank of India (July 1, 2018–June 30, 2019), ¶1.1, https://rbidocs.rbi.org.in/rdocs/Publications/PDFs/AR201820190FB8B9072F984910A9FC7BA568B634D8.PDF.
39. *The Banking Ombudsman Scheme, 2006* (as *amended* in July 1, 2017), Reserve Bank of India, https://rbidocs.rbi.org.in/rdocs/Content/PDFs/BOS2006_2302017.pdf (hereinafter "Banking Ombudsman Scheme").
40. *Id.*, at Clause 4.
41. *Id.*
42. *Id.*, at Annexure I. *See also*, Frequently Asked Questions: Banking Ombudsman Scheme, 2006, Reserve Bank of India (July 14, 2017), https://m.rbi.org.in/Scripts/FAQView.aspx?Id=24.
43. Banking Ombudsman Scheme, *supra* note 39, Clause 7(1).
44. *Id.*, Clause 6(1).
45. *Id.*, Clause 7(3).
46. *Id.*, Clause 7(2).
47. *Id.*

- The primary function of the Ombudsman is to facilitate the satisfaction of grievances or settlement by agreement.[48] The Ombudsman also has the power to mediate or conciliate the dispute between the bank and the aggrieved party.[49]
- Procedure for filing complaint is specified in Clause 9 of the 2006 Scheme.
- An authorized representative can make a complaint on behalf of another person, but such authorization cannot be to an advocate.[50]
- The complaint is to be made to the Ombudsman within whose jurisdiction the office or branch of the bank against which complaint is made is situated,[51] apart from issues regarding credit cards or centralized services, in which case the complaint is to be filed with the Ombudsman within whose jurisdiction the billing address of the customer is situated.[52]
- One of the conditions precedent for making a complaint with the Ombudsman is that a written representation should have been made to the bank on the issue and the complainant should not have received any reply on the representation within one month from the complaint or where the complainant is dissatisfied with the bank's reply.[53]
- The complaints can be made to the Ombudsman within one year from the date of reply or lapse of one month as stated above.
- The Ombudsman has power to call for information from the parties.[54]
- The Ombudsman should attempt a settlement agreement between the bank and the complainant through mediation or conciliation.[55]
- If the dispute is not settled within a specific period, the Ombudsman can pass an award.[56] The bank is required to comply with such an award.[57]
- Appeal from the Ombudsman's decision is as per Clause 14 of the 2006 Scheme.
- A complaint can be filed on the Ombudsman portal as well through email.[58]

The working of the Ombudsman Scheme has shown a positive trend. The Ombudsman Scheme has led to a cost-effective method of resolution of consumer grievances. Instead of pushing parties to courts, the RBI has ensured that an escalation mechanism is followed: at the first instance, the bank can satisfy the consumer by addressing his grievance, and in case of failure to do so, the consumer can approach the Ombudsman who can conciliate or mediate. In case of failure of conciliation or mediation, the Ombudsman can pass an award.

48. *Id.*
49. *Id.*
50. Banking Ombudsman Scheme, *supra* note 39, Clause 9(1).
51. *Id.*
52. *Id.*
53. Banking Ombudsman Scheme, *supra* note 39, Clause 9(3).
54. *Id.*, Clause 10.
55. *Id.*, Clause 11(1).
56. *Id.*, Clause 12(1).
57. *Id.*, Clause 12(9).
58. *Complaints*, Reserve Bank of India, https://www.rbi.org.in/Scripts/Complaints.aspx.

The Annual Report of the RBI on the said scheme shows a continuous increase in the number of complaints to the Ombudsman year-on-year and a high rate of disposal at 96.46% in 2017–2018 and 94.03% in 2018–2019.[59] The number of complaints pending for more than three months was about 1.55% of the total complaints in 2016–2017, 0.34% in 2017–2018, and 0.51% in 2018–2019,[60] showing an efficient and expeditious system. Further research is necessary to examine if the figures reflect the ground reality, but the statistics suggest an effective resolution of disputes through amicable methods.

[F] Taxation

In February 2021, the Central Government announced the introduction of a DRC to resolve taxation disputes amicably.[61] While pending disputes are being resolved or adjudicated, it was considered important that there are fewer disputes from fresh assessments in the future. Hence, to provide early tax certainty to small and medium taxpayers, the government has proposed introducing a new scheme for preventing new disputes and settling the issue at the initial stage.

The new scheme is proposed to be incorporated in a new section 245MA of the Income Tax Act 1961 (IT Act) and has the following features:

- The Central Government shall constitute one or more DRCs.
- The DRC shall resolve disputes of such persons or class of person that the Board of Advance Rulings shall specify (to be constituted under the Finance Act, 2021). The assessee would have an option to opt for or not opt for the dispute resolution through the DRC.
- Only those disputes where the returned income is INR 50 lakhs or less (if there is a return) and the aggregate amount of variation proposed in a specified order is INR 10 lakhs or less shall be eligible to be considered by the DRC.
- Suppose the specified order is based on a search initiated under section 132 or requisition made under section 132A or a survey initiated under 133A or information received under an agreement referred to in section 90 or section 90A of the IT Act. In that case, such specified order shall not be eligible for being considered by the DRC.
- The assessee would not be eligible for the benefit of this provision if there is detention, prosecution, or conviction under various laws as specified in the proposed section.
- The Board will prescribe some other conditions in due course, which would also need to be satisfied for being eligible under this provision.
- The DRC, subject to such conditions as may be prescribed, shall have the powers to reduce or waive any penalty imposable under the IT Act or grant

59. *Id.*
60. *Id.*
61. Speech of Nirmala Sitaraman, Minister of Finance, *on Budget 2021-2021*, Government of India (Feb. 1, 2021), ¶¶155–157, https://www.indiabudget.gov.in/doc/Budget_Speech.pdf.

immunity from prosecution for any offense under the IT Act in case of a person whose dispute is resolved under this provision.

By way of the Finance Act, 2021, the Central Government will be empowered to make a scheme by Notification in the Official Gazette for dispute resolution under this provision. It appears that such a scheme could provide for mediation by the DRC.[62] If the DRC is empowered to mediate or conciliate tax disputes, that could lead to a quicker settlement of tax disputes, especially considering the requirement of the use of technology to reduce the physical interface between the assessee and the tax authorities.

§8.03 ADR IN PSUs

Lately, Central Public Sector Undertakings (CPSUs) have adopted the ADR policies as a part of their internal rules relating to litigation management. Some CPSUs such as Oil and Natural Gas Corporation Ltd. (ONGC) have been using a certain specialized form of ADR mechanisms for a long time.[63] But the past few years have shown a new trend in CPSU dispute resolution, with such entities readily adopting amicable resolution methods.[64]

[A] PSU Policies on ADR

Some key features on conciliation-related policies that are common to various PSUs are synthesized in the segment below.

First, the number of conciliators depends on the pecuniary value of the claim or counterclaim involved (whichever is higher). In other words, the number of conciliators is fixed depending on the quantum of disputes, although the amounts vary between PSUs:

62. *See*, e.g., Status Quo Signals Stability in Tax Regime: Experts, OUTLOOK (Feb. 1, 2021, 9:28 PM), https://www.outlookindia.com/newsscroll/status-quo-signals-stability-in-tax-regime-experts/2021648.
63. *See*, e.g., J.K. Bodha, *Dispute Resolution Mechanisms in ONGC*, BUSINESS PARTNERS' MEET 2013 (July 20–21, 2013), p. 11, https://www.ongcindia.com/wps/wcm/connect/4059fb8c-3e6b-492e-ab8e-771338f96015/Legal_Services.pdf?MOD=AJPERES&CONVERT_TO=url&CACHEID=ROOTWORKSPACE-4059fb8c-3e6b-492e-ab8e-771338f96015-lZnjVSs (hereinafter "OEC Presentation").
64. *See*, e.g., Indian Oil Corporation Limited Conciliation Rules, 2014 *(Revised: September 2018)*, https://www.iocl.com/download/ConciliationRules.pdf (hereinafter "IOC Conciliation Rules"); Bharat Heavy Electricals Limited, Conciliation Scheme, 2018, http://www.bhel.com/pdf/Brief_Procedure_under_BHEL_Conciliation_Scheme-06-10-18.pdf (hereinafter "BHEL Conciliation Scheme 2018").

Ser.	*PSU*	*Amount (INR)*	*No. of Conciliators*
1.	Bharat Heavy Electricals Ltd.[65]	Up to 5 crores	1
		Above 5 crores	3
2.	Gas Authority of India Ltd.	Up to 5 crores	1
		Above 5 crores	3
3.	Indian Oil Corporation Ltd.	Up to 1 crore	1
		Above 1 crore up to 10 crores	2
		Above 20 crores	3
4.	Neyveli Lignite Corporation Ltd.[66]	Up to 3 crores	1
		Above 3 crores	3

Second, PSUs having a conciliation policy maintain a panel of conciliators. But there are divergences in practice regarding whether a party can opt for conciliators beyond the panel maintained by the PSU. For instance, Neyveli Lignite Corporation Ltd. allows parties to select a conciliator outside the panel under its conciliation rules.[67] On the contrary, Bharat Heavy Electricals Ltd., under its conciliation scheme, does not contemplate such a possibility.

Third, advocates are not permitted to participate in the conciliation proceedings to represent the party, although they are permitted to appoint their in-house legal counsels to present their case.[68]

As for some other common features, the fee to be paid for the conciliation is required to be shared equally between the parties;[69] and the conciliation proceedings are to be kept confidential.[70]

65. *See* BHEL Conciliation Scheme 2018, *supra* note 65, Clause 29.
66. *See* Neyveli Lignite Corporation Conciliation Rules 2017, https://www.nlcindia.in/new_website/tenders/NLC_Concilation_Rules.pdf (hereinafter "NLC Conciliation Rules").
67. *Id.*, Clause 6(c).
68. *See*, e.g., GAIL (India) Limited Conciliation Rules, 2010, rules 8(a) and 8(b), https://gailonline.com/pdf/others/GAIL_(INDIA)_LIMITED_CONCILIATION_RULES_2010.pdf (hereinafter "GAIL Conciliation Rules"); IOC Conciliation Rules, *supra* note 64, rule 7(h). Such prohibition of advocates from appearing on behalf of parties in conciliation/mediation is not uncommon. In opposition, a group of advocates had written to the Bar Council of India objecting to the prohibition. *See* Kritika Krishnamurthy et al., Representation on Undue Restriction on Advocate to Appear in Conciliation Proceedings (Sept. 25, 2020), https://www.legaleraonline.com/wp-content/uploads/2020/09/Representation-on-undue-restriction-on-Advocates-.pdf. It is pertinent to note that some international arbitration rules similarly restrict the participation of advocates. *See*, e.g., GAFTA Arbitration Rules No. 125, Clause 4.8og, https://www.gafta.com/write/MediaUploads/Contracts/2016/125_2016.pdf.
69. *See*, e.g., IOC Conciliation Rules, *supra* note 64, rule 12(g); BHEL Conciliation Scheme, *supra* note 65, Clause 26; GAIL Conciliation Rules, *supra* note 68, rule 11(c) & (d).
70. *See*, e.g., BHEL Conciliation Scheme, Clause 29; GAIL Conciliation Rules, *supra* note 68, rule 15; NLC Conciliation Rules, *supra* note 66, rule 15; IOC Conciliation Rules, *supra* note 64, rule 15.

[B] ONGC Outside Experts Committee

ONGC constituted an Outside Experts Committee (OEC) in 1998,[71] which is still considered a pioneer among PSU schemes to implementing conciliation to resolve disputes. Some of its key features are as follows:[72]

- Conciliation proceedings conducted by the OEC are consensual.
- The requesting or initiating party must give a 30-day notice to ONGC mentioning points of disputes and claim amount.
- The request for conciliation is then put up internally before the Chief Managing Director (CMD) of ONGC for approval.
- On approval from the CMD, the OEC consisting of a three-member panel is constituted. The panel has cross-sectoral expertise, including technical, legal, and financial.
- The conciliation proceedings are required to be completed within 8–10 weeks.
- The parties are themselves required to present their case, and advocates are not allowed to participate.
- The parties are to submit documentary evidence supporting their claim, and oral evidence is not permitted.
- OEC can make nonbinding recommendations.
- Matters relating to OEC's conciliation proceedings are confidential.[73]
- Costs are shared equally between the parties.[74]
- Arbitration or litigation proceedings are required to be kept in abeyance during conciliation proceedings.[75]

Statistics (available up to December 2014) on the use of OEC's conciliation proceeding show a significant impact of conciliation policy on claims against ONGC.[76] A total of about 125 cases were referred to OEC. Among these 125 cases, 87 cases were settled based on the OEC's recommendations/proposals; this constitutes about 70% of the cases. Among the cases that could not be successfully resolved (29), the settlement proposals of OEC were rejected by the contractor in 12 cases and by ONGC in about 17 cases. The remaining 9 cases are shown under consideration by ONGC (as shown in the data available till December 2014).

[C] Micro and Small Enterprises

The Micro, Small, and Medium Enterprises Development Act 2006 (MSMED Act) was a radical development that introduced the resolution of disputes involving micro, small

71. *See* OEC Presentation, *supra* note 63.
72. *Id.*, at p. 12. *See also*, Oil and Natural Gas Corp. Ltd., *Revised Guidelines for Conciliation Through Outside Expert Committee (OEC)* (No. MAT/PMC/13(186)1/2016, Dec. 29, 2016).
73. *See* OEC Presentation, *supra* note 63, p. 14.
74. *Id.*, p. 15.
75. *Id.*, p. 16.
76. *Id.*, p. 18.

and medium enterprises, among which many such enterprises have government entities as their clients or customers.

Chapter V of the MSMED Act provides for dispute resolution through a mechanism of mediation, conciliation, and arbitration, for settling disputes regarding the delay in payment to micro and small enterprises. The Act imposes an exorbitant interest in delay in payment and creates a forum for micro and small enterprises to file complaints before the Facilitation Council has jurisdiction.[77]

On receipt of such a reference or complaint, the Facilitation Council shall either conduct conciliation in the matter or seek the assistance of any institution or center providing ADR services by referring to such an institution for conducting the conciliation. Part III of the ACA applies to such a dispute as if the conciliation were initiated under Part III. If the conciliation fails, and no settlement is reached between the parties, section 18 of the MSMED Act empowers the Facilitation Council to either take up the dispute for arbitration or refer it to any institution or center providing such services. Here too, the ACA provisions apply to the disputes as if the arbitration was pursuant to an arbitration agreement under section 7(1) of the ACA. *See* Chapter on Mediating Commercial Disputes for more on conciliation under the MSMED Act.

The Facilitation Councils had initially faced many stumbling blocks concerning administration and functioning. Over the years, however, there has been a substantial improvement in the way cases are handled, mainly owing to the support provided to the Councils by the courts and the Ministry of Micro, Small, and Medium Enterprises (MMSME). In particular, the MMSME introduced a "Samadhan" portal, where micro and small enterprises can initiate and manage their payment disputes.[78]

As regards government entities, the following statistics (as available on July 1, 2020) are indicative of the impact of conciliatory methods in disputes involving government entities:[79]

- Among the 46,742 cases filed by micro and small enterprises, about 10,781 (23%) have been against government entities.[80]
- Among the 10,781 cases that have been filed against government entities, 3,058 cases (38%) have resulted in an outcome, which is either a part or complete acceptance of amount claimed by the micro or small enterprise, or complete rejection of the claim, or a mutual settlement on other terms:

77. Micro, Small and Medium Enterprises Development Act, 2006, §18(1).
78. *MSME Samadhan*, MINISTRY OF MICRO SMALL & MEDIUM ENTERPRISES, https://samadhaan.msme.gov.in/MyMsme/MSEFC/MSEFC_Welcome.aspx.
79. Statistics provided on the official website of MSME Samadhan at, https://samadhaan.msme.gov.in/ (on filed with the authors).
80. The government entities/respondents include Central Ministries, Central Departments, Central PSUs, Railway Zones, Railway Divisions, Ordnance Factory, State Governments, and State PSUs.

Particulars of the 3,058 Cases	*Number*
Cases where there is either a part or complete acceptance of amount claimed	683
Cases where the claim is completely rejected	1,215
Cases where the claim is mutually settled on other terms	1,160
Total	**3,058**

- The remaining 7,723 cases (62% among the 10,781 involving a government entity) are pending.

It is commonly understood that settlement in government-related disputes and most of the dues payable to micro and small enterprises are usually from the government.[81] Given that, the percentage of disputes settled through the Facilitation Council is promising.

§8.04 MEDIATING GOVERNMENT DISPUTES: ISSUES AND CONCERNS

[A] Decision-Making in the Government

Critical to the success or failure of the mediation (or conciliation) is the manner of decision-making in government entities. The processes of mediation entail decision-making on various issues such as the decision to:

- accept mediation, as opposed to the traditional mode of dispute resolution, as in litigation or arbitration;
- appoint an official or a group of officials (as in a Committee) to represent the government entity in the mediation;
- make submissions on the merits of the dispute;
- make a settlement offer (or respond to one) and make concessions;
- accept or reject a settlement offer;
- sign a settlement agreement; and
- file a consent decree (or award) on the settlement terms, where procedurally possible (and warranted).

The nature of consensual dispute resolution processes entails active decision-making by the government entity. There are broadly three stages in any government decision-making: (1) proposal, (2) recommendation, and (3) approval. Consonant with these three stages, various authorities are involved in the process: the proposing

81. NITI Aayog, *Designing the Future of Dispute Resolution: The ODR Policy Plan for India 51* (NITI Aayog Expert Committee on ODR, 2020), https://niti.gov.in/sites/default/files/2020-10/Draft-ODR-Report-NITI-Aayog-Committee.pdf.

authority,[82] the recommending authority, the finance department, and the approving authority. The approving authority is the authority endowed with the power to decide, as per the relevant delegation of powers. However, the finance department of each government entity is generally endowed with the power of financial concurrence. In sum, four fundamental aspects are government decision-making: proposal, recommendation, financial concurrence, and approval.

A decision involves more than one department; such a decision is taken by different departments through interdepartmental consultations.[83] For instance, deciding whether to accept a mediation or conciliation proposal might have cross-departmental implications, such as financial, technical, commercial, and legal.

In resolving disputes through mediation or conciliation, there is a requirement for internal decisions to be made at various stages of the said processes, often with a small window of time available. A small window is due to the typical three to six months to complete the conciliation or mediation process.[84]

Thus, given the number of authorities involved, maneuvering a dispute through conciliation or mediation is a humongous task for a government entity. After that, to get a settlement proposal or negotiated draft settlement reach its logical conclusion of a final settlement agreement is equally challenging. Further, a settlement proposal, even if accepted and executed as a settlement agreement, is subject to review by various overseers such as internal auditors, the office of the Comptroller and Auditor General of India (CAG),[85] Lokpal,[86] the Central Vigilance Commission (CVC),[87] and other similar authorities. Hence, there is a tendency in government entities to opt for "risk-averse" avenues by letting courts decide disputes rather than proposing and agreeing upon consensual settlements.

[B] Authority to Propose and Settle

A critical distinction (generally accepted) between mediation and conciliation is that in mediation, the mediator facilitates an amicable resolution between the parties without

82. A "Dealing Officer," in Central Government parlance. *See* Department of Administrative Reforms and Public Grievances, *Central Secretariat Manual of Office Procedure*, Clause 7.1 (2019) (hereinafter "CSMOP 2019").
83. *Id.*, at Clause 4.3; GAIL Conciliation Rules, *supra* note 68, rule 17.
84. Most of the policies in place contemplate completion of conciliation/mediation within three months of initiation, which is extendable by the parties.
85. CAG is the apex authority responsible for external and internal audits of the expenses of the Central and State Governments.
86. Lokpal is established under the Lokpal and Lokayuktas Act 2013 to inquire and investigate into allegations of corruption against public functionaries who fall within the scope and ambit of the above Act.
87. CVC is the apex vigilance institution, free of control from any executive authority, monitoring all vigilance activity under the Central Government and advising various authorities in Central Government organizations in planning, executing, reviewing and reforming their vigilant work. Consequent upon promulgation of an Ordinance by the President, the Central Vigilance Commission has been made a multimember Commission with "statutory status." The CVC Bill was passed by both the houses of Parliament in 2003 as the Central Vigilance Commission Act 2003 (No. 45 of 2003) came into effect from that date.

proposing any settlement on her own. On the other hand, in conciliation, the conciliator can propose settlements, which the parties may or may not agree with.

This distinction is of considerable significance for the efficacy of the appropriate DRM for the settlement of government disputes. Mediation is a dispute resolution process that entails parties exchanging settlement offers with each other and the acceptance or rejection of such offers. For that reason, mediation may not suit decision-making in the government, particularly given the dynamic nature of the proposals being exchanged between the parties.

Every time a proposal is made by the other side, a decision as to whether it has to be accepted, rejected, or a counterproposal is to be made has to be taken. These actions require approval from the approving or competent authority in the government, unless such authority is also at the negotiating table. It may not be possible for the competent authority to participate in all the mediation sessions and decide thereon. However, conciliation is a better prospect because there is scope for nonbinding proposals from the conciliator, which is up to the parties to accept it or not. When a conciliator proposes a settlement for resolving any dispute, it would after that be subject to the approval, rejection, or counterproposal of the competent authority as per the decision-making process noted above.

[C] Case Management

A major handicap faced by several government departments and authorities is the absence of appropriate staff to manage and coordinate the disputes (and dispute resolution) faced by the department or authority. For example, when facing a dispute, a government department or authority usually must expend its project and technical personnel (or its contract administrators) to closely monitor, pursue, and administer the dispute-related issues. Not only does this affect the progress and commitment to any ongoing projects, but such personnel is neither qualified nor trained to do so.

Hence, there is a need to appoint a nodal officer in every department at the Joint Secretary level to coordinate effective handling of disputes and dispute resolution processes. This was considered in the "Action Plan to Reduce Government Litigation" by the Department of Justice in 2017.[88] The recommendations were:

- appointment of a nodal officer in every department at the Joint Secretary level to coordinate effective resolution of the disputes;
- nodal officer to regularly monitor the status of the cases;
- promotion of ADR mechanisms and, in particular, mediation as the preferred form of dispute resolution in service-related matters;
- avoidance of any unnecessary filing of appeals (as a routine matter), except where there is a substantial policy in issue;

88. *See* Department of Justice, *Action Plan to Reduce Government Litigation* (June 13, 2017), p. 15, https://doj.gov.in/sites/default/files/action%20plan.pdf.

- creation of an intuitional ADR mechanism, to be included in case of a reference to either arbitration or mediation; and
- withdrawal (and mandatory settlement, in the authors' view) of any vexatious litigation.

The authors consider that engaging legal professionals would have substantial input in these processes, the dispute, and the process. It is not uncommon that government entities engage legal consultants/advisors on a contractual basis, even if they cannot get sanctions for the recruitment of legally trained officials.

The authors consider that engaging legal professionals would have substantial input in these processes, the dispute, and the process. It is not uncommon that government entities engage legal consultants/advisors on a contractual basis, despite (or given) the absence of any specific sanction for recruiting in-house lawyers. The proposed nodal officer (along with a legal consultant) will provide all-around management of claims and disputes at governing, enabling its project and technical personnel to devote more time and resources toward the projects and assignments.

[D] Mediation Institutions and Lack of Research

There exists a considerable lack of research on consensual dispute processes employed in government disputes and their success rates. This is perhaps due to the confidential nature of the process. Regular publication of data relating to settlement through consensual processes can go a long way in ensuring transparency in the working of conciliation or mediation vis-à-vis government disputes. Although different government entities are likely to have their policies regarding ADR processes, the efficacy of such policies and how these are implemented in the letter and spirit assume great significance. It is in this context that data regarding ADR processes employed by the government entities is crucial.

[E] Other Issues and Concerns

Other than the procedure and implementation-related issues that pervade conciliatory means of settling government disputes, other systemic issues have inhibited the use of consensual dispute resolution.

A 2015 report by the Ministry of Defense identified some of the main causes for the rising graph of litigation (especially appeals) in service and pension matters. These causal reasons, we think, are universal in some sense. The report categorized them as:[89] (i) government's default reaction to appeal lost litigation; (ii) perception that a "government policy" is sacrosanct; (iii) perception that the litigant is acting against the interests of the State; (iv) pressure to win cases and incidence of ego-fueled litigation

89. MINISTRY OF DEFENCE, RAKSHA MANTRI'S COMMITTEE OF EXPERTS REVIEW OF SERVICE AND PENSION MATTERS INCLUDING POTENTIAL DISPUTES, MINIMIZING LITIGATION AND STRENGTHENING INSTITUTIONAL MECHANISMS RELATED TO REDRESSAL OF GRIEVANCES (2015), https://www.mod.gov.in/sites/default/files/Reportc051020.pdf.

by government officers; and (v) lack of uniformity of implementation in cases which have attained finality.

Nevertheless, as discussed in the sections above, interesting developments have occurred in the past few years, especially the constitution of conciliation committees in several infrastructure and energy sectors such as highways, roadways, and others. Although the statistical performance of these conciliation committees remains to be empirically and/or qualitatively assessed, it appears that contractors have begun using these mechanisms extensively, especially during the COVID-19 crisis.

Given the mediation or conciliation's potential in unlocking the cash flow (that would otherwise be stuck in protracted litigation), conciliation has been particularly viewed by the construction industry as a method to improve liquidity in the interest of the project.[90] It would be interesting to see how disputes involving government entities were settled by the conciliation committees and the procedure adopted. The processes involved could be documented, studied, categorized, and best practices could be derived.

For instance, keeping privilege in mind, in a case under the Public Premises (Eviction of Unauthorised Occupants) Act 1971 (PP Act), after the conclusion of the arguments, the appellants and the PSU arrived at a negotiated settlement. Under the settlement terms, the PSU was to pay monies to the appellants, and the appellants were to vacate the properties. Upon vacation and demolition, the PSU was to construct an important public project.

Accordingly, statements were recorded, and the appeals were disposed of. To secure the PSU interests, the appellants executed indemnity bonds in order that their legal heirs do not sue the PSU for excess monies (than what has already been agreed to be paid by the PSU to the appellants). The issue of indemnification gains immense significance in settlements. This is especially true in the context of PSUs since the money at stake is public money.

One interesting issue that arose was related to the spellings of some of the appellants' names. In the statements, orders, payment instruments, and demand drafts, the spellings of the appellants were the same as mentioned in the memorandum of parties in the appeal. However, some of the appellants could not realize the demand drafts since their names were spelled differently in their respective bank records. Remedying these issues would now mean a revival of the appeals, clarificatory orders to issue demand drafts as per the spelling of appellants' names in their respective bank records. Without this, the PSU would be in no position to make the payments, as that would give rise to audit-related concerns. The lesson is that even a minor issue such as the spelling of a beneficiary's name can have a chilling effect on settlements.

These teething issues must not, however, lead one to think of these settlements as redundant. Had the parties taken the litigation route instead of a mutual settlement, then irrespective of the outcome, there would have been further challenges, which

---

90. *See* Amritha Pillai, *Road Developers Take Conciliation Route for Claims Amid Liquidity Crunch*, Business Standard (Oct. 13, 2020, 8:38 PM), https://www.business-standard.com/article/companies/road-developers-take-conciliation-route-for-claims-amid-liquidity-crunch-120101301287_1.html.

could have escalated up to Supreme Court. It would not be out of place to mention that before the PSU invoked PP Act, many of the appellants had multiple rounds of litigation about the subject properties in varying contexts.

§8.05 GOVERNMENT POLICIES ON DISPUTES

[A] National Litigation Policy

In 1974, the Supreme Court of India made some critical remarks (which are often quoted) about the absence of a litigation policy in India:[91]

> [...] I feel impelled to make a few observations not on the merits but governmental disposition to litigation, the present case being symptomatic of a serious deficiency. In this country the State is the largest litigant today and the huge expenditure involved makes a big draft on the public exchequer. In the context of expanding dimensions of State activity and responsibility, is it unfair to expect finer sense and sensibility in its litigation policy, the absence of which, in the present case, has led the Railway callously and cantankerously to resist an action by its own employee, a small man, by urging a mere technical plea which has been pursued right up to the summit Court here and has been negatived in the judgment just pronounced.

The sentiment has been echoed in several judgments, emphasized the need for a sensible litigation policy. In one such case, the Supreme Court observed:[92]

> We like to emphasize that Governments must be made accountable by Parliamentary social audit for wasteful litigative expenditure inflicted on the community by inaction. [...] An opportunity for setting the dispute through arbitration was thrown away by sheer inaction. A litigative policy for the State involves settlement of governmental disputes with citizens in a sense of conciliation rather than in a fighting mood. Indeed, it should be a directive on the part of the State to empower its law officer to take steps to compose disputes rather than continue them in Court. We are constrained to make these observations because much of the litigation in which Governments are involved adds to the case load accumulation in Courts for which there is public criticism. We hope that a more responsive spirit will be brought to bear upon governmental litigation so as to avoid waste of public money and promote expeditious work in Courts of cases which deserve to be attended to.

The Law Commission of India echoed such need for a litigation policy in its 126th Report on "Government and Public Sector Undertaking Litigation Policy and Strategies." It expressed the need for a policy to avoid or reduce litigation to bring down the load on the court system resulting in a reduction of expenses on judicial setup. Actioning on the sentiments being expressed by the courts and the Law Commission, the Ministry of Law and Justice held a national consultation for strengthening the judiciary toward reducing pendency and delay in October 2009. There, a resolution

91. Dilbagh Rai v. Union of India & Ors., AIR 1974 SC 130.
92. State of Punjab v. Geeta Iron & Brass Works Ltd. (1978) 1 SCC 68, ¶4.

was undertaken to frame a National Litigation Policy (NLP) to promote responsible litigation.

This was followed by an NLP in 2010, formulated by the Department of Legal Affairs (DLA). However, the said policy could not be implemented. The NLP is still under consideration of the government intending to bring pendency and reduce government litigation.[93]

[B] Government Versus Government

In respect of court cases between one department of the government with other or between one department of the government and PSU, the Supreme Court observed the following:[94]

> It was not contemplated by the framers of the Constitution or CPC that two departments of a State or the Union of India will fight litigation in a court of law. It is neither appropriate nor permissible for two department of a state or the Union of India to fight litigation in a court of law. Indeed, such a course cannot but be detrimental to the public interest as it also entails avoidable wastage of public money and time. Various departments of the Government are its limbs and, therefore, they must act in coordination and not in confrontation. Filing of a writ petition by one department against the other by invoking the extraordinary jurisdiction of the High Court is not only against the propriety and policy as it smacks of indiscipline but is also contrary to the basic concept of law which requires that for suing or being sued, there must be either a natural or a juristic person. The States/ Union of India must evolve a mechanism to set at rest all interdepartmental controversies at the level of the Government and such matters should not be carried to a court of law for resolution of the controversy.

On government versus government disputes, the 126th Report of the Law Commission had recommended mandatory arbitration for resolving disputes between public enterprises. Following this recommendation, the Central Government constituted the High-Power Committee (or the Committee of Disputes) in 1991. It made it compulsory for all disputes between two government entities to be examined by the High-Powered Committee before proceeding to a court or tribunal for adjudication.[95]

Though the High-Power Committee was a laudable initiative to reduce government litigation and avoid wastage of government resources, it had failed to achieve it

---

93. *See National Litigation Policy, 2010*, https://www.scribd.com/document/300845780/National-Litigation-Policy-2010. On many occasions, the government has considered releasing updated versions of the Policy. Recently, the Central Government submitted before the Delhi High Court that it would soon release the Policy. *See* Department of Legal Affairs, *Status Note on National Litigation Policy*, https://legalaffairs.gov.in/sites/default/files/status%20note%20on%20nlp_0_0.pdf; Revised National Litigation Policy under Process, Centre tells HC, OUTLOOK: THE NEWS SCROLL (Jan. 13, 2021, 6:28 PM), https://www.outlookindia.com/newsscroll/revised-national-litigation-policy-under-process-centre-tells-hc/2009787.
94. Chief Conservator of Forests, Government of Andhra Pradesh v. Collector & Ors. (2003) 3 SCC 472.
95. *See* DIRECT TAXES REGIONAL TRAINING INSTITUTE, MANUAL FOR FILING APPEALS IN HIGH COURT AND SUPREME COURT (2011), http://www.nadt.gov.in/writereaddata/MenuContentImages/streamlining%20of%20Appeals%20Manual%20for%20NWR634729497354353682.pdf.

in practice. The Committee, as per the Supreme Court, had only caused a delay in litigation and, on occasion, has given clearance to one body while denying it to another on the same set of facts.[96]

For these reasons, the Committee was decommissioned.[97] Reflecting the same sentiment as the Supreme Court, in 2018, the Union Cabinet approved the strengthening of the mechanism for resolving commercial disputes of Central Public Sector Enterprises (CPSEs) *inter se* and between CPSEs and other government departments. The Cabinet decision was based on the recommendations of the Committee of Secretaries, which will put in place an institutionalized mechanism within the government for a speedy resolution of commercial disputes of CPSEs without the matter being referred to adversarial modes of dispute resolution.

As per the Cabinet decision, a new two-tier mechanism will be put in place of the existing Permanent Machinery of Arbitration to resolve commercial disputes (excluding disputes concerning the railways, IT, custom and excise departments) between CPSEs *inter se* and CPSEs and government departments.

At the first instance (tier one), such commercial disputes will be referred to a Committee comprising of Secretaries of the administrative ministries or departments to which the disputing CPSEs or parties belong and Secretary of the DLA. The financial advisors of the two concerned administrative ministries or departments will represent the dispute's issues before the Committee. If the two disputing parties belong to the same ministry or department, the Committee will comprise the Secretary of the administrative ministry or department concerned, Secretary of DLA, and Secretary of the Department of Public Enterprises (DPE). In such cases, the matter may be represented before the Committee by the financial advisors and one Joint Secretary of that ministry or department.

Further, in case of a dispute between CPSE and a State Government's department or organization, the Committee will be comprised of the Secretary of the ministry or department of the Union to which the CPSE belongs, the Secretary of DLA, and a senior officer nominated by the Chief Secretary of the concerned State. In such cases, the matter may be represented before the Committee by the concerned Principal Secretary of the State Government's Department or Organization.

At the second instance (tier two), if the dispute remains unresolved, even after consideration by the above Committee, the same will be referred to the Cabinet Secretary, whose decision will be final and binding on all concerned. If the disputes are disposed of promptly, a schedule of three months is prescribed for tier one.

---

96. *See* Electronics Corporation of India Ltd. v. Union of India & Ors., Civil Appeal No. 1883 of 2011 (arising out of SLP (C) No. 2583 of 2009) (Order, Feb. 2, 2011) (PSE and the Ministries/Departments of the Central Govt. do not require the permission of the Committee on Disputes in Cabinet Secretariat before approaching the courts and Tribunals. The Committee, accordingly, stands wound up).
97. Cabinet Secretariat, *Settlement of Disputes Between One Central Government Department and Another and One Central Government Department and Central Government Public Enterprises and Public Enterprises and Another* (No. A-12031/01/2011-Ad.I, Sept. 1, 2011), https://cabsec.gov.in/files/committeondisputes/codsep2011.pdf.

In this regard, the DPE has also issued detailed guidelines, i.e., the Administrative Mechanism for Resolution of CPSEs Disputes (AMRCD).[98] The guidelines promote the resolution of disputes through mutual efforts to resolve commercial disputes, thereby, reducing the number of litigations and avoiding wastage of public money. In 2020, the AMRCD mechanism applied to disputes (other than those related to taxation) and extended to all ministries and departments.

§8.06 CONCLUSION

In the past decade, there have been rapid strides by India in promoting ADR processes. Government entities, too, have come a long way in considering the ADR process instead of traditional forms of dispute resolution. Now that ADR processes (including mediation or conciliation) are more or less acceptable in government disputes,[99] the implementation of these ADR processes must catch up. We say this because most government contracts have provisions for multitier dispute resolution, requiring that the parties first negotiate/consult before engaging in adversarial dispute resolution processes like arbitration. However, such clauses requiring negotiation, consultation, mediation, or conciliation find it impossible to be implemented, given the administrative and procedural hurdles typical to government entities.

For starters, it would do well for government entities to have a clear policy on their use of ADR and a system or procedure for responding to proposals and executing settlement agreements under ADR processes. Those policies could include the constitution of third-party neutrals (arbitrators, mediators, and conciliators), qualifications of the neutrals, the panel's strength, the procedure for settlement of disputes through ADR, the manner of settlement of disputes, and so on.

There is a special need for policies concerning the way settlement proposals are to be dealt with by the government entity and the criteria (cost-benefit analysis) and procedure for its acceptance or rejection. Such policies eliminate the exercise of any wide discretionary powers, which could be called in question later by auditing and vigilance authorities. This, in turn, would greatly minimize the potential for corrupt practices.

Further, it would do well for government entities to publish data periodically (annually/half-yearly) on various aspects of the working or implementation of ADR processes. For example:

- total number of disputes referred to adjudication (litigation or arbitration) versus the disputes referred to conciliation or mediation and their value;

98. Department of Public Enterprises, *Settlement of Commercial Disputes Between Central Public Sector Enterprises (CPSEs) Inter Se and CPSE(s) and Government Department(s)/Organization(s): Administrative Mechanism for Resolution of CPSEs Disputes (AMRCD)* (F. No. 4(1)/2013-DPE(GM)/FTS-1835, May 22, 2018), https://dpe.gov.in/sites/default/files/R-171-merged.pdf. *See also*, DPE-GM-05/0003/2019-FTS-10937 (Feb. 20, 2020), https://dpe.gov.in/sites/default/files/FTS-10937-ALL.pdf.

99. *See* Department of Justice, *Action Plan to Reduce Government Litigation* (June 13, 2017), p. 15, https://doj.gov.in/sites/default/files/action%20plan.pdf.

- time taken from reference till completion of conciliation or mediation proceedings versus the stipulated period for conclusion of conciliation proceedings;
- value of disputes claimed versus the value of disputes settled;
- time taken from execution of settlement agreement to payment or satisfaction of any obligations under the settlement agreement;
- number of disputes in which the recommendations of the conciliation committee were accepted by both parties, which settled the disputes between the parties;
- number of disputes in which the contractor rejected the recommendations of the conciliation committee; and
- the number of disputes in which the government entity rejected recommendations of the conciliation committee.

Such statistics and empirical data would encourage research and development of consensual modes of dispute settlement involving government entities. At the very least, such data would enable an objective assessment of the performance of the respective government entities vis-a-vis resolution of their disputes through ADR processes. With such data, NITI Aayog (or the Arbitration Council of India)[100] may even publish annual rankings of government entities that have performed the best in managing disputes. This would potentially nudge other government entities toward more comprehensive dispute management systems, including a focused approach to settling disputes using conciliatory means.

As an illustration, PSUs are already rated annually through a Memorandum of Understanding (MoU) system. MoU is a mutually negotiated agreement between the CPSEs and the Government of India. Under this agreement, the CPSE undertakes to achieve the targets set in the agreement at the beginning of the year. As per the decision of the High-Powered Committee on MoU headed by the Cabinet Secretary, all CPSEs are required to sign MoUs with their administrative ministries or the holding companies. The principal components of the parameters used for performance evaluation are financial (static) (50%) and nonfinancial (50%). The nonfinancial component constitutes dynamic parameters (30%), enterprise-specific parameters (10%), and sector-specific parameter (10%).

This rating system seeks to assess PSUs on the anvil of "efficacy towards the fulfillment of core objectives for which these [PSUs] have been constituted."[101] Although there is a sub/specific parameter called "managing contracts efficiently," there are no points allocated to employment ADR processes and/or their outcomes. Hence, there is simply no incentive system in the MoU ratings for PSUs to engage in conciliatory processes to resolve their disputes. But it would be greatly beneficial for the DPE to provide necessary incentives to PSUs to engage and enter settlements through conciliation or mediation by providing ADR in the MoU ratings.

100. *See* Arbitration & Conciliation (Amendment) Act, 2019, §43D (dealing with the duties and functions of the Arbitration Council of India).
101. Ministry of Heavy Industries & Public Enterprises, *MoU Guidelines for the Year 2021-22 and Onwards* (No.M-03/0003/2020 DPE (MoU), Feb. 16, 2021), https://dpemou.nic.in/MOUFiles/MoU_Guidelines_16022021.pdf.

CHAPTER 9

Mediating Investor-State Disputes

*Harshad Pathak & Pratyush Panjwani**

§9.01 INTRODUCTION

Even though the first case of investor-State dispute settlement (ISDS) occurred as far back as in 1864 when Ferdinand de Lesseps' *Compagnie de Suez* and the Arab Republic of Egypt arbitrated a dispute regarding the digging of the Suez Canal,[1] ISDS (as we know it today) nonetheless remains relatively nascent.

Traditionally, bilateral investment treaties (BITs) envisaged dispute resolution via diplomatic protection offered by the foreign investor's home State and called for disputes to be resolved inter-State, i.e., between the home and the host States.[2] One of the first steps toward legitimizing ISDS was establishing the International Centre for Settlement of Investment Disputes (ICSID) under the 1965 Convention on the Settlement of Investment Disputes between States and Nationals of Other States (ICSID Convention).[3] Since then, several arbitral institutions have also forayed into ISDS. As a result, ISDS gained popularity swiftly, evidenced by ICSID's registry with 40 new cases every year in the last decade.[4]

* The able assistance of Sahil Malhotra (National Law University—Delhi) is greatly appreciated, particularly in assimilating information regarding India's investment treaty obligations and disputes.

1. Jason Webb Yackee, *The First Investor-State Arbitration? The Suez Canal Dispute of 1864 and Some Reflections on the Historiography of International Investment Law*, *in* INTERNATIONAL INVESTMENT LAW AND HISTORY 89 et seq. (Edward Elgar Publishing 2018).
2. *See* Treaty between the Federal Republic of Germany and Pakistan for the Promotion and Protection of Investments (with Protocol and exchange of notes), Art. 11, Ger.-Pak., Nov. 25, 1959, 457 U.N.T.S. 24.
3. Convention on the Settlement of Investment Disputes between States and Nationals of Other States, Mar. 18, 1965, 575 U.N.T.S. 159 (hereinafter "ICSID Convention").
4. Int'l Ctr. for Settlement of Inv. Disp. (ICSID), *New issue of the ICSID Caseload – Statistics published (Issue 2018-1)* (Feb. 2, 2018); Int'l Ctr. for Settlement of Inv. Disp. (ICSID), *ICSID Releases Fiscal Year 2020 Caseload Statistics* (Aug. 13, 2020).

Despite the increasing popularity of ISDS, mediation or conciliation (used interchangeably in this chapter) has not had a similar journey. It remains marginalized and largely unexplored, especially considering that the first ISDS treaty arbitration award on merits was pronounced in 1990,[5] but the first ICSID arbitration registered in 1972 was amicably settled and discontinued.[6] This chapter accords much-needed attention to mediation between the stakeholders of ISDS, i.e., the investor and the State, more so in the context of the Indian regime of ISDS.

India's tryst with mediation in ISDS is a curious one. Through an empirical analysis, the authors examine the myriad ways in which India has conditioned its consent to ISDS arbitration. Almost all India's investment treaties (IITs) require litigants to attempt to reach an amicable resolution before commencing arbitration. A number of these treaties also provide an optional recourse to conciliation. Notwithstanding these provisions, and based on the limited data publicly available, it appears that India's treaty practice does not translate to an increased usage of mediation in the resolution of India's disputes with its foreign investors.

§9.02 MEDIATION IN ISDS

While expressing his discontent with ISDS arbitration in a conference in 2004, little did Metalclad Corporation's Chief Executive Officer, Mr. Grant Kesler, know that despite having won what he called a "hollow victory," his statement would end up as a foundational stone in the literature relating to mediation in ISDS.[7] His belated desire to have explored "political options" instead of commencing arbitration proceedings against Mexico under the now-defunct North American Free Trade Agreement (NAFTA) is interpreted as "hinting, at least in part, that before the arbitration started, his company had hoped to build on existing friendships ... in Mexico" to arrive at an amicable settlement.[8]

Consistent with Mr. Kesler's sentiment, the authors endeavor to independently examine the potential utility of mediation in ISDS. But two remarks are warranted to begin with. *First*, there are ample success stories of mediation to resolve commercial disputes, and perhaps a similar claim can be made for inter-State or State-State mediation.[9] Despite this, mediation is not considered a mainstream technique in ISDS.

---

5. Asian Agric. Prod. Ltd. v. Republic of Sri Lanka, ICSID Case No. ARB/87/3, Final Award (June 27, 1990).
6. Holiday Inns S.A. and others v. Kingdom of Morocco, ICSID Case No. ARB/72/1, Order Taking Note of the Discontinuance (Oct. 17, 1978), 1 ICSID Rep. 645 (1993); Pierre Lalive, *The First "World Bank" Arbitration (Holiday Inns v. Morocco): Some Legal Problems*, 51 Brit. Y.B. Int'l L. 123 (1981).
7. Jack Coe, Jr., *Should Mediation of Investment Disputes Be Encouraged, and, If So, by Whom and How?, in* Contemporary Issues in International Arbitration and Mediation: The Fordham Papers 2009 339 (Brill | Nijhoff 2010). *See also* Shu Shang, *Implementing Investor-State Mediation in China's Next Generation Investment Treaties, in* China's International Investment Strategy: Bilateral, Regional, and Global Law and Policy 504 (Oxford University Press 2019).
8. Coe, Jr., *supra* note 7, at 340.
9. John Collier & Vaughan Lowe, The Settlement of Disputes in International Law: Institutions and Procedures 27–31 (Oxford University Press 1999).

As per ICSID's recent Caseload Statistics, around 35% of all arbitration proceedings initiated with the ICSID since 1966 have either resulted in a settlement or been discontinued for other reasons.[10] Within these 35% cases (which do not include the conciliation proceedings initiated with ICSID), 49% of cases discontinued at the request of both parties, and 13% cases recorded a settlement in the award.[11]

Second, it is perhaps fair to mention (though not definitively) that there are diverging opinions about whether mediation ought to become a conventional avenue of dispute settlement in ISDS.

On the one hand, it is considered that despite the polarization of the international investment law (IIL) framework, the interests of an investor and a State often overlap. For instance, unless an investment is expropriated, the investor and the State may have a common interest in continuing the investment. One of the "often-expressed desire[s]" of the disputants is "preserving the long-term link between the investor and the host State."[12]

ISDS parties are also interested in a "swift, cost-effective and final settlement of the disputes,"[13] which may make mediation an enticing proposition for all stakeholders.[14] Further, considering the complexities of an ISDS dispute, stakeholders themselves often prefer amicable "solutions based on parties' interests" in place of the legal and economic hassle associated with obtaining remedies under international and domestic law.[15] This is supplemented by the fact that mediation bestows confidentiality,[16] unlike the transparency requirements in ISDS arbitration and may encourage parties to discuss politically sensitive issues without apprehending reputational concerns.

ISDS mediation comes with its own set of obstacles. The absence of a concrete legal framework to ensure the enforceability of the ultimate result is oft-cited.[17] This is even though using mediation "implies the expectation of a high possibility of voluntary conformity" because it is the parties themselves that mutually shape their solution.[18]

This obstacle may now stand eased. On September 12, 2020, the 2018 United Nations Convention on International Settlement Agreements Resulting from Mediation (Singapore Convention) entered into force. The Convention requires, among other things, that "[e]ach Party to the Convention shall enforce a settlement agreement"

10. Int'l Ctr. for Settlement of Inv. Disp. (ICSID), *The ICSID Caseload—Statistics: Issue 2020-2*, 13 (Jan. 28, 2021).
11. *Id.*, 14.
12. Barton Legum et al., *Rules for Investor-State Mediation: Draft Prepared by the International Bar Association State Mediation Subcommittee*, *in* PROSPECTS IN INTERNATIONAL INVESTMENT LAW AND POLICY 265, 265–266 (Cambridge University Press 2013).
13. *Id.*, at 265–266.
14. ADR Center et al., *The Cost of Non ADR: Surveying and Showing the Actual Costs of Intra-Community Commercial Litigation*, 49 (Survey Data Report, June 9, 2010).
15. Chunlei Zhao, *Investor-State Mediation in a China-EU Bilateral Investment Treaty: Talking about Being in the Right Place at the Right Time*, 17 CHINESE J. INT'L L. 111, 114 (2017).
16. *Id.*, at 131–132.
17. Silvia Constain, *Mediation in Investor-State Dispute Settlement: Government Policy and the Changing Landscape*, 29 ICSID REV.—FOREIGN INV. L. J. 25, 37 (2014).
18. *Id.*, at 133.

resulting from mediation.[19] One hopes that the Singapore Convention will achieve the enforcement of settlement agreements what the New York Convention has achieved for the enforcement of arbitral awards. But if the life of the New York Convention has taught something, it is that the entry into force of such instruments, while a landmark occasion, may nonetheless give rise to myriad legal issues that are unknown today.

Among other obstacles to ISDS mediation are its enhanced confidentiality provisions. Unlike typical commercial disputes, ISDS often entails issues of public interest which creates a fear that "particularly irresponsible or culpable behavior by one or both parties may escape detection."[20] Ironically, the very allure of mediation also serves as its weakness from a systemic perspective. And while one may envisage solutions to address this fear, such as making the settlement agreement public,[21] it is difficult to craft a solution to a systemic lack of trust resulting from excessive opacity.

In this background, the chapter explores how mediation can transition from the marginalized to the mainstream in the ISDS discourse. As a starting point, we examine the relevance of legal instruments in treaties, institutional rules, and soft law sources, followed by procedures in ISDS mediations.

[A] International Treaties

The obligation to attempt amicable settlements before commencing arbitration proceedings for a designated period (often referred to as the "cooling-off period") is a routine treaty provision. Such provisions have been criticized for being unrealistic since litigants, particularly the host State, would likely "lack sufficient information at that early juncture to meaningfully participate" in the envisaged negotiations.[22] At the same time, these cooling-off periods (usually ranging from three to six months) may often be too short of achieving a resolution.[23] Consequently, despite being generally regarded as a mandatory precursor to arbitration, these treaty provisions are often relegated to inconsequential pre-arbitral steps that precede the initiation of arbitration. Occasionally, parties even "tend to waste cooling-off periods by turning the temperature up, not down, and concentrating on arbitration, not settlement."[24]

Hence, for much time, it has been believed that ISDS in "BITs are not designed with mediation in mind; they often make no mention of collaborative third-party procedures."[25] That being said, the appreciation of ISDS mediation is convalescent.

19. Singapore Convention, Art. 3.
20. Coe, Jr., *supra* note 7, at 349.
21. *See* EU-Singapore FTA, annex 6, Arts. 4.6, 6.3; EU-Vietnam FTA, annex 10, Arts. 4.6, 6.3.
22. Jack Coe, Jr., *Settlement of Investor-State Disputes Through Mediation: Preliminary Remarks on Processes, Problems and Prospects*, *in* Enforcement of Arbitral Awards Against Sovereigns 73, 95 (Juris Net 2009).
23. U.N. Conf. on Trade and Dev. (UNCTAD), Investor–State Disputes: Prevention and Alternatives to Arbitration, at 41, U.N. Sales No. E.10.II.D.11 (2010).
24. Wolf von Kumberg et al., *Enabling Early Settlement in Investor-State Arbitration: The Time to Introduce Mediation Has Come*, 28 ICSID Rev.—Foreign Inv. L. J. 133, 135–136 (2014).
25. Coe, Jr., *supra* note 22, at 94.

There is a growing trend of investment treaties that now include comprehensive provisions on investor-State mediation.

For instance, the Closer Economic Partnership Arrangement between Mainland China and Hong Kong (which entered into force in 2017) provides the option of resolving investor-State disputes through mediation with a "mediation institute" in either Hong Kong or the Mainland. However, it does not include the option of pursuing arbitration.[26] Before this, the ASEAN Comprehensive Investment Agreement, which entered into force in 2012, included the option of investor-State conciliation, which could be pursued "at any time" irrespective of the consultation obligation during the cooling-off period or the pendency of arbitration proceedings.[27]

In North America, the recent Canada-United States-Mexico Agreement, which entered into force in July 2020 and replaced NAFTA, contains a more elaborate version of the consultation and negotiation than its predecessor-NAFTA.[28] It requires the disputants to "initially seek to resolve the dispute through consultation and negotiation, which may include the use of non-binding, third party procedures, such as good offices, conciliation, or mediation."[29] Similar provisions are present in other Free Trade Agreements (FTAs) by the US, such as the Singapore-US FTA[30] and the Dominion Republic-Central America FTA.[31]

The leading trend of ISDS mediation provisions can be seen in the European Union's (EU's) FTAs. The most important ones are the Comprehensive and Economic Trade Agreement (CETA) (provisionally entered into force in September 2017),[32] the EU-Singapore FTA (entered into force in November 2019),[33] and the EU-Vietnam FTA (entered into force in July 2020).[34] Each of these FTAs provides detailed provisions on the mediation of investor-State disputes "at any time" in the dispute resolution process, i.e., including but not limited to before the initiation of arbitration proceedings.[35] Thus, this mediation process operates in conjunction with, and not instead of, the cooling-off period for amicable consultants that are dealt with under separate provisions.[36] The provisions for mediation in each of these FTAs are identical in many respects. As an

26. Mainland and Hong Kong Closer Economic Partnership Arrangement Arts. 19, 20, China-H.K., June 28, 2017.
27. ASEAN Comprehensive Investment Agreement Art. 30, Feb. 26, 2009.
28. North American Free Trade Agreement Art. 1118, Can.-Mex.-U.S., Dec. 17, 1992, 32 I.L.M. 289 (1993).
29. Canada-United States-Mexico Agreement Art. 14.D.2, Can.-Mex.-U.S., Nov. 30, 2018.
30. United States—Singapore Free Trade Agreement Art. 15.14. Sing.-U.S., May 6, 2003, Hein's No. KAV 6376.
31. Dominican Republic—Central America—United States Free Trade Agreement Art. 10.15, Aug. 5, 2004, Hein's No. KAV 7157.
32. *See* Comprehensive and Economic Trade Agreement, EU-Canada, Oct. 30, 2016 (hereinafter "CETA").
33. *See* Free Trade Agreement between the European Union and the Republic of Singapore, EU-Singapore, Oct. 19, 2018 (hereinafter "EU-Singapore FTA").
34. *See* Free Trade Agreement between the European Union and the Socialist Republic of Vietnam, EU-Vietnam, June 30, 2019 (hereinafter "EU-Vietnam FTA").
35. CETA, *supra* note 32, at Art. 8.20; EU-Singapore FTA, *supra* note 33, at Art. 3.4; EU-Vietnam FTA, *supra* note 34, at Art. 3.31.
36. CETA, *supra* note 32, at Art. 8.19; EU-Singapore FTA, *supra* note 33, at Arts. 3.2, 3.3; EU-Vietnam FTA, *supra* note 34, at Arts. 3.29, 3.30.

example, the provision from the EU-Singapore FTA is quoted below, to the extent relevant:[37]

> ARTICLE 3.4—Mediation and Alternative Dispute Resolution
> 1. The disputing parties may at any time, including prior to the delivery of a notice of intent, agree to have recourse to mediation.
> 2. Recourse to mediation is voluntary and without prejudice to the legal position of either disputing party.
> 3. Recourse to mediation may be governed by the rules set out in Annex 6 (Mediation Mechanism for Disputes between Investors and Parties) or such other rules as the disputing parties may agree. Any time limit mentioned in Annex 6 (Mediation Mechanism for Disputes between Investors and Parties) may be modified by mutual agreement between the disputing parties.
> 4. The mediator shall be appointed by agreement of the disputing parties or in accordance with Article 3 (Selection of the Mediator) of Annex 6 (Mediation Mechanism for Disputes between Investors and Parties). Mediators shall comply with Annex 7 (Code of Conduct for Members of the Tribunal, the Appeal Tribunal and Mediators).
> 5. The disputing parties shall endeavour to reach a mutually agreed solution within sixty days from the appointment of the mediator.

Furthermore, these FTAs contain annexes on "Mediation Mechanism for Disputes Between Investors and Parties"[38] (labeled as "Rules of Procedure for Mediation" in CETA,[39] which also applies to State-State mediation). It contains detailed rules on mediation, from the selection of the mediator to the implementation of the mutually agreed solution.[40] Under these rules, a mediator may offer advice and propose a solution to consider the disputing parties who may accept or reject the proposed solution or agree on a different solution. However, the mediator shall not advise or comment on the consistency of the measure at issue with the FTA.[41] Hence, it appears that the role of the mediator is circumscribed under EU FTAs as being more facilitative, as opposed to evaluative. There are also annexes providing the "Code of Conduct" for mediators, ensuring the ethical integrity of the process.[42]

Overall, these treaty provisions provide a robust foundation for mediation in ISDS.[43] Such provisions are intended to become commonplace in further EU FTAs and

---

37. CETA, *supra* note 32, at Art. 8.20; EU-Singapore FTA, *supra* note 33, at Art. 3.4; EU-Vietnam FTA, *supra* note 34, at Art. 3.31.
38. EU-Singapore FTA, *supra* note 33, at annex 6; EU-Vietnam FTA, *supra* note 34, at annex 10.
39. CETA, *supra* note 32, at annex 29-C.
40. *Id.*, at Arts. 2–5; EU-Singapore FTA, *supra* note 33, at annex 6, Arts. 2–5; EU-Vietnam FTA, *supra* note 34, at annex 10, Arts. 2–5.
41. CETA, *supra* note 32, at annex 29-C, Art. 4.3; EU-Singapore FTA, *supra* note 33, at annex 6, Art. 4.3; EU-Vietnam FTA, *supra* note 34, at annex 10, Art. 4.3.
42. CETA, *supra* note 32, at annex 29-B; EU-Singapore FTA, *supra* note 33, at annex 7; EU-Vietnam FTA, *supra* note 34, at annex 11.
43. Chester Brown & Phoebe Winch, *The Confidentiality and Transparency Debate in Commercial and Investment Mediation*, *in* Mediation in International Commercial and Investment Disputes 321, 338 (Oxford University Press 2019); Elsa Sardinha, *Towards a New Horizon in Investor-State Dispute Settlement? Reflections on the Investment Tribunal System in the Comprehensive Economic Trade Agreement (CETA)*, 54 Can. Y.B. Int'l L. 311, 337–338 (2017).

have become increasingly common in Asia.[44] It promises a bright future for mediation in ISDS. Of course, it remains to be seen how these provisions are put into motion by investors and States, and for that purpose, arbitral (or other) institutions may play a key role.

[B] Institutions, Rules, and Guidelines

Among the various institutions that have taken steps toward mediation in ISDS, ICSID stands out as a leader.[45] The International Chamber of Commerce (ICC) has its own set of mediation rules,[46] under which investor-State disputes have been mediated, such as the *Odebrecht-Tecnimont-Estrella consortium v. Corporación Dominicana de Empresas Eléctricas Estatales*, which resulted in a successful settlement.[47] Similarly, other institutions, such as the Permanent Court of Arbitration (PCA)[48] and the Stockholm Chamber of Commerce (SCC),[49] also have their respective mediation or conciliation rules. However, the most prominent use of mediation in ISDS has been under the administration of the ICSID.

Chapter III of the ICSID Convention deals with conciliation of investor-State disputes. In this regard, the ICSID Conciliation Rules were first adopted together with the Arbitration Rules in September 1967, and since then have been amended thrice. The ICSID Conciliation Rules have been used successfully on multiple occasions to arrive at amicable settlements.

The first successful conciliation happened in 1985 in *Tesoro Petroleum Corporation v. Trinidad and Tobago*.[50] Since then, the ICSID Conciliation facilities have been used successfully on multiple occasions by States, such as in the case of *SEDITEX Engineering v. Madagascar (II)*,[51] *TG World Petroleum Ltd. v. Niger*,[52] *Togo Electicité v. Togo*,[53] *Shareholders of SESAM v. Central African Republic*,[54] *Société d'Energie et d'Eau du Gabon v. Gabonese Republic*,[55] *Republic of Equatorial Guinea v. CMS Energy Corporation & Ors.*[56] (under the ICSID Additional Facility Conciliation Rules) and

44. *See* generally Zhao, *supra* note 15.
45. Int'l Ctr. for Settlement of Inv. Disp. (ICSID), *Possible Improvements of the Framework for ICSID Arbitration*, 13 (Discussion Paper, 2004); Matthew Gearing & Autumn Ellis, *Reforming ICSID*, 6(1) INT'L ARB. Q. L. REV. 19, 29 (2005).
46. Int'l Chamber of Com. (ICC), Mediation Rules (2014) (in effect from Jan. 1, 2014).
47. Cosmo Sanderson, *Billion-Dollar Odebrecht Dispute Settled Through Mediation*, GLOB. ARB. REV. (Mar. 18, 2020), https://globalarbitrationreview.com/article/1216389/billion-dollar-odebrecht-dispute-settled-through-mediation.
48. Permanent Ct. of Arb. (PCA), Optional Conciliation Rules (1996) (in effect from July 1, 1996).
49. Arb. Inst. of the Stockholm Chamber of Com. (SCC), Mediation Rules (2014) (in effect from Jan. 1, 2014).
50. Lester Nurick & Stephen Schnably, *The First ICSID Conciliation: Tesoro Petroleum Corporation v. Trinidad and Tobago*, 1 ICSID REV.—FOREIGN INV. L. J. 340 (1986).
51. ICSID Case No. CONC/94/1 (July 19, 1996).
52. ICSID Case No. CONC/03/1 (Apr. 8, 2005).
53. ICSID Case No. CONC/05/1 (Apr. 6, 2006).
54. ICSID Case No. CONC/07/1 (Aug. 13, 2008).
55. ICSID Case No. CONC/18/1 (Sept. 19, 2018).
56. ICSID Case No. CONC(AF)/12/2 (May 12, 2005).

recently in *Barrick (Niugini) Limited v. Independent State of Papua New Guinea.*[57] While details of these conciliation proceedings are not publicly available, we can make at least two remarks in their regard.

First, from a statistical perspective, a vast majority of the successful conciliation proceedings under ICSID appear to involve the African States. This trend was recognized by Marie-Andrée Ngwe and Marion Deligny Malchair,[58] who note that 9 out of the 12 conciliation cases recorded by ICSID involved the African States. Such skewed usage of ICSID's conciliation facilities by developing the African States reflects their proclivity to resolve investment disputes amicably and puts into perspective the inhibitions expressed by some about the disinclination of States to participate in mediations or conciliations allegedly due to the lack of ministerial organization.

If the alleged lack of ministerial organization were, indeed, one contributing factor, such disorganization would presumably have affected developing countries more than the seemingly more sophisticated economies. However, the relatively uninhibited use of ICSID's conciliation facilities by the African States indicates the contrary. It suggests that some of the States are already sitting on the negotiation table despite any such inhibitions because they desire and the attitude to settle. To then borrow words from Marie-Andrée Ngwe and Marion Deligny Malchair, there is, thus, a need to reflect upon the position of mediation in the overall reform of the ISDS regime.[59]

Second, from a procedural point of view, a conciliator's role under the ICSID's Conciliation facilities appears to be a relatively active one, particularly in comparison with his role usually envisaged in ISDS. For instance, in the first concluded conciliation proceedings under the ICSID Conciliation Rules, the conciliator "conceive[d] that his task in these proceedings is to examine the contentions raised by the parties, to clarify the issues, and to endeavor to evaluate their respective merits and the likelihood of their being accepted, or rejected, in arbitration or court proceedings, in the hope that such evaluation may assist the parties in reaching an agreed settlement."[60]

This evaluative assistance in helping parties arrive at a settlement aligns with how Article 34(1) of the ICSID Convention describes the conciliator's role when it states that:

> It shall be the duty of the [Conciliation] Commission to clarify the issues in dispute between the parties and to endeavor to bring about agreement between them upon mutually acceptable terms. To that end, the Commission may at any stage of the proceedings and from time to time recommend terms of settlement to the parties. The parties shall cooperate in good faith with the Commission in order to enable the Commission to carry out its functions, and shall give their most serious consideration to its recommendations.

57. ICSID Case No. CONC/20/1 (Apr. 9, 2021).
58. Marie-Andree Ngwe & Marion Deligny Malchair, *La propension des Etats africains à résoudre leurs litiges d'investissement à l'amiable*, 34 ICSID Rev.—Foreign Inv. L. J. 388 (2019).
59. *Id.*, at 407–408 (*"le besoin d'intégrer une réflexion sur la conciliation et la médiation dans la réforme globale du système de règlement des différends d'investissements"*).
60. Nurick & Schnably, *supra* note 50, at 348.

After the conciliation process, the ICSID Conciliation Rules require the conciliator to "draw up its report noting the issues in dispute and recording that the parties have reached agreement."[61]

As mentioned, such evaluative assistance during the conciliation process indicates an active involvement on the part of the conciliator, especially when compared against how the mediation procedure has been designed under the currently available rules or guidelines relating to the mediation. In this regard, particularly notable are the ICSID's draft Mediation Rules, the latest version published in February 2020,[62] and the International Bar Association (IBA) Mediation Rules for investor-State Mediation 2012.[63] The ICSID's draft Mediation Rules, which are awaiting ICSID Member States' approval, define the mediator's role, among other things, as follows:[64]

> The mediator shall assist the parties in reaching a mutually acceptable resolution of all or part of the issues in dispute. The mediator does not have the authority to impose a resolution of the dispute on the parties.

The IBA Mediation Rules define the mediator's role in, *inter alia*, the following terms:[65]

1. The mediator shall be guided by principles of fairness, objectivity, independence and impartiality.
2. The mediator shall not have the authority to impose on the parties any partial or complete settlement of the differences or disputes.
3. Following consultation with the parties, the mediator may take decisions with regard to the procedural conduct of the mediation, including the language(s) of the mediation and the place, the format, times and dates of the mediation sessions.
4. In conducting the mediation and in taking procedural decisions, the mediator shall take into account the wishes of the parties, the circumstances of the case and the overall goal of a cost-efficient and timely settlement of the differences or disputes.

After the mediation process, the ICSID's draft Mediation Rules require the mediator to "issue a notice of termination of the mediation" containing "a summary of the procedural steps and the basis for termination of the mediation," as opposed to an evaluative report that the conciliator is required to issue under the ICSID Conciliation Rules.[66]

This basis of termination of proceedings could be, among other things: "(a) a notice from the parties that they have signed a settlement agreement; (b) a notice from

61. Int'l Ctr. for Settlement of Inv. Disp. (ICSID), Rules of Procedure for Conciliation Proceedings (Conciliation Rules), ICSID/15/Rev. 1, rule 30(1) (2006) (in effect from Apr. 10, 2006).
62. Int'l Ctr. for Settlement of Inv. Disp. (ICSID), *Proposals for Amendment of the ICSID Rules*, ICSID Mediation Rules, rule 17(1) (Working Paper No. 4, 2020) (hereinafter "ICSID Working Paper No. 4").
63. Int'l Bar Ass'n (IBA), Mediation Comm., IBA Rules for Investor-State Mediation, Art. 10.3 (2012) (hereinafter "IBA Mediation Rules").
64. ICSID Working Paper No. 4, *supra* note 62, at rule 17(1).
65. IBA Mediation Rules, *supra* note 63, at Art. 7.1.
66. Frauke Nitschke, *The IBA's Investor-State Mediation Rules and the ICSID Dispute Settlement Framework*, 29 ICSID Rev.—Foreign Inv. L. J. 112, 127 (2014).

the parties that they have agreed to terminate the mediation; (c) a notice of withdrawal by any party, unless the remaining parties agree to continue the mediation; [or] (d) a determination by the mediator that there is no likelihood of resolution through the mediation."[67] A similar procedure for termination is envisaged in the IBA Mediation Rules.[68]

Accordingly, it appears that the "guiding principle" behind the IBA Mediation Rules was "to provide for a minimum degree of formality ... so as to facilitate recourse to this means of dispute settlement by parties."[69] In the context of a mediator's role, some scholars have argued that a mediation should follow a more formalistic rights-based approach instead of a flexible interest-based approach due to the involvement of matters of public interest. In this regard, it is considered that a mediator's final aim should further be to "ascertain who is in the right."[70] However, the ICSID's draft Mediation Rules and the IBA Mediation Rules reflect an altogether distinct approach, with the principles of "flexibility and party autonomy" constituting the foundation of mediation under these Rules.[71]

In a comprehensive comment on the IBA Mediation Rules, it has been proposed that between the evaluative style of mediation (where the mediator is more actively involved in suggesting settlement options and rendering opinions relating to "how mediators believe adjudicators decide or what is equitable under the circumstances") and the facilitative style of mediation (where the mediator's role is relegated to being a facilitator enabling the disputants to solve their problems), ISDS cases can be resolved latterly. This is even though ISDS cases involve elements of public interest.[72] We agree with the proposition.

The hallmark of mediation is that it offers control to the disputants over the procedure and the result, and there is no reason why this characteristic feature should suffer in ISDS cases. To the extent that there are concerns relating to confidentiality due to the involvement of public interest matters, as discussed above, there are some scalable corrective measures. These measures focus on ensuring transparency of the outcome of the mediation process after the dispute has been settled, without interfering with the dispute settlement procedures per se.

In the above context, there are ample reasons to be optimistic about the role of mediation in ISDS. There has already been one successful mediation conducted under the IBA Mediation Rules in *Systra SA v. Philippines*.[73] The Energy Charter Conference

67. ICSID Working Paper No. 4, *supra* note 62, at rule 22.
68. IBA Mediation Rules, *supra* note 63, at Art. 11.
69. Legum et al., *supra* note 12, at 267.
70. Belen Olmos Giupponi, *Investment Mediation and Regional Economic Integration Organizations: The European Union and the Central American Integration System in Comparative Perspective*, 34 Conflict Resol. Q. 119, 123 (2016).
71. Susan Franck, *Using Investor-State Mediation Rules to Promote Conflict Management: An Introductory Guide*, 29 ICSID Rev.—Foreign Inv. L. J. 66, 80 (2014).
72. *Id.*, at 73–74.
73. Luke Eric Peterson, *In an Apparent First, Investor and Host-State Agree to Try Mediation under IBA Rules to Resolve an Investment Treaty Dispute*, IA Rep. (Apr. 14, 2006), https://www.iareporter.com/articles/in-an-apparent-first-investor-and-host-state-agree-to-try-mediation-under-iba-rules-to-resolve-an-investment-treaty-dispute/.

has also endorsed the "Guide on Investment Mediation" published in 2016, which is intended to encourage the Contracting Parties to consider using mediation voluntarily as one of the options at any stage of the dispute. These developments, coupled with the ICSID and the IBA efforts, demonstrate that the stakeholders are taking the future of mediation in ISDS seriously.

[C] Mixing Modes in ISDS

Undoubtedly, neither the ICSID's draft Mediation Rules nor the IBA Mediation Rules operate in exclusion of the arbitration dispute resolution processes, but instead are complementary to these processes.[74] Thus, it is implied that mediation can be pursued by the investor and the State before, after, or simultaneous to an ongoing arbitration.

Although it is theoretically possible to pursue conciliation and arbitration proceedings simultaneously,[75] the ICSID setup requires the initiator of any one of these proceedings to specifically indicate to the ICSID "whether [its request] relates to a conciliation or an arbitration proceeding."[76] Similarly, the Energy Charter Secretariat has also clarified that under Article 26 of the Energy Charter Treaty 1994, an investor has to choose whether to pursue conciliation or arbitration proceedings, with the pursuit of the former not barring the investor from pursuing the latter subsequently.[77]

Concerning mediation, investment treaties also acknowledge the flexibility associated with the place of mediation in the dispute resolution process, which is evident from the use of the expression "at any time" to qualify mediation in the EU's recent FTAs discussed above.[78] Accordingly, it appears that mediation can be pursued at multiple junctures and in multiple manners in the ISDS process. Three such junctures where mediation can be pursued between the investor and the State are identified below.

First, mediation can be pursued as a precursor to forthcoming arbitration proceedings, if any—commonly referred to as the med-arb model.[79] This is equally applicable to ISDS. The investor and the State can first try and resolve their dispute amicably through mediation and if that is unsuccessful, either party can consider pursuing arbitration. Theoretically, this procedure can either be integrated with the cooling-off period in investment treaties or be conducted on an ad hoc basis while the cooling-off period is running or otherwise.[80] Of course, if the mediation is pursued in good faith and with the right attitude, this option could likely result in a successful

74. Nitschke, *supra* note 66, at 128.
75. Jack Coe, Jr., *Toward a Complementary Use of Conciliation in Investor-State Disputes: A Preliminary Sketch*, 12 U.C. DAVIS J. INT'L L. & POL'Y 7, 42–43 (2005).
76. Int'l Ctr. for Settlement of Inv. Disp. (ICSID), Rules of Procedure for the Institution of Conciliation and Arbitration Proceedings (Institution Rules), ICSID/15, rule 1(1) (2006).
77. Energy Charter Conf., Adoption by correspondence of the Guide on Investment Mediation, ¶2.2, CC 560/CCDEC201612 (2016).
78. CETA, *supra* note 32, at Art. 8.20; EU-Singapore FTA, *supra* note 33, at Art. 3.4; EU-Vietnam FTA, *supra* note 34, at Art. 3.31.
79. Coe, Jr., *supra* note 22, at 95.
80. Nitschke, *supra* note 66, at 128–129.

outcome, rendering arbitration unnecessary. But if that is not the case, mediation succumbs to its chief weakness of being perceived as a delay tactic.[81]

Second, mediation can also be pursued in parallel with arbitration proceedings. Article 2(4) of the IBA Mediation Rules was drafted, keeping this possibility in mind. It specifically provides that "[m]ediation under these rules may take place at any time, regardless of whether court, arbitration, or other dispute resolution proceedings have been initiated."[82] Indeed, given that as many as 35% of the ICSID arbitration proceedings are discontinued after initiation—most as a result of ad hoc settlements—it may be beneficial to concretize such settlement procedures and use the IBA Mediation Rules (or the ICSID's Mediation Rules, once they are adopted) for arriving at such settlements.[83] Mediation on the substance of the dispute, while the arbitration proceedings are ongoing, creates (at the very least) an opportunity for the disputants to refine their claims and defenses, which could, in turn, result in "higher quality submissions, and better use of the tribunal's time."[84]

Third, mediation may be used as a procedural tool to aid the arbitration process. There are various avenues available during an arbitration process wherein a mediator can be tasked to step in to resolve incidental procedural issues. For instance, a mediator may be well placed to narrow down the parties' document production requests, which, in practice, often end up being extremely extensive and, on occasions, repetitive. Similarly, it has been suggested that mediators can intervene to resolve issues such as the designation of the seat of the arbitration if it is in dispute.[85]

Rule 21(2) of the ICSID Arbitration Rules provides another such avenue: "[a]t the request of the parties, a pre-hearing conference between the Tribunal and the parties, duly represented by their authorized representatives, may be held to consider the issues in dispute to reach an amicable settlement."[86] Such a prehearing conference to arrive at an amicable settlement has been used on one occasion, where the tribunal president functioned as a mediator and facilitated the narrowing down of disputed issues, which helped streamline the arbitration process.[87]

Based on the above, it is apparent that the flexibility associated with mediation enables it to be used in ISDS in various ways, either before or in association with the arbitration or conciliation proceedings. Mediation is always available as a freestanding dispute resolution mechanism, which may be pursued regardless of initiating arbitration proceedings. Such use of mediation and conciliation is desirable from an attitudinal and a systemic perspective. That said, while steps, in leaps and bounds, have been taken in the past decade to make mediation a more mainstream dispute settlement avenue, there are other areas requiring improvement. Critically, until the position of

81. Coe, Jr., *supra* note 75, at 32.
82. IBA Mediation Rules, *supra* note 63, at Art. 2.4.
83. Nitschke, *supra* note 66, at 130-131.
84. Coe, Jr., *supra* note 75, at 19.
85. *Id.*, at 19-20.
86. Nitschke, *supra* note 66, at 130-131.
87. Eloise Obadia, *How Proactive Arbitrators Really Are in Conducting Arbitral Proceedings: An ICSID Perspective*, 16 News from ICSID 8, 10 (1999).

mediation is fully crystalized in ISDS, their use as precursors or supplements to ISDS arbitrations will remain an intriguing area of study and practice.

In this context, and mindful of the global practices, we now turn to analyze India's tryst with mediation in the ISDS regime.

§9.03 FRAMEWORK OF IITs

To analyze India's tryst with mediation and conciliation in ISDS, one must begin by assessing IITs. India signed its first BIT in 1994 with the UK,[88] which was likely influenced by its Model BIT of 1993. Since then, India has published two Model Texts of its BIT or Bilateral Investment Promotion and Protection Agreements (BIPAs) in 2003 and 2016, respectively.[89]

India had entered into investment treaties with at least 84 countries, but it terminated at least 58 in 2017.[90] More recently, in 2019, India withdrew from the negotiations surrounding the Regional Comprehensive Economic Partnership, which also contained a chapter on investments.

Throughout this tumultuous relationship between India and investment treaties, how did India engage with mediation of its investment disputes? Despite the burgeoning scholarship on India's approach to IIL and its increasing emphasis on alternative dispute resolution mechanisms in the context of commercial disputes, this question is rarely addressed in the context of ISDS. Nevertheless, we assess this by first examining the conditional nature of India's consent to arbitrate as contained in various BITs and, *second*, by verifying as to what extent, if at all, do these conditions focus on mediation requirements.

[A] India's Conditional Consent to Arbitration

Consent is the cornerstone of arbitration. An arbitral tribunal's jurisdiction is confined to those disputes that fall within the scope of the parties' consent, and investment treaty tribunals are not an exception to this rule.[91]

In the context of ISDS, a host State's consent to arbitrate foreign investors' investment disputes can be contained in a contract, a domestic investment protection law, or a BIT. However, in the latter two instances, the dispute settlement provisions

---

88. Agreement between the Government of the United Kingdom of Great Britain and Northern Ireland and the Government of the Republic of India, India-U.K., Mar. 14, 1994, Treaty Series No. 27 (1995).
89. Govt. of India, Indian Model Text of BIPA (2003) (hereinafter "2003 Model Indian BIT"); Govt. of India, Model Text for the Indian Bilateral Investment Treaty (2016) (hereinafter "2016 Model Indian BIT").
90. Alison Ross, *India's Termination of BITs to Begin*, Glob. Arb. Rev. (Mar. 22, 2017), https://globalarbitrationreview.com/indias-termination-of-bits-begin; Prabhash Ranjan, *As India's New Bilateral Investment Strategy Sputters out, the Secrecy and Opaqueness Must Go*, The Wire (May 1, 2017).
91. *See* generally Jan Paulsson, *Arbitration Without Privity*, 10 ICSID Rev.—Foreign Inv. L. J. 232 (1995).

contained in domestic law or a BIT are not arbitration agreements per se, even if they provide for ISDS. Instead, these provisions represent a host State's unilateral offer (or standing offer) made to all existing and future investors to settle their investment disputes by employing arbitration, subject to any conditions stated therein.

Thus, upon the occurrence of any investment dispute, an investor can accept the host State's unilateral offer to arbitrate, such as by sending a notice of arbitration to commence arbitration. The host State's offer to arbitrate is contained in a BIT; the resultant arbitration is referred to as an investment treaty arbitration proceeding.

Within this framework, it is well accepted that a host State's consent to arbitrate need not be absolute. A host State can attach any conditions to its arbitral consent and requires that each of these conditions is necessarily fulfilled before the arbitral process can commence. Likewise, a host State is also competent to limit the scope of its arbitral consent by excluding certain subject matters that it does not wish to refer to arbitration. That being said, an arbitral tribunal may be asked to determine whether a particular condition included in an investment treaty constitutes a condition attached to a State's arbitral consent and, therefore, a question of jurisdiction. In such circumstances, a tribunal's determination can deviate from the position of a host State. For instance, despite the objections taken by several States, arbitral tribunals routinely interpret the pre-arbitration step of good faith negotiations between the disputants as merely a procedural requirement (a question of admissibility and not a question of jurisdiction).[92]

We will illustrate the above premise by reference to the provision for ISDS contained in the 2003 Indian Model Text of BIPA (2003 Model BIT) and the 2016 Model Text for the Indian BIT (2016 Model BIT).

Article 9 of the 2003 Model BIT provided a three-tiered mechanism for ISDS:

> (1) Any dispute between an investor of one Contracting Party and the other Contracting Party in relation to an investment of the former under this Agreement shall, as far as possible, be settled amicably through negotiations between the parties to the dispute.
> (2) Any such dispute which has not been amicably settled within a period of six months may, if both Parties agree, be submitted:
>   (a) for resolution, in accordance with the law of the Contracting Party which has admitted the investment to that Contracting Party's competent judicial, arbitral or administrative bodies; or
>   (b) to International conciliation under the Conciliation Rules of the United Nations Commission on International Trade Law.
> (3) Should the Parties fail to agree on a dispute settlement procedure provided under paragraph (2) of this Article or where a dispute is referred to conciliation but conciliation proceedings are terminated other than by signing of a settlement agreement, the dispute may be referred to Arbitration.

92. *See*, e.g., Anatolie Stati, Gabriel Stati, Ascom Grp. SA & Terra Raf Trans Traiding Ltd. v. Republic of Kaz., SCC Case No. 116/2010, Award, ¶829 (Dec. 19, 2013); Ethyl Corp. v. Gov't of Can., UNCITRAL Ad Hoc Tribunal, Award on Jurisdiction, ¶¶76–77 (June 24, 1998), 7 ICSID Rep. 12 (1999); SGS Société Générale de Surveillance S.A. v. Islamic Republic of Pak., ICSID Case No. ARB/01/13, Decision on Jurisdiction, ¶184 (Aug. 6, 2003).

Accordingly, before commencing arbitration under Article 9(3) of the 2003 Model BIT, an investor must first attempt to settle the dispute amicably through negotiations for a cooling-off period of at least six months. If these attempts are unsuccessful, both parties have the option to jointly refer the dispute to any of the two avenues stated in Article 9(2), including international conciliation under the Conciliation Rules of the UNCITRAL. If no such agreement is forthcoming, or if the parties' attempt to conciliate is unsuccessful, then only in such scenario can the investor commence arbitration, as long as the dispute raised by it is "in relation to [its] investment."[93]

Apart from these preconditions, and a general requirement that the instrument shall apply to investments made in accordance with India's laws and regulations,[94] the 2003 Model BIT does not contain any other conditions attached to India's consent to arbitrate. In summary, it reflects India's supposed preference at the time to not attach fetters to its arbitral consent.

In stark contrast to the above framework, ISDS in the 2016 Model BIT contains several preconditions attached to India's consent to arbitrate and further requirements that limit the scope of such consent. To enumerate a few:

(1) Article 13.2 states that the chapter on the "Settlement of Disputes Between an Investor and a Party" "shall only apply to a dispute between a Party and an investor of the other Party with respect to its investment, arising out of an alleged breach of an obligation of a Party under Chapter II of this Treaty, other than the obligation under Articles 9 and 10 of this Treaty." This excludes any claims premised on an alleged breach by India of its obligations under domestic law, as opposed to a treaty obligation.

(2) Article 13.3 clarifies that "[a] Tribunal constituted under this Chapter shall only decide claims in respect of a breach of this Treaty as set out in Chapter II, except under Articles 9 and 10, and not disputes arising solely from an alleged breach of a contract between a Party and an investor."

(3) Article 13.4 provides that "[a]n investor may not submit a claim to arbitration under this Chapter if the investment has been made through fraudulent misrepresentation, concealment, corruption, money laundering or conduct amounting to an abuse of process or similar illegal mechanisms."

(4) Article 13.5 provides that "a Tribunal constituted under this Chapter shall not have the jurisdiction to (i) review the merits of a decision made by a judicial authority of the Parties; or (ii) accept jurisdiction over any claim that is or has been subject of an arbitration under Chapter V."

(5) Article 15.1 on "Condition Precedent to Submission of a Claim to Arbitration" obligates an investor to exhaust its local remedies before the relevant domestic courts or administrative bodies in India before commencing the arbitral process. In this regard, Article 15.2 clarifies that arbitration may only commence "after exhausting all judicial and administrative remedies relating

93. 2003 Model Indian BIT, *supra* note 89, at Art. 9(1).
94. *Id.*, at Art. 2.

to the measure underlying the claim for at least a period of five years from the date on which the investor first acquired knowledge of the measure in question."

(6) Article 15.5(i) provides a limitation constraint, which allows recourse to arbitration only if "not more than six (6) years have elapsed from the date on which the disputing investor first acquired, or should have first acquired, knowledge of the measure in question and knowledge that the disputing investor with respect to its investment, had incurred loss or damage as a result."

(7) Article 2.4 prescribes certain general exclusions, stating that "[t]his Treaty shall not apply to (i) any measure by a local government; (ii) any law or measure regarding taxation, including measures taken to enforce taxation obligations [...] (iii) the issuance of compulsory licenses granted in relation to intellectual property rights, or to the revocation, limitation or creation of intellectual property rights, to the extent that such issuance, revocation, limitation or creation is consistent with the international obligations of Parties under the WTO Agreement; (iv) government procurement by a Party; (v) subsidies or grants provided by a Party; [as well as] (vi) services supplied in the exercise of governmental authority by the relevant body or authority of a Party [...] which is not supplied on a commercial basis."

The above requirements are additive to a minimum cooling-off period of six months, in which the parties are required to use their best efforts to resolve the dispute amicably through meaningful consultation, negotiation, or other third-party procedures.[95]

The 2016 Model BIT is ultimately only indicative of what India construes as an ideal BIT for itself. It only guides India's future treaty negotiations and is not a treaty in itself. Yet, some of the provisions contained in the 2016 Model BIT have already found a place in recent treaties concluded by India.

For instance, Article 10(1) of the India-Japan Comprehensive Economic Partnership Agreement, concluded before the 2016 Model BIT, already stipulated that "the provisions of this Agreement [including the investment chapter] shall not apply to any taxation measures."[96] Similarly, the 2018 India-Belarus BIT and the 2019 India-Kyrgyz Republic BIT mimic the content of the 2016 Model BIT.

The above considerations allow us to infer some preliminary conclusions. Evidently, between 2003 and 2016, there was a radical shift in India's approach toward ISDS and its arbitral consent nature and scope. Learning from its ISDS experience in *White Industries v. Republic of India* (*White Industries*),[97] and presumably concerned by an increasing number of investment proceedings initiated against it after 2010, India

95. 2016 Model Indian BIT, *supra* note 89, at Art. 15.4.
96. Comprehensive Economic Partnership Agreement between the Republic of India and Japan Art. 10, India-Japan, Feb. 16, 2011, 2862 U.N.T.S. 3.
97. *See*, e.g., White Indus. Austl. Ltd. v. Republic of India, UNCITRAL Ad Hoc Tribunal, Final Award (Nov. 30, 2011).

took a policy decision to condition its consent to arbitrate on the fulfillment of multiple condition precedents. It also chose to explicitly exclude certain categories of disputes, most notably those relating to taxation measures,[98] that it considered unsuited for investment treaty arbitration. As noted by commentators, "the combined reading of the qualifications on ISDS that the 2016 Model BIT contains makes it very difficult, if not impossible, for the foreign investor to make effective use of the ISDS mechanism."[99] This appears to be the objective that India had in mind.

This poses the question: To what extent do IITs mandate, or at least encourage, an investor to resolve its investment dispute through mediation? Dealt in the subsequent segment, the answer is rather disappointing.

[B] Mapping IITs

We analyzed ISDS provisions in 91 of IITs, beginning from the 1994 India-UK BIT. For convenience and to discern any policy trends, these treaties were divided into three Phases based on the year they were signed.

Phase I includes 35 treaties signed before 2000; Phase II includes 43 treaties signed between 2000 and 2009; finally, Phase III includes 13 treaties signed between 2000 and January 2020.

This classification of IITs into three Phases reveals that since 2010, India has been reluctant to sign new IITs, which is consistent with its discontent with the ISDS regime after the adverse investment award in *White Industries*. There, the tribunal had held that "the Indian judicial system's inability to deal with White's jurisdictional claim in over nine years, and the Supreme Court [of India's] inability to hear White's jurisdictional appeal for over five years amounts to undue delay and constitutes a breach of India's voluntarily assumed obligation of providing White with 'effective means' of asserting claims and enforcing rights."[100]

In analyzing the 91 BITs, we had a twofold objective. *One*, to ascertain the significance (or lack thereof) of conciliatory modes of dispute settlement, i.e., negotiations, mediation, or conciliation, in the ISDS framework provided for in IITs. *Two*, to ascertain the extent to which India's consent to arbitrate investment claims is contingent upon adherence to a conciliatory mode of dispute settlement. This, in turn, provides us a benchmark for examining India's experience in ISDS proceedings. It is, however, pertinent to clarify three confines regarding the scope of our analysis of 91 IITs.

> *First*, we acknowledge that India terminated many of the 91 IITs analyzed. These treaties are nonetheless relevant for this analysis. This is because all

98. Nissan Motor Co. Ltd. v. Republic of India, PCA Case No. 2017-37, Decision on Jurisdiction (Apr. 29, 2019).
99. Prabhash Ranjan & Pushkar Anand, *The 2016 Model Indian Bilateral Investment Treaty: A Critical Deconstruction*, 38 NW J. INT'L L. & BUS. 1, 51 (2017).
100. White Indus. Austl. Ltd. v. Republic of India, *supra* note 97, at ¶11.4.19.

such terminated treaties contain a "sunset clause," which extends their application for a specified number of years beyond its termination date.[101]

Second, we note that though some of the IITs were signed, they are not yet in force. This includes the 2009 India-Colombia BIT, the 2010 India-Congo BIT, the 2014 ASEAN-India Investment Agreement, the 2018 India-Belarus BIT, and the 2019 India-Kyrgyz Republic and the 2020 India-Brazil BIT. But this is immaterial to the present analysis, which aims to ascertain the significance of mediation in India's broader treaty framework. Thus, the mere fact that these treaties were negotiated and signed by India is sufficient to justify their inclusion.

Third, we have excluded the content of the 2003 and 2016 Model BITs, which were referred to above. Although these instruments indicate India's unilateral expectations from BITs, they are not binding instruments and cannot be classified as IITs.

[1] Mediation for Amicable Settlement

Consistent with the 2003 and 2016 Model Indian BITs, almost all of the analyzed IITs obligate investors to engage in consultation and negotiations to arrive at an amicable settlement for at least six months before commencing arbitration. This practice remained constant across Phases I, II, and III.

The sole exception in this regard can be found in the 1997 India-France BIT; Article 9 of which provides the following mechanism:[102]

> (1) Any dispute concerning the investment occurring between one Contracting Party and an investor of the other Contracting Party shall, if possible, be settled amicably between the two parties concerned.
> (2) Any such dispute which has not been amicably settled within a period of six months from written notification of a claim may be su[b]mitted [sic] to international conciliation under the Conciliation Rules of the United Nations Commission on International Trade Law, if the parties so agree.
> (3) Notwithstanding paragraph 2, [sic] the dispute may be referred to arbitration *at any time* as follows ...

While Article 9(1) of the 1997 India-France BIT requires the parties to attempt to settle their dispute amicably, if possible, it does not specify a precise duration for which the parties must continue with their attempts. Critically, Article 9(3) appears to allow an investor to commence arbitration "at any time" and "notwithstanding" the effect of the conciliation option provided in Article 9(2) of the BIT. One may interpret these

101. *See*, e.g., Agreement between the Government of the Republic of India and the Government of the Republic of Korea on the Promotion and Protection of Investments Art. 11.2, India-S. Kor., Feb. 26, 1996, 1942 U.N.T.S. 2000.

102. Accord entre le Gouvernement de la Republique Francaise et le Gouvernement de la Republique D'Inde sur L'Encouragement et la Protection Reciproques des Investissements Art. 9, Fr.-India, Sept. 2, 1997 (emphasis added). *See* Louis Dreyfus Armateurs SAS v. Republic of India, PCA Case No. 2014-26, Decision on Jurisdiction, ¶26 (Dec. 22, 2015).

provisions to construe that India's consent to arbitrate in Article 9(3) of the BIT is independent of, and not contingent on, the negotiation requirement in Article 9(1).

The arbitral tribunal in *Louis Dreyfus Armateurs SAS v. Republic of India* interpreted Article 9(3) of the 1997 India-France BIT similarly. It reasoned that:[103]

> The ordinary meaning of "at any time" is exactly what it says, namely that there is no temporal restriction on the commencement of arbitration proceedings, such as that expressed in the context of conciliation [...] The conclusion is also supported by the transition language between Articles 9(2) and 9(3) [...] Taken in conjunction with "at any time," the clear import of the "notwithstanding" language is that any temporal pre-condition on invoking the mechanism offered in Article 9(2) does not apply to invoking the different mechanism offered in Article 9(3).

Accordingly, the above analysis reveals that barring the 1997 India-France BIT, India's consent to arbitrate in IITs has consistently been conditional. Despite a difference in articulation, 90 out of 91 IITs require parties to engage in negotiations/consultations for an amicable settlement, for a specified duration, before allowing recourse to arbitration.

[2] Mediation of Investment Disputes

Unlike the requirement of negotiations/consultations for an amicable settlement, India did not adopt a uniform approach concerning allowing conciliation of investment disputes. That being said, one can witness certain commonalities across the three Phases of IITs.

i. No Recourse to Mediation

Out of the 35 IITs signed during Phase I, 8 treaties do not provide any explicit recourse to conciliation. This includes the 1996 India-Korea BIT, the 1997 India-Spain BIT, and the 1998 India-Mauritius BIT, to name a few. This trend continued in Phase II. Out of the 43 IITs signed during Phase II, another 9 treaties do not provide any explicit recourse to conciliation. For example, this includes the India-Hungary BIT 2003, the India-Saudi Arabia BIT 2006, and the India Greece BIT 2007. Lastly, out of the 13 IITs signed during Phase III, 5 treaties do not provide any explicit recourse to conciliation. This includes the India-Latvia BIT 2010, the India-UAE BIT 2013, and the India-Belarus BIT 2018.

As such, cumulatively, out of the 91 IITs analyzed, 22 treaties do not provide any "explicit" recourse to conciliation. We say "explicit" since some treaties, such as the 2018 India-Belarus BIT, allow parties to adopt any "third-party procedures" while using their best efforts to resolve the dispute amicably.[104] While these provisions may potentially allow the parties to mediate/conciliate investment disputes, their ambit

103. Louis Dreyfus Armateurs SAS v. Republic of India, *supra* note 102, at ¶¶83–84.
104. Treaty between the Republic of Belarus and the Republic of India on Investments Art. 15.4, Belr.-India, Sept. 24, 2018.

remains unclear, especially if juxtaposed against other IITs that explicitly provide an option to mediate/conciliate. We do not construe such provisions as providing a clear recourse to mediation/conciliation since third-party procedures would particularly need further agreement between the parties (like the appointment of a mediator, procedural rules, implementation of the settlement agreement, etc.).

ii. Optional Recourse to Mediation

A majority of the IITs analyzed provide an optional recourse to conciliation of investment disputes, either at the unilateral discretion of investors (unilateral conciliation) or with both parties (joint conciliation). We note that a unilateral conciliation is no less than an oxymoron since conciliation is a voluntary process by nature (hence, doubting its practicality, from both the investor and the State).

For instance, Article 9(2)(c) of the 1995 India-Italy BIT 1995 states that if negotiations for settlement are unsuccessful, "the investor may at his choice [...] submit the dispute for settlement to [...] an ad hoc Conciliation."[105] This can be contrasted with Article 9(2) of the 1995 India-Tajikistan BIT, which provides recourse to international conciliation only "if both parties agree."[106] As such, the authors construe these two optional recourses to conciliation distinctly.

About unilateral conciliation, out of the 35 IITs signed during Phase I, 5 treaties grant investors the option to commence conciliation without seeking India's approval. Likewise, out of the 43 IITs signed during Phase II, another 5 treaties grant investors the option to commence conciliation unilaterally. Finally, out of the 13 IITs signed during Phase III, 5 treaties grant investors a unilateral option to commence conciliation. In total, out of the 91 IITs analyzed by the authors, 15 treaties allow investors to unilaterally commence conciliation for resolution of their investment disputes, irrespective of India's consent to conciliate.

That being said, a far larger number of IITs provide an optional recourse to conciliation, *albeit* with the consent of both parties. Out of 35 IITs signed during Phase I, 22 treaties allow for joint conciliation. Likewise, out of 43 IITs signed during Phase II, 29 treaties allow for joint conciliation. However, there appears to be a downward trend during Phase III, where out of the 13 IITs signed by India, only 3 treaties provide for joint conciliation. Yet, out of a total of 91 IITs analyzed by the authors, 54 treaties allow joint conciliation.

Cumulatively, out of the 91 IITs signed across all the three Phases, 69 treaties allow some form of optional recourse to conciliation, whereas the remaining 22 treaties do not explicitly reference conciliation.

---

105. Agreement between the Government of the Italian Republic and the Government of the Republic of India on the Promotion and Protection of Investments Art. 9(2)(c), India-It., Nov. 23, 1995.
106. Agreement between the Government of the Republic of India and the Government of the Republic of Tajikistan for the Promotion and Protection of Investments Art. 9(2)(c), India-Taj., Dec. 12, 1995.

iii. Mandatory Mediation

Finally, none of the 91 IITs analyzed by the authors obligate an investor to attempt conciliation before commencing arbitration. To put it differently, India's consent to arbitrate indicated in any of these IITs is not contingent on the adherence to a mandatory conciliation. For Phase I and Phase II treaties, this is likely to result from an inadvertent lack of emphasis on the availability of conciliatory mechanisms for the settlement of investment disputes. However, India's approach did not change during Phase III, even when the Government of India had made a conscious decision to attach several conditions to its consent to arbitrate in the 2016 Model BIT.

This is not surprising. A recent study revealed that though there are more than three thousand investment treaties, only two of these, i.e., the 2019 Hong Kong-UAE BIT and the 2019 Indonesia-Australia CEPA (IA-CEPA), appear to provide for conciliation as a mandatory precondition for arbitration.[107] For example, Article 14.23 of the IA-CEPA states:[108]

> If the dispute cannot be resolved within 180 days from the date of receipt by the disputing Party of the written request for consultations, the disputing Party may initiate a conciliation process, which shall be mandatory for the disputing investor, with a view towards reaching an amicable settlement. Such a conciliation process shall be initiated by a written request delivered by the disputing Party to the disputing investor.

Consistent with this provision, a disputing investor may commence arbitration under Article 14.24 only where "consultations have not resolved an investment dispute following Article 14.22 or conciliation following Article 14.23."[109] However, the same cannot be said about the 2019 Hong Kong-UAE BIT with equal certainty, considered by some as providing for a mandatory conciliation requirement.[110] Article 8(3) of this BIT provides that:[111]

> (3) When required by the Contracting Party, if the dispute cannot be settled amicably within six months from the date of receipt of the written notice, it shall be submitted to the competent authorities of that Contracting Party or arbitration centres thereof for conciliation.

The use of the word "shall" suggests that if the attempts to reach an amicable settlement do not succeed within the six months cooling-off period, conciliation is mandatory if required by the host State. Yet, Article 8(5) allows an investor to commence arbitration in two seemingly distinct scenarios, i.e., if the dispute cannot be

107. Ana Ubilava, *Mandatory Investor-State Conciliation in New International Investment Treaties: Innovation and Interpretation*, KLUWER MEDIATION BLOG (Sept. 5, 2020).
108. Indonesia-Australia Comprehensive Economic Partnership Agreement Art. 14.23, Austl.-Indon., Mar. 4, 2019.
109. *Id.*, at Art. 14.24.
110. Ubilava, *supra* note 107.
111. Agreement between the Government of the Hong Kong Special Administrative Region of the People's Republic of China and the Government of the United Arab Emirates for the Promotion and Reciprocal Protection of Investments Art. 8(3), H.K.-U.A.E., June 16, 2019.

settled amicably within six months from: (i) the date of receipt of the written notice or (ii) the start of the conciliation referred to in Article 8(3).[112] This suggests that an investor may commence arbitration immediately upon the expiry of the six-month cooling-off period.

Likewise, Article 17 of the 1981 Agreement on Promotion, Protection, and Guarantee of Investments among Member States of the Organisation of the Islamic Conference (OIC Investment Agreement) is considered by some to provide for mandatory conciliation. But even this claim is subject to scrutiny. While Article 17(1) of the OIC Investment Agreement does allow for conciliation of investment disputes,[113] the subsequent provision that details the process of conciliation appears to apply only "[i]n case the parties to the dispute agree on conciliation."[114]

Nonetheless, the above provisions clarify that India's reluctance to embrace the requirement of mandatory conciliation is certainly not anomalous. Rather, it is consistent with the fact that mandatory conciliation in ISDS is yet to become a staple provision internationally.

[3] Other Third-Party Procedures

While India's approach toward mediation of investment disputes lacks uniformity, there is no similar concern regarding the possibility of mediating investment disputes. Across the three Phases, none of the 91 IITs analyzed provide an explicit recourse to mediation.

Again, using the word "explicit" is deliberate because some IITs, such as the India-BLEU BIT 1997, allow parties to seek "expert advice from a third party" as part of the requirement to engage in negotiations for amicable settlement.[115] Similarly, some IITs, such as the India-Korea Comprehensive Economic Partnership Agreement 2009, make generic references to "non-binding third party procedures."[116] While these provisions may potentially allow the parties to mediate investment disputes, their ambit remains unclear. Therefore, as was the case with conciliation, the authors do not construe such provisions as providing a clear recourse to mediation.

Even concerning mediation, India's approach is consistent with global practice. Recent studies indicate that while most investment treaties do not provide recourse to mediation, no investment treaty makes mediation mandatory.[117]

---

112. *Id.*, at Art. 8.
113. Agreement on Promotion, Protection and Guarantee of Investments among Member States of the Organisation of the Islamic Conference Art. 17(1), June 5, 1981.
114. *Id.*, at Art. 17(1).
115. Accord entre l'Union économique belgo-luxembourgeoise et le Gouvernement de la République de l'Inde concernant l'encouragement et la protection des investissements Art. 9(1), Belg.-India-Lux., Oct. 31, 1997.
116. Comprehensive Economic Partnership Agreement between the Government of the Republic of India and the Government of the Republic of Korea Art. 10.21(2), India-S. Kor., Aug. 7, 2009.
117. Catherine Kessedjian et al., *Mediation in Future Investor-State Dispute Settlement* (Acad. F. on ISDS Concept Paper No. 2020/16, 2020).

[C] Sub-conclusions

Given the above discussion, it is possible to derive a few conclusions.

Since signing its first BIT in 1994, India's consent to arbitrate in IITs is conditioned on the parties attempting to resolve their investment disputes through negotiations or consultations. While Article 9 of the 1997 India-France BIT remains an exception to this norm, no similar provision is found in India's subsequent investment treaties.

Across all three Phases, none of the IITs obligate the parties to mandatorily refer their investment dispute to mediation as a precondition for commencing arbitration. But most of the IITs provide an optional recourse to conciliation, either at the investor's discretion or with the consent of both parties. The IITs signed by India are not averse, at least in theory, to settle investment disputes through a conciliatory mechanism like mediation.

In the next segment, we examine whether this partial nod to conciliatory mechanisms in IITs has influenced India's ISDS experience and, if so, to what extent.

§9.04 NAVIGATING INDIA'S ISDS EXPERIENCE

[A] Investment Claims Against India

Considering all IITs (barring one) obligate the parties to engage in consultation/negotiation for an amicable settlement, and considering a majority of these also allow recourse to conciliation, one may cautiously expect a fair number of ISDS claims filed against India to have been settled amicably. To verify whether this expectation holds true, we examined the following 26 investment claims filed against India between 2003 and 2020 on the basis of the limited information that is available in the public domain. This includes each case where the investor sent a formal notice of the dispute to the Government of India, even if it did not ultimately result in the commencement of arbitration proceedings:

No.	*Particulars*	*Year*	*Treaty*	*Status*
1.	*Bechtel Enterprises Holdings, Inc. and GE Structured Finance v. The Government of India*	2003	India-Mauritius BIT 1998	Amicably Settled
2.	*Standard Chartered Bank v. Republic of India*	2004	India-United Kingdom BIT 1994	Amicably Settled
3.	*ANZEF Limited v. Republic of India*	2004	India-United Kingdom BIT 1994	Amicably Settled
4.	*BNP Paribas v. Republic of India*	2004	India-France BIT 1997	Amicably Settled

No.	*Particulars*	*Year*	*Treaty*	*Status*
5.	*Credit Lyonnais S.A. v. Republic of India*	2004	India-France BIT 1997	Amicably Settled
6.	*ABN Amro NV v. Republic of India*	2004	India-Netherlands BIT 1995	Amicably Settled
7.	*Offshore Power Production C.V., Travamark Two BV, EFS India-Energy B.V., Enron BV, and Indian Power Investments BV v. Republic of India*	2004	India-Netherlands BIT 1995	Amicably Settled
8.	*Credit Suisse First Boston v. Republic of India*	2004	India-Switzerland BIT 1997	Amicably Settled
9.	*Erste Bank Der Oesterreichischen Sparkassen AG v. Republic of India*	2004	India-Austria BIT 1999	Amicably Settled
10.	*White Industries Australia Limited v. Republic of India*	2010	India-Australia BIT 1999	Decided Against India
11.	*CC/Devas (Mauritius) Limited, Devas Employees Mauritius Private Limited, and Telecom Devas Mauritius Limited v. Republic of India* PCA Case No. 2013-09	2012	India-Mauritius BIT 1998	Decided Against India
12.	*Maxim Naumchenko, Andrey Poluektov, and Tenoch Holdings Limited v. Republic of India* PCA Case No. 2013-23	2012	India-Cyprus BIT 2002 India-Russia BIT 1994	Decided in Favor of India
13.	*Deutsche Telekom AG v. Republic of India* PCA Case No. 2014-10	2013	India-Germany BIT 1995	Decided Against India
14.	*Khaitan Holdings Mauritius Limited v. Republic of India* PCA Case No. 2018-50	2013	India-Mauritius BIT 1998	Pending
15.	*Louis Dreyfus Armateurs SAS v. Republic of India* PCA Case No. 2014-26	2014	India-France BIT 1997	Decided in Favor of India
16.	*Vodafone International Holdings BV v. Republic of India (I)* PCA Case No. 2016-35	2014	India-Netherlands BIT 1995	Decided Against India

No.	Particulars	Year	Treaty	Status
17.	*Cairn Energy PLC and Cairn UK Holdings Limited v. Republic of India* PCA Case No. 2016-7	2015	India-United Kingdom BIT 1994	Decided Against India
18.	*Astro and South Asia Entertainment v. Republic of India*	2016	India-United Kingdom BIT 1994 India-Mauritius BIT 1998	Discontinued by the Investor
19.	*Ras-Al-Khaimah Investment Authority v. Republic of India*	2016	India-UAE BIT 2013	Pending
20.	*Strategic Infrasol Foodstuff LLC and The Joint Venture of Thakur Family Trust, UAE with Ace Hospitality Management DMCC, UAE v. Republic of India*	2016	India-UAE BIT 2013	Pending
21.	*Vedanta Resources PLC v. Republic of India*	2016	India-United Kingdom BIT 1994	Pending
22.	*Carissa Investments LLC v. Republic of India*	2017	India-Mauritius BIT 1998	Pending
23.	*Nissan Motor Co., Limited v. Republic of India*	2017	India Japan CEPA 2011	Amicably Settled
24.	*Vodafone Group Plc and Vodafone Consolidated Holdings Limited v. Republic of India (II)*	2017	India-United Kingdom BIT 1994	Pending
25.	*Korea Western Power Co. v. Republic of India*	2019	India Korea BIT 1996 India-Korea CEPA 2009	Pending
26.	*GPIX LLC v. Republic of India*	2020	India-Mauritius BIT 1998	Pending

An analysis of these cases reveals some interesting findings. Out of the 26 cases analyzed, 18 cases have concluded, whereas 8 remain pending. Out of the 18 concluded cases, 10 cases were amicably settled, the investor discontinued 1 case, 5 cases resulted in an award against India, and 2 cases were decided in favor of India.

On the face of it, the above data evidences India's tendency to amicably settle investment disputes wherever considered possible. This inference is also consistent with the findings of the preceding section, which suggest that IITs either obligate or encourage the disputing parties to utilize conciliatory mechanisms to arrive at an amicable settlement. However, these inferences need to be viewed in the appropriate context.

First, 9 of the 18 concluded ISDS cases against India, i.e., serial numbers 1–9 in the above table, related to the Dabhol Power Project in Maharashtra, India. Although distinct entities initiated these cases under separate BITs, they nonetheless concerned the same underlying dispute. Therefore, the amicable settlement reached in these 9 distinct cases was essentially a result of only 1 investment dispute settlement.

If one construes these 9 cases as reflective of 1 comprehensive investment claim against India and correspondingly interprets the 18 concluded cases to denote a total of 10 investment disputes or claims, the results of the analysis paint a different picture. Out of the 10 concluded investment disputes or claims, only 2 claims (those relating to the Dabhol Power Project and *Nissan Motor Co., Limited v. Republic of India*) were amicably settled. The rest of the data remains the same; in as much as 1 investment claim was discontinued by the investor, 5 investment claims resulted in an award against India, and 2 investment claims were dismissed in favor of India.

These revised numbers are consistent with the global estimates, which indicate that "23% of all known cases (from 1987 to 2018) have settled and 10% have been discontinued."[118]

Second, it is questionable whether India or the investor relies on the specific provisions on negotiation/consultation or conciliation in IITs to arrive at an amicable settlement. The procedural history of several ISDS cases against India suggests the contrary. For instance, in *Deutsche Telekom AG v. Republic of India*, the investor had sent a notice of the dispute to the Prime Minister of India on May 15, 2012, indicating the existence of a treaty dispute. However, it only received a response on behalf of the Government of India on December 16, 2012, i.e., after more than six months, stating that the notice of dispute was premature.[119] This cycle was replicated in 2013,[120] but India did not express any willingness to engage in negotiations/consultations.

Similarly, in *Strategic Infrasol Foodstuff LLC and The Joint Venture of Thakur Family Trust, UAE with Ace Hospitality Management DMCC, UAE v. Republic of India*, it appears that the investor had sent a notice of the dispute to India under Article 10(4) of the 2013 India-UAE BIT, requesting to commence negotiations for amicable settlement.[121] However, it did not receive any response on behalf of India.[122] Likewise, the procedural history in *White Industries* reveals that although the investor had offered to meet with India to negotiate an amicable resolution on two separate occasions, it did not receive any response from India on either occasion.[123] It is also doubtful whether,

118. *Id.*
119. Deutsche Telekom AG v. Republic of India, PCA Case No. 2014-10, Interim Award, ¶95 (Dec. 13, 2017).
120. *Id.*, at ¶96.
121. Strategic Infrasol Foodstuff LLC and The Joint Venture of Thakur Fam. Tr., U.A.E. with Ace Hospitality Mgmt. DMCC, U.A.E. v. Republic of India, UNCITRAL Ad Hoc Tribunal, Notice of Arbitration, ¶56 (Oct. 8, 2015).
122. *Id.*, at ¶57.
123. White Indus. Austl. Ltd. v. Republic of India, *supra* note 97, ¶3.2.64.

barring the dispute underlying *Vodafone International Holdings BV v. Republic of India (I)*,[124] any of the remaining investment disputes were subjected to a conciliation process as envisaged by the various IITs.

Hence, although India has shown some proclivity to amicably settle the investment disputes raised by its investors, such attempts may not necessarily be following the specific provisions contained in IITs. Instead, these attempts may take the form of independent negotiations that occur in parallel to an arbitration proceeding.

[B] Political Impediments to Mediation in ISDS

The above discussion shows that active pursuit of amicable settlement in ISDS remains an anomalous proposition. While the precise reasons for this lack of proclivity to settle disputes may vary from case to case, it is not difficult to delineate certain general obstacles that inhibit the disputing parties, i.e., the State and the investor, from actively pursuing settlement through mediation.

A survey conducted by the NUS Centre for International Law between 2016 and 2018 revealed that the majority (70%) of participants believed that the State is more reluctant to settle disputes. Although the sample space of the survey was limited (97 participants; 47 respondents),[125] the findings are interesting to note, particularly because they align with a scholarly opinion on this issue.

As per the survey, the most common obstacle from the States' perspective is the desire to defer responsibility for decision-making to a third party on the ground that "[a] State might find it easier to sell" to parliament and public opinion the need to comply with a binding award, and hence "prefer to have an international tribunal tell it to pay."[126]

Another factor that emerges from the NUS Centre's survey is that States fear coming across as "weak or branded as puppets of foreign interests" if they are too amenable to settle without aggressively defending an arbitration claim.[127] As Michael Reisman points out, this may particularly be the case "in States in which active political oppositions are waiting for an opportunity to pounce on the incumbents for having 'betrayed' the national patrimony by settling with an investor, modalities other than transparent third-party decisions can undermine or even bring down governments."[128]

A third inhibiting factor brought out in the NUS Centre's survey is the "structure of the State, such as the existence of multiple stakeholders."[129] As mentioned, each of these factors has also been identified by scholars in academic writings.[130]

124. Remya Nair, *Vodafone Initiates Investment Arbitration Against India*, MINT (May 7, 2014).
125. Seraphina Chew, Lucy Reed & J. Christopher Thomas QC, *Report: Survey on Obstacles to Settlement of Investor-State Disputes*, NUS Centre for International Law Working Paper 18/01 (September 2018), 1.
126. *Id.*, at 13, 16.
127. *Id.*, at 17–18.
128. W. Michael Reisman, *International Investment Arbitration and ADR: Married but Best Living Apart*, 24 ICSID REV.—FOREIGN INV. L. J. 185, 191 (2009).
129. Chew, Reed & Thomas QC, *supra* note 125, at 15.
130. Coe, Jr., *supra* note 7, at 348.

It is difficult to confirm whether (and to what extent) these political and structural impediments inhibit India's proclivity to engage in amicable settlements with investors. Keeping this speculative exercise aside, the authors do consider these commonly identified impediments to be worth addressing.

It has been suggested that the inhibition stemming from internal governmental complexities, such as the involvement of multiple ministries or the lack of a united front, can be resolved by designating a centralized "lead agency" that has the "explicit mandate to negotiate a possible settlement with investors" either by itself or via third-party neutrals,[131] or has the mandate to provide a forum for investor-State discussions in general.

Concretizing these designations by appropriate legislation or in a treaty will help in the long run to ensure that mediation is perceived as a formalized dispute settlement process. For instance, the CETA creates a Committee on Services and Investment, which is a centralized agency whose mandate ranges from, among other things, "provid[ing] a forum for the [Contracting] Parties to consult on issues related to [the Investment] Chapter" to drafting the procedural rules for investor-State mediation.[132] The availability of such a treaty-based centralized agency, or a corresponding legislation-based domestic agency, will go a long way to quell political oppositions and untie the government officials' hands "regarding negotiating settlements with foreign investors" without appearing too weak to settle.[133]

From the side of the investor, the reluctance to mediate may be attributable, among other factors, to the lack of faith in the host State to negotiate in good faith and the ease of justifying decisions by authoritative third parties, such as arbitrators, to shareholders and others, as opposed to agreed-upon outcomes resulting from settlement. The investor-specific impediments may also be alleviated with the States taking concrete steps to make mediation more mainstream and formal. As Professor Jack Coe Jr. points out, "[m]ediation will not assume a significant role in the investor-State dispute process, unless States find virtue in the process sufficient to warrant the effort" to undertake steps that will give mediation the stamp of legitimacy.[134]

That said, it is also obvious that the propriety of mediation will vary from case to case and investor to investor. For instance, in a situation where the investor is inclined to continue its business activities in the host State, there is a greater desire on both sides to arrive at a settlement than in a situation where the investor is not so inclined either due to its investment having been expropriated or otherwise. As pointed out by the Cochairs of the IBA State Mediation Subcommittee, tasked with drafting the IBA Mediation Rules, one of the "often-expressed desire[s]" of disputing parties is "preserving the long-term link between the investor and the host state."[135] This is unsurprising since, at its very core, an investor's right to profit shares significant territorial overlap with a State's objective of economic growth. If the ultimate desire of

131. Constain, *supra* note 17, at 34.
132. CETA, *supra* note 32, at Arts. 8.20 and 8.44.
133. Constain, *supra* note 17, at 33–36.
134. Coe, Jr., *supra* note 7, at 354.
135. Legum et al., *supra* note 12, at 265–266.

the disputing parties is to maintain or indeed improve the relationship between the investor and the host State, mediation "holds great [*sic*] potential."[136]

§9.05 CONCLUDING REMARKS

India has had a checkered relationship with the mediation of investor-State disputes. While it has settled at least two disputes amicably with investors, it has not taken any concrete steps toward formalizing the avenue for mediation. None of India's IITs mandate mediation or conciliation as a precursor to arbitration. Likewise, India has not shown any inclination to adopt any other procedures that would alleviate the investors' hesitation or the internal political hurdles in the pursuit of mediation.

Taking steps to make mediation more accessible, for instance, by legislatively authorizing a lead agency to negotiate settlements with investors, will be beneficial, not the least, because it may serve to reduce the time and cost burden of investor-State arbitrations, of which India has seen many.

India's relationship with ISDS mediation is by no means exceptional. The ISDS fraternity, in general, is still in the process of recognizing mediation as a legitimate alternative to arbitration. In this regard, in 2020, a large obstacle pertaining to the lack of a legal framework for the enforcement of settlement agreements has been crossed with the entry into force of the Singapore Convention. This, in all likelihood, also holds true for ISDS mediation. The UNCITRAL's Working Group on ISDS reform clarified recently that the applicability of the Singapore Convention could be "tailor[ed] … in a flexible manner, including in the context of [ISDS],"[137] unless, of course, States specifically restrict the applicability of the Singapore Convention in this regard by way of a declaration (as has been done by Iran, Belarus and Saudi Arabia).

Other impediments often cited by stakeholders and scholars may occasionally be overstated in that they are reflective more of subliminal insecurities than of legal hurdles. For instance, the ease with which developing countries in Africa or elsewhere have successfully resolved disputes through conciliation belies the claim that dispute resolution mechanisms such as mediation and conciliation suffer at the hand of the lack of interministerial or intra-ministerial structures in governments. Similarly, investors' disinclination to mediate disputes with States may ultimately boil down to their state of mind and perception of mediation as a dispute resolution mechanism.

Overall, now that the Singapore Convention has entered into force, if the ISDS fraternity, including arbitration institutions, concentrates on spreading awareness of mediation while enabling certain necessary organizational adjustments on a case-by-case basis, a solid foundation can be laid to foster and protect the credibility of ISDS mediation.

---

136. Coe, Jr., *supra* note 7, at 347.

137. U.N. Comm. on Int'l Trade L., *Summary of the intersessional regional meeting on investor-State dispute settlement reform submitted by the Government of the Dominican Republic*, at ¶ 54, A/CN.9/WG.III/WP.160 (Feb. 27, 2019).

CHAPTER 10

Mediating Family Disputes

A.J. Jawad & Nisshant Laroia

§10.01 INTRODUCTORY REMARKS

All matters relating to or arising from a family relationship fall under India's ken of family law. This includes marriage, divorce, restitution of conjugal rights, custody of children, alimony and maintenance, division of assets, succession and inheritance, the partition of property, and so on. Among these areas, a significant segment of family disputes pertains to or arise from marriage or matrimony—a personal relationship that forms the building block of society. This chapter's primary focus is exactly that; we are concerned with the subject matters that fall in the purview of a family court's jurisdiction.[1] Thus, other loose forms of family disputes that manifest as disputes within a Hindu Undivided Family, business disputes among family members, a conflict between siblings, etc., are not the central theme of this chapter (though one may practically apply to them the principles of family mediation discussed herein).

When addressing this theme of mediating family disputes, a broad categorization is necessary to grasp the avenues in which such mediations take place vis-à-vis family disputes (though the principled approach may be universally applicable). The first, of course, is the mediation of family disputes in private settings, which is possible in all matters, except those that would either require a decretal status (like divorce) or concern familial relations, freedom, or personal liberty and lives (like restitution of conjugal rights, or family disputes in the vague sense). But for such disputes, as well as family disputes of the "general" sense (like conflicts between siblings, or among parents and children, etc.), private mediation may still be considered a means of repairing relationships, reinstating harmony, etc., though not necessarily a means of achieving an enforceable settlement (i.e., as a contract simpliciter, or an award on

1. Family Courts Act, 1984, § 7 (jurisdiction of family courts).

agreed terms in case of conciliation). In cases like divorce by mutual consent, the mediated settlement will be required to file a joint petition for divorce before a family court,[2] wherein the settlement may contain parties' agreement on important issues relating to child custody, alimony and maintenance, property and assets, and the like.

Court-annexed mediation (referrals from the family court under section 89 of the Code of Civil Procedure or CPC) is another avenue where family disputes may be resolved through amicable means.[3] But, at the same time, parties may decide to mediate aspects of their dispute parallelly, without a specific referral of the family court. In which case, if parties can arrive at a settlement, the same may be presented before the court. Having said that, such avenues are rather seldom utilized by family courts, due to either the nonexistence of court-annexed mediation centers in family courts or the existence of special provisions for counselors in family courts. Speaking of which, the counselors are yet another avenue of mediation of family disputes, who can employ conciliatory tools and techniques (as an impartial third party) to assist parties in resolving their conflicts.

This chapter nudges all the avenues mentioned above in discussing the theme of mediating family disputes, starting with understanding the sociocultural aspects in Indian marriages (as matrimonial conflicts constitute the most significant chunk of family disputes). We then dive into the Family Courts Act (FCA), 1984, to understand the procedures adopted by family courts, the role of counselors, and the possibility of settlements through counselors and proactive family courts. This is followed by identifying the drawbacks of litigating family disputes and the deficiencies in family courts that render adversarial modes often deleterious, given the nature of family conflict and the parties' needs and interests. Then, the chapter leads into a discourse on private avenues for mediation with the specific example of the Delhi Dispute Resolution Society (DDRS) (which also sets an example of pre-institution mediation in divorce matters by mutual consent). Lastly, the chapter gives coverage of the style of mediation and the relevant skills well suited for family disputes.

§10.02 SOCIOCULTURAL ASPECTS IN INDIAN MARRIAGES

In India, marriage is a complex institution and has a different perspective in different religions and cultures. Its concept, the rituals performed during the ceremony, and relational dynamics, are all governed by factors like religion, customs, traditions, and social mores. And in a society composed of myriad cultures, languages, and traditions, it would be impractical and arbitrary to deal with all of them with the same bracket and ignore its diversity. Hence, in order to grasp the gamut of issues that arise in family

2. *See*, e.g., Hindu Marriage Act, 1976, §13B(1) (a petition for dissolution of marriage by a decree of divorce may be presented to the district court by both the parties to a marriage together).
3. Family Courts Act, 1984, § 10 (the provisions of the Code of Civil Procedure, 1908 shall apply to the suits and proceedings before a family court, and for the purposes of the said provisions of the Code, a family court shall be deemed to be a civil court and shall have all the powers of such court).

disputes (particularly, matrimonial), it is necessary that mediators, conciliators, counselors, etc., consider marriage from the perspective of religion, culture, and socioeconomic considerations.

For instance, there are some overarching similarities notwithstanding the fundamental differences between marriages under different religious beliefs. One such commonality is the ubiquitous joint family. Though the joint family concept is a characteristic of the Hindu society, other communities follow it in the general sense, and it is, therefore, common to find two or even three generations of a family living together in a common, shared household (usually, on some ancestral property).

With the change in socioeconomic circumstances, joint family households are in decline while somehow continuing to have the hierarchical structure seen within a joint family. Though children marry and move out to their own home, the authority of the elders in the family continues to influence to a large extent. Hence, one can say that even in modern India, a large percentage of marriages are still arranged (and is strongly believed in).

Dowry, similarly, has a pervading impact on the community in general, whether Hindu or not. It is a payment made in cash and/or in-kind by the bride's family to the groom's family at the time of the marriage. It has its foundation in the traditional upper caste practices of *Kanyadhan* and *Stridhan*.[4] *Stridhan* was a sort of premortem inheritance given by the bride's family to their daughter since she would not be entitled to inherit the family estate.[5]

Stridhan may also have been a sort of compensation to the groom's family for bringing the bride into their family since an orthodox view was that women had little or no role in the market economy and were dependent upon their husbands and in-laws.[6] Unfortunately, what was originally conceived as a mode of overcoming the succession barrier (*Stridhan* also being considered as the father's fair assessment of his daughter's share in his property, which was gifted to her at the time of the marriage) has now transformed into a symbol of status even though personal laws now entitle daughters inheritance. Hence, disagreement (or perceived noncompliance) affects the families' honor and is a potential source of long-drawn conflicts between the spouses and their respective families. In the context of family disputes, this is a classic breeding ground for a host of conflicts, grudges, and grievances that are often ignored/avoided in the excitement of marriage but reappear with much contempt.

Overall, there are three aspects of Indian sociocultural and marriage systems, which give us an essential understanding that is directly or indirectly relevant to family conflicts.[7]

First, that there is a strict regulation on sexual relationships outside marriage. A person who indulges in premarital sex is considered to bring shame to the family and

---

4. *See* Padma Srinivasan & Gary Lee, *The Dowry System in Northern India: Women's Attitudes and Social Change*, 66 J. MARRIAGE & FAMILY 1108–1117 (2004) (that dowry has strong roots in tradition).
5. *See id.*
6. *Id.*
7. *See* Premchand Dommaraju, *Divorce and Separation in India*, 42(2) POPULATION & DEV. REV. 195–223 (2016).

corrupt her caste's purity and sanctity. The infamous *Khap Panchayats*, for instance, are those extrajudicial caste councils (with no official government recognition or authority) that intervene in situations where there is a (perceived) transgression of caste and cultural norms called *Parampara* (tradition) and *Maryadha* (modesty, dignity, limit) of the clan or the caste and hand down punishments like fines, social ostracism, public humiliation, and expulsion from the village.

Second, in general, parents (and the family) play an essential role in spouse selection since marriage is seen as affecting the status of the family and lineage. And even though its degree has declined in the present times with increasing autonomy among the people, a considerable weight continues to be given to caste and class norms.

The *third* is the issue of remarriages. While remarriages are not uncommon, remarriage of a woman societally conferred a lower status than the remarriage of a man. Interestingly, these traditions and customs trace their origin to the *Vedic* era. And the shared cultural history of the subcontinent has resulted in these traditions and customs permeating through all the other communities and groups in India.

§10.03 FAMILY COURTS ACT 1984

[A] Background

In its 54th Report in 1973, the Law Commission of India had strongly recommended the need for special handling of matters pertaining to divorce. Again, in its 59th Report, the Law Commission stressed that in dealing with family disputes, the courts ought to adopt an approach radically different from that adopted in ordinary civil proceedings and that it should make reasonable efforts for settlement before the commencement of trial.

Consequent to these recommendations of the Law Commission, Order XXXII-A was incorporated in the CPC 1908 by way of an amendment in 1976. It codified a different approach where matters concerned the family, including the need to bring about an amicable settlement. It provided a special procedure to be adopted in suits or proceedings concerning the family.

However, the FCA 1984 shifted the paradigm in the resolution of family disputes, which were treated at par with other civil and commercial courts. It provided for establishing family courts intending to promote conciliation and secure speedy settlement of disputes relating to marriage and family affairs and for matters connected therewith by adopting an approach radically different from that adopted in ordinary civil proceedings. One such fine distinction is the elimination of rigid rules of procedure and the involvement of gender sensitized personnel, including judges, social workers, counselors, and other trained staff, who are expected to induce a conciliatory approach between the parties to a family dispute.

The functioning of family courts under the FCA is heavily governed by the rules framed by the respective High Courts, State Governments, and the Central Government.[8] These rules enable family courts to carry out the purposes of the FCA, e.g., the Delhi Family Court Rules 1996 (amended in 2011), or the High Court of Andhra Pradesh Family Courts (Court) Rules, 2005. Among the two, the latter is more extensive in its coverage of processes and procedures.

[B] Jurisdiction

Under section 7 of the FCA, family courts have the jurisdiction exercisable by any district court or any subordinate civil court in suits and proceedings of the nature dealt with in Explanation to section 7(1). Accordingly, the following subjects come under the purview of the FCA:

- Decree for nullity of marriage.
- Restitution of conjugal rights.
- Judicial separation.
- Dissolution of marriage.
- Declaration of the matrimonial status of any person.
- Matrimonial property matters.
- Claim of maintenance.
- Guardianship.
- Custody of children.
- Access to children.
- Application for an injunction in matrimonial matters.
- Custody of children, guardianship, legitimacy of a child under the Hindu Minority and Guardianship Act, 1956.

These are essentially all the subject matters that constitute "family disputes," in which regard a mediated or conciliated settlement is possible under the overarching framework of a family court or the FCA. In this regard, the Supreme Court has emphasized the need for mediation (as well as directed the setting up of mediation help desks):[9]

> In terms of Section 9 of the Family Courts Act, the Family Courts shall make all efforts to settle the matrimonial disputes through mediation. Even if the Counsellors submit a failure report, the Family Courts shall, with the consent of the parties, refer the matter to the mediation centre. In such a case, however, the Family Courts shall set a reasonable time limit for mediation centres to complete the process of mediation because otherwise the resolution of the disputes by the

8. Family Courts Act, 1984, §§ 21–23.
9. *See* K. Srinivas Rao v. D. A. Deepa (2013) 5 SCC 226 (court expressed the need to use mediation, which could have avoided the escalation of the dispute and things would not have been ugly. If the parties could have taken the help of a neutral person to understand the dispute better, they could have arrived at an amicable solution. Court also held that dowry cases being noncompoundable offenses can also be referred for mediation).

Family Court get delayed. In a given case, if there is good chance of settlement, the Family Court in its discretion, can always extend the time limit.

But, in all such cases before the family courts, nothing stops parties from trying mediation in parallel, with, without (or in addition to) a court referral to mediation or a counselor. The terms of the agreement may then be presented before the court to be converted into a decree. Here lies the great advantage of private mediation for family disputes before family courts.

As mentioned earlier, the same subject matters may be well suited for private mediation (or conciliation under the Arbitration and Conciliation Act 1996), except where a settlement would not legally necessitate a decretal status (like in the case of divorce, which requires a judicial recognition), or where the nature of dispute does not relate familial relations, freedom, or personal liberty and lives (such restitution of conjugal rights).

Hence, it is possible that the spectrum of mediatable family disputes can be perceived widely with the inclusion of family disputes in the loose sense (such as conflicts between spouses, siblings, and with parents) which by nature involve familial relations, freedom, or personal liberty and lives of the parties. However, in such cases, mediation may be considered a means of healing a conflict, not one that necessarily results in an enforceable settlement (as either a contract simpliciter or an award on agreed terms in case of conciliation). While no case laws contain a discourse on these issues, the authors posit such a standard given the public policy issues involved in matters where the nature of dispute concerns familial relations, freedom, or personal liberty and lives.[10] Further, such disputes can also be those that require a decretal status of the court, as in the case of divorce or restitution of conjugal rights.

But when considering mediatable family disputes that are (by nature) transactional, like disputes relating to the division of property or maintenance or alimony issues, a mediated settlement may be considered an enforceable one (as either a contract simpliciter or an award on agreed terms in case of conciliation)[11] whether before, during, or after family court proceedings.[12]

10. *See*, e.g., Sundar Sahu Gountia v. Chamra Sahu Gountia, AIR 1954 Ori 80 (an agreement calculated to prevent a person from enjoying a fundamental right and which compels him not seek redress in a court of law is bad and unlawful); Annie Besant v. G Narayaniah, AIR 1914 PC 41 (a guardianship being sacred, trust, he cannot, during his lifetime, substitute another to be the guardian. He may, in his discretion as a guardian, entrust the custody and education of his children to another. But the authority is essentially a revocable one and if the welfare of the children requires it, he can take such custody and education in his own hands notwithstanding any contract to the contrary. The court's decision shows how far the agreement acted upon will be enforced); Victor Justin Walter v. Marie Josephine Walter, AIR 1928 Cal 600 (an agreement by the father to give up entirely the custody and control of his child to the mother was held void); Mohinder Singh v. Ravneet Kaur, AIR 2007 P&H 49 (parents cannot by agreement between themselves take away rights of minor children to maintenance).
11. Arbitration and Conciliation Act, 1996, § 74. For a detailed discussion, *see* Chapter on the Law of Conciliation. There is no commercial reservation as such that is applicable in case of domestic conciliations, i.e., conciliation between two domestic parties.
12. *See*, e.g., Muniammal v. Raja, AIR 1978 Mad 103, 108 (an agreement by a wife in consideration of a lump sum payment not to claim maintenance from the husband is not opposed to public policy); Vemuru Venkata Krishnayya v. Vemuru Lakshmamma, AIR 1944 Mad 17 (a contract by

There are also several family-related matters that fall outside the scope of a family court's jurisdiction, such as the following, principally because they do not arise out of a matrimonial relationship; in which cases, the possibility of mediation (privately or under the purview of the court) would have to be considered on the anvil of the substantive laws, procedures, and policy considerations.

Hence, family courts exercise a vital jurisdiction in the entire court system in India, one that concerns and impacts the culture, social institutions, and social development.[13] At its core, family disputes are, after all, unlike any other dispute, necessitating a unique address, given the existence of factors like "motivation, sentiments, social compulsion, personal liabilities, and responsibilities of the parties, the view of two parties regarding life in general and to the institution of marriage in particular, the security of the future life, so on and so forth."[14]

In this, the prominent role of family courts is to discover a solution instead of breaking the family relations.[15] It is the mandate of the law (as also the social obligation of a judge of the family court) to make an earnest attempt for reconciliation, using counseling and conciliation as a method of achieving the ultimate object of the FCA—the preservation of the family.[16]

[C] Procedure

Chapter IV of the FCA deals with the procedure to be followed by family courts in deciding cases before it. Section 9 mandates that in every action before it, the courts shall endeavor in the first instance, where it is possible to do considering the nature and circumstances of the case, assist and persuade the parties to arrive at a settlement in respect of the subject matter of the suit action. For this purpose, a family court may,

---

a wife to suspend the operation of her maintenance decree for some time to give opportunity to her husband to prove his willingness to maintain her properly was considered valid in law); A E Thirumal Naidu v. Rajammal, AIR 1968 Mad 201 (a postnuptial agreement of separation between the husband and wife, providing for maintenance of wife, was not considered opposed to public policy or the principles of Hindu law); Gogineni Subbayya v. Goggineni Govindamma, AIR 1945 Mad 36 (court held valid an agreement made on their reconcilIation after separation, if it contemplates a future separation and a promise for maintenance in that event); Narayan v. Laxman, AIR 1925 Nag 111 (the husband entering into an agreement for the return of the expenses spent in the marriage, upon his consenting to divorce the wife, is not void). *See also*, Ranjit Kaur v. Pavittar Singh, 1992 Cri LK 262 (an agreement by which the wife surrenders her right to maintenance may not per se be illegal but it cannot be given effect to as it negates the statutory right conferred under section 125 of the Code of Criminal Procedure, 1973).

13. *See generally*, International Federation for Family Development, *The Crucial Role of Families* (NGO in Special Consultative Status with ECOSOC), https://www.un.org/ecosoc/sites/www.un.org.ecosoc/files/files/en/integration/2017/IFFD.pdf.
14. *See* Smt. Hina Singh v. Satya Kumar Singh, AIR 2007 Jhar 34, ¶ 16 (that matrimonial disputes are distinct from other types of disputes on account of presence of certain factors which are not found in other disputes).
15. *See id.*
16. *See* Jagraj Singh v. Birpal Kaur, AIR 2007 SC 2083. *See also*, Government of India, *Report of the Committee on the Empower of Women on Functioning of Family Courts* (Parliament, 2001) (the basic concept of family courts emerged from the convictions that the family being a social institution, disputes connected with family breakdown, divorce, maintenance, custody of children, etc., need to be viewed from the social rather than legal perspective).

subject to any rules made by the High Court, follow such procedure as it may deem fit (including adjourning the proceedings until the settlement is reached).[17] In this regard, in *Gurubachan Kaur v. Preetam Singh*,[18] the Allahabad High Court has held that:

> 9. [...] A duty has been imposed under Section 9 of the Family Courts Act to make all possible endeavour [...]. [...] Family Courts should work in a spirit of dedication to settle the matter by negotiation and all possible methods of persuasion so that the marriage may be preserved. [...] [Petitions before the Family Court] should not turn into an ordinary civil court as seen by us while sitting in this jurisdiction and dispose of the matter as expeditiously as possible and adjournments should be restricted. The proceedings must be held in camera and the advantage of provisions of Family Court Act be taken fully with respect to the association of social welfare agencies.

Section 10 of the FCA deals with the procedure to be followed by family courts, empowering the courts to lay down its own procedure "with a view to arriving at a settlement in respect of the subject-matter of the suit or proceedings or at the truth of the facts alleged by the one party and denied by the other." These provisions make it incumbent upon family courts to see that the parties are assisted and persuaded to come to a settlement, for which family courts may employ appropriate settlement procedures.

Section 13 of FCA also dispenses with the appearance of Advocates, giving parties the platform to directly represent themselves. In practice, however, there are obvious concerns with such exclusion of Advocates, who as "mediation lawyers" can assist family courts to achieve their goal and purpose under the FCA. Without the Advocates, there may be circumstances where litigants are left to the mercy of court clerks to help them. The court can nevertheless allow Advocates on either side to appear only as amicus curiae if it is considered necessary in the interest of justice.

It also seems possible for a party before family courts to file a petition seeking permission of the court to engage an Advocate for legal assistance, which the court may or may not allow. Where it so allowed, the Advocate would be required to file his *Vakalatnama* and do all that is necessary for his client in the conduct of that case.[19] But if the court concludes that an Advocate is a cause of some obstruction, the court can immediately cancel the *Vakalatnama* and follow the mandate of the legislature rather than prolonging the matrimonial dispute and its agony.[20]

In the conduct of proceedings under the FCA, family courts (under section 14 of the FCA) may receive as evidence any report, statement, documents, information, or matter for its opinion and assist it in dealing effectually with a dispute, whether or not

17. *See* Family Courts Act, 1984, § 10(3).
18. AIR 1998 All 140. *See also*, Hindu Marriage Act, 1955, § 23(2) (mandating court to attempt reconciliation between the parties); Code Civ. Proc., Order XXXII-A, rule 3.
19. *See* S Venkataraman v. L Vijayasarathan (1996) SCC OnLine Mad 408; *See also*, Komal S Padukone v. Principal Judge, Family Court, Bangalore, AIR 1999 Kar 427 (if one side has been permitted to be represented by an Advocate, the family court should not refuse permission to the other side to be represented by an Advocate).
20. Gurubachan Kaur v. Preetam Singh, AIR 1998 All 140, ¶ 18 (the time spent cannot be regained or recalled and youth can be restored; hence, the court should also keep in mind the settlement of the parties by negotiation).

the same would be otherwise relevant or admissible under the Indian Evidence Act, 1872. This gives family courts a wide field in deciding family disputes, which is why it would not be proper for a judge of a family court to leave every filing in the hands of the parties who may not be conversant with the court's procedures or the evidentiary requirements and standards.[21] A family court may also call witnesses (including grown-up children) to understand the nature of the dispute and encourage reconciliation between the parties.[22] All in all, the rigor of the Indian Evidence Act 1872 is not applicable in the acceptance or admissibility of evidence by family courts.[23]

Though the FCA has transformed the landscape of resolution of family disputes in courts, its adversarial nature has primarily endured, particularly when one considers the fault-based grounds of divorce under applicable substantive laws (which usually ends up in a full-fledged trial). After all, the FCA is not a self-contained Act; it has to be read along with other applicable substantive laws. This, the authors think, will inevitably lead to a dilution of the very objective of family courts, exacerbating the tensions and obviating possibilities of reconciliation. At the end of it, parties can potentially lose their control over the trajectory of the dispute resolution process.

[D] Decree

As per section 18 of the FCA, a decree or an order of the family court has the same force and effect as a decree or an order of the civil court, which is executable in the same manner as is prescribed under CPC. And an order passed by the family court under Chapter IX of the Code of Criminal Procedure 1973 is executable in the manner prescribed for executing such order by said Code. In either case, a decree or an order may be executed either by the same family court which passed it or by another family court or an ordinary civil court, to which it is sent for execution.

Under section 19 of the FCA, an appeal shall lie from every judgment or an order of a family court to the High Court both on facts and on law, except in case of interlocutory orders. Importantly, however, no appeal lies where the family court has passed a decree or an order with the parties' consent (a decree on agreed terms). Such terms may arrive through several ways as envisaged in this chapter: a pre-institution mediated settlement that is submitted before the family court by way of a joint petition (as in the case of divorce by mutual consent); parallel private mediation while the dispute is before the family court; a referral under section 89 of the CPC (which includes mediation, conciliation, judicial settlement, and arbitration); or through the conciliatory efforts of the counselor.

21. *See* Manohar Lal Agrawal v. Santosh & Ors, MANU/RH/0162/1993.
22. *See id.*
23. *See* Narayana Roy v. Jamuna Dey (Roy), AIR 2010 Gau 75.

[E] Counseling

Under section 6, the State Government, in consultation with the High Court, must provide counselors to assist family courts in discharging its functions. Family courts often have counseling centers attached to them, with each center impaneling several counselors as determined by the High Court.[24]

Counseling is foundational to the whole structure and procedure of family courts. In fact, in selecting persons for appointment as judges, the FCA expressly states under section 4(4) that "every endeavor shall be made to ensure that persons committed to the need to protect and preserve the institution of marriage and to promote the welfare of children and qualified by reason of their experience and expertise to promote the settlement of disputes by conciliation and counseling are selected."

In the authors' view, the role of counselors should not only be understood as limited to counseling but also considered to extend to employing mediation/conciliation and encouraging mutual settlement between the parties (wherever feasible). In family disputes, counseling and conciliation can have a synergy that can have a "bridging effect" on the parties and create opportunities for the parties to arrive at a settlement. This is also why a judge of a family court is expected to have such experience and expertise, so he too may proactively do counseling or conciliation when he considers it appropriate, or where counseling (by a court-appoint counselor) has failed at the initial stages. In practice, judges may shy away from personally counseling the parties when the case has come up for a trial or because none of the family court rules provide for judges employing counseling or conciliation.

Counselors play an essential role in resolving family disputes under the FCA, making their selections, qualifications, continuing training, etc., of significance in the administration of justice in the family courts. From time to time, family courts call upon the assistance of counselors by referring the dispute to them[25] or by requiring the counselors to submit a report that would assist the court in its decision-making or its conciliatory efforts. Presently, there are no uniform rules as to what procedures have to be adopted by a family court judge (or by the counselors) when dealing with family disputes.

Generally, counselors may fix appointments with the parties, requiring them to attend.[26] If either of the parties fails to attend on that date, the counselor may fix another date. But if the default continues, the counselor may submit a report to the family court for the court's consideration. Where parties attend the counselor's invitation, the counselor may assist and advise the parties about settlement and/or apply conciliatory techniques.[27] Again, there is conspicuous silence in the rules, the FCA, and case law on how counselors should be expected to conduct the conciliation

24. *See*, e.g., Delhi Family Court Rules, 1996, rules 9–11 (on counseling centers, appointment of counselors, and qualifications of counselors).
25. *See* Leela Mahadeo Joshi v. Mahadeo Sitaram Joshi (1990) Mah LJ 1267 ("Provisions regarding reference to Counsellor does not mean that parties must be forced against their wishes or interest to patch up a marriage which cannot be mended").
26. *See*, e.g., High Court of Andhra Pradesh Family Courts (Court) Rules, 2005, rule 18.
27. *See id.*

and achieve a settlement between the parties.[28] There is also no uniformity or consistency in the rules passed by various States regarding how counselors and judges are to conciliate. This induces an undesirable ad hoc-ism that runs counter to the object and purpose of the FCA.

Nevertheless, there can be a straightforward extension of the principle of Part III of the Arbitration and Conciliation Act 1996 in the settlement efforts of either the family court or the counselor. Another source of inspiration may benefit from Lok Adalats, which principles have been laid down by the Supreme Court in *B P Moideen Sevamandir v. A M Kutty Hassan.*[29] In this case, the apex court laid down the principles to be borne in mind by members of the Lok Adalat in the absence of rules. The court first equated and then extended the understanding of conciliations under the Arbitration & Conciliation Act, 1996, to the functioning of the Lok Adalat.[30] On this basis, Daniel Mathew may be credited for synthesizing six principles that family courts and counselors must adopt when attempting settlement:[31]

> 1. [They] should assist the parties in an independent and impartial manner to reach an amicable settlement of their dispute;
> 2. [They should] be guided by the principles of objectivity, fairness and justice, giving due consideration to, among other things, the rights and obligations of the parties and the circumstances surrounding the dispute, while assisting the parties;
> 3. [If they are] of the opinion that a settlement seems unlikely, at any stage of the proceedings [they] may suggest plausible areas/issues of agreement and encourage discussions on settlement. Such suggestions need not be in writing and need not be accompanied by a statement of the reasons;
> 4. [As] regards matters discussed during attempts of settlement, they cannot be relied upon or used as evidence in any adversarial proceeding before the family court. This would in particular extend to view and suggestions expressed by a party as regards a possible settlement, admissions made by any party, proposals made by the counsellor or judge of the family court as the case may be, and sentiments expressed by any party as regards these proposals;
> 5. At no point of time should any pressure, threat, force, or coercion be visited on the litigant to settlement their dispute against their wishes;
> 6. [They] must clearly desist from finding fault with a particular litigant if the matter is not conciliated, so as not to prejudice themselves when they adjudicate the matter. In such an instance what happened during conciliation or parties' behaviour during conciliation would become completely irrelevant.
>
> (internal citations omitted)

Where the parties have arrived at a settlement before the counselor relating to the dispute or any part thereof, such settlement is required to be reduced in writing, read

28. *See* FLAVIA AGNES II, MARRIAGE, DIVORCE AND MATRIMONIAL LITIGATION 300 (2011) (hereinafter "AGNES") (the author notes that initially there was no clarity in the counselor's role, which led a widespread disparity in the assumption of a counselor's role).
29. (2009) 2 SCC 198.
30. *Id.*, at ¶ 11.
31. Daniel Mathew, *Arriving at a Settlement under Family Courts Act, 1984: Deconstructing the Role of the Judge of the Family Court and Counsellor*, 56(3) J. INDIAN L. INSTITUTE 376, 383 (2014).

over and explained to the parties, signed by the parties, countersigned by the counselor, and filed before the family court.[32]

In the discharge of his duties, a counselor may also decide to visit parties at their home or interview their relatives, friends, and acquaintances to better under their conflict. In the discharge of their duties, counselors may also assist an organization, institution, or agency. The counselor's report may contain observations about the living conditions/environment of the parties, their personalities, nature of relationships, income and standard of living, educational status of the parties, status in society, etc.[33] Often, the counselor's report notes the reason for the failure of conciliation and the party responsible for it.[34] Generally, however, the information gathered by the counselor, any statement made before the counselor, or any notes or report prepared by the counselor, is treated as confidential.[35] Accordingly, a counselor cannot be called upon to disclose the information statements, notes, or report to any court,[36] except with the consent of both the parties or to the extent it is needed in the court's efforts to arrive at a settlement.[37]

But even though section 6 of the FCA provides for the assistance of counselors to courts, the counseling process has unfortunately not received adequate regard. There is a paucity of literature on counseling and training for counselors (particularly marriage counselors) in counseling and conciliation. Further, a notable survey among marriage counselors revealed that while the counselors considered individual factors, relational factors, as well as the family and socioeconomic influences, counselors did not seem to be exploring other factors such as religious differences, violence, abuse, and dowry, which are frequent in divorce actions.[38] There were significant differences

32. *See*, e.g., High Court of Andhra Pradesh Family Courts (Court) Rules, 2005, rule 23.
33. *See id.*, at rule 18.
34. *See* Durga Prasanna Tripathy v. Arundhati Tripathy, AIR 2005 SC 3297 (the report was not only made available but was referred to in detail by the appellate courts. The court then attempted to adjudicate the matter on merit in view of relevant applicable law).
35. *Id.*, at rule 20 (such notes of report or statements or any material lying with the counselor shall be kept in sealed cover by the counselor and shall not form a part of evidence before the court but form part of record. If the case is reported in the journals, the information can be used for research or education after obtaining permission from the High Court).
36. *Id.*, at rule 20 (the counselor shall not be permitted to give evidence in any court in respect of the information, statements, notes, or report. Provided that the counselor shall submit to the court a report relating to the home environment of the parties concerned their personalities and their relationship with the child or children in order to assist the court in deciding the question of custody, guardianship of the child or children of the marriage, and provided further that the counselor shall submit to the court a report relating to home environment income, standard of living of the party or parties concerned in order to assist the court in determining the amount of maintenance or alimony to be granted to one of the parties).
37. *Id.*, at rule 26 (court may call for report as regards efforts made). *See* Perry Kansagra v. Smriti Madan Kansagra (2019) 20 SCC 753 (where the scope of mediation is the solution of a child parenting issue, report by a mediator or a child counselor concerning the behavior and attitude of the child would not fall within the bar of confidentiality for the reason no information shared by the couple is being brought on record. The mandate of section 12 of the Family Courts Act, 1984 cannot be lost sight of).
38. *See* Chetna Duggal, Sujata Sriram & Kriti Jain, *Marriage Counsellors' Reflections on the Counselling Process in Family Courts in India*, 63(4) PSYCHOLOGICAL STUDIES 365 (2018) (the present study used an exploratory research design to understand marriage counselors' perspectives on the process of counseling in family courts. Fifty-six marriage counselors completed

in assessing factors, which foster diversity in perspectives, risk a lack of uniformity or universal standard in counseling. It has also been observed that some family courts have not sufficient counselors or that the counselors kept on frequently changing.[39] In many cases, the counselors join on a part-time basis or are not adequately trained in counseling or conciliation methods.[40]

§10.04 DRAWBACKS OF LITIGATING FAMILY DISPUTES

Litigating family disputes (i.e., before family courts) exasperates the conflict and vexes parties with high cost, mental distress, and physical affliction of the parties involved (including the children, who are likely to be most affected by the growing acrimony in family relationships). And it is often the case that the adversarial system forces parties off the edge, complicating the conflict to the point of no return. For instance, the peculiarity among all divorce laws in India is that marriages can be dissolved only on fault-based grounds, except for dissolution of the marriage by mutual consent[41] or irretrievable breakdown of marriage,[42] existing under the Hindu Marriages Act 1955

open-ended questionnaires on counseling assessment, goals, interventions, and the influence of the presence of children on the couple counseling process. Findings suggested that there was a lack of uniformity in the counseling approaches used by marriage counselors. Additionally, marriage counselors reported not being equipped to address some intrapersonal and interpersonal concerns that emerged in the counseling process, despite identifying them. Based on the findings, the paper recommends the need for a unifying framework for training and practice for marriage counselors working with couples in family courts to conceptualize couples' concerns as well as guide their goals and interventions. The paper underscores the need for acknowledging sociocultural influences, reflective practice, and client feedback in the process of counseling).

39. *See* Namita Singh Jamwal, *Have Family Courts Lived up to Expectations?*, Mainstream (Vol XLVII No. 12, Mar. 7, 2009), https://www.mainstreamweekly.net/article1205.html.
40. *See* Agnes, *supra* note 28, at pp. 299–305 (for a critical appraisal of the working of counselors in different States).
41. *See* Smt. Sureshta Devi v. Om Prakash (1991) 2 SCC 25 (the court explained the grounds for dissolution of marriage, in that: (i) parties have been living separately for a period of one year immediately preceding the petition; (ii) parties have not been able to live together and irreconcilable; and (iii) parties have mutually agreed that the marriage should be dissolved).
42. *See* Paras Diwan, Hindu Law 563 (2nd ed., 2005) (irretrievable breakdown of marriage can be defined as such failure in the matrimonial relationship or such circumstances adverse to that relationship that no reasonable probability remains of the spouses remaining together as husband and wife for mutual comfort and support); Law Commission of India, Report No. 71 (1978) ("The situation that exists when either or both spouses are no longer able or willing to live with each other, thereby destroying their husband and wife relationship with no hope of resumption of spousal duties"). *See also*, Rishikesh Sharma v. Saroj Sharma (2006) 12 SCALE 282 (court observed that the wife was living separately from the year 1981 and the marriage had broken down irretrievably with no possibility of the parties living together again. Court thought it would not be possible for the parties to live together and, therefore, the best course was to dissolve the marriage by passing a decree of divorce); Munish Kakkar v. Nidhi Kakkar (2020) 14 SCC 657 (court dissolved a marriage by exercising its inherent powers under Art. 142 of the Constitution, although it admitted that there is no statutory law to recognize the irretrievable breakdown of marriage as a divorce ground in India). Cf. Vishnu Dutt Sharma v. Manju Sharma, 2009 (3) SCALE 425 (court denied giving divorce on the grounds of irretrievable breakdown because it was not mentioned in Hindu Marriage Act, 1955).

and the Special Marriages Act 1954. These fault-based grounds for divorce include cruelty, desertion, adultery, impotence, and communicable disease.

Thus, interestingly, petitions for divorce (except where the divorce is by mutual consent) must necessarily feature faults and allegations against the spouse, which opens the Pandora's Box, spewing bitterness and nearly irreversible damage to the relationship and the emotional and psychological well-being of the parties. This is aggravated by the usual criminal complaints, like cruelty under section 498-A of the Indian Penal Code 1860, dowry demands under Dowry Prohibition Act 1961, domestic violence under the Protection of Women from Domestic Violence Act 2005, which in most cases result in arrest upon the filing of an FIR. Under such circumstances, the real issues are often forgotten or forsaken.[43]

Adversarial processes do not have the amplitude to deal with the parties' emotional predicament, meaning that the legal system does not recognize or respond to the emotions such as anger, grief, disappointment, anxiety, and sadness felt by the parties. While proceedings before courts do provide some protection to the vital social interest in marriage and the family and give a reference point by which to arrive at some sort of resolution,[44] there is little or no scope for any sort of healing to set in or to examine outcomes that would be less damaging to the parties' emotional well-being. In the words of Jethro K. Lieberman (applicable in the context of family disputes):[45]

> Important and as effective as the adversary system can be, it is not without a deleterious side. It can be a hugely inefficient means of uncovering facts; its relentless formalities and ceaseless opportunities for splitting hairs are time consuming and expensive. It is not available therefore to everyone, and if it is the only system for obtaining redress then justice cannot be done. For that reason, it may mislead us as a society into supposing that its availability is a guarantee of safety. Litigation is not a panacea; social policies are not necessarily carried out merely because there is an avenue open to some ...
>
> Moreover, like every other human system, litigation is subject to regular abuse. The limitations of semantics, the fallibility of memory, the will to prevaricate, all contribute to unpredict-ability. The outcome is never certain, and litigation is therefore frequently an exercise in anguish and futility. As a mechanism to instil in people a fiduciary regard for others, it can be effective. But for all that it does not often treat well those who are ensnared in it. Litigation, and especially the trial itself, can be unremittingly harsh. Lawyers are often adversaries not only of each other but of their clients; some kinds of litigation are prolonged (and even initiated) solely to ensure the lawyers sufficient billable hours to earn a decent or even a handsome living. The process can be psychologically harmful, hurting

43. *See generally*, K. Srinivas Rao v. D. A. Deepa (2013) 5 SCC 226 (when any case occurs under section 489A of IPC, the Supreme Court directed criminal court not to deal with such complaints unless the matter is dealt by the mediation. But where the cruelty amounts to be a very rigorous and a dangerous one, the criminal courts can take up the case without referring it to the meditation. Further, lower courts and/or mediation centers set up their own personal clinics so that matrimonial disputes can be resolved using mediation without the involvement of court).
44. *See generally*, Thomas E. Carbonneau, *A Consideration of Alternatives to Divorce Litigation*, Univ. Ill. L. Rev. 1119 (hereinafter "Carbonneau").
45. Jethro K. Lieberman, The Litigious Society 171 (1981).

self-esteem as well as pocketbook. Other modes of resolving disputes and solving problems bear scrutiny.

The adversarial process is not equipped to deal with the hostilities that string along with divorce proceedings. Neither the substantive law nor the procedural rules are designed to coalesce the legal rights with the emotions and relationships. The legal requirement of plead accusations and prove the fault of the other, in order to justify a relief of divorce, compels parties to anchor themselves on contentious grounds—often with distorted, vindictive statements showing oneself as the victim to the perpetrator's actions. This not only takes root in the psyche of the parties[46] but also percolates into future relationships, stirring child custody issues as well as parental and financial responsibilities. Thus, contentious proceedings not only have the potential to leave scars that hurt and fester but also impact innocent children (and family members) who too take a hit in the cross fire.

Besides the general drawbacks of litigating family disputes, the Family Court Act, 1984 (or the functioning of family courts) is not without serious glitches. In Indian society, it is customary for women to leave their matrimonial homes. But in a case of domestic violence, a woman would need to depend upon her parental home or look for an alternative shelter. And even though she has the right of residence, its efficacy has constantly been in doubt.[47]

Then again, whether a woman gets maintenance during a separation or after divorce depends on her ability to prove her husband's means. It is no secret that in a society like India, women are often unaware of their husband's business affairs, investment, or sources of income, making it a hell of a task to prove the husband's income. Family courts must be endowed with investigative powers that can compel disclosures of income and assets for passing appropriate orders of maintenance. Only recently, the Supreme Court framed key guidelines for the proper enforcement of maintenance orders, in that both parties would be required to file an affidavit disclosing assets and liabilities (which would subject a misrepresentation to contempt of court and proceeding under sections 195 and 340 of the Code of Criminal Procedure, 1973).[48] Yet, there are no clear guidelines or procedures about ascertaining maintenance amounts (in that, taking assistance of NGOs, social workers, etc.) or about

46. *See generally*, Carbonneau, *supra* note 44.
47. *See* Satish Chander Ahuja v. Sneha Ahuja, 2020 SCC OnLine SC 841 (court held that respondent in a proceeding under Domestic Violence Act can be any relative of the husband and in event, the shared household belongs to any relative of the husband with whom in a domestic relationship the woman has lived, the conditions mentioned in section 2(s) are satisfied and the said house will become a shared household. This overruled an earlier judgment of the court in SR Batra v. Taruna Batra (2007) 3 SCC 169, where it was held that the wife is entitled only to claim a right to residence in a shared household and a shared household would only mean the house belonging to or taken on rent by the husband, or the house which belongs to the joint family of which the husband is a member). *See also*, Ramachandra Warrior v. Jayasree (2021) SCC OnLine Ker 1444 (a divorced wife would not be entitled to the right of residence conferred under section 17 of the Protection of Women from Domestic Violence Act).
48. *See* Rajnesh v. Neha & Anr. (2020) SCC OnLine SC 941 (court observed that inappropriate disclosures of true income of both the parties create difficultly for family courts to grant maintenance and because of which it becomes difficult for the claimant to get essentials for survival not only after the judgment but also during the pendency of judgment).

depositing maintenance in the family court to avoid any undue delay and ensure timely payments.

Nevertheless, reaching a consensus on family conflicts through mediation is not without challenge. In matters of child custody, for instance, each one thinks that he or she is better suited to provide the best care for the child. Each parent projects the other as callous, less loving, and incompetent to rear a child, and such an approach takes over into misguided negotiation. Similarly, in matters of quantum of maintenance, parties project themselves as devoid of means that they cannot provide for themselves. Cognitive biases like anchoring,[49] reactive devaluation,[50] and the endowment effect[51] are few examples of the inhibitors that play out in family mediations. But the mediator is aware of such possibilities and trained and equipped to handle such conflicts with kid gloves.

§10.05 MEDIATING FAMILY DISPUTES

For a holistic resolution of any family conflict, three kinds of satisfaction are required. First, procedural satisfaction; i.e., the procedure should be such that all parties to the conflict should get an equal opportunity to present their version of the dispute and advance their respective claims. Second, substantive satisfaction, i.e., the outcome of the process, should be such that all sides to the conflict get what they need through substantive relief. And third, emotional satisfaction; i.e., the parties should come out of the process feeling vindicated and satisfied that their feelings have been understood and their fears and concerns have been addressed.

While satisfaction is well explainable in theory, conflicts cannot always be defined in the binaries of right and wrong. There are many shades of grey in between. This is particularly so for family disputes. There are many nuances to such conflicts that can be confounding if sought to be dealt with from the perspective of faultfinding. Adjudicatory processes, however, by their very design, only focus on these binaries leading to an expensive and protracted journey of establishing wrongdoing at the cost of nuances that define the human condition.

In any matrimonial dispute, the first intervention takes place at the family level, where the elders of the family step in to try and resolve the issues. But it is no mystery that family members may be biased and sometimes may also be a cause (directly or indirectly) of the conflict. Nonadjudicatory or conciliatory processes like mediation are, thus, most appropriate for resolving family disputes. It emphasizes a collaborative approach to discuss the issues of relationship, parenting, finances, and so on, in a less formal atmosphere, giving space to parties to express their emotions in a safe environment, focusing on individual rationality and responsibility in the decision-making process. The process is designed to imbibe trust in the mediator and confidence in the parties to enable parties to vent their emotions, give voice to their feelings, and

49. To cling to one's first offer to evaluate all subsequent proposals.
50. Running down the other party's offer.
51. Overvaluing one's own capabilities as a parent or overvaluing one's own property offered for settlement of a claim or as an exchange.

express their deepest anxieties and concerns in a safe environment. This empowers parties to negotiate as equals and work out a conclusion that best serves their (as well as their children or family's) interests.

Conciliatory processes also have the added functional capability to work as an appendage to the legal system, providing divorcing couples with a structured opportunity to reach a consensual agreement on their divorce's parent and financial consequences. Since matters of status and capacity fall in the domain of public policy, the formal pronouncement of divorce remains in the jurisdictional province of the courts. Mediation, however, provides a humane framework for resolving difficulties that attend to the formal dissolution of marriage more amicably and harmoniously.[52]

Mediation may be broadly described as a voluntary, confidential, without prejudice, nonadjudicatory, and conciliatory process in which a trained neutral facilitates the negotiation between disputing parties to bring about a mutually acceptable resolution to the dispute. While thoroughly discussed elsewhere in the book, these attributes may be revisited briefly with their finer nuances in the context of family disputes.

[A] Voluntary Process

Voluntary participation of the parties in the mediation process is a *sine qua non* as the very essence of mediation is to endow the parties with the feeling that they own the process to solve their problems and it is their responsibility to solve it with the assistance of a trained neutral. While in court systems, disputes are mandatorily referred to mediation (and while it may also be necessary to goad the parties to come to the negotiating table), once there, it is their free will to either go through the process or withdraw from it without being visited by any legal consequences of such withdrawal (a "see you in court" scenario comes to mind).

Thus, there is a fundamental difference between mandating parties to mediate and requiring them to think about the possible benefits of mediating their dispute. Often parties (and their Advocates) may not be fully aware of the process or its advantages in the context of the dispute at hand. Hence, though mandatory mediation may have an element of compulsion in getting the parties to participate in the process, there is no compromise on their willingness to conclude (whether it results in a mediated settlement or not).

The term "voluntary" does not only concern the parties' participation in the process but also features the voluntariness in determining the outcome—self-determination makes up for one of the cornerstones of mediation. Settlements in mediation are a product of direct negotiations between the parties, which necessarily involves evaluating the pros and cons of the conflict being ended by a settlement.

Case study

In a case involving several connected disputes relating to divorce (on the division of property, custody of the children, and allocation of shares in the family business), a

52. *See generally*, Carbonneau, *supra* note 44.

couple had been advised by their Advocates to inform the mediator that owing to the complexity of the disputes pending before different courts, the reference to mediation in the child custody matter alone would not serve any purpose. Hence, as soon as the parties entered the mediation room, they informed the mediator that though they agreed to appear before the mediator in deference to the court's directions, they have been advised that it would not be conducive to proceed with the mediation for the said reason. The mediator politely said, "I respect your decision not to proceed with the mediation. But if you can bear with me for a few minutes, let me explain how the process works and what you can expect out of it. If you still feel it will not be helpful, you may withdraw." The mediator explained how the process worked and the possibility of settling all the offshoot disputes in parallel litigations. Hearing this, both parties and their Advocates agreed to go through the processes, having better understood its potential in the context of their dispute.

The key takeaway from this case study is that the parties' decision to participate in mediation was motivated by the advantages of the process—as explained by the mediator—rather than a legal compulsion to do so. In this manner, they would also have been instilled with a responsibility to engage meaningfully with their conflict throughout to find outcomes that truly address their needs and interests. If compelled to participate in mediation—while unconvinced of its advantages—parties may well have carried their earlier attitude of only engaging cursorily with the process and putting their best efforts in the multiple ongoing litigations instead.

[B] Confidentiality

There are two tiers of confidentiality in mediation. The first tier is the confidentiality of the process itself. This is the confidentiality that covers the entire mediation process and binds everyone—the mediator, the parties, and the Advocates—from disclosing any information to the outside world or using any information acquired through the mediation process in any other legal proceedings. The second tier of confidentiality is the one that binds the mediator from disclosing any information obtained from either party in the private sessions to the other party unless expressly requested by the party so communicating the information. There is another principle that works hand in hand with confidentiality called privilege. It provides that confidential communications are not admissible in court. These are protections that are well laid out in the rules applicable to a mediation referred by a family court.

Confidentiality is an essential ethic in mediation since parties are directly participating and sharing information that they would not otherwise disclose, making pragmatic legal sense to protect such information. That apart, there is a definite psychological and emotional advantage in creating a safe and secure environment for parties to share confidential information, to trust the mediator with such information, and have faith in the process itself. While generally crucial to the mediation process, confidentiality is undeniable importance to the mediation of family disputes where the source conflict may commonly arise out of personal and sensitive matters such as religious practices, compatibility, and intimacy.

Frequently, some motivating forces behind suit actions may be legally irrelevant but exceptionally important in understanding conflicts and facilitating resolution. Often, clients disclose certain private events, perceptions, and issues to their Advocates (only after having entered mediation) that they would not have disclosed earlier or would have wanted anyone to know since the efforts until would have been to fit facts into a legal formula for claiming legal reliefs. But, in mediation, for parties to explain their concerns and fears is often critically important to facilitate the resolution of the underlying conflict. Hence, if confidentiality were not afforded, the mediation process, the mediator's role, and the potential for resolution would have been significantly meaningless and hollow.

Case study

In a divorce action, the wife was seeking divorce on the ground of cruelty by the husband. This was buttressed with allegations of verbal and physical abuse, drunken behavior, and philandering. The private/caucus sessions with both the husband and the wife revealed that they had different religious beliefs: the wife was a Christian, and the husband was a Hindu. The wife's parents had been against the marriage but later came around. But when a girl child was born to the couple, religion became a cause of dissension. The wife's parents were very keen that the child should be brought up as a Christian and that the husband should also convert to Christianity. Though a Hindu by birth, the husband was an atheist and wanted his daughter to grow up as a free thinker. The parents had put a lot of pressure on the wife to prevail upon her husband to convert to Christianity, and when she failed to convince him, they convinced her to withdraw from the marriage. These facts were not known to the Advocate until several private sessions happened in the mediation. The wife was keen to keep her real motivation confidential. The wife finally came around to accepting and aligning with her husband's point of view. In the end, but for the assurance of confidentiality, the wife would have never confided about the root cause of the conflict.

[C] Without Prejudice

Without prejudice is a term with legal connotation signifying that any statement, admission, or offer would not be binding unless and until it leads to a mutually acceptable agreement. It is a corollary of confidentiality. In mediation, it would mean that parties can feel free to make any statements, admissions, and offers without the fear that these may be held against them either in the mediation or in any other proceedings that may follow if the mediation fails.

The reason for this is simple. Parties, whether with their Advocates or not, can talk openly about issues without prejudice. Therefore, the mediator can challenge parties' assumptions and expectations and understand what each party wants or needs to bring the dispute to a conclusion. Thus, anything disclosed during the mediation is done to facilitate an agreement and cannot be used in the court later. But once a mediated agreement is reached, parties are bound by the same and cannot renege on their solemn commitments.

Case study

In a very hostile case for divorce and custody of minor children, a mediated agreement was reached between the husband and the wife. The terms were that the wife would transfer one of her properties to the husband, and the husband would agree to consent to dissolve the marriage under section 13(B) of the Hindu Marriage Act 1955. The agreement was filed before the court along with the petition under section 13B. The wife fulfilled her part of the commitment. However, the husband reneged on his promise and sought to withdraw his consent given under section 13(B). While the contentious proceedings were pending before the court, the husband had a change of heart following their children's intervention and decided to abide by the agreement. Fortunately, for the parties, in this case, the matter was resolved amicably, and there was a finding by the court as to whether a party could renege from an agreement (in relation to the dissolution of marriage) once it has attained finality and a party has performed its part of the obligations.

As to whether a party can withdraw its consent in a proceeding under section 13(B) of the Hindu Marriage Act, there were divergent views among the High Courts, which the Supreme Court finally settled in *Sureshta Devi v. Om Prakash* ("*Sureshta Devi*").[53] It was held that consent could not be withdrawn after the settlement had been drawn. But these judgments have not been in the context of the requisite consent under section 13(B) being given in a mediated settlement (even though the ratio in *Sureshta Devi* can reasonably extend to mediated settlement agreements).

§10.06 MEDIATION STYLES FOR FAMILY DISPUTES

A brief discussion of mediation styles in the context of family disputes widens our appreciation of the chapter's theme. There are (at least) three contemporary styles appropriate for family disputes: facilitative, transformative, and narrative (as they are popularly known). In India, facilitative mediation may be the most applied model to family disputes, but there is great potential in adopting the other models. Understanding the fluidity in the dynamics of family disputes in mediation, a good mediator of family disputes must have the right tool kit and skill set (handpicked from various styles) to match the circumstances of the dispute and the parties in it.

[A] Facilitative Mediation

The facilitative model of mediation is considered pragmatic and tuned to be a problem-solving process. While popularly applied in commercial disputes, it also has relevance for family disputes, particularly where the parties aim to end the relationship and go separate ways with a settlement in hand.

53. AIR 1992 SC 1904.

The model usually prescribes a defined stagewise process, starting with the opening statement, agenda-setting, information gathering, issue identification, brainstorming, negotiations, and finally, the conclusion (with or without a settlement). Practically, there are no such obvious demarcations of stages; the process flows (with the mediator at its helm), and so stages may reappear or shuffle around, depending on how the mediation progresses. For example, parties may develop their agenda again in the subsequent stages, as more and more information is exchanged and the underlying interests are understood. For more discussion on the facilitative model, *see* Chapter on the Role and Approach of the Mediator.

[B] Transformative Mediation

The transformative model of mediation aspires to transform parties from a perceived state of weakness to strength while improving the relational context of the dispute.[54] Under this model, mediation is considered a process in which a third party works with parties in conflict to help them change the quality of their conflict interaction from negative and destructive to positive and constructive, as they explore and discuss issues and possibilities of resolution.[55]

This model has the unique potential for changing the parties' mindset in conflict by generating two important dynamic effects: empowerment and recognition. It empowers by restoring the parties' sense of their value and making decisions; it grants recognition by evoking empathy, acknowledgment, and understanding of each situation, views, and emotions.[56] It is considered that focusing on empowerment and recognition (as in transformative mediation) typically results in settlements that the parties build, whereas focusing on settlement (as in a facilitative model) usually results in ignoring empowerment and recognition.[57]

A matrimonial relationship involves a close and intimate interaction between individuals who come together from (possibly) two different environments—cultural, familial, societal, and psychological. When in conflict, it is not unusual that they find themselves in a state of powerlessness and alienated from the other. This inescapably leads to a sense of hostility, suspicion, and anger toward the other person because our neurophysiological response to conflict affects our experience of/interaction with others in virtually every context in which it occurs.[58] The effort in transformative mediation transforms their destructive conflict interaction into a more positive one (to the greatest possible degree) so that parties can move on with their lives constructively, whether together or apart.[59] In this, "the mediator's role is to help the parties make positive interactional shifts (empowerment and recognition shifts) by supporting the

54. *See* ROBERT A. BARUCH BUSH & JOSEPH P. FOLGER, THE PROMISE OF MEDIATION: RESPONDING TO CONFLICT THROUGH EMPOWERMENT AND RECOGNITION 82–83 (1994) (hereinafter "BUSH & FOLGER").
55. *Id.*
56. *Id.*
57. *Id.*
58. *Id.*
59. *Id.*

exercise of their capacities for strength and responsiveness, through their deliberation, decision making, communication, perspective-taking, and other party activities."[60]

[C] Narrative Mediation

Also called the "storying process," the idea is that in a narration, people tend to organize their experiences in story form to make sense of their lives and relationships:[61]

> People grow up amid a multitude of competing narratives that help shape how they see themselves and others. They tell stories about themselves and about others. They act both out of and into these stories, shaping the direction of the ongoing plot as they do so. Descriptions of problems are typically told in narrative terms. Such problem narratives have often been rehearsed and elaborated over and over again by participants in a conflict.

In this mediation style, the emphasis is not to view stories from the perspective of whether it is true or false; instead, the aim is to understand how the story creates a reality for the parties (not whether the story reports the reality accurately). This is because "events cannot be known independently of the dominant narratives held by the knower."[62] The mediator, therefore, does not seek an objective account of what happened but, instead, validates the stories which the parties experienced in the conflict and then sets out the points where these stories might come to crossroads.[63]

There is much potential in cultural narratives that express people's experiences of transitioning from marriage to divorce.[64] Divorce becomes ugly because many couples experience it as a "transgression against the social imperative to remain married to the same person for the whole of one's adult life."[65] Separation can be viewed as an experience of deep betrayal of such cultural norms of marriage as a sanctuary of love, safety, security, success, and permanence. This leads the parties to experience a range of emotions from guilt and shame to anger and desire for revenge. Hence, court systems are insufficient to provide a holistic opportunity and remedy to divorcing couples, who innately desire dignity and self-respect in their transition from married to single.[66] In that, narrative mediation focuses on "leading from behind" to encourage parties to self-identify solutions, rather than "leading from the front," which assumes a sort of expert's approach to resolving the conflict (which is potentially deconstructive).[67] As a result of the narrative approach, i.e., having heard each other's narration

60. *Id.*
61. *See* John Winslade & Gerald Monk, *Narrative Mediation: A New Approach to Conflict Resolution*, Research Gate (January 2000), https://www.researchgate.net/publication/240132907_Narrative_Mediation_A_New_Approach_to_Conflict_Resolution.
62. *Id.*
63. *Id.*
64. *See generally*, John Winslade & Gerald D. Monk, Practising Narrative Mediation: Loosening the Grip of Conflict (2008).
65. *Id.*
66. *Id.*
67. *Id.*

and perspective, it is considered that the number of desirable outcomes rise exponentially and giving both parties the opportunities to benefit from it.

§10.07 RELEVANT SKILLS FOR MEDIATING FAMILY DISPUTES

Family mediation, and more particularly divorce mediations, involves a high degree of emotions compared to other kinds of disputes. Thus, family mediators are required to be trained at least in three broad areas: legal aspects, process skills, and (most importantly) handling emotions and communication.[68] A mediator should know family law; understand the impact of family conflict on spouses, children, parents, child development, child abuse, and domestic abuse; and have the appropriate education and training in the process of mediation. In divorce mediations, emotional and interpersonal issues are intertwined with legal issues. Thus, to deal with the psychological structure of divorce and the parties' needs, a mediator should have "a solid background of training and experience in the behavioral sciences."[69]

The Model Standards of Practice for Family and Divorce Mediation (adopted by the American Bar Association) provide a reasonable standard for considering family mediation in India. The Model Standards aim to promote public confidence in an evolving, interdisciplinary profession by defining good mediation practice. It identified the following essential areas of knowledge and training for mediators:

- know family law;
- have knowledge of and training in the impact of family conflict on parents, children, and other participants, including knowledge of child development, domestic abuse, and child abuse and neglect;
- have education and training specific to the process of mediation; and
- be able to recognize the impact of culture and diversity.

These standards recognize the diverse knowledge and disciplines that family mediators must bring to their practice.[70] Beyond these three broad areas, it is also important (especially in a multicultural and pluralistic society like India) that a mediator can recognize the dynamics of cultural, social, religious, and economic diversities in the context of family relationships. Further, in divorce mediations, for instance, where emotional and interpersonal issues arise in high degrees, mediators must also have "a solid background of training and experience in the behavioral sciences."[71]

68. *See generally*, Amiram Elwork & Mervin R. Smucker, *Developing Training and Practice Standards for Custody Mediators*, 26(2) FAMILY COURT REV. 21 (1988); Robert McWhinney, *Issues in the Provision and Practice of Family Mediation*, 26(2) FAMILY COURT REV. 33 (1988).
69. *Id.*
70. *See generally*, Archie Zariski et al., *Standing on the Shoulders of Giants: Artistry, Expertise and Professionalism in Mediation and the Role of Higher Education* (Working Paper), https://www.researchgate.net/publication/268413269_Standing_on_the_Shoulders_of_Giants_Artistry_Expertise_and_Professionalism_in_Mediation_and_the_Role_of_Higher_Education_Working_Paper.
71. *See id.*

In India, however, no such specialized training or qualifications are prescribed or recognized. There are no "counselor mediators" in the family courts, and the counselors do not conduct mediation. Almost all the mediators in the family courts in India are Advocates who are cleared to conduct mediations after undergoing a basic 40-hour mediation training program prescribed by Supreme Court's Mediation and Conciliation Project Committee (MCPC).

It is also relevant to understand the Indian context that somewhat undergirds family mediations in India. There is a cultural, statutory, and judicial imperative to "preserve the sanctity of the marriage" at all costs; much of this is reflected in the approach of mediators to matrimonial mediations. For example, section 14 of the Hindu Marriage Act of 1955 initially prescribed a three-year waiting period (from marriage date) before filing a divorce petition. However, the Hindu Marriage (Amendment) Act 1976 changed this period to one year (except in case of extreme hardship or depravity).[72] But before the court disposes of any such petition for divorce before the expiry of one year from the date of marriage, the court is required to consider the interest of any children of the marriage and the reasonable probability of reconciliation.

Therefore, only in cases where the court is satisfied that it would be impossible for the parties to continue the relationship and that no chance of reunion remains (such as in the case of cruelty)[73] the court may grant leave to file a petition for divorce before the expiry of one year from the date of marriage. However, this waiver of the statutory period is at the court's discretion, varying from case to case.[74] Generally, it remains the court's duty to not entertain any such divorce petitions by giving the parties a reasonable opportunity for reconciliation. In this regard, the Madras High Court has held:[75]

> The multiplicity of proceedings should be avoided and obliterated. No doubt, the sanctity of the marriage should be preserved. Soon after the marriage, without taking steps for reconciliation, etc., and having sufficient time for reflection, they should not be allowed to approach the Court for divorce and in the meantime, one other aspect, this Court has to see.

The Bombay High Court took a similar view concerning giving parties sufficient time for reconciliation. It held:[76]

> With this pious thinking, the marriage tie be continued till the last breath of the spouse and should not be untied during the subsistence of their marriage, therefore, even under the provisions of the Hindu Marriage Act, some provisions are incorporated to maintain the sanctity of the social institution. The object of section 14 of the Hindu Marriage Act, 1955 is that—section 14 provides restrictions presumably designed to prevent hasty recourse to legal proceedings before the parties have made a real effort to save their marriage from disaster. It is grounded on public policy because marriage is the very foundation of civil society, and no

72. Hindu Marriage (Amendment) Act, 1976, § 9.
73. *See* Priyanka Maity v. Sabyasachi Maity, 2012 SCC OnLine Cal 4657.
74. *See* Amardeep Singh v. Harveen Kaur (2017) 8 SCC 746; In re Vishnudas H. and Ors. (2020) SCC OnLine Ker 3141.
75. *See* G. Ganesh Babu v. A. P. Arthi (2013) 2 Mad LJ 481, ¶ 34.
76. Suresh Nathmal Rathi v. State of Maharashtra, 1991 Mah LJ 1106, ¶ 17.

> part of the laws and institutions of a country can be of more vital importance to its subjects than those which regulate the manner and conditions of forming and, if necessary, of dissolving the marriage contract.

The legislature's intention in providing such limitation in the filing of matrimonial suit is grounded in public policy, restricting any hasty recourse to legal proceedings without any real effort to save the marriage.[77] Courts do not waiver from the strict requirement of section 14 unless, of course, the parties have made a case of exceptional hardship or depravity.[78]

Section 29 of the Special Marriage Act 1954 also applies the same standard as section 14 of the Hindu Marriage Act 1955.[79] On this, the Kerala High Court held the following:[80]

> On an appreciation of the language in Section 29 of the Act and the interpretation given in afore cited decisions to an analogous provision, i.e., Sec. 14 of the Hindu Marriage Act, we are of the firm opinion that, to present a petition for divorce before the expiry of one year from the date of marriage, leave of the Court has to be obtained, as contemplated under Section 29 of the Act, even if the prayer for divorce is an alternative relief; if not, the Court has the discretion to order the decree to be effective only after one year from the date of marriage, and in case the petitioner has obtained leave by misrepresentation or concealment, the Court may also dismiss the petition.

Hence, the pith for incorporating section 29 of the Special Marriage Act 1954 was to discourage a spouse from taking legal recourse to snap the marital bond hastily and irrationally.[81] And even if the court is satisfied that the petitioner has suffered exceptional hardship or that there is exceptional depravity on the part of the respondent, after considering the interest of any children in the marriage and the reasonable probability of reconciliation before the cessation of one year, the court may decide to grant leave to present the petition.[82]

Lastly, private mediations in the arena of family disputes are still at a nascent stage. But to ensure uniformity and quality of service to end users, there is a need to prescribe standards of qualification for family mediators and a transparent system of accreditation to discourage persons with insufficient training and experience.

§10.08 DDRS EXAMPLE

DDRS, a registered society and pro bono mediation center, was set up in collaboration with Delhi and Delhi High Court in 2009. As one of the first community mediation centers, it offers a platform for pre-litigation mediation in India, i.e., before filing a suit

77. *See* Smt. Debaleena Bhawal v. Chirajit Paresh Chandra Bhawal, AIR 1967 Mad 423, ¶ 25; Meganatha Nayagar v. Shrimathi Shusheela (1956) SCC OnLine Mad 320.
78. *See* Sakshi v. Abhinandan Sharma, 2014 SCC OnLine P&H 23365, ¶ 10.
79. *See* Mr. X v. Mrs. Y (2009) SCC OnLine Bom 1850.
80. Kavya Prakash K. v. Sujith V. J., AIR 2020 Ker 165, ¶ 20.
81. *Id.*
82. *Id.*

in court. But DDRS also has a record of accepting cases during and post-litigation proceedings.

DDRS accepts all types of civil and petty criminal matters, whether or not pending in court. Specifically, with regards to family disputes, DDRS accepts the request of mediation pertaining to parent-child, parenting (child custody, visitation, support), child welfare, adult guardianship, restitution of conjugal rights, divorce, domestic violence, maintenance, etc.

The mediation centers spread all across Delhi are managed and supervised by trained mediators and other administrative officials. As for the procedure, any party (or both) to a dispute, irrespective of whether it is pending in court, can approach a DDRS center for mediation services. To initiate proceedings, the party is required to write the complaint, briefly setting out the facts of the matter, and sign. This complaint is then submitted to the center, along with a self-attested photo identification proof and address(es) of the opposite party. Upon receipt of these documents, the center assigns the matter to a mediator and sends an invitation to mediate to the opposite party.

Mediators impaneled at the DDRS center are generally senior lawyers, bureaucrats, and judges who have undergone 40-hour mediation training prescribed by the MCPC of the Supreme Court of India. Mediators are assigned a particular day of the week, and then mediations accepted on that day are referred to these mediators.

The general period for settling a matter is three months. If the parties reach an agreement within the period, the settlement agreement is drawn up. In case the period exceeds, the mediator can choose to close the matter as not settled. However, if the parties feel that they would like to mediate further, the mediator can extend beyond the three months.

In case of a settlement, parties receive an authenticated copy of the signed settlement agreement, which is also explained in their vernacular. This settlement agreement takes the form of a binding contract between the parties. In case of breach of the settlement agreement, the aggrieved party may approach the courts for breach. And if a matter is referred from a court, a police station, or a Crime Against Women cell, the respective authority or center is notified of the settlement so that any further steps may be taken. For instance, in case of court actions, mediation referred by the court, the settlement may be used to withdraw ongoing proceedings or be converted into a decree on agreed terms (especially where the settlement requires a decretal status).

§10.09 CONCLUDING REMARKS

With changing social mores and economic advancement of the Indian society, marital relationships are being redefined, and their dynamics and expectations are undergoing a sea change. The approach to matrimonial disputes needs a relook. Mediators must find themselves with new insights into these generational changes and shift the focus onto the welfare of the individual rather than only the sanctity of the marriage and societal expectations.

CHAPTER 11

E-Mediation

*Ishana Tripathi**

§11.01 THE CONTEXT

In India, from March 2020 onward (the postcrisis era), there has been a push toward enhancing digital courtrooms and procedures to adapt to online modes. In 2020, with the COVID-19 pandemic, a singular focus was creating a digital landscape for case resolution that led to an extensive conversation relating to online dispute resolution (ODR) that considered all processes of case resolution, i.e., litigation, arbitration, and mediation. However, it did consider e-mediation as uniquely different from physical mediation.

This chapter considers March 22, 2020,[1] as the reference for precrisis and postcrisis scenarios for e-mediation. When considering the precrisis scenario, the discourse was noticeably inclined toward physical mediation if it were to succeed or be effective.[2] This is owed mainly to the "let's talk face-to-face" approach of bargaining predominant in India.[3] Similarly, the discourse would have also made a case for e-mediation in court-annexed programs, especially in light of existing State-funded

* The author is thankful to all the ODR and mediation evangelists, who supported this chapter with their conversations, questionnaire responses, and general support. Specifically, the author thanks Poornima Hatti (Partner, Samvad Partners), Chittu Nagarajan (Founder, ODRworld; Co-founder, Modria.com), Vikas Mahendra (Partner, Keystone Partners; Co-founder, CORD), and Badrivishal Kinhal (Co-founder, CORD), who agreed to be interviewed that helped augment this chapter. The author also thanks Mr. Sushant Chandra, Advocate, Allahabad High Court, for his insight and ground support.

1. March 22, 2020, is the date on which the first nationwide lockdown was announced in India as a consequence of the COVID-19 pandemic.
2. *See* Paula Young, *Online Mediation: Its Uses and Limitations*, MEDIATE.COM, https://www.mediate.com/articles/young4.cfm.
3. *See* Ashok Panikkar et al., *Adapting the MGA for Negotiating with Indian Counterparts*, ASIALINK BUSINESS (2015), https://www.cbi.org/assets/resource/reports/5.4%20India%20Brief.pdf.

settlement forums that have mediation facilities, such as the Lok Adalats,[4] and institutions, such as the Delhi Dispute Resolution Society (*Sehmati*).[5]

Today, in the post-crisis scenario, ODR is "the" operative means for courts, arbitrations, mediations, and commercial negotiations. Hence, this chapter's discussion manifests and captures the shift *from* using technology as "one of the options" *to* using technology as a necessity and norm.

In recent times, ODR aggregators[6] offering digital arbitration and mediation services have gained much importance. Joining the race are private-public collaborations for online arbitration and mediation services, which have become a popular venture even though they showed hesitation in the precrisis era.[7]

While all dispute resolution processes and stakeholders (judges, advocates, ADR service providers, disputants, case managers, etc.) are amidst developing adaption strategies to ensure that case resolution is unhampered, mediation (a front-runner in using technology, particularly in international mediation) has neither sufficiently found a relevant/interested audience nor use through digital means. Hence, it is worth considering if (and how) e-mediation is separate from in-person mediation and whether a typology of cases naturally suits either of them.[8]

In that context, this chapter provides a definition and distinction between online and in-person mediation, focusing on pre-and post-crisis scenarios.[9] It also delves into the legal framework for e-mediation, as distinct from ODR. Finally, it provides an overview of the existing infrastructure, such as digital platforms and the resolution success of mediation through digital means while referencing "use cases" indicating potential dispute resolution through e-mediation.

---

4. Lok Adalats are quasi-judicial bodies created for the purpose of nonadversarial case resolution under the Legal Services Authorities Act, 1987. Lok Adalats provide a forum for settlement and speedy redressal. Lok Adalats have been a part of the pilot project to digitize pretrial mediation and settlement, particularly, owing to the efficiency and infrastructure issues that have been raised as concerns while making assessment of Lok Adalat functioning and usage. *See* Loknath Mohapatra et al., *Analysis of the Functioning of the Lok Adalats in the Eastern Region of India: A Comparative Report* (Department of Justice, 2019), https://doj.gov.in/sites/default/files/OJA.pdf (hereinafter "Lok Adalat Eastern Region Report").
5. "Sehmati" is the online mediation platform of Delhi Dispute Resolution Society (DDRS). DDRS is an initiative of Department of Law. It accepts not only matters pending before courts, consumer forums, and other bodies, but also pre-litigation cases and community mediation matters. Before taking legal recourse to courts, police, etc., parties can approach a DDRS center (or make an online reference with Sehmati) for an amicable resolution of the conflict or dispute.
6. The year 2020 saw the surfacing (and resurfacing) of many private aggregators providing e-ADR services. *See Online Dispute Resolution Through Mediation, Arbitration, Conciliation, Etc.*, Department of Justice, Ministry of Law, https://doj.gov.in/sites/default/files/firm%20details.pdf (hereinafter "DOJ List of ODR Service Providers").
7. *See* Deepika Kinhal et al., ODR: The Future of Dispute Resolution in India (Vidhi Centre for Legal Policy, July 28, 2020), https://vidhilegalpolicy.in/wp-content/uploads/2020/07/200727_The-future-of-dispute-resolution-in-India_Final-Version.pdf.
8. *See* NITI Aayog, *Stakeholder Notes, Catalyzing Online Dispute Resolution in India*, NITI Aayog (June 12, 2020), http://niti.gov.in/catalyzing-online-dispute-resolution-india.
9. The date distinction is in the context of statistics, consolidated recommendations, and conclusions that are provided in this chapter. This is also to provide a view of how mediation through digital platforms is being used post March 2020.

[A] Physical to Virtual

The mediation movement found its formal footing in India when the first court-annexed mediation programs were established in 2002.[10] It started with implementing the Civil Procedure (Amendment) Act 1999, which came into effect on July 1, 2002. As a next step, the Supreme Court, with the combined effect of three landmark cases, *Salem Advocate Bar Association v. Union of India* ("*Salem Bar I*"[11] and "*Salem II*")[12] and *Afcons Infrastructure Ltd. & Anr. v. Cherian Varkey Construction Co. (P) Ltd. & Ors.* ("*Afcons*"),[13] upheld the constitutionality of section 89 of the Code of Civil Procedure 1908 (CPC), promulgated mediation rules for court-annexed programs, and delved into the aspects of the application of mediation.

Given drafting errors pointed out in *Afcons*, section 89 of the CPC also underwent corrections and readjustments.[14] The provision is extracted below for the author's emphasis on certain specific terms:

> 89. Settlement of Disputes Outside the Court.—
> (1) Where it appears to the court that *there exist elements of a settlement which may be acceptable to the parties*, the court *shall formulate the terms of settlement and give them to the parties for their observations and after receiving the observations of the parties*, the court may reformulate the terms of a possible settlement and refer the same for:—(a) arbitration; (b) conciliation; (c) [mediation] including settlement through Lok Adalat: or (d) [judicial settlement].
> (2) Where a dispute has been referred—(a) for arbitration or *conciliation*, the *provisions of the Arbitration and Conciliation Act, 1996 (26 of 1996) shall apply* as if the proceedings for arbitration or *conciliation were referred for settlement* under the provisions of that Act; [...]
> (c) for [mediation], the court shall *refer the same to a suitable institution or person* and such institution or person shall be deemed to be a Lok Adalat and all the provisions of the Legal Services Authority Act, 1987 (39 of 1987) shall apply as if the dispute were referred to a Lok Adalat under the provisions of that Act; [...]
>
> (emphasis supplied)

On a literal interpretation, section 89 was engineered toward the settlement of certain types of cases, and it placed a duty on the courts to determine elements of settlement before referring the matter to any of the specified processes. Moreover, arbitration (an adjudicative process) and conciliation (a nonadjudicative process), both of which require the parties' consent, were also brought within the purview of court referrals for settlement under section 89 of the CPC.

The conciliation framework under the Arbitration and Conciliation Act, 1996 ("Arbitration Act") is more evaluative, where the conciliator facilitates a compromise

10. Madras and Karnataka High Courts were the first, followed by the Delhi High Court.
11. Salem Advocate Bar Association v. Union of India (Salem I) (2003) 1 SCC 49.
12. Salem Advocate Bar Association v. Union of India (Salem II) (2005) 6 SCC 344.
13. Afcons Infrastructure Ltd. & Anr. v. Cherian Varkey Construction Co. (P) Ltd. & Ors., 2010 (8) SCC 24 (hereinafter "Afcons").
14. *Id.*, at ¶ 19.

between the parties and can also provide (nonbinding) settlement proposals for the parties' consideration. In contrast, mediation is considered entirely facilitative and without the interventionist approach of a conciliation. One can trace back conciliation's evaluative feature to the Industrial Disputes Act, 1947 (ID Act).[15]

However, these statutes (or statutory provisions), including court-annexed mediation rules, do not envisage electronic modes of mediation. Nor do they offer any structure/provision for parties to use mediation through digital means. Thus, it is not far-fetched to posit that the premise of dispute resolution under these statutes (or statutory provisions) has been (conceptually) based on physical presence.

Further, it is also evident that mediation in India has primarily needed court sanctions (a referral from the court) before parties can sit across the table to mediate. This is not to say that parties are not free to mediate whenever they wish to, but mediation in India is commonly triggered only upon a discretionary court sanction under the existing framework.

We, therefore, come to an important juncture and must ask: where does e-mediation fit?

In India, the need for (and inception of) digital case resolution is closely connected with consumerism. With the advent of e-commerce and globalization, the need for digital payments and banking increased. This parallelly needed a setup that enabled consumers to swiftly resolve payment and product-related disputes, to name a few. Around the same time, the beginnings of a start-up culture were witnessed, and intellectual property (IP) discoveries and innovations increased. It also led to increased registration in trademarks, copyrights, and digital designs, as well as related disputes.[16] In that context, technology was a natural means to create ease of resolution, which focused on negotiation, settlement, and mediation. These developments necessitated the consideration of mediation's suitability, besides ODR.

In *Afcons*, in 2010, the Supreme Court identified various case/subject matters in which mediation could be used. With that, the court presented a starting point for what e-mediation "could" also be utilized. An obvious next step was to understand how technology could step in to supplement case resolution through mediation. This was predominantly born out of a need for an efficient business model of resolution. Although, in the consumer and banking sectors, many prior (and parallel) developments had already been implemented that included efficient and effective means of case resolution. In *Afcons*, the following illustrative list of suitable cases is indicative for e-mediation:[17]

(i) All cases relating to *trade, commerce and contracts*, including
   - disputes arising out of contracts (including all money claims);
   - disputes relating to specific performance;
   - disputes between suppliers and customers;

15. Now repealed and replaced by the Industrial Relations Code, 2020.
16. For example, Modria®, which spun out of the offices of eBay and PayPal. *See also*, WIPO Online Case Administration Tools, WORLD INTELLECTUAL PROPERTY ORGANIZATIONS, https://www.wipo.int/amc/en/eadr/.
17. Afcons, *supra* note 13, at ¶ 28.

- disputes between *bankers and customers*;
- disputes between developers/builders and customers;
- disputes between landlords and tenants/licensor and licensees;
- disputes between insurer and insured.

(ii) All cases arising from strained or soured relationships, including
- disputes relating to matrimonial causes, maintenance, custody of children;
- disputes relating to partition/division among family members/co-parceners/co-owners; and
- disputes relating to partnership among partners.

(iii) All cases where there is a need for continuation of the pre-existing relationship in spite of the disputes, including
- disputes between neighbours (relating to easementary rights, encroachments, nuisance etc.);
- disputes between employers and employees;
- disputes among members of societies/associations/Apartment owners Associations;

(iv) All cases relating to tortious liability including
- claims for compensation in motor accidents/other accidents; and

(v) All *consumer disputes* including
- disputes where a trader/supplier/manufacturer/service provider is keen to maintain his business/professional reputation and credibility or product popularity.

Afcons, hence, considered banking and consumer disputes (key fields of coverage in this chapter) to be suitable for mediation. This is primarily owed to the early adoption of technology to develop digital banking and online shopping. Moreover, most cases in these sectors are transactive and quantifiable in relation to defective products, credit card nonpayments, loan defaults, etc., and thus most suitable to mediation online. Why then were these cases not shifted to online resolution? We now explore the skepticism in moving digital, in taking mediation online.

[B] Skepticism in Moving Online

As a process, mediation has both evangelists and skeptics. The former, in particular, fall into two categories: the first type synonymize mediation with litigious processes and think of them to be part of the same structure for reaching a win-lose outcome, and the second type is those who have tried the process but emerged dissatisfied with either the infrastructure or the mediator driving the resolution process, thus rejected the viability of the process. A consequence of both types is a dismissal of the process since success is often measured not just by settlement rates but also by the user experience and mutual satisfaction of the outcome (whether it led to a settlement or just a conclusion without a settlement).

While mediation is party-driven, it is necessary to accept that without the infrastructural support and quality mediators at the helm of the process, mediation copes with much resistance (particularly at a pretrial stage when parties are charged). Equally, it is also necessary for parties (and advocates) to come to terms with the process of mediation and appreciate its use.

In this backdrop, we consider to what degree (and in what way) do the issues, concerns, and contentions of in-person mediation transpose onto online mediations, in addition to the technology adaptation and accessibility concerns. We make this expedition since the author (and this chapter) postulates a distinction between e-mediation and in-person mediation. Such emphasis is laid because mediation online is expected to have a definite and separate practice and process, infrastructure requirements, mediator and case manager qualifications, governing framework of the procedure, and enforcement rules.

Further, since the Indian mediation regime is visibly heavily dependent on court referrals or court sanctions, the author chooses to discuss the chapter's theme more in the context of the court or tribunal-annexed programs (or State-funded forums) because such mediations presumably constitute the large majority of mediation practice in India. While the past six years have also seen the establishment of some private service providers, there are no consolidated statistics or detailed individual statistics maintained by any institution. Moreover, whether any of these private service providers are enlisted or have received court referrals is also unavailable.

The following two examples set the stage:

Illustration 1: *Absence of infrastructure and no reference to private service providers*

> In April 2020, in a transfer petition before the Supreme Court,[18] the advocate requested online mediation through court-annexed or private service providers recognized by the Department of Justice (DOJ).[19] The court rejected the request with the observation that infrastructure was absent in a particular State and the lack of facilities available with the opposing party. Further, while bringing to the notice of the court the list of service providers by the DOJ, the court observed that it did not know the details and efficiencies of the mediation service providers and that, therefore, it would not set a precedent for it.

Illustration 2: *Quality of the mediator and technological barriers*

> In July 2020, in another transfer petition before the Supreme Court, the advocate's request for online mediation was accepted. The court referred the matter to mediation through the court-provided online facilities and not the private service providers set out in the DOJ List of ODR Service Providers. The court facilities involved creating a Whatsapp group by the court registry with the mediation assignment, with the lawyers only. Accordingly, a mediator was appointed, and a first date was fixed.
>
> In the first session, a link was shared, and only one party and advocate adopted the video. At the start of the session, the mediator did not provide an opening statement, nor did the mediator set down the process of mediation. Further, one of the parties was absent, who was represented by an advocate who did not make a visual representation.

18. Transfer petitions are petitions where a case being adjudicated in one State can be transferred to another State by the Supreme Court on certain grounds.
19. *See* DOJ List of ODR Service Providers, *supra* note 6.

> The mediator tried to connect with the party telephonically, but the party chose not to join the online platform. The mediator allowed the advocates to be present, even during private sessions, and could not use the separate window technology on the platform provided.
>
> One party refused to appear through the virtual court platform being used by the mediator for any joint session. The advocate created points of reference, and the mediator set no agenda or terms.
>
> Throughout the two-week mediation process, one party changed positions and options too frequently, and even the advocate was replaced midway through the mediation process. In addition, the mediator provided no information of any dates of meetings and caucuses but indicated to one party to draft a term of settlement, which was left unsigned at the end of it. Suffice to say, the mediation was inconclusive.

Both the above illustrations were cases involving ongoing matrimonial proceedings. Through these Illustrations, the author highlights the "macro" issues relating to the ease of use, the efficiency of time and cost, and the availability of proper technology and training to conduct the mediation. At the "micro" level, the author highlights issues concerning the credibility of e-mediation and the availability of expert drivers (mediators).

The Illustrations also highlight the need to separate in-person mediation from e-mediation, conceptually and in practice. E-mediation requires its own identity as a process. And since it would be insufficient to say that mediations conducted on an online platform qualify as online mediation, the following working definition may be a helpful adoption:

> E-mediation is a digital process conducted on a specifically designed virtual platform that is accessible, user friendly, and led by a qualified third-party neutral (the mediator) who uses the technology to facilitate an amicable resolution of specific disputes to reach an online settlement that is enforceable.

The online mediation definition has some distinctive elements that may be considered as having four pockets (as depicted in *Figure 11.1: E-Mediation Issue Wheel*): digital economy, credibility, expertise, and enforcement. The *E-Mediation Issue Wheel* forms a reference for the subsequent discourse on issues, suggestions, and legal frameworks concerning e-mediation.

Figure 11.1 E-Mediation Issue Wheel

§11.02 THE E-MEDIATION ISSUE WHEEL

In India, the in-person mediation process, in general, has been riddled with inefficiencies and ineffectiveness in various sectoral cases, which has led to the development of sector-specific platforms and focused solutions. In this regard, the banking and domain name (IP) sectors have been the forerunners in digital innovation and technology adaptation. The following section enters a discourse on the four pockets of the *E-Mediation Issue Wheel,* which indicate a systemic adaption of e-mediation.

[A] Digital Economy and Infrastructure

An essential functional part of e-mediation is its "e" element. Hence, to make e-mediation services available, the technology should first be accessible. Accordingly, the following preliminary questions emerge: what is the infrastructure needed for e-mediation, how (or by whom) should it be developed, and what is the target audience of such e-mediation services?

[1] Digital Platform

Private service providers have been better equipped to digitize mediation (particularly since they fixate their services for a target audience/sector, like banking, consumer, etc.). However, it is not so in court-annexed mediation programs (whether pre-or post-crisis eras), which takes a general/one-size-fits-all approach, making it a Herculean task. And given that court-annexed mediations are heavily dependent on both court facilities and court sanctions, the use of e-mediation suffers directly from the cascading effect of underdeveloped e-courts.

As in *Illustration 1*, digital infrastructure not only is an issue in the courtroom but also trickles down in mediation. The concern is not unfounded but is rather evident in the enormous network of the judicial system in India from top to bottom, including courts, tribunals, statutory forums, and settlement bodies (like Lok Adalats). In such an extensive network, universal standard digitization is a key concern. In the post-crisis era, even though courts, tribunals, and quasi-judicial forums, at all the levels, have been able to digitize in some manner (e.g., e-filings, e-hearings, etc.), it cannot be claimed either that there is effective digitization or that there is digitization for all stages of judicial/quasi-judicial proceedings (e.g., evidentiary hearings).

Recognizing the need for a robust e-courts network, in November 2019,[20] the former Chief Justice of India, Justice Sharad Bobde, while launching the Neural Machine Translation tool, made the following remark that hints at the insufficiency of digitization:

> While technology has enabled us to go paperless in *many courts* and *go digital, if not all the way then substantially*, in *many courts*, we now have the benefit of modern artificial intelligence tools that will assist in improving the efficiency of our justice system through sophisticated and contextual automation of existing repetitive non-judicial tasks and functions to reduce pendency, expedite judicial adjudication and create more time for judges to resolve complex cases.
>
> (emphasis supplied)

Even in 2021, most States have not been able to adopt an effective virtual courtroom. Most subordinate and trial courts have failed to function properly as e-courts, for example, absence of a proper system for the taking of evidence digitally (as in testimonies, direct and cross-examination, etc.). However, while digital evidence has had infrastructural hurdles in litigation, it has been efficiently adapted in arbitrations, particularly institutional arbitration, given the flexibility and relaxation of the rules of evidence.[21] Moreover, criminal courts, especially during the onslaught of the pandemic, functioned very sporadically, and on most occasions were compelled to conduct physical hearings.

The post-crisis era revealed India's instinctive inability to transition into and use digital means effectively, which is basically why the adoption of e-mediation has not been systemic. With such challenges, a continuous process like mediation, which as a concept has already been struggling to catch on in a nondigital environment, has staggered. With the rise of cases in the post-crisis era, even at the Supreme Court,[22] "settlement" is an important mantra in the wake of pendency of cases. But it is hard to tell whether it is working; there is simply no data.

---

20. *See* Chief Justice of India, Justice Sharad Bobde, *Constitution Day Speech*, THE PRINT (Nov. 26, 2019), https://theprint.in/judiciary/ai-can-improve-judicial-systems-efficiency-full-text-of-cji-bobdes-constitution-day-speech/326893/.
21. *See, e.g.*, Shakti Bhog v. Kola Shipping (2009) 2 SCC 134, ¶ 90; Trimex International Fze. v. Vedanta Aluminum Ltd., 2010 (3) SCC 1, ¶¶ 6–9.
22. *See* SHREYA TRIPATHI & TARIKA JAIN, SUPREME COURT'S CASELOAD DURING COVID-19 (APRIL 2020): A LOOK AT THE NUMBERS (July 20, 2020), https://vidhilegalpolicy.in/research/supreme-courts-caseload-during-covid-19-april-2020-a-look-at-the-numbers/.

[2] Referrals to E-Mediation

In the post-crisis era, though tardy, case referrals to mediation have continued. In terms of statistics, the National Judicial Data Grid, a data initiative of the e-courts project of the Supreme Court,[23] shows the pendency in various High Courts to be a total of approximately 5.8 million cases, with an increase in pendency from the previous year as represented in *Table 11.1*. Similarly, the total pendency in the district and local courts is approximately 38.5 million cases, with a substantial increase in pendency from the previous year, as depicted in *Table 11.2*.

Table 11.1 Pendency in High Courts (as of May 10, 2021)

Particulars/Pendency Years	*Civil*	*Criminal*	*Total*
0–1 Years	661,694 (15.9%)	351,430 (21.3%)	1,013,124 (17.43%)
1–3 Years	1,056,657 (25.39%)	430,006 (26.07%)	1,486,663 (25.58%)
3–5 Years	678,756 (16.31%)	223,511 (13.55%)	902,267 (15.52%)
5–10 Years	867,058 (20.83%)	296,265 (17.96%)	1,163,323 (20.02%)
10–20 Years	713,860 (17.15%)	289,760 (17.56%)	1,003,620 (17.27%)
20–30 Years	109,424 (2.6%)	41,903 (2.6%)	151,327 (2.6%)
Above 30 Years	75,043 (1.8%)	16,866 (1.02%)	91,909 (1.58%)
Total	**4,162,492**	**1,649,741**	**5,812,233**
Cases Instituted in April 2021	57,313	45,800	103,113
Cases Disposed in April 2021	35,952	28,930	64,882

23. The National Judicial Data Grid was developed as a part of the e-courts project established by the Supreme Court of India. The e-courts project was conceptualized under the National Policy and Action Plan for Implementation of Information and Communication Technology in the Indian Judiciary 2005 and is funded by the Department of Justice. *See* National Judicial Data Grid (District and Taluka Courts of India), https://njdg.ecourts.gov.in/njdgnew/index.php.

Table 11.2 Pendency in District Courts (as of May 10, 2021)

Particulars	*Civil*	*Criminal*	*Total*
0–1 Years	2,757,832 (26.79%)	7,644,253 (27.17%)	10,402,085 (27.07%)
1–3 Years	3,440,675 (33.43%)	8,723,651 (31.01%)	12,164,326 (31.66%)
3–5 Years	1,713,074 (16.64%)	4,668,823 (16.6%)	6,381,897 (16.61%)
5–10 Years	1,663,321 (16.16%)	4,483,153 (15.94%)	6,146,474 (16%)
10–20 Years	562,488 (5.47%)	2,172,763 (7.72%)	2,735,251 (7.12%)
20–30 Years	117,201 (1.28%)	374,107 (1.28%)	491,308 (1.28%)
Above 30 Years	37,813 (0.37%)	65,037 (0.23%)	102,850 (0.27%)
Total	**10,292,404**	**28,131,787**	**38,424,191**
Cases Instituted April 2021	184,992	726,789	911,781
Cases Disposed in April 2021	133,683	540,951	674,634

Against such a mounting caseload, mediation is easily one of the best and effective ways to unclog the court system. It is also an opportunity for e-mediation.

During the post-crisis era, when comparing the number of mediations conducted by settlement bodies such as the Lok Adalats, the numbers demonstrate a considerable disparity in the referrals to (and settlement by) court-annexed mediations. From April 2019 to March 2020, approximately 1.3 million cases were closed and settled in Lok Adalats,[24] whereas only 95,000 cases (approx.) were closed and settled through mediations across mediation centers in India.[25] From April 2020 to December 2020, around 1 million cases were settled through e-Lok Adalats, which were also run-on platforms by private service providers.[26] However, only 33,000 cases (approx.) were closed and settled in court-annexed mediation centers across India.[27]

In comparing these figures (though statistics on court-annexed mediations are grossly limited), court-annexed mediations have fallen behind due to the

24. *Disposal of National Lok Adalat,* National Legal Services Authority, https://nalsa.gov.in/lok-adalat/national-lok-adalat.
25. *ADR and Mediation Statistical Information,* National Legal Services Authority, https://nalsa.gov.in/uploads/pdf/2020/09/04/04_09_2020_962011885.pdf.
26. *See* PIB Delhi, *Over 10 Lakh Cases Worth Settlement Value of Nearly ₹3228 Cr. Disposed of in Last National Lok Adalat of the Year 2020 Organised Through Both Virtual and Physical Mode,* Ministry of Law & Justice (Dec. 17, 2020, 12:02 PM), https://pib.gov.in/PressReleaseIframePage.aspx?PRID=1681363.
27. *Statistical Snapshot 2020,* National Legal Services Authority, https://nalsa.gov.in/library/statistical-snapshot/statistical-snapshot-2020.

ineffectiveness/inefficiency or absence of proper digital means in courts.[28] Court-sanctioned digital platforms for e-mediations are still far from reality. Even the High Courts of certain States with large populations and pending cases (such as Bihar and Uttar Pradesh)[29] have not fully implemented a digital process for e-filing and online hearings.[30] Online mediation cannot thrive in such conditions.

Interestingly, during the onslaught of the pandemic, efforts were made to move back to physical modes, owing to the absence of proper access among advocates and parties and ineffectiveness/inefficiencies of the e-courts system. Thus, in the post-crisis era, erratic court functioning has had a cascading effect on the number of cases referred to mediation and the number of cases mediated, demonstrating a general inability among courts, practitioners, and users to transpose from physical to virtual mediation.

[3] Digital Access and Localization

While access to the internet is outside the scope of this chapter, it must also be posited as to whom should e-mediation be made available; should it be accessible at the grassroots,[31] or only in urban areas,[32] or both? This is not an unfounded question to raise since grassroots in India have had severe limitations in internet access and digital awareness. Thus, from an infrastructural standpoint, there is a need to recognize the absence of internet accessibility.

At the grassroots, digital awareness projects such as *Gyandoot*,[33] Wired Village,[34] *Bhoomi*,[35] and Information Village Research,[36] have boosted internet access and awareness, helping forums like Nyaya Panchayats in online case settlements in various States. However, while the localization of these projects has helped bridge the digital

28. For instance, the cause list of the Delhi High Court's mediation center showcased a reduced number of cases, nonassignment of mediators, and an average of 60 days spent in mediation (research on file with the author).
29. *See National Judicial Data Grid (District and Taluka Courts of India)*, https://njdg.ecourts.gov.in/njdgnew/index.php (select Uttar Pradesh for details).
30. The information has been gathered by interviewing practicing advocates of various High Courts on virtual court functioning, updated as on Apr. 10, 2021.
31. *See* D.L. Seth, *Knowledge Power and Action: Challenges Facing the Grassroots Movements for Alternative Development*, Centre for Social Studies (July 2000), http://www.css.ac.in/download/ip_desai_lecture/IPD-12.pdf (Seth identifies grassroots in India as remote, underdeveloped and without access to basic amenities parts of various States).
32. The term "urban" is used as per the terms used in the Indian Census. *See Terms Used in Indian Censuses*, Ministry of Home Affairs, https://censusindia.gov.in/data_products/library/indian_perceptive_link/census_terms_link/censusterms.html.
33. *See Gyandoot Project: ICT Initiative in the District of Dhar, Madhya Pradesh*, The World Bank, http://documents1.worldbank.org/curated/en/621851468267614396/pdf/514530WP0IN0Gy10Box342028B01PUBLIC1.pdf.
34. *See* Venkatamallu Thadaboina, *ICT and Rural Development: A Study of Warana Wired Village Project in India*, 16 Transit. Stud. Rev. 560–570 (2009).
35. *See* Rajeev Chawla & Subhash Bhatnagar, *Online Delivery of Land Titles to Rural Farmers in Karnataka, India*, The World Bank, https://documents1.worldbank.org/curated/pt/209541468774682650/pdf/308280IN0Bhoomi01see0also0307591.pdf.
36. *See* M.S. Swaminathan Research Foundation's, *Information Village Research Project (IVRP), Union Territory of Pondicherry*, The World Bank, https://documents1.worldbank.org/curated/en/107871468040601362/pdf/514570WP0IN0MS10Box342028B01PUBLIC1.pdf.

divide and cancel basic mistrust in technology, most parts of India still need such initiatives so that communities can have digital awareness and access. Further, this inquiry must be considered on the premise and understanding that access to ODR is as much part of access to justice. But the absence of universally effective technology in the post-crisis era has been glaring, which is consequential for court-annexed e-mediations.

Digital access is also incomplete without access in local languages. India is highly diversified by languages beyond English, which is the official language of the courts. Hence, e-mediation services cannot be considered truly accessible across all urban and rural regions if it is only available in English.

It is also not enough for courts and legal services authorities associated with the Supreme Court or High Courts to develop the requisite infrastructure for e-mediation. It is crucial for lower courts (which suffer a colossal pendency of cases), tribunals, and bodies such as Nyaya Panchayats to participate in the development and digitization of mediation at their level so that issues like local language may be addressed. As mediation provides parties an equal platform to voice their side of a case, it must also be in the language they can effectively communicate in. To achieve this, local language experts and digital translation capacities can be developed so that parties can participate effectively in e-mediations. This, of course, must be in parallel with the expansion of internet services to enable the possibility of e-mediation services in the first place.

Creating an effective, fully capable, and accessible online platform for dispute resolution is a costly ordeal. The budget of the e-courts project demonstrates this.[37] A credible e-mediation system demands a particular focus on a platform to provide for the dynamics encountered in a mediation process. This is indeed an opportunity for private-public partnerships, which have beneficial by products like enhancing credibility and a greater pool of mediator expertise.

[B] Credibility

Imparting credibility to e-mediation requires the endorsement of all its stakeholders, like judges, mediators, advocates, government bodies, and the parties or users themselves. Courts, in particular, must provide suitable online platforms with proper infrastructural setup and connectivity. In addition, judges must enable the process by identifying specific cases suitable for referral to e-mediation (instead of in-person mediation only).

When referred to e-mediation, mediators must be skilled in using e-mediation platforms (having a grasp of the elements that play out in a digital platform to facilitate the process). The mediators must also coach parties in the use of technology. And even though such a role would be beyond the mediator's role as a facilitator, it would be necessary to enable effective participation—something unique to a mediator's role in

37. *See* Shalini Seetharam & Sumathi Chandrashekaran, *E-courts in India: From Policy Formation to Implementation*, Vidhi Centre for Legal Policy 14 (July 2016), https://vidhilegalpolicy.in/wp-content/uploads/2019/05/eCourtsinIndia_Vidhi.pdf.

an e-mediation (in comparison to in-person mediations). While courts and mediators play an implementation role, parties must also be willing to participate, supported by their advocates, who must be obligated to provide certain mandatory information to their clients about e-mediation or the online process.

E-mediation, unfortunately, has not had the attention it deserves as compared to ODR vis-à-vis litigation, arbitration, and e-Lok Adalats, which is often a breeding ground for party reluctance, mediator unpreparedness, and hesitance from the court to refer disputes to e-mediation. Moreover, while investments into and discourse on ODR vis-à-vis litigation, arbitration, and Lok Adalats have been prevalent and galvanized,[38] there has been only little reform or specific focus on e-mediation.

To lend credibility and distinct identity to the process of e-mediation, the author posits that not all cases identified by the Supreme Court in *Afcons* may be suitable for e-mediation. Hence, to develop credibility, court-annexed programs should, as a matter of policy, classify cases where e-mediation should be preferred (over physical mediation) and referred upon parties' choices. This emphasis on "party choice" for referrals to e-mediation is generally aligned with the way courts have also adopted online modes based on parties' consent.[39]

When identifying cases preferred for e-mediation, it must be considered exclusive of in-person mediation (on the premise that both are different from each other). The exclusivity is emphasized because e-mediation is often clubbed with other ODR methods, causing a dilution and loss of individuality of e-mediation. This is why the application of mediation is often restricted to in-person mediation (not online).

To legitimize and increase the use of e-mediation, private service providers must be approved for use by court-annexed mediation programs. A collaborative approach must be introduced, so that court-annexed programs can first benefit from the private digital infrastructure. It also widens the choice of mediators, who can use technology, are equipped with different language and communication skill sets, and have diverse backgrounds. This is necessary since a pool of qualified, trained, and experienced mediators are crucial to the development e-mediation process and practice (which should, as far as possible, not accept part-time mediators). In order to configure this pool of mediators, a strict ethical code must be imposed, domain expertise must be emphasized in mediator selection, and technology-related skills must be mandated for e-mediation purposes.

Focused digital infrastructure, credibility, and expertise together can be introduced by way of a pilot project. Fortunately, lessons may be learned from the introduction of e-Lok Adalats for settlements which moved Lok Adalats to fully online

38. *See* NITI Aayog, *Designing the Future of Dispute Resolution: The ODR Policy Plan for India* 7 (October 2020), https://niti.gov.in/sites/default/files/2020-10/Draft-ODR-Report-NITI-Aayog-Committee.pdf.
39. *See* State of Maharashtra v. Praful Desai (2003) 4 SCC 601 (Supreme Court gave legal recognition to recording evidence by videoconferencing if both parties consent to it). *See also*, Supreme Court of India, *Guidelines for Court Functioning Through Video Conferencing During COVID-19 Pandemic* (Suo Motu Writ (Civil) No. 5/2020, Apr. 6, 2020), https://main.sci.gov.in/supremecourt/2020/10853/10853_2020_0_1_21588_Judgement_06-Apr-2020.pdf.

platforms.[40] Around 27 e-Lok Adalats were organized, in June 2020, in 15 different States, as a real-time response to the pandemic crisis and the need for settlements, given the increasing caseload.[41] E-Lok Adalat is one such innovation where technology has been used to its maximum advantage, delivering justice at people's doorstep. It is also cost-effective as it largely excludes organizational expenses.

However, Lok Adalats are not for resolving disputes. They are for settling them without facilitation, marking a stark difference in the process. Lok Adalats require limited human interference in the form of an adjudicator to settle the case, unlike mediation. The technology and the human element must be in sync for e-mediation to find credibility as a process. A virtual room for e-mediations should be sufficiently equipped to disassociate from the process since individuals need to trust the technology and the process.

[C] Expertise

In e-mediation, while technology and design play a role in making the virtual room accessible for a user, mediator expertise is also key. And when considering court-annexed programs, there has been a general concern about the quality of mediators, besides user experience and satisfaction of outcomes.

In India, mediations that result from "party choice" are limited, and even corporate culture does not mandate mediation as the first choice of dispute resolution.[42] This has hindered the effective use of mediation which has, in turn, supported pendency and delayed/affected the adoption of e-mediation. Besides, parties, advocates, and mediators have also failed to make the grade in adopting online tools.

E-mediation, being a virtual process, requires adaptation/conditioning of the process in a virtual form. Therefore, it is not a matter of squeezing in-person mediation methods into a virtual format. E.g., a mediator's opening statements must include navigating the online platform, explaining the digital needs/requirements to ensure smooth functioning of the process, communications tips, housekeeping rules, etc. Further, mediators will also need to equip themselves for using digital platforms in local languages to establish a safe space and enhance communication skills.

The success of e-mediation also needs case management expertise, which is a human resource investment required in court-annexed programs to manage and administer e-mediation cases. For this, training manuals for e-mediation will be needed for implementation, particularly for those segments of the e-mediation process that are novel or different from the usual in-person mediation. The Mediation and Conciliation

40. *See* NALSA, *Statistical Snapshot 2020*, NATIONAL LEGAL SERVICES AUTHORITY, https://nalsa.gov.in/library/statistical-snapshot/statistical-snapshot-2020.
41. *See* PIB Delhi, *27 E-Lok Adalats organized in 15 States leading to disposal of 2.51 lakh cases from June to October, 2020*, MINISTRY OF LAW & JUSTICE (Nov. 23, 2020, 2:17 PM), https://pib.gov.in/PressReleasePage.aspx?PRID=1675059. *See, e.g.*, Gujarat State Legal Services Authority, *Standard Operating Procedure e-Lok Adalat*, https://images.assettype.com/barandbench/2020-09/05de01a6-4059-4a79-9ed5-fd4a136400d7/E_Lok_Adalat_SOP.pdf.
42. This is based on individual and case management experience and informal conversations with corporate counsels of leading law firms.

Project Committee (MCPC) of the Supreme Court has developed several manuals in the past for India's court-annexed mediation program. Similarly, a manual on e-mediation may also be taken up as a specific project by the MCPC, identifying the typology of cases suitable for e-mediation. Ultimately, the abovementioned aspects would need to be stitched together into a fully capable case management system for e-mediations under court-annexed programs.

While the e-courts project envisages a mediation module, it does not delve into the particulars of the process or training. Mediation case management is integrated with the court's case management, which advisably must be developed with some particular focus (at least) so that e-mediation is not made dependent on the functioning of e-courts.

[D] Enforcement

Key resistance to trying mediation that a court does not sanction (private mediation) has been the enforcement of the mediation's outcome. This has trickled into private mediation, and very instances exist where a court has referred a case to private mediation service providers.

It is also questionable as to whether the mediation process conducted outside a court-annexed program has any recognition in law. Unlike mediation under private settings, a settlement agreement resulting from a court-annexed mediation receives the recognition of the referral court and is enforceable as a decree on agreed terms ("consent decree").[43] For a more detailed discussion, *see* Chapter on court-annexed mediation. E-mediation could suffer from similar concerns of a lack of recognition and enforcement of the process or the outcome.

To circumvent the gap, private mediations have placed reliance on Part III of the Arbitration Act by endorsing so in the settlement agreement that the process (actually) proceeded as a conciliation under Part III of the Arbitration and Conciliation Act. This is done to make private mediation settlements enforceable as an award on agreed terms (consent award) under section 74 of the Arbitration Act. While this has provided some impetus to private mediation, it is still primarily based on fictional/indirect means without any case law recognizing such practice. For example, in *Shri Ravi Aggarwal v. Shri Anil Jagota,*[44] the Delhi High Court refused to enforce a mediated settlement agreement (resulting from a private mediation), which was sought to be enforced/implemented under section 74 of the Arbitration and Conciliation Act (read with sections 30 and 36). The court reasoned that Part III of the Arbitration and Conciliation Act only applied to settlement agreements that resulted from conciliation proceedings under the law and not otherwise. Hence, without recognition of a resolution through a private service provider, private-public partnerships cannot also manifest.

43. *See Statistical Snapshot 2020,* National Legal Services Authority, https://nalsa.gov.in/library/statistical-snapshot/statistical-snapshot-2020.
44. Shri Ravi Aggarwal v. Shri Anil Jagota (2009) SCC Online Del 1475.

Concerning the signing of settlement agreements using digital or electronic signatures, the Information Technology Act 2000 (IT Act)[45] adopts the international standards laid down in the UNCITRAL Model Law on E-Commerce to validate contracts and authenticity of signatures using electronic authentication techniques.[46] Most regulators and compliance bodies now use electronic signatures for instruments like contracts, wills, trusts, and negotiable instruments. They are also used by some court-annexed mediation centers and e-Lok Adalats.[47] Hence, a digital or electronic signature is a valid option available for e-mediated settlement agreements.

In the context of the *E-Mediation Issue Wheel*, the following concluding remarks may be drawn from the discourse above:

(i) Identified sectors and suitable cases for e-mediation need to be separated and considered distinctly from in-person mediation. To simply transpose in-person mediation onto an online platform is not a viable solution. E-mediation needs to be considered a unique and distinct process given the levels of human interaction needed, rather than merely consolidating it with ODR generally. Taking stock of examples can be a starting point. In particular, §11.03 *infra* takes stock of various sectors, cases, and methods that have successfully adopted e-mediation (or other similar methods).

(ii) Infrastructural development of e-mediation must contemplate an effective and fully capable online platform, including possible private-public collaborations. Capacity building in the form of technologically trained mediators and case managers is also essential. In addition, it requires the creation of a pool of mediators in association with private mediation service providers.

§11.03 USE CASE STUDIES IN INDIA

E-mediation must find use cases to support sector-specific implementation. The following sectors have developed and adopted in-house, regulated, specific, and private solutions for case resolutions. The use cases in this segment indicate the specific types of cases or subject matters that invite a compelling preference for the use of e-mediation. These cases have also attempted to address the pockets of the *E-Mediation Issue Wheel* for a specific target audience and gained much success, thus, making a case against universalization of the process. For each use case, the first step is usually adopting technology and creating user trust, followed by the implementation of a nonadjudicative case resolution method.

45. Information Technology Act, 2000, §§ 4–5.

46. *See* Nishith Desai Associates, The Information Technology Act 3 (Chamber of Income Tax Consultants, November 2001), http://www.nishithdesai.com/fileadmin/user_upload/pdfs/The_information_Technology_act.pdf.

47. *See* Delhi State Legal Services Authority, *E-Lok Adalat Standard Operating Protocol*, https://delhicourts.nic.in/Circulars/Sep20/8b.pdf, ¶ 11.

[A] Banking and Recovery

The banking sector in India has been an early adopter of technology and a front-runner in going paperless through the digital banking movement. With the advent of e-commerce payment systems, such as Paytm, Google Pay, PhonePe, and others, online payment is the new norm. Thus, the settlement of cases involving payments through an effective online digital resolution framework is simply a corollary. Banking services such as sanctioning loans, fraudulent and unauthorized withdrawals, and honoring bank guarantees are some of such disputes that can be resolved through an officer known as the ombudsman.

Through conciliation or mediation, the ombudsman endeavors to promote a settlement of the complaint between the complainant and the bank. If the terms of the settlement are acceptable to the parties as a full and final settlement of the complaint, the ombudsman passes an order as per the terms of the settlement, which are binding on the bank and the complainant. The Banking Ombudsman Scheme 2006 (BOS) provides for the entire scheme of resolution of disputes.[48] Section 7(2) of the BOS states that:

> The Banking Ombudsman shall receive and consider complaints relating to the deficiencies in banking or other services filed on the grounds mentioned in clause 8 irrespective of the pecuniary value of the deficiency in service complained and facilitate their satisfaction or settlement by agreement or through conciliation and mediation between the bank concerned and the aggrieved parties or by passing an Award as per the provisions of the Scheme.

Interestingly, the ombudsman scheme has a hybrid nature, in that the ombudsman can also pass an award as per the provision of the BOS. Thus, the ombudsman first plays the role of the mediator or a conciliator. But if the parties do not settle, the ombudsman wears the hat of an adjudicator and passes an award.[49] The ombudsman model for identified cases may be a starting point for implementing e-mediation using existing infrastructure. The BOS supports an entirely digital complaint management system,[50] monitored by the Reserve Bank of India (RBI), and the settlement process is (primarily) documents-only and binding on the parties.

As the BOS was not serving its purposes effectively/efficiently in terms of consumer-related cases in banking services, the Payment and Settlement Systems Act 2007 (PSS Act) was passed, providing for the regulation and supervision of payment systems in India. Under PSS Act, the RBI constituted the Board for Regulation and Supervision of Payment and Settlement Systems (BPSS) to discharge its duties and functions under the PSS Act. The PSS Act and the regulations under it cover matters like

48. The Banking Ombudsman Scheme 2006 was introduced under section 35A of the Banking Regulation Act, 1949, by the Reserve Bank of India, with effect from 1995.
49. *See* the Ombudsman Scheme for Digital Transactions, 2019, https://cms.rbi.org.in/cms/Documents/en-US/The%20Ombudsman%20Scheme%20for%20Digital%20Transactions_FAQ.pdf (*see* FAQ no. 16).
50. *See* *Complaint Management System*, Reserve Bank of India, https://cms.rbi.org.in/cms/IndexPage.aspx?aspxerrorpath=/cms/cms/indexpage.aspx.

form of application for authorization for commencing/carrying on a payment system and grant of authorization, payment instructions, and determination of standards of payment systems, furnishing of returns, documents, and other information, furnishing of accounts and balance sheets by the system provider, etc. In this regard, the PSS Act lays down an elaborate mechanism for resolving disputes between system participants in a payment system, between a system participant and a system provider, and between system providers through a digital platform.

The PSS Act requires the system provider to make provision in its rules or regulations to create a panel to decide disputes between system participants. Where any system participant is dissatisfied with the panel's decision, or where disputes arise between system participant and system provider or between system providers, such disputes are required to be referred to the RBI for adjudication, whose decision shall be final and binding on the parties. In cases the RBI, in its capacity as either a system participant or system provider, is itself a party to the dispute, there is a provision (under section 24) for referring such cases to the Central Government for adjudication.

In 2010, a dispute resolution framework was envisaged, which was modeled on the hearing and settlement method under the ID Act.[51] The framework creates a separate process from the banking ombudsman under BOS.

In the ODR drive, banks have played a crucial role, collaborating with private service providers/aggregators in furthering online means of settlements and case resolutions. Although e-mediation has not gained any statistical use or specific support, the ombudsman method is structured as a mediation model. One may speculate that since arbitration is now time-bound under section 29A of the Arbitration Act, mediation has likely stepped down the ladder of preferred dispute resolution choices in the banking sector. A shortage in human resources for mediations is perhaps another reason for its lower preference than arbitration.

The BOS, if adopted digitally, would be a starting point for e-mediation of cases in recoveries related to small and individual businesses. The experience of e-mediation under the BOS could influence the banking sector to develop the e mediation model in other cases involving, or related to, the banking sector. For example, while there has been a steady increase of settlements in bankruptcy and insolvency disputes, mediation (or even e-mediation) remains an unexplored avenue. *See* Chapter on mediating company, insolvency, and banking disputes discussing the possible avenues where mediation may be applied.

[B] Consumer and Commercial

With the liberalization of investments in e-commerce between 2008 and 2012, there was a steep increase in consumer complaints and cases, which resulted in stressed consumer forums. While Lok Adalats accepted cases relating to refunds, delayed

51. *See* C. Padmanabhan, *Dispute Resolution Mechanism under the Payment and Settlement Systems Act, 2007*, Reserve Bank of India (DPSS.CO.CHD.No.654/ 03.01.03 / 2010–2011, Sept. 24, 2010), https://rbidocs.rbi.org.in/rdocs/Notification/PDFs/CDPSSC0910.PDF.

deliveries, etc., the process of referrals to Lok Adalats took a fair number of hearings, spanning over three to six months, resulting in consumer dissatisfaction and strain on the existing infrastructure of quasi-judicial bodies.[52]

Hence, online complaint and redressal portals were developed in-house for case resolution. The most effective model, which was tested at a pilot level, was the banking ombudsman model (particularly for credit card cases) adopted by the American e-commerce giant, eBay. The eBay model sought to implement online settlement and case management of consumer and product-related cases and found success.[53]

To meet the "e" requirements of commerce, a formal framework for resolving consumer disputes online was introduced in the precrisis era under the Consumer Protection Act 2019 (CPA), which introduced consumer mediation cells that would resolve consumer grievances using technological solutions. The CPA addresses enforcement (like electronic signatures) by referencing the provisions of the IT Act. All in all, in the precrisis era, consumer cases were identified as appropriate for e-resolution.

Under the CPA, the dispute resolution procedure contemplates that a complaint (at the first instance) is first made to the district forums, which are local consumer tribunals set up in different cities. Thereafter, the first appeal would lie before a State consumer forum (one in each State), and the second appeal would lie before the national consumer forum, followed by a final appeal to the Supreme Court. A reference to mediation can be made at any stage. The Consumer Protection (Mediation) Regulations 2020 detail the process for mediating consumer disputes. However, there is no mention of using online platforms in either the Act or the regulations, even though the filing system is fully digital.

Mediation in consumer cases has been high, and the post-crisis era mainly has seen a high disposal rate. *Table 11.3* shows the statistics on the disposal of consumer cases, which represents a high percentage of disposal rate. Most consumer cases are disposed of through Lok Adalats and mediation (including referrals to recognized mediation institutions like Delhi Dispute Resolution Society). However, since consumer mediation cells are a new addition to the consumer dispute redressal system, there is currently no data available about their use.

Table 11.3 Disposal Rate of Consumer Cases

Name of Agency	*Cases Filed Since 1986*	*Cases Disposed as on March 24, 2021*	*Cases Pending*	*Disposal Rate (%)*
National Commission	137,725	116,368	21,357	84.49%

52. *See*, e.g., Lok Adalat Eastern Region Report, *supra* note 4, at p. 106 (other such studies undertaken indicate a docket in the Lok Adalats in relation to consumer cases).

53. *See Resolution Centre*, EBAY, https://resolutioncenter.ebay.com/. *See also*, eBay, *User Guide: Tips to Avoid and Manage Disputes*, http://pics.ebay.com/aw/pics/in/pdf/sellercentral/handling-buyer-disputes.pdf.

Name of Agency	*Cases Filed Since 1986*	*Cases Disposed as on March 24, 2021*	*Cases Pending*	*Disposal Rate (%)*
State Commissions	966,812	842,337	124,475	87.13%
District Commissions	4,437,941	4,039,375	398,566	91.02%
Total	**5,542,478**	**4,998,080**	**544,398**	**90.18%**

Similarly, both the Commercial Courts Act 2015 (CCA) and the Companies Act 2013 (CA 2013) envisage a mediation referral mechanism for case resolution under its respective rules, i.e., the Commercial Courts (Pre-Institution Mediation & Settlement) Rules 2018 and the Companies (Mediation and Conciliation) Rules 2016. The CCA provides for mandatory pre-institution mediation, and the CA 2013 relies on the tribunal's discretionary referral to mediation. Even though statistics have been provided on the functioning of the commercial court, there is simply no demarcation as to whether (and how many) cases were disposed of through pre-institution mediation.

In the post-crisis era, a key conversation is the protection of small and medium scale businesses. From a sector-specific perspective, for micro and small enterprises (MSEs), contractual disputes undergo a conciliation process through the "MSME Samadhaan—Delayed Payment Monitoring System." However, there is no data or details on whether (and the number of) cases followed the online process or if they independently closed cases through a mutual settlement. As per the statistical information provided, out of approximately 77,000 cases filed since the inception of the Micro, Small, and Medium Enterprises Development Act 2006, approximately 7,000 were mutually settled, of which approximately 6,700 were disposed of by the MSE Facilitation Council.[54] However, it is unclear whether this was through the online platform, e-mediation, or physical mediation.

The timing to adopt a fully digital model may be right, given that the MSEs are well versed with technology and that legislative and policy support has been frequent.

[C] IP and Trade

Growing commerce and consumers have spiked innovation and development of intellectual property rights (IPR), but that has not been without a rise in disputes and conflicts. IPR cases typically include patent, copyright, trademark, and domain name-related disputes. In India, IPR case resolution has been moving toward digitization

54. *MSME Samadhaan: Delayed Payment Monitoring System*, Ministry of Micro Small and Medium Enterprises, https://samadhaan.msme.gov.in/MyMsme/MSEFC/MSEFC_Welcome.aspx.

since the precrisis era,[55] for instance, through virtual conferencing facilities (in 2016–2017) at the Patent Office, which was an impetus to higher case closure rates.[56]

The digital resolution movement for IPR cases started with domain name cases by the World Intellectual Property Organization (WIPO). In terms of suitability, WIPO identifies the following to be best suited for resolution by in-person mediation and e-mediation: licensing agreements (e.g., trademarks, patents, copyright, software), research and development agreements, technology transfer agreements, distribution agreements, franchising agreements, IT agreements, data processing agreements, joint venture agreements, consultancy agreements, art marketing agreements, TV distribution and formats, film production, copyright collective management, cases arising out of agreements in settlement of prior court litigation.[57]

Even though there is limited data on in-person mediation in IPR cases in India, in-person mediation and hybrid mediations have generally been successful. The following segments discuss the specific types of IPR cases.

[1] Patent Cases

Patent suits are generally complex. Hence, a mixed-mode method is often seen at play in patent infringement suits. Roche-Cipla[58] and Merck-Glenmark[59] disputes are two classic examples. The Roche-Cipla dispute was mediated in-person through a court referral, and the Merck-Glenmark dispute was mediated in-person by party-choice. In particular, the Roche-Cipla mediation of "agree to disagree" indicated that perhaps voluntariness in entering mediation is key to the process if a resolution is to be expected. The consent of both parties in entering mediation is suggested to be a better means of finding resolution and making better use of the nonadversarial processes.[60]

Patent issues often give rise to license negotiations. Due to the limited lifespan of a patent, more often than not, the patentee is willing to offer licenses for the use of its patents, inviting the implementors to the table to negotiate, to either make a deal or settle a dispute. Here certain disclosures of commercial secrets contained in license agreements in open court can be a severe cause of concern for the patentee. Courts have tried to tackle this problem by setting up confidentiality clubs, whereby only

55. The author is thankful to Vrinda Bagaria, Associate, Singh & Singh Law Firm, for her subject matter knowledge, research references and support.
56. *See* Vadali Rambabu, Modernisation of Intellectual Property Offices in India Ideas from the Experience of the Japan Patent Office, https://ipindia.gov.in/writereaddata/images/pdf/report-tambhu-vadal-march-2007.pdf.
57. *See WIPO Caseload Summary*, World Intellectual Property Organization, https://www.wipo.int/amc/en/center/caseload.html.
58. *See* Shamnad Basheer, *Roche vs Cipla: Pondering the Puzzle*, Spicy IP (Sept. 11, 2012), https://spicyip.com/2012/09/roche-vs-cipla-pondering-puzzle.html.
59. *See* Madhulika Vishwanathan, *Merck: Glenmark to Mediate in Januvia (Sitagliptin) Patent Infringement Case*, Spicy IP, https://spicyip.com/2014/07/merck-glenmark-to-mediate-in-januvia-sitagliptin-patent-infringement-case.html.
60. *See* Shamnad Bhasheer, *Andhyarujina vs Adversariality: A Legal Lesson for Life*, Spicy IP (Apr. 4, 2017), https://spicyip.com/2017/04/andhyarujina-vs-adversariality-a-legal-lesson-for-life.html.

members of the club (limited to advocates and experts appointed by the parties) can look at the documents relating to the disputes.[61] No representative or employee of the concerned parties is allowed to be part of the club. However, before a confidentiality club can be constituted, the cause must pass the muster of satisfying the court about the confidential sensitivity of the document. Moreover, since the matter proceeds before an open court, parties run the risk of public disclosure of sensitive information if the court does agree with the confidential nature of the documents in question.

Hence, there is a strong inclination among companies to gravitate toward settling their disputes[62] rather than entering (or prolonging) litigation proceedings. Given that these cases involve multiple stakeholders from different jurisdictions, several meetings, discussions, and negotiations are conducted online, and the settlement agreements are signed digitally. In such scenarios, closed-door mediation, or even e-mediation, is well suited to serve the needs of the parties involved.

[2] *Trademark and Domain Cases*

With the advent of e-commerce, anyone can be a seller. However, with that comes frequent instances of the sale of counterfeit goods online. As mandated by the IT (Intermediaries Guidelines) Rules 2011,[63] e-commerce entities must provide Grievance Redressal Officers ('GRO') to address disputes of IP owners who identify the sale of counterfeit goods on the internet.

This movement has been powered by the increasing e-commerce and the need for swift and effective digital consumer complaint redressal. While the consumer courts (and now also Lok Adalats) are trying to run purely on virtual modes by partnering with private service providers, the eBay example is a leader in this field,[64] given the high efficiency of over 60 million cases that eBay's resolution tool has resolved.[65] While the banking sector in India (particularly in credit card cases) has adopted such resolution tools, it remains very private and specific, unable to find wider application

61. *See*, e.g., Telefonaktiebolaget LM Ericsson (Publ) v. Xiaomi Technology & Ors, 4 2017 SCC OnLine Del 11069 where the court on the facts of the case permitted the establishment of a confidentiality club. *See also*, Amendments to the Delhi High Court (Original Side) Rules, 2018 (Chapter VII Rule 17 on confidentiality clubs).
62. *See*, e.g., Telefonaktiebolaget LM Ericsson (Publ) v. Xiaomi Technology & Ors., 4 2017 SCC OnLine Del 11069; Dolby International AB v. GDN Enterprises Pvt. Ltd., 1 Order dated Aug. 4, 2017, by a learned Single Judge in IA 6911/2017 in CS (Comm) 1425/2016; Interdigital Technology Corporation & Ors. v. Xiaomi Corporation & Ors. I.A. 6447/2020 in CS(COMM) 296/2020.
63. Created by the Central Government, in exercise of the powers conferred by clause (zg) of subsection (2) of section 87 read with subsection (2) of section 79 of the Information Technology Act, 2000.
64. *See* Colin Rule, *Resolving Disputes in the World's Largest Marketplace*, AC Resolution 8 (Fall 2008), http://colinrule.com/writing/acr2008.pdf (based on this personal experience, Colin Rule writes about SquareTrade, a pilot program that resolved several million eBay disputes through online mediation. However, there was a need to keep data and information in relation to eBay confidential; therefore, eBay made the decision to bring ODR in-house and hired a person dedicated to dispute resolution between buyers and sellers).
65. *See eBay-Style Online Courts Could Resolve Smaller Claims*, BBC News (Feb. 16, 2015), https://www.bbc.com/news/uk-31483099.

or adaptability. Many other e-commerce giants like Flipkart and Snapdeal have attempted to follow suit but have been unable to capture the Indian market in swift case resolution (besides the refund, return, or exchange options available to a dissatisfied/aggrieved customer).

E-commerce websites frequently comply with the trademark owner's request and remove disputed listings that violate IPR, thus, bringing an end to the trademark controversy. However, occasionally, e-commerce websites may also refuse to exercise their discretion to remove a disputed listing, leading to the institution of suits. In such cases, the e-commerce entities assert the safe harbor provisions under the IT Act, which the Supreme Court has expounded in *Shreya Singhal v. Union of India.*[66]

Since trademark, by its very nature, is an identifier of the business, rights claimed over domain names also get covered under trademark law. However, there is no specific provision dealing with the same, and they are dealt with under the law relating to passing off. Concerning domain names, cybersquatting is a practice where domain names bearing names of existing companies are registered by various individuals and then sold back to the same company for a profit when the company wishes to set up its website. Domain names, often called online trademarks or e-trademarks, are registered on a first-come, first-serve basis and, as such, need to be protected, for which a person or entity holding such rights requires an appropriate dispute resolution forum or mechanism.

In India, domain name cases have been identified as further clogging the judicial system (which is already overburdened). There has been some chatter about developing a separate domain name disputes policy to combat issues such as cybersquatting, but that is still in the pipeline and may take several months before it is a reality. Nevertheless, declogging the system is a priority in which domain name cases can be in the lead. Their suitability is reflected in WIPO's caseload statistics, wherein domain name cases have the highest success rates of resolution through mediation, followed closely by copyright cases.[67] Despite the viability, there has been no move toward e-mediation, and a focus on a virtual formal court system continues.

[3] Copyright and Others

Given the struggles of court-annexed mediation programs, IPR cases are often directed for resolution by industry associations or bodies with an internal (specialized) ADR forum for their members (much like trade and commerce cases), who use hybrid methods of online and in-person meetings.[68]

An example of the use of in-person mediations in a copyright dispute is the case of a designer, Vaishali Shadagule, who accused Sanjay Garg (Founder of Raw Mango)

66. Shreya Singhal v. Union of India (2015) 5 SCC 1, ¶¶ 116–119. *See also*, Christian Louboutin Sas v. Nakul Bajaj & Ors. (2018) 253 DLT 728, ¶¶ 9–10.
67. *WIPO Caseload Summary*, World Intellectual Property Organization, https://www.wipo.int/amc/en/center/caseload.html.
68. *See*, e.g., Mediation, International Trademark Association, https://www.inta.org/resources/mediation/.

of plagiarism. Garg filed a defamation suit and, while the matter was pending, the parties mediated before the Fashion Development Council of India. The matter was resolved in mediation, and this was within four working days of the institution of the suit.[69] Open success stories give in-person mediation some visibility and traction. However, users/parties continue to rely on the courts to make referrals rather than mediation being the first (appropriate) choice.

What is also needed are suitable policies to implement platforms, including those used internationally, like the WIPO platform, and integrate e-mediation of IPR cases through various administrative offices concerning IPR.

[D] Personal Injury, Matrimonial and Others

There has been a move to digitize matters concerning motor vehicle accidents and traffic violations, where penalties/fines (for instance) can be paid online.[70] Moreover, the Supreme Court has also recognized and suggested a need for a mandatory and first-mediation approach in motor vehicle accidents and traffic violation cases.[71]

In cases of matrimonial or family disputes, where mediation has been mandatory in certain States,[72] courts seem to have taken the view that e-mediation is a party-choice and parties can choose not to proceed with the option, thus, making a clear distinction between in-person and online mediations. Moreover, matrimonial or family disputes being highly fragile and emotionally sensitive may be better suited to in-person mediations (again drawing a clear distinction between in-person and online mediations). Thus, instead of being a replacement, online family mediations may be considered an addition to the already existing face-to-face approach of mediations to provide parties with any potential benefits (e.g., in cases where parties are living, studying, or working abroad).

§11.04 END CASE AND TAKEAWAYS

Internationally, a key driver of rapid growth and globalization can be attributed to the rising number of individuals connected to the internet. Statistically, in comparison to the 1990s, reports from the early 2000s show that at least one-fifth of the world's population is connected to the internet. In another recent update on mobile internet

69. *See* Prarthana Patnaik, *The New Age of IP Mediation in India*, Spicy IP (July 26, 2018), https://spicyip.com/2018/07/the-new-age-of-ip-mediation-in-india.html.
70. M. R. Krishna Murthi v. New India Assurance Co. Ltd., (2020) 15 SCC 493. *See also*, *District-Level Motor Accident Mediation Cells to be Inaugurated on Aug 10*, The Hindu (Aug. 8, 2020, 6:45 PM), https://www.thehindu.com/news/cities/Madurai/district-level-motor-accident-mediation-cells-to-be-inaugurated-on-aug-10/article28906932.ece.
71. *See* Saradha Kumar, *Mediation in Motor Accident Cases*, Samhita-CAMP Mediation Series-18, https://www.sharadasc.com/wp-content/uploads/2019/07/Mediation-in-Motor-Accident-Cases-SCSA.pdf.
72. *See* Family Court Act, 1984, § 9. *See also*, Krishnaprasad, *HC to Family Courts: Don't Avoid Mediation in Matrimonial Disputes*, The Hindu, https://www.thehindu.com/news/cities/bangalore/hc-to-family-courts-dont-avoid-mediation-in-matrimonial-disputes/article6670266.ece.

users, China has reported its internet users as around 650 million persons, and India has approximately 560 million users.[73]

In 2010, the UNCITRAL General Assembly raised questions regarding the accommodation of international electronic commerce, inconsistent mechanisms, and the development of regional ODR systems.[74] This initiated discourse on developing generic rules and model laws that would enable business-to-business and business-to-consumer cases to be resolved in a cost-effective and time-bound manner. The UNCITRAL General Assembly (in December 2016) spelled out what would entail "online" resolution; it offered technical notes catering to cross-border issues that were seen to be a substantial increase among "nation-states."[75] It defined ODR to mean a broad spectrum of resolution tools available digitally, including mediation and conciliation. The principle observed in the technical notes was that:

> ODR ought to be simple, fast and efficient, in order to be able to be used in a "real world setting," including that it should not impose costs, delays and burdens that are disproportionate to the economic value at stake.

Similarly, the World Bank Guidelines on ADR include ODR as one of the options and emphasized the suitability of different e-resolution tools for different processes.[76]

In this context, the development of e-mediation internationally has seen focused implementation, separate from physical mediation. However, the e-mediation movement in India needs to identify the specific types of cases appropriate for e-mediation, which must be implemented pretrial on a mandatory basis. The Supreme Court has been petitioned to mandate pretrial mediation in some instances in the post-crisis era, given the growing docket.[77]

While a roadmap for ODR has been developed, the time may be suitable for carving out a niche for e-mediation for cases concerning IPR, banking, recovery, consumer, and commercial disputes. A macro/mass policy for ODR will not allow the e-mediation process to emerge independently in its unique terms. However, this must be supplemented by suitable infrastructure and increased awareness among users (and their advocates). Given the issues surrounding cost and effectiveness, privatization with public sanctions under the court and tribunal-annexed programs may be the best start. In addition, new consumer and company mediation regulations may be enacted

73. *See* McKinsey Global Institute, Digital India (March 2019). *See also*, Sandhya Keelery, *Internet Usage in India: Statistics & Facts*, Statista, https://www.statista.com/topics/2157/internet-usage-in-india/.
74. *See* UN General Assembly, *Report of Working Group III (Online Dispute Resolution) on the work of its twenty-second session (Vienna, 13-17 December 2010)*, UNCITRAL (A/CN.9/716, Jan. 17, 2011), https://undocs.org/en/A/CN.9/716%20.
75. *UNCITRAL Technical Notes on Online Disputes Resolution*, United Nations Commission on International Trade Law (2017), https://uncitral.un.org/sites/uncitral.un.org/files/media-documents/uncitral/en/v1700382_english_technical_notes_on_odr.pdf.
76. Investment Climate Advisory Services of the World Bank Group, Alternative Dispute Resolution Guidelines (June 2011), http://documents1.worldbank.org/curated/en/108381468170047697/pdf/707630ESW0P1160BLIC00153220ADRG0Web.pdf.
77. *See* PIL Petition filed in Youth Bar Association & Ors. v. Union of India & Ors., https://www.livelaw.in/pdf_upload/pdf_upload-378275.pdf.

which contemplate online resolution and mandate impaneled mediators to retain tech skills to conduct e-mediations.

The e-courts roadmap, as it stands, does not envisage the adoption of e-mediation,[78] despite the rise in pendency of cases in the post-crisis era (i.e., since March 2020). But a model must be promulgated, and necessary amendments must be made (in statutes, rules, and regulation) that incorporate physical and online mediations separately, as showcased in *Figure 11.2*.

Figure 11.2 Roadmap for E-Mediation in India

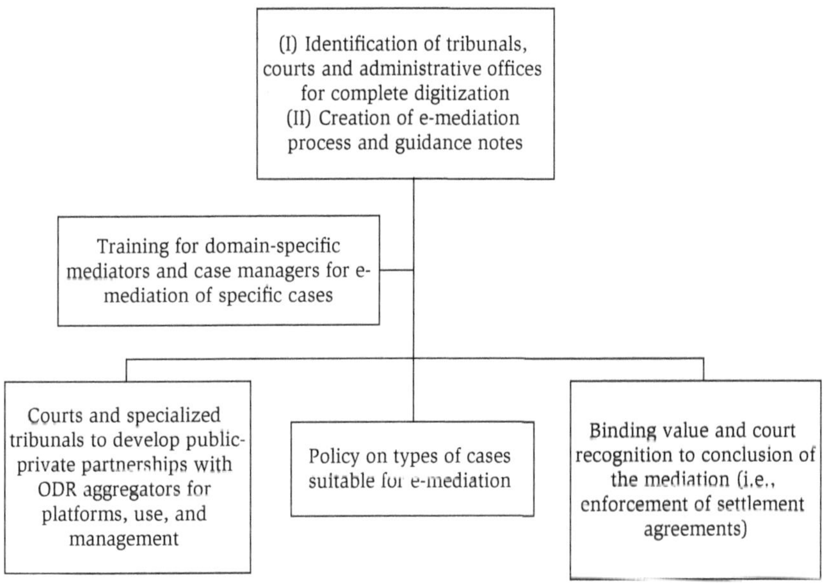

78. *See E-Courts Project: About Us*, ECOURTS SERVICES: DISTRICT AND TALUKA COURTS OF INDIA, https://services.ecourts.gov.in/ecourtindia_v6/static/about-us.php.

CHAPTER 12

Community Mediation and Citizen Empowerment*

*Kudrat Dev & Ajay Kumar Pandey**

§12.01 INTRODUCTION

The term "community" in India is not just a description for groups of people with specific characteristics but is a way and system of living through social interdependence, which is continually being imagined, invented, and reinvented.[1] The culture and system of the community have transcended into diverse systems from "Gram Sabhas"[2] to "Khap Panchayats"[3] to "Mohalla Sabhas."[4]

Community mediation has been prevalent in India under different names and in diverse forms. It is a *myth* that community mediation has been exported to India from the west.[5] Although arguably, certain European and western models from the UK and US, particularly, may have revived both the interest in community mediation and the institutionalization of mediation in India through legal reforms. Few studies exist on

* The able assistance of Balapragatha M is greatly appreciated.

1. A "community" is constituted by a set of practices, a series of "performances," through which claims are made about collective and intersubjective identities. *See generally*, Anne Hardgrove, *Community and Public Culture: The Marwaris in Calcutta 1897-1997*, HARDGROVE/COMMUNITY AND PUBLIC CULTURE, http://www.gutenberg-e.org/haa01/frames/fhaa02.html.
2. *See* INDIA CONST. Art. 243A.
3. *See generally*, Vijender Singh Beniwal, *An Appraisal of Khap Panchayats: Issues and Concerns*, in PANCHAYATI RAJ AND RURAL DEVELOPMENT (Japdeep Singh & Anju Beniwal eds., 2015); Guruswamy Menaka & Singh Aditya, *Accessing Injustice: The Gram Nyayalayas Act, 2008*, 45(43) ECON. & POL. WKLY. 19 (2010).
4. *See generally*, Manish Sisodia, *Delhi Government's Revolutionary Initiative*, MOHALLA SABHA, http://mohallasabha.delhi.gov.in/.
5. *See* Bert Suykens & Danielle Stein, *Whoever Has the Stick Guides the Buffalo: Neutrality, Party Politics and Authority Formation in Community Mediation in the Central and West Terai, Nepal*, 11(1) J. SOUTH-ASIAN DEV. 88, 93 (2016).

community mediation in India[6] and Asia more generally.[7] However, research and documentation on community mediation in India are urgently required for two reasons: first, the *myth* needs to be dispelled with evidence; and second, the hope for citizen empowerment through community mediation in India is more likely to be fulfilled through learnings from Indian community mediation systems, as opposed to reliance on research dominated by western examples.

§12.02 ORIGIN OF COMMUNITY MEDIATION AND ITS RE-ENERGIZERS IN INDIA

[A] Origin of Community Mediation in India and Its Underlying Value

There is demonstrable evidence that Indian citizens have been heavily relying upon mediation to resolve their disputes.[8] Indeed, India, like many other village societies,[9] has been taking mediatory assistance of elders or peacemakers.[10] Indigenous dispute resolution practices at the community level,[11] such as *Parishads, Kula, Shreni*, and *Uga*,[12] predate the Anglo-Saxon legal systems introduced after colonization.[13] However, there is a lack of official records about these processes, which is attributable to colonization.[14]

Several village societies have had informal groups of elders to mediate disputes. However, the first formal institution in India is that of the *Pancha* (body of five men with a head called the *Sarpanch*) in India.[15] Before British colonialism, in the *panchayat* system, designated village elders assisted in resolving community disputes, including repayment of the debt, domestic violence, theft, infertility, religious discords, and business problems, which continue even today.[16] Like with many social institutions, the genesis of the panchayat is unknown. Before the thirteenth century, social organizations and charities were linked to religious obligations; therefore, the temples

---

6. *See* James A. Wall et al., *Indian and U.S. Community Mediation*, https://ssrn.com/abstract=398160 (hereinafter "Wall").
7. *See* Craig Valters, *Building Justice and Peace from Below? Supporting Community Dispute Resolution in Asia*, Working Politically in Practice Series—Case Study No. 9, 23 (2016) (hereinafter "Valters").
8. *See* Wall, *supra* note 6, at 1-10. *See also* S.K. Chauhan, *Status, Power, and Institutions in Rural Communications in Upper Assam*, in North East India: A Sociological Study 67-76 (S.M. Dubey ed., 1978).
9. *See generally*, D.W. Augsburger, Conflict Mediation Across Cultures: Pathways and Patterns (1992).
10. *See* Wall, *supra* note 6, at 3; S.E. Merry, *Mediation in Non-industrialized Societies*, in Mediation Research 68-90 (K. Kressel & D.G. Pruitt eds., 1989) (hereinafter "Merry").
11. *See* Valters, *supra* note 7, at 4.
12. *See* Mediation Training Manual of India, The Mediation and Conciliation Project Committee, 4, https://main.sci.gov.in/pdf/mediation/MT%20MANUAL%20OF%20INDIA.pdf (hereinafter "MCPC Training Manual").
13. *Id.*, at 1-5.
14. *Id.*, at 1-3.
15. *See* Wall, *supra* note 6, at 1-10; Merry, *supra* note 10.
16. *See generally*, Anil Xavier, *Meditation: Its Origin & Growth in India*, 27 Hamline J. Pub. L. & Pol'y 275 (2006) (hereinafter "Xavier").

became the first centers for social services and, under this system, panchayats evolved and became independent social institutions. The *Panchas* ask questions, suggest concessions, and make their decision.[17] However, the *Panchas* also encourage self-determination in saving face in public and maintaining relationships, usually by conducting private meetings.[18]

Conversely, panchayat mediation has been criticized as inquisitional, authoritarian, male-dominated, and can turn into an arbitration.[19] Consequently, this suggests that the real dispute is left unaddressed due to the public nature of the proceedings, which turns it to be more about public perception than meeting the parties' needs. The informal and private community mediation system of village elders or a private meeting with the *Sarpanch* was also male-dominated, but conceivably aimed at addressing the real conflict by reorienting the parties toward each other in the safe place with "greater potential for parties to admit faults, cooperate, and to develop a genuine commitment to the process."[20] As of date, not every State panchayat law provides for dispute resolution by such *panchayats*.

Before India's independence, the Bihar Provincial Government had set up five experimental *Gram Katchahri* to complement the existing *Gram Panchayats*. After independence, the *Gram Katchahri* was recognized by statute.[21] These *Katchahri* are formed with the underlining feature that "*gaonka samasya gao me niptaiye*" (let the village's problems be settled in the village itself).[22] The modern *Gram Katchahri* is a rural dispute resolution forum of five: headed by a *Sarpanch* and four other elected *Panchas* (members). *Gram Katchahri* is supported by *Nyay Mitra* (law graduates) and *Nyay Sachiva* (volunteers) to help the forum understand and implement its own rules and powers. The *Gram Katchahri* is considered a success as they are efficiently used by local communities, given that a *Katchahri* can "dispense justice with sensitivity to local social conditions."[23] Equally, the reservation of seats for women also contributes to their success.[24]

Nyaya Panchayats have existed since ancient times and have played a very important role in dispute resolution in villages.[25] The Nyaya Panchayat Bill 2009 shows that *Nyaya Panchayats* represent a decentralized dispute redressal system through

17. *See* Wall, *supra* note 6, at 10.
18. *See id.*, at 17.
19. *Id.*, at 7, 10.
20. *Id.*, at 8.
21. *See* The Bihar Panchayat Raj Act 2006, amended by The Bihar Panchayat Raj (Amendment) Act 2016.
22. *See* Jorge Luis Alva-Luperdi & Farah Zahir, *Delivering Rural Justice Through Community-Owned Courts in Bihar, India*, World Bank Blogs (Apr. 25, 2018), https://blogs.worldbank.org/endpovertyinsouthasia/delivering-rural-justice-through-community-owned-courts-bihar-india#_ftn1.
23. *Id.*
24. *See* The Bihar Panchayat Raj Act 2006, §91 (Reservation of seats).
25. Videh Upadhyay, *A Study to Review and Strengthen Nyaya Panchayat in India: Including Aspects of Constitutionality of Nyaya Panchayats with Reference to the Nyaya Panchayat Bill, 2009*, Samarthan-Centre For Development Support and 3E Law (May 2011), https://www.panchayat.gov.in/documents/20126/0/A + STUDY + TO + REVIEW + AND + STRENGTHEN + NYAYA.pdf.

mediation and conciliation at the grassroots level, which requires institutionalized with the local people's involvement. However, the Bill has not yet been enacted for issues of its constitutional validity.

The majority of community mediation and community dispute resolution systems have been male-dominated and criticized for not addressing women's issues and concerns.[26] However, a few examples of systems with active female involvement include: the *Shailishi Adalats* established in West Bengal, wherein one-third seats are reserved for females;[27] the *Mahila Adalat* by the All-India Muslim Women's Personal Law Board that was first established in Lucknow in 2005 and is predominantly run by females;[28] and others such as *Madar Sanagm* established in 1997 by the Tamil Nadu State Legal Aid Authority,[29] *Mahila Panchayat*, and *Mahila Sabhas.*[30]

Shailishi Adalat, for instance, is considered to boost women's self-confidence as it encourages the role of women in public places through a public hearing on issues including domestic violence. The facilitator, or *Shailishidaari*, who is the main activist, ensures that a decision is reached after a discussion.[31] *Shailishidaari* enables understanding of the nature of compulsion that both disputants face with a closer view on the complexities of breaking and establishing relationships.[32] However, *Shailishi Adalats* are not free from criticism for alleged trial by status, power play, and disproportional punishments.[33]

Unfortunately, the full extent of Indian values and traditions of community mediation cannot be conclusively defined because of a lack of records.[34] Indeed, there is a lack of information on informal or unreported community mediation mechanisms or any dynamic cultural changes specific to regions. Despite such obscured origin and incomplete history of community mediation in India, it is generally accepted that historically justice was accessible through a local bottom-up structure by which

26. *See generally*, PREM CHOWDHRY, CONTENTIOUS MARRIAGES, ELOPING COUPLES: GENDER, CASTE AND PATRIARCHY IN NORTHERN INDIA (2007); ERIN P. MOORE, GENDER, LAW, AND RESISTANCE IN INDIA (1998); ERIN P. MOORE, GENDER, POWER, AND LEGAL PLURALISM: RAJASTHAN, INDIA 522–542 (1993); Karine Bates, *The Indian Legal System: A Unique Combination of Traditions, Practices and Modern Values*, in COMMUNICATION, CULTURE AND CONFRONTATION 69–98 (Vibodh Parthasarathi et al. eds., 2010).
27. *See* Shramajibee Mahila Samity, *"Shalishi" in West Bengal a Community-Based Response to Domestic Violence*, 38(17) ECON. & POL. WKLY. 1665, 1668 (2003) (hereinafter "Samity").
28. Sylvia Vatuk, *The "Women's Court" in India: An Alternative Dispute Resolution Body for Women in Distress*, 45(1) J. LEGAL PLURALISM & UNOFFICIAL L. 76, 89 (2013).
29. *Id.*, at 85.
30. *Id.*, at 76.
31. *See* Samity, *supra* note 27, at 1668.
32. *See generally*, Jayati Gupta, *Women, Land and Law: Dispute Resolution at the Village Level*, in DOWRY AND INHERITANCE (S. Basu ed., 2005).
33. *See Bengal's Injustice League*, NATIONAL LEGAL RESEARCH DESK (Jan. 26, 2014), https://nlrd.org/bengals-injustice-league/; Jaideep Mazumdar, *The Injustice of Justice*, TIMES OF INDIA (Jan. 26, 2004, 6:45 PM), https://timesofindia.indiatimes.com/home/sunday-times/deep-focus/The-injustice-of-justice/articleshow/29385084.cms; Jamia Miilia Islamia, *Discriminative and Derogatory Practice Against Women by Khap Panchayats, Shalishi Adalats and Kangaroo Courts in India: An Empirical Study in the States of Haryana, Uttar Pradesh, West Bengal and Rajasthan*, NATIONAL COMMISSION FOR WOMEN, http://ncw.nic.in/sites/default/files/ReportbyJamiaMilia.pdf.
34. *See* MCPC Training Manual, *supra* note 12, at 1–3.

members of the community resolved their disputes amicably and arrived at decisions to realize justice or *Nyaya*.[35]

[B] Rejuvenating Community Mediation in India

Several obstacles such as unawareness about the effectiveness of mediation,[36] the dearth of trained mediators (which is interrelated with the unavailability of mediation trainers), deficient financial aid for mediators and mediation centers, and the lack of a specific law on mediation have greatly inhibited mediation's potential for growth.[37] Neutralizing communication skills, powerful bargaining strategies, facilitated negotiation, and other tools can strengthen the system's capacity to bring justice to society.[38] The potential of citizen empowerment and access to justice through community mediation is yet to be achieved and maximized. This is supported and rejuvenated by a few important pillars: formalism and backing from law and the State; bottom-up community involvement led by the youth; and increased use of technology.

[1] Formalism and Backing from the State

In addition to court-annexed mediation centers, which have played a pivotal role in legitimizing mediation (albeit in the shadow of the courts), government mediation centers such as the Delhi Dispute Resolution Society (DDRS) have rejuvenated community mediation locally in Delhi. Generally, mediation has received support from recent legislative enactments and the judiciary, promulgated mediation as a useful dispute resolution mechanism. This has greatly emphasized the need for a law on mediation[39] and perhaps even led to large-scale community disputes referred to mediation, such as the *Ayodhya* case.[40]

[2] Bottom-Up Community Involvement Led by the Youth

The Indian Institute of Arbitration & Mediation (IIAM) community mediation clinics launched in 2009 in southern India were remodeled as People's Mediation Centres ('PMC') in July 2018, reinitiated as a people's movement.[41] Under the initiative, community members, who are not advocates, are eligible (and encouraged) to be

35. *See id.*, at 4. *See generally*, AMARTYA SEN, THE IDEA OF JUSTICE 20–23, 67–72, 354, 413 (2009) (hereinafter "SEN"); S. MURLIDHAR, LAW, POVERTY AND LEGAL AID: ACCESS TO CRIMINAL JUSTICE (2004) (hereinafter "MURLIDHAR").
36. *See* GAURANG ASHUTOSH THAKER, ROLE OF MEDIATION AS AN EFFECTIVE TOOL OF DISPENSATION OF JUSTICE 229 (2013) (hereinafter "THAKER").
37. *See generally* Xavier, *supra* note 16; THAKER, *supra* note 36, at 219.
38. *See generally*, Hiram E. Chodosh, *Mediating Mediation in India*, https://lawcommissionofindia.nic.in/adr_conf/chodosh4.pdf.
39. *See* M R Krishna Murthi v. New India Assurance Co. Ltd., 2019 SCC OnLine SC 315, ¶4.
40. *See* M. Siddiq v. Mahant Suresh Das, 2019 SCC OnLine 1440.
41. *People's Mediation Centres*, INDIAN INSTITUTE OF ARBITRATION & MEDIATION, https://www.arbitrationindia.com/pmc.html.

trained as mediators. This paves the way to opening mediation to the community (which is perceived to be dominated by advocates).

Leading legal education institutions such as the National Law School of India University, V. M. Salgaocar College of Law (VMSCL), and O.P. Jindal Global University (JGU) have channelized the power of youth through legal-aid clinics,[42] despite the challenges of clinical legal education.[43] VMSCL students have promoted mediation on community issues such as garbage disposal and traffic problems. The Youth Conflict Management and Community Mediation Initiative's (YCM) collaboration with JGU, Sonipat began in August 2019.[44] It is a collaboration between students from diverse streams, young professionals, the university, and the local community, culminating in YCM JGU, India's first youth-run conflict management and community mediation center. It has been developed as a model to be replicated across educational institutions in India, not just limited to legal education institutions because the aim is twofold. First to tap into diverse youth as change-leaders and community-mobilizers who build a diverse youth network across India. Second to build a culture where dispute resolution skills are life skills for everyone, and dispute prevention skills are life skills for everyone, not just advocates.

[3] Technology as a Driver

Technology and Online Dispute Resolution mechanisms enable mediation in many ways, especially in the COVID-19 pandemic era. DDRS initiated online mediation and tele-mediation in April 2020 due to the pandemic in the context of community mediation.[45] People's Mediation Society (PMS) too launched the PeaceGate Resolution App in collaboration with the IIAM, whereby any citizen or community member in India can approach a PMC. and request mediation by submitting an online mediation form or by registering a dispute on the PeaceGate App.

These rejuvenators of community mediation are positive milestones in the movement to ultimately achieve citizen empowerment through a self-sufficient, independent system.[46] YCM is addressing the need to open access to a language "beyond

---

42. *Legal Services Clinic,* NATIONAL LAW SCHOOL OF INDIA UNIVERSITY, https://www.nls.ac.in/information/students/student-bar-association/legal-services-clinic/; *Legal Aid Society,* V M SALGAOCAR COLLEGE OF LAW, https://www.vmslaw.edu.in/legal-aid-society/#: ~ :text = Salgaocar%20College%20of%20Law%20Legal,Legal%20Aid%20in%20their%20Panchayat; *Legal Aid Clinic,* JINDAL GLOBAL LAW SCHOOL, https://jgu.edu.in/jgls/legal-aid-clinic/.
43. *See* Meher Dev, *The Global Clinical Movement: Educating Lawyers for Social Justice,* 11 JINDAL GLOBAL L. REV. 409–439 (2020) (reviewing THE GLOBAL CLINICAL MOVEMENT: EDUCATING LAWYERS FOR SOCIAL JUSTICE (Frank S. Bloch ed., 2011)).
44. *About YCM,* YCM INDIA, https://www.ycmindia.org/.
45. *See Online Mediation,* DELHI DISPUTE RESOLUTION SOCIETY, http://mediation.delhigovt.nic.in/wps/wcm/connect/doit_ddrs/DELHI + DISPUTES + RESOLUTION + SOCIETY/Home/Online + Mediation.
46. *See* Joseph Folger & Robert Baruch Bush, *Transformative Mediation,* 2(1) INT'L J. CONFLICT ENGAGEMENT & RESOL. 20, 29 (2014) (hereinafter "Folger & Bush").

law"[47] and to revive the culture of community in the process of reviving community mediation. This is based on the Gandhian value that "the way you fight and the goal for which you are fighting are the same."[48]

§12.03 COMPARISON OF STATE INSTITUTIONALIZED COMMUNITY MEDIATION VERSUS CITIZEN-RUN COMMUNITY MEDIATION: FORMALISM OR INFORMALISM?

The dichotomous roots of community mediation can be seen in community mediation as a State response to inefficiencies of the court system (a court-focused movement) and as an opportunity for citizen participation for self-determination and governance (a community-focused movement).[49] Community mediation in India is broadly based on such dichotomy in two forms in terms of structure. The State runs one, and citizens or communities themselves run the other.

Whether formalism or informalism is best suited for community mediation in India has not been examined with real examples, even though it is a determinative factor in the success of these community mediation initiatives. As initiatives to promote and strengthen community mediation, DDRS State-run community mediation centers were launched in 2009 in Delhi, the IIAM community mediation clinics were also launched in 2009 in southern India and later remodeled as P.M.C.s in July 2018. The YCM JGU collaboration began in August 2019 in Sonipat. State and citizen initiatives are striving to promote and benefit from community mediation.

This part examines whether formalism or informalism is best suited for community mediation by analyzing: key advantages and disadvantages of State involvement, role and incentives of the mediator, style(s) appropriate for community mediation, and matters appropriate for community mediation.

[A] Key Advantages and Disadvantages of State Involvement

State-run or -connected mediation forms, on the one hand, provide legitimacy but, on the other, face resistance for interference in citizens' lives. Localized mediation forms can facilitate the expansion of sovereign power through informal governance and siphon discontent from the courts.[50] Institutionalization of community mediation raises the concern that mediation flows from the funder, i.e., the State. The State uses the rhetoric of anti-formal courts to persuade parties to appreciate mediation's benefits.

47. *See* Linda Mulcahy, *The Devil and the Deep Blue Sea? A Critique of the Ability of Community Mediation to Suppress and Facilitate Participation in Civil Life*, 27(1) J. L. & Soc'y 133, 146 (2000) (hereinafter "Mulcahy").
48. *See generally*, Mark Juergensmeyer, Gandhi's Way: A Handbook of Conflict Resolution (2003).
49. *See generally*, Scott Bradley & Melinda Smith, *Community Mediation: Reflections on a Quarter Century of Practice*, 17 Mediation Q. 315–317 (2000).
50. *See* Samia Bano, *Introduction*, in Women, Mediation and Religious Arbitration: Thinking Through Gender and Justice in Family Law Disputes 3 (Samia Bano ed., 2017).

Despite the critique of State involvement in community mediation, legal elites and peacemakers behind the modern emergence of mediation share the view that mediation can enhance the quality of justice. However, access is a prerequisite to achieving quality justice. Access may mean removing geographical and financial barriers.[51] State involvement has the potential to make such access a reality. An example of such access is the DDRS, with its several (16 presently) mediation centers across Delhi provide free mediation services to citizens. On the other hand, citizen-run community mediation faces the challenges of funding, quality assurance, and maintaining workloads.

[B] Role and Incentives of the Mediator

In State-run community mediation centers, there is no clarity about the involvement of locals or residents as mediators and, hence, the only localization factor is the center's geographical location. Such reality indicates the absence of the "feminine search for context"[52] in mediation which can be addressed by the active participation of local community members as trained mediators who would have the advantage of contextual particularity.[53] However, apprehension of bias and lack of neutrality may be valid concerns if local disputes are mediated by mediators having a close connection to the community to which the disputants belong.

Success in State-run mediation centers may just mean: (i) a high settlement rate, as mediators are incentivized with additional remuneration for the same; and (ii) a reduction of courts' caseload. Such success entails diluting community mediation's goals of citizen empowerment and often results in a limited questioning of mediation in the patriarchal paradigm,[54] where success is understood in a "binary" sense[55] (settled or not-settled). However, citizen-run community mediation centers can define success beyond this binary such as: (i) whether parties to the dispute have reoriented in their relationship based on the transformative mediation approach and (ii) whether parties are equipped with conflict management skills to take ownership of the present dispute and prevent future disputes from arising.

[C] Mediator Style Most Appropriate for Community Mediation

In the context of community mediation, transformative mediation has been recognized as a style that: (i) supports a party-driven settlement focus as opposed to a mediator-driven settlement focus; (ii) enables a transformation through a relational orientation

51. *See* Valters, *supra* note 7, at 8.
52. *See* Kate McCabe, *A Forum for Women's Voices: Mediation Through a Feminist Jurisprudential Lens*, 21 New-Illinois U. L. Rev. 459, 477 (2001) (hereinafter "McCabe").
53. *See* U. Kalpagam, *Perspectives for a Grassroots Feminist Theory*, 37(47) Econ. & Pol. Wkly. 4686, 4687–4688 (2002) (hereinafter "Kalpagam").
54. *See* McCabe, *supra* note 52, at 468.
55. *See generally*, Marvin Astrada & Scott Astrada, *Re-examining the Integrity of the Binary: Politics, Identity, and Law*, 17(2) U. Maryland L. J. Race, Religion, Gender & Class, 173, 182, 187–188 (2017).

between the disputants; and (iii) supports empowerment and recognition of diverse perspectives among community members as parties retain control on the outcome.[56]

Some have gone beyond evaluative, facilitative, and transformative mediation models and coined activist mediation—a style that employs interventionist techniques to equalize the balance of power between parties to enable justice (in process and substance).[57] Consider, for instance, that an activist mediator may invite the parties to define principles of equality and justice and then abide by such principles throughout the mediation process, all the way to the settlement (if reached).

Either way, the goals of transformative and activist mediation are like the goals of the community justice mediation movement because it values parties' right to self-determination and recognition, empowering individuals to collectively involve as a community to change social power structures, foster a "purer democracy,"[58] and invite self-governance. Thus, transformative mediation may be the most appropriate style for community mediation.

However, a community mediator must resist the urge to defend or assist on an assumption of power imbalance or an assumption that the mediation participants cannot address the same.[59] The interventionist techniques may raise an apprehension of bias (mediator's interest in the outcome), but at the same time, silence can lead to the same. Hence, it is important to discuss equality and justice as guiding principles with the mediation participants (as a part of the process) at the start of the mediation. This way, the widely debated risk in the informalism of community mediation (about no equality and justice in the outcomes) stands mitigated by reinforcing the process.

"Authentic" self-determination cannot be divorced from voluntary consent and informed decision-making. Hence, the mediator's interest in authentic self-determination cannot be labeled as averse to neutrality. This is easier said than done, and a mediator's neutrality may still be questioned. But what remains important is an exercise of discretion on a case-to-case basis. The safest approach would be to expect good faith from both the parties, and when an outcome or proposal is suggested, a party may ask themselves: would it be fair if the other party had proposed this to me? Then in the true sense, community mediation will become an open space for "authentic" application of the evolving principles of equality and justice, which are stagnated or constrained in the legal systems, and community mediators will not be perceived as "conflict stoppers."[60]

Evaluative mediation has been criticized for being top-down with heavy reliance on the mediator, while transformative mediation has been criticized for being too ideal,

---

56. *See* Folger & Bush, *supra* note 46. *See generally*, ROBERT BARUCH BUSH & JOESPH FOLGER, THE PROMISE OF MEDIATION: RESPONDING TO CONFLICT THROUGH EMPOWERMENT AND RECOGNITION (1994).
57. Isabelle R. Gunning, *Know Justice, Know Peace: Further Reflections on Justice, Equality and Impartiality in Settlement Oriented and Transformative Mediations*, 5 CARDOZO J. CONFLICT RESOL. 87, 90 (2004) (hereinafter "Isabelle").
58. *See* Arby Aiwazian, *Transformative Mediation: Empowering the Oppressed Voices of a Multicultural City to Foster Strong Democracy*, 11 SCHOLAR 31, 33, 55 (2008) (hereinafter "Aiwazian").
59. *See* Isabelle, *supra* note 57, at 91–93.
60. *Id.*, at 95.

and facilitative mediation for being too time-consuming.[61] Evaluative and facilitative mediation attribute too much value to legal information and outcomes, while transformative mediation serves more of a nurturing role in preserving an amicable and lasting resolution. Thus, the most appropriate style for community mediation is the one that will allow parties the best opportunity to exercise their respective rights of self-determination.[62]

In the context of State-run community mediation, the risk is that authentic self-determination may not be the determinative factor for employing a particular mediation style. The State's "gate-keeping," covetousness (for mediators) to steer solutions and discussions in a selective direction, coerced participation vide procedures sending "request to appear" (like court summons), and cost-time efficiency goals all end up diluting community empowerment goals.[63]

In the context of citizen-run community mediation, the expectation for authentic self-determination as the determinative factor for employing a particular mediation style and the expectation for a space for "participatory democracy through self-governance"[64] is understudied and not fully explored.

[D] Matters Appropriate for Community Mediation

The term "community mediation" can be misleading if understood as a space for resolution of community and neighborhood disputes alone since many community mediation centers across the globe accept a wider scope to include "family, custody and divorce referrals; school and juvenile matters; victim-offender mediations; hospital collections; inter-group conflicts, such as those within religious congregations or business and non-profit entities; and environmental and land use issues."[65] DDRS, for instance, lists the following cases appropriate for community mediation: consumer, family, neighborhood, commercial, school, government, religious and petty compoundable offenses. P.M.C. lists any civil, commercial, contractual, business or family disputes as appropriate for community mediation and excludes questions of public law and non-compoundable criminal offenses.

In community mediation, "often the State is implicated in the cause of the disputes."[66] "Cases by or against the government having elements of settlement" are an explicit category under matters suitable for mediation.[67] But in disputes involving the government as a party, normally, no officer will take up the responsibility for

61. *See* Aiwazian, *supra* note 58, at 41.
62. *See* Samuel J. Imperati, *Mediator Practice Models: The Intersection of Ethics and Stylistic Practices in Mediation*, 33 Willamette L. Rev. 703, 712–715 (1997).
63. *See* Timothy Hedeen, *Institutionalizing Community Mediation: Can Dispute Resolution of, by, and for the People Long Endure*, 108(1) Penn St. L. Rev. 265, 271–273 (2003).
64. *See* Aiwazian, *supra* note 58, at 55.
65. *See* Becky L. Jacobs, *Volunteers: The Power of Community Mediation*, 11 Nevada L. J. 481, 482 (2011) (hereinafter "Jacobs").
66. *See* Mulcahy, *supra* note 47, at 143.
67. *See* Anil Xavier, *People's Mediation Centres: Promoting Local Mediation in India*, Global Pound Conference-Series (June 29, 2018), https://imimediation.org/2018/06/29/peoples-mediation-centres-promoting-local-mediation-in-india/.

settlement, and as such, mediation may not be effective. From a feminist perspective, however, the question remains: is the State using community mediation to preserve family unity or promote informalism by keeping family disputes private (perpetuating inequalities and power imbalance)?[68]

It is difficult to exhaustively define what matters are appropriate for community mediation as there cannot be a one-size-fits-all approach. However, disputes that define our core societal values should make it to court for larger public engagement and involvement.[69]

Thus, the attraction toward "government-sanctioned legitimacy and repulsion from governmental co-optation" is simultaneous, which creates an "oscillating space."[70] The US National Association of Community Mediation characterizes community mediation as:[71] "(1) the use of trained community volunteers as the primary providers of mediation services; volunteers are not required to have academic or professional credentials; (2) a private non-profit or public agency, or program thereof, with a governing/advisory board; (3) mediators, staff and governing/advisory board are representative of the diversity of the community served; (4) providing direct access of mediation to the public through self-referral and striving to reduce barriers to service including physical, linguistic, cultural, programmatic and economic; (5) providing service to clients regardless of their ability to pay; (6) initiating, facilitating and educating for collaborative community relationships to effect positive systemic change; (7) engaging in public awareness and educational activities about the values and practices of mediation; (8) providing a forum for dispute resolution at the early stages of the conflict; and (9) providing an alternative to the judicial system at any stage of the conflict."

Such characterization shows the hybrid space and understanding of community mediation that emerges out of and exists in both a court-focused and community-focused movement. Along these lines, further research is warranted on citizens' preferences toward formalism, informalism, or a hybrid for mediation in India. Citizen satisfaction toward DDRS (emerging out of a court-focused movement) and P.M.C. and Y.C.M. (emerging from a community-focused movement) is certainly a starting point.

§12.04 COMMUNITY MEDIATION IN ACTION: EXAMPLE OF A STATE-RUN COMMUNITY MEDIATION CENTER AND A CITIZEN-RUN COMMUNITY MEDIATION CENTER

There are few empirical studies on community mediation in Asia, including India,[72] and this part examines the working of DDRS and P.M.C. closely. The goals of DDRS and

68. *See generally*, Trina Grillo, *The Mediation Alternative—Process Dangers for Women*, 100 YALE L. J. 1545, 1569, 1592 (1991) (hereinafter "Grillo").
69. *See* Isabelle, *supra* note 57, at 89.
70. *See* Timothy Hedeen, *Institutionalizing Community Mediation: Can Dispute Resolution of, by, and for the People Long Endure*, 108(1) Penn State Law Review 265, 271–273,275 (2003).
71. *See* Jacobs, *supra* note 65, at 482.
72. *See* Valters, *supra* note 7.

P.M.C., such as citizen empowerment and "social harmony," are examined to question the extent of community mediation as an "alternative" to the court system and the extent of State involvement. The process of mediation and the procedure followed by a community mediation center reveal the goals of community mediation in practice. Thus, DDRS and P.M.C.'s community mediation initiatives are examined here to understand community mediation in action. Lastly, key challenges and drivers are examined as lessons learned by P.M.S. and DDRS in their decade-long journeys.

[A] Goals of Community Mediation and Extent of State Involvement

DDRS and P.M.C. both have common goals of citizen empowerment, self-empowerment, and social harmony. At DDRS, the goals are to empower the public to resolve disputes amicably; make people build relationships, create a stronger and safer society; reduce the backlog of cases from courts; reduce litigation costs, and promote greater public satisfaction legal system. P.M.C.'s mission is to rekindle the age-old pattern of giving and take to reweave healthy families and communities and allow courts to deal with severe cases.

Thus, both DDRS and P.M.S. draw a comparison to courts while defining the goals and benefits of community mediation. Such comparison may be necessary to explain the difference between the modes of dispute resolution available to the citizens approaching the community mediation center, especially those who are learning about mediation for the first time or who misunderstand mediation to be litigation or arbitration.

However, this may strengthen the notion that community mediation is an "alternative" dispute resolution mechanism subordinate to the court system. Nevertheless, DDRS' mission is that community mediation centers become the most effective forum for the resolution of all disputes, and P.M.S.'s mission is to build a people's movement to revive a culture based on the realization that "if we can create disputes, we can also resolve them."[73]

A key distinction between P.M.S. and DDRS, as expected in any citizen-run and State-run community mediation initiative, is the characteristic of State involvement. DDRS has State involvement: (i) at an organizational level, it is funded and run by the Government of Delhi; (ii) at the judiciary level, it has the backing of the High Court of Delhi; (iii) at the referral level, many cases are referred by public authorities, judicial and quasi-judicial authorities; and (iv) at the level of the dispute, it mediates cases where the government is involved. On the other hand, P.M.C. does not have State involvement, organizational, judicial, or referral level. However, P.M.C. draws its legitimacy through IIAM, which government ministries recognize as it is enlisted with the Department of Justice to assist in the out-of-court resolution of disputes through mediation.

73. *People's Mediation Centres*, INDIAN INSTITUTE OF ARBITRATION & MEDIATION, https://www.arbitrationindia.com/pmc.html.

Thus, examples of P.M.C. and DDRS indicate that State involvement has its own pros for the sake of legitimacy and referrals. But it has cons, such as the State's motive to achieve higher settlement rates.

[B] Community Mediation Centers in Action

DDRS and P.M.C.'s community mediation initiatives have made over a decade-long journey in reviving and promoting community mediation in India.

[1] Approaching the Community Mediation Center

Any citizen or community member can approach P.M.S. and request mediation by submitting a mediation form online on their website or registering a dispute on the PeaceGate Resolution App. Any resident in Delhi, or a citizen who has a dispute with a resident in Delhi, can approach DDRS with a request for mediation or contact public authorities such as the crimes against women cells, consumer forums, or district courts, who then refer the matter to DDRS. P.M.C., being privately run, does not receive referrals from public authorities. DDRS has permanent physical infrastructure for community mediation centers in various districts of Delhi, and disputants can walk in to initiate a mediation. P.M.C. runs five mediation centers with full physical infrastructure in Kerala, and over 98 spaces across India, affiliated with it and are either owned or run by mediators whom it impanels.[74]

P.M.C. and DDRS both entertain mediation requests regardless of whether the mediation has been contractually agreed or not by the disputants. The request for mediation simply requires details such as a description of the dispute and details of the other party in case only one party (or side) has approached the community mediation center. P.M.C. and DDRS both consider community mediation as a service to society. P.M.C. charges subsidized rates for community mediation services and provides free mediation services on a case-to-case basis.[75] DDRS promotes community mediation as a free of cost initiative but charges a nominal fee to financial institutions and companies. DDRS uses the "comparison to the courts" strategy, emphasizing cost implications, promoting mediation, and explaining how mediation is different from litigation.

[2] Community Mediators: Impanelment Criteria, Recommended Mediation Style, and Allocation of Matters

DDRS empanels senior advocates, bureaucrats, and judges, who have undergone mediation training prescribed by the Mediation and Conciliation Project Committee

74. Interview of Matthew P J (Administrator of People's Mediation Center) on May 22, 2020, and Feb. 1, 2021 (on file with the authors) (hereinafter "Interview of Matthew P J").
75. *IIAM Community Mediation Fee Schedule*, Indian Institute of Arbitration & Mediation, https://www.arbitrationindia.com/pdf/cms_fee.pdf (INR 100 for registration and INR 500 per session of three hours).

(MCPC) of the Supreme Court of India, in addition to respectable citizens of the locality and public-spirited persons who have undergone the 40-hour mediation training at DDRS. At P.M.C., both advocates and non-advocates are eligible to be impaneled after being trained as mediators by an institute recognized by P.M.C., or a 10-hour training for community members to become community mediators or the 40-hour mediation training conducted by IIAM.

P.M.C. and DDRS both conduct training for mediators to follow a facilitative approach to mediation, even though mediators exercise their discretion on the style of mediation on a case-to-case basis. At the point this was investigated, P.M.C. had approximately 51 impaneled community mediators, out of which 13% are advocates and 33% are females, and DDRS had approximately 68 impaneled mediators, out of which 34% are females. The administrative staff at DDRS allocates matters to mediators based on their expertise and availability as a fixed schedule is maintained. At P.M.C., in some cases, the administrative staff nominates the mediator, and in others, the parties can choose a mediator available at their location.[76]

[3] Mediation Procedure and Rules

P.M.C. follows the IIAM Mediation Rules, which are drafted based on the International Mediation Institute (I.M.I.) Guidelines. At P.M.C., the average timeline for completing a mediation is one month.[77] DDRS, on the other hand, follows the mediation procedure as per the guidance of the Delhi High Court Mediation and Conciliation Rules 2004. Both at P.M.C. and DDRS, the internal procedure is followed to maintain a mediation status report and mediation completion report shared with the parties. Additionally, both institutions collect feedback from parties about the mediator and the process.[78]

At DDRS, the average timeline for completing a mediation is 3–4 sessions of 30–60 minutes, spread over one week to a month. Both at P.M.C. and DDRS, parties are free to engage and bring along an advocate or a legal representative. But, in the context of community mediations, there is a chance that the involvement of advocates runs the risk of the process becoming more law-centric, thus, disempowering communities.

[4] Mediated Settlement Agreements

At DDRS and P.M.C., in case of resolution of a dispute, the mediator assists the parties at their request in making a settlement agreement.[79] At P.M.C., the settlement agreements are drafted to be covered by Part III of the Arbitration & Conciliation Act 1996 to be enforceable and binding as per sections 73 and 74 of the Act. At DDRS, parties receive a verified copy of the signed settlement agreement, and in cases where

76. Interview of Matthew P J, *supra* note 74.
77. *Id.*
78. *Id.*
79. PMC Brochure, INDIAN INSTITUTE OF ARBITRATION AND MEDIATION, https://www.arbitrationindia.com/pdf/brochure_pmc.pdf.

the parties were referred to mediation through a referral authority, such referral authority is notified.

[C] Key Challenges and Drivers

P.M.C. and DDRS have overcome challenges and found new drivers. The key challenges faced by them concern funding, sustainability, and the lack of awareness about mediation. US studies reveal that most community mediation centers report financial stability as the most significant concern for both their centers and the broader field.[80] This may be the case in India as well.

Other key challenges include the lack of representative character among impaneled mediators vis-à-vis the communities in which they mediate (which would include language and cultural barriers). However, there are solutions such as implementing co-mediation where at least one of the two mediators is from the community, and the involvement of community volunteers. The use of technology can reduce operational costs or funding and increase outreach-cum-access. Like conflict management and coaching, capacity-building programs can empower members of the community with dispute resolution and dispute prevention skills and dilute the challenges. It is conceivable that a specific law on community mediation could potentially eliminate most of these challenges.

[1] Lack of Representativeness of Community Mediators

When community mediators have nothing in common with the communities (for instance, age, gender, income, ethnicity, literacy, education, religious affiliation, and spoken languages), concerns emerge regarding their fairness and effectiveness. A homogeneous category of advocates as community mediators cannot represent the community members they mediate between. However, there is a general bias in favor of advocates given their evaluation skills and knowledge of law (since there is some expectation of ensuring fair outcome under the law).[81] Despite the arguably majoritarian view, a mediator's process expertise makes a mediator effective.[82]

Citizen participation through volunteer mediators can be the real power of community mediation. It would provide cost-effective services through accessible citizen mediators and increase "compliance efforts"[83] of settlement agreements for two reasons. First, citizens as users and providers of mediation will be invested in the real

80. *See* Jacobs, *supra* note 65, at 482; T. Hedeen & P.G. Coy, *Community Mediation and the Court System: The Ties That Bind*, 17(4) MEDIATION Q. 351–367 (2000) (the issue of funding is fundamental to any social service, even one that relies heavily on volunteer labor, and the need for stable and diverse funding streams is repeated through the literature on community mediation).
81. *See* Nancy A. Welsh, *You've Got Your Mother's Laugh: What Bankruptcy Mediation Can Learn from the Her/History of Divorce and Child Custody Mediation*, 17 AM. BANKR. INST. L. REV. 427, 590 (2009).
82. *See* Jacobs, *supra* note 65, at 490.
83. *Id.*, at 486.

impact of a citizen-run mediation center, and second, belongingness to the same community or locality will bring in the sense of co-accountability. However, there exists an inherent bias against "non-advocate mediators," and concerns have been raised especially from within the legal communities on the capability of "non-advocate mediators."[84] Recruiting volunteer mediators, training them, and maintaining a fixed qualified pool of motivated volunteer mediators may be challenging. However, personal pride contributes to society, improvement in personal communication, and dispute resolution skills are motivating factors.

Paralegal Volunteers (P.L.V.) Scheme by the National Legal Services Authority is recommended to be utilized as a potential resource to educate and mobilize communities for community mediation as P.L.V.s are intermediaries bridging the gap between the common people and the Legal Services Institutions for access to justice.[85] Inclusion of youth volunteers, law students, and partnerships with law schools can address concerns of quality, accessibility, and resources, in addition to ensuring diversity/representativeness of community mediators.

Co-mediation (i.e., where two mediators jointly facilitate a mediation process) is not mandatorily present concerning P.M.C. or DDRS. It can be a key driver of community mediation as it provides the skills, experiences, and creativity of two mediators. However, for co-mediation to be successful, selecting pairs must be a careful process, which should be revisited periodically. It serves good to couple experienced mediators with less experienced (or volunteer) ones for capacity building. Co-mediation may not be the preferred choice for some mediators as they would prefer to focus their efforts on the parties and the mediation process instead of consuming time coordinating with the co-mediator.[86] Co-mediation could also increase costs if both the mediators charge fees, yet it is prevalent in different parts of the world owing to its benefits. For instance, in the Philippines and Japan, multiple mediators collectively resolve community disputes.[87]

[2] Lack of Funding and Constraints to Outreach-cum-Access

The emergence of technology-mediated dispute resolution as an efficient and cost-effective means of resolving disputes illustrates the significant impact the technology revolution has had.[88] In the Indian context, P.M.C.'s PeaceGate App is an example of

84. *Id.*, at 488. *See also* Welsh, *supra* note 81, at 438. The Family Courts Act 1984 debars parties to be represented by advocates in mediation (section 13). The Consumer Protection Regulations 2005 require consumer forums to be people-friendly forums (Regulations 3 and 4).
85. Scheme for Para-Legal Volunteers, NATIONAL LEGAL SERVICES AUTHORITY, https://nalsa.gov.in/acts-rules/preventive-strategic-legal-services-schemes/scheme-for-para-legal-volunteers.
86. *See* Gill Marvel P. Tabucanon et al., *Philippine Community Mediation, Katarungang Pambarangay*, 2 J. DISP. RESOL. 501, 512 (2008) (hereinafter "Tabucanon").
87. *Id.*
88. *See generally*, David Allen Larson, *Brother, Can You Spare a Dime: Technology Can Reduce Dispute Resolution Costs When Times Are Tough and Improve Outcomes*, 11 NEVADA L. J. 523 (2011).

using technology to reduce operational costs and increase outreach. P.M.C.s' Administrator stated that: "It is a first of its kind Dispute Resolution App—empowering people to resolve disputes by way of negotiation, mediation or arbitration. Now a person can register his dispute in a P.M.C., select a mediator and schedule the mediation meeting using the Peacegate Application and all this can be done at the ease of clicking a button in your smartphone!"[89]

P.M.C.'s PeaceGate App is also an example of using technology to increase outreach by the involvement of volunteers through a unique time banking system. As per the P.M.C.'s Administrator:[90]

> Time Banking is a reciprocity-based service system in which hours are credited in the Time Account of the holder. In a time-banking environment, people receive time credits when they provide a service to another member of the timebank (and the member receiving the service is debited an equal amount). Anytime you can redeem your time credit for availing any services in return free—for you, your friends, relatives, or others for whom you would like to get a service.

Such initiatives by P.M.C. promote inclusive participation and enable awareness of mediation as a more cultured way of handling and resolving disputes.

[3] Adoption of Conflict Management and Coaching

The terms "conflict" and "dispute" have different meanings. The former is an inevitable tension that arises when humans interact and may not necessarily transform into a dispute. A conflict may transform into a dispute only when one human resorts to blaming, naming, and claiming from another human.[91] A dispute is a social construct. Its emergence, as well as transformation, is a neglected topic in the sociology of law.[92] Conflict coaching for enabling conflict management skills, i.e., identifying the real point of conflict coupled with the self-awareness to manage its subsequent transformations, can break the cycle of disputes and nail the point of conflict management.

Y.C.M., Wandsworth Mediation Service (London), and DDRS are some examples of institutions that have provided conflict coaching as a service. DDRS, for instance, explains that it brings it closer to the goal of reducing non-starter mediation cases, particularly cases where mediation does not begin as one of the parties is unwilling to engage in mediation. These examples show how conflict coaching can be integrated into the community mediation service as it furthers the mediation goal of citizen empowerment. Moreover, once the dispute is identified, the conflict coaching service can trace back the dispute to the underlying, real conflict. The example of Y.C.M. and its conflict identification and management goals illustrate that conflict management skills can be beneficial in two ways. *It may help trace* back the dispute to the

89. Interview of Matthew P J, *supra* note 74.
90. *PeaceGate Time Banking*, INDIAN INSTITUTE OF ARBITRATION & MEDIATION, https://www.arbitrationindia.com/time_bank.html.
91. *See generally*, William L.F. Felstiner et al., *The Emergence and Transformation of Disputes Naming Blaming Claiming*, 15(3–4) L. & SOC'Y REV. 631 (1980–1981).
92. *Id.*, at 632.

underlying, *real* conflict in cases where the dispute has already arisen. *Two*, it helps proactively identify the conflict through self-awareness to manage its subsequent transformations, including the possibility of it transforming into a dispute.

In other words, it is a two-way conflict identification and management approach. This is recommended to be adopted by community mediation initiatives in India because it is a mechanism for authentic citizen empowerment through conflict management, dispute resolution, and dispute prevention skills. In turn, this reduces dependency on community mediation centers and the State judiciary as parties will be skilled and prepared, i.e., "self-dependent," to deal with a future conflict or dispute situation they might face.

[4] Law on Community Mediation as a Driver

A law to govern community mediation (which is already a prevalent system of dispute resolution) can help to overcome the challenges of community mediation. For instance, in the Philippines, a law was passed on community mediation (*Katarungang Pambarangay*), which recognized the tradition of community dispute resolution with the aims of speedy administration of justice, implementation of the constitutional mandate to preserve and develop Filipino culture and strengthen the family as a basic social institution.[93] Moreover, mandating mediation before filing a case before a court has boosted community mediation in the Philippines.[94] Adopting these examples can be a step forward for promoting community mediation in India as well.

The pre-litigation mediation requirement under Indian laws such as the Commercial Courts Act 2015 can be explored to be fulfilled by directing the same toward community mediation centers, such as DDRS and P.M.C. However, the notion of mandatory mediation is an oxymoron and may well defeat the core value of voluntariness in mediation.[95]

§12.05 ACCESS TO JUSTICE AND CITIZEN EMPOWERMENT: THE TWIN-AIMS OF COMMUNITY MEDIATION

Globally, community mediation initiatives predominantly have the twin aim of access to justice and citizen empowerment.

[A] Access to Justice Through Mediation Versus Adjudication

The Constitution of India 1950 provides that the State shall ensure that the legal system promotes justice by providing equal opportunity, and opportunities for securing justice

93. *See* Tabucanon, *supra* note 86.
94. *Id.*
95. *See generally*, Michael Bartlet, *Mandatory Mediation, and the Rule of Law*, 1(1) AMICUS CURIAE 50, 52 (Series 2, 2019).

are not denied to any citizen owing to socioeconomic disabilities.[96] Defining justice and access to justice have been an endless challenge in India.

Access to justice developed as a human right with India's emergence as a welfare State facing widespread non-actualization of rights.[97] As a product of the social contract between the State and its members, access to justice is a top-down operation,[98] wherein the existence of institutions such as the judiciary dispenses justice or *Nyaya.*[99] India has consistently failed to provide access to justice.[100] Statistics at the time of our investigation showed that 37 million cases are pending before the judiciary,[101] the government is a litigant in 46% of these cases, and litigants spend INR 300 billion annually to attend courts.[102]

Recommendations continue to repose faith in the State and the judiciary to remedy obstructions to access justice by making laws accessible and comprehensible for legal empowerment, ensuring high-quality and affordable legal aid, and streamlining courts' case management processes.[103]

The public interest litigation system developed by the Indian judiciary (which minimized procedural formalities) has been a milestone measure for making justice accessible.[104] Such measures coupled with constitutional provisions illustrate how the welfare State is arguably the duty holder[105] to provide access to justice vis-à-vis the citizens as of right holders.[106] The judiciary is the supreme provider of justice,[107] glorified in the Indian Supreme Court's title: "the world's most powerful court"[108] having constitutional power to do complete justice.[109] India's access to the justice system is a top-bottom structure where reforms are focused more on achieving "access" to justice, i.e., legal representation or legal aid and less access to "justice."[110]

96. INDIA CONST., Art. 39-A.
97. *See* Pratiksha Baxi, *Access to Justice and Rule-of (Good) Law: The Cunning of Judicial Reform in India,* 2(2) INDIAN J. HUM. DEV. 1, 5 (2007) (hereinafter "Baxi").
98. *See* Rebecca Sandefur, *Access to Civil Justice and Race, Class and Gender Inequality,* 34 ANNUAL REV. SOCIOLOGY, 339, 344 (2008) (hereinafter "Sandefur").
99. SEN, *supra* note 35, at 20–23, 67–72, 354.
100. *See* Sandefur, *supra* note 98, at 2–3.
101. *National Juridical Data Grid,* NATIONAL INFORMATICS CENTRE (Mar. 12, 2021), http://njdg.ecourts.gov.in/njdg_public/main.php.
102. *See* Sriparna Chaudhuri, *The Winding Road to Justice in India,* MINT (Jan. 24, 2018), https://www.livemint.com/Opinion/pPyGzS0Y7PXmIqI9CBIaMJ/The-winding-road-to-justice-in-India.html.
103. *Id.*
104. *See generally,* ANUJ BHUWANIA, COURTING THE PEOPLE: PUBLIC INTEREST LITIGATION IN POST-EMERGENCY INDIA (2017).
105. INDIA CONST., Ch. II; INDIA CONST., preamble; INDIA CONST., Arts. 38, 39-A, and 41 (Directive Principles).
106. INDIA CONST., Ch. III (Art. 21 on the right to life and liberty).
107. INDIA CONST., Arts. 32 and 226.
108. Indira Jaising, *An Outsider, Inside,* in MAKING A DIFFERENCE: MEMOIRS FROM THE WOMEN'S MOVEMENT IN INDIA 257 (Rukmani Menon ed., 2011).
109. INDIA CONST., Art. 142(1).
110. *See* Baxi, *supra* note 97, at 2.

The judiciary dispenses "formal justice"[111] by deciding the values and standards to be applied to human interactions, including conflicts,[112] solely based on "legal merits,"[113] disregarding that the strictest application of law can do the gravest injustice.[114] Patriarchy is deeply rooted in the judiciary's access to justice structure in two senses. First, the law's content is based on a binary of wrong and right from the male perspective.[115] The drafters and envisaged beneficiaries of laws are predominantly men.[116] Second, the adversarial style is adopted for adjudication dictated by the ethic of justice, i.e., claiming your right against a wrong.[117]

Alternative dispute resolution (A.D.R.) was not intended to be an "alternative" to a top-bottom patriarchal structure of "access" to justice by being a bottom-up, non-patriarchal structure for access to "justice." A.D.R. was advanced to address the failure in "access" to justice in a narrow sense,[118] to provide a time and cost-efficient dispute resolution system.

As opposed to formal justice, in mediation, parties are invited to act creatively in crafting an outcome with their sense of justice by choosing values/standards not limited to law-creative justice.[119] As opposed to generalization in adjudication, mediation provides for particularization by taking broader considerations into account, including emotions.[120] Mediation has been termed the feminization of the legal system,[121] as a departure from the adversarial, patriarchal legal system as it is a non-adversarial, empowering approach where disputants endeavor to achieve a mutually acceptable solution.[122] Adjudication is based on the patriarchal conceptions of hierarchy and rationality, where reason means the reasonable man.[123] At the same time, mediation encourages dialogue by invoking concern of responsibility and self-determination using the ethic of care and cooperation where persons are seen as members in a network of relationships, not opponents. It is pertinent to briefly note two fundamental critiques: (i) mediation is not meant for justice yet fairness is a part of every dispute resolution process; and (ii) disputing without the force of law benefits the

---

111. *See generally*, Carrie Menkel-Meadow, *Regulation of Dispute Resolution in the United States of America: From the Formal to the Informal to the Semi-formal*, in REGULATING DISPUTE RESOLUTION: ADR AND ACCESS TO JUSTICE AT THE CROSSROADS (Felix Steffek et al. eds., 2013).
112. *Id.*, at 773.
113. *Id.*, at 767.
114. *Id.*, at 766.
115. *See* CAROL GILLIGAN, IN A DIFFERENT VOICE: PSYCHOLOGICAL THEORY AND WOMEN'S DEVELOPMENT 5–8 (1982).
116. *See* Robin West, *Jurisprudence and Gender*, 55 UNIV. OF CHICAGO L. REV. 1, 60 (1988).
117. *Id.*
118. *See generally*, SEN, *supra* note 35.
119. *See generally*, CLARK BRYAN, LAWYERS AND MEDIATION 139, 151 (2012).
120. *Id.* at 768.
121. *See* Deborah Rubin, *Re-Feminizing Mediation Globally*, 12 NYC L. REV. 355 (2009) (hereinafter "Rubin").
122. *See* Janet Rifkin, *Mediation from a Feminist Perspective: Promise and Problems*, 2(1) L. & INEQUALITY J. 21, 23–25 (1984).
123. *Id.*

stronger party, even though the strictest application of law can do the gravest injustice.[124]

[B] Potential of Citizen Empowerment Through Community Mediation

Empowerment means citizens take control of the resolution process and their lives to transform dependencies.[125] Citizen empowerment, especially women empowerment, means a speak-for-yourself approach, challenging socialized stereotypes.[126] Achieving and improving empowerment has been focused in a macrostructural context owing to global thinking and failing to recognize the importance of thinking locally.[127] The strategic need for empowerment questions how an increasingly shrinking local excludes disadvantaged citizens and women whose accessibility and effective participation are constrained by poverty, family roles, working lives, education, and skills.[128] Moreover, "authentic" empowerment warrants more profound research on the essentials of "authentic" self-determination, especially in dispute resolution through community mediation and informed decision-making.[129]

In contrast, in an adjudication system by courts, the language of the law alienates the common citizen, and the formal and adversarial structure intimidates the citizens. The knowledge of the law is in the hands of privileged judges and advocates, which is inaccessible to most citizens.[130] An illustration is how litigants themselves are asked to sit in India's last row of the courtrooms. An example of such an exclusion and disempowerment is the authors' experience in a family court in Delhi with the insignia, "Seats are Reserved for Advocates," whereas the Family Courts Act 1984 (section 13) restricts the participation of advocates in mediation. An empowering and inclusive approach would have reserved seats for the parties. The adjudication system is structured to support the dependency of the citizens seeking resolution of their disputes, not citizen empowerment.

Community mediation has the potential for citizen empowerment, broadly in three ways. *First*, training community members as mediators results in the inclusion of the marginalized common citizen in mediation, which furthers citizen empowerment and representation.[131] *Second*, community members participate in the mediation process intending to develop their sustainable solutions. Most scholars advocate for the

124. *See* Bert Suykens and Danielle Stein, *Whoever has the Stick Guides the Buffalo: Neutrality, Party Politics and Authority Formation in Community Mediation in the Central and West Terai, Nepal*, 11(1) J. OF SOUTH-ASIAN DEV. 88, 93 (2016).
125. *See* Kalpagam, *supra* note 53, at 4692.
126. *See* McCabe, *supra* note 52, at 471, 480.
127. Kalpagam, *supra* note 53, at 4691.
128. *Id.*
129. *See* Isabelle, *supra* note 57, at 93.
130. *See generally*, Krishna Agrawal, *Justice Dispensation through the Alternative Dispute Resolution System in India*, 2(2) RUSSIAN L. J. 65 (2014); James Boyd White, *The Invisible Discourse of the Law: Reflections on Legal Literacy and General Education*, 54 UNIV. COLORADO L. REV. 143, 144–45 (1983).
131. *See* Jacobs, *supra* note 65, at 490.

opportunity of citizen participation and empowerment provided by community mediation by educating people to resolve future disputes without reliance and dependency on courts. *Third*, community members run community mediation centers with the democratic goal of creating an unfettered community space for participation. Thus, community mediators "improve their communities in unquantifiable ways, including instilling and modeling a sense of social justice, self-reliance, and a spirit of volunteerism."[132]

Transformative mediation aims at party self-determination, recognition, empowering individuals to collective community involvement to change social power structures, and fostering a purer democracy. Thus, the use of transformative mediation, which defines self-determination as "empowerment," can achieve the full meaning of citizen empowerment in community mediation. Moreover, it ensures empowerment through self-determination even if a settlement is arrived at or not.

The hope is that community mediation is an open space for "authentic" application of the evolving principles of equality and justice, which are stagnated or constrained in the legal systems.

[C] Other Motives of Community Mediation

"Empowerment processes are not a zero-sum game" and have contextual complications.[133] Moreover, community mediation has been criticized and perceived as "conflict stoppers."[134]

For instance, the infamous *Khap Panchayats* are patriarchal, unelected, upper-caste village men who police morality at the community level. However, the question is, does that really constitute community mediation? Some feminists are skeptical of mediation as an empowering "forum for women"[135] as it may have ulterior motives of informalizing less important matters having racial, class, and "gender implications"[136] and is equally becoming corrupted by patriarchy and formalism.[137]

There is skepticism that the main aim of community mediation is clearing court dockets, which was the first motivation for promoting mediation in India, followed by being a segment in the multi-door[138] courthouse system, affording second class justice.[139] The real challenge then lies in finding and determining what is appropriate for community mediation and what is fit for adjudication.

---

132. *Id.* at 487–88.
133. *See* Isabelle, *supra* note 57, at 12.
134. *Id.*, at 95.
135. *See* Grillo, *supra* note at 68, 1592.
136. *See* Rubin, *supra* note 121, at 360.
137. *See* Leda Cooks & Claudia Hale, *A Feminist Approach to the Empowerment of Women Mediators*, 3 Discourse & Soc'y J. 277, 297 (1992).
138. *See generally*, John Lande, *Shifting the Focus from the Myth of "The Vanishing Trial" to Complex Conflict Management Systems, or I Learned Almost Everything I Need to Know About Conflict Resolution from Marc Galanter*, 6 Cardozo J. Conflict Resol. 191 (2005).
139. *See generally*, Rubin, *supra* note 121, at 355.

Community mediation can rejuvenate the self-reliant communities of the past within modern societies. The choice of the dispute resolution system reflects on a particular society's values. An oversimplistic categorization of certain *Indian-ess* in mediation positioned as opposed to *westernization* may be used strategically to appeal to the masses. Regardless of such categorization, the tradition of grassroot and bottom-up approach to dispute resolution through mediation is resurfacing in new community mediation forms such as the DDRS, the P.M.S., and Y.C.M. However, the example of the patriarchal and regressive *Khap Panchayats* has shown how a grass-roots system does injustice. Thus, it is pertinent to re-question: can community mediation always enable citizen empowerment, social transformation, and justice?

Community mediation programs endeavor changes in intangible areas such as perceptions, trust, cooperation, and relationships. It is assumed that such changes, if they arise between the parties, will also transfer to the society, despite the absence of a binding norm or precedent as in adjudication. For social change, an approach of "conflict transformation" will have to be adopted, recognizing conflict as an inevitable outcome of social interaction and focusing on the transition of conflict into positive outcomes.[140]

Globally, scant attention has been paid to mediation's effect on its users. Disregarding what happens to people must be a central concern for justice. Thus, a more comprehensive research is required in India on citizens' experiences and evaluations of justice and access to justice through citizen empowerment driven by mediation.

§12.06 CONCLUSION: FUTURE OF COMMUNITY MEDIATION IN INDIA

Community mediation is an evolving pluralistic movement in law and culture, prevalent in both ancient and contemporary forms in India. There are concerns regarding community mediation's ability to meet the aims of citizen empowerment and access to justice, beginning with the root of how these terms are defined. However, the community mediation movement in India should not be written off because: (i) it enables the democratic goal of creating an unfettered community space for citizen participation; (ii) it can be a conduit for collective voicing of dissatisfaction regarding recurring disputes with the State or social situations; (iii) it encourages the marginal-ized common citizens' participation as mediators; (iv) it provides an opportunity for creative justice based on self-determination; and (v) it can enable imbibing of skills for dispute prevention-cum-resolution for future cases with reduced dependency on the State. Community mediation can transform citizens' dormant power and responsibility into a dynamic form of service and justice.

The future of community mediation in India is promising and can bring about a cultural level realization that if we can create disputes, we can also resolve them. There is immense hope in unreported and reported community mediation initiatives such as

140. *See* Anna Snyder & Stephanie Stobbe, Critical Aspects of Gender in Conflict Resolution, Peacebuilding, and Social Movements 22 (2011).

the DDRS and P.M.S. and growing youth-led initiatives such as the Y.C.M. Despite the diversities of these community mediation initiatives, such as the runners being the State or a private charitable organization or youth collectives, the real hope is that the common goal of "authentic" citizen empowerment will be pursued as the critical goal of community mediation. If there is any need to create unity in diversity in community mediation initiatives, it is to have a united goal of authentic citizen empowerment.

[A] Feminism and Localization Framework to Test Authenticity of Community Mediation

It is pertinent to emphasize the difference between the popular understanding of feminism and localization and how these terms are being used in this part. First, equal inclusion of men and women in mediation is a positive step for structural representation but is not the "perfect solution" for ensuring non-patriarchy, and the *Shailishi Adalats* are an example of the same. Second, the local is not constituted based on ethnicity, caste, class, and gender but instead by contingent factors that bring together a group of people in materiality and sociality in a common local. This counters the argument of non-cohesive communities in cities.

Feminism has faced the challenge of being a pluralistic movement of social and cultural change or evolution in a larger context, which mediation is now facing. Hence, the comparison to learning from feminism is warranted especially given its commonalities with the mediation of: (i) self-determination; (ii) reinterpretation of power; (iii) introduction of values from the private sphere into public life; and (iv) localization/contextualization.

Despite the feminist critique, mediation and feminism both have commonalities as they both criticize the adversarial style of dispute resolution and traditional power politics, and both emphasize the "interests of all parties and the relationships among parties." Transformative mediation is the only one that openly acknowledges its basis in feminist values. However, mediation, in general, embodies them as well.

Self-determination and voluntariness in mediation are similar to the feminist approach of speak-for-yourself or "competence power"[141] as seen through various struggles, including rape law reforms and consent. Structural Feminists critique how a structure supports systemic injustice, which in the context of mediation hits the debate on whether the mediator's responsibility is to ensure fairness in the process and not the outcome, or how interventionist can a mediator be to ensure power balance between the disputants. Ten sources of power recognized in mediation are formal authority, expert/information power, associational power, resource power, procedural power, sanction power, nuisance power, habitual power, moral power, and personal power. However, transformative mediation has not integrated power in its discourse fully.

141. Independent strength, ability, autonomy, self-determination, control over one's own life rather than the lives of others, competence to deal with one's environment out of one's own energies and resources, rather than based on dependence.

In the context of transformative community mediation, the need for mediators to understand the interpersonal dimensions of conflict, to preserve relationships above and beyond the need to reach agreement and recognition of interconnectedness and interdependency, also known as empathy, has been emphasized. Thus, values consigned to private life are brought into the public sphere of mediation by a third party, as seen in the feminist value on the ethic of care. Furthermore, "each conflict is unique, and the outcome must emerge from the uniqueness of that particular relationship, not relying on precedent or law," which is similar to the feminist values of local contextualization and acceptance of the non-homogenous truth.

Moreover, community mediation can be tested for promoting authentic empowerment by examining community mediation centers in India for the existence and implementation of feminist values. The critique of defining core elements is essentialism. However, foundational elements have to be identified for theoretical analysis.[142] There is a need for "re-feminization" of corrupted mediation using feminist principles of self-determination, non-adversarial and non-hierarchal dialogue.

A preliminary analysis of feminist values in mediation in India indicates that mediation is a hybrid socio-legal process and a fluid practice traversing through multiple sociocultural contexts and legalities. The actual subjective construction of space and norms of mediation define mediation. Thus, feminist values are recommended to be used as the foundation before setting up mediation structures and reforming existing mediation structures for bottom-up, non-patriarchal, non-adversarial, and empowering mediation processes rather than only being used for academic critique.

Transformative mediation along with feminist values is recommended as the best way forward for community mediation as it ensures the goal of empowerment through self-determination and such self-determination in itself is a step of social change. However, mediation needs to come to terms with the "needs of a heterogeneous, multicultural society will give rise to more diversity in the shape of mediation" even though there is formalism or some push through some institutionalization and practices of community mediation initiatives for uniformity.

[B] Recommendations for the Community Mediation Movement in India

There is no doubt that feminism is an ally of mediation and can strengthen the community mediation movement. The following recommendations can further strengthen community mediation in India, particularly: (i) the use of technology; (ii) youth leadership and volunteer involvement; (iii) the use of conflict management as an approach; and (iv) partnerships including with the State.

The recommendations above are practical strategies to strengthen the community mediation movement in India. However, in the authors' view, the continual

142. *See* Anne Phillips, *What's Wrong with Essentialism?*, 11(1) SCANDINAVIAN J. SOCIAL THEORY 47, 48–50, 56 (2010).

success of community mediation lies in defining the one-value-and-one-goal of community mediation. The key to the success of community mediation lies in living the value of establishing a human connection based on recognizing universal needs and feelings of human beings that transcend the socioeconomic differences, including status, race, religion, caste, gender, sex, and sexual orientation (the "Human Connection").[143] "When you make the connection, the problem usually solves itself,"[144] and if not, then at least the Human Connection, which is established between two disputants, positively transforms the nature of their relationship beyond being disputants.

Thus, the main recommendation to have Human Connection as the underlying spirit of the Indian community mediation movement is threefold: (i) live the goal of establishing Human Connection in the structure and running of community mediation centers; (ii) practice the goal of establishing Human Connection while promoting and reviving community mediation in India with different stakeholders especially those who are skeptical of the value addition of community mediation; and (iii) define the main role of a community mediator as a facilitator for establishing Human Connection between the disputants.

Such recommendations come with a consciousness that learning and applying Human Connection in mediation or in the way we co-live as humans will take time. It invites resistance as it challenges deep conditioning or the status quo of: (i) looking at mediation as space or process for participants to give up something and reach a compromise as opposed to space for using the power of Human Connection to reach a place of satisfaction for both the participants regardless of arriving at a solution; and (ii) looking at disputes through the lens of wrongness-rightness as opposed to the lens of Human Connection that questions, "What human needs are unmet which led to a dispute or even used of violence," or "What can disputants do to recognize each other's needs and then contribute to meeting of such needs."[145]

The voice and power of the citizens will be determinative in community mediation's continual journey to establish Human Connection, the one-goal-and-one-value of community mediation for realizing authentic citizen empowerment. Such authentic citizen empowerment would mean facilitating the citizens to realize the power within themselves. In the context of community mediation, it would mean enabling their agency as effective users of mediation, runners of community mediation centers, and leaders of India's culture where dispute prevention and dispute resolution are common life skills everyone is equipped with. Empirical research using a perceptual approach to understand the citizens' perspective and preferences concerning community mediation is lacking in India and is the need of the hour for community mediation in India to be an authentic people's movement.

---

143. *See* Marshal Rosenberg, Conflict Resolution and Mediation, Non-violent Communication: A Language of Life Ch. 11 (2015).
144. *Id.*
145. *Id.*

CHAPTER 13
Mixed-Mode Dispute Resolution

Gracious Timothy Dunna & Kabir Duggal

§13.01 INTRODUCTION

Mixing the modes of dispute resolution or mixed-mode dispute resolution is simply the hybridization of the adjudicative (arbitration or litigation) and settlement-based processes (mediation, conciliation, negotiation). In these times, business perspectives and strategies have become complex and transnational to an unprecedented degree in response to the development of international markets and the infrastructures that serve them. Coupled with that, commercial disputes have also originated and completed their course among forces that make them distinctive and often exceedingly costly, time-drawn, and damaging to the business. Stand-alone arbitration or mediation is perhaps not sufficient at all times.

The hybridization of dispute resolution processes has a unique advantage, giving us the best of both worlds (so to speak). In the national survey results of the Global Pound Conference held at Chandigarh on May 12–13, 2017, when asked "the most effective commercial dispute resolution processes," the voting results showed that the top choice was "Combining adjudicative and non-adjudicative processes (e.g., arbitration/litigation with mediation/conciliation)." However, for long, dispute resolution processes have lacked effective integration between adjudicative and consensual (or settlement-based) processes, considered isolated; thus, making for an unsystematic patchwork dispute resolution process. Enter mixed-mode dispute resolution, such processes come in various well-structured shapes and sizes, as considered in the subsequent paragraphs. These are Med-Arb, Arb-Med, Arb-Med-Arb (AMA), parallel processes, and multitier dispute resolution.

Within the legal system in India (whether judicial or arbitral), parties can utilize a structure to better resolve their disputes or make them more efficient. Further, there is some cross-pollination among various jurisdictions when considering mixed-mode in the arbitral system vis-à-vis mediation, particularly due to UNCITRAL's efforts to bring uniformity among jurisdictions through the UNCITRAL Model Law on International Commercial Arbitration (hereinafter "Model Law on Arbitration"). This existing cross-pollination among jurisdictions is indeed further influenced by the unifying effect of treaties like the UN Convention on Enforcement of Foreign Arbitral Awards 1958 (hereinafter "New York Convention") and the recent UN Convention on International Settlement Agreement Resulting from Mediation (hereinafter "Singapore Convention").

Ultimately, the parties have the power to create dispute resolution procedures by carefully crafting their dispute resolution clauses; that is by "party autonomy" to agree on a suitable mixed-mode method, along with other matters like the governing substantive law, the appointment of neutrals (third-party arbitrator or mediator), institutional rules/ad hoc procedures, etc. This kind of flexibility is not present to the same extent in national court systems when we talk about mixed-mode dispute resolution because the procedures are largely predetermined as per the governing rules promulgated by courts or the appropriate government (central or State). However, the bigger need is for parties (and advocates equally) to better understand the mixing of modes in order to better implement the procedures to disputes.

Given arbitration's advantages over litigation, it is not surprising that arbitration has emerged as an important fixture in international business. Nevertheless, there is scope to improve that structure with the infusion of settlement-based processes for the purposes of better outcomes. Here, "better outcomes" may mean different things to different beneficiaries. However, the point of mixing modes of dispute resolution is that in seeking to fulfill client goals and priorities through effective conflict management, neither arbitration nor mediation should not be considered in isolation. Among "better outcomes," it would also include reducing dissatisfied parties from trying to have a second bite at the cherry and alleviating settlement outcomes' enforceability.

§13.02 LEGAL FRAMEWORK

[A] Section 30 of Arbitration Act

Section 30 of the Arbitration and Conciliation Act 1996 (hereinafter "Arbitration Act") sets the foremost example of mixed-mode dispute resolution, which functions within the arbitration proceedings. Section 30 provides:

> 30. Settlement.—(1) It is *not incompatible with an arbitration agreement for an arbitral tribunal to encourage settlement of the dispute and, with the agreement of the parties, the arbitral tribunal may use mediation, conciliation or other procedures* at any time during the arbitral proceedings to encourage settlement.
>
> (2) If, during arbitral proceedings, the parties settle the dispute, the arbitral tribunal shall terminate the proceedings and, if requested by the parties and not objected to by the arbitral tribunal, record the settlement in the form of an arbitral award on agreed terms.
>
> (3) An arbitral award on agreed terms shall be made in accordance with Section 31 and shall state that it is an arbitral award.

> (4) An arbitral award on agreed terms shall have the same status and effect as any other arbitral award on the substance of the dispute.
>
> (emphasis supplied)

Section 30 of the Arbitration Act is the adoption of Article 30 of the Model Law on Arbitration. However, the Indian provision goes two steps forward than Article 30, which merely provides:

> Article 30—Settlement
>
> (1) If, during arbitral proceedings, the parties settle the dispute, the arbitral tribunal shall terminate the proceedings and, *if requested by the parties* and not objected to by the arbitral tribunal, record the settlement in the form of an arbitral award on agreed terms.
>
> (2) An award on agreed terms shall be made in accordance with the provisions of article 31 and shall state that it is an award. Such an award has the same status and effect as any other award on the merits of the case.

Hence, unlike section 30 of the Arbitration Act, the Model Law provision nowhere expressly gives an arbitral tribunal the mandate to encourage settlement of disputes and specifically use mediation, conciliation, or other procedures, with the parties' agreement. Nor is there any restriction, if it so agreed between the parties, that a tribunal itself changes hats to mediate the matter (wholly or partly), rather than referring it to a separate mediator/panel of mediators. In this regard, the uniqueness of Indian law, i.e., resolution of disputes at the behest of the tribunal, is quite exemplary and was not always present in Indian law when we visit the erstwhile Arbitration Act 1940.

[1] Award on Agreed Terms

Section 30 of the Arbitration Act deals with an arbitral award on agreed terms or, simply put, a consent award based on the settlement's terms. One can question from the language used in section 30(2) whether only one of the parties can submit a request before the tribunal to record the settlement in the form of a consent award. However, a compromise represents the will of all the parties, and an acceptance to a settlement may very well be conditional to the terms not being recorded as a consent award. Sure, if a settlement has already been drawn between the parties and one party requests the tribunal based on some evidence that declares the other party's will to record the terms as a consent award, then perhaps there may be a reasonable case.

In this regard, an arbitral tribunal is given complete authority to record the settlement terms, without any particular requirement as to whether the settlement concerns the entire dispute or only a part thereof. Moreover, there is no requirement for the tribunal to record any reasons under section 31 of the Arbitration Act since the award is made on the terms agreed between the parties, thus, precluding the need for reasons.[1] Any which way, such a settlement is essentially the compromise between

1. *See* Mafatlal Securities Ltd. v. Birla Sun-Life Securities Ltd. (2002) 2 Arb LR 304, ¶ 5.

both the parties that brings an end to the dispute, wholly or partly (leaving the rest to be decided on its merits by the arbitral tribunal). But such a settlement cannot be one-sided and would need to showcase a mutual compromise.[2]

Once a settlement (not some Memorandum of Understanding or such nonbinding instrument) is drawn and delivered as a consent award, under subsection 30(3), this consent award shall have the same status and effect as any other award on the merits of the case,[3] hence, offering the same finality as in the case of arbitral awards and practically no recourse, save for the narrow grounds of annulment under section 34 (as is typically still available in case of arbitral awards). A consent award is therefore final and binding on the parties (including persons claiming through or under such party),[4] and it shall be enforceable in accordance with the provisions of the Code of Civil Procedure 1908 (CPC), in the same manner as if it were a decree of the court.[5]

Additionally, before delivering the consent award, a tribunal may also give due regard to the parties' conduct and the resulting settlement when considering the issue of costs under section 31A(3) of the Arbitration Act (on the regime for costs), which would continue to apply, irrespective of whether the award was delivered on agreed terms or the merit.

[2] Role of the Tribunal

In the entire scheme of things under section 30, the role of the tribunal under section 30 of the Arbitration Act is an important one since it is the tribunal that will record the terms and deliver a consent award under its signatures (give its seal of approval, as it were). In this regard, section 30(2) of the Arbitration Act does give a tribunal the discretion to refuse the recording of the terms as a consent award. Here, the statute does not indicate as to whether a tribunal is required to record reasons or not. However, the safer postulation is that the tribunal should record its reasons to discharge its duties as a quasi-judicial body (unless, of course, there is some overriding public policy-related reasoning behind the tribunal's decision to not record the terms of the settlement).

Furthermore, some parameters about this discretion to refuse can be drawn from explanation (i) of section 34(2)(b)(ii) of the Arbitration Act, which states that the award would be in conflict with the public policy of India if the making of the award was induced or affected by fraud or corruption,[6] e.g., where the settlement constitutes

2. *See* Malpati Sevasangh v. Gujarat State Khadi & Village Industries Board, 2004 (2) Arb LR 521, ¶¶ 21–26.
3. *See* Mysore Cement Ltd. v. Svedala Barmac Ltd. (2003) 10 SCC 375, ¶ 16. *See also*, Morgan Securities & Credits Pvt. Ltd. v. Morepen Laboratories Ltd., 2006 (3) Arb LR 159, ¶¶ 15–18 (distinction removed between award on agreed terms and award on merits).
4. *See* Haresh Dayaram Thakur v. State of Maharashtra & Ors. (2000) 6 SCC 179, ¶ 19.
5. Arbitration & Conciliation Act, 1996, §36.
6. *See* Kiyue Co. Ltd. v. Aquagen International Pte. Ltd., [2003] 3 SLR 130, ¶ 11 (Sg.) ("It is manifestly wrong for a controlling shareholder to sue its subsidiary and then order it not to defend. On this fact alone, equity is against it. And that is not all. It appears that the company had received legal advice to the effect that the claim ought to be resisted").

a part of elaborate tax fraud by the parties. The same standard also reflects in the analogous provisions under the CPC, discussed in the Chapter on Court-Annexed Mediations. In brief, according to the principles entailing Order XXIII rule 3 of the CPC, a court must satisfy itself that there is a lawful agreement adjusting the suit and whether the agreement is vitiated by grounds such as illegality, fraud, and misrepresentation. If the settlement, for instance, was arrived at fraudulently, the court which entertained the compromise petition may refuse to pass a consent decree in terms of the settlement.[7]

[3] Termination of Proceedings

Once parties have settled and brought an end to their dispute on the whole (whether pursuant to section 30 of the Arbitration Act or not, i.e., even without the tribunal's cognizance), section 30(2) read with section 32(2) makes it amply clear that the arbitral tribunal shall terminate the proceeding. Though the parties come to a settlement without the tribunal ever being aware of any such settlement talks between the parties, it would still be necessary for the parties to notify the tribunal about the settlement (if any) for the tribunal to terminate the proceedings.

Once aware and notified about the settlement, the tribunal shall go so far as to record the terms of settlement only if it is so requested by the parties—giving parties the autonomy to convert their settlement terms into a consent decree (mainly for an advantage in enforcement).

As in section 32(3) of the Arbitration Act, with the termination of proceedings, the arbitral tribunal's mandate also comes to an end, rendering the tribunal *functus officio*. And even though section 32(3) does contemplate residual powers under sections 33 and 34(4) of the Arbitration Act (for correction/interpretation and remand, respectively), these provisions do not conceive any application in a scenario where a consent award is rendered.

[4] Practical Application

Part III of the Arbitration Act provides for conciliation. However, it does not envisage a pre-dispute agreement to conciliate. In other words, Indian law does not permit a conciliation agreement for future disputes, given the inherent quality of conciliation being a voluntary process.[8] However, this limitation is assuaged by section 30 of the Arbitration Act, which is available to parties (and to the tribunal) by virtue of a pre-dispute arbitration agreement or arbitration agreement for future disputes.

Thus, where the parties, lawyers, and the tribunal are well aware and equipped (and willing) to undergo conciliatory processes, the dispute resolution process can be enhanced multifold by mixing modes that can potentially help resolve at least such parts of the dispute that are emitting settlement vibes. But even if a settlement could

7. *See* Banwari Lal v. Chando Devi & Anr. (1993) 1 SCC 581, ¶7, ¶14.
8. *See* Visa International Ltd. v. Continental Resources (USA) Ltd. (2009) 2 SCC 55, ¶ 27.

not materialize, the process would still benefit the parties in understanding each other's perspectives; narrowing down the issues for contentious proceedings; paving the way for partial resolutions on negotiable issues; and removing any negative/regretful feeling about taking a contentious course of action without wounding the existing relationship.

Most importantly, a consent award gives parties a straightforward execution of the settlement terms since challenges to enforcement (brought by defaulter) may be cumbersome (in terms of both time and cost). Default situations may particularly arise where there is some element of future performance, e.g., payment by installments or a future obligation to be carried out by one party. In case of a default, a consent award brings immediate implementation by way of execution proceedings in the appropriate, with a very high threshold to seek a refusal of enforcement (such that the consent award was induced or affected by fraud or corruption).

In the case of an international commercial arbitration seated in India, where it becomes essential for one party to enforce the consent award in a foreign jurisdiction, a party may well enforce the consent award through the New York Convention by bringing an enforcement action in the courts of a signatory State.

[B] Section 73 of Arbitration Act

Section 73 of the Arbitration provides that the settlement agreement signed by the parties in dispute shall be final and binding on the parties, which agreement would need to be authenticated/signed by the conciliator.

But to reach an agreement on the settlement, when it appears to the conciliator that there exist elements of the settlement that may be acceptable to the parties, he is required to formulate the terms of a possible settlement and submit them to the settlement parties for their observations. Upon receiving observations of the parties, the conciliator may reformulate the term of a possible settlement in view of the observations by the parties.

Once the parties reach an agreement on the settlement, they may draw up and sign a written settlement agreement, which is thereafter signed/endorsed by the conciliator. The parties may also request the conciliator to draw up (or assist parties in drawing up) the settlement agreement.[9] This is final and binding on the parties (and those claiming through or under them)[10] and attains the status and legal sanctity of an arbitral award under section 74 of the Arbitration Act.

Similarly, under Article 17 of the 2018 Model Law, courts have the substantive obligation to enforce a settlement agreement (subject to exceptions, of course). Nevertheless, how a State enforces a settlement agreement (i.e., the rules of procedure) will be within its discretion. Article 17 further covers the scenario where a settlement agreement might be raised in defense against a claim in a court. Namely, that by meeting all the conditions under the Model Law, a party seeking relief would be able to

9. *See* Haresh Dayaram Thakur v. State of Maharashtra & Ors., AIR 2000 SC 2281, ¶¶ 19–20.
10. *See* Mysore Cements Ltd. v. Svedala Barmac Ltd., AIR 2003 SC 3493, ¶ 12.

prove that the dispute had been settled. Here again, the rules of procedure are the prerogative of the State.

[C] Section 80 of Arbitration Act

Section 80 of the Arbitration Act defines the role of a conciliator in proceeding other than the conciliation itself. It states that:

> 80. Role of conciliator in other proceedings.—Unless otherwise agreed by the parties—
>
> (a) the conciliator shall not act as an arbitrator or as a representative or counsel of a party in any arbitral or judicial proceedings in respect of a dispute that is the subject of the conciliation proceedings.

Hence, the default rule is that a conciliator is prohibited from acting as an arbitrator, or as a representative or counsel of a party in any arbitration, regarding a dispute which is the subject matter of the conciliation proceedings. However, parties have been given the freedom to agree otherwise,[11] deviating from Article 19 of the UNCITRAL Conciliation Rules 1980, making the default rule mandatory. While much has been discussed on this issue in the Chapter on the Law of Conciliation, the policy of this provision (assuming a conciliation fails) is to preclude any potential bias that a conciliator may carry into the subsequent proceedings, where a party may be seriously prejudiced.

It is, however, ambiguous as to whether such an agreement can be entered into pre-dispute, i.e., for future disputes. This ambiguity arises since pre-dispute conciliation clauses are not enforceable;[12] however, that is limited to parties' participation in conciliation proceedings (section 62 of the Arbitration Act). At the same time, there is also no prohibition that parties cannot put down a written (unenforceable) agreement that can receive the parties' confirmation after the dispute has arisen, either by conduct or by writing. Thereby, parties may indeed enter into multitier or mixed-mode clauses wherein a conciliator's role may be stipulated to act as an arbitrator in any arbitration regarding a dispute that is the subject of the conciliation.

[D] Section 89 of the CPC

Section 89 of the CPC is the wellspring of Appropriate Dispute Resolution (ADR) (and mixed-mode dispute resolution) under the litigation regime, supplemented by rules 1A–1C of Order X of CPC. It deals with and encourages the settlement of disputes.[13]

11. *See generally*, Rules on the Efficient Conduct of Proceedings in International Arbitration (Prague Rules), Art. 9(2) ("Upon the prior written consent of all parties, any member of the arbitral tribunal may also act as a mediator to assist in the amicable settlement of the case").
12. *See* Visa International Ltd. v. Continental Resources (USA) Ltd. (2009) 2 SCC 55, ¶ 27.
13. *See* Surinder Kaur & Ors v. Pritam Singh & Ors (2008) 154 DLT 598, ¶ 8.

Even though section 89 uses the phrase "outside of court," it does not mean that processes commenced through this provision go outside the stream of the court when a reference is made to nonadjudicatory processes (except arbitration wherein the case would go outside the stream of the court). And so, the court retains its control and jurisdiction over the case, even when the matter is undergoing any of these nonadjudicatory processes like mediation, conciliation, Lok Adalat,[14] or judicial settlement.[15] This is because where a settlement could not be reached, the case would ultimately go to trial. If parties can arrive at a settlement (wholly or partially), the judicial system would still come into play to end the court action by recording the terms of the settlement,[16] or continuing the proceeding into trial concerning such issues which could not be settled.

There are five different alternatives provided by section 89, consisting of one adjudicatory (i.e., arbitration) and four nonadjudicatory processes (i.e., conciliation, Lok Adalat, mediation, and judicial settlement). In providing these alternatives, the Supreme Court observed many drafting errors, and consequently, provided a coherent interpretation and suggested several amendments to expunge the errors and deficiencies.[17] Thus, when analyzing considering section 89, we must note that the Supreme Court interchanged the word "mediation" in section 89(2)(d) of CPC with the words "judicial settlement" in section 89(2)(c) of CPC. This change is not yet reflected in any enactment or amendment. Hence, section 89 now reads thus:

> 89. Settlement of disputes outside the Court.—
> (1) Where it appears to the Court that there exist elements of a settlement which may be acceptable to the parties, the Court shall formulate the terms of settlement and give them to the parties for their observations and after receiving the observations of the parties, the Court may reformulate the terms of a possible settlement and refer the same for:—
> (a) arbitration;
> (b) conciliation;
> (c) judicial settlement including settlement through Lok Adalat; or
> (d) mediation.
> (2) Were a dispute has been referred—
> (a) for arbitration or conciliation, the provisions of the Arbitration and Conciliation Act, 1996 (26 of 1996) shall apply as if the proceedings for arbitration or conciliation were referred for settlement under the provisions of that Act;
> (b) to Lok Adalat, the Court shall refer the same to the Lok Adalat in accordance with the provisions of sub-section (1) of section 20 of the Legal Services Authority Act, 1987 (39 of 1987) and all other provisions of that Act shall .apply in respect of the dispute so referred to the Lok Adalat;

14. Lok Adalat is a forum where disputes/cases pending in the courts or at pre-litigation stage are settled or compromised amicably. Lok Adalats have been given statutory status under the Legal Services Authorities Act, 1987.
15. *See* Afcons Infrastructure Ltd. v. Cherian Varkey Construction Co. Pvt. Ltd. (2010) 8 SCC 24, ¶ 38 (hereinafter "Afcons").
16. *Id.*
17. *See id.*, at ¶¶ 13 and 25.

(c) for [mediation], the Court shall refer the same to a suitable institution or person and such institution or person shall be deemed to be a Lok Adalat and all the provisions of the Legal Services Authority Act, 1987 (39 of 1987) shall apply as if the dispute were referred to a Lok Adalat under the provisions of that Act;

(d) for [judicial settlement], the Court shall effect a compromise between the parties and shall follow such procedure as may be prescribed.

[1] Judicial Settlement

Judicial settlement is where the court brings about a compromise between the parties. It is not exactly clear what this process entails and what the court's role is when proceeding on this basis. Thus, the only attempt to understand (though brief) was in the *Afcons Infrastructure Ltd. v. Cherian Varkey Construction Co. Pvt. Ltd.* ("*Afcons Infrastructure*"), where it is observed in the context of United States (US) practice that "'[j]udicial settlement' is a term in vogue in the USA referring to a settlement of a civil case with the help of a Judge who is not assigned to adjudicate upon the dispute."[18]

Hence, one may reasonably say that judicial settlement under section 89 is conceived as a distinct process where the sitting judge (other than the referral judge) plays an active role in resolving a dispute. If the court feels that a suggestion or guidance by a judge would be appropriate, it can refer the dispute to that judge for a judicial settlement.[19] As such, judicial settlement is not governed by any statute, and the court will follow such procedure as may be prescribed by appropriate rules.[20] Though no such appropriate rules have been prescribed, one may source some guidance from the functioning of a Lok Adalat (since proceedings before a Lok Adalat are deemed judicial). For instance, section 20(4) of the Legal Services Authorities Act 1987 (LSA) stipulates that every Lok Adalat shall, while determining any reference before it, act with utmost expedition to arrive at a compromise or settlement between the parties and shall be guided by the principles of justice, equity, fair play, and other legal principles. Similarly, as in the case of Permanent Lok Adalats (PLAs) under section 27C(7) of the LSA, it may formulate the terms of a possible settlement of the dispute and give it to the parties for their observations.

What is important is that the court system does embrace a form of mixed-mode dispute resolution, integrating a settlement-based process into an adjudicatory process, giving a court or judge the authority to bring about a settlement between the parties. While there are no published instances in practice, there is nevertheless a clear statutory permit for the courts to exercise a settlement-based approach.

18. *Id.*, at ¶12.
19. *Id.*, at ¶36.
20. *Id.*, at ¶¶ 29–30.

[2] Mediation

Court-annexed mediation under section 89 has been discussed in detail in the respective chapter. Briefly, when a matter is considered suitable or appropriate for mediation,[21] a court may (having regard to the nature of the case) refer the parties to mediation. Particularly, if the suit is complicated or lengthy, mediation is preferred among Lok Adalat and judicial settlement.[22] While mediation is deemed to be a reference to Lok Adalat, this is only for limited purposes, and any mediated settlement (except such matters which are not the subject matter of the suit/proceedings) is made into a consent decree by applying the principles of rule 3 of Order XXIII of the CPC. However, if no settlement is reached between the parties, the matter returns to the court for trial.[23]

The procedures, however, take a different route when there are settlements on issues beyond the subject matter of the court's proceedings.[24] In such cases, the settlement has a Lok Adalat settlement status under section 21 of the LSA (and accordingly a deemed decree of the court).[25] As a matter of procedure, the Lok Adalat settlement award is also to be placed before the referral court for recording it and disposal on its term,[26] since mediation is after all nonstatutory and it stands on a different footing; hence, the *imprimatur* of the referring court is required to make it effective. It is acknowledged that there may be some difference of opinion in that there is no such distinction in procedures when the settled issues are beyond the subject matter of the court's proceedings. At the same time, there is also no clarity about the uniform practice followed by courts.

Because a reference to mediation is deemed a reference to Lok Adalat in accordance with section 89(2)(c) of the CPC and because the said clause states that all provisions of the LSA shall apply, the general view is that a mediator, therefore, assumes the powers of a Lok Adalat and, in turn, a civil court under section 22 of the LSA. This fundamentally contradicts the concept of mediation, and, hence, there is an inherent inconsistency here that needs correction by the legislature. Nevertheless, its effect in practice seems to have been circumvented by ignoring the ramifications of section 89(2)(c), which is also reasonable since the import "all provisions" of the LSA

---

21. *Id.*, at ¶27.
22. *Id.*, at ¶36.
23. *Id.*, at ¶ 43 (h). *See also*, Legal Services Authority Act, 1987, §19(5) and §20(1) (discussing the Act's source of jurisdiction and reference of settlement).
24. *Id.*, at ¶ 40 ("such settlement" refers to the paragraph above at ¶39).
25. *Id.*, at ¶ 29, 30.
26. *Id.*, at ¶ 39. *See also*, LAW COMMISSION OF INDIA, REPORT NO. 238 ¶ 5.3 (2011), https://lawcommissionofindia.nic.in/reports/report238.pdf ("... Therefore, the more appropriate course would be to require the mediator to submit the terms of settlement reached as a result of mediation to the court so that the court, after due scrutiny, can pass a decree in accordance with the compromise arrived at between the parties. Accordingly, we propose to recast the provision relating to mediation. Secondly, it is not necessary to provide that the award of Lok Adalat or the settlement arrived at through conciliation should be forwarded to the referring court for passing a decree on the same lines, notwithstanding certain observations made by the Hon'ble Supreme Court in paragraph 38 of Afcons ...") (hereinafter "LCI Report 238").

should be considered in the context of mediation (keeping in mind the conceptual nature of the process and the role of a mediator):

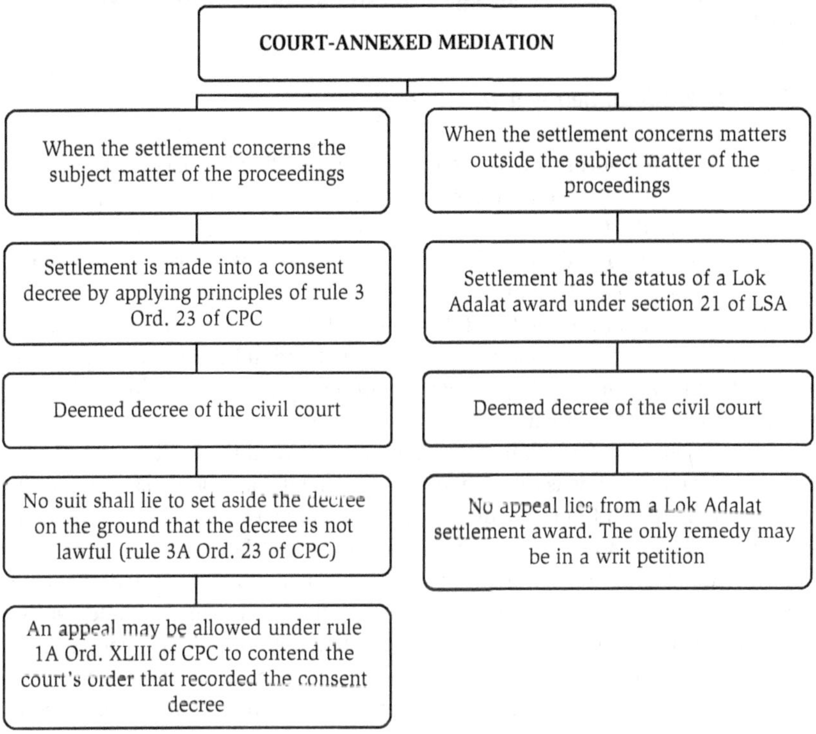

[3] Conciliation

Where a court refers the dispute to conciliation, section 89(2)(a) stipulates that the provision of the Arbitration Act would apply (specifically sections 65–81) as if the conciliation was initiated under the said Act. The only difference in conciliation (as opposed to a referral to mediation) is that a reference to conciliation is only possible when the parties give consent.[27] This is because of section 62 of the Arbitration Act, which requires that the responding party accepts an invitation.

A conciliation referral has a straightforward approach and result. If at the end of the process parties arrive at a conciliated settlement, it attains the status of a consent award under sections 74 and 30 of the Arbitration Act (which is enforceable in the same manner as if it were a decree of the court under section 36 of the Act). The terms would have to be placed before the referral court for recording it and disposal on its term,[28] though it would not be necessary to forward the terms of the settlement to the referring

27. *See* Afcons, *supra* note 15, at ¶¶ 35–36.
28. *Id.*, at ¶ 28.

court for passing a decree on the same lines,[29] given the effect of sections 74 and 30 of the Arbitration Act. Meaning that conciliation does not technically require the seal of the court, but it is returned to the court to formally end the court action.[30] However, in case the settlement efforts fail, the matter is returned to the court for framing of issues and trial.[31]

[4] Lok Adalat Settlement

Lok Adalat is an ADR forum where disputes/cases pending in the court of law or at the pre-litigation stage are settled/compromised amicably. Lok Adalats have been given statutory status under the LSA 1987. Under LSA, the award (decision) made by the Lok Adalats is deemed to be a decree of a civil court and is final and binding on all parties, and no appeal against such an award lies before any court of law. If the parties are not satisfied with the award of the Lok Adalat, though there is no provision for an appeal against such an award, parties are free to initiate litigation by approaching the court of appropriate jurisdiction by filing a case by following the required procedure, in the exercise of their right to litigate.

There is no court fee payable when a matter is filed in a Lok Adalat. If a matter pending in the court of law is referred to the Lok Adalat and is settled subsequently, the court fee originally paid in the court on the complaints/petition is also refunded back to the parties. The persons deciding the cases in the Lok Adalats are called the Members of the Lok Adalats, they have the role of statutory conciliators only and do not have any judicial role; therefore, they can only persuade the parties to conclude settling the dispute outside the court in the Lok Adalat and shall not pressurize or coerce any of the parties to compromise or settle cases or matters either directly or indirectly. The Lok Adalat shall not decide the matter so referred at its instance. Instead, the same would be decided based on the compromise or settlement between the parties. The members shall assist the parties independently and impartially in their attempt to reach an amicable settlement of their dispute.

Lok Adalats have been organized at different levels: National Authority level, State Authority level (by the State Legal Service Authority), at the High Court level (by the High Court Legal Services Committee), at the District level (by the District Legal Services Authority), and the Taluka level (by the Taluk Legal Services Committee). The composition of any Lok Adalat is according to its level. Mobile Lok Adalats are also organized in various parts of the country, which travel from one location to another to resolve disputes to facilitate the resolution of disputes through this mechanism.

Reference to a Lok Adalat under section 89(2)(b) of the CPC is generally considered appropriate where the dispute is not complicated and easily sortable or can be settled by applying clear-cut legal principles. Once a reference is made to a Lok Adalat, the procedures under the LSA come into play, although the court continues to

29. *See* LCI Report 238, *supra* note 26.
30. *See* Afcons, *supra* note 15, at ¶ 38.
31. *Id.*, at ¶ 35.

retain control and jurisdiction over the case referred to Lok Adalat. Hence, the Lok Adalat settlement/award is required to be placed before the court for recording it and disposal on its terms. Although the Lok Adalat award does not technically require the court's seal, it is returned to the court to formally end the court action. In practice, a referring court on receipt of intimation from a Lok Adalat records the factum of settlement leading to a Lok Adalat and closes the case in the presence of the parties or their counsel formal order or decree is passed.[32]

Under section 19(5) of the LSA, a Lok Adalat has the jurisdiction to "determine" and "arrive at a compromise or settlement between the parties" on any matter which falls within the court's jurisdiction for which the Lok Adalat is organized. The LSA becomes ambiguous as to the exact role of a Lok Adalat when it says "determine." One may understand it to mean that Lok Adalat should determine *ex aequo et bono* (or as *amiable compositeur*) since a Lok Adalat is to be "guided by the principles of justice, equity, fair play, and other legal principles."[33] Section 22 of the LSA specially deems the proceedings before a Lok Adalat as judicial proceedings and sets out a Lok Adalat's powers for holding any determination, such as: (a) the summoning and enforcing the attendance of any witness and examining him on oath; (b) the discovery and production of any document; (c) the reception of evidence on affidavits; (d) the requisitioning of any public record or document or copy of such record or document from any court or office; and (e) such other matters as may be prescribed.

Ultimately, party autonomy and self-determination seem to be given precedence. In that, where the Lok Adalat makes no settlement award on the ground that no compromise or settlement could be arrived at between the parties, the case is returned to the court for disposal according to the law.[34]

Where a Lok Adalat settlement award is reached, it is deemed a civil court decree.[35] It is final and binding on all the parties to the dispute, and no appeal shall lie to any court against the award,[36] which leaves parties with only extraordinary remedies like a special leave petition or a writ petition. A Lok Adalat's award is executable as a decree of a court.[37]

Regarding the Lok Adalat administrative procedures, the Supreme Court has recommended that Lok Adalats have a uniform procedure, prescribed registers and standardized formats of awards, and permanent records of awards to avoid misuse or abuse ADR process.[38] Accordingly, it was suggested that the National Legal Services Authority (NALSA) should issue uniform guidelines for the effective functioning of the Lok Adalats.[39] In the meanwhile, however, the Supreme Court held that the principles

32. *See* LCI Report 238, *supra* note 26, ¶ 5.3 (observes that on inquiring from some District Judges/Secretaries and Legal Services Authorities, the Chairman of LCI came to know that as the existing practice).
33. Legal Services Authority Act, 1987, §20(4).
34. *Id.*, §20(5) and §20(7).
35. *Id.*, §21(1).
36. *Id.*, §21(2).
37. *See* B. P. Moideen Sevamandir and Anr. v. A. M. Kutty Hassan (2009) 2 SCC 198, ¶¶ 7–8.
38. *Id.*, ¶¶ 12–13.
39. *Id.*

underlying sections 67 (role of conciliators), 75 (confidentiality), and 86 (admissibility of evidence in other proceedings) might be treated as guidelines till uniform guidelines are issued by NALSA.[40]

As per section 18(1) of the LSA, a Lok Adalat has jurisdiction to determine and to arrive at a compromise or settlement between the parties to a dispute in respect of: (a) any case pending before any court; and (b) any dispute which has not been brought before any court and is likely to be filed before the court[41]—provided, however, that any matter relating to divorce or an offense not compoundable under the law is outside the scope of a Lok Adalat.

[E] Permanent Lok Adalats

The LSA, under Chapter VI-A of the Act, separately establishes PLAs with specific jurisdiction over enumerated public utility service issues, which include:[42] (i) transport service for the carriage of passengers or goods by air, road, or water; (ii) postal, telegraph or telephone service; (iii) supply of power, light or water to the public by any establishment; (iv) system of public conservancy or sanitation; (v) service in hospital or dispensary; (vi) insurance service; and any other service which the government may include. Besides enumerated subjects, LSA stipulates a pecuniary limit to PLA's jurisdiction at INR 10 lakhs (increasable by the government in consultation with the NALSA/Central Authority).

PLAs are unique for their hybrid model, which first requires it to attempt conciliation (including formulating settlement options), and only on its failure shall a PLA proceed to decide the dispute on its merit (but on principles of natural justice, objectivity, fair play, equity and other principles of justice). Meaning, the same forum acts as both the conciliator and the adjudicator, even though a PLA is deemed to be a civil court, and the proceedings before it is deemed to be judicial proceedings. This model of "one forum two roles" is also seen in the context of the Micro and Small Enterprise Facilitation Council (Facilitation Council) under the Micro, Small, and Medium Enterprises Development Act 2006 (MSMED).

A PLA takes cognizance of a matter on the application of a disputing party.[43] Once such an application has been made, no party to that application can invoke the jurisdiction of any court (perhaps with the intent to give no scope for parallel litigation and bringing the focus entirely to the conciliation before PLA).[44] Once an application is made, the PLA follows an elaborate conciliation procedure (which resembles the procedure under Part III of the Arbitration Act):

40. *Id.*
41. The State and District Authority on receipt of an application from any one of the parties at a pre-litigation stage may refer such matter to the Lok Adalat for amicable settlement of the dispute for which notice would then be issued to the other party.
42. Legal Services Authority Act, 1987, §22A.
43. *Id.*, §22C(1).
44. *Id.*, §22C(2).

- PLA shall direct each party to file before it a written statement, stating therein the facts and nature of the dispute, points or issues in such dispute and grounds relied upon, any document and other evidence in support of each party's case.[45]
- PLA may require any party to file an additional statement before it at any stage of the conciliation proceedings;[46] it shall be the duty of every party to cooperate in good faith to comply with any direction of the PLA to produce evidence and other related documents.[47]
- PLA shall conduct conciliation proceedings in such manner as it thinks appropriate taking into account the circumstances of the dispute;[48] it shall assist parties in their attempt to reach an amicable settlement independently and impartially.[49]
- If PLA is of the opinion that there exist elements of a settlement which may be acceptable to the parties, it may formulate the terms of a possible settlement of the dispute and give to the parties concerned for their observations.[50]
- If a settlement is reached, parties shall sign the settlement, and the PLA shall pass an award in terms thereof and furnish a copy to each party.[51]
- If parties fail to reach an agreement, the PLA shall decide the dispute on its merits;[52] in doing so, it shall be guided by the principles of natural justice, objectivity, fair play, equity, and other principles of justice, and shall not be bound by CPC and the Indian Evidence Act 1872;[53] when deciding on the merits, it shall do so by a majority of the persons constituting the PLA.[54]

A PLA award (whether a settlement award or an award on merits) is final and binding on the parties and persons claiming under them,[55] and it cannot be called in question in any original suit, application, or execution proceeding.[56] Every award of the PLA is a deemed decree of a civil court, and, for execution purposes, the PLA can transmit the PLA award to a civil court having local jurisdiction, which shall execute it as if it were a decree made by that court.[57] In essence, a PLA seeks to achieve a hybrid purpose; it speaks of not only conciliation qua conciliatory means but also conciliation qua determination.[58]

45. *Id.*, §22C(3)(a).
46. *Id.*, §22C(3)(b).
47. *Id.*, §22C(6).
48. *Id.*, §22C(4).
49. *Id.*, §22C(5).
50. *Id.*, §22C(7).
51. *Id.*, §22C(7).
52. *Id.*, §22C(8).
53. *Id.*, §22D.
54. *Id.*, §22E(3).
55. *Id.*, §22E(1).
56. *Id.*, §22E(4).
57. *Id.*, §22E(5).
58. *See* United India Insurance Ltd. v. Ajay Sinha and Anr. (2008) 7 SCC 454, ¶ 24.

§13.03 FORMS OF MIXED-MODE DISPUTE RESOLUTION

Given the contracting freedom under Indian law and the general framework of dispute resolution discussed above, it is possible to conceive various forms of mixed-modes to resolving disputes. The combination/hybrid models discussed here may be considered to be the typical understanding of these models (with endless possibilities in the hands of the parties to tailor the process according to their needs).[59]

[A] Med-Arb

Med-Arb refers to a mixed-mode process where the parties engage in mediation, first followed by arbitration for issues that remain unresolved, all with the help of a single neutral who wears the hats of both a mediator and an arbitrator consecutively. In Med-Arb, the mediator charged with facilitating the settlement of disputes shifts to the role of adjudicator. Thus, where mediation is unsuccessful in resolving some or all disputes, the mediator "changes hats" and takes on the arbitrator's role to render a binding decision (hence referred to as Med-Arb).[60]

Such procedures include variants such as mediation and last-offer arbitration, in which the arbitral discretion of the neutral is limited to adopting one or the other of the parties' final offers in his award.

Among the pros, Med-Arb has an immense potential to save time and cost. Since parties invest much time communicating their dispute to the mediator, the mediator becomes well educated about the technicalities and issues surrounding the dispute, making him an ideal arbitrator (as someone who is already aware of the facts and circumstances of the case).

Med-Arb also encourages (or even pushes) the parties to resolve the dispute, knowing that the mediator will later render an award as an arbitrator. The psychological motivation to settle is (arguably) a beneficial driver for settlements. But one may also argue that it would be like using the "big stick" approach—to speak softly but carry a big stick that undermines self-determination. On the flip side, candid discussions by a party may influence the mediator-turned-arbitrator to award a less beneficial decision (hence, limiting a party's candor during mediation). Such mediation is more likely to fail.

---

59. For example, would it be better to follow up an unsuccessful mediation with arbitration (as the outcome in the former is voluntary, whereas the latter is not) if multitier clauses would prevent parties from genuinely participating in the mediation process and instead doing the bare minimum with the intention of arbitrating their disputes later?
60. *See*, e.g., Spruce Envtl. Techs., Inc. v. Festa Radon Techs., Co., 370 F.Supp. 3d 275 (D. Mass. 2019) (it was argued that the contractual stipulation to arbitrate before the same neutral who mediated the dispute was invalid as a matter of public policy because it violated Massachusetts' mediation privilege statute. The court, however, disagreed, suggesting that a party may waive its privilege rights). *See also*, Mahindra Lifespace Developers Ltd. v. The New Great Eastern Spinning and Weaving Company Ltd., 2009 (111) Bom LR 2048 (discussing section 80 of the Arbitration Act and that the role played by the neutral was more of a mediator).

There is also a fundamental change in the role of the neutral—one that amplifies the cons of Arb-Med and potentially compromises neutrality and impartiality of the neutral. Mediators often caucus with each party to encourage candid and full-ranging discussions. These discussions are ex parte, revealing facts that may never be shared with, or subject to challenge by, the other side. Such factors may be influential upon the mediator-turned-arbitrator's mind. That is why advocates must address whether and how the arbitrator will separate factual statements and other impressions formed during the mediation from the evidence presented in arbitration.

From the parties' point of view, when the mediator transforms into the arbitrator, a party may tend to no longer have a fear of an adverse adjudication, instead of imagining that the mediator-turned-arbitrator continues to have the same understanding, empathy, and insight about the needs and interest of the party. But such a party would be making a big mistake.

Even though the procedure packs in a substantial advantage, it would be legally untenable under Indian law (unless, of course, the statute provides for it, as in the case of the PLA or the Facilitation Council under the MSMED Act). The reason being that arbitration can only be invoked from a dispute and not a settlement, and thus a settlement cannot lead to the appointment of a tribunal.[61] Even at the UNCITRAL, a model legislative provision in this regard was rejected for the same reason.[62]

There may be some creative ways of circumventing this legal impediment by providing procedures that a settlement shall be put into writing after the arbitration is invoked and a tribunal has been constituted. This would require that parties arrive at some agreement in principle before invoking arbitration. Hence, if parties successfully put their settlement in writing, the tribunal may then record the settlement in the form of an arbitral award on agreed terms under section 30 of the Arbitration Act. But if parties fail, arbitration proceedings can seamlessly proceed thereon.

The Indian Institute of Arbitration & Mediation (IIAM) subscribes to a different approach. IIAM's suggested Med-Arb clause stipulates mediation under IIAM Mediation Rules, which in turn state that "while formulating the settlement, [if] the parties request the mediator that they would like to give finality and enforceability for the MSA, the parties agree that the mediation process shall be considered as conciliation, and agree to give the [mediated settlement agreement] the status of a settlement agreement executed as under section 73 of the [Arbitration Act], and thereby having the same status as that of an arbitral award and can be executed and enforced as a decree of a court."[63] Thus, IIAM prefers to redirect the process in a different direction in the event parties successfully arrive at a settlement. But on its failure (as provided in

61. *See* Arbitration & Conciliation Act, 1996, § 61 ("this Part shall apply to conciliation of disputes arising out of legal relationship"). *See generally*, K K Modi v. K N Modi, 1998 AIR SC 1297 ("Therefore our courts have laid emphasis on (1) existence of disputes as against intention to avoid future disputes"); M/s Earth and Air Films Pvt Ltd. v. M. T. Vasudevan Nair (2019) SCC OnLine Ker 4701, ¶ 10 ("Merely because the notice was not responded, it cannot be said that no dispute existed. [...] [dispute or difference existed between them").
62. *See* Official Records of the General Assembly, Fifty-seventh Session, Supplement No. 17 (A/57/17), ¶121 (hereinafter "UNGA A/57/17").
63. IIAM Mediation Rules, Art. 12(d).

the IIAM's suggested Med-Arb clause), such dispute or difference is referred to and determined by arbitration by IIAM in accordance with its Arbitration Rules and in accordance with the Arbitration Act.

[B] Arb-Med

Arb-Med contemplates a neutral shifting his role from an arbitrator to a mediator or conciliator. The arbitrator switches hats after the award is ready for pronouncement but sealed instead of revealing its contents to the parties. The arbitrator, thereafter, acts as a mediator or conciliator in order to try to help the parties attain an amicable settlement of disputes; if mediation or conciliation fails to produce a full resolution, the neutral pronounces the award, carrying his final and binding decision on the merits.

Simply put, much of Arb-Med's pros are the mitigation of Med-Arb's practical, legal, and ethical quandaries (particularly concerning the single neutral changing hats). Nothing under Indian law prohibits parties from agreeing to Arb-Med procedures.

Particularly, Arb-Med avoids the problem of ex parte evidence in Med-Arb. Often Arb-Med is perceived to be futile since a party who believes to have the upper hand in the arbitration would never be amenable (or yield) to a settlement. However, parties may still have considerable intangibles (like commercial relations, future prospects, etc.), which would otherwise not be achieved by way of an arbitral award (even if it were a favorable one). In Arb-Med, rather than pronouncing the decision, the arbitrator applies the knowledge gained during the arbitration to mediate the dispute. This can potentially result in creative solutions, especially since the arbitrator is well aware of the arbitral award's worst-case scenario. The binding award is pronounced only when the mediation fails (and all practical settlement efforts are lost).

[C] Baseball Arbitration

Baseball (or final offer, or pendulum) arbitration is a form of the arbitration process involving reasonable proposals from the parties in delivering a binding arbitral award. In baseball arbitration, the arbitrator's award has to be equal to one or the other of the final offers submitted by the parties.[64] Among the variants, final offer arbitrations are used to resolve salary disputes in major league baseball. It offers a potentially quick, informal, final, and binding resolution to a dispute, stimulating the parties to make more reasonable/perceptible offers and realistic concessions/demands.[65] This way, parties also curb any risk of unfair decisions.

64. *See generally*, Benjamin A. Tulis, *Final Offer "Baseball" Arbitration: Contexts, Mechanics and Applications*, 20 SETON HALL J. SPORTS & ENTER. L. 86 (2010).
65. *See* Michael Carrell & Richard Bales, *Considering Final Offer Arbitration to Resolve Public Sector Impasses in Times of Concession Bargaining*, 28 OHIO ST. J. DISP. RESOL. 1, 31 (2013).

Baseball arbitration also provides a useful option for the construction industry, say for quantification of additional cost and/or time for admitted excusable and compensable delay.

"Bracketed awards" are also similar. It involves setting predetermined upper and lower limits for an award of damages.[66] Accordingly, if the arbitrator renders an award between the limits, it is enforceable in the amount rendered. An award above the agreed range or below the agreed limit is enforceable at the respective limits. Again, parties can avoid the risk of an unfair award.

Again, nothing under Indian law prohibits parties from agreeing to a baseball or bracketed arbitration. This is particularly so since, under section 28(2) of the Arbitration Act, an arbitral tribunal can decide *ex aequo et bono* or as *amiable compositeur* if the parties have expressly authorized it to do so. Further, under section 31(3)(a) of the Act, the arbitral award does not require reasons to be stated if parties agree. Hence, Advocates must give careful consideration when drafting a package baseball arbitration clause.

[D] Arb-Med-Arb

In AMA, the neutral simply resumes his arbitral role (i.e., after having first commenced the process as an arbitrator and changing hats to a mediator or conciliator). However, the first step in AMA (arbitration) is merely a trigger necessitated before referring the dispute mediation for two reasons: (1) it allows the parties to take advantage of the New York Convention, in case parties do reach a settlement and require an enforceable consent award; (2) only Med-Arb (without the first Arb) invokes a jurisprudential hurdle: that there cannot be escalation from mediation to arbitration if the mediation is successful and the dispute ends. For example, *see* IIAM's AMA Procedure under its Arbitration Rules (revised w.e.f. October 1, 2020).

The enforceability of settlement agreements resulting from international commercial conciliation/mediation had been a concern in the past. The concern was germane to mediation cases of cross-border disputes, which had no means of cross-border enforcement (given the then lack of international convention). With AMA, mediating parties had the possibility of a settlement that could be enforced under the New York Convention by converting it into an award on agreed terms.

However, the Singapore Convention in force (i.e., the UN Convention on International Settlement Agreement Resulting from Mediation) has made AMA substantially redundant.[67] Nevertheless, AMA is still an effective process that augments the legal untenability of Med-Arb under Indian law. This is because the arbitration procedures kick in when the dispute is in existence, which is immediately directed to mediation after the invocation of arbitration. From which point, the matter is redirected

---

66. *See* Jay Folberg, Dwight Golann, Thomas J. Stipanowich & Lisa Kloppenberg, Resolving Disputes: Theory, Practice & Law 599 (2d ed., 2010).
67. *See* Gracious Timothy, *The Downside of Arb-Med-Arb Procedures*, Mediate India, https://www.mediate.com/articles/TimothyG2.cfm (critiquing Arb-Med-Arb procedures and emphasizing need for the UN Convention).

to arbitration, either with a settlement to be converted into a consent award or without the settlement to proceed with the arbitration on the merits.

Under Indian law, AMA procedures are perfectly valid, and no prohibition (direct or indirect) exists. For instance, IIAM Arbitration Rules offer parties the choice to opt AMA Procedure. IIAM recommends the following clause for incorporation by parties into their contracts:

> Any dispute, difference or controversy arising out of or in connection with this contract, including any question regarding its existence, operation, termination, validity or breach thereof shall be referred to and finally resolved by arbitration as per the Arbitration Act, and shall be conducted by the Indian Institute of Arbitration & Mediation, in accordance with their Arbitration Rules ("IIAM Arbitration Rules") for the time being in force.
>
> It is further agreed that following the commencement of arbitration, the parties will attempt in good faith to resolve such dispute, difference or controversy through mediation, as per the IIAM Arb-Med-Arb Procedure for the time being in force. Any settlement reached in the course of mediation shall be referred to the arbitral tribunal appointed by IIAM and may be made a consent award on agreed terms.

[E] Multitier/Escalation

Multitier dispute resolution is where parties stipulate one or more (sometimes time-bound) pre-arbitral settlement procedures to be satisfied before commencing the arbitration. Such procedures may include conciliatory or adjudicatory processes, either as the sole step or as successive steps. To a large extent, multitier or escalation dispute resolution procedure is similar Med-Arb, except that it does not contemplate single neutral or swapping of hats.[68] Separate individuals play the mediator and arbitrator roles, hence, mitigating any perceived ethical risks.

Multitier or escalation clauses should be encouraged given that they potentially act as an antidote to the considerable costs, time, and effort involved in a contentious arbitration proceeding. A typical multitier procedure starts with negotiation or consultations, then escalates to facilitated negotiation (mediation or conciliation), and lastly, knocks on the proverbial arbitration door. A typical multitier clause may look like the sample provided below:

> 1. Any dispute, difference, controversy, or claim (together referred as "dispute") arising out of or in connection with this Agreement, the disputing party shall provide a Notice of Dispute to the other party, setting out the details of the dispute. The dispute shall be settled in good faith by negotiations within a period 30 days from the date of receipt of Notice of Dispute.

68. *See*, e.g., Stanislaus Prabakaran & Anr. v. B.N. Saravanan, Madras High Court, O.P.No. 777 of 2014 (June 5, 2015) ("[...] the dispute is referred to the Mediation and Conciliation Centre, Madras High Court for mediation [...]. The mediator will endeavour to resolve the dispute within a maximum period of two (2) months from the first date fixed for him or any extended period granted by this Court. 3. In the eventuality of there being failure of mediation, the dispute will be referred to the Arbitrator. However, the arbitration proceedings will not take place till the finalisation of mediation in terms aforesaid").

2. If negotiations fail, the dispute shall be settled in good faith by conciliation within a period of 60 days, or until such time the parties agree in writing. [Insert Name], [Insert Designation/Position], shall be the conciliator. The party initiating conciliation shall send to the named conciliator and the other party a written invitation to conciliate, and the other party shall accept such invitation. In case the named conciliator is unable to perform his functions, or for other reasons fails to act, the conciliator shall be appointed by [Designation of an Independent Organization or an Individual] within 21 days of such request being made by either party.
3. If conciliation fails, the dispute shall be referred to and determined by arbitration in [New Delhi], the seat of arbitration. The party invoking the arbitration ("Claimant") shall give to the named arbitrator and the other party ("Respondent") a Notice of Arbitration, which shall include:
   (i) a demand that the Dispute be referred to arbitration;
   (ii) the names and addresses of the parties;
   (iii) a reference to this arbitration clause; and
   (iv) a description of the nature and circumstances of the dispute giving rise to the claim(s) and a statement of the relief sought including, so far is possible, an indication of any amount(s) claimed.
3. [Insert Designation/Position], shall be the sole arbitrator. In case the named sole arbitrator is unable to perform his functions, or for other reasons fails to act, the sole arbitrator shall be appointed by [Designation of an Independent Organization or an Individual] within 21 days of such request being made by either party.
4. As soon as practicable after the sole arbitrator enters upon the reference, the sole arbitrator shall convene a meeting with the parties or their representatives to determine the procedure to be followed in the arbitration, including identifying the relevant issues and possible settlements of such issues. The following procedural matters shall in any event be taken as agreed:
   (i) the language of the arbitration shall be English; and
   (ii) the tribunal may in its discretion hold a hearing and make an award in relation to any preliminary issue at the request of either party and shall do so at the joint request of both parties.

[1] Enforceability of Multitier Dispute Resolution Clauses

Whether a multitier clause is considered mandatory or merely permissive (or aspirational) has a significant bearing. The judicial verdict on this question remains as "clear as dishwater." However, based on the decisions of Indian courts,[69] a well-drafted multitier clause is likely to be enforced (perhaps more likely where the pre-arbitral

69. *See*, e.g., M K Shah Engineers v. State of Madhya Pradesh (1992) 2 SCC 594 (the court considered whether an award could be set aside if certain "procedural pre-requisites" were not achieved. The court held that such conditions were "essential" and necessarily had to be observed. However, it was found that the parties had, by conduct, waived this procedural precondition); S K Jain v. State of Haryana & Anr. (2009) 4 SCC 357 (tribunal refused to assume jurisdiction on the basis that the appellant had not complied with certain "mandatory requirements." The petition against the tribunal's decision was dismissed on the basis that the language of the arbitration clause required prior satisfaction of certain conditions); Oriental Insurance Co. v. M/s Narbheram Power & Steel Pvt. (2018) 6 SCC 534 (court held arbitration clauses must be construed "strictly," therefore, requiring completion of the "pre-conditions" to arbitration. The

procedure is adjudicatory, like a Dispute Adjudication Board (DAB)). Under Indian law, the enforceability of multitier dispute resolution clauses is dependent on: (a) language of the clause;[70] (b) conduct of the parties; and (c) waiver if any. Language-wise, if the clause were to stipulate a good faith requirement, a period of time, a written notice, a named-mediator, or a specific process like mediation or conciliation, such a clause is likely to be enforced by the courts.[71]

Postulating the likely enforceability of a multitier clause, the general outcomes of such enforceability may be: (a) a tribunal may not enter a reference for lack of jurisdiction, as a result of premature invocation; (b) a tribunal may suspend the proceedings until parties have exhausted the pre-arbitral procedure(s); (c) a court may refuse to appoint an arbitrator; or (d) a court, when seized of an action which is the subject matter an arbitration agreement, may refer parties to arbitration, subject to compliance with any pre-arbitral procedure(s). In that, propositions (a) and (b) are

arbitration agreement was considered to be "hedged with a conditionality" and the nonfulfillment of the "pre-condition" rendered the dispute "non-arbitrable." However, even though the existence of an arbitration agreement was not disputed, the court found that the arbitration agreement could be "activated" or "kindled" upon the completion of the preconditions, and the same was "sine qua non for triggering the arbitration clause"); United India Insurance Co. Ltd. & Anr. v. Hyundai Engineering and Construction Co. Ltd. & Ors. (2018) 17 SCC 607 (court held arbitration clauses must be construed "strictly," therefore, requiring completion of the "pre-conditions" to arbitration); Demerara Distilleries (P) Ltd. v. Demerara Distilleries Ltd. (2015) 13 SCC 610 (court found that objections relating to the appointment application being "pre-mature" did not merit "any serious consideration." It was held that various correspondence between the parties indicated that any mutual discussions or mediation would be an "empty formality"); M/s ICOMM Tele Ltd. v. Punjab State Water Supply & Sewerage Board & Anr. (2019) 4 SCC 401 (court struck down a precondition requiring a deposit of 10% of the claimed amount as it found this obligation to be "arbitrary," making the process "ineffective" and "expensive"); Municipal Corporation of Greater Bombay v. Atlanta Infrastructure Ltd., 2006 (2) Arb LR 93 Bom (court declined to set aside an award on the ground of violations of pre-arbitral steps as it found that the satisfaction of such procedures was not mandatory under the dispute resolution clause); Ravindra Kumar Verma v. M/s BPTP Ltd. & Anr. (2014) SCC OnLine Del 6602 (court held that prior requirements before referring a dispute to arbitration are "only directory and not mandatory"); Sikand Construction Co. v. State Bank of India, ILR 1979 Delhi 364 (court held that the procedure/precondition has to be only taken as a directory and not a mandatory requirement); Saraswati Construction Co. v. East Delhi Co-Operative Group (1995) DLT 343 (court held that the procedure/precondition has to be only taken as a directory and not a mandatory requirement); Union of India v. M/s Baga Brother & Anr., 2017 SCC OnLine Del 8989, ¶¶ 8–11 (court held that the procedure/precondition has to be only taken as a directory and not a mandatory requirement); Siemens Ltd. v. Jindal India Thermal Power Ltd. (2018) SCC OnLine Del 7158 (court held that the procedure/precondition has to be only taken as a directory and not a mandatory requirement); Sarvesh Security Services Pvt. Ltd. v. Managing Director, DSIIDC (2018) SCC OnLine Del 7996 (court held that the procedure/precondition has to be only taken as a directory and not a mandatory requirement).

70. S Kumar Construction Co. & Anr. v. Municipal Corp. of Greater Bombay (2017) SCC OnLine Bom 130 (court found that the cases which held such procedures to be compulsory were decided on the basis of a differently worded arbitration clause, and thus could be distinguished on facts. Court held that such procedures could be mandatory and go to the jurisdiction of the tribunal depending on the language of the arbitration clause).
71. *See* Sun Security Services v. Babasaheb Bhimrao Ambedkar University (2014) SCC OnLine 16608 (pre-arbitral settlement mechanism cannot be interpreted to be an absolute bar). *See also*, Emirates Trading Agency LLC v. Prime Mineral Exports Pvt Ltd., [2014] EWHC 2104 (Comm), ¶¶ 64, 65–73.

directly applicable to emergency arbitration (EA) since an emergency arbitrator has the authority to determine its jurisdiction.

[2] Interactions with EA

Multitier clauses (as may be in the case of Med-Arb) also have an interesting bearing on the ability of a party to secure interim relief(s) of protection from imminent injuries in an EA. The motif of EA is to provide an avenue to parties seeking an urgent relief of protection that cannot wait for the tribunal's constitution or cognizance of the court. However, a potential conflict arises when a multitier clause assumes mandatory status, making emergency relief dependent on pre-arbitral compliance, rendering an EA redundant.[72] The pursuit of redeeming an EA from such a challenge could be time and energy-consuming, or perhaps even unnecessary given the nature of EA—the justifications follow.

Analogical scenario in court actions

Court actions often contemplate similar situations where interim measures of the protection may be necessary to preserve the parties' rights, such as the preservation of evidence or assets or the granting of an interim injunction.

Section 12-A of the Commercial Courts, Commercial Division and Commercial Appellate Division of High Courts Act, 2015 ("Commercial Courts Act") mandates that parties exhaust the remedy of pre-institution mediation before initiating court proceedings. This mandatory rule comes with the limited exception that parties may institute a suit if it contemplates an urgent interim relief. Interestingly, section 12A does not presuppose only interim relief but "urgent" interim relief. Thus, only if the case is one of urgency, the court may entertain the suit contemplating such relief and make such orders as it considers necessary to preserve the subject matter of the dispute.

Actions under the Commercial Court Act are, of course, not predicated on any agreement, as in the case of arbitration proceedings which require a specific invocation under section 21 of the Arbitration and Conciliation Act 1996 ("1996 Act"). The exhaustion of any pre-arbitral procedure would typically be considered conditional to the initiation of arbitration proceedings or a tribunal's proper jurisdiction (or, at the least, bar admissibility). Thus, the invocation of the arbitration agreement may be rendered premature for that reason.

On the other hand, a party may seek interim measures of protection from courts under section 9 of the Arbitration Act (adopting Article 9 of the UNCITRAL Model Law). That, however, is not dependent on an invocation of the arbitration agreement under section 21 of the Arbitration Act. A court may afford to grant interim reliefs, whether or not the arbitration agreement has been invoked, but it comes with the mandate that the arbitral proceedings shall be commenced within 90 days from the date of such order or within such further time as the court may determine.

72. The authors thank Juhi Gupta for her personal views and academic discussions with the authors, which added much value to the discussion here in this section (on file with the authors).

Nonetheless, it is common ground that there can be situations where the need for interim relief, for example, in the form of a freezing injunction, is so urgent that an Application before the court under section 9 of the Arbitration Act may be inexpedient. Such situations would demand EA under the applicable institutional arbitration rules, which can create complications of sorts discussed here if they coexist with multitier dispute resolution provisions.

Justification 1: Resorting to arbitration when necessary to preserve rights (a Model Law principle)

Taking a cue from court analogies, a similar consideration may apply in the case of EA. If not expressly prohibited, one must necessarily be allowed to take the resort of EA. Thus, where parties have agreed to negotiate, mediate, or conciliate (or adjudicate, say using DAB) and have expressly undertaken not to initiate (during a specified period or until a specified event has occurred) arbitral proceedings, such an undertaking must not be given effect by the tribunal (or the court) when a party seeks to preserve its rights through urgent interim relief.

This position reflects in Article 14 of the UNCITRAL Model Law on Mediation 2018 (following Article 13 of the Model Law on Conciliation 2002). The *travaux préparatoires* suggest a general consensus among the drafters that limiting the parties' right to initiate arbitral proceedings might, in certain situations, discourage parties from entering into agreements to conciliate or mediate.[73] The probable circumstances that may require a party to initiate arbitration would typically include the need for interim measures of protection or to avoid the expiration of a limitation period.[74]

The chances are that provisions like the Model Law may be inadequate to address the conflicting motifs that we are discussing here. Take, for instance, the Arbitration Act contains a similar provision in section 77, which states:

> The parties shall not initiate, during the conciliation proceedings, any arbitral or judicial proceedings in respect of a dispute that is the subject-matter of the conciliation proceedings except that a party may initiate arbitral or judicial proceedings where, in his opinion, such proceedings are necessary for preserving his rights.

Section 77 of the Arbitration Act only applies to conciliations under Part III of the 1996 Act, and it does not apply to negotiation, DABs, or even mediations (since mediation and conciliations are legally distinct under Indian law). Similar chasms and schism may prevail in other jurisdictions (particularly, Model Law jurisdictions), indicating the need for a general rule to develop (legislatively or judicially). Otherwise, if multitier clauses are read mandatorily, disregarding EA's purpose, it may result in serious and grave prejudice to a party.[75]

---

73. *See* UNGA A/57/17, *supra* note 62, ¶ 112.
74. *See id.*, ¶ 117.
75. *See generally*, Ravindra Kumar Verma v. M/s BPTP Ltd & Anr. (2015) 147 DRJ 175, ¶¶ 8–12 (if the arbitration clause is read in a mandatory manner with respect to a prior requirement to be complied with before invoking arbitration, the same can result in serious and grave prejudice to a party).

In principle, any inadmissibility or refusal to enter a reference, arising as a consequence of enforcing a pre-arbitral procedure, must only concern claims on the merit before the tribunal (whether EA or a regular tribunal) and not when it concerns "urgent" interim relief—such practice must be developed and adopted by tribunals, domestic or international. Such a standard is postulated here with the idea that a tribunal (in ad hoc arbitrations, or where EA provisions are absent) may well enter reference (even in the presence of mandatory pre-arbitral procedures) to the extent (or with caution) that it will only determine any "urgent" interim measure of protection, deferring the rest of the substantive arbitral proceedings until such time the pre-arbitral procedures are laterally exhausted. The goal is specific: to protect the subject matter of the dispute through an urgent interim measure, which may be considered a parallel objective along with the pre-arbitral mandatory efforts.

Justification 2: Harmonious interpretation of the conflicting motifs

The provisions for EA in the arbitration rules vis-à-vis the provision for pre-arbitral procedures under the arbitration agreement, though conflicting, may be reconciled by applying the harmonious-reading canon of interpretation, duly described in that "one part is not to be allowed to defeat another, if by any reasonable construction the two can be made to stand together."[76]

Thus, a tribunal (in EA, or otherwise in regular proceedings) would have to read harmoniously to give effect to both provisions and not render either one redundant. This is possible by considering the provision for emergency measures as a carve-out to the pre-arbitral procedures. In other words, neither provision is specific in comparison with the other; i.e., both provisions hold the same level of generality. The apparent conflict does not render the provisions irreconcilable, such that neither provision should be given effect.

Justification 3: Whether EA is "arbitration" at all may also depend on the institutional rules (besides the statutory or judicial recognition)

Typically, an application seeking emergency relief is either filed concurrently with or following the Request for Arbitration. Interestingly, for example, a different approach is adopted by Article 75.7 of Japanese Commercial Arbitration Association (JCAA) Arbitration Rules, whereby the Request may be delayed by 10 days (or more, subject to JCAA's extension under Article 77.7).

Similarly, Article 1(6) of Appendix V of the International Chamber of Commerce Rules allows a delay of 10 days (unless the emergency arbitrator determines that a longer period is necessary). Such temporal consideration of the Request is critical (at least in the Indian perspective, given the legal consequences of section 21 of the Arbitration Act). Theoretically, if the Request is delayed by 10 days from the Application for EA, the EA may not be considered "arbitration," at least, for Indian law since the invocation of the arbitration agreement would not have technically happened with

76. *See* THOMAS M. COOLEY, A TREATISE ON THE CONSTITUTIONAL LIMITATIONS WHICH REST UPON THE LEGISLATIVE POWER OF THE STATES OF THE AMERICAN UNION 58 (1868).

the application for EA. And since this view critically assumes that EA is not "arbitration," an emergency arbitrator may (under such circumstances) conveniently disregard any issues concerning mandatory pre-arbitral procedures.

[F] Parallel Processes

Where facilitated negotiations (mediation or conciliation) occur in parallel to ongoing litigation or arbitration, the situation is commonly called parallel processes. Among its variations (and according to conventional wisdom), what happens in mediation, including the very fact of mediation, is not shared with the judges or arbitrator. For example, the Centre for Mediation and Arbitration of Paris (CMAP), under its "Simultaneous Med-Arb Rules," offers mediation simultaneously with the arbitration. The mediation and arbitration occur independently of one another, and CMAP does not allow the mediator to know the name(s) of the arbitrator(s) and vice versa. The mediator and the arbitrator(s) are forbidden to discuss the matter between themselves should they happen to know one another.

Another variant of parallel processes is the Concurrent Mediation-Arbitration by the International Institute for Conflict Prevention and Resolution (CPR), which allows the parties to agree that they will attempt to settle any dispute that is the subject of arbitration by confidential mediation conducted during the pendency of the arbitration.[77] The mediation is pursuant to the CPR Mediation Procedure and in accordance with the CPR Protocol for Concurrent Mediation-Arbitration. But unlike CMAP, the mediator and the tribunal may confer with each other regarding scheduling to facilitate a timely and efficient mediation. However, the tribunal is not informed about any settlement offers or other statements made during the settlement negotiations or mediation (unless, of course, both parties consent). The parties are required to provide the mediator with the procedural timetable adopted in the arbitration and inform the mediator of any material developments in the arbitration, including further orders and directions by the tribunal that will likely affect the opportunity for a negotiated settlement. Such procedures, allowing a limited exchange of information, uniquely curtail unnecessary duplication of cost and effort in the two parallel processes.

A similar example exists under Article 29.1 of the Delhi International Arbitration Center Arbitration Rules 2018, which provides the following:

> 29.1 Parties to an arbitration agreement may, at any time before the commencement of the arbitration proceedings or while the arbitration proceedings are in progress, opt for mediation, and request the arbitral tribunal to put the arbitration proceedings on hold to enable the parties to resolve their disputes amicably.
>
> 29.2 The parties should convey their request to the Arbitral Tribunal, or if the Arbitral Tribunal is not in session, to the Coordinator.

77. *Concurrent Mediation-Arbitration Clauses and Protocol*, International Institute for Conflict Prevention and Resolution (CPR), https://www.cpradr.org/resource-center/protocols-guidelines/concurrent-mediation-arbitration-clauses-and-protocol.

29.3 The arbitral tribunal shall accept the request of the parties and keep in abeyance the arbitration proceedings, relegating the parties to Med-Arb.

§13.04 MIXED-MODE TASK FORCE

The International Mediation Institute (IMI) constituted a Mixed-Mode Task Force, in collaboration with the College of Commercial Arbitrators and the Straus Institute for Dispute Resolution, Pepperdine University Caruso School of Law (Straus Institute).[78] The Task Force has been examining and seeking to develop model standards and criteria for ways of combining different dispute resolution processes that may involve the interplay between public or private adjudicative systems (e.g., litigation, arbitration, or adjudication) with nonadjudicative methods that involve the use of a neutral (e.g., conciliation, or mediation), whether in parallel, sequentially or as integrated processes.[79] This is becoming increasingly important to understand and have the required clarity (and uniformity, wherever practical).

The Task Force was conceived to work in two phases: phase one includes the investigation of standards and practices relating to mixed-mode scenarios in different countries and regions, which would be explored in detail, compared, and contrasted; phase two includes developing best practices and other informational tools for the guidance of dispute resolution professionals and legal practitioners, courts, legislators and standard-makers. To achieve the goals in the respective phases, the Task Force has been composed of six Working Groups (WG), with a specific theme and an international membership from different legal cultures. The end product of this Task Force will give us an extensive written report providing:[80] working definitions of a wide variety of dispute resolution and conflict management approaches in use around the globe; an in-depth treatment of current approaches to the variety of mixed-mode scenarios, comparing and contrasting approaches developed in different cultures and legal systems; and best practices or guidelines aimed at practitioners, dispute resolution professionals, business users, and others.

The Mixed-Mode Task Force is unique in that it is investigating and analyzing the mixing of modes more systemically (than just commenting on typical mechanisms like Arb-Med, Med-Arb, and so on). Six scenarios (making the six themes for each WG) describe the scope of the Task Force, which is the base on which the Task Force has made much progress. Prof. Thomas Stipanowich and Veronique Fraser have extensively captured the work of the Task Force in their article called "The International Task Force on Mixed Mode Dispute Resolution: Exploring the Interplay Between

78. Both the authors are members of the Task Force.
79. *Mixed Mode Task Force*, International Mediation Institute, https://imimediation.org/about/who-are-imi/mixed-mode-task-force/
80. *Memo on the Task Force and Project*, International Task Force on Mixed Mode Dispute Resolution (Apr. 5, 2016), https://imimediation.org/download/184/mixed-mode-task-force-documents/3806/integrating-mediation-into-arbitration_why-it-works-in-china.pdf.

Mediation, Evaluation, and Arbitration in Commercial Cases,"[81] and so, the following only briefly examines the various WG themes—and their relevance to the Indian mixed-mode framework.

[A] Mediators Using Nonbinding Evaluation as a Means of Encouraging Settlement

One of the most common forms of mixed-mode practice occurs when mediators or conciliators engage in evaluation forms and use nonevaluative techniques and approaches. In the Indian context, this is expressly provided for conciliation under section 73 of the Arbitration Act and PLA. But this is not only statute-based, and parties can agree to the same in their mediation agreement.

Under Indian law, a defining difference ascribed to conciliation is that a conciliator is more proactive than a mediator. The Civil Procedure Alternative Dispute Resolution and Mediation Rules 2003 (ADR Rules)[82] demarcated conciliation as follows:

> Settlement by "conciliation" means the process by which a conciliator who is appointed by parties or by the court, as the case may be, conciliates the dispute between the parties to the suit by the application of the provisions of 1996 Act insofar as they relate to conciliation, and in particular, in exercise of his powers under Sections 67 and 73 of 1996 Act, *by making proposals for a settlement of the dispute and by formulating or reformulating the terms of a possible settlement; and has a greater role than a mediator.*
>
> (emphasis supplied)

However, there is no consistency in what should constitute "evaluative" or "evaluation" and whether the making proposals/options can be considered "evaluative" by nature. Such consistency is necessary since it directly concerns mediator-ethics (knowing where to draw the line or understanding party expectations).

[B] Mediators "Setting the Stage" for Adjudication and Other Dispute Resolution Options

Often, discussions around the role of mediators or conciliators are focused on resolving the substantive issues (those concerning the dispute or the merits of the case).

81. Thomas J. Stipanowich & Véronique Fraser, *The International Task Force on Mixed Mode Dispute Resolution: Exploring the Interplay Between Mediation, Evaluation and Arbitration in Commercial Cases*, 40(3) FORDHAM INT'L L. J. 839 (2017).
82. The ADR Rules were prepared by a Committee headed by a former Judge of Supreme Court and the then Chairman of the Law Commission of India, Justice M. Jagannadha Rao. In Salem Advocate Bar Association, T.N. v. Union of India (Salem II) (2005) 6 SCC 344, the Supreme Court observed that the model rules devised by Committee, with or without modification, may be adopted by the High Courts concerned for giving effect to section 89(2)(d) of Code of Civil Procedure, 1908. Accordingly, the Mediation Rules of all High Court are based on the ADR Rules prepared by the Committee.

However, mediators bring much more to the table with mediation's application to process management—concerning the mediation process and concerning alternative approaches that may be necessary or appropriate steps in the final resolution of disputes. Meaning, mediators can help parties "set the stage" for adjudication of a dispute by working with parties to tailor procedures for arbitration or litigation.

A variety of sub-scenarios are conceivable, for which the WG has provided a draft checklist for process design. This is provided in Appendix 1. For example., where mediation fails (wholly or partly), a mediator may continue to facilitate agreement on appropriate arbitration procedures ("guided choice") or assist parties in the joint-selection of the arbitrator(s).

The WG explains that "guided choice" encourages parties to retain a process facilitator as early as possible (which may even be before any dispute arises). The "guiding mediator" basically mediates procedural issues to protect the confidentiality of the parties' communications, enabling them to explore the most appropriate method for resolving their dispute. A sample clause developed by the WG is provided in Appendix 2. The sample clause provides for a default method of resolving disputes (i.e., mediation followed by arbitration) if the Guiding Mediator's use on process issues is not accepted or implemented. Though this clause is drafted with the inclusion of institutions, it may be adapted for ad hoc mediation and arbitration instead (or developed further as suited).

[C] Neutrals "Changing Hats"

Mediators shifting to the role of arbitrator (Med-Arb), or arbitrators shifting to the role of mediator (Arb-Med), are not a common phenomenon in India. Although uncommon in arbitration practice, we have already seen the possibility of Med-Arb in the PLA and the Facilitation Council under the MSMED Act, and that it is permissible (if parties agree) under section 80 of the Arbitration Act.

Arb-Med and Med-Arb continue to be controversial internationally—with the debate centering on whether it is appropriate for neutrals who assist parties in a settlement-based process to shift roles and become adjudicators, or vice versa. But what must be understood is that cultural traditions and legal backgrounds drive perceptions about these approaches.

[D] Arbitrators "Setting the Stage" for Settlement

An arbitral tribunal is generally understood to have wide authority on procedural matters, which discretion is sourced statutorily from the Arbitration Act. However, in exercising such authority, arbitrators often play a facilitative role by discussing with counsels to formulate an agreement between the parties about the arbitration procedures.

This is often employed in the first meeting (a case management conference) to fix a broad procedural framework of the arbitration. And in the event no agreement can be reached on a particular procedural matter, arbitrators typically resolve the issue by making a determination.

The precise dynamics of arbitrators' management of procedural matters might be differently understood, depending on general practice or legal traditions that fall from the judicial system (given the predominance of retired judges as arbitrators).

Besides procedural aspects within adjudication, there are some important issues and questions surrounding arbitrators' (or judges') roles in helping parties settle the dispute through mediation or conciliation (or, at least, set the stage for settlement). Though this is essentially permissible under section 30 of the Arbitration Act, arbitrators view their role as strictly adjudicatory and regard settlement as a collateral prospect. However, the shift in perception is quite recent, with the increasing cross-pollination of arbitral practice, exchange of ideas, and dual training as both arbitrator and mediator.

Truly, in understanding an arbitrator's role, one often overlooks the impact or influence that various procedural determinations have on substantive matters, such as a determination on the production of documents/information which causes a significant concern to parties about their merits, or a ruling on dispositive motions which dispose of an aspect(s) of the dispute. These may indeed be viewed as settlement drivers, giving a cue (or a clue) to the parties (and arbitrators) to get their feet wet.

There are many other creative ways in which arbitrators can set the stage for settlement, which is only limited by self-perpetuating procedural creativity. For instance, arbitrators may sometimes advance the use of mediation by working with the parties to arrange "mediation windows" in the procedural schedule of the arbitration, or arbitrator may offer their preliminary views (with the consent of the parties) and thereby encourage or provoke settlement on issues in dispute.

Conveniently, the Task Force has laid down specific sub-scenario in an attempt to sum up the possibilities of arbitrator setting the stage for settlement:

- arbitrators setting the stage for settlement of substantive disputes by handling key procedural issue(s) (like production requests and dispositive motions);
- arbitrators setting the stage for settlement of substantive disputes by either mediating or promoting the use of mediation; and
- arbitrators setting the stage for settlement of substantive disputes by issuing preliminary views, etc.

[E] Arbitrators Rendering Decisions Based on a Settlement Agreement

During the arbitration proceedings, if parties settle on all or some disputes, parties may notify the tribunal, requesting for the settlement to be converted into an award on agreed terms (i.e., a consent award). This has a practical advantage since it allows parties to avail direct enforcement of the consent award as if it were a court decree. The Indian context of this scenario has been discussed at length in the earlier segment of this chapter.

[F] Possible Interactions Between Adjudicative and Nonadjudicative Neutrals

When parties are engaged in multiple separate dispute resolution processes (parallel processes) in the course of resolving a particular dispute, and each of these processes has separate neutral(s), this scenario conceives interaction between these neutrals. Beyond a doubt, many permutations and combinations are practicable dependent on several moving parts, such as the sequential order of processes, the role of neutrals, the level of permissible interaction and its mode; confidentiality, and so on.

Two helpful examples (by Edna Sussman, a Task Force member) may be given a thought to understand this scenario more intently. Edna was appointed as an arbitrator in a dispute regarding a law firm's split. Since she strongly felt that the matter could be settled, she suggested that the parties use the erstwhile emergency arbitrator as the mediator since he was now well acquainted with the details of the case (similar to an Arb-Med model). The parties did appoint the EA as the mediator. Edna said that she would have liked to tell the EA/mediator what production of documents would be helpful in the mediation but felt constrained from communicating with the EA/mediator. The case did not settle with the EA/mediator, but Edna ultimately took over the mediation, serving as a mediator with the informed consent of parties which would allow her to serve as the arbitrator if the mediation did not yield a settlement. The matter ultimately settled with Edna, and perhaps it could have made a difference if there were interactions between the EA/mediator and Edna on issues that would have encouraged an earlier settlement.

In another example, Edna handled a case involving billions of dollars of Argentine debt held by hedge funds. The mediator worked "hand-in-glove" (as the mediator described it) with the judge, who issued rulings to assist the mediation process, setting deadlines and consequences if the parties did not resolve. The judge and the mediator were in constant touch and working to provoke a settlement between the parties, and, as it were, all the disputed issues (but one) were settled.

§13.05 CONCLUSION

Mixed-mode dispute resolution, as a phenomenon, has witnessed gradual growth in India (though still nascent, when compared with some advanced jurisdictions like the US). Besides the rampant lack of awareness among ADR users, one key factor is the absence of a large pool of advocates (or neutrals) who play a dual role as an arbitration cum mediation practitioner (or arbitrator cum mediator case of neutrals). Once such duality among advocates and neutrals becomes common, it would be followed by a more regular adoption of mixed-mode by users, policies on best practices, jurisprudence, and more inclusive development of ADR in India.

APPENDIX 1: DRAFT CHECKLIST OF ISSUES FOR PROCESS DESIGN (BY THE MIXED-MODE TASK FORCE)

The following points are suggested as a checklist of issues when seeking to design an ADR process. They are not intended as a comprehensive or compulsory list, but only as an aid to a Guiding Mediator or other process facilitator for discussion with the parties and their advisors (e.g., legal counsel). Please feel free to add any additional concepts/words you think should appear in this checklist, which could be useful for designing an ADR or Mixed-Mode process, or for overcoming any impasses in a negotiation or dispute. Please note that the numbering provided is only a suggestion to assist in grouping topics. It should not be given any particular importance. The checklist is intended primarily for discussion purposes only, when seeking to design an appropriate process early on in a dispute. It is important to verify with the parties and their advisors what their experience and views are regarding different ADR processes, and whether they have any initial preferences.

1. Process History
   - 1.1. Type of dispute (e.g., contractual, tortious, family, commercial, civil, investor-state, etc.).
   - 1.2. Duration of the process to date.
   - 1.3. Past attempts to settle: any prior negotiations? Mediations? Judicial settlement conferences?
   - 1.4. Current stage of litigation/arbitration/dispute?
   - 1.5. Attitudes, concerns and reactions to seeking early dispute resolution or the early intervention of a neutral?
2. Party/Advisor Information
   - 2.1. Who are the key stakeholders and potential participants involved in resolving the dispute?
   - 2.2. What are their likely preferences or points of resistance to early process design?
   - 2.3. Size and structure of the parties (e.g., individuals, SMEs, small family-owned business, privately owned corporation, publicly owned corporation, etc.).
   - 2.4. Size and structure of parties' law firms or advisors (if any).
   - 2.5. The participants' backgrounds (e.g., educational, professional, business, cultural)?
   - 2.6. Who are the key decision-makers in each team (business and legal)?
   - 2.7. Familiarity with different types of ADR processes (e.g., mediation, conciliation or arbitration)?
   - 2.8. Have the disputants and their respective advisors jointly considered all their alternatives fully (e.g., best, worst, and reasonable alternatives, including from cost, time, outcome, risks and consequences perspectives)? Would they like a neutral to help in these assessments early on?
   - 2.9. Language and communication issues?

- 2.10. The need for simplicity?
- 2.11. Views and preferences regarding information exchange and the need for accessing evidence?
- 2.12. Financial means of the parties (e.g., either party claiming insolvency/bankruptcy potential—collection issues)?
- 2.13. Decision-making structures or bodies of the parties.
- 2.14. Presumed interests (e.g., business, reputational, etc.) of the disputants?
- 2.15. Power ratio as between the disputants?
- 2.16. Relational issues: is a continuing relationship of any kind between the parties a possibility?
- 2.17. Emotional issues?
- 2.18. Social issues?
- 2.19. Are there unrelated business needs that either party might meet for the other party?
- 2.20. Dynamics between decision-makers?
- 2.21. Willingness of legal advisors to engage?
- 2.22. Process recommendation of parties and counselors?

3. Financial & Third-Party information
   - 3.1. The value of the dispute.
   - 3.2. Expected or budgeted cost of pending or default proceedings (e.g., litigation or arbitration)?
   - 3.3. Insurance?
   - 3.4. Third-party financing?
   - 3.5. Financial pressures from third parties/stakeholders?
   - 3.6. Tax or regulatory issues (e.g., affecting the dispute or its outcome?).
   - 3.7. Need for forensic expertise?
4. Timing
   - 4.1. Time constraints, deadlines and timing? (Are there concerns this process may be too soon/too late?)
   - 4.2. Should some issues be prioritized and addressed first?
   - 4.3. Duration of intended ADR process(es).
   - 4.4. Desired outcome date.
   - 4.5. Availabilities of key participants.
   - 4.6. Timing logistics (e.g., use of Doodle polls).
5. Venue
   - 5.1. Impact of venue and process on information exchange (e.g., entitlement to discovery)?
   - 5.2. Impact on group dynamics (e.g., neutrality, business setting, hotel, big city, rural, off-site & team-building activities)?
   - 5.3. Geographical constraints?
   - 5.4. Special requirements.
   - 5.5. Confidentiality.
   - 5.6. Configuration of rooms and seating plans.
   - 5.7. Support (food, projectors, flipcharts, accommodation, etc.).

6. Constraints
    6.1. Cost/budget constraints? (How do they relate to the value of the dispute?)
    6.2. Evidentiary constraints?
    6.3. Geographical constraints?
    6.4. Cultural constraints?
    6.5. Religious constraints?
    6.6. Psychological constraints?
    6.7. Insurance constraints?
    6.8. Stakeholder constraints?
7. Social and Emotional factors
    7.1. Propensity of dispute to escalate?
    7.2. Impact of process on cognitive, emotional and/or social factors?
    7.3. Uncertainties and fears associated with a settlement or perceptions of weakness?
    7.4. Group dynamics: one group, many groups, in-group, out-of-group, status issues, etc.?
    7.5. Meals (joint or separate), breaks, and dietary issues?
8. Process design
    8.1. Negotiation style (e.g., positional or interests-based).
    8.2. Range of topics the parties are willing to discuss.
    8.3. Judicial or arbitral framework within which the dispute is occurring (e.g., access to adjudicative neutrals, recognition of nonjudicial/ADR processes)?
    8.4. Who wishes to participate?
    8.5. Need for experts?
    8.6. Number of participants?
    8.7. Language issues?
    8.8. Joint assessments of alternatives (BATNA/WATNA/RATNA assessments)?
    8.9. Need to identify values?
    8.10. Need to identify interests?
    8.11. Need to identify metrics?
    8.12. Need to set a precedent/jurisprudence?
    8.13. Are there any dispositive legal, factual or other issues that should be resolved in a focused manner?
    8.14. Are there likely to be recurring disputes? Is this part of a bigger issue?
    8.15. Need to identify new or more options?
    8.16. Likely impact, timeline and complications of such a process (e.g., its enforceability or consequences)?
    8.17. Need for information exchange before parties/insurers/experts/other key stakeholders can assess positions?
    8.18. How to expedite exchange of needed information as opposed to any usual local "discovery"/"disclosure" requirements? What if these needs are not obvious? Is a special master needed?

8.19. The need for confidentiality/transparency of the process or any outcome, as well as any information exchanged or submitted.

9. Outcome
   9.1. The need for a (written) settlement agreement or terms sheet/heads of agreement?
   9.2. The need for an award/adjudicative decision (whether reasoned or unreasoned)?
   9.3. The need for a precedent.
   9.4. The need for possible future settlement processes (for the settlement or other future issues).
   9.5. Closure and closing rituals.
   9.6. Enforceability of outcome (e.g., in other jurisdictions)?
   9.7. Communication of outcome & confidentiality.
10. Any other factors?
   10.1. Please add your own thoughts to this checklist.

What other variables/concepts/factors may be missing in this list? Please add your own ideas. Should some of the above categories be regrouped? Would it be helpful to have different checklists for the parties and their advisors? Please send all feedback to laura.kaster@gmail.com and jlack@lawtech.ch.

APPENDIX 2: DRAFT "GUIDED CHOICE" CLAUSE FOR A GUIDING MEDIATOR (BY THE MIXED-MODE TASK FORCE)

The primary purpose of this possible clause is to encourage parties to retain a process facilitator as early as possible (which may even be before any dispute arises). It is proposed that the facilitator (referred to here as a "**Guiding Mediator**") should be granted the status of a mediator on procedural issues, to protect the confidentiality of the parties' communications, enabling them to explore with the Guiding Mediator the most appropriate[83] method and/or mixed-mode of dispute resolution for assisting the parties to resolve any dispute. This clause provides for a default method of resolving disputes (mediation followed by arbitration) in case the use of a Guiding Mediator on process issues is not accepted or implemented.

This default method is an optional provision, however, as litigation in the courts of a mutually acceptable jurisdiction may be preferable in some cases. The possibility of eliminating the default mediation and arbitration provisions provided in this clause should be considered in each case. Furthermore, although this clause has been drafted with institutional mediation and arbitration rules in mind, these proceedings could be ad hoc instead. Overall, this model clause should be viewed only as a possible starting point and modified in accordance with whatever is deemed most appropriate in each case. Please send all feedback regarding this clause to laura.kaster@gmail.com and to jlack@lawtech.ch. Possible Appropriate Dispute Resolution (ADR) clause for the appointment of a Guiding Mediator:

CLAUSE No. __: GUIDED DISPUTE RESOLUTION

a) Guided Mediation: Any disagreement or dispute between the parties arising out of or relating to this agreement, including its formation, related documents and any non-contractual claims, shall be resolved as quickly and efficiently as possible by mutual consent using the most appropriate form of dispute resolution available for that disagreement or dispute (e.g., negotiation, mediation, conciliation, litigation or arbitration) or a combination of such processes as agreed to by the parties. The parties [shall/may][84] jointly retain a neutral, independent and impartial mediator to focus initially on process issues (the "**Guiding Mediator**").[85] The Guiding Mediator will help the parties to design an optimal process for achieving an early and mutually-acceptable resolution. The optimal process should be efficient and cost-effective, taking into consideration relationships and commercial interests, as well as other important factors identified by the parties (e.g., enforceability, remedies, deadlines,

83. "Appropriate" in this context includes a broad range of parameters that best address the parties' needs, taking into consideration such factors as cost, time, relationships, confidentiality, impact on stakeholders, enforceability, propensity of the conflict to escalate, reputational issues, etc.
84. Whether the appointment of a Guiding Mediator should be compulsory or optional is something to be discussed in advance. It is recommended that there should be a clear commitment to do so (i.e., using "shall" instead of "may" as otherwise it may be difficult to get consensus on doing so).
85. Rather than use the term "Process Facilitator," which may connote the sense of an additional process or cost, the Working Group recommends referring to this person as a "Guiding Mediator," to clarify that the role of this neutral may not only be to do process design, but that they can also assist in overcoming early impasse or acting as a mediator on substantive issues.

etc.)[86] The Guiding Mediator shall maintain strict confidentiality regarding all aspects of the process, including any private conferences with parties and/or their attorneys. The Guiding Mediator may provide non-binding recommendations on process issues. The parties agree that any information they or their attorneys exchange or provide to the Guiding Mediator and/or other parties or stakeholders as part of this appropriate dispute resolution process will be treated as confidential and immune from discovery or disclosure.[87] The Guiding Mediator shall be granted mediation privilege and professional secrecy status as a mediator to ensure that all information exchanged or provided pursuant to this process shall be legally privileged and immune from disclosure or discovery to the extent possible under applicable laws. Once appointed, the Guiding Mediator may act as a mediator and/or arbitrator in any subsequent proceedings with the prior written consent of all the parties involved in those proceedings.[88] If a Guiding Mediator was not retained within [thirty (30)][89] days from the date of first request for the appointment of a Guiding Mediator by a party, or if no other process or ADR neutral has been agreed to or appointed by that date by mutual consent of all the parties involved in the dispute, the substantive matters in dispute shall be settled by mediation [in accordance with the rules of the [NAME OF INSTITUTION] in effect at that date].[90]

b) Arbitration: If the dispute is not fully resolved by [mediation] within [ninety (90)][91] days from the date a party first requested the appointment of the Guided Mediator or [sixty (60)] days from the appointment of the Guided Mediator as the substantive matters mediator or of another mediator as provided for above (whichever period is longer), any dispute arising out of or relating to this agreement or this dispute resolution clause, including the making, breach, termination or validity thereof, shall be finally resolved by binding [expedited][92] arbitration [by a sole arbitrator], [in accordance with the rules of the [INSERT NAME OF INSTITUTION] in effect at that date],[93] unless all of the parties agree in writing to another process.

86. A list of factors to take into consideration when designing a dispute resolution process is available on IMI's website at https://www.imimediation.org/about-imi/who-are-imi/mixed-mode-task-force/.
87. It may be worth drafting a confidentiality agreement to this effect, including the inability for the Guiding Mediator to be summoned as a witness, especially if the seat of the proceedings does not automatically recognize mediation privilege.
88. It is suggested that an additional waiver be signed by all of the disputants involved if the Guiding Mediator will also have a further role, especially if (s)he will act as an arbitrator. The issue of any influential information heard in caucuses should also be addressed (please consider only relying on such information if it has been disclosed with the disclosing party's consent).
89. It is suggested that clear deadlines be set by which the appointment of a Guiding Mediator should have occurred. This provision, however, is optional. The suggestion of 30 days and 60 days in this section is something for the parties to review and are only suggestions.
90. The choice of the mediation (or other first process) being ad hoc or institutional mediation is also something to be discussed and reviewed on a case-by-case basis.
91. An adequate amount of time should be provided before initiating the second stage (in this case, arbitration).
92. Certain institutions have specific provisions for expedited arbitration, which normally entail a sole arbitrator as well as reduced pleadings/hearings and a faster deadline for the issuing of an award.
93. Once again, the arbitration may be ad hoc or institutional. This is something for the parties to discuss and decide in each case. The parties and their counsel should also check the rules of any institutions used to verify that they have complied with the requirements for the same person acting as mediator and arbitrator, if they have chosen to do so.

c) Seat & Language of any Proceedings: The seat of any proceedings shall be [INSERT CITY NAME AND COUNTRY] although meetings may physically take place elsewhere or by Internet by mutual consent of the parties. The language of any proceedings shall be [INSERT LANGUAGE]. [Nothing in these provisions shall preclude a party from reasonably seeking emergency or injunctive relief before any court or arbitral tribunal of competent jurisdiction of its choice anywhere in the world].[94]

94. This is an optional provision.

CHAPTER 14
Cross-Border Enforcement of International Mediated Settlement Agreements and the Singapore Convention

Gracious Timothy Dunna & Jatan Rodrigues

§14.01 INTRODUCTORY REMARKS

In recent years, the Indian legal community has seen a strong policy focus on mediation for the settlement of disputes. This focus has manifested in several ways, including through legislation requiring parties to try mediation before initiating commercial litigation,[1] compulsory teaching of mediation in Indian law schools,[2] and a committee of professionals working under the aegis of the Supreme Court to promote the practice of mediation in India.[3] In a recent judgment, the Supreme Court even acknowledged this policy focus, referring to it as the "mediation movement" and, consequently, expressing the need for stand alone legislation on mediation to pursue this focus.[4]

But for international commercial mediations to be truly viable, the outcome of mediation—a mediated settlement agreement—must have a supporting framework for its enforcement and, in particular, there should be no barriers for enforceability across State borders. Indeed, one of the principal hindrances to the popular use of mediation for international commercial disputes is the lack of an international legal regime for the

1. *See, e.g.*, Commercial Courts Act, 2015, §12A (Pre-Institution Mediation and Settlement).
2. *See* Rintu Mariam Biju, *Mediation with Conciliation to Be a Compulsory Subject in Law Colleges from Academic Year 2020-2021: BCI*, BAR AND BENCH (Aug. 15, 2020, 2:35 PM), https://www.barandbench.com/news/lawschools/bci-mediation-with-conciliation-compulsory-subject-law-colleges-academic-year-2020-2021.
3. *See* Mediation and Conciliation Project Committee, *Brochure*, https://main.sci.gov.in/pdf/mediation/Brochure%20-%20MCPC.pdf.
4. *See* Krishna Murthi v. New India Assurance Co. Ltd. (2019) SCC OnLine SC 315, ¶29.

enforceability of settlement agreements.[5] Nevertheless, this lack of an international regime has (almost) phased out, and change has dawned with the advent of the (United Nations) UN Convention on International Settlement Agreements Resulting from Mediation (the "Convention").

Given the importance of enforceability of settlement agreements in furthering the overall policy promoting the use of mediation, this chapter focuses on two themes: *one*, the existing framework in India for cross-border enforcement of mediated settlement agreements; and, *two*, the salient features of the Singapore Convention in a bid to make a case for India's expeditious adoption of the Convention. Following the present introduction, the next segment of this chapter appraises the legislative framework on conciliation in India and explores whether it is viable for the cross-border enforcement of settlement agreements arising out of mediations. The third segment examines the indirect mechanisms for enforcement evolved by users of mediation over time. In the end, the chapter sets out the salient features of the Singapore Convention, with a call to action for India to ratify the Convention.

§14.02 GOVERNING FRAMEWORK FOR INTERNATIONAL MEDIATED SETTLEMENT AGREEMENT

This section's focus is to appraise whether there is a viable legislative framework governing cross-border enforcement of mediated settlement agreements arising out of international commercial mediations governed by foreign law (hereinafter "iMSA"). And such "international" mediations are those where (at least) one party is Indian. The inquiry here tests India's law on conciliation under Part III of the Arbitration and Conciliation Act 1996 (ACA), particularly whether it is viable for the cross-border enforcement of iMSAs.

However, a subtle distinction is necessary to be drawn at the outset; that Part III's applicability is to be questioned by understanding two given scenarios.

One, where parties to an international commercial mediation/conciliation specifically designate or refer to Part III of the ACA (be it international commercial conciliation between foreign and Indian parties or between foreign parties). In such cases, if the governing law of the conciliation is chosen by parties to be Part III, the settlement agreement reached through such conciliation would be enforceable in India as an arbitral award on agreed terms (by virtue of section 74 of the ACA). This does not concern this chapter's theme (but is discussed in the Chapter on the Law of Conciliation).

Two, where parties to an international commercial mediation/conciliation do not specifically designate Part III as the governing law and where the mediation/conciliation is governed by a law other than Part III. In such cases, a question arises

5. *See* Edna Sussman, *The Singapore Convention: Promoting the Enforcement and Recognition of International Mediated Settlement Agreements*, 3 ICC Bulletin 42, 44–45 (2018) (the author shares the results of three research surveys where respondents state that they would be more likely to use mediation had there been an effective cross-border enforcement mechanism) (hereinafter "Sussman").

about the cross-border enforceability of such iMSAs: whether there is any existing framework under Indian law that opens a channel for enforcing settlement agreements that result from such international commercial conciliations/mediation. In other words, where an international commercial conciliation/mediation has no specific reference to Part III, the proceedings would be dehors Part III, leaving the settlement's enforceability in the open. This is the crux of this chapter.

Part III of the ACA—among other things—prescribes the enforcement of settlement agreements arising out of conciliation.[6] Section 74 provides that a settlement agreement arising out of a conciliation "shall have the same status and effect as if it is an arbitral award"[7] and thereby creates a legal fiction that equates the legal effects produced by such a conciliated settlement to that of a "consent award."[8]

As such, section 74 has occasionally been invoked by parties to argue the enforceability of settlements arising out of conciliation as an arbitral award. A recent example of this is the case of *Anuradha SA Investments LLC v. Parsvnath Developers Limited*, wherein a settlement agreement was sought to be enforced through section 74 and was granted enforcement.[9] This was a case of international commercial conciliation, given that one party was a Mauritian company and the other was Indian. Further, in this case, the conciliation was governed by Part III of the ACA.[10]

Hence, nothing under Part III of the ACA would extend the fiction under section 74 to an iMSA resulting from mediation or conciliation governed by foreign law; and so, in such cases, Part III should not be read as a viable mechanism for cross-border enforcement. As held by the Delhi High Court in *Ravi Aggarwal v. Anil Jagota*, section 74 is only applicable regarding conciliations commenced under section 62 of the ACA. Thus, there is no question of enforcement of any mediated settlement arising out of private mediation.[11] Section 62 mandates the exchange of a proposal to conciliate and its acceptance, both in writing,[12] hence, implying a specific designation, reference, or application, of Part III of the ACA.

In conclusion, Part III of the ACA was not enacted for this purpose, i.e., enforcement of iMSAs resulting from conciliations and mediations governed by foreign law.

Beyond that, there is also the current divide in Indian law between "mediation" and "conciliation" and whether this divide is contagious to a conciliation/mediation governed by a law other than Part III of the ACA. Section 61 of the ACA simply states

6. The focus of the present chapter is on cross-border enforcement and necessarily only provisions of Part III relevant to this theme are discussed presently. For a fuller understanding of the provisions of Part III, *see* Chapter on the Law of Conciliation.
7. *See* Arbitration and Conciliation Act, 1996, §74.
8. *See* Futuristics Offshore Services and Chemicals Ltd. v. Oil and Natural Gas Corporation Ltd. (2012) SCC OnLine Bom 1432, ¶¶11–12.
9. (2017) SCC OnLine Del 7970. However, it should be noted that the main issue before the court were a maintainability objection as to whether a settlement agreement was required to be stamped or not.
10. *Id.*, ¶12.
11. Ravi Aggarwal v. Anil Jagota (2009) SCC OnLine 1475, ¶8.
12. Arbitration and Conciliation Act, 1996, §62.

that Part III "shall apply to conciliation of disputes arising out of legal relationship."[13] However, the term "conciliation" is nowhere defined within the text of the legislation. Neither has any superior court in India defined the term in the context of the chapter's theme, hence, the controversy. For a detailed discussion, *see* Chapter 1 on Introduction to Mediation and Conciliation in India.

But for this chapter, the authors reasonably assume that this divide is only superfluous in mediation or conciliation proceedings governed by foreign law. This is primarily because mediation as a process may be known by different names and be fundamentally the same.

§14.03 EXISTING APPROACHES FOR ENFORCEMENT OF AN IMSA

As discussed, the legislation on conciliation is not a viable mechanism for the enforcement of iMSAs that result from mediations governed by foreign law. Most jurisdictions also do not fare much better in this area. However, over time, alternative dispute resolution (ADR) users have evolved various indirect legal mechanisms, founded in other branches of law, and fashioned them to enforce such iMSAs. Typically, these include enforcing iMSAs as consent decrees, consent awards, or as contracts simpliciter.[14] These mechanisms—their advantages and inadequacies—are discussed hereunder.

[A] Enforcement as Consent Decrees

This enforcement gateway has two requirements: the first is that an iMSA is recorded as a decree of the court, and the second is its enforcement through the fora of enforcing courts in India.

Settlement agreements may be recorded as a decree of the court in various ways. An example of this is a settlement agreement pursuant to court-annexed mediation; i.e., the court refers litigants in international litigation to mediation and, thereafter, records the terms of parties' settlement as a decree of the court. For more on this issue, *see* Chapter on Court-Annexed Mediation. The principle in foreign jurisdictions is generally the same. The methods themselves would differ from jurisdiction to jurisdiction. However, what is ultimately important for the operation of this indirect mechanism of enforcement is that a settlement agreement is recorded as a decree of the court (a "consent decree") by some legal process.

Once a settlement agreement is recorded as a consent decree by the foreign court, a party may approach the courts in India to seek enforcement of the consent decree as a judgment of the foreign court.[15] Section 44-A of the Code of Civil Procedures 1908 (CPC) encapsulates India's law on the recognition and enforcement of foreign decrees.

13. *Id.*, §61.
14. *See* Clemens Treichl, *The Singapore Convention: Towards a Universal Standard for the Recognition and Enforcement of International Settlement Agreements?*, 11(3) J. INT'L DISP. SETTLE. 409, 413–417 (2020) (hereinafter "Treichl"). *See also*, Sussman, *supra* note 5, at pp. 45–46.
15. *See* CODE CIV. PROC., §2(6) (foreign judgment means the judgment of a foreign court).

Accordingly, a foreign decree may be executed in India if it was made by the "superior Courts of any reciprocating territory"[16] and is conclusive on the matter or dispute for the purposes of section 13 of the CPC.[17] Two limitations, however, make this gateway narrow.

First, section 44A of the CPC is applicable only in case of money decrees. Explanation 2 of section 44A of CPC states that:

> Explanation 2. "Decree" with reference to a superior Court means any decree or judgment of such Court *under which a sum of money is payable*, not being a sum payable in respect of taxes or other charges of a like nature or in respect of a fine or other penalty, but shall in no case include an arbitration award, even if such an award is enforceable as a decree or judgment.
>
> (emphasis supplied)

This is a serious limitation since a settlement agreement often includes obligations that are not money related. Without that, this gateway may prove impractical on most occasions.

Second, and while this is not topical to iMSAs or mediation itself, is the requirement that a foreign decree must originate from a reciprocating territory. This is especially problematic in the context of India as only 12 jurisdictions are recognized as reciprocating territories by India.[18] While it is debatable whether such recognition of reciprocal territories can be discounted on the grounds of comity, the fact of the matter is that many trading jurisdictions are missing from this list, making it unviable as an indirect method for the enforcement of settlement agreements.

Arguably, the above two limitations can be circumvented when considering the possibility of enforcing such consent decrees under common law principles as a matter of enforcing the obligations imposed by a foreign court.[19] Time and again, Indian courts

16. *See id.*, §44A(1).
17. *Id.*, §13 (a foreign judgment shall be conclusive as to any matter thereby directly adjudicated upon between the same parties or between parties under whom they or any of them claim litigating under the same title except where any of the 6 grounds under section 13 apply). *See generally*, Gracious Dunna, *Introducing "Public Policy" to Enforcement of Foreign Judgments: Lessons from the Law of Arbitration*, 15(2) TRANSNAT'L DISP. MGMT. (February 2018) (discussing enforcement of foreign judgments and expansive language of the grounds that create an unfavorable regime for enforcement of foreign judgments in India) (hereinafter "Dunna").
18. *See* C. Muralidhara, Suman Katarki, Princy Ponnan & Vedanayaki Kiran D., *Enforcement of Judgments and Arbitral Awards in India: Overview, Practical Law Country Q&A*, PRACTICAL LAW, https://uk.practicallaw.thomsonreuters.com/9-619-4568?transitionType=Default&contextData=(sc.Default)&firstPage=true&OWSessionId=8f5f5b9e87a94d8e9f941c98c7e74a65&skipAnonymous=true (these include Malaysia; New Zealand and Cooks Island; Burma; The Colony of Aden; United Kingdom; Fiji; Hong Kong; Singapore; Trinidad and Tobago; Papua New Guinea; Bangladesh; Ontario, Canada).
19. *See* Sankaran Govindan v. Lakshmi Bharathi & Ors. (1975) 3 SCC 351, 368. *See also*, Y Narasimha Rao v. Y Venkata Lakshmi (1991) 3 SCC 451, 459 (the courts in India fall back upon precedents which have taken their inspiration from the English rules of private international law). *See generally*, Chormal Balchand v. Kasturchand, AIR 1938 Cal 511, 514; Smt. Satya v. Shri Teja Singh (1975) 1 SCC 120, 124.

have recognized the principle of comity, by which due respect must be given to a decree passed by foreign courts.[20] This is a facet of private international law.

Another way to circumvent the above limitations would be to institute a fresh suit before Indian courts and cite the settlement agreement—that formed the basis of a foreign consent decree—as evidence of liability and/or obligation. This, for example, was the approach before the Bombay High Court in *HSBC Bank, USA v. Silverline Technologies Ltd.*, where a party sought to enforce a New York Southern District Court decree which recorded a settlement agreement between the disputing parties.[21] The court creatively passed a "judgment on admissions" under Order XII, Rule 6 of the CPC, by reasoning that the settlement agreement that formed part of the record was an admission of liability and, thus, the court could enter judgment on that basis alone.[22]

[B] Enforcement as Consent Awards

A more popular gateway mechanism discussed is the cross-border enforcement of iMSAs by way of an arbitral award on agreed terms ("consent award"). A consent award refers to an arbitral award rendered by an arbitral tribunal that records the terms of settlement arrived at by the disputing parties to an arbitration. A consent award is not a determination made by the tribunal, yet most arbitration legislations globally recognize a consent award to produce the same legal effects as an award passed on the merits.[23] As will be seen, this is perhaps a more viable indirect mechanism for cross-border enforcement of iMSAs, though it is not without drawbacks.

There are two paths leading to this gateway of enforcement, coming from two species of international commercial arbitrations (ICAs) recognized by the ACA: one which is seated in India and carried out according to the provisions of Part I of the ACA (but with the requirement that at least one party to the arbitration is foreign);[24] and the other seated outside India, which results in a foreign award enforceable through the UN Convention on the Recognition and Enforcement of Foreign Arbitral Awards (the "New York Convention"). Such an ICA is dealt with under Part II of the ACA.[25]

[1] ICA Seated in India

Under Part I of the ACA, consent awards are made capable of enforcement in India by virtue of section 30(4) of the ACA, which provides that "[a]n arbitral award on agreed

20. *See* Alcon Electronics Pvt Ltd. v. Celem S.A. of FOS 34320 Roujan, France, & Anr (2017) 2 SCC 253, ¶ 19 (court gave effect to an English judgment by applying the principles of comity). *See also*, Dunna, *supra* note 17, pp. 2-3.
21. 2006(3) Mh LJ 107 (hereinafter "HSBC Bank").
22. *See id.*, at ¶¶ 19–20. *See* Code Civ. Proc., Order XII, Rule 6 (a rule of Indian civil procedure which permits civil courts in India to pass judgment on the basis of party admissions—in pleadings or in documents—without the need for an elaborate trial and arguments).
23. Gary Born, *International Commercial Arbitration* 3274–3275 (2021) (hereinafter "Born").
24. Arbitration and Conciliation Act, 1996, §2(1)(f).
25. Although certain provisions of Part I apply to a foreign-seated international commercial arbitration as well. *See* Arbitration and Conciliation Act, 1996, § 2(2).

terms shall have the same status and effect as any other arbitral award on the substance of the dispute." In this context, "agreed terms" may arise out of a negotiation, mediation, conciliation, or any other amicable dispute resolution processes that parties may adopt.[26]

However, merely entering into a settlement during the pendency of arbitration is insufficient for enforcement; it is also essential that the arbitral tribunal records the settlement agreement as an arbitral award. Under section 30(2) of the ACA, this is possible only when the parties request it to the arbitration and it is not objected to by the tribunal. To put it differently, if parties to arbitration settle, then the tribunal must mandatorily discontinue the arbitration and discretionarily record the settlement (as a consent award) on the request of the parties unless the tribunal has any objections to the making of a consent award.[27]

Practically, the requirement of a tribunal's acquiescence, as to the recording of the settlement agreement as a consent award, is perhaps one of the drawbacks of this means of achieving enforceability of iMSAs. Nevertheless, most arbitrators would be slow to refuse the making of a consent award, save for instances of illegality, unconscionability, or the like.

Procedurally, to implement this method of achieving enforceability of iMSAs, specific procedures are often opted by the parties, like Arb-Med, Med-Arb, Arb-Med-Arb, parallel processes, etc. Under any of these special procedures, an iMSA results from a mediation within an overarching arbitration process or procedure. This ensures that the iMSA exploits the enforceability mechanism available to an arbitral award under the ACA. The concept of Arb-Med-Arb, now provided by various institutions, has been the most effective (procedurally) in paying attention to the needs of ADR users. It created the possibility of an enforceable iMSA by converting it into an arbitral award on agreed terms and, thus, filled a gaping hole.

But just as a consent award is capable of enforcement as a conventional arbitral award, it is also subject to annulment under section 34 of the ACA.[28] For a discussion on special procedures, *see* Chapter on Mixed-Mode Dispute Resolution, and for a discussion on setting aside of consent awards, *see* Chapter on Law of Conciliation in India (under the commentary on sections 73 and 74).

[2] ICA Seated Outside India

Part II of the ACA applies to foreign awards arising out of ICA. In this context, a foreign award refers to an arbitral award made in any New York Convention jurisdiction and under the relevant implementing legislation in that jurisdiction.[29] Thus, the provisions

26. Arbitration and Conciliation Act, 1996, §30(1).
27. *Id.*, §30(2).
28. *See*, e.g., Surinder Kumar Beri v. Deepak Beri (2018) SCC OnLine Del 9371, ¶¶ 23–34 (the court set aside a consent award in which the arbitrator added certain directions in the consent award beyond the terms of the parties' settlement agreement).
29. *See* Sasan Power Ltd. v. North American Coal Corporation (India) Pvt Ltd. (2016) 10 SCC 813, ¶ 34 (Geneva Convention awards are also covered under Part II under sections 53–60 of the ACA;

of Part II cover the enforcement—in India—of arbitral awards seated outside India. Sections 44–49 of Part II specifically give effect to the New York Convention in India.

Notably, Part II of the ACA does not have an equivalent provision to section 30(4) under Part I, as discussed earlier. And the applicability of Part I to foreign-seated arbitrations is limited to the granting of court-ordered interim relief under section 9; court assistance in taking evidence under section 27; and appeals to order refusing a reference to arbitration under section 37(1)(a).[30] Nevertheless, an uncontested view is that an arbitral award as referenced in the New York Convention also includes consent awards.[31] Thus, by logical extension, an arbitral award referenced in Part II of the ACA would also include consent awards as Part II gives effect to the New York Convention.

There is a clear corollary between setting aside a consent award (from an ICA seated in India) under section 34 and refusing the enforcement of a foreign consent award (from an ICA seated abroad) under section 48. Foreign consent awards are also subject to refusal of recognition and enforcement under section 48 of the ACA, which grounds are similar to those under section 34.[32] This is, of course, welcome as it ensures some judicial scrutiny over consent awards. And as will be seen in the following segments of this chapter, the grounds for the refusal of enforcement of settlement agreements under the Singapore Convention are somewhat similar to the grounds for the refusal to enforce arbitral awards under Part II of the ACA New York Convention.

Although there has been no notable treatment regarding the enforcement of a foreign consent award by any Indian court to date, the attractiveness of this mechanism is that iMSAs can avail of the impressively successful regime on the cross-border enforcement of foreign arbitral awards created by the New York Convention.[33] However, where the juridical seat is in a jurisdiction that has adopted the Model Law on Arbitration,[34] a likely drawback (as in the case of section 30(2) of the ACA) is the discretion of the foreign arbitral tribunal to record the settlement. Article 30(1) of the Model Law provides that a consent award shall be drawn only when the parties request it to the arbitration, and it is not objected to by the tribunal. Hence, in such cases where the Model Law on Arbitration applies, foreign arbitral tribunals must be willing to make a consent award on agreed terms, though—as discussed above—they too would be slow to refusing it, save for instances of illegality, unconscionability, or the like.

---

however, these are not discussed due to their limited relevance to both the topic at hand and international arbitration practice more generally).

30. Arbitration and Conciliation Act, 1996, § 2(2).
31. *See* Born, *supra* note 23, pp. 3274–3275.
32. On the setting aside of consent awards, it is relevant to *see* Chapter on Law of Conciliation in India (under the commentary on sections 73 and 74).
33. The New York Convention as on Mar. 25, 2021, has 168 state parties thereby making it one of the most successful multilateral treaties in existence. *See Convention on the Recognition and Enforcement of Foreign Arbitral Award*, United Nations Treaty Collection (Status as at: 02-05-2021 09:15:43 EDT), https://treaties.un.org/Pages/ViewDetails.aspx?src=IND&mtdsg_no=XXII-1&chapter=22&clang=_en.
34. UNCITRAL Model Law on International Commercial Arbitration 1985 (amended in 2006) (hereinafter "Model Law on Arbitration").

[C] Enforcement as a Contract Simpliciter

Unlike the preceding gateways, enforcing a settlement agreement as a contract does not rely on the operation of legal fictions that treat an iMSA with the same status and effect a decree or award on agreed terms. Rather, disputing parties simply enter into a contract capturing the terms of settlement arrived at through mediation. And in the event of any breach of the terms, the innocent party can move a court seeking relief for breach of contract. This is the simplest of the indirect enforcement mechanisms.

However, it is also (arguably) the most ineffective. The principle is that contracts are incapable of bringing finality to the dispute.[35] Thus, where a party to iMSA is unwilling to comply with its terms, then the only recourse possible is to sue for breach of contract, which entails a relitigation of the dispute purported to be settled through mediation. Admittedly, such scenarios deter parties from mediating their disputes, inclining their favor toward processes with binding outcomes like arbitration.

Parties can, of course, create several inbuilt redressal mechanisms that both deter a party from a breach of the settlement agreement and compensate the injured party without ever knocking the court's door or invoking an arbitration clause. For example, parties could peg bank guarantees (BGs) along with important obligations, the failure of which by one party would allow the other party to invoke a BG. An injured party may, by similar means, create necessary safety nets in case of a breach. However, this is completely dependent on negotiations and the contract drafting skills of the advocates representing the parties.

Additionally, enforcing iMSAs as contracts can be jurisdictionally limiting since the court where the action for breach is brought may simply lack territorial or subject-matter jurisdiction over that contract—the iMSA.[36] This is likely to deter parties from opting for mediation. It is not uncommon for award holders to seek enforcement in multiple jurisdictions, aside from the award debtor's place of business or where the cause of action occurred (the place with the closest connection). Again, this is completely dependent on negotiations and the contract drafting skills of the advocates representing the parties to ensure that the settlement agreement sufficiently addresses future disputes and jurisdictional issues. Notably, there is a lack of Indian case law specifically engaging with iMSAs under the law of contracts.

In conclusion, the indirect mechanisms evolved over time are not viable for ADR users to truly embrace mediation to resolve international commercial disputes. Perhaps, there can be some optimism in the mechanism of enforcing iMSAs as arbitration awards, but not without the connected drawbacks. Nevertheless, the very emergence of these indirect mechanisms indicates the aspirations of the mediation community to build an international legal regime for the cross-border enforcement of iMSA—an aspiration that has now manifested in the Singapore Convention.

---

35. *See* Treichl, *supra* note 14, pp. 413–414 (the author notes that contracts cannot produce res judicata effects).
36. *See id.*, at p. 414.

§14.04 SINGAPORE CONVENTION ON MEDIATION

The Singapore Convention—as it is popularly known—is a UN multilateral treaty on the recognition and enforcement of iMSAs. Suffice to say, the advent of the Singapore Convention will greatly alleviate the present inadequacies with the existing approaches to cross-border enforcement of settlement agreements and, thus, is appropriately considered a "game-changer" for promoting the use of international mediation.[37] The Convention opened for signature on August 7, 2019, and has had 53 signatories and 6 ratifications.[38]

Much has been written about the process that produced the Convention and the evidence of the need for a cross-border enforcement instrument like the Singapore Convention.[39] Thereupon, the ensuing paragraphs explore certain key provisions and features of the Singapore Convention in-depth and why India should adopt the Convention in its pursuit of promoting the use of mediation for the resolution of international commercial disputes.

[A] Object and Purpose

Preamble

The Parties to this Convention,

Recognizing the value for international trade of mediation as a method for settling commercial disputes in which the parties in dispute request a third person or persons to assist them in their attempt to settle the dispute amicably,

Noting that mediation is increasingly used in international and domestic commercial practice as an alternative to litigation,

Considering that the use of mediation results in significant benefits, such as reducing the instances where a dispute leads to the termination of a commercial relationship, facilitating the administration of international transactions by commercial parties and producing savings in the administration of justice by States,

Convinced that the establishment of a framework for international settlement agreements resulting from mediation that is acceptable to States with different

37. *See* K.C. Vijayan & Cara Wong, *Convention a Game-Changer: Industry Players*, THE STRAITS TIMES (Aug. 7, 2019, 5:00 AM), https://www.straitstimes.com/singapore/convention-a-game-changer-industry-players.

38. *See* United Nations Convention on International Settlement Agreements Resulting from Mediation, UNITED NATIONS TREATY COLLECTION (Status as at: 02-05-2021 09:15:43 EDT), https://treaties.un.org/pages/ViewDetails.aspx?src=TREATY&mtdsg_no=XXII-4&chapter=22&clang=_en.

39. *See* SINGAPORE MEDIATION CONVENTION REFERENCE BOOK 1001–1148 (Nicholas Gliagias ed., 2019).

legal, social and economic systems would contribute to the development of harmonious international economic relations.

The Convention's Preamble and the Working Group process make it clear that the object and purpose of the Convention is "the establishment of a framework" for iMSAs that will, in turn, promote the use of mediation for the resolution of international commercial disputes.[40] A further objective is that the Convention intends to make mediation as mainstream as arbitration for commercial disputes. One can infer this from the Preamble's text that "mediation is increasingly used [...] as an alternative to litigation."[41]

The Convention's emphasis is on the creation of an international legal regime governing cross-border enforcement of iMSAs. The emphasis being on cross-border enforcement, many key aspects of the mediation process—such as commencement of proceedings, the appointment of mediators, and confidentiality—are not covered by the Convention and are instead left to other instruments such as the UNCITRAL Model Law on International Commercial Mediation ("Model Law") and soft law contained in institutional rules, mediator codes, etc.

Similarly, the Convention does not reference or address the enforceability of mediation agreements. As rightly noted by commentators, parties may well agree to a range of matters in their iMSA that go beyond their contractual arrangements and thus may have otherwise been limited to the scope of reference contained in a mediation agreement.[42] This contrasts with the New York Convention[43] but reflects that the decision to participate in mediation is voluntary.

[B] Scope

Article 1. Scope of application

1. This Convention applies to an agreement resulting from mediation and concluded in writing by parties to resolve a commercial dispute ("settlement agreement") which, at the time of its conclusion, is international in that:
   (a) At least two parties to the settlement agreement have their places of business in different States; or

40. *See* Timothy Schnabel, *The Singapore Convention on Mediation: A Framework for the Cross-Border Recognition and Enforcement of Mediated Settlements*, 19 Pepp. Disp. Resol. L.J. 1, 2 (2019) (hereinafter "Schnabel").
41. Nadja M. Alexander & Shouyu Chong, *The Singapore Convention on Mediation: A Commentary* 9 (2019) (hereinafter "Alexander & Chong").
42. *See id.*, at pp. 1, 17; Schnabel, *supra* note 40, at 14 (that usually dispute resolution clauses—particularly references to arbitration—are worded in a manner suggesting that the terms of reference are limited to issues arising under the Contract between parties).
43. *See* New York Convention, 1958, Art. II.

(b) The State in which the parties to the settlement agreement have their places of business is different from either:
   (i) The State in which a substantial part of the obligations under the settlement agreement is performed; or
   (ii) The State with which the subject matter of the settlement agreement is most closely connected.

2. This Convention does not apply to settlement agreements:
   (a) Concluded to resolve a dispute arising from transactions engaged in by one of the parties (a consumer) for personal, family or household purposes;
   (b) Relating to family, inheritance or employment law.
3. This Convention does not apply to:
   (a) Settlement agreements:
      (i) That have been approved by a court or concluded in the course of proceedings before a court; and
      (ii) That are enforceable as a judgment in the State of that court;
   (b) Settlement agreements that have been recorded and are enforceable as an arbitral award.

Article 2. Definitions

1. For the purposes of article 1, paragraph 1:
   (a) If a party has more than one place of business, the relevant place of business is that which has the closest relationship to the dispute resolved by the settlement agreement, having regard to the circumstances known to, or contemplated by, the parties at the time of the conclusion of the settlement agreement;
   (b) If a party does not have a place of business, reference is to be made to the party's habitual residence.
2. A settlement agreement is "in writing" if its content is recorded in any form. The requirement that a settlement agreement be in writing is met by an electronic communication if the information contained therein is accessible so as to be useable for subsequent reference.
3. "Mediation" means a process, irrespective of the expression used or the basis upon which the process is carried out, whereby parties attempt to reach an amicable settlement of their dispute with the assistance of a third person or persons ("the mediator") lacking the authority to impose a solution upon the parties to the dispute.

For iMSAs to avail of the enforcement regime created by the Convention, four essentials must be present:

(i) it must be the outcome of a "mediation";
(ii) it must be in "writing";

(iii) it must be "international" in nature; and
(iv) the underlying dispute it resolves must be "commercial" in nature.

[1] iMSA Must Be the Outcome of a "Mediation"

A "mediation" in the context of the Convention refers to a "process [...] whereby parties attempt to reach an amicable settlement of their dispute with the assistance of a third person or persons ('the mediator') lacking the authority to impose a solution upon the parties to the dispute."[44] This definition makes it apparent that three requirements must be met for a process to qualify as a "mediation" as per the Convention that:

(i) parties pursue an amicable settlement of their dispute;
(ii) they do so with the assistance of a mediator, who is a third person and *ipso facto* not a party to the dispute; and
(iii) the mediator does not have the power to impose a particular outcome on the parties.

A standout element of this definition is that it holds good "irrespective of the expression used or the basis upon which the process is carried out."[45] Indeed, parties—or domestic law—may accord any name to the processes in which they participate; however, if the process is within the definition of "mediation" under Article 2(3), the Convention shall then apply to the iMSA. This is particularly important in the Indian context, given that Part III of the ACA concerns the enforcement of settlement agreements arising out of "conciliation," but its application to mediation is doubtful.

[2] iMSA Must Be "In Writing"

An iMSA must also be "in writing" for the Convention to apply. This writing requirement has also been considered expansively under the Convention. In order to meet this requirement, the settlement must be "recorded in any form."[46] Additionally, this requirement may also be fulfilled "by an electronic communication if the information contained therein is accessible to be useable for subsequent reference."[47] Including electronic communications within the writing requirement will likely further modern mediation practices, such as e-mediation or virtual mediation.

[3] iMSA Must Be "International" in Character

The Convention requires that an iMSA possesses an "international" character. A settlement meets this requirement where "[a]t least two parties to the settlement

44. Singapore Convention 2018, Art. 2(3).
45. *Id.*, Art. 2(3).
46. *Id.*, Art. 2(2).
47. *Id.*, Art. 2(2).

agreement have their places of business in different States" or "[t]he State in which the parties to the settlement agreement have their places of business is different from" the State where "a substantial part of the obligations under the settlement agreement is performed" or where "the subject matter of the settlement agreement is most closely connected."[48] Notably, the Convention prescribes a requirement of internationality based on the location of the party's commercial activities and thus does not envision any concept analogous to a "seat" under the arbitration law.[49]

Further, the Convention also considers the realities of modern-day commerce and clarifies the meaning of the term "international" (qua iMSAs) where parties have more than one place of business or where a party does not have a place of business. In the first situation, the place of business as prescribed under Article 1(1) is "that which has the closest relationship to the dispute resolved by the settlement agreement."[50] Whereas, in the second situation, the place of business is a "party's habitual residence."[51]

[4] The Underlying Dispute Must Be "Commercial" in Nature

The "commercial" requirement relates to the underlying dispute, which is a slight contrast to the preceding essential, which relates to attributes of the iMSA itself. Essentially, the "international" settlement recorded "in writing" and arising out of a "mediation" must have been made to resolve a dispute that is "commercial" in nature. Unlike the preceding elements, "commercial" has not been defined under the Singapore Convention. However, the Convention does expressly exclude certain subject matters from its scope and applicability. These excluded subject matters include consumer disputes, family matters, and employment disputes.[52]

Even though the term "commercial" is undefined in the Convention, an accurate international understanding of the term may be achieved by referencing the definition contained in the 2018 Model Law on International Commercial Mediation and International Settlement Agreements Resulting from Mediation ("Model Law on Mediation"). The footnote to Articles 1(1) states that:

> The term "commercial" should be given a wide interpretation so as to cover matters arising from all relationships of a commercial nature, whether contractual or not. Relationships of a commercial nature include, but are not limited to, the following transactions: any trade transaction for the supply or exchange of goods

48. *Id.*, Art. 1(1)(a) and Art. 1(1)(b).
49. *See* Shouyu Chong & Felix Steffek, *Enforcement of International Settlement Agreements Resulting from Mediation under the Singapore Convention: Private International Law Issues in Perspective*, 31 Sg. Acad. L.J. 448, 456 (2019) (hereinafter "Chong & Steffek").
50. Singapore Convention 2018, Art. 2(1)(a).
51. *Id.*, Art. 2(1)(b). Given the requirement that all disputes are commercial and its connotation that there must be some business transaction, it is difficult to envision an example of scenarios where a party does not have a place of business. *See*, Schnabel, *supra* note 40, at p. 21 ("[This] rule is unlikely to be practically relevant given that the Convention is limited to commercial, non-consumer disputes").
52. Singapore Convention 2018, Art. 1(2).

> or services; distribution agreement; commercial representation or agency; factoring; leasing; construction of works; consulting; engineering; licensing; investment; financing; banking; insurance; exploitation agreement or concession; joint venture and other forms of industrial or business cooperation; and carriage of goods or passengers by air, sea, rail or road.

As is apparent, the Model Law on Mediation accords a very wide definition to the term "conciliation" that includes a variety of commercial scenarios from which disputes could arise. This expansive understanding of "commercial" is likewise consistent with the term's meaning in the arbitration context and the New York Convention.[53]

[5] Exclusions from Scope of Application

The Convention excludes from its scope of application iMSAs based on their enforceability under different legal regimes. Settlement agreements recorded as a decree or judgment of a court and enforceable in the jurisdiction where enforcement is sought excluded from availing the Convention's mechanism.[54]

Notably, the mere recording of a settlement agreement as a decree or judgment of a court (a consent decree) is not enough to exclude an iMSA from the Convention's purview. It is also necessary that such consent decree be capable of recognition and enforcement in the jurisdiction where enforcement is sought. This is particularly useful in the context of India, given the limitations of enforcing iMSAs recorded as a decree of a foreign court, as discussed in the segments above.

Similarly, the Convention also excludes from its scope settlement agreements enforceable as an arbitral award on agreed terms under the New York Convention or another such international instrument/mechanism.[55] The decision to exclude such settlement agreements—while welcome—was not without contest during the Working Group process. Indeed, certain delegations debated the exclusions holding that it would not be problematic if the same settlement agreement could be enforced through multiple regimes, and it was for enforcing fora to resolve conflicts, if any.[56] Nevertheless, the ultimate compromise in excluding settlement agreements recorded as decrees or consent awards is welcome. It avoids conflicts between the enforcement regimes created by the Singapore Convention and the existing indirect mechanisms of enforcement available to parties, as discussed in the segments above. As discussed, the existing indirect mechanisms are far from viable, and it is a wise decision to avoid dilution of the uniform and international regime sought to be created by the Convention.

---

53. *See* Hans Bagner, *Article I, in* Recognition and Enforcement of Foreign Awards: A Global Commentary on the New York Convention 33-35 (Herbert Kronke et al. eds., 2010).
54. Singapore Convention 2018, Art. 1(3)(a).
55. *Id.*, Art. 1(3)(b).
56. *See* Khory McCormick & Sharon S.M. Ong, *Through the Looking Glass: An Insider's Perspective into the Making of the Singapore Convention on Mediation*, 31 SG. ACAD. L.J. 520, 535-537 (2019) (hereinafter "McCormick & Ong").

[C] Enforcement

Article 3. General principles

1. Each Party to the Convention shall enforce a settlement agreement in accordance with its rules of procedure and under the conditions laid down in this Convention.
2. If a dispute arises concerning a matter that a party claims was already resolved by a settlement agreement, a Party to the Convention shall allow the party to invoke the settlement agreement in accordance with its rules of procedure and under the conditions laid down in this Convention, in order to prove that the matter has already been resolved.

A key aspect of the Singapore Convention is how enforcement is effected. The operation of the enforcement mechanism is contained in Article 3 and is best understood by drawing on the "sword" and "shield" metaphor originating from the UNCITRAL Working Group II.[57] Notably, the Convention avoids using the term "recognition" in Article 3 or anywhere else. This contrasts with the New York Convention and emanates from the varying meaning accorded to the term in different jurisdictions—an issue that was in contention during the Working Group process but ultimately resolved by adopting a "functional description" of its enforcement mechanism.[58]

Article 3(1) acts as a "sword" to the extent that it allows a party to approach a competent authority in the jurisdiction where enforcement is sought and avail of the authority's sanctionative powers—typically, attachment of property, freezing of assets, etc.—to ensure compliance with the terms of the iMSA.[59] Further, the Convention leaves it to the discretion of States to device the particulars of the procedural law through which such enforcement may be effected under Article 3(1).

In contrast, Article 3(2) operates as a "shield." Essentially, it bars a party from relitigating a dispute settled by mediation and recorded as a settlement agreement recognized by the Convention.[60] Thus, when an authority in a particular jurisdiction is faced with an action concerning a dispute already resolved by mediation, such authority is required by the Convention to treat the matter as already resolved. The effect of this "shield" is that it has the potential to remedy the problem of relitigating issues settled by mediation.

57. *See* Schnabel, *supra* note 40, at footnote 216.
58. *See* McCormick & Ong, *supra* note 56, at pp. 533–535 (some of the concerns with the use of the term "recognition" were that in some jurisdictions the term is used in relation to State actions and cannot be conferred on private agreements. Similarly, delegations from Civil Law systems raised the issue that enforcing fora in their jurisdictions would be confined to an examination of the settlement agreement alone when faced with an enforcement action and thus would not be able to examine extrinsic evidence in determining grounds for refusal).
59. *See* Alexander & Chong, *supra* note 41, at pp. 70–72.
60. Singapore Convention 2018, Art. 3(2).

Article 4. Requirements for reliance on settlement agreements

1. A party relying on a settlement agreement under this Convention shall supply to the competent authority of the Party to the Convention where relief is sought:
   (a) The settlement agreement signed by the parties;
   (b) Evidence that the settlement agreement resulted from mediation, such as:
      (i) The mediator's signature on the settlement agreement;
      (ii) A document signed by the mediator indicating that the mediation was carried out;
      (iii) An attestation by the institution that administered the mediation; or
      (iv) In the absence of (i), (ii) or (iii), any other evidence acceptable to the competent authority.
2. The requirement that a settlement agreement shall be signed by the parties or, where applicable, the mediator is met in relation to an electronic communication if:
   (a) A method is used to identify the parties or the mediator and to indicate the parties' or mediator's intention in respect of the information contained in the electronic communication; and
   (b) The method used is either:
      (i) As reliable as appropriate for the purpose for which the electronic communication was generated or communicated, in the light of all the circumstances, including any relevant agreement; or
      (ii) Proven in fact to have fulfilled the functions described in subparagraph (a) above, by itself or together with further evidence.

Furthermore, Article 4 of the Convention prescribes certain form requirements that must be observed by a party wishing to enforce an iMSA—as either a "sword" or a "shield"—under the Convention. Thus, a party intending to enforce an iMSA must present to a competent authority in the enforcement jurisdiction a "settlement agreement signed by the parties,"[61] along with "[e]vidence that the settlement agreement resulted from mediation."[62]

The first requirement that an iMSA must be signed is straightforward and recognizes "electronic communication(s)" for the signature requirement.[63] Whereas,

61. *Id.*, Art. 4(1)(a).
62. *Id.*, Art. 4(1)(b).
63. *Id.*, Art. 4(2).

evidence to meet the second requirement (evidence of mediation) may be adduced in four ways:[64]

(i) through the "mediator's signature on the settlement agreement" itself; or
(ii) the mediator's signature on any other document signifying that mediation did occur between disputing parties; or
(iii) a document provided by a mediation institution attesting that mediation occurred between the parties in the case of an institutional mediation; or
(iv) "Any other evidence acceptable" to a competent authority faced with an enforcement action.

The first three forms of evidence are particularly delimited and envision specific circumstances. However, the fourth form of evidence is particularly pro-enforcement and envisions circumstances where the first three forms of evidence are unavailable. It allows a competent authority faced with enforcement action to accept any other evidence in its discretion to give effect to an iMSA and thereby ensure that the object and purpose of the Convention are not defeated for want of strict evidentiary requirements.

[D] Grounds for Refusal of Enforcement

Article 5. Grounds for refusing to grant relief

1. The competent authority of the Party to the Convention where relief is sought under article 4 may refuse to grant relief at the request of the party against whom the relief is sought only if that party furnishes to the competent authority proof that:
   (a) A party to the settlement agreement was under some incapacity;
   (b) The settlement agreement sought to be relied upon:
      (i) Is null and void, inoperative or incapable of being performed under the law to which the parties have validly subjected it or, failing any indication thereon, under the law deemed applicable by the competent authority of the Party to the Convention where relief is sought under article 4;
      (ii) Is not binding, or is not final, according to its terms; or
      (iii) Has been subsequently modified;
   (c) The obligations in the settlement agreement:
      (i) Have been performed; or
      (ii) Are not clear or comprehensible;
   (d) Granting relief would be contrary to the terms of the settlement agreement;

64. *Id.*, Art. 4(1)(b)(i)–(iv).

> (e) There was a serious breach by the mediator of standards applicable to the mediator or the mediation without which breach that party would not have entered into the settlement agreement; or
> (f) There was a failure by the mediator to disclose to the parties circumstances that raise justifiable doubts as to the mediator's impartiality or independence and such failure to disclose had a material impact or undue influence on a party without which failure that party would not have entered into the settlement agreement.
>
> 2. The competent authority of the Party to the Convention where relief is sought under article 4 may also refuse to grant relief if it finds that:
>   (a) Granting relief would be contrary to the public policy of that Party; or
>   (b) The subject matter of the dispute is not capable of settlement by mediation under the law of that Party.

The Convention, in Article 5, prescribes eight grounds by which the Contracting States can refuse to enforce an iMSA to which the Convention applies:[65] however, it may be more insightful to classify and discuss these grounds under four categories:

(i) contractual grounds;
(ii) performance-related grounds relating to the performance of the settlement agreement;
(iii) mediator-conduct grounds; and
(iv) public interest grounds.

The contractual grounds and public interest grounds (by and large) draw parallelly from analogous grounds under the New York Convention, whereas the grounds relating to the performance of the settlement agreement and mediator-conduct grounds are germane to mediation.

It is worth noting here that the obligation to refuse enforcement in certain circumstances is a discretionary one, which is evident from the use of "may refuse to grant relief" and "may also refuse to grant relief" used in sections (1) and (2) of Article 5 (rather than the use of mandatory languages, like "shall"). This reflects the pro-enforcement bearing of the Singapore Convention. However, a word of caution is in order. In a recent judgment, the Supreme Court interpreted identical phrases to have a mandatory connotation—particularly when public interest norms are at stake—despite the use of the word "may" in the context of the refusal of enforcement of an arbitral award under section 48 of the ACA (which is based on Article V of the New York Convention).[66]

65. *Id.*, Art. 5.
66. *See* Vijay Karia & Ors. v. Prysmian Cavi E Sistemi SRL & Ors. (2020) 11 SCC 1, ¶¶ 58–59.

[1] Contractual Grounds

Contractual grounds for refusal envision two scenarios. The first involves situations where "[a] party to [a] settlement agreement [is] under some incapacity,"[67] and the second is where the settlement agreement "[i]s null and void, inoperative or incapable of being performed under the law" applicable to it.[68] Neither of these terms has been defined under the Singapore Convention. However, these terms may be thought of in the contractual sense under the applicable law. This would be the logical conclusion, drawing a parallel from the analogous grounds for refusing enforcement of foreign arbitral awards under the New York Convention.[69]

As such, the term "incapacity" has acquired the connotation of contractual capacity.[70] Under the New York Convention, the foundation of an agreement to arbitrate is contractual. Similarly, the foundation of iMSA between parties is also contractual. Thus, a forum faced with an action to enforce an iMSA may refuse the enforcement where a party to the iMSA lacks contractual capacity.[71] For example, where a party is a minor or lacks soundness of mind. Similarly, the words "null and void," "inoperative," and "incapable of being performed" also point to the contractual validity of the iMSA. Accordingly, iMSAs that are null and void, or inoperative, or incapable of being performed are generally recognized as invalid under the applicable law of contract.

In dealing with the Convention's contractual grounds for refusing the enforcement of iMSA, the following two potential choice-of-law issues emerge.

[i] Determining the Law Applicable to the Formation of iMSA, i.e., to the Capacity of the Parties under Article 5(1)(a)

Issues concerning forming an iMSA—a party's capacity to enter an iMSA—must be understood and determined under the law that governed or applied to the parties to the process by which the parties entered a settlement. This is wholly different from the law applicable to the settlement itself or the law applicable to the parties' agreement to mediate (though, in either case, it is possible that one may be the same as the other, under the given circumstances).

Commentators have suggested the use of Gary Born's validation principle.[72] According to the principle, an arbitration agreement should be considered validly formed if the parties have the capacity to contract under any of the laws applicable to

67. Singapore Convention 2018, Art. 5(1)(a).
68. *Id.*, Art. 5(1)(b)(i).
69. New York Convention 1958, Art. (V)(1)(a).
70. *See* Redfern and Hunter on International Arbitration 81 (2015).
71. *See* Schnabel, *supra* note 40, at p. 44 (that this ground "encompasses various contract law concepts"). For examples of situations under each category, *see* Alexander & Chong, *supra* note 41, at pp. 93–98.
72. *See* Alexander & Chong, *supra* note 41, at pp. 89–90; Chong & Steffek, *supra* note 49, pp. 479–480.

the transaction,[73] the rationale being that parties' contractual arrangements should take precedence over domestic law.[74] Alternatively, commentators also suggest the application of the doctrine of renvoi to determine formation issues.[75] The doctrine of renvoi is applicable in circumstances where a court is faced with a dispute involving a foreign element and applies the conflict-of-law rules of that foreign jurisdiction—whose law is in question—to determine the law applicable to the issue before it—which may well be the law of either State or even a third State.[76]

But both, the validation principle and the doctrine of renvoi, in the authors' view, are extraneous and unsuited in the context of the law applicable to the formation of iMSA.

For example, where parties to an iMSA belong to two different States, application of the validation principle concludes that iMSA should be considered validly formed if either party has the capacity to contract under the law of either State. To further illustrate this example, a party to an iMSA may not have the capacity to contract under its national law, but if they have the capacity under the other party's personal law, then the iMSA should be considered as validly formed. But validation principle has not received judicial acceptance internationally. A Singapore court rejected the validation principle as its application ignores the intention of the parties in favor of ensuring the validity of the arbitration agreement "come what may."[77] At the same time, the court observed that Article V(1)(a) of the New York Convention required that the validity of the arbitration agreement be tested against the applicable law indicated by the parties.[78]

Similarly, much criticism can be leveled against the suitability of renvoi in the present context and generally.[79] For starters, the doctrine of renvoi has been rejected as forming part of Indian conflict-of-law rules.[80] But even if it were to apply, the problem we face is in deciding what should be the starting point of a renvoi analysis to the question of the parties' capacity: should it be the law that governs the agreement to mediate, or the law the governs the mediation or the party's national law? Renvoi is also prone to *circulus inextricabulus* (a loop of remissions from forum to forum); it is dependent on anticipating a forum's approach under its law; it fails to promote uniformity in approach (which is a vision of private international law).

One approach emanates from "Dicey, Morris, and Collins on Conflict of Laws," which is set out in the context of capacity to enter contracts simpliciter.[81] It proposes that the parties' capacity may be governed by either the law applicable to the contract

73. *See* Born, *supra* note 23, at 3817.
74. *See id.*, at 670.
75. *See* Alexander & Chong, *supra* note 41, at pp. 89–90.
76. Dicey, Morris and Collins on the Conflict of Laws 4R-001–4-004 (Lord Collins of Mapesbury & Jonathan Harris eds., 2018) (hereinafter "Dicey, Morris & Collins").
77. BNA v. BNB, [2019] SGHC 142, ¶¶ 52–56.
78. *Id.*, at ¶¶ 65–66.
79. *See*, e.g., David Alexander Hughes, *The Insolubility of "Renvoi" and It Consequences*, 6 J. Priv. Int'l L. 195 (2010).
80. *See* V.C. Govindaraj, *The Conflict of Laws In India: Inter-Territorial and Inter-Personal Conflict* 36–37 (2019).
81. *See* Dicey, Morris & Collins, *supra* note 76, at 32R-168–32-177.

or a party's personal law, which validates the contract's formation. In a way, this leads to a narrower version of Born's validation principle. A problem with this rule (fairly acknowledged by the authors) becomes apparent where the formation of the contract is invalidated under the law applicable to the contract but not under the party's personal law. The rationale, however, for giving effect to contracts in such cases based on a party's personal law alone is that if the party's home State does not deem it necessary to protect a party from entering contracts, then the local law of the place of contracting should not be concerned with the party's capacity either.[82] In the topical context of iMSAs, the problem with this approach is the possible influence of a third law—the law governing the mediation (which is beside the parties' personal law and the law applicable to the mediation agreement).

The authors, thus, posit that the law applicable to the formation of iMSA—i.e., the capacity of the parties—should be the law of the State, whose law governs the mediation. This is the only rationale since we are concerned with the process under/within which parties apply their capacity to enter settlements. Neither the law applicable to the agreement to mediate nor the law applicable to the ultimate settlement can influence the mediation process or the parties' ability to enter settlements in the mediation. One could allege that the authors' approach introduces a place or seat-like concept into international mediation through the back door by using the law governing the mediation as a "proverbial compass," to point to the State whose law should apply to the formation of iMSA, i.e., to the capacity of the parties under Article 5(1)(a). This is exactly what is intended. But this is not a reliance on the place of mediation itself and is intended to avoid the legal pandemonium of other approaches by infusing certainty and uniformity.

Nevertheless, there may also be situations where there is no discernible law governing the mediation, to begin with. Consider, for example, a United States (US) party enters a contract with an Indian party, the performance of which is entirely within the territory of India. A dispute arises, which the parties resolve through mediation resulting in a settlement agreement (an iMSA). But at no point do the parties indicate the law governing the mediation.[83] Under the settlement, the US party has agreed to pay a certain sum to the Indian party. The Indian party initiates enforcement proceedings against the US party and its assets in, say, Singapore. Let us also say that the US party invokes Article 5(1)(a) of the Convention to defend the enforcement action, that it was under some incapacity. To determine the law governing this issue, the authors posit a "three-step progressive principle."

The *first* step involves discovering the law governing the mediation expressly chosen by parties to identify the State whose law would govern the issue of capacity. This is a logical/natural starting point given that the law the parties subject the mediation to would indicate their intention as to what law should govern their capacities to enter into a settlement agreement.

82. *Id.*, at 32-177.

83. As discussed at section §14.02 *supra*, this is a mandatory requirement for Part III of the ACA to apply.

But if there is no express choice of such law governing the mediation, courts must avoid the tendency to import such law from the place of mediation. This is because a place could simply be a venue of convenience for the parties (or the mediator) for the mediation, without any intention to apply the local law to the proceedings. Also, in the case of virtual mediations, a place of mediation would have no meaning.

Hence, the *second* step would be to consider the law governing the mediation agreement as to the law that also governs the mediation; that parties would have intended that the same State's law apply to the mediation as well, further evincing the parties' intention as to the law that should govern their capacities to enter settlements.

Finally, step *three*, if there is no agreement to mediate—as the Convention does not envision such agreements as necessary—then issues of capacity may be tested according to the Dicey, Morris, and Collins rule—i.e., the settlement will be considered to have been validly formed if a party possesses capacity either under their personal law or under the law applicable to the settlement agreement.

[ii] Determining the Law Applicable to the iMSA Itself (Governing Substantive Issues like the Voidness, or Inoperativeness of the iMSA, under Article 5(1)(b)(i))

Similarly, a question arises about ascertaining the law applicable to the iMSA itself for determining whether the settlement is "null and void," "inoperative," or "incapable of being performed." The Convention, in this regard, envisions a two-part choice-of-law rule.[84]

Where parties themselves have indicated a particular law, then an enforcing forum must test the validity of the settlement agreement under Article 5(1)(b)(i) under that law expressly chosen by parties to apply to the settlement itself. But where no such indication exists, it is upon the enforcing forum to determine the law applicable to the settlement agreement.

The text of Article 5(1)(b) does not provide any insight into how an enforcing forum may go about this choice-of-law determination. However, Article 5(1)(b) is founded on the sub current of contractual validity. Thus, it would be appropriate to determine the law applicable to the settlement agreement based on the "closest and most real connection test"—a widely accepted test for determining the proper law of contract absent any indication of party choice.[85] By applying this test, an enforcement forum would principally have to determine the place where the settlement agreement was made and apply the law of those jurisdictions, respectively.[86]

---

84. Singapore Convention 2018, Art. 5(1)(b) ("The settlement agreement sought to be relied upon: (i) Is null and void, inoperative or incapable of being performed under the law to which the parties have validly subjected it or, failing any indication thereon, under the law deemed applicable by the competent authority of the Party to the Convention where relief is sought [...]").
85. *See* CHITTY ON CONTRACTS 30-013 (Hugh Beale ed., 2020) (hereinafter "CHITTY").
86. But depending on the facts, this could also lead to the application of a law other than the place where the settlement agreement was made. For example, the law of the place where the obligations in the settlement agreement are to be performed. *See id.*, ¶ 30-013.

[2] Performance-Related (of the Settlement Agreement) Grounds

There are five grounds for refusal of enforcement which relate to the performance of the settlement agreement.

The *first* ground under this category is that an iMSA may be refused enforcement where it is not "binding [or] final, according to its terms."[87] Indeed, one scenario that may attract refusal under Article (5)(1)(b)(i) is Schnabel's example that the settlement itself contains an express stipulation that it is not final and binding (say a nonbinding memorandum of understanding or a mere agreement to agree).[88] Likewise, this ground may also be attracted where there has only been an exchange of drafts between parties (say, for reworking the wordings of certain terms) but no intention to hold oneself bound by it either principally or otherwise. This is why (for example), Article 12(a) of the Model Law on Mediation provides that mediation proceedings are terminated by the "conclusion of a settlement agreement by the parties," recognizing that such conclusion would only occur when the settlement agreement is considered final by all the parties, in that parties express to be bound by putting their signatures (for instance).

Under the *second* ground of this category, an iMSA may be refused enforcement where the settlement "[h]as been subsequently modified."[89] Just as with the foregoing ground, it preserves the finality of the outcome of a mediation, as captured in the settlement; only the final and ultimate agreement between parties should be enforceable. Thus, where the terms are modified or additional terms are agreed upon by parties, the iMSA may be refused enforcement.

In this regard, the Singapore Convention is unclear about two glaring issues: (i) it does not indicate whether the modified iMSA will have the benefit of the Convention's enforcement regime; (ii) what is the acceptable degree/extent of modification that would not affect the enforceability of the iMSA.

In the strict sense, the Convention's purpose would be lost if the parties modify an iMSA for minor reasons, and the courts refuse to enforce on the ground of modification. There can be modifications that can relate to simple clerical or typographical errors or (slightly controversial) modifications to bring better clarity regarding the settlement, which would otherwise have a different/wrong meaning. In the view of the authors, modifications that correct and/or clarify the terms and do not fly in the face of the overall settlement, or contradict its overall meaning and purpose, should not render the iMSA unenforceable under Article 5(1)(b)(iii) of the Convention. The modified and the original iMSA somewhat merge and should be considered as one and the same.

But suppose the modifications were not so (i.e., corrections, clarifications, etc.), the Convention is clear that the original iMSA would not be enforceable. In that case, a question arises whether the modified iMSA that resulted from negotiations (or another agreement modifying the iMSA) can still be enforced under the Convention. In

87. Singapore Convention 2018, Art. 5(1)(b)(ii).
88. *See* Schnabel, *supra* note 40, at pp. 45-46.
89. Singapore Convention 2018, Art. 5(1)(b)(iii).

other words, can a modified iMSA (with substantially or materially modified terms of the settlement) still have the benefit of the Convention's enforcement regime? The authors doubt it.

Practically, however, enforcing fora should consider adopting a view that gives effect to the purpose of the Singapore Convention, allowing parties to modify their iMSAs through subsequent agreements (whether negotiated or mediated, whether material or minor) and give effect to modified iMSAs. Else, the corollary effect would be that both the original iMSA and the modified iMSA would be left marooned and unenforceable, rendering the parties' efforts in mediation redundant. Consequently, parties would be legally expected to satisfy an empty formality of engaging a mediator to modify an iMSA that they were perfectly capable of addressing on their own at that point. Thus, it would be advisable for enforcing fora not to refuse enforcement of such subsequent settlement agreements solely because the modifications may have been arrived bilaterally between parties and not with the assistance of a mediator.

The *third* in this category of grounds is where the terms of the iMSA have already been performed.[90] This ground envisions scenarios where parties to an iMSA voluntarily perform their part of the settlement agreement and consequently requires that enforcement is refused qua such iMSA that has already been performed. For example, Party A agrees to pay Party B a sum of INR 1,00,000 according to their settlement agreement, and Party A voluntarily does so after the mediation; then, it would not be proper and just for Party B to initiate enforcement proceedings to recover that same ₹1,00,000. Given that party autonomy over the outcome is a salient feature of mediation, it is not unlikely that a considerable amount of iMSAs will be voluntarily complied with. And as such, this ground for refusal ensures that parties cannot enforce iMSAs that have already been performed (eliminating double recovery, for instance). Of course, where only some part of the iMSA has been complied with, then there is nothing in Article 5(1)(c)(i) to suggest that enforcement cannot be sought against unperformed obligations.

The *fourth* ground of refusal is where the terms of the iMSA "[a]re not clear or comprehensible."[91] An enforcing court may refuse the enforcement of settlement where it cannot determine the obligations the settlement imposes on the parties.[92] However, this ground may not be attracted in cases of mere ambiguity or unsatisfactory drafting.[93]

The *fifth* (and final) ground under this category states that enforcement may be refused if enforcement of the iMSA would itself be "contrary to the terms of the settlement."[94] This ground (for example) would be attracted when the settlement provides for force majeure circumstances that excuse the nonperformance by a party,

90. *Id.*, Art. 5(1)(c)(i).
91. *Id.*, Art. 5(1)(c)(ii).
92. *See* Schnabel, *supra* note 40, at p. 48.
93. *Id.*
94. Singapore Convention 2018, Art. 5(1)(d).

thus, rendering the enforcement of any obligation under the settlement terms antithetical to the settlement itself.[95]

[3] Mediator-Conduct-Related Grounds

Both grounds relating to mediator conduct emphasize the importance of the mediator's role in the process. Thus, an iMSA may be refused enforcement where:

(i) there was a serious breach by the mediator of standards applicable to the mediator, or the mediation, without which breach that party would not have entered the settlement;[96] or

(ii) there was a failure by the mediator to disclose to the parties circumstances that raise justifiable doubts as to the mediator's impartiality, or independence and such failure to disclose had a material impact or undue influence on a party without which failure that party would not have entered the settlement.[97]

As can be seen, both these grounds have a dual feature, both of which are necessary for refusal of enforcement. First, it is the requirement of a breach on the part of the mediator of ethical standards, and on the second, it is the requirement that that breach caused parties to enter into a settlement that they otherwise would not have entered.

The inclusion of these grounds was hotly contested during the Working Group process with the debate qua Article 5(1)(e) centering on the reasons that: *one*, a party entering into a settlement agreement without free consent is already a ground for refusal under Article 5(1)(b)(i) which deals with contractual invalidity of the settlement agreement. *Two*, mediation is a voluntary process allowing a party dissatisfied with a mediator's conduct free to walk away at any time.[98] Similarly, the debate against Article 5(1)(f) centers around the issue that it was not customary for mediators to make disclosures in some jurisdictions.[99] Nevertheless, these grounds were retained in the final text of the Convention and serve the purposes of emphasizing the importance of appropriate mediator practices in the mediation process.

It is apparent from the above that the motif is to preserve the sanctity of the mediation process without sacrificing its flexibility, by which mediators may use a repertoire of tools, techniques, and tactics to facilitate a resolution between the parties. This is why a refusal of enforcement is possible only if there is a substantial discrepancy on the part of the mediator that would amount to a breach of any applicable mediator or mediation standard (without which breach that party would not have entered the settlement). In other words, the mere fact of a substantial deviation from any applicable mediator or mediation standard is not in and of itself a ground for

95. *See* Alexander & Chong, *supra* note 41, at p. 108.
96. *See* Singapore Convention 2018, Art. 5(1)(e).
97. *Id.*, Art. 5(1)(f).
98. *See* McCormick & Ong, *supra* note 56, at 540–543.
99. *See id.*, at 543–544.

refusing enforcement, but that there must also be some causation between such deviation and the parties' decision or willingness to enter a settlement. A substantial breach of applicable (ethical) standards, without an adverse consequence to a party to the settlement, cannot on its own be insufficient to attract a refusal of enforcement.

A question, however, arises about the applicable standards. These standards may have a variety of sources, given the circumstances of the case. For example, these standards may come from:[100]

(i) national law (statute and/or judicial law) of the State, whose law governs the mediation proceedings;
(ii) practice directions, rules, or regulations, issues by a superior court of the State to apply mediation proceedings that fall in the purview of the Singapore Convention;
(iii) rules and/or code of conduct applied by a mediation institution/center that administered the mediation, or in whose panel the mediator is a member;
(iv) rules and/or code of conduct applied by the parties by incorporating soft laws or guidelines in the agreement to mediate to govern the mediator and process; or
(v) rules and/or code of conduct applied to the mediator (or the mediation institution) by accrediting body or standards organization (like the International Mediation Institute or the Singapore International Mediation Institute).

Hence, any given scenario can potentially have multiple ethical standards governing the mediator and the mediation process. The other tension that is likely to arise is between the accrediting bodies or standards organizations and the enforcing courts about how such ethical standards are to be interpreted and applied. While the former creates these standards (and perhaps are best placed to comment on their interpretation), the latter has the final word on their interpretation and application.

To truly develop a sound and consistent jurisprudence on this topic, it is hoped that the early precedents are pronounced by courts, with some consultation with the mediation institutions and the accrediting bodies or standards organization. An example falls from *Halliburton Co. v. Chubb Bermuda Insurance Ltd.* of the UK Supreme Court, which clarified the effect of nondisclosure of circumstances of independence and impartiality as to arbitral appointments.[101] The proceedings involved amicus curiae submissions from five leading arbitration institutions—including oral arguments from the International Court of Arbitration of the International Chamber of Commerce and the London Court of International Arbitration—given the nature of the question at stake that concerned international arbitration practice at large.

Nondisclosure of "circumstances that raise justifiable doubts as to the mediator's impartiality or independence" may also invite refusal of enforcement under Article 5(1)(f) of the Convention. Drawing from arbitration law, the terms "independence"

100. *See* Alexander & Chong, *supra* note 41, at 114–124.
101. *See* Halliburton Company v. Chubb Bermuda Insurance Ltd (formerly known as Ace Bermuda Insurance Ltd) (2020) UKSC 48.

and "impartiality" generally refer to scenarios where there is some conflict of interest between the disputing parties and the arbitrator.[102] Thus, the presence of Article 5(1)(f) imposes a duty on the mediator acting in a Convention mediation to disclose if there exist justifiable doubts as to their impartiality or independence. More so, the provision also requires that such nondisclosure has a material impact or undue influence on a party, without which that party would not have entered the settlement. Hence, it is the mediator's nondisclosure of such circumstances, its material impact or undue influence on a party, as well as the causation between such nondisclosure and that party's decision or willingness to enter the settlement, that together attracts a refusal of enforcement under Article 5(1)(f) of the Convention.

Furthermore, given the multiplicity of potentially applicable ethical standards, there would also be no universality and consistency to it; such that would promote the harmonization/uniformity among the States (which is, after all, the core aim of both the instruments from the UN, the Singapore Convention and the Model Law on Mediation).

[4] Public Interest-Related Grounds

Enforcement may also be refused where enforcing an iMSA "would be contrary to the public policy" of the enforcement jurisdiction,[103] or where the underlying dispute—which the settlement agreement resolves—is itself "not capable of settlement by mediation under the law" of the enforcement jurisdiction.[104] A key difference between the grounds under this category, vis-à-vis the preceding three categories, is that an enforcing court may refuse enforcement *suo sponte*.[105] Notably, both the public interest-related grounds must be examined under the law/public policy of the enforcing forum.[106] The Singapore Convention does not tread any new ground under this category when compared with the New York Convention; public policy and arbitrability have long been recognized as grounds for the refusal of enforcement of foreign arbitral awards under the New York Convention. This is the position in India as well, and it is likely that the grounds under Article 5(2) of the Singapore Convention will be

102. *See generally*, International Bar Association, Guidelines on Conflicts of Interest in International Arbitration (2014) (for examples of scenarios "that raise justifiable doubts as to the [...] impartiality or independence" in the context of international arbitration).
103. Singapore Convention 2018, Art. 5(2)(a).
104. *Id.*, Art. 5(2)(b).
105. This difference emerges from the use of the words "The competent authority ... may refuse to grant relief at the request of the party against whom the relief is sought ..." in Art. 5(1) compared with the words "The competent authority ... may also refuse to grant relief *if it finds*" in Art. 5(2).
106. This is plainly evident from the text "[g]ranting relief would be contrary to the *public policy of that Party*" and "[t]he subject matter of the dispute is *not capable of settlement by mediation under the law of that Party*." In context, the phrase "that Party" refers to the enforcement forum of a contracting state.

interpreted similarly to their arbitration counterparts by Indian courts,[107] given the common content of the provisions of the two sister Conventions.

[E] Discretion to Adjourn in the Event of Parallel Enforcement Proceedings

> **Article 6. Parallel applications or claims**
>
> If an application or a claim relating to a settlement agreement has been made to a court, an arbitral tribunal or any other competent authority which may affect the relief being sought under article 4, the competent authority of the Party to the Convention where such relief is sought may, if it considers it proper, adjourn the decision and may also, on the request of a party, order the other party to give suitable security.

The Convention permits enforcing fora to adjourn enforcement proceedings before it, where the same iMSA sought to be enforced is already subject to an enforcement proceeding relating to the Convention in a different jurisdiction—one that is also party to the Convention.[108]

Some commentators view this as an "implied ground" for refusal. The idea is that the fact of refusal of enforcement by an enforcing forum in one jurisdiction creates a ground for refusal for the subsequent fora facing an enforcement proceeding qua the same iMSA.[109] However, the text of the Convention does not read so. The authors view that the Convention's provision in this regard has the effect of allowing the enforcing fora a certain discretion to exercise procedural economy, thus, allowing it to defer to the decision made in prior enforcement proceedings by other enforcing fora. For example, a challenge to set aside an iMSA on the ground of the mediator's misconduct may require findings of fact to be carried out. But in such instances, it may be reasonable under the principles of comity (perhaps procedurally economical) to give deference to a decision of another court that has decided the matter with due process.

107. For the content of "public policy" under Indian arbitration law, *see* Ssangyong Engineering and Construction Ltd. v. National Highway Authority of India (NHAI) (2019) 15 SCC 131, ¶¶ 35–37; Associate Builders v. Delhi Development Authority (2015) 3 SCC 49, ¶¶ 18, 27, 30, 36–38. Similarly, for a test as to which disputes are "arbitrable" under Indian law, *see* Vidya Drolia & Ors. v. Durga Trading Corporation (2020) SCC OnLine 1018, ¶¶ 60–61. While the authors are mindful of the fact that the Supreme Court, in Afcons Infrastructure Limited & Anr. v. Cherian Varkey Construction Co. Pvt. Ltd. (2010) 8 SCC 24, ¶¶ 27–28, proposed a list of disputes capable of being settled by mediation, the list concerned specifically court-annexed mediations and included family disputes and consumer disputes which are specifically excluded from "Convention mediations." Thus, it is more appropriate to approach the issue of disputes capable of settlement of mediation under Indian law by drawing analogies with the content of arbitrability under Indian arbitration law.

108. Singapore Convention 2018, Art. 6.

109. *See* Chong & Steffek, *supra* note 49, at pp. 576–478; *see* Alexander & Chong, *supra* note 41, pp. 150–153.

Nevertheless, this cannot suggest that this is a new ground in and of itself. Rather it only allows for discovering a ground for refusal of enforcement as determined in prior enforcement proceedings. Such deference would be limited only to the grounds under Article 5(1) and not Article 5(2) since that is likely to differ from jurisdiction to jurisdiction.[110]

[F] Reservations

Article 8. Reservations

1. A Party to the Convention may declare that:
   (a) It shall not apply this Convention to settlement agreements to which it is a party, or to which any governmental agencies or any person acting on behalf of a governmental agency is a party, to the extent specified in the declaration;
   (b) It shall apply this Convention only to the extent that the parties to the settlement agreement have agreed to the application of the Convention.
2. No reservations are permitted except those expressly authorized in this article.
3. Reservations may be made by a Party to the Convention at any time. Reservations made at the time of signature shall be subject to confirmation upon ratification, acceptance or approval. Such reservations shall take effect simultaneously with the entry into force of this Convention in respect of the Party to the Convention concerned. Reservations made at the time of ratification, acceptance or approval of this Convention or accession thereto, or at the time of making a declaration under article 13 shall take effect simultaneously with the entry into force of this Convention in respect of the Party to the Convention concerned. Reservations deposited after the entry into force of the Convention for that Party to the Convention shall take effect six months after the date of the deposit.
4. Reservations and their confirmations shall be deposited with the depositary.
5. Any Party to the Convention that makes a reservation under this Convention may withdraw it at any time. Such withdrawals are to be deposited with the depositary, and shall take effect six months after deposit.

110. Commentators putting forth the "implied ground" theory also limit its availability to the grounds in Art. 5(1), however, for apparently different reasons. *See* Chong & Steffek, *supra* note 49, at pp. 477–478; Alexander & Chong, *supra* note 41, pp. 151–152.

Article 8(1) of the Convention allows the Contracting States to make reservations about the applicability of the Convention within their territory.[111] Reservations may only be made on the two grounds provided under Article 8(1).[112] The *first* reservation is that a State may exclude the Convention's applicability toward settlement agreements to which it is a party or its entities and officials.[113]

The phrase "to the extent specified in the declaration" further suggests that this reservation may be applied to varying degrees. Some State agencies or officials may be parties to iMSA, whereas others may not be. The option to exclude the State and its entities appears to be a teleological exercise to encourage States to sign up to the Convention and not be dissuaded on account of the Convention's applicability to iMSAs involving the State.[114] Out of the States that have signed the Convention, three have opted to make a reservation on this ground.[115] This may be of particular concern to proponents of the settlement of investor-State disputes through mediation.

The second reservation is more controversial and allows States to limit the Convention's applicability to only those iMSAs where parties expressly stipulate that the Convention shall apply to their settlement agreement.[116] The inclusion of this reservation was met with considerable controversy.[117] One side of the debate was that mediation is a voluntary process, and thus, choosing for the Convention to apply should also be a voluntary act.[118] Conversely, it was debated that parties to a settlement agreement would enter into it with the intention that it could be enforced.[119] Ultimately, a compromise is evident from Article 8(1)(b), which allows contracting states to exclude the automatic application of the Convention.[120] This reservation is particularly problematic as it can only hinder the development of an effective international regime for the cross-border enforcement of iMSAs. There are at least two problems with reservations on this ground.

One is that parties may simply fail to make the Convention applicable to their settlements out of ignorance, which would frustrate the Convention's purpose for nothing more than a lack of awareness about the Convention.[121] And *two*, this is likely to encourage forum shopping as parties would simply attempt to enforce their settlements in jurisdictions that do not make a reservation on this ground. However, no reservation on this ground has been made by any of the States that have signed the Convention until now, and it would be wise for States not to make this reservation to properly give effect to an international regime of mediation.

111. Singapore Convention 2018, Art. 8(1).
112. *Id.*, Art. 8(2) ("No reservations are permitted except those expressly authorized in this article").
113. *Id.*, Art. 8(1)(a).
114. *See* Schnabel, *supra* note 40, at 55–56.
115. As on May 5, 2021, Belarus, Iran, and Saudi Arabia have made said reservations.
116. Article 8(1)(b).
117. *See* McCormick & Ong, *supra* note 56, at pp. 537–540.
118. *See id.*, at 538.
119. *See id.*, at 538.
120. *See id.*, at 538.
121. *See* Alexander & Chong, *supra* note 41, pp. 164–165 (the authors cite empirical research which suggests that parties are likely to prefer status quo in the State rather than themselves making the decision to opt in or out of a particular mode of dispute resolution).

[G] Additional Provisions of the Convention

[1] Conflicts with Other Laws or Treaties

> **Article 7. Other laws or treaties**
>
> This Convention shall not deprive any interested party of any right it may have to avail itself of a settlement agreement in the manner and to the extent allowed by the law or the treaties of the Party to the Convention where such settlement agreement is sought to be relied upon.

The Convention allows parties to enforce their settlement agreement through any other treaty regimes or laws that may be applicable.[122] Essentially, this provision will ensure the avoidance of norm conflicts between other treaties or laws and the Singapore Convention. This is of no consequence to India since India is not a party to any other similar treaty and does not have any domestic law that runs contrary to the Convention's provisions.

[2] Convention to Apply to iMSAs Concluded after Entry into Force

> **Article 9. Effect on settlement agreements**
>
> The Convention and any reservation or withdrawal thereof shall apply only to settlement agreements concluded after the date when the Convention, reservation or withdrawal thereof enters into force for the Party to the Convention concerned.

The Convention also provides that it shall apply to iMSAs entered into after its entry into force in the enforcing jurisdiction.[123] This suggests that settlement agreements entered into before adopting the Convention by a particular State will not be enforceable in that State.

122. Singapore Convention 2018, Art. 7.
123. *Id.*, Art. 9.

[3] *Depositary and Modes of Adopting the Convention*

Article 10. Depositary

The Secretary-General of the United Nations is hereby designated as the depositary of this Convention.

Article 11. Signature, ratification, acceptance, approval, accession

1. This Convention is open for signature by all States in Singapore, on August 7 2019, and thereafter at United Nations Headquarters in New York.
2. This Convention is subject to ratification, acceptance or approval by the signatories.
3. This Convention is open for accession by all States that are not signatories as from the date it is open for signature.
4. Instruments of ratification, acceptance, approval or accession are to be deposited with the depositary.

The designated depository of the Convention is the UN Secretary-General.[124] States may adopt the Convention by the process of ratification, acceptance, approval, or accession, and such "instruments of ratification, acceptance, approval or accession are to be deposited with the depositary."[125]

[4] *Applicability of the Convention to REIOs and Territorial Units*

Article 12. Participation by regional economic integration organizations

1. A regional economic integration organization that is constituted by sovereign States and has competence over certain matters governed by this Convention may similarly sign, ratify, accept, approve or accede to this Convention. The regional economic integration organization shall in that case have the rights and obligations of a Party to the Convention, to the extent that that organization has competence over matters governed by this Convention. Where the number of Parties to the Convention is relevant in this Convention, the regional economic integration organization shall not count as a Party to the Convention in addition to its member States that are Parties to the Convention.

124. *Id.*, Art. 10.
125. *Id.*, Art. 11(4).

2. The regional economic integration organization shall, at the time of signature, ratification, acceptance, approval or accession, make a declaration to the depositary specifying the matters governed by this Convention in respect of which competence has been transferred to that organization by its member States. The regional economic integration organization shall promptly notify the depositary of any changes to the distribution of competence, including new transfers of competence, specified in the declaration under this paragraph.
3. Any reference to a "Party to the Convention," "Parties to the Convention," a "State" or "States" in this Convention applies equally to a regional economic integration organization where the context so requires.
4. This Convention shall not prevail over conflicting rules of a regional economic integration organization, whether such rules were adopted or entered into force before or after this Convention: (a) if, under article 4, relief is sought in a State that is member of such an organization and all the States relevant under article 1, paragraph 1, are members of such an organization; or (b) as concerns the recognition or enforcement of judgments between member States of such an organization.

The Convention allows for a Regional Economic Integration Organization (REIO) to adopt the Convention if it has the competence to do so.[126] An REIO is essentially a collection of States such as the European Union or ASEAN. If the States comprising an REIO have conferred upon it competence to enter into the Singapore Convention, then the REIO can do so on behalf of its Member States. An interesting aspect about an REIO contracting into the Convention is that the REIO (as a whole) becomes a member, including its Member States.[127] Thus, a consequence that arises is that an iMSA, if granted enforcement (or refused enforcement), would be affected throughout the territory of the REIO and not the individual State in which the enforcement action was brought. In any case, this is of limited interest to India, as India is not a party to any REIOs.

Article 13. Non-unified legal systems

1. If a Party to the Convention has two or more territorial units in which different systems of law are applicable in relation to the matters dealt with in this Convention, it may, at the time of signature, ratification, acceptance, approval or accession, declare that this Convention is to extend to all its territorial units or only to one or more of them, and may amend its declaration by submitting another declaration at any time.

126. *Id.*, Art. 12(1).
127. *Id.*, Art. 12(3).

2. These declarations are to be notified to the depositary and are to state expressly the territorial units to which the Convention extends.
3. If a Party to the Convention has two or more territorial units in which different systems of law are applicable in relation to the matters dealt with in this Convention: (a) Any reference to the law or rule of procedure of a State shall be construed as referring, where appropriate, to the law or rule of procedure in force in the relevant territorial unit; (b) Any reference to the place of business in a State shall be construed as referring, where appropriate, to the place of business in the relevant territorial unit; (c) Any reference to the competent authority of the State shall be construed as referring, where appropriate, to the competent authority in the relevant territorial unit.
4. If a Party to the Convention makes no declaration under paragraph 1 of this article, the Convention is to extend to all territorial units of that State.

Similarly, where a State intending to contract into the Convention comprises more than one territorial unit, the Convention permits States to adopt the Convention selectively over particular territorial units by a declaration to that effect.[128] A prime example of a State with different territorial units is the United Kingdom, with England and Wales, Scotland, and Northern Ireland all having separate legal systems and administration. A State may make a declaration concerning the Convention's applicability to its territorial units at the time of adoption or at any time thereafter by notifying the depository. Here again, this provision is of limited interest to India.

[5] Entry into Force

Article 14. Entry into force

1. This Convention shall enter into force six months after deposit of the third instrument of ratification, acceptance, approval or accession.
2. When a State ratifies, accepts, approves or accedes to this Convention after the deposit of the third instrument of ratification, acceptance, approval or accession, this Convention shall enter into force in respect of that State six months after the date of the deposit of its instrument of ratification, acceptance, approval or accession. The Convention shall enter into force for a territorial unit to which this Convention has been extended in accordance with article 13 six months after the notification of the declaration referred to in that article.

128. *Id.*, Art. 13.

The Convention shall enter into a force for a particular State six months after the deposit of the third instrument of ratification, acceptance, approval, or accession.[129] After this, the Convention becomes legally binding on States that have adopted it, and enforcement of settlement agreements as per its provisions will have to be observed.

[6] Procedure and Effect of Amendments and Denunciations

Article 15. Amendment

1. Any Party to the Convention may propose an amendment to the present Convention by submitting it to the Secretary-General of the United Nations. The Secretary-General shall thereupon communicate the proposed amendment to the Parties to the Convention with a request that they indicate whether they favor a conference of Parties to the Convention for the purpose of considering and voting upon the proposal. In the event that within four months from the date of such communication at least one-third of the Parties to the Convention favor such a conference, the Secretary-General shall convene the conference under the auspices of the United Nations.
2. The conference of Parties to the Convention shall make every effort to achieve consensus on each amendment. If all efforts at consensus are exhausted and no consensus is reached, the amendment shall, as a last resort, require for its adoption a two-thirds majority vote of the Parties to the Convention present and voting at the conference.
3. An adopted amendment shall be submitted by the depositary to all the Parties to the Convention for ratification, acceptance or approval.
4. An adopted amendment shall enter into force six months after the date of deposit of the third instrument of ratification, acceptance or approval. When an amendment enters into force, it shall be binding on those Parties to the Convention that have expressed consent to be bound by it.
5. When a Party to the Convention ratifies, accepts or approves an amendment following the deposit of the third instrument of ratification, acceptance or approval, the amendment shall enter into force in respect of that Party to the Convention six months after the date of the deposit of its instrument of ratification, acceptance or approval.

The Convention may also be amended on the proposal of any of its Contracting States.[130] In this regard, the Convention prescribes a five-step process. *First*, any contracting state may propose an amendment. *Second*, all contracting states vote on whether they favor the conference for deliberating amendment. *Third*, if one-third of

129. *Id.*, Art. 14.
130. *Id.*, Art. 15.

contracting states vote in favor of a conference, the Secretary-General must convene a conference to deliberate potential amendments. *Fourth*, all contracting states attempt to reach a consensus on proposed amendments. And *Fifth*, if no such consensus is reached, amendments will be made based on a two-thirds vote. Following this process, the Convention shall stand amended. However, the amended Convention will not automatically be binding on contracting states. States—to do so—would have to adopt the amended Convention specifically. Equally, the amended Convention would only enter into force six months after three states adopt it.

Article 16. Denunciations

1. A Party to the Convention may denounce this Convention by a formal notification in writing addressed to the depositary. The denunciation may be limited to certain territorial units of a non-unified legal system to which this Convention applies.
2. The denunciation shall take effect 12 months after the notification is received by the depositary. Where a longer period for the denunciation to take effect is specified in the notification, the denunciation shall take effect upon the expiration of such longer period after the notification is received by the depositary. The Convention shall continue to apply to settlement agreements concluded before the denunciation takes effect.

Likewise, the Convention may also be denounced by the Contracting States through a written notice to the depositary.[131] Once the notice is received, a 12-month sunset period applies before the denouncing State ceases to be bound by the Convention's provisions.[132]

[II] Next Steps for India's Adoption of the Singapore Convention

India was one of 46 states that signed the Convention on the day it was opened for signing in Singapore. However, for the Convention to enter into force for India and be applied within its territory, there must be domestic legislation passed by Parliament to that effect.[133] Nevertheless, it is worth noting that an unratified—but signed—treaty also creates an obligation on a State "not to defeat the object and purpose of a treaty prior to its entry into force."[134] This rule is somewhat recognized under Indian constitutional law as well to the extent that Indian courts are required to give effect to

131. *Id.*, Art. 16.
132. *Id.*, Art. 16(2).
133. India Const., Art. 253.
134. This rule of international law is reflected in Art. 18 of the Vienna Convention on the Law of Treaties. While India is not a signatory to the Convention, Art. 18 is accepted as a reflection of general international law. *See* Paul V. McDade, *The Interim Obligation Between Signature and Ratification of a Treaty*, 32 Netherlands Int'l L. Rev. 5, 27–28 (1985).

applicable rules of international law provided there is no conflicting domestic legislation.[135] In this regard, an Indian court would be bound to give effect to iMSAs covered by the Convention's scope as there is no contrary domestic legislation on cross-border enforcement. As seen in the segments above, domestic legislation governing cross-border enforcement of iMSAs is unviable at best and absent at worst, but it is not contrary to the provisions of the Singapore Convention.

The best way for India—or any other State—to adopt the Convention is to directly implement the Model Law on Mediation. One of the significant points of contention within the UNCITRAL Working was what instrument should be prepared by it—whether a multilateral treaty or a model law. Ultimately, a compromise was achieved, resulting in the simultaneous preparation of both a multilateral treaty and the Model Law.[136] As such, the Model Law mirrors the relevant provisions of the Convention. Article 16 of the Model Law, which deals with the scope of applicability to iMSAs, mirrors Articles 1 and 2 of the Convention. Similarly, the operation of the enforcement mechanism and form requirements for an enforcement action are identical in content between Articles 17 and 18 of the Model Law and Articles 3 and 4 of the Convention. Lastly, the grounds of refusal of enforcement in Article 19 of the Model Law mirror the grounds in Article 5 of the Convention.

Thus, it is clear that the Model Law is an instrument intended to further the Convention, and adoption of the Model Law is just what is needed—any more, or any less is likely to frustrate uniformity of the international legal regime for cross-border enforcement of iMSAs sought to be created by the Convention.

§14.05 CONCLUSION

In recapitulation, India does not have any viable legislative mechanism for cross-border enforcement of iMSAs. Neither do the alternative enforcement mechanisms evolved over time offer any viable solutions, albeit apart from enforcing settlements as consent awards (which is not without its flaws).

This great chasm in the effective means for cross-border enforcement of iMSAs is at variance with India's demonstrated policy interest in promoting mediation. However, the advent of the Singapore Convention has a singular significance for India—that India must ratify the Singapore Convention expeditiously, to further its pursuit of promoting mediation.

135. *See* National Legal Services Authority v. Union of India & Ors. (2014) 5 SCC 438, ¶¶ 54–60.
136. *See* McCormick & Ong, *supra* note 56, at 545–546.

CHAPTER 15

Law of Conciliation

Gracious Timothy Dunna & Manisha T. Karia

§15.01 INTRODUCTION

The conciliation process has had recognition under various specific statutes in India to resolve the dispute under such statutes, such as the Industrial Dispute Act 1947.[1] However, it was seemingly unable to gain popularity for lack of any general enactment on conciliation. A conciliation-specific law was enacted under Part III (sections 61–81) of the Arbitration and Conciliation Act 1996 (ACA), which sets out the procedural and substantive law on conciliation.

The term "conciliation" is not defined under the ACA; however, it has been defined by the Supreme Court as a:[2]

> [...] process by which a conciliator who is appointed by parties or by the Court, as the case may be, conciliates the disputes between the parties to the suit by the application of the provisions of the Arbitration and Conciliation Act, 1996 (26 of 1996) ..., and in particular, in exercise of his powers under sections 67 and 73 of that Act, by making proposals for a settlement of the dispute and by formulating or reformulating the terms of a possible settlement; and has a greater role than a mediator.

One may understand various attributes about conciliation through this definition, reflecting many provisions of Part III of the ACA, which are all expounded in the subsequent segments of this chapter. In another case law, the Supreme Court considered that while the ACA did not define conciliation, the functions of a conciliator (in section 67) revealed much about the process generally:[3] that he shall assist parties

1. Now consolidated and amended in and by the Industrial Relations Code 2020.
2. Salem Advocate Bar Association, T.N. (I) v. Union of India (2003) 1 SCC 49 (hereinafter "Salem (I)").
3. United India Insurance Ltd. v. Ajay Sinha & Anr. (2008) 7 SCC 454.

independently and impartially; that he shall be guided by principles of objectivity, fairness, and justice, giving consideration, among other things, to the rights and obligations of the parties, the usages of the trade concerned and the circumstances surrounding the dispute, including any previous business practices between the parties; that he shall take into account "the circumstances of the case, the wishes that the parties may express, including a request for oral statements"; and that he may propose settlement options.

Part III is essentially based on the UN Commission on International Trade Law Conciliation Rules of 1980 ("1980 UNCITRAL Rules"), even though these rules were not meant to be a model law for legislative enactment. The Rules were prepared to offer parties an internationally harmonized set of procedural rules suited for international commercial disputes. Many institutions have also followed the 1980 UNCITRAL Rules as a model for their own rules for institutional conciliation or mediation services.

After ACA was enacted in 1996, UNCITRAL published a Model Law on International Commercial Conciliation in 2002 ("Model Law on Conciliation") intending to contribute to a harmonized legal framework for the fair and efficient settlement disputes arising in international commercial relations. This effort was furthered with the UN Convention on International Settlement Agreements Resulting from Mediation (also known as the "Singapore Convention"). The UNCITRAL Commission adopted amendments to the UNCITRAL Model Law on Conciliation 2002 and re-casted it in the form of UNCITRAL Model Law on International Commercial Mediation and International Settlement Agreements Resulting from Mediation 2018 ("Model Law on Mediation" or "2018 Model Law"). The Model Law on Mediation now defines "mediation" as:[4]

> [...] a process, whether referred to by the expression mediation, conciliation or an expression of similar import, whereby parties request a third person or persons ("the mediator") to assist them in their attempt to reach an amicable settlement of their dispute arising out of or relating to a contractual or other legal relationship. The mediator does not have the authority to impose upon the parties a solution to the dispute.

Accordingly, the 2018 Model Law provides for a wide, all-encompassing definition that inspires uniformity and generates greater predictability and certainty in the use of mediation (especially for international commercial disputes). But also, this Model Law serves a dual purpose: (i) be the basis for enacting legislation on mediation; and (ii) be the basis for implementing the Singapore Convention, thereby assisting States in modernizing their statutory laws on mediation.

Interestingly, UNCITRAL had historically used the term "conciliation" in its previously adopted texts and documents, understanding the terms "conciliation" and "mediation" to be interchangeable. But in amending the Model Law on Conciliation, UNCITRAL embraced the term "mediation" instead, to adapt to the actual and practical use of the terms and the expectation that this change will facilitate the promotion

4. UNCITRAL Model Law on International Commercial Mediation and International Settlement Agreements Resulting from Mediation, Art. 1, para. 3 (hereinafter "Model Law on Mediation").

heighten the visibility of the Model Law. Ultimately, the change in terminology does not have any substantive or conceptual implications.

While India's adoption of the Model Law on Mediation (to amend the existing Part III of ACA and/or implement the Singapore Convention) is awaited, Part III of ACA continues to be the existing law on conciliation addressing the procedural aspects of the process, including the appointment of conciliators, commencement and termination of conciliation, the conduct of the conciliation, communication between the conciliator and other parties, confidentiality and admissibility of evidence in other proceedings as well as post-conciliation issues, such as the conciliator acting as arbitrator and enforceability of settlement agreements. However, reports suggest that various committees have prepared the draft legislations under the aegis of the Law Commission and the Supreme Court to recommend implementing the Model Law on Mediation (and along with it, the Singapore Convention).[5] The most significant reason for adopting the Model Law is to make Indian law as transparent and familiar as possible for foreign parties, lawyers, and mediators, who participate in mediation in other jurisdictions (especially those that have adopted the Model Law).

§15.02 BACKGROUND OF CONCILIATION IN INDIA

In the beginning, the term "conciliation" appeared in the Industrial Disputes Act 1947 (IDA, now the Industrial Relations Code 2020 or "IRC"). Despite using the "conciliation" terminology, the authors differ from the legislature's use of this term to describe the process under the IDA or IRC since a Conciliation Officer is vested with various powers as with a civil court under the Civil Procedure Code 1908. At best, conciliation under the IDA or IRC has a hybrid formulation that reflects both adjudicatory and conciliatory features (a quasi-adjudication or quasi-conciliation process).

A conciliatory model also appears in the Hindu Marriage Act 1955 (section 14(2)) and the Special Marriage Act 1954 (section 29(2)) that when considering leave to present a petition for divorce (before the completion of a year from the date of marriage), the court must have regard to the reasonable probability of reconciliation between the parties. This also echoes in the Preamble of the Family Courts Act 1984 that the Family Courts were established to promote conciliation and secure speedy settlement of disputes relating to marriage and family affairs.

The Real Estate (Regulation and Development) Act 2016 (RERA) also espouses conciliation,[6] giving the RERA Authority powers to make recommendations to the government to facilitate amicable conciliation of disputes between the promoters and allottees through dispute settlement forums set up by the consumer or promoter associations. In light of such recommendations, state governments (like Maharashtra)

5. *See* Ajmer Singh, *Supreme Court Forms Committee to Draft Mediation Law, Will Send to Government*, THE ECONOMIC TIME (Jan. 19, 2020, 11:40 PM), THE ECONOMIC TIME (Jan. 19, 2020, 11:40 PM), https://economictimes.indiatimes.com/news/politics-and-nation/supreme court-forms-committee-to-draft-mediation-law-will-send-to-government/printarticle/73394043.cms.
6. Real Estate (Regulation and Development) Act 2016, §32(2).

can set up a Conciliation Committee so that conciliatory proceedings can take place between promoters and home buyers.

Moreover, the Law Commission of India has time and again reported on conciliation/mediation in India, suggesting expansive ideas of incorporating conciliation as part and parcel of the dispute resolution system in India.[7] The list on the use and adoption of conciliation in India goes on with Lok Adalats, court-annexed mediation, Companies Mediation and Conciliation Rules 2016, and Facilitation Councils for micro and small enterprises, all of which provide conciliatory mechanisms for amicable settlement of the disputes.

To discuss a variety of themes, while this Book has used "mediation" and "conciliation" interchangeably, Part III of the ACA is strictly in respect of conciliation (and not mediation). We consider it necessary to draw this distinction here, given the legal connotations the terms carry and their project's legal ramifications. For instance, in a case before the Delhi High Court, the court refused to enforce a mediated settlement agreement (resulting from a private mediation), which was sought to be enforced/implemented under section 74 of the ACA (read with sections 30 and 36).[8] The court was of the opinion that Part III of the ACA only applied to settlement agreements that resulted from conciliation proceedings under the ACA.

§15.03 UN INSTRUMENTS ON MEDIATION

[A] Singapore Convention

The Singapore Convention was adopted on June 26, 2018, by the UNCITRAL and opened for signatures on August 7, 2019. A total of 53 States have signed the Convention, and 6 have given their explicit consent in the form of an instrument of ratification, acceptance, approval, or accession. The Convention's objective is to make a mediated settlement agreement in any international commercial disputes enforceable. Such a remedy was absent previously for the lack of an international instrument, discouraging parties from opting mediation for international disputes (or leaving parties to use other methods like Arb-Med-Arb to achieve enforceability for a settlement). The following puts the Convention in a nutshell.

Article 1 describes the peripheral limits of the Convention. It lays down the requirements necessary for a settlement agreement to fall within the Convention's scope, and it illustrates the exclusions. It is made applicable to an agreement that is the result of mediation, meaning that it must be the outcome of mediation (not merely a negotiated settlement). This settlement agreement is required to be in writing.

---

7. *See*, e.g., LAW COMMISSION OF INDIA, REPORT NO. 14, VOL-I (1958), https://lawcommissionofindia.nic.in/1-50/Report14Vol1.pdf (Ch. 11 discussing delays in civil proceedings); LAW COMMISSION OF INDIA, REPORT NO. 77 (1978), https://lawcommissionofindia.nic.in/51-100/Report77.pdf (Ch. 8 discussing conciliation).
8. *See* Shri Ravi Aggarwal v. Shri Anil Jagota (2009) SCC OnLine Del 1475.

The Convention requires that disputes be "commercial"[9] in nature and mediated agreements pertaining to "personal, family, or household purposes" or "family, inheritance or employment law." Furthermore, the Convention does not apply to those agreements that are either approved by a court or are enforceable as a judgment/decree or an arbitral award in a court.

The temporal determination of a settlement agreement's "internationality" is considered at the time of the conclusion of that settlement agreement. The Convention sets a simple and intelligible criterion for determining the internationality of a settlement agreement, which is primarily based on the place of business of the parties.

Article 2 is explanatory, spelling out what the Convention means by the "place of business" of a party, the writing requirement, and the process of "mediation."

As per Article 3, State Parties to the Convention have the substantive obligation to enforce a settlement agreement (subject to the exceptions, of course). Nevertheless, how a State Party enforces a settlement agreement (i.e., the rules of procedure) is left to the complete discretion of the party to the Convention. Besides, Article 3 also addresses the situation where a settlement agreement might be raised in defense against a claim. Namely, that by meeting all the conditions laid down in the Convention, a party seeking relief would thereby be able to prove that the dispute had been settled. In other words, a party would be entitled to rely on the settlement agreement for seeking a preclusion or bar on the initiation of any new proceeding on the same cause of action.

Article 4 of the Convention is intended to encompass the right of a party to both seek enforcement and invoke a settlement agreement. However, to rely on the settlement agreement, the party seeking to rely on the settlement agreement must satisfy the Convention's requirements provided in Article 4.

In addition to providing that a settlement agreement is to be "signed" by the parties, the Convention requires that parties provide evidence that the settlement agreement resulted from mediation. Such evidence may include a mediator's signature on the settlement agreement or a separate declaration by the mediator or a mediation institution/center, which would attest to the mediator's involvement in the mediation process. In that context, the mediator's signature or attestation would simply be to prove its involvement in the process and should not be construed as an endorsement of the settlement agreement nor an indication that the mediator was a party to the settlement agreement. Lastly, in the absence of any of the suggested evidence, any other evidence acceptable to the competent authority may be produced as well.

Article 5 of the Convention enumerates the grounds based on which enforcement by a particular State may be refused by a competent authority of the enforcing States. The grounds for refusal have been classified into substantive grounds, grounds relating

9. The Convention does not go further to define what is "commercial," but the Model Law on Mediation proposes that the term "commercial" should be given a broad interpretation to cover matters arising from all commercial relationships, whether contractual or not. This is likely to include investor-State disputes as well, although the Delhi High Court has held that "commercial" would not include investor-State relationship since such relationship is rooted in public international law. *See* Union of India v. Vodafone Group Plc, 2018 SCC OnLine Del 8842; Union of India v. Khaitan Holdings (Mauritius) Ltd., 2019 SCC OnLine Del 6755.

to the terms of the settlement agreement, grounds relating to the mediator's conduct and process, and *suo moto*/sua sponte grounds.

Under Article 6, the Convention grants discretion to the competent authority (court) to adjourn the decision and/or order security in situations where the decision of another court or arbitral tribunal may affect the relief being sought before it. The provision applies to both when enforcement of a settlement agreement is sought and when a settlement agreement is invoked as a defense.

Article 7 of the Convention merely encapsulates a party's entitlement to avail itself of other laws or treaties to which the Contracting State may be a party.

Article 8 of the Convention provides State Parties with the option to make the following reservations: (i) application of the Convention to settlement agreements to which the government or any government entity is a party; and (ii) autonomy of the parties as to the application of the Convention to their settlement agreement (i.e., providing opt-in and opt-out for private parties). Generally, the rest of the provisions on reservations in Article 8 deal with the applicable reservation's temporal determinations, confirmation, and deposition with the depositary and withdrawals.

Article 9 of the Convention designates the Secretary-General of the UN as the depositary of the Convention. This is followed by Article 10 on signature, ratification, acceptance, approval, and accession. The participation by any Regional Economic Integration Organization (REIO) is dealt with under Article 11. In this regard, the Convention facilitates REIO and Member States in becoming a party to the Convention. Under Article 11(4), relief would be sought before not only a competent authority of a State that is a member of REIO but also all members of the REIO, depending on the recognition or enforcement of judgments as between Member States of the REIO. Thus, an important aspect of Article 11(4) is that when a party invoking a settlement agreement in a court of a Member State of REIO is not granted relief under the Convention, such a judgment by the court will circulate within the REIO, and that party would no longer be able to rely on the settlement agreement in a court of another Member State of the REIO. Thus, in practice, a party would be able to seek relief in only one Member State of the REIO.

Article 12 of the Convention permits Parties to the Convention to declare that the Convention would extend to all its territorial limits or only to one or more of them. State Parties may make such declaration at the time of signature, ratification, acceptance, approval, or accession. Moreover, Parties to the Convention shall be free to amend its declaration by submitting another declaration at any time. This is a well-established and standard provision that features private international law instruments.

Article 13 states that the Convention shall enter into force six months after the date of deposit of the third instrument of ratification, acceptance, approval, or accession. As of September 12, 2020, India is yet to ratify the Singapore Convention in accordance with Article 253 of the Constitution of India[10] by passing an enactment ratifying the Convention.

10. India Const., Art. 253.

[B] Model Law on Mediation

The Model Law on Mediation can be used as a basis for enacting legislation on mediation, including implementing the Singapore Convention. Through the Model Law, one can expect the adoption of a uniform set of procedural (and substantive) rules, in addition to the enforcement of mediated settlement agreements. The 2018 Model Law has three Sections.

Section 1 of the Model Law (containing general provisions from Articles 1 to 2) applies to the entire Model Law, providing the scope of the entire instrument, a definition to the term "mediation," and setting the general principles that must govern the application of the Model Law instrument. Under section 1, States wishing to enact the Model Law to apply to domestic and international mediation may also do so by deleting certain provisions from the instrument. And this can be done without violating any of the obligations under the Singapore Convention. Thus, the Model Law provides enough flexibility to States which wish to have a much broader instrument.

Section 2 of the Model Law on Mediation (containing Articles 3–15) addresses all aspects relating to international commercial mediation. Section 2 of the 2018 Model Law is almost entirely picked out from the 2002 Model Law on Conciliation. Importantly, section 2 prescribes when "mediation" may be considered "international." It essentially follows the pattern adopted by the Singapore Convention basing the internationality on the place of business/nationality of the parties to the conciliation (although, as per Article 1, the Convention is about when a settlement agreement is international). It should be well noted that while under Article 3, the Model Law considers the internationality of the "mediation," basing it on the agreement to mediate (and not the mediated settlement agreement), under Article 16, the Model Law considers the internationality of the mediated "settlement agreement."

Accordingly, Article 15 (which belongs in section 2 of the Model Law) provides for the binding and enforceable nature of the settlement agreements, including those settlement agreements that may be domestic but resulting from "international commercial mediation." And Article 16 (which belongs to section 3) applies to "settlement agreements" that are "international." Hence, since section 2 of the Model Law addresses international commercial mediation, the internationality would need to be assessed at the conclusion of the agreement to mediate (as provided by Article 3 of the Model Law). Since section 3 addresses enforcement of settlement agreement, the internationality would need to be assessed at the conclusion of the settlement agreement (as provided by Article 16 of the Model and Article 1 of the Singapore Convention). One possibility that the latter caters to is situations where there might not necessarily be an agreement to mediate between the parties (although the Model Law has an expansive definition under Article 16, whereby the writing requirement is also met by electronic communication).

Section 3 of the Model Law addresses all aspects concerning the enforcement of international settlement agreements resulting from mediation that have been concluded in "writing" and resolving a "commercial" dispute. Section 3 also provides options to grant States the flexibility or reflect the reservations provided under the

Singapore Convention. Accordingly, a State may consider enacting this section to apply to settlement agreements, irrespective of whether they resulted from mediation. Of course, some necessary adjustments would have to be made to the relevant Articles when adopting the Model Law. Further, a State may consider enacting section 3 to apply only where the parties to the settlement agreement agreed to its application. This reflects Article 8(1)(b) of the Singapore Convention, which gives parties the autonomy to opt in or opt out.

While India is yet to adopt the Model Law on Mediation and ratify the Singapore Convention, the Model Law's relevance is little in the Indian context. Nevertheless, as part of the section-wise commentary in the subsequent segment, we refer to the 2018 Model Law to better understand either the limitation or primacy of Part III of the ACA. And even if the 2018 Model Law refers to mediation, it refers to it synonymously to conciliation—the authors take that as *apropos* for this commentary on Part III.

§15.04 COMMENTARY ON PART III

The procedure laid down in Part III supports and preserves conciliation's core characteristics: conciliation is voluntary, nonadversarial, flexible, and less formal, autonomous, and self-determining for parties, confidential, interest-oriented (instead of rights-oriented), expeditious and cost-effective, and so on. For this, a conciliator is given the discretion to conduct the proceedings and not be bound by any specific code or statute on procedure/evidence. In doing so, he may offer settlement options/recommendations which may be acceptable to the parties. And ultimately, Part III provides equal status and effect as an arbitral award to any settlement agreement arrived by the parties because of the conciliation. In the authors' view, procedural flexibility and the status of a conciliated settlement agreement form the crucible of conciliation under Part III of the ACA.

As described in ACA's Preamble, Part III adopts the UNCITRAL Conciliation Rules 1980 ("UNCITRAL Rules"). Where a dispute arises in the context of international commercial relations and the parties seek an amicable settlement of that dispute by recourse to conciliation, Part III provides for it.

As regards "international commercial conciliation," it is given the same meaning as the expression "international commercial arbitration."[11] Accordingly, "international commercial conciliation" means a conciliation relating to disputes arising out of legal relationships, whether contractual or not, considered as "commercial" under the law in force in India and where at least one of the parties is:

(i) an individual who is national of, or habitually resident in, any country other than India; or
(ii) a body corporate which is incorporated in any country other than India; or

11. Arbitration & Conciliation Act 1996, §1(2) Explanation and §2(1)(f).

(iii) an association or a body of individuals whose central management and control is exercised in any country other than India; or
(iv) the Government of a foreign country.

Therefore, the internationality factor depends on the place of business/ nationality of the parties in the conciliation. While the ACA is not clear, the temporal point of such internationality should be at the time of execution of the agreement to conciliate (not at the time of execution of the settlement agreement), given that section 62 requires that the invitation and its acceptance be in writing; only then conciliation proceedings commenced under Part III of the ACA.

At the same time, Part III of ACA does not contain any provision that it would apply only to conciliations that take "place" in India (or any such concept of juridical seat or territoriality as may be found concerning arbitrations). As such, where the governing law of conciliation is (or chosen by parties to be) Part III of the ACA, a settlement agreement reached through conciliation, which is conducted and executed outside India, should be enforceable in India on the same basis as any domestically conducted conciliation and its resulting settlement agreement.[12] This reflects a rule of India's private international law concerning recognition and enforcement of an agreement to conciliate and/or a conciliated settlement agreement.

There is, however, some doubt as to whether Part III of the ACA would apply without a specific designation or reference to Part III of the ACA (be it domestic conciliation between Indian parties, international commercial conciliation between foreign and Indian parties, or international commercial conciliation between foreign parties). The authors view that a specific designation or reference to Part III of the ACA is necessary for Part III to apply as the governing law to the process. For more, *see* the discussion under section 62 in this chapter.

Finally, a situation may be contemplated where parties in a dispute seek the intervention of a third person in an ad hoc setting without specifically designating it as "conciliation" and without being aware of the purview of ACA. It raises the question if the parties would be bound by the provision of Part III of the ACA (such as section 75 on confidentiality or section 81 on the admissibility of evidence in other proceedings). While Part III of the ACA does not provide a straitjacket answer, it should reasonably be negative since the parties' understanding, intention, and expectations as to the process should provide the footing to apply Part III. Moreover, section 62 requires that the invitation and acceptance to invitation be in writing; only then conciliation proceedings commence as per section 62(2). But this may be viewed differently by those subscribing to the school of thought that "mediation" and "conciliation" are synonymic, that any ad hoc setting does not specify the process or the third-party intervention as "conciliation" would nevertheless be governed by Part III of the ACA.

Moreover, it seems that there is a dichotomy in the law of conciliation as regards the "commercial" reservation. The reservation is applicable only in respect of international conciliation, not domestic. The 2018 Model Law also applies only to settlement

12. *See* Anuradha SA Investments LLC v. Parsvnath Developers Ltd. (2017) SCC OnLine Del 7970.

agreements reached in international "commercial" mediation. But the term "commercial" is used expansively to cover all relationships of commercial nature, whether contractual or not.[13] This would include, but not limited to, any trade transaction for the supply or exchange of goods or services; distribution agreement; commercial representation or agency; factoring; leasing; construction of works; consulting; engineering; licensing; investment; financing; banking; insurance; exploitation agreement or concession; joint venture and other forms of industrial or business cooperation; and carriage of goods or passengers by air, sea, rail or road. The restriction to commercial matters not only is a reflection of the traditional mandate of UNCITRAL but also acknowledges that conciliation of noncommercial matters touches upon policy issues that do not readily lend themselves to universal harmonization (leaving it to the State to either accept or reject the commercial reservation).[14]

In the Indian context, the High Court of Gujarat is often quoted to have construed the "commercial" reservation as being of the "largest import" encompassing "all the business and trade transactions in any of their forms."[15] In the same vein, the Supreme Court of India has held that the term "commercial" has to be "construed broadly having regard to the manifold activities which are an integral part of international trade today."[16] Such expansive meaning of the expression "commercial" may include investment dispute within its ambit since at least the underlying context of such disputes is commercial in nature. However, the position taken by the court seems to go the opposite direction in excluding investment disputes from the ambit of "commercial."[17]

[A] Application and Scope of Conciliation (Section 61)

> 61. Application and scope—
>
> (1) Save as otherwise provided by any law for the time being in force and unless the parties have otherwise agreed, this Part shall apply to conciliation of disputes arising out of legal relationship, whether contractual or not and to all proceedings relating thereto.
> (2) This Part shall not apply where by virtue of any law for the time being in force certain disputes may not be submitted to conciliation.

Section 61 of ACA delineates the application and scope of conciliation, and it mirrors Article 1 of the UNCITRAL Rules. As stated in section 61(1), Part III only extends to

13. *See* Model Law on Mediation, *supra* note 4.
14. UN General Assembly, *Report of the Working Group on Arbitration on the Work of its Thirty-Fifth Session (Vienna, 19-30 November 2001)*, UNCITRAL ¶ 88 (A/CN.9/506, Dec. 21, 2001), https://undocs.org/en/A/CN.9/506 (hereinafter "UNGA A/CN.9/506").
15. Union of India & Ors. v. Lief Hoegh & Co & Ors., AIR 1983 Guj 34.
16. R. M. Investment and Trading Co. (P) Ltd. v. Boeing Co. (1994) 4 SCC 541, 546.
17. Cf. Union of India v. Vodafone Group PLC United Kingdom, 2017 S.C.C. OnLine Del 9930, ¶¶ 89–91; Union of India v. Khaitan Holdings (Mauritius) Limited, 2019 S.C.C. OnLine Del 6755, ¶ 29.

disputes arising out of a legal relationship, whether contractual or not, and all proceedings relating to it. A "dispute" may describe giving one party the right to sue and the other party the liability to be sued.[18] For example, under a construction contract, a dispute is considered to arise when:[19] (a) one party makes a claim against the other (which may be a claim, as defined in the contract, or a matter to be determined by the engineer under the contract, or otherwise); (b) the other party rejects the claim in whole or in part; and (c) the first party does not acquiesce (by giving a notice of dispute, or its equivalent).

Further, section 61(2) provides that Part III shall not apply where certain disputes may not be submitted to conciliation under any law for the time being into force. We may call this "conciliability" (analogous to "arbitrability"), i.e., whether a subject matter is conciliable or not. Examples of subject matters that are not arbitrable under Indian law include disputes pertaining to criminal offenses, matrimonial matters, guardianship, insolvency, antitrust and competition laws, registration and ownership of intellectual property rights, bribery, corruption, and fraud.[20]

Further, the Supreme Court of India recently proposed a "fourfold" test to determine disputes capable of settlement through arbitration:[21]

(1) when cause of action and subject matter of the dispute relate to actions in rem that do not pertain to subordinate rights in personam that arise from rights in rem;
(2) when cause of action and subject matter of the dispute affect third-party rights; have erga omnes effect; require centralized adjudication, and mutual adjudication would not be appropriate and enforceable;
(3) when cause of action and subject matter of the dispute relate to inalienable sovereign and public interest functions of the State and hence mutual adjudication would be unenforceable; and
(4) when the subject matter of the dispute is expressly or by necessary implication nonarbitrable as per mandatory statute(s).

These examples of arbitrability and the Supreme Court's test propounded are likely to be equally applicable to determining "conciliability" under Indian law.

Article 16 of the Model Law lays down specific exclusions from the purview of the instrument in the same manner as that of Article 1 of the Singapore Convention. The Model Law excludes subject matters like consumer transactions and family, inheritance, and employment law. Lastly, concerning settlement agreements concluded in the course of adjudicative proceedings (judicial or arbitral), if the proceedings have begun, and the parties were able to settle through mediation without any assistance of the

18. *See* Black's Law Dictionary 540 (Bryan A. Gardner ed., 2009) ("A conflict or controversy, esp. one that has given rise to a particular lawsuit").
19. *See*, e.g., FIDIC Conditions of Contract for Construction for Building and Engineering Works Designed by the Employer 1.1.29 (2nd ed., 2017).
20. *See* Booz Allen and Hamilton Inc. v. SBI Home Finance Ltd. and Ors. (2011) 5 SCC 532, ¶ 36; A. Ayyasamy v. A. Paramasivam and Ors. (2016) 10 SCC 386, ¶ 14.
21. Vidya Drolia and Ors. v. Durga Trading Corporation (2020) SCC OnLine SC 1018, ¶ 60.

court or arbitrator, such settlement agreements would fall outside the scope of the Model Law as long as the settlement agreement was enforceable as a judgment or award in the State where proceedings began. Similarly, settlement agreements reached during adjudicative proceedings but not recorded as judicial or arbitral decisions would fall outside the scope of the Model Law as long as the settlement agreement was enforceable as a judgment or award in the State where proceedings took place.

Neither the ACA nor the 2018 Model Law mentions a "place of conciliation" or "place of mediation." This is likely so because "place" is somewhat an artificial idea as a basis of triggering the application of the Model Law.[22]

[B] Invitation, Acceptance for Conciliation and Commencement (Section 62)

> 62. Commencement of conciliation proceedings—
>
> (1) The party initiating conciliation shall send to the other party a written invitation to conciliate under this Part, briefly identifying the subject of the dispute.
> (2) Conciliation proceedings, shall commence when the other party accepts in writing the invitation to conciliate.
> (3) If the other party rejects the invitation, there will be no conciliation proceedings.
> (4) If the party initiating conciliation does not receive a reply within thirty days from the date on which he sends the invitation, or within such other period of time as specified in the invitation, he may elect to treat this as a rejection of the invitation to conciliate and if he so elects, he shall inform in writing the other party accordingly.

As per section 62, a conciliation is initiated with the acceptance of an invitation to conciliate. Any party can initiate these proceedings by inviting the other party in writing, providing a brief background of the subject matter and the dispute at hand. Importantly, the proceedings commence when the other party accepts the proposal in writing. Upon reaching an agreement to settle disputes via conciliation, the conciliator is appointed by mutual agreement. Section 62, therefore, considers the intention of the parties to conciliate after the dispute has arisen.

But, under section 62(4) of the ACA, if the requesting party does not receive an acceptance to his invitation within 30 days from the day he sent the invitation (or within such time specified in the invitation), the requesting party has two options: (i) he may either elect to treat it as an acceptance; or (ii) he may elect to treat it as a rejection, and if he elects so, he is required to inform the other party. In a way, the

22. *See* UNGA A/CN.9/506, *supra* note 14, ¶ 88.

purpose of section 62(4) is to provide some certainty in a situation where it is unclear whether a party is willing to conciliate by giving the requesting party the option to elect.

As per the writing requirement under section 62, it would not always be necessary that the parties should sign it. Like an arbitration agreement (under section 7 of the ACA), an agreement to conciliate can be contained in an exchange of letter, telex, or other means of telecommunication that provide a record of an agreement or an exchange of statement which an agreement to conciliate is evidenced.[23]

Section 62 does not provide anything regarding the withdrawal of an invitation to conciliate. It would be reasonable to consider that a party would be free to withdraw its invitation until its acceptance based on the principles of contract law under sections 3 to 5 of the Indian Contract Act 1872. But given that conciliation is voluntary, a party would be free to withdraw from conciliation at any point, making this issue moot. In essence, participation in conciliation is voluntary, and it is up to the parties (their autonomy) to agree and settle. If not, a party has the liberty to withdraw from the conciliation at any time. Hence, unlike arbitration, conciliation does not require any prior written agreement between parties on which basis conciliation may be invoked/initiated. Once invited to conciliate, the responding party is simply required to convey its acceptance or rejection within 30 days of the invitation's receipt.

Part III of the ACA, however, does not contemplate a pre-dispute agreement to conciliate (or to conciliate future disputes) and, therefore, such agreements are considered unenforceable.[24] Part III only provides for an agreement to refer disputes to conciliation once a dispute has arisen. Hence, Part III does not deal with the obligation of parties to conciliate, and, in the case of a multitier dispute resolution, conciliation may not be considered mandatory as a pre-arbitral step. Nevertheless, conciliation may still become mandatory if it were contractually made a conditional pre-arbitral step (without which the consent to arbitration would be nonexistent). This again distinguishes the invocation of conciliation from that of arbitration (wherein parties may agree to refer future disputes to arbitration). Parenthetically, section 89 of the Code of Civil Procedure 1908 (CPC) provides another avenue whereby parties may be referred to conciliation by the court. But there, too, the parties' consent is mandatory by virtue of section 62 of the ACA.

Finally, a situation may be contemplated where parties in a dispute seek the intervention of a third person in an ad hoc setting without specifically designating it as "conciliation" under Part III of the ACA and without being aware of the purview of

---

23. *See*, e.g., Jugal Kishore Rameshwardas v. Goolbai Hormusji, AIR 1955 SC 812. *See also*, UP Rajkiya Nirman Nigam Ltd. v. Indure (P) Ltd. & Ors., AIR 1996 SC 1373 (where one of the parties to the arbitration agreement has singed it and the others have knowledge of the existence of such an agreement, they would be deemed to have given their consent); Rickmers Verwaltung Gmbh v. Indian Oil Corp. Ltd. (1999) 1 SCC 11 ("Unless from the correspondence, it can unequivocally and clearly emerge that the parties were ad idem to the terms, it cannot be said that an agreement had come into existence between them through correspondence ... [For e.g., if the correspondence] shows that there had been meeting of mind between the parties and they had actually reached an agreement upon all material terms ...").
24. *See* Visa International Ltd. v. Continental Resources (USA) Ltd. (2009) 2 SCC 55, ¶ 27.

ACA. That further raises the question whether the parties would be bound by the provision of Part III of the ACA (such as section 75 on confidentiality or section 81 on the admissibility of evidence in other proceedings). While Part III of the ACA does not provide a straightjacket answer, it should reasonably be negative since the parties' understanding, intention, and expectations as to the process should provide the footing to apply Part III. Moreover, section 62 requires that the invitation and acceptance to invitation be in writing; only then conciliation proceedings commence as per section 62(2). But even then, an invitation and its acceptance can be devoid of any designation or reference to Part III of the ACA, and the applicability of Part III would still be an abyss.

At least two other practical and legal difficulties are foreseeable if a specific designation or reference to Part III of the ACA is not considered to be legally mandatory. *One*, in international commercial conciliation, where (at least) one party is foreign, there is no rational way of determining the application of Part III of the ACA, except where parties have designated so. Conciliation, unlike arbitration, has no concept of a juridical seat or place of arbitration. Similarly, choice of court clauses cannot also shed any light on the issue. *Two*, if a specific designation or reference to Part III is not considered to be legally mandatory, courts would be manifestly ignoring the legal and statutory distinction between a private mediation and conciliation under Part III (since there is, after all, not much of a practical difference between the two processes). But this mandatory requirement of designating Part III may be viewed differently by those subscribing to the school of thought that "mediation" and "conciliation" are synonymic, which is also why Part III of the ACA would nevertheless govern any ad hoc setting which does specify the process or the third-party intervention as "conciliation."

[C] Number of Conciliators and Appointment (Sections 63 and 64)

63. Number of conciliators—

(1) There shall be one conciliator unless the parties agree that there shall be two or three conciliators.
(2) Where there is more than one conciliator, they ought, as a general rule, to act jointly.

64. Appointment of conciliators—

(1) Subject to sub-section (2)—(a) in conciliation proceedings, with one conciliator, the parties may agree on the name of a sole conciliator;
    (b) in conciliation proceedings with two conciliators, each party may appoint one conciliator;

(c) in conciliation proceedings with three conciliators, each party may appoint one conciliator and the parties may agree on the name of the third conciliator who shall act as the presiding conciliator.

(2) Parties may enlist the assistance of a suitable institution or person in connection with the appointment of conciliators, and in particular—(a) a party may request such an institution or person to recommend the names of suitable individuals to act as conciliator; or

(b) the parties may agree that the appointment of one or more conciliators be made directly by such an institution or person:

> Provided that in recommending or appointing individuals to act as conciliator, the institution or person shall have regard to such considerations as are likely to secure the appointment of an independent and impartial conciliator and, with respect to a sole or third conciliator, shall take into account the advisability of appointing a conciliator of a nationality other than the nationalities of the parties.

As per section 63 of the ACA, conciliation may be conducted by a maximum of three conciliators. However, by default, the number of conciliators is one (unless parties agree to either two or three conciliators). Thus, the term "conciliation" has a broad notion of a proceeding in which a person (or a panel of persons) conciliates the parties' dispute.

As for procedure for appointment, in conciliation with one conciliator, the parties may agree on the name of a sole conciliator; two conciliators, each party may appoint one conciliator; three conciliators, each party may appoint one conciliator, and the parties may agree on the name of the third conciliator who shall act as the presiding conciliator. Where more than one conciliator is appointed, the panel of conciliators is required to act jointly, with independence and impartiality.

This is a departure from the 2018 and 2002 Model Laws (Article 6 and Article 5, respectively), which encourage the parties to mutually agree on the selection of each conciliator unless a different procedure has been agreed upon by the parties. The intent was to encourage the parties to collaborate and foster greater control and confidence in the conciliation process.[25] In the absence of an agreement by the parties on selecting a conciliator, the Model Law provides that reference may be made to an institution or a third person. In this regard, it would seem that section 64 of ACA takes a more practical approach for expeditious conciliation proceedings, rather than making an ideal expectation that parties will mutually agree on each conciliator.

Section 64(2) makes a subtle reference to possible institutional conciliation. To appoint a conciliator or a panel, parties may take the support of an institution/center (or an individual). A party may request either such an institution or person to

25. *See* UNGA A/CN.9/506, *supra* note 14, ¶ 88.

recommend the names of suitable individuals to act as conciliator, or parties may agree that the appointment of one or more conciliators will be directly made by such an institution (or person). In recommending or appointing a conciliator or a panel, the institution (or person) needs to regard the independence and impartiality of the potential conciliator. And, particularly in the case of international conciliations, when recommending or appointing the sole conciliator or the presiding conciliator, the conciliator's nationality (against the nationality of the parties) should be considered.

Section 64 of the ACA, however, is critically deficient in comparison to Model Law provisions. Unlike Article 6 of the 2018 Model Law, the person who is approached in connection with his or her possible appointment as a conciliator does not have any specific obligation to disclose any circumstances likely to give rise to justifiable doubts as to his or her impartiality or independence. This is neither at the stage of appointment nor throughout the proceedings. This is why it may be particularly important to consider conciliation under the rules of an institution, which rules would impose such an obligation upon the conciliator. Indirectly, however, the ACA (under section 67(1)) does oblige a conciliator to assist the parties independently and impartially in their attempt to reach an amicable settlement of their dispute. Be that as it may, a failure to disclose would not, in and of itself, create a ground for setting aside an award on agreed terms (a consent award) under section 34 of the ACA,[26] unless the allegations rise to the level of violating the public policy of India (say, fraud or corruption; violation of the fundamental policy of Indian law; or notions of justice).

While the 2018 Model Law does require disclosure by the conciliator, there is no provision to address the consequences that might result from the failure to make such a disclosure. Does the conciliation proceeding become null and void? The prevailing view was that the consequence of such failure to disclose should be left to the enacting State's local law.[27]

[D] Submission of Statement to Conciliator (Section 65)

> 65. Submission of statements to conciliator—
>
> (1) The conciliator, upon his appointment, may request each party to submit to him a brief written statement describing the general nature of the dispute and the points at issue. Each party shall send a copy of such statement to the other party.
>
> (2) The conciliator may request each party to submit to him a further written statement of his position and the facts and grounds in support thereof, supplemented by any documents and other evidence that such party

26. *See* UN General Assembly, *Report of the United Nations Commission on International Trade Law on its Thirty-Fifth Session 17-28 June 2002*, UNCITRAL ¶¶ 50, 157 (A/57/17, July 18, 2002), https://documents-dds-ny.un.org/doc/UNDOC/GEN/V02/565/81/PDF/V0256581.pdf?OpenElement (hereinafter "UNGA A/57/17").
27. *See* UNGA A/CN.9/506, *supra* note 14, ¶ 65.

deems appropriate. The party shall send a copy of such statement, documents and other evidence to the other party.

(3) At any stage of the conciliation proceedings, the conciliator may request a party to submit to him such additional information as he deems appropriate.

Explanation—In this section and all the following sections of this Part, the term "conciliator" applies to a sole conciliator, two or three conciliators, as the case may be.

Section 65(1) provides that the conciliator, once appointed, may request each party to submit to him a brief written statement describing the general nature of the dispute and the points at issue. This is to be exchanged between the parties.

In terms of sections 65(2) and 65(3), the conciliator may seek further clarity on the issue at hand, requesting the parties to submit any additional information or a further written statement of the party's position, along with the facts and grounds which support his position, as well as any documents and other evidence that supplement the party's position. The conciliator may request so at any stage of conciliation proceedings, and the same is to be exchanged between the parties.

These statements are generally referred to as "statements of positions and interests" or "position papers," in which parties set out the issues and grounds of their claim/case and support it with documents. This becomes a useful tool for a conciliator to understand the dispute and catch up with the pace of the parties in conflict. It also enables a conciliator's effort to formulate agreeable proposals to facilitate settlements. With that goal in mind, a conciliator may also request parties to provide specific information in their position papers, like a party's factual perspective or counter-perspective, any previous offers or counteroffers, the status of the contractual relations, views on the merits of a claim, etc.

[E] Conciliator Not Bound by Procedural Law (Section 66)

66. Conciliator not bound by certain enactments—

The conciliator is not bound by the Code of Civil Procedure, 1908 (5 of 1908) or the Indian Evidence Act, 1872 (1 of 1872).

Section 66 of ACA gives conciliators flexibility and discretion in conducting the conciliation proceedings. It frees the conciliator from being bound by rigidity and formalism of the CPC and the Indian Evidence Act 1872 and, hence, preserves the true nature of the process. Hence, e.g., there is no such mandate to hear witnesses. The conciliator may conduct the proceedings in such a manner as the conciliator considers appropriate, considering the circumstances of the case, any wishes that the parties may express, and the need for a speedy settlement of the dispute.

By no means should this mean that parties cannot set the procedure. The parties are free to agree on how the mediation is to be conducted by reference to a set of rules or otherwise. This is possible by referring the dispute to an institution/center (like the International Chamber of Commerce) or incorporating ad hoc rules (like the UNCITRAL Rules).

In any case (even though Part III does not specify so), the conciliator in conducting the proceedings should seek to maintain "fair treatment" of the parties and, in so doing, shall take into account the circumstances of the case. This is made into a specific requirement under Article 7(3) of the 2018 Model Law, which would cover the notion of equality of treatment when dealing with the parties. However, "fair treatment" should not be understood mechanically, as in spending equal time (literally) in the caucus with each party. The conciliator may explain this to the parties in advance, that there may be differences (real and perceived) in the time spent with each party but that it would all be to understand all issues, interests, and possibilities for settlement.[28]

Under Article 7 of the 2018 Model Law (Article 6 of 2002 Model Law), the parties are free to agree on how the conciliation is to be conducted. It further recognizes the role of the conciliator who, while observing the will of the parties, may shape the process as he considers appropriate.

Though conciliators are given substantial freedom in the conduct of conciliation proceedings, Part III of the ACA lacks in providing any immunity to the conciliator (or the institution). Without such insulation, conciliators are (unfortunately) exposed to civil liability for alleged wrongdoing during the conciliation. Nevertheless, the rules of various institutions add this layer of protection for conciliators (and the institution itself), making institutional conciliation more appealing in the interest of progressiveness and development in the practice of conciliation.

[F] Role of Conciliator (Section 67)

67. Role of conciliator—

(1) The conciliator shall assist the parties in an independent and impartial manner in their attempt to reach an amicable settlement of their dispute.
(2) The conciliator shall be guided by principles of objectivity, fairness and justice, giving consideration to, among other things, the rights and obligations of the parties, the usages of the trade concerned and the circumstances surrounding the dispute, including any previous business practices between the parties.
(3) The conciliator may conduct the conciliation proceedings in such a manner as he considers appropriate, taking into account the circumstances of the case, the wishes the parties may express, including any

28. *See* UN General Assembly, *Draft Guide to Enactment and Use of the UNCITRAL Model Law on International Commercial Conciliation*, UNCITRAL ¶ 55 (A/CN.9/514, May 27, 2002) (hereinafter "UNGA A/CN.9/514").

request by a party that the conciliator hear oral statements, and the need for a speedy settlement of the dispute.

(4) The conciliator may, at any stage of the conciliation proceedings, make proposals for a settlement of the dispute. Such proposals need not be in writing and need not be accompanied by a statement of the reasons thereof.

Section 67 of ACA explains (though limitedly) the role of a conciliator. First and foremost, a conciliator is obligated to assist the parties independently and impartially.

Despite proceedings being informal and flexible, a conciliator must be guided by principles of fairness, objectivity, and justice. He must also consider the rights and obligations of the parties, the usages of the trade concerned, and the circumstances surrounding the dispute, including any previous business practices between the parties. However, this approach to the conciliator's role provides only the legal boundaries but not a practical one. This nevertheless gives the conciliator the desired freehand to conduct the proceedings as he deems fit, under the above considerations.

At any stage of the proceedings, the conciliator may make proposals for a settlement of the dispute. Such proposals need not be in writing and need not be accompanied by any reasons. Hence, the conciliator may adopt either a facilitative or an evaluative approach to resolve the dispute with the parties' sanction. Whether, to what extent and at which stage the conciliator may make any such proposal will depend on many factors, including the parties' wishes and the conciliator's techniques most conducive to a settlement. Both the 2002 and 2018 Model Laws provide for such a possibility on the part of the conciliator.

[G] Administrative Assistance (Section 68)

68. Administrative assistance—

In order to facilitate the conduct of the conciliation proceedings, the parties, or the conciliator with the consent of the parties, may arrange for administrative assistance by a suitable institution or person.

In order to facilitate the conduct of the conciliation proceedings, the parties, or the conciliator, with the consent of the parties, may arrange for administrative assistance by a suitable institution or person. Section 68 promotes the use of institutional conciliation, statutorily recognizing the beneficial role of an institution in assisting the conduct of conciliation proceedings.

Though there are cost implications in conducting an institutional conciliation, parties to conciliations usually access real benefits in adopting a tried and tested institutional rules and a process that a respected ADR provider administers. These benefits are particularly true in the case of international conciliations. Institutional administrative support becomes imperative because complexities often accompany international commercial disputes (multiple time zones, cultures, languages, participants, etc.). Such support is rendered in the form of case management services, which continue throughout the proceedings, even after the appointment of the conciliator (or panel of conciliators). An institution, for instance, plays a vital role in the selection of a conciliator (or panel of conciliators) when there is a disagreement between the parties about the appropriate person or when the parties do not know how to find one (one who is both qualified, competent, and suitable for their case).

[H] Communication and Venue (Section 69)

> 69. Communication between conciliator and parties—
>
> (1) The conciliator may invite the parties to meet him or may communicate with them orally or in writing. He may meet or communicate with the parties together or with each of them separately.
> (2) Unless the parties have agreed upon the place where meetings with the conciliator are to be held, such place shall be determined by the conciliator, after consultation with the parties, having regard to the circumstances of the conciliation proceedings.

Sections 69–76 set out certain procedural matters about the conciliation proceedings. Under section 69, the conciliator has the discretion to invite the parties to meet, communicate orally or in writing, and he may meet jointly or separately. The conciliator can also decide the place of meeting after he has consulted the parties and considered the circumstances of the case. There is no proscription on conducting the proceedings virtually (online conciliation).

Except where the parties have expressly agreed to restrict separate meetings, separate meetings between the conciliator and the parties are, in practice, so usual that a conciliator is presumed to be free to use this technique. Section 69 puts this issue beyond doubt. As a matter of practice, conciliators routinely brief the parties (and the advocates) about using this tool to avoid any negative perception.

[I] Disclosure of Information (Section 70)

> 70. Disclosure of information—
>
> When the conciliator receives factual information concerning the dispute from a party, he shall disclose the substance of that information to the other party in

> order that the other party may have the opportunity to present any explanation which he considers appropriate:
>
> Provided that when a party gives any information to the conciliator subject to a specific condition that it be kept confidential, the conciliator shall not disclose that information to the other party.

One of the most important features of conciliation is confidentiality, and this comes in layers for conciliation: (i) confidentiality between the conciliator and a party (section 70); (ii) confidentiality among or between all participants of the conciliation (section 75); and (iii) confidentiality as in the inadmissibility of any evidence or statements (including proposals) made in any other arbitral/judicial proceedings on the same subject as the conciliation (section 81) and that the parties shall not present a conciliator as a witness in any arbitral/judicial proceedings (section 80).

While section 69 allows a conciliator to meet and communicate with each party separately (private session), section 70 prohibits the conciliator from revealing to the other party any fact or information disclosed to the conciliator in a private session with a specific condition that it be kept confidential. In other words, when the conciliator receives information concerning the dispute from a party, he is required to (*shall*) disclose the substance of that information to the other party in order that the other party may have the opportunity to present any explanation which he considers appropriate. The words "substance of that information," as used in section 70, reflect that conciliators do have to communicate the literal content of any information received from the parties. But when a party gives any information to the conciliator subject to a specific condition that it is kept confidential, the conciliator shall not disclose it to the other party.

Article 9 of the 2018 Model Law, however, assumes a significant difference. It uses the phrase "may disclose" as against the phrase "shall disclose" in section 70, showing that the Model Law prefers giving discretion to the conciliator about disclosing any information. However, in practice, conciliators often brief the party in a private session that he would not be revealing anything to the other side unless the party is okay with it. This way, conciliators try to win the party's trust, encouraging him to be completely open and frank in private sessions.

Lastly, in using the term "information," section 70 implies a broad notion that would enclose every communication exchanged between a party and the conciliator. It is, however, unsure whether this would cover any communications or information that might have been exchanged before the commencement of the conciliation. Nevertheless, best practice would suggest that conciliators (and mediation advocates) brief the parties about such potential issues to ensure parties take informed decisions about disclosing information.

[J] Cooperation of the Parties and Suggestions (Sections 71 and 72)

> 71. Co-operation of parties with conciliator—
>
> The parties shall in good faith co-operate with the conciliator and, in particular, shall endeavour to comply with requests by the conciliator to submit written materials, provide evidence and attend meetings.
>
> 72. Suggestions by parties for settlement of dispute—
>
> Each party may, on his own initiative or at the invitation of the conciliator, submit to the conciliator suggestions for the settlement of the dispute.

The key to a successful conciliation is the legitimate approach of the parties toward the settlement of the dispute. Hence, section 71 requires (by casting a duty on the parties) that parties cooperate in good faith with the conciliator and, in particular, endeavor to comply with the conciliator's request to furnish written statements, supporting evidence, and attend meetings. In its absence, it would be challenging for the conciliator to support parties for an amicable settlement.

While the 2018 Model Law does not capture such a provision, it is understood that conciliation is a voluntary process, and the party will choose to cooperate if they are willingly participating. Essentially, ACA imposes a good faith obligation upon the parties when participating in conciliation proceedings, which provides a layer of ethics to the proceedings. But since such an obligation exists, there must also be some consequences or sanctions for a party's failure to comply with such good faith obligation. One such possible consequence can be in the form of an unfavorable determination on costs, as under section 31A(3)(d) of the ACA, wherein a court or arbitral tribunal shall have regard of whether any reasonable offers to settle the dispute were made but refused.

Complementarily, section 72 of the ACA encourages suggestions/proposals by parties to settle a dispute. Hence, each party may, on his initiative or at the invitation of the conciliator, submit to the conciliator suggestions for the settlement of the dispute. In presenting a settlement proposal, parties would still be bound by their good faith obligation under section 71. Hence, if a party includes unreasonable stipulations in a settlement offer, he would be breaching his obligation to participate and cooperate in good faith. And so, he will not be in a position to say that the other side acted unreasonably in refusing to accept it, thus, for example, subjecting himself to an unfavorable order on costs under section 31A(3) of the ACA.[29] On this issue of costs, it is helpful to refer to the Halsey principles, derived from *Halsey v. Milton Keynes General*

29. Hence, a party who refuses to consider ADR following an invitation from the court, or the other side, would be doing so at risk of a costs sanction. *See generally*, Dunnett v. Railtrack Plc, [2002] EWCA Civ 302; Halsey v. Milton Keynes General NHS Trust, [2004] EWCA Civ 576; Jarrom and Shepherd v. Sellars, [2007] EWHC 1366 (Ch).

NHS Trust,[30] where the United Kingdom Court of Appeal considered if a refusal to mediate should give rise to costs sanctions. To deprive a successful party of any of its costs (on the grounds that it refused to agree to mediate) was considered an exception to the usual rule that costs follow the event, the burden being on the unsuccessful party to show that the successful party acted unreasonably in refusing to mediate. In determining whether a party acted unreasonably, the following considerations (Halsey principles) are factored: the nature of the dispute; the merits of the case; other settlement options; costs of mediation; delay; prospects of success; and other factors (like judicial encouragement, or the further need for expert evidence).

[K] Settlement Agreement (Section 73)

> 73. Settlement agreement—
>
> (1) When it appears to the conciliator that there exist elements of a settlement which may be acceptable to the parties, he shall formulate the terms of a possible settlement and submit them to the parties for their observations. After receiving the observations of the parties, the conciliator may reformulate the terms of a possible settlement in the light of such observations.
> (2) If the parties reach agreement on a settlement of the dispute, they may draw up and sign a written settlement agreement. If requested by the parties, the conciliator may draw up, or assist the parties in drawing up, the settlement agreement.
> (3) When the parties sign the settlement agreement, it shall be final and binding on the parties and persons claiming under them respectively.
> (4) The conciliator shall authenticate the settlement agreement and furnish a copy thereof to each of the parties.

Section 73 of the ACA provides that the settlement agreement signed by the parties in dispute shall be final and binding on the parties, which agreement would need to be authenticated/signed by the conciliator. A settlement comes about when parties manage to reach a mutually acceptable compromise of the dispute that has arisen between them. And, simply put, such a settlement is no less binding and final than if the parties had asked the court to determine the dispute for them. Finality is a by-product of the settlement, which brings an end to the dispute and the conciliation proceedings (unless, of course, the parties have agreed that the dispute can be resuscitated in certain circumstances or for grounds like fraud and/or corruption).[31]

30. [2004] EWCA Civ 576.
31. *See generally*, Zurich Insurance Company Plc v. Hayward, [2011] EWCA Civ 641 (a settlement agreement that had been embodied in a Tomlin order was not considered to be final because the settlement was found to have been induced by fraudulent misrepresentation).

But generally, the parties will not be able to start a new action relating to that dispute. Thus, for instance, if a creditor settles the debt for less than the full amount by accepting payment in "full and final settlement," the creditor loses his ability to settle for more and/or lose its ability to pursue a claim against the debtor for the balance of the debt.

In order to reach an agreement on the settlement, when it appears to the conciliator that there exist elements of the settlement which may be acceptable to the parties, the conciliator may formulate the terms of a possible settlement and submit them to the parties for their observations. Upon receiving observations of the parties, the conciliator may reformulate the term of a possible settlement in view of the observations by the parties.

Once the parties reach an agreement on the settlement, they may draw up and sign a written settlement agreement, which is thereafter signed/endorsed by the conciliator. The parties may also request the conciliator to draw up (or assist parties in drawing up) the settlement agreement.[32] This is final and binding on the parties (and those claiming through or under them)[33] and attains the status and legal sanctity of an arbitral award under section 74 of the ACA.

Similarly, under Article 17 of the 2018 Model Law, courts have the substantive obligation to enforce a settlement agreement (subject to exceptions, of course). Nevertheless, how a State enforces a settlement agreement (i.e., the rules of procedure) will be within its discretion. Article 17 further covers the scenario where a settlement agreement might be raised in defense against a claim in a court. Namely, that by meeting all the conditions under the Model Law, a party seeking relief would be able to prove that the dispute had been settled. Here again, the rules of procedure are the prerogative of the State.

Besides the issues and matters that have been settled fully and finally by way of the settlement agreement, it does not necessarily mean that a party cannot litigate a matter that it failed to deal with in the conciliation proceedings. However, if the court referred the conciliation (or even mediation) in a court proceeding under section 89 of the CPC, the question will arise whether the court should allow the party to litigate that matter in the future. If a party brings a fresh claim regarding such a matter which could have been raised in the previous compromised proceedings, the court must regard this as abuse of process and prevent subsequent litigation as res judicata under section 11 of the CPC.

32. Arbitration and Conciliation Act 1996, §73(2) ("If requested by the parties, the conciliator may draw up, or assist the parties in drawing up, the settlement agreement"). *See also*, Haresh Dayaram Thakur v. State of Maharashtra & Ors., AIR 2000 SC 2281 (holding that provisions of the Act manifest that a conciliator is a person who is to assist the parties to settle the dispute between them amicably. He has wide powers to decide the procedure to be followed by him, untrammeled by the procedural laws). *See generally*, Anuradha SA Investments LLC & Anr. v. Parsvnath Developers Ltd. & Ors, 2017 (4) Arb LR 72 (Del).
33. A settlement may affect a third party. Such party may also enforce a term of the settlement if the settlement expressly provides that he may, or if the term purports to confer a benefit on him and it cannot be shown that the parties did not intend the term to be enforceable by him. And if such third party is intended, the third party should be (as a matter of good practice) clearly identified in the settlement agreement.

Furthermore, in conciliations, there is always a likelihood that parties negotiate a settlement on unrelated claims (say, claims arising out of the different agreement) to create an all-encompassing, comprehensive settlement of the disputes between them. In doing so, parties create enough connection between such claims to give rise to an equitable set-off, even though the negotiation was held "without prejudice."[34] If an equitable set-off is not intended, then parties must specify so.

Given that a conciliated settlement agreement is contractual by nature (and given the status and effect of a consent award), it is arguable that the law of contract would nevertheless apply for the settlement agreement to first come into existence. This would include the rules of formation of a contract and the requirements of a valid contract. Some of these are as follows:

- A dispute must be in existence, which is capable of settlement by conciliation.[35]
- There must be a consideration.[36]
- The settlement must be certain (and not vague).[37]
- There must be an intention to create a binding compromise. E.g., it must not be a mere memorandum of understanding, or the use of the words "subject to contract" may be used to rebut the presumption of contractual intent.[38]
- Parties to the settlement agreement must be competent to contract and of sound mind to contract.[39]

Thus, in defending an action to enforce a conciliated settlement as a consent award, a party may be allowed to invoke the abovementioned (or other) contractual defenses to establish that the conciliated settlement is void (or voidable) under the grounds in Chapter II of the Indian Contract Act 1872. Without a valid conciliated settlement in existence, there would be no question of a consent award. Nevertheless, since the settlement process involved a third party, neutral conciliator, courts should (as a matter of policy) prefer not to undo the stitches to invalidate the settlement. After

34. *See generally* Addax Bank BSC v. Wellesley Partners LLP [2010] EWHC 1904 (QB).
35. *See* Arbitration & Conciliation Act, 1996, §61 ("this Part shall apply to conciliation of disputes arising out of legal relationship"). *See generally*, K K Modi v. K N Modi, 1998 AIR SC 1297 ("Therefore our courts have laid emphasis on (1) existence of disputes as against intention to avoid future disputes"); M/s Earth and Air Films Pvt. Ltd. v. M. T. Vasudevan Nair, 2019 SCC OnLine Ker 4701, ¶10 ("Merely because the notice was not responded, it cannot be said that no dispute existed. [...] [dispute or difference existed between them").
36. Indian Contract Act, 1872, §25. *See generally*, Simantob v. Shavleyan, [2019] EWCA Civ 1105 (Court of Appeal held that a forbearance to raise a defense that was later found to be without legal merit may constitute sufficient consideration to support a contract); Crystal Palace FC (2000) Ltd. v. Iain Dowie, [2008] EWHC 240 (QB) (illustrates how careful solicitors need to be when negotiating a settlement on their clients' behalf, especially when the negotiations are being carried out orally. Solicitors need to be especially careful to make it clear whether they are making a conditional offer or an unconditional offer).
37. Indian Contract Act, 1872, §29.
38. *See generally*, Shirley Jackson & Ors. v. Subhash Kanji Thakrar & Ors., [2007] EWHC 271 (TCC), ¶ 30 (where, for whatever reason, a binding compromise has not been reached, it is wholly illegitimate for the court to try and fill in the gaps, in order to achieve a result that the parties themselves did not intend).
39. Indian Contract Act, 1872, §§ 11–12.

all, the settlement was not arrived at through mere negotiations but by conciliation proceedings under a governing law that minimizes the risks of a void or voidable settlement outcome.

[L] Status and Effect of Settlement Agreement (Section 74)

> 74. Status and effect of settlement agreement—
>
> The settlement agreement shall have the same status and effect as if it is an arbitral award on agreed terms on the substance of the dispute rendered by an arbitral tribunal under section 30.

Section 74 provides that the settlement agreement shall have the same status and effect as an arbitral award rendered under section 30 of the ACA (i.e., an award on agreed terms or "consent award"). Hence, a conciliated settlement agreement has statutory recognition under Indian law, which shall be directly enforceable under section 36 of the ACA in accordance with the provisions of the CPC, in the same manner as if it were a decree of the court. The attractiveness of conciliation in India is unique as it enjoys a regime of expedited enforcement like an arbitral award.

The status and effect of the settlement agreement as if it is an arbitral award should be understood as a mandatory provision from which parties can contract out. It would otherwise result in an absurdity that strips "conciliation" under Part III from its very essence or lifeblood that causes a conciliated settlement to be consequential (and qualitatively more than just a negotiated agreement).

A "consent award" can be challenged on the same grounds assailing arbitral award under section 34 of the ACA, but this should be considered limited to only certain grounds available under section 34 that can be related to a conciliated settlement agreement:

(i) section 34(2)(a)(i): where a party was under some incapacity; or
(ii) section 34(2)(b)(i): where the subject matter of the dispute is not capable of settlement by arbitration/conciliation under the law for the time being in force (read with Section 61(2) whereby Part III shall not apply to what is not conciliable); or
(iii) section 34(2)(b)(ii): where the arbitral award conflicts with the public policy of India.

Hence, a consent award (which is a settlement agreement) cannot be easily challenged under section 34, given that the primary basis of the grounds is for setting aside arbitral awards. It causes absurd results (for example) when a settlement agreement is challenged on the ground that the petitioner was not given an equal opportunity to be heard. These grounds do not translate easily to mediation and conciliation.

While the scope of section 34 of the ACA may be limited in terms of setting aside an award on agreed terms, it is postulated by the authors that a party may still validly rely on the defenses under the law of contract that would establish a conflict with the public policy of India under section 34(2)(b)(ii) of the ACA. Accordingly, a party should rely on grounds, such as where the settlement agreement is both void and voidable under Chapter II of the Indian Contract Act 1872. That said, as a matter of policy, a challenge to an arbitral award on agreed terms (consent award) must be understood to be very limited, with a high threshold. Such a threshold, in the context of dispute settlement, is necessary to ensure finality that insists the end of a dispute, particularly given the involvement of a third party, impartial, and independent conciliator who has facilitated a conciliated settlement—which is, qualitatively, somewhat higher than a mere negotiated settlement. Courts should (as a matter of policy) prefer not to unlock and invalidate a settlement that is an outcome of structured facilitation by a conciliator under Part III of the ACA (and not an outcome of simple negotiations between the parties that may breed more risk of a void or voidable settlement outcome).

Unlike the ACA, Article 19 of the 2018 Model Law covers extensive grounds for refusing the enforcement of the settlement agreement, which are all tuned toward a conciliated settlement (unlike section 34, which is largely meant for arbitration/arbitral awards). Like the Singapore Convention, the grounds for refusal have been classified into the following:

(1) Substantive grounds:
   (i) incapacity of a party to the settlement agreement, or
   (ii) settlement agreement being null and void, inoperative or incapable of being performed (under applicable law).
(2) Grounds relating to the terms of the settlement agreement:
   (i) settlement agreement is not binding, or is not final, according to its terms, or
   (ii) settlement agreement has been subsequently modified, or
   (iii) obligations in the settlement agreement:
      - have been performed; or
      - are not clear or comprehensible, or
   (iv) granting relief would be contrary to the terms of the settlement agreement.
(3) Grounds relating to the mediator's conduct and the process:
   (i) serious breach by the mediator of standards applicable to the mediator or the mediation, or
   (ii) failure by the mediator to disclose to the parties circumstances that raise justifiable doubts as to the mediator's impartiality or independence.
(4) Sua sponte grounds (invocable by the competent authority or a requesting party):

(i) granting relief would be contrary to the public policy of the State Party; or

(ii) the subject matter of the dispute is not capable of settlement by mediation under the law of the State Party.

The requirement to stamp conciliated settlement agreements for enforcement has divergent views from the Delhi and Karnataka High Courts. The Karnataka High Court holds the view that since a conciliated settlement agreement has the same status and effect as an arbitral award, stamp duty (as chargeable on an arbitral award)[40] would also have to be paid for the settlement agreement.[41] *Au contraire*, the Delhi High Court has held that a legal fiction cannot be extended beyond the purpose for which it is created and, accordingly, section 74 of ACA creates a legal fiction to elevate the status and effect of a conciliated settlement agreement to an arbitral award to enable enforcement of such agreements without any further adjudication/litigation. Relying on a judgment of the Supreme Court's constitutional bench,[42] the Delhi High Court held that legal fiction could not be extended to other statutes. It is not as if the settlement ceases to be an agreement that was voluntarily entered into between the parties and instead becomes an arbitral award; it merely has the status and effect of an arbitral award under the ACA for enforcement.

Article 18 of the 2018 Model Law, in addition to providing a settlement agreement that is "signed" by the parties, requires that parties must provide evidence that the settlement agreement resulted from mediation (and not simply a negotiated settlement). Such evidence may include a mediator's signature on the settlement agreement or a separate declaration by the mediator or a mediation institution/center, which would attest to the mediator's involvement in the mediation process. This is necessary for a party to rely on the settlement agreement to either enforce it or defense against an action to prove that the matter has already been resolved/settled.

It should be considered that a signature or an attestation by the mediator would simply be to prove its involvement in the process and should not be construed as an endorsement of the settlement agreement nor an indication that the mediator was a party to the settlement agreement. And in the absence of any of the suggested evidence, any other evidence acceptable to the competent authority may be produced as well. However, the Singapore Convention further expands on how the requirement that a settlement agreement shall be signed by the parties or, where applicable, the mediator is met concerning electronic communication.

Furthermore, Article 19 of the 2018 Model Law grants discretion to the competent authority to adjourn the decision and/or order security in situations where the decision of another court or arbitral tribunal may affect the relief being sought before it. The provision applies to both when enforcement of a settlement agreement is sought and when a settlement agreement is invoked as a defense.

40. Stamp Act, 1899, Art. 12 schedule I (specifying the stamp duty payable on an arbitral award).
41. ILR 2008 Kar 3850.
42. *See* Bengal Immunity Company Limited v. State of Bihar, AIR 1955 SC 661.

[M] Confidentiality (Section 75)

> 75. Confidentiality—Notwithstanding anything contained in any other law for the time being in force, the conciliator and the parties shall keep confidential all matters relating to the conciliation proceedings. Confidentiality shall extend also to the settlement agreement, except where its disclosure is necessary for purposes of implementation and enforcement.

Section 75 of the ACA appears as a nonobstante provision, which casts an absolute duty on the conciliator(s) and the parties/participants to keep all matters relating to the conciliation proceedings confidential. The words "all matters relating to the conciliation" are broad enough to cover any information disclosed/exchanged during the conciliation proceedings, as well as the substance and the result of those proceedings. This would include discussions concerning the desirability of conciliation, the terms of an agreement to conciliate, the choice of conciliators, an invitation to conciliate, and the acceptance or rejection of such an invitation. The protection of confidentiality under section 75 prevails despite any other law in force.

Hence, anything disclosed, discussed, or proposed by the parties before the mediator cannot be recorded, much less divulged. The ethos of mediation bars any disclosure of communications and writings associated with the mediation. This is how parties are encouraged during mediation to engage in honest discussions as regards their problems. For example, in matrimonial disputes, these honest discussions often give rise to a better understanding between the couple. Spouses are emboldened to forget and forgive. But if anyone is under the apprehension that a well-meant, open discussion will be subsequently used against him, it would hamper unreserved considerations between the parties. An atmosphere of mutual trust warrants complete confidentiality.

Regarding the related issue of confidentiality of mediation proceedings under section 89 of the CPC, the Supreme Court has held that they are confidential.[43]

A related aspect is the application of the "without prejudice" in settlement negotiations. Generally, communications are often conditioned as "without prejudice" to protect the author of the letter or the document. But such additions do not always provide blanket protection against any liabilities. There are exceptions to this rule. Genuine settlement negotiations are usually treated as "without prejudice," irrespective of whether the phrase "without prejudice" was used. Therefore, in negotiation scenarios, it would simply not be permissible to use them in court as evidence of admissions against the party's interests that made the admissions. Although, an

43. *See* Moti Ram v. Ashok Kumar & Ors. (2011) 1 SCC 466. Cf. Perry Kansagra v. Smriti Madan Kansagra (2019) 20 SCC 753 (but where the scope of mediation is the solution of a child parenting issue, report by a mediator or a child counsellor concerning the behavior and attitude of the child would not fall within the bar of confidentiality for the reason no information shared by the couple is being brought on record. The mandate of section 12 of the Family Courts Act, 1984 cannot be lost sight of).

exception may be where it is necessary to ascertain whether the parties have concluded a settlement or not.[44] A conciliation is, after all, a without prejudice negotiation,[45] and the "without prejudice" rules (including its exceptions) would also apply in the context of conciliation under Part III of the ACA.

Confidentiality under section 75 also extends to the settlement agreement, except where its disclosure is necessary to implement and enforce the settlement agreement. This may include a court action to set aside an award on agreed terms or to set up a defense that the matter has already been resolved, or if it is required of the conciliator or the parties to reveal information about a threat that a person will suffer death or substantial bodily harm if the information is not disclosed, or (similarly) if it is required of the conciliator or the parties to disclose as it would be in the public interest (for example) to alert the public about a health or environmental or safety risk.[46]

Even though section 75 does not provide an illustrative or exhaustive list of possible exceptions to the general rule on confidentiality, a court considering an allegation that a party (or the conciliator) did not comply with section 75 would need to balance the competing interests.[47] It would also need consideration for any evidence of the parties' conduct that shows whether they had, or did not have, an understanding that a conciliation existed and consequently whether confidentiality was expected. *See* discussion under section 62, *infra*.

[N] Termination of Conciliation Proceedings (Section 76)

> 76. Termination of conciliation proceedings—
>
> The conciliation proceedings shall be terminated—(a) by the signing of the settlement agreement by the parties, on the date of the agreement; or

44. *See generally*, Unilever Plc v. Proctor & Gamble Co., [2000] 1 WLR. *See also* Manna v. Central Manchester University Hospitals NHS Foundation Trust, [2017] EWCA Civ 12 (that the defendant's conduct in negotiations should not attract any sanction in costs and said that, in his view, a judge should be very slow to entertain a discussion as to whether parties to litigation have negotiated in a reasonable manner. Such an inquiry opens the prospect of undesirable and wasteful satellite litigation, as the reasonableness of a negotiating stance will usually depend upon a careful evaluation of the respective states of knowledge of the parties).
45. *See* Reed Executive Plc v. Reed Business Information Ltd [2004] EWCA Civ 887 (no distinction should be drawn between party-to-party negotiations and negotiations conducted within a mediation. Both are to be treated as subject to the without prejudice rule). *See also*, Brown v. Rice & Ors., [2007] EWHC 625 (Ch) (communications during the mediation process could be admitted as evidence to establish whether a settlement had been reached).
46. *See* UNGA A/CN.9/514, *supra* note 28, ¶ 60.
47. *See*, e.g., Perry Kansagra v. Smriti Madan Kansagra (2019) 20 SCC 753 (that the normal principle of confidentiality will not apply in matters concerning custody or guardianship issues and the court, in the best interest of the child, must be equipped with all the material touching upon relevant issues in order to render complete justice. This departure from confidentially is consistent with the underlined theme of the Family Court Act, in general, and section 12 of the said, in particular).

(b) by a written declaration of the conciliator, after consultation with the parties, to the effect that further efforts at conciliation are no longer justified, on the date of the declaration; or

(c) by a written declaration of the parties addressed to the conciliator to the effect that the conciliation proceedings are terminated, on the date of the declaration; or

(d) by a written declaration of a party to the other party and the conciliator, if appointed, to the effect that the conciliation proceedings are terminated, on the date of the declaration.

Section 76 of the ACA provides for situations/conditions when conciliation proceedings shall be terminated. The following four circumstances are provided for:

(i) on the conclusion of the settlement agreement by the parties (on the date of the agreement). It contemplates a successful conciliation that results in the settlement of a dispute. But the provision uses the expression "conclusion" instead of "singing," which opens the possibility of settlement being entered in a form other than a signed document, viz., exchange of emails, or oral agreement;[48]

(ii) by a written declaration of the conciliator, after consultation with the parties, to the effect that further efforts at conciliation are no longer justified (on the date of the written declaration). This should also cover cases of abandonment by the parties (whether express or implied by the conduct). For example, it would be reasonable for a conciliator to consider further efforts futile if a party expresses most negatively that any prospects of conciliation are nil, or if a party refuses to consult or meet with the conciliator. The words "after consultation with the parties" should be interpreted rather limitedly to include only those cases where the conciliator has contacted the parties in an attempt to consult but receives no response. A conciliator must have the discretion to bring a conciliation to an end when it would be futile to proceed;

(iii) by a written declaration of the parties addressed to the conciliator to the effect that the mediation proceedings are terminated (on the date of the written declaration); or

(iv) by a written declaration of a party to the other party or parties and the conciliator, if appointed, to the effect that the conciliation proceedings are terminated (on the date of the declaration).

In addition to the grounds of termination specified in section 76, the ACA also contemplates termination under section 79(3), wherein if the deposits toward conciliation costs are not paid in full by both parties within 30 days of the instruction to do so, the conciliator may suspend the proceedings or may make a written declaration of

48. *See* UNGA A/CN.9/506, *supra* note 14, ¶ 88.

termination of the proceedings to the parties. Accordingly, the termination would be effective on the date of said declaration.

[O] Resort to Arbitration or Judicial Proceedings (Section 77)

> 77. Resort to arbitral or judicial proceedings—
>
> The parties shall not initiate, during the conciliation proceedings, any arbitral or judicial proceedings in respect of a dispute that is the subject-matter of the conciliation proceedings except that a party may initiate arbitral or judicial proceedings where, in his opinion, such proceedings are necessary for preserving his rights.

Section 77 of the ACA concerns parallel proceedings alongside conciliation. It prohibits parties from initiating any arbitral/judicial proceedings regarding the disputes, which is the subject matter of conciliation proceedings during the pendency of such conciliation proceedings. However, this prohibition is subject to the exception that where a party to the conciliation is of the opinion that arbitral/judicial proceedings are necessary for preserving his rights, the bar would not apply.

The words "in his opinion" (as in, the party's opinion) have an interesting connotation. The provision is based on the assumption that parties will effectively limit themselves in good faith to initiating arbitral or court proceedings in circumstances where such proceedings are truly necessary to preserve their rights.[49]

As per section 77, an action for emergency measures or urgent interim reliefs would not be affected by any conciliation proceeding commenced. Else, the entire purpose of a mechanism for urgent interim reliefs would be rendered redundant.[50] Thus, section 77 of the ACA reassures a harmonious working between parallel conciliatory and adjudicatory proceedings (which are only seemingly opposing) by considering the provision for urgent interim reliefs as a carve-out to the bar under section 77.

Article 14 of the 2018 Model Law provides similarly. However, its scope is much larger than section 77 in important ways. *First*, Article 14 contemplates not only ongoing mediations but also a pre-commencement scenario. Hence, where the parties have agreed to mediate and have expressly undertaken not to initiate arbitral/judicial proceedings concerning an existing or future dispute, such an undertaking shall be given effect by the arbitral tribunal or the court until the terms of the undertaking have been complied with, except to the extent necessary for a party, in its opinion, to

49. *See* UNGA A/CN.9/514, *supra* note 28, ¶ 76; UNGA A/57/17, *supra* note 26, ¶117.
50. *See* Charles Jarrosson, *Observations on Poire v. Tripier*, 19(3) Arb. Int'l 363, 366 (2003) (such a solution to seek an interim measure of protection was reserved by the Cour de Cassation); Ravindra Kumar Verma v. M/s BPTP Ltd & Anr. (2015) 147 DRJ 175, ¶¶ 8–12 (if the arbitration clause is read in a mandatory manner with respect to a prior requirement to be complied with before invoking arbitration, the same can result in serious and grave prejudice to a party).

preserve its rights. *Second*, Article 14 of the Model Law also provides that any initiation of arbitral/court proceedings shall not of itself be regarded as a waiver of the agreement to mediate or as a termination of the mediation proceedings.

Section 77 (or any other provision under Part III) provides nothing on the suspension of the limitation period. Until 2019, the position under Indian law was clear that there is no exclusion of the limitation period for conciliation (or negotiation, or mediation) under any of the provisions of the Limitation Act 1963 (including section 14 on the exclusion of time of proceeding bona fide in court without jurisdiction).[51] However, in *Geo Miller v. Rajasthan Vidyut Utpadan Nigam Ltd.* ("*Geo Miller*"),[52] the Supreme Court held that the time spent in "good faith" settlement discussions/ negotiations might be excluded to compute the limitation period for reference of the dispute to arbitration. However, this Supreme Court seems to have been only in the context of family disputes and only in respect of negotiations (not conciliation or other ADR processes like mediation or Dispute Resolution Boards, etc.).[53]

Hence, it would be reasonable to understand post-dispute negotiations in respect of a commercial dispute will be outside the purview of *Geo Miller*, as would conciliations under Part III of the ACA, which explicitly allows a party (under section 77) to invoke arbitral/judicial proceedings where it necessary for preserving his rights. Moreover, no law expressly bars parties from contractually extending the limitation period under the Limitation Act 1963.[54] Such an agreement would not be hit by section 28 of the Contract Act (only agreements that limit the period of limitation would be void).[55]

On this issue, the Model Law recommends a footnoted provision (for optional use) on the suspension of the limitation period. The following text is suggested:

> Article X. Suspension of limitation period
> 1. When the conciliation proceedings commence, the running of the limitation period regarding the claim that is the subject matter of the conciliation is suspended.
> 2. Where the conciliation proceedings have terminated without a settlement agreement, the limitation period resumes running from the time the conciliation ended without a settlement agreement.

There was strong opposition to retaining this article in the main text since it raised complex technical issues and would be difficult to incorporate into national

51. *See* Union of India v. M/s Baga Brother &Anr., 2017 SCC OnLine Del 8989, ¶¶ 8-11.
52. 2019 SCC OnLine SC 1137.
53. *Id.*, at ¶ 27.
54. Limitation Act, 1963, §3 (the provision does not deal expressly with consequences of agreements which contract around or alter the law of the limitation or the limitation periods prescribed in the said law. Section 3(1) reads: "Subject to the provisions contained in sections 4 to 24 (inclusive), every suit instituted, appeal preferred, and application made after the prescribed period shall be dismissed, although limitation has not been set up as a defence").
55. Indian Contract Act, 1872, §28 (the provision expressly bars agreements that limit the time within which a party may enforce its rights. The relevant portion of section 28 provides: "Every agreement- (b) ... which limits the time within which he may thus enforce his rights ... is void to that extent").

procedural regimes that took different approaches.[56] For example, it would require a high degree of precision as to what constituted the commencement of conciliation proceedings; but at the same time, requiring such a degree of precision could disregard the fundamentally informal and flexible nature of conciliation. Moreover, this would create a sort of expectations regarding its procedural implications that could potentially render it a mechanical requirement.

[P] Costs and Deposits (Sections 78 and 79)

78. Costs—

(1) Upon termination of the conciliation proceedings, the conciliator shall fix the costs of the conciliation and give written notice thereof to the parties.

(2) For the purpose of sub-section (1), "costs" means reasonable costs relating to—(a) the fee and expenses of the conciliator and witnesses requested by the conciliator with the consent of the parties;

(b) any expert advice requested by the conciliator with the consent of the parties;

(c) any assistance provided pursuant to clause (b) of sub-section (2) of section 64 and section 68.

(d) any other expenses incurred in connection with the conciliation proceedings and the settlement agreement.

(3) The costs shall be borne equally by the parties unless the settlement agreement provides for a different apportionment. All other expenses incurred by a party shall be borne by that party.

79. Deposits—

(1) The conciliator may direct each party to deposit an equal amount as an advance for the costs referred to in sub-section (2) of section 78 which he expects will be incurred.

(2) During the course of the conciliation proceedings, the conciliator may direct supplementary deposits in an equal amount from each party.

(3) If the required deposits under sub-sections (1) and (2) are not paid in full by both parties within thirty days, the conciliator may suspend the proceedings or may make a written declaration of termination of the proceedings to the parties, effective on the date of that declaration.

56. *See* UNGA A/CN.9/506, *supra* note 14, ¶¶ 93–94; *see* UNGA A/CN.9/514, *supra* note 28, ¶ 44.

(4) Upon termination of the conciliation proceedings, the conciliator shall render an accounting to the parties of the deposits received and shall return any unexpended balance to the parties.

Section 78 of the ACA requires that the conciliator fixes a reasonable cost of conciliation proceedings upon the termination of conciliation proceedings and give written notice to the parties. The provision explains the term "costs" as: (a) the fee and expenses of the conciliator and witnesses requested by the conciliator with the consent of the parties; (b) any expert advice requested by the conciliator with the consent of the parties; (c) any assistance provided pursuant to sections 64 and 68; and (d) any other expenses incurred in connection with the conciliation proceedings and the settlement agreement.

Section 78(3) also mandates that the costs be borne equally by the parties unless the settlement agreement provides for a different apportionment. All other expenses incurred by a party shall be borne by that party. In a way, the provision encourages an equal sharing of the burden of costs by enabling cooperation between the parties in this regard.

Further, section 78(3) of the ACA Act provides that the conciliator may direct each party to deposit an estimated equal amount in advance toward the costs. In case required, the conciliator may direct parties to deposit supplementary costs. The conciliator can suspend the proceedings in case parties fail to deposit the cost within 30 days of the instruction. Alternatively, the conciliation proceedings may be terminated by a written declaration of the failure to deposit (effective on the date of such written declaration). On termination proceedings, a conciliator is obligated to render accounts of the deposits received by him during the conciliation proceedings and return any unexpended balance to the parties.

[Q] Role of Conciliator in Other Proceedings (Section 80)

80. Role of conciliator in other proceedings—

Unless otherwise agreed by the parties—(a) the conciliator shall not act as an arbitrator or as a representative or counsel of a party in any arbitral or judicial proceeding in respect of a dispute that is the subject of the conciliation proceedings;

(b) the conciliator shall not be presented by the parties as a witness in any arbitral or judicial proceedings.

Section 80(a) categorically provides that the conciliator shall not act as an arbitrator or as a representative or counsel of a party in any arbitral/judicial proceedings regarding a dispute that is the subject of conciliation proceedings. This default rule can, of course, be modified by an agreement of the parties. Further, section 80(b) states that the parties shall not present a conciliator as witnesses in any arbitral/judicial proceedings. Hence, it avoids any conflict of interest and prejudice to the parties.

One issue that section 80 does not cover is that of an arbitrator changing hats and assuming the role of a mediator. Although, on closer look, section 30 of the ACA is indicative of this, i.e., allowing the possibility of an arbitrator turning into a mediator. For more on neutrals changing hats, *see* Chapter on Mixed-Mode Dispute Resolution, *infra*.

[R] Admissibility of Evidence in Other Proceedings (Section 81)

81. Admissibility of evidence in other proceedings—

The parties shall not rely on or introduce as evidence in arbitral or judicial proceedings, whether or not such proceedings relate to the dispute that is the subject of the conciliation proceedings—

(a) views expressed or suggestions made by the other party in respect of a possible settlement of the dispute;
(b) admissions made by the other party in the course of the conciliation proceedings;
(c) proposals made by the conciliator;
(d) the fact that the other party had indicated his willingness to accept a proposal for settlement made by the conciliator.

Section 81 restricts the use, reliance, or introduction of anything from the conciliation proceedings as evidence in any arbitral/judicial proceedings, whether or not such arbitral/judicial proceedings relating to the dispute are the subject of the conciliation proceedings. Hence, the scope of section 81 extends not only to subsequent proceedings related to the conciliation but also to subsequent unrelated proceedings.

The provision enumerates various matters, which shall be considered inadmissible as evidence and include: (a) views expressed or suggestions made by the other party in respect of a possible settlement of the dispute; (b) admissions made by the other party in the course of the conciliation proceedings; (c) proposals made by the conciliator; (d) the fact that the other party had indicated his willingness to accept a proposal for settlement made by the conciliator. Reasonably, section 81 is intended to apply broadly to the range of information or evidence, whether it appears in the form of a written document, an oral statement, or electronic messages.

Considering the scope matters that are inadmissible as evidence in other proceedings, a clear distinction is warranted between documents that are prepared solely for purposes of the conciliation proceedings and those that are not. Often documents, reports, statements, etc., are prepared, not specifically for the conciliation but for other purposes and/or would have existed before the conciliation. By presenting these in the conciliation proceedings, it should not be understood that the party has forfeited its use in any subsequent proceedings or otherwise made it inadmissible. That would be absurd. Only such documents should be considered inadmissible, which are prepared solely for the conciliation proceedings. These would include not only statements of the parties but also, for example, witness statements and expert opinions.

The 2018 Model Law, in Article 11(5), illustrates a simple test: evidence that is otherwise admissible in arbitral or judicial proceedings would not become inadmissible as a consequence of having been used in a conciliation. In other words, only statements (views, proposals, etc.) made in conciliation proceedings, as enumerated in section 81, should be inadmissible, but the inadmissibility should not extend to any underlying evidence that may have given rise to those statements.[57] For example, in a dispute concerning a contract of carriage of goods by sea, a bill of lading would be admissible to prove the shipper's name, notwithstanding its prior use in a conciliation.

Relatedly, section 81 is also vacuous on the implication of presenting a privileged document in conciliation (which may or may not be solely for the conciliation). For example, in written communication between a client and his advocate, which is protected by privilege but can be waived, the client relies on the privileged document in a proceeding. To facilitate a settlement, if at all a privileged document is used, the court would need to balance the competing interests involved but, ultimately, side with the integrity and confidentiality of the process (meant to facilitate a mutually agreeable settlement). Accordingly, the use of a privileged document in conciliation proceedings should not be considered by courts as a waiver of the privilege.[58]

The motif of this provision is to protect the core characteristic of conciliation, which is its open forum that encourages parties to be forthcoming and approach settlements using concessions and admissions. Hence, the offers before a conciliator cannot be treated as an admission by a party and by their very nature are without prejudice to the respective rights and contentions of the offeror.[59]

If there are insidious encroachments on confidentiality, a free and fair settlement may never reach, thus stultifying the object sought to be achieved by Part III of the ACA.[60] But for section 81 to play out, the process must specifically be conciliation, and there must be a conciliator.[61] For example, section 81 would not be attracted where an arbitrator did not change hats and play the role of a conciliator or mediator but merely recorded an offer and counteroffer.[62] Similarly, a Commissioner's Report, which did not contain any suggestions of conciliation or how the matter could be resolved between the parties, could not be excluded by virtue of section 81.[63] And even though

57. *See* UNGA A/CN.9/514, *supra* note 28, ¶ 67.
58. *Id.*, at ¶ 68.
59. *See* Syndicate Bank v. B.N. Pandey, 2010 SCC OnLine Del 2250, ¶¶ 7, 8, and 11.
60. *See* Govind Prasad Sharma v. Doon Valley Officers Cooperative Housing Society Ltd. (2018) 11 SCC 501, ¶ 7.
61. *See* ITI Ltd. v. Par Pressings, 2011 SCC OnLine Del 3853, ¶ 35.
62. *See* Bombay Colour Lab v. Jindal Photo Films Ltd., 2009 SCC OnLine Del 3909, ¶ 12.
63. *See* Gajanan Sakaram Taleigaonkar v. Raghurai Tamba (2007), paras. 5-6.

the Commissioner was appointed in the conciliation proceedings, what was considered important is the role he was expected to play.[64]

The 2018 Model Law similarly provides for this under Article 11 but is more extensive and wider in scope. It not only includes the mediator but also "any third person," which would also comprise witnesses, experts, and those involved in the administration of the mediation proceedings (like a mediation institution or center). Article 11 states that they shall not be introduced as evidence or give any testimony or evidence on matters including any invitation by a party to engage in mediation proceedings or the fact that a party was willing to participate in mediation proceedings; or any document prepared solely for purposes of the mediation proceedings. The bar placed is irrespective of the form of the information or evidence enumerated under Article 11.

The Model Law also places a corresponding bar on courts/arbitral tribunals—that such evidence or testimony shall not be ordered by an arbitral tribunal, court, or other competent governmental authority. And that if such information is offered as evidence in contravention of the article, that evidence shall be treated as inadmissible. However, Article 11 of the Model Law also makes some exceptions. Accordingly, only such information may be disclosed or admitted in evidence to the extent required under the law or for implementation or enforcement of a settlement agreement. But evidence that is otherwise admissible in arbitral, judicial, or similar proceedings does not become inadmissible due to having been used in a mediation.

64. *Id.*

CHAPTER 16
Ready, Set, Mediate: *For the Mediator*

Judith B. Ittig & Gracious Timothy Dunna

I never blame myself when I'm not hitting. I just blame the bat and if it keeps up, I change bats. After all, if I know it isn't my fault that I'm not hitting, how can I get mad at myself?

—Yogi Berra

§16.01 INTRODUCTION

There is a lot to be learned from watching others mediate. But unless a mediator is still practicing as a mediation advocate, it is highly unlikely that the mediator will have opportunities to observe other mediators and the successful techniques and approaches they use.

This chapter addresses the techniques and approaches that experienced mediators have found to be most valuable in their preparation for a mediation. These subjects have not been given much attention, but they are critically important. The mediator's preparation for mediation is essential because it allows the mediator to fully devote all the mediator's abilities to the parties at the mediation session and give them every assistance to resolve their disputes.

The roadmap to mediation outlined in this chapter should enable a mediator to appropriately execute the managerial and administrative tasks of arranging a mediation and handle the challenges that regularly arise in mediation.

§16.02 RULES OF THE ROLE

[A] What You Are as a Mediator

You are neutral, impartial, a facilitator, in some cases an evaluator, and a confidant to the parties who claim to want to resolve their disputes but who need assistance from an independent third party to help them communicate with each other and fashion a resolution that will be acceptable to all.

The term "acceptable" is important to understand. The mediator's resolution helps the parties reach may not be one the parties feel is just or equitable, and it may not be the most satisfactory to the parties, but they are willing to accept it to terminate their disputes.

The challenge all mediators face is how to remain neutral. It is relatively easy to appear impartial. All you need to do is treat all parties fairly and respectfully and assist each of them as best you can to promote their positions. But, as you learn about their situations and evaluate what you have learned, the mediator develops his/her views about the legal foundation and factual basis of the parties' positions. Need you put those views aside?

In certain fields of mediation practice, such as commercial disputes, it is common for parties to appoint mediators who can take on an evaluative role. Beyond facilitating the parties' interactions, an evaluative mediator presents the parties with his/her evaluation of the merits of their arguments and helps the parties determine the strength and weaknesses of their arguments for relief. Although the evaluative approach is less common in India, mediators engage in varieties of evaluations such as reality testing and clearing an impasse.

What you are as a mediator is defined by the role you are willing to assume and whether the parties are agreeable to that role. Part of your mediation preparation is determining the parameters of your assignment and then being faithful to that unless you and the parties agree on a change. Depending on the important objectives to the parties, be they resolving the disputes/claims, repairing the relationship, or ending their association, different approaches may be needed.

[B] What You Are Not as a Mediator

You are not the parties' advocate, advisor, or any party's representative. In order to make sure the parties understand that limitation, many mediators include a disclaimer in their mediation agreement that makes it clear that the parties will not rely on them for legal advice or validation of their position. The following clause, or something very much like it, frequently appears in mediation agreements and should be suitably considered by mediators:

> The parties understand that the mediator is acting exclusively in a neutral capacity, does not provide legal advice, and is not acting as an advocate or an advisor for any party to the mediation. The mediator facilitates the negotiations but may not force the parties to agree or impose her views of what the agreement should be. A party

> whom an advocate does not represent may consult with an advocate at any time during the mediation and are encouraged to do so. The parties acknowledge that the mediator has informed them that each party should have any draft settlement agreement reviewed by an advocate or waive that opportunity before an agreement is executed.

Some mediators go further and include an additional clause in their mediation agreements, along the following lines:

> The parties acknowledge that the mediator has consulted with them before the beginning of the mediation session about the nature of the mediation process, the limitations on the use of the mediator's evaluation, the mediator's approach, style and subject matter expertise, and the parties' expectations regarding the mediation process. The parties agree that the mediator may use evaluative techniques in this mediation if the mediator believes that such an evaluative method will be helpful and appropriate. The parties agree that they will not rely upon the mediator for any legal advice related to this dispute.

The parties need to know what you are promising to do and what constraints there may be in your role as mediator. Part of the mediator's preparation for the mediation is making certain that this information is communicated to the parties at the outset of the mediation. Sample mediation agreements are provided in Appendices 1 and 2.

§16.03 LEANING INTO MEDIATION

[A] Pre-mediation Chores

Before the mediation session date, there is much for the mediator to do personally. Not only does the mediator need to be educated about the issues that are in conflict but also should the mediator learn about the procedural posture of the dispute. Are the parties currently or soon to be in litigation or arbitration? Have they undertaken a prior, but failed, mediation? Are they in mediation voluntarily, or have they been ordered to mediate by a court or a requirement in their contract?

It is vitally important to find out if the parties have sufficient information about the disputes. Have the parties engaged in discovery? If so, have they learned enough to engage in meaningful negotiation? If not, what information should the mediator assist the parties in obtaining before the mediation session? The mediator can usefully help the parties establish a protocol for the exchange of information.

Who will attend the mediation session is a vitally important question that the mediator should pose. Ensure that the parties agree that the persons with knowledge of the dispute and those with authority to resolve the dispute and bind the parties will be present, or at least available for consultation, at the mediation session.

Ask the parties how they would prefer to begin the mediation session. Do they each want to present a detailed introduction or complete presentation of the facts and their position, or would they prefer a brief introduction or no opening presentation at all? When the parties have exchanged mediation statements, the mediator should find out whether there are sufficient reasons to take the time for opening statements.

As an alternative to the parties' giving an opening presentation, the mediator could explain his understanding of the disputes that need to be addressed and introduce the topics to be discussed. The benefits of this alternative are that the mediator can demonstrate his command of the material facts and disputed issues, and the parties can add or clarify that understanding.

How the parties describe the opening presentation can give the mediator insights into how cooperative the parties can be with each other, the level of emotion and hard feelings that may exist, and the general respect they may or may not have for one another or some of the mediation attendees. What they say or do not say about the opening presentation helps inform your decision on whether to proceed with joint sessions or keep the parties separated and begin immediately with private caucuses.

Finally, the mediator needs to emphasize to the parties the importance of properly educating the mediator about the dispute in advance of the mediation session. Ask the parties about the documents they will be providing and whether they will be exchanging the mediation statements and other materials that they submit to you. Feel free to invite the parties to send confidential notes and materials to you "for the mediator's eyes only." The freedom to have separate, private discussions with each party before the mediation session is an important aspect of mediation that differs from litigation and arbitration. Those separate conferences are a way for the mediator to learn about aspects of the dispute that often are not contained in more formal, written submissions to the mediator.

A basic checklist for a pre-mediation conference with the parties is provided below. You are encouraged to amend or revise this checklist as you see fit for different types of mediations.

Checklist for Pre-mediation Session Conference

(i) Discuss the dispute's procedural posture, including whether:
  - the parties are currently in litigation or arbitration;
  - the judge or arbitrator ordered mediation or mediation is compelled by the parties' contract;
  - the parties have already engaged in extensive evidentiary submissions.

(ii) Discuss whether a limited, informal exchange of documents and information may lead to a more productive mediation and, if so, establish a framework for that exchange.

(iii) Identify the attendees to the mediation session and clarify the participants' respective roles, including:
  - which of the participants have the authority to resolve the dispute; and
  - whether anyone with possible influence over the decision-maker should also attend.

(iv) Determine the contents, scheduling, and parameters to exchange any pre-mediation submissions requested by the mediator.

(v) Be sure the parties know that a mediator can speak privately and separately with them before the mediation commences. Arrange meetings, telephone conferences, or virtual platform conferences with each party as advisable. You may also give the parties your contact information and let them know they are permitted to contact you separately in advance of the mediation.
(vi) Set the date and start time of the mediation session.
(vii) Ensure that all participants know that the mediation may require their attendance for longer than normal working hours and that they commit to staying engaged in the mediation for the duration.
(viii) Discuss how the mediation will be commenced. Will the parties make opening presentations of some length, or would they prefer to give brief introductory statements?
(ix) Identify the locations from which each participant is attending the mediation.
(x) If a remote platform will be used for some or all participants, make those arrangements. Note that participants unfamiliar with the technology may want to have a practice or test session in advance of the mediation.
(xi) For mediations conducted remotely by a virtual platform, establish and review the features of the remote platform and the protocols to which the participants must adhere during the virtual mediation session. Typical protocols require that each participant have a strong and reliable internet connection, that each participant is in a private space during the mediation with no distractions, that persons who are not listed as attendees cannot be present with them during the mediation, and that they may not record the mediation session.
(xii) If the mediation is being administered by the mediator alone without the assistance of an administering body, describe your billing practice and make sure the parties understand that you will be sending them an engagement agreement that they must sign in advance of the mediation.

[B] Parties and Advocates Getting to Know You

Some mediators begin the mediation with an introduction about their knowledge of the field of law at issue and their broad experience as mediators. But it is a challenge to talk about yourself without appearing to be boastful and seemingly self-important. Bear in mind that in cases where the parties and their advocates have more experience than the mediator, a recitation of your experience and knowledge can be underwhelming. Also, as the parties and their advocates are most interested in their dispute, not the mediator's accomplishments, the mediator's introduction about his/her background may be perceived as not getting to the problem at hand.

Training programs for mediators commonly teach mediators to begin the mediation session with opening statements of introduction highlighting the mediator's experience. We think there is a more effective way, although we recognize that the most appropriate method is occasionally dependent on the parties' circumstances, and cultural perceptions.[1]

Most of us have a firmer memory of answers we have sought, as opposed to information that is delivered to us before we are readied to receive it. When a person asks a question of a mediator, for example, "how many mediations have you conducted and what types of issues were in dispute," the questioner is curious and will pay attention to the response from the mediator. On the other hand, when the mediator recites a resume of mediation experience without being asked, it is likely that the parties are not really attentive.

Opening remarks by the mediator about his/her qualifications and experience are being delivered to parties when they may be least interested. Their focus at that point is mainly on why they are there and what the process is going to do for them. They are not receptive to having the mediator promote his skills before they have seen the mediator perform.

As the mediation progresses and the mediator has private conversations with the parties, numerous opportunities will arise to tell the parties about your prior experiences with similar issues and disputes. By that time, the parties will be more at ease with you, and they are likely to be genuinely interested in you and your background. You then may be able to relate experiences that help the parties understand and deal with their predicaments.

Responding to parties' inquiries is far less self-promotional than opening the mediation session with a synopsis of your CV. Highlighting your own experiences in an introduction may work at cross-purposes if the parties believe they have more experience than you. You do not want to reduce your influence and put yourself at an immediate disadvantage. Sharing your experiences with the parties when it pertains to the situation and responding to the parties' natural curiosity about you as they work with you on settlement are valuable ways to cement their trust in you.

There are two other ways for the parties and their advocates to get to know you. First, arrive at the mediation session early enough to introduce yourself to each party separately. They are likely to be in separate rooms at this time, and visiting them for a few minutes in advance of the mediation session lets you give them an informal "hello" and discuss how the session will start. We know of several mediators who like to have breakfast or dinner beforehand with each party, not necessarily to talk about the dispute but to get to know one another. Second, as the mediation progresses, we find that parties and their advocates begin to make their inquiries to the mediator about his/her background. Because generally, people are most attentive when they have asked the questions, the mediator will have their interest when this curiosity surfaces.

1. It should be recognized, however, that some parties (given their cultural background or personal perceptions) want to be reassured that the one mediating their dispute is accomplished and illustrious and accordingly be convinced about the mediator's competence and trustworthiness.

[C] Getting to Know Parties and Advocates

One approach that works well is to use "mediation downtime" to converse with the parties about their interests and work. During the mediation session, there are bound to be times when the mediator is waiting while a party has a confidential discussion with counsel or others back in the home office. Use this time not only to let the other party know what is being discussed in the other room but also to engage them in general conversation.

These general conversations can help you learn behind the scenes information about their priorities for settlement and their manner of analysis of settlement offers. When there is more than one representative from a party or multiple interests in the room, for example, insurers and their clients and experts for the party, the mediator needs to find out who the real decision-maker is and what influences the others have in decision-making. General conversations with the group can reveal to the mediator: Who defers to whom, who exhibits leadership qualities, who is likely to be the more stubborn or intransigent in his views.

The important point is that the mediator should take advantage of every opportunity—every break in the mediation, every lunchtime, every caucus—to get to know the parties/party representatives, their advocates, and their other advisors. What the mediator learns about them as individuals will be of immense help in figuring out what is meaningful to them in the negotiations and how they will absorb and deal with the information the mediator will be conveying throughout the mediation session.

§16.04 MEDIATOR AT THE GATE

[A] Expressing Neutrality and Impartiality

The mediator's knowledge and experience with the subject matter of the dispute and your track record of successful negotiations need to be communicated to the parties and their advocates. This information is important to the disputants—it gives them a basis for trusting the mediator, and it promotes the parties' confidence that spending their time in mediation will prove worthwhile.

The mediator's opening statement is an important phase. In the opening statement, the mediator can demonstrate his understanding of the dispute and begin to direct the parties to the areas of discussion that are most likely to lead to resolution. "Salting the dish" shows that you know what the problems are, and you are giving the parties and their advocates a way to orient themselves to the purpose of the mediation—to look to a future with their dispute behind them.

At the outset of every mediation, it is important to tell the parties that you will be neutral and impartial in your dealings with everyone. It is equally essential to demonstrate your continuing neutrality/impartiality throughout the session. How do you do that?

Parties are very conscious of the amount of time you spend separately with them and the others, and they often draw inaccurate conclusions about how you divide your time. Some think that the more time you spend with them means that you are trying to get them to compromise and the less you are working with the other party to get them to meet the demands. Others think the opposite—that the more time you spend with the other side, the more helpful you are to them.

Overcoming these concerns is part of your job as a mediator. Explain to the parties at the outset and throughout the mediation that the distribution of your time with one party or another is not intended to slight or benefit anyone but is a measure of a lot of factors, which include the number of persons who need to be consulted for each side, the number of issues that have to be addressed, the difficulty of certain issues, the variety of paces that different people use to communicate, etc. Keep in mind that your conduct (physical cues/nonverbal communication) is being scrutinized by the participants, positively and negatively. For instance, when in a caucus, leaning gently toward the party reflects attentive listening, or turning your chair and body toward the party reinforces the commitment to give the party your undivided attention.

When expressing concerns about a party's position on an issue, you can demonstrate neutrality by posing the concerns as those of the other side, not as your own. For example, rather than saying to a party, "The amount you are claiming for extra work is not consistent with the schedule of values in the contract," you could instead say, "The other side has raised concerns about how you are valuing your extra work, and they need to know if and why it differs from the BOQ or itemized values in the contract for that type of work." Describing the problem as the other party's (not yours) allows the party to see the problems he is encountering with his calculations without concluding that you have become impartial.

Asking questions, probing a party's strengths and weaknesses in its position can be done neutrally. Instead of criticizing the position, help the party analyze from the other side's perspective. This approach is evaluative, but instead of being adversarial, it enables each party to see the problems the other side has with the issues, gives them the means to address those problems, and provides you with information and analysis that you can take back to the other side.

[B] Mediator's Commitment to the Process and the Parties

Mediators undertake commitments to the process and the parties when they enter a mediation. Mediators promise dedication, persistence, confidentiality, and impartiality.

Parties and their advocates highly value dedication and persistence, so much so that one mediator has said that when the parties hire me, they hire me for life! If the mediation session ends without a settlement being reached, that does not mean the mediator's work is over.

First, you should document with the parties any interim or partial agreements (or agreements in principle) that they have reached. Doing so gives a starting point for continued discussions.

Second, check in with them after the mediation session. Some time for reflection and possibly consultation with others whom the parties trust may have resulted in continued interest in the negotiations.

Third, as the mediator, you may have reflected after the session on points that could have been made or emphasized that could open the parties' thinking about reengaging. Do not be hesitant about contacting the parties to discuss these thoughts.

Some of our mediations have taken over a year to resolve. Some have even had to fail before they could be restarted and settled. In many of those cases, there were no additional in-person mediation sessions but multiple telephone conferences and emails to keep the negotiations (or the thought process) active and moving forward.

[C] Mental and Physical Challenges

In mediation, there is rarely any downtime for the mediator, and if there is, the mediator should use it to engage the parties in some way. Mediators find themselves going from caucus room to caucus room, bringing parties together when useful, and engaging with individuals or "executive" groups they have formed to address particular problems. There is either little or no opportunity to take a break, have a meal, or time to contemplate.

Most mediation sessions take many hours, even days of work. The expenditure of the mental energy required of a mediator can be as physically exhausting as a demanding workout.

Mediators know about these challenges, and they also know that the parties and their advocates are experiencing the same reactions to the pace and stress of mediation, but they do not all know how to cope with them. Here are some suggestions.

Keep parties informed/give homework

One of the stresses for the parties in mediation is the amount of downtime they must endure. People differ considerably in how they process information, how much explanation they need, how quickly they can react to new information about the dispute, and proposals for resolution. These considerations can result in the mediator spending a great deal of time with the parties separately.

When these separate sessions are lengthy, the other party is wondering: What is transpiring; if this mediation is advancing; are they wasting their time? The following are some suggestions to help parties cope with downtime:

- Explain that it may take longer for you to work with one party or the other as the mediation progresses. Acknowledge that you understand that in today's world, they have devices that enable them to do other work or entertain themselves, but that you will do your best to limit these idle periods.
- Check in with the idle party regularly. If you will be out of their room for a time, make it a point to return periodically and let them know what is happening and how long you predict the separate caucus will last.

- Give the idle party something to do that will aid the negotiations. This "homework" may be obtaining some additional information from others who are not present at the mediation or compiling a chart or timeline or other summaries that may help the other party analyze more effectively. If you are nearing the end of the mediation session with a resolution in sight, ask them to begin drafting the settlement agreement. We are not proposing "make work." Rather, there are usually information, positions, and/or arguments that can be discussed, compiled, consulted about, or obtained while you are engaged with the other party in a separate caucus. Keeping everyone busy and focused on resolving the dispute pays off because the more the parties dedicate their energy to finding a resolution, the more they have invested in devising a settlement outcome.

Get out of the space

Take a party or the advocate(s) for a walk around the block, or if there is a lobby or outside courtyard space, go sit there with them for a conversation about the dispute in a different setting.

Here is an illustration: Late in the day, as dusk was falling, the mediator happened by chance to see the CEO on her way to the elevator—the CEO had had enough and had just decided to leave for good. Seeing she was upset, the mediator led her to an empty, darkened room, sat her down, and said, "What is really going on? I know mediation is stressful, but you seem to be having a particularly bad reaction to this negotiation. Let us talk about it—and everything you tell me will be just between us."

Maybe it was those words, maybe it was the safe place she now found herself in, but whatever the reason she proceeded to describe her past personal conflicts with the other side's CEO, all of which might have seemed irrelevant to the dispute but all of which caused her to not want to deal with him any longer.

The dispute was settled within the next two hours. Why? Because the mediator gave her the opportunity to vent her frustrations, expose her feelings (in a setting different from a typical mediation room), and find a way to get past them to end the conflict.

Make sure you and the parties have lunch/dinner breaks

It has been often said that the best way to settlement is to keep the parties uncomfortable, without food or breaks. That can work, but why do it? It is difficult for parties to be away from their normal work life to engage in mediation, a situation that they find already foreign and uncomfortable. What is more, they often have to endure lengthy periods with little to do, while the mediator works with the other side. There is tension enough in the mediation process without having to create unnecessary hardship for the parties. A break for food with the mediator, if possible, can be an opportunity to engage the parties in a more casual way, which can often recharge them to look for different ways to resolve the dispute.

Change the dynamic

You do not have to spend all of your time as a mediator talking about the dispute. Find out what the party's interests are, how they affect his/her work life and decision-making.

Here is an illustration: The mediator and the party started discussing a popular TV game show in which the contestants were faced with a series of decision points—they could stop the game and keep their winnings up to that point, or they could continue the game with the prospect of either larger winnings or losing everything.

Because both the mediator and the party liked watching this game show, the mediator turned the conversation to strategic thinking: When should a contestant stop the game and keep his winnings? Is it wise to try to win the top prize money, or is it a better strategy to quit when the winnings reach a certain dollar value?

In a different way, the mediator was really asking if that party was willing to risk not taking a sound offer in favor of not settling and hoping to recover everything he was asking for in a court trial and how far did he think a good businessperson should go before determining that the money being offered was sufficient. Shortly thereafter, the party settled for a good deal, even though he did not get everything he had sought in his mediation demand.

Successful businesspeople know that it can make sense to get a good deal rather than risk no deal to get the best one. "The best is the enemy of the good" analysis helped the party see that the very same strategic thinking he used for the game show was the way he operated his business.

Deal with the discordant

Recognize that internal discord often exists within a party and take measures to deal with it. One approach is to divide the party representatives into smaller groups with specific tasks to perform. Forming an executive committee of only some of the party representatives can be helpful so long as everyone agrees that this executive committee will have the ultimate authority or at least that its recommendations will be given great weight. A more aggressive path is to find a way to dismiss the discordant person from the discussions. This approach can often work with experts or lower-tier management personnel who can be excluded from continuing negotiations on the grounds that their contributions have been made and considered.

Take, and give, the time that is needed

Working to settlement is not a rigid process with a built-in clock of a few hours or a day. If the parties need more time to, say, process the information they have obtained in mediation, consult with others, or spend more effort delving into matters at issue, then continue the mediation to another session. Those later sessions can be in person, by email, by telephone—or even all three methods—and the time interval between the mediation and the follow-up need not be immediate.

Here is an illustration: Year-end is an opportune time for parties to close out disputes. Many businesses like to book a settlement disbursement before the tax year ends. In the last quarter of the year, mediators can contact parties whose disputes did not settle and check in to see if there is an interest in reengaging.

This kind of "check-in" call is usually well received. Many settlements not obtainable earlier in the year have resulted from the desire to settle accounts before year-end. It also often happens that after leaving a mediation session with no settlement reached, the parties place that dispute on the back burner while they turn their attention to more pressing business and personal matters. Checking in with them after a time can reenergize their interest in the settlement negotiations. Your persistence shows them that you are a reliable ally in helping them resolve a problem.

[D] Prepping Yourself

Mediation is physically exhausting and mentally challenging for the mediator. In addition to the preparation that a mediator does in advance of the mediation session to understand the background of the dispute, the parties' interests and concerns, and potential settlement options, the mediator must undertake personal preparation to ready his/her mind and spirit.

Just before the mediation session begins, mediators feel internal mind and body pressures—they get "butterflies," they are nervous, some are fearful that they will not be able to resolve the dispute, others say they worry about how the parties and their advocates will perceive and react to them. There is no litany of things that you know you should do that will resolve a dispute. Insecurities arise because you never know exactly what you are confronting, and when it is over, and the dispute has been resolved, you are not always certain about what techniques solved the problems.

We have asked mediators from many different backgrounds, fields of practice, and locales to tell us what they do to prepare themselves. Initially, when we asked this question, they focused their answers on substantive preparation—what they did to become sufficiently knowledgeable about the dispute they had undertaken to resolve. But when we pressed them to reveal what they did for themselves, to make themselves ready, every one of them was stumped, at first. Then, as we asked the same question in different ways and queried them about what they did in an hour or two before they entered the mediation session, each one revealed that he/she had a routine that they had not even thought much about before we inquired.

Here are some of the responses we received:

- Several mediators said they meditated. They went to a quiet place, alone for a time, sometimes for up to an hour, and tried to calm themselves and find a zone of peacefulness. Not all meditated in any structured way or had studied meditation techniques, but they all were looking to escape for a short time to a quieter world.
- Some mediators reported that they engaged in physical activity, such as running/jogging or working out, to expend their nervous energy and feel physically fit.

- A fewer number, but a sizeable group, said they gave themselves a "pep talk." Those pep talks took many forms. Some mediators posed in front of mirrors and told themselves—for some, out loud, or for others, silently—that they were fully ready and able to do the mediator's job and resolve the dispute. Others just had an internal conversation with themselves. All were basically saying to themselves, "I can do this. I know what I need to know, and I will find out what I have to do to obtain a settlement. I am ready!"

Research shows that silently repeating a phrase to yourself, such as "I can do it," is very effective when it comes to shoring up your brain's reaction time.[2] World-class athletes use a mantra like this one for mental motivation—sports psychologists call this "self-talk."[3] But forcing positive self-talk can be self-defeating. Instead (and perhaps more suitable to you as a mediator), offer yourself gentle instructions rather than purely motivational, overzealous monologues:

- One mediator says that she practices her voice and gestures in the hour before the mediation session by making a video of a sample opening statement on her smartphone. When she plays back the video, she watches carefully for voice modulation and what she calls "verbal tics" and repetitive gestures. Did she say "umm" too much, "okay" whenever she finished a thought, or play with her hair, touch her face, or fiddle with her glasses? She says the video makes her conscious of these annoying habits, and she is then primed to dispense with them when she meets with the parties.
- Some felt the need to energize themselves by listening to loud rock n' roll music in the car on the way to the mediation session.
- Others reported that before every mediation, they review Jon Lang's "The Pocket Mediator." This monograph summarizes the mediator's role and emphasizes some of the strategies that mediators use to resolve disputes. Reviewing this pocket guide helps these mediators focus on the various parts of mediation and reminds them of steps they should take in preparation for the mediation and during the mediation session.

No matter what method they had, these mediators had developed a routine that they relied upon to get mentally and physically prepared. They are convinced that they had to be confident before turning their full attention to the disputants.

Successful mediators immerse themselves in the process of mediation. They are not thinking about themselves; they think about the disputed issues, the parties' reactions, and what they can do to advance the discussions toward settlement.

2. *See* Elaine Mead, *What Is Positive Self-Talk?*, POSITIVE PSYCHOLOGY (Feb. 18, 2021), https://positivepsychology.com/positive-self talk/#: ~ :text = Positive%20self%2Dtalk%20isn't,from%20it%20for%20next%20time.
3. *See* Judy L. Van Raalte & Andrew Vincent, *Self-Talk in Sport and Performance*, OXFORD RESEARCH ENCYCLOPEDIAS—PSYCHOLOGY (Mar. 29, 2017), https://doi.org/10.1093/acrefore/9780190236557.013.157; Antonis Hatzigeorgiadis et al., *Self-Talk and Sport Performance: A Meta-Analysis*, 6(4) PERSPECT PSYCHOL SCI. 348–356 (2011).

The mediators who developed routines for their preparedness used a method that worked for them to get outside themselves. Their meditations, pep talks, or physical activities helped them feel centered and ready to take on the mediation challenges. Once they entered the mediation room, they were ready to concentrate, not on themselves, but everything important to settlement.

§16.05 THE ROAD LESS TRAVELED TO MEDIATION

[A] Location of the Mediation

The ideal location of the mediation session is neutral territory—away from the competing demands of a party's office environment. But, if the mediation is held in a party's office or advocate's law firm, ask to have a separate room set aside for you. It is helpful to have a separate space that you can use for meetings with an individual or part of a group.

Some mediators prefer using their facilities. We know of mediators who have created very accommodating spaces, some with outside patios and even soothing water features. Other mediators would rather not be the host so they can avoid disruption to their coworkers or the responsibility of seeing to the comfort of the attendees.

Think about what you prefer and what scene would work best for each mediation. These days, there are various dedicated facilities for alternative dispute resolution, which can be hired at the shared cost of the parties.

Here is an interesting illustration: For years, one of us brought her Labrador Retriever to her office every day. Every mediation held there resulted in a settlement, except only one—it will never be clear whether the dog's presence was a factor, but it was certain that one party did not like dogs, which had to be banished to an upper floor for the day. For everyone else, the dog was a calming influence, a welcome diversion, and a topic of conversation, indeed an icebreaker, for those who had pets of their own.

[B] Seating Arrangement

When most parties enter the meeting room, they choose a side and align themselves—each of the advocates sitting along one row of the table with their party representatives. Consider mixing them up, or at least have them circle the ends of the table with the mediator in the middle. This concept, well known to Sun Tzu,[4] is referred to as "mixing the flags."

4. Sun Tzu was a Chinese general, military strategist, writer and philosopher who lived in the Eastern Zhou period of ancient China. Sun Tzu is traditionally credited as the author of *The Art of War*, an influential work of military strategy that has affected both Western and East Asian philosophy and military thinking.

If you cannot mix everyone up at the beginning of the mediation session, such opportunities may arise as the session progresses. Consider the following two examples.

In one example, 10 parties were present for mediation about traffic control standards for roads in different jurisdictions in one country. One of us, as the mediator, identified several different issues that needed to be addressed and agreed upon by all the parties to resolve their disputes.

The mediator divided the parties into groups, with each group to address one of the issues and report its findings and conclusions to all the parties later in the day. The mediator asked the parties to agree in advance that they would accept the recommendations of each group unless there was an overwhelming obstacle to doing so.

The groups, comprised of representatives from the various parties (here the "flags" were mixed), all reported their conclusions and recommended protocols, which all parties found to be satisfactory. The disputes, which would have taken much time to resolve had they been addressed by all party representatives, were resolved in one day of mediation.

In another example, the employer and contractor (Joint Venture (JV) partners) had dredging and tree-cutting license issues. Without a resolution on these issues, their claims for extension of time and additional costs could not have been addressed. The employer initially thought that it would only negotiate with the lead partner of the JV. However, the mediator suggested (and the employer agreed) that the JV partners address the issues with their counterparts. The participants were grouped accordingly and were instructed to reconvene with their outcomes. This format proved successful in resolving the dispute, and it saved time and cost, increasing the efficiency of the mediation.

[C] Medium of the Mediator

In addition to seating the parties, their advocates, and their advisors, give thought throughout the mediation day to where you will sit. Most mediators begin the session at the head of the conference table, and that makes sense to establish authority and leadership.

Some mediators take the view that in a joint session, it is important to be impassive, looking straight ahead down the rectangular conference table and not showing any implicit favoritism by positioning themselves, so their body is not aligned toward either party. Others think that they should use their body language and facial expressions to show that they are attentive to the party or advocate who is speaking. There is no right or wrong way. But think about the nonverbal messages you are sending and adjust your physical self accordingly.

As the mediation session progresses, you should consider moving around. When in caucus, you may want to position yourself opposite the party and advocate, or stand for a time, or possibly sit next to a party representative or the advocate. Locating/placing yourself appropriately, vis-à-vis the other players, can send a nonverbal message along with what you are saying.

[D] Facilities

Ensure that the facilities you use for the mediation session have the technology you may need when it comes time for the settlement agreement to be drafted. Will there be secretarial assistance throughout the day? If the mediation session extends beyond normal business hours, will there be access to computers and a copy machine and someone who knows how to operate them?

Are the doors locked after hours so that access to restrooms is restricted? What about parking? Is there security for the building and garage after normal business hours? Make it part of your job to know whether any inconveniences will be experienced if the mediation session takes longer than the business day.

[E] Secretary

Like the appointment of an arbitral or tribunal secretary in international arbitrations, a mediator may consider appointing a junior mediator to assist him or the mediation panel if there is more than one mediator.

The secretary's role can include: (i) organizational and administrative tasks in setting up the mediation session as well as assisting the parties with any virtual platform use; (ii) review and summary of parties' documents and mediation statements along with needed research; (iii) note-taking during deliberations; (iv) memorializing proposals; and (v) reviewing the settlement agreement for basic compliances and coverage of agreed issues.

Besides the potential benefits in efficiency and cost savings that a secretary can bring to the mediation process, it is also a commendable way to benefit young mediators in developing their practice.

[F] Virtual Mediation

"Hysteresis" refers to an event in the economy that persists into the future, even after the factors that led to that event have been removed. The drastic shift in India and in many other nations in 2020 to virtual modes of conducting mediation sessions will likely continue for various objective and subjective reasons.

Mediators need to understand the salient features and limitations of remote platforms. While the virtual process remains substantially the same as any in-person mediation, the conversion of the format impacts its modalities and raises new requirements to fulfill.

A basic prerequisite for a virtual mediation must be a reliable and suitable platform to conduct the mediation session online. Mediators need to learn how to operate the platform with breakout rooms, waiting rooms, screen-sharing, and default mute and video options. Consider using at least two devices to pull up documents for easy reference and other multitasking purposes.

Take steps to ensure that there will be no recording of any kind and issue written and oral instructions to this effect. Occasionally, a viewer may see or hear things that were not supposed to be shared. Discuss in advance how participants should respond if that situation occurs. For instance, it may be agreed that upon such a disclosure, the participants will immediately refrain from listening or viewing and must immediately alert the mediator and/or the other party.

Use virtual breakout rooms with caution, being mindful about which participants should be inside/outside the created rooms to preserve confidentiality and privilege. If there is no "virtual knock" feature when someone enters a room, the sudden entrance can be awkward. Minimize the risk of such unexpected appearances by agreeing to a protocol: that participants (including the mediator) will announce in the chatbox before entering a room; or that participants will drop a text in a group chat (e.g., a WhatsApp group) to indicate his/her intention to enter the room.

Mediation sessions can be lengthy, creating a high chance of on-screen fatigue that may cause participants to lose attention or affect their decision-making. Consider taking regular breaks, reducing the amount of screen sharing, recommending that participants have access to hard copies of the mediation statements and documents for reference purposes, and adopting a dress code that is more informal than it would be in an in-person proceeding.

With the internet being so widely available, its users often work from public places such as coffee shops or airports, or they may be situated at home without a separate office space and where they may be interrupted by family members, visitors, or pets. Caution all mediation attendees that they should make every effort to avoid interruptions by family members, visitors, or pets. Insist that mediation attendees do not participate in the mediation from a public space and that persons not part of the mediation cannot be present with them or hear or see the communications. They need to ensure that they will be able to give everyone in the mediation their uninterrupted attention at all times.

§16.06 MEDIATOR'S MUSES

Ideal mediators possess and demonstrate several traits that make them our muses. These mediators are:

- Receptive and Curious: The participants must find you receptive and curious. You may use encouraging statements ("what you said makes things clear" or "that's useful information") or acknowledge their positions to reinforce their trust in you and the process ("I see your point" or "I understand what you are saying").
- Active Listeners: Listening actively is being a patient listener and comprehending what has been said. You can demonstrate that you actively listen by summarizing what you heard, reflecting (restatement of feelings and emotions in terms of the party's experience), or reframing (to help parties move from positions to interests to problem-solving).
- Good at Analyzing People and Positions: Effective mediators watch for and learn from an individual's subtle clues and signs that show whether the person

agrees, is disengaged, or is hostile. They also have developed a good sense of why a position is being taken, whether that position is nonnegotiable, and whether further discussion about that position will be fruitful with the mediator or with the opposing party. This ability derives from experience, not only in mediation but also from life experience in general.

- Creative Thinkers: Always be thinking about different ways to approach the dispute and its resolution. For example, is there another person not at the mediation who could be useful if invited to consult with and advise a party? Is it possible to set up a payment schedule rather than a lump sum payment? Could a party be enticed to settle at a lower amount if the party could share in recovery from future litigation or arbitration against someone else?
- Capable of Not Injecting Their Egos into the Dispute: It is not uncommon for parties to express anger, impatience, and disappointment and target the mediator with those complaints. A party may say: "Why are you letting this mediation take so long?" or "I don't think you are telling the other side what they need to know in order to settle." Of course, these are direct attacks on the mediator, but your response should not be defensive or retaliatory. Rather, explain to the complainer what you have been doing, why there is resistance from the other party, and treat these complaints as an opportunity for a collaborative discussion about what other approaches might be effective. Mediators who take criticisms personally lose the ability to be neutral, and they lose the control that they must exert to resolve the dispute.

§16.07 STAYING IN

[A] What to Do When You Are Not Working?

With all the demands on the mediator during a session, it seems unlikely that there will be much downtime for the mediator. But it often happens that the mediator is caught with little to do while a party has a private discussion.

When you cannot work with the party who wants some private time, this downtime should be used to advantage. The mediator has several options for how to fill this vacant space. The mediator could use that interval to report to the other party what is going on in the other room. Letting the other party know that private discussions are taking place helps them understand the pace of the mediation. The mediator can also use that time to go back to the other party to discuss the options being considered and whether anything new has been learned or thought of while the mediator was absent from that room.

If the parties see that you are working all the time, they often will respond with more commitment to the process themselves. It is difficult for parties to sit through long intervals of quiet time when the mediator is working with others. That is when hopelessness can set in. Keep their interest level high by engaging with them as often as possible, even if it is only to pop into their room when you have a break from discussions with the other party.

[B] What to Do When "It" Is Not Working?

It is helpful to tell the parties that you are open to altering the course of the mediation if progress is not being made and that you will welcome the parties' suggestions about other ways to advance the negotiations. Simply setting the problematic issues aside and working on the next steps or less difficult issues can result in interim agreements that lead to a dialogue on the entire dispute.

Periodically asking the parties whether the discussions are productive can open them to thinking about different avenues of approaching the dispute. This type of strategizing with the parties and their advocates can effectively restart their enthusiasm for resolving the dispute.

However, some situations need more than one mediation session to resolve. Perhaps the parties realize that more information-gathering is needed, or certain events must occur, such as a court ruling on a dispositive motion before negotiations should resume.

Avoid the trap of framing yourself to be responsible, which can (consciously or subconsciously) cause many mediators to falter. You must refrain from becoming frantic, desperate about failure, pushing/enforcing your suggestions upon the parties, and even inviting arguments/altercations. Stay calm. Parties who can raise a dispute need to know they are equally capable of resolving it (a burden that they must bear). As a mediator, you must trust the process and drive it effectively.

[C] Mediator's Proposal

If you have been able to narrow a monetary dispute to a range where settlement is likely, but the parties have not been able to agree, consider making a mediator's proposal. When suggesting this idea, explain how your proposal would be conveyed and that the agreement of all parties would be required for the proposal to be adopted as a settlement.

Commonly, the mediator's proposals are offered separately to each party, with each of them to notify the mediator, usually by a deadline, whether it would accept the proposal if the other party or parties accepted it as well. If all parties agree, the dispute is settled on the terms of the proposal. Where there are multiple parties, the mediator can keep each party's view blind, not revealing to other parties whether that party would have accepted it or not.

Mediators should think about how they will decide upon their proposal and explain it to the parties. Is the proposal based on the merits of the claims, is it the mediator's judgment of a fair settlement, or is it the mediator's decision to recommend a settlement that has a good chance of being accepted by the parties?

There are a variety of types of mediator proposals. Usually, they are nonbinding, but the parties could agree in advance to accept the result the mediator recommends. The proposal need not be a specific figure or set of terms of the settlement. Instead, it could be a range in which the final figure should fall or terms of the settlement with alternatives or options.

Be aware that there are dangers to the mediation with the mediator's proposal. Confidence in the mediator's judgment and impartiality could be weakened if a party thinks the proposal is unrealistic or demonstrates ignorance of the dispute or the parties' contract or other agreements. A party who interprets the mediator's proposal as too generous to the other party may conclude that the mediator has not been neutral.

Mediator proposals can be effective when offered with the full support of the parties, the timing is appropriate, and the proposals are thoughtfully prepared. If, however, the mediator's proposal is not accepted, the mediation need not end. In some instances, the mediator's proposal becomes a basis for further negotiations at the mediation session or the continuation of the mediation later.

[D] Continuing the Mediation

If the mediation needs to be continued, make certain that all the participants take time to decide on the next steps. Either memorialize them in writing at the close of the mediation session or, at least, send the parties confirmation of what will be done with a timeline.

Then, check in regularly to be sure that the next steps are being taken. If they are not, then find out why and, if necessary, amend the protocol. It is easy for parties and their advocates to return to the demands of their work and allow the mediation to simmer. Without the intervention of the mediator, the willingness to work on resolution can fade. A mediator must find ways to engage and drive the parties and their advocates in a positive direction.

It is also worth reminding the parties to approach the continuation of mediation with an open mind. Obviously, if the parties reach an agreement and the dispute is settled, the mediation is successful. However, if a settlement is not reached (or partly reached), the mediation may still have been valuable if it has resulted in a narrowing of issues in the case or if it has led the parties to understand their own and each other's case better, or if it helps to pave the way for settlement at a later stage in the proceedings.

[E] Documenting What Has Been Accomplished

Even a handwritten recitation of what has been accomplished is better than having no record. There is a tendency for parties who have left a mediation session unfinished to return to their original postures in the dispute. Nailing down what has been agreed to, even if those agreements are tentative/in principle and dependent on resolving the remaining items in dispute, may help forestall parties reposition themselves.

[F] Figure Out What Needs to Be Changed to Arrive at Settlement

The decision to terminate a mediation session, but keep the negotiations ongoing, is a point where the mediator's creativity is essential.

Talk to the advocates to elicit their ideas about what is needed to reenergize the negotiations. Are there other paths to a settlement that have not been explored? Are they and their clients still committed to resolving? If not, what changed? If so, what other avenues might be explored?

Do your mulling over the dispute. By now, you will have learned so much about what motivates each party, the hurdles they face, and other strategies that may need further exploration. Sharing your thoughts with the parties and the advocates may well aid you in developing a settlement structure that has appeal.

§16.08 CONCLUSION

This chapter has been all about you, the mediator—not the types of disputes the mediator may encounter, but how to present your best version of a mediator and resolve obstacles to settlement. Although mediators are not decision-makers, like arbitrators or judges, they are regarded by the parties as the negotiation leaders. Anything and everything you can do to gain their respect, win their trust, and direct the discussions are essential to resolving the dispute.

In India and many other countries and locales, mediation is underutilized and a reluctant choice for various reasons. Perhaps, it has been used too late or too early for the dispute, or through the wrong person/advocate/party team, or in the wrong environment, or without the requisite preparation or willingness to give it an honest and serious try. Consider the thoughts, experiences, and suggestions included in this chapter to expand your thinking about what you can do so you and the disputants will be ready and set to mediate to resolution.

APPENDIX 1: SAMPLE MEDIATION AGREEMENT 1

This agreement is dated [DATE].
PARTIES

(1) [NAME AND ADDRESS] (Party 1)
(2) [NAME AND ADDRESS] (Party 2)
(3) [NAME AND ADDRESS] (Mediator)

BACKGROUND

A dispute has arisen between the parties concerning [DESCRIPTION OF THE DISPUTE (the Dispute)].

By signing this agreement, Party 1 and Party 2 (the parties) agree to mediate their dispute on the terms and conditions set forth in this Agreement.

The mediator has agreed to facilitate the negotiations between the parties to help resolve their dispute.

AGREED TERMS

1. AUTHORITY
   1.1 The mediation shall be held and conducted according to this Agreement.
   1.2 The parties, by signing this Agreement, declare and affirm that they have the authority to settle the dispute and commit to the settlement terms.
2. PLACE AND TIME OF THE MEDIATION

   The mediation will take place at [PLACE] beginning at [TIME]. Any further meetings/sessions shall be arranged by the mediator with the consent of the parties.
3. LANGUAGE

   The language of the mediation shall be English. The parties will agree to produce English translations at the party's expense, submitting a document that is not written originally in English.
4. ROLE OF THE MEDIATOR
   4.1 The mediator is independent of and impartial to Party 1 and Party 2.
   4.2 The mediator acknowledges that the mediator has disclosed any prior contacts with all persons who will participate in the mediation, including the parties, their advocates and other representatives, and their experts and consultants. Prior contacts, if any, have been waived by the parties.
   4.3 The parties have satisfied themselves that the mediator is impartial and neutral and agree that the mediator will not be liable to the parties for any acts unless they are proved to be grossly negligent or with malice.

4.4 If, during the mediation, the mediator becomes aware of any circumstances that might reasonably be considered to affect the mediator's capacity to act impartially, the mediator will immediately inform the parties.

4.5 The parties recognize that the mediator will not offer legal advice or act as a legal advisor to either of them.

4.6 The mediator will not make decisions for the parties or impose a solution on them unless the parties mutually request that the mediator does so.

5. CONDUCT OF THE MEDIATION

5.1 The mediation shall be conducted in a manner that the mediator considers appropriate by taking the circumstances of the case and wishes of the parties into account. These steps may include:

(a) the exchange between the parties and provision to the mediator of written statements of the matters in dispute and supporting documents; and

(b) separate preliminary discussions with the mediator, by telephone, virtual platform, or in person, before the mediation.

5.2 The parties may have one or more persons, including those legally qualified, to assist and advise them in the mediation.

5.3 The mediator may obtain assistance or advice from a qualified person or expert with the parties' consent. The parties will bear the expenses incurred.

5.4 Each party and its representatives shall act in good faith and use their best endeavors to comply with the mediator's requests.

5.5 Each party shall, at the mediator's request, deliver or cause to be delivered such instruments and other documents at such times and places as are reasonably necessary or desirable.

5.6 The parties reserve their legal rights regarding the issues in dispute in the mediation that are not the subject of a settlement agreement between them.

6. MEDIATION FEES, EXPENSES, AND COSTS

6.1 The mediator's fee will be [AMOUNT]. The administrative fee will be [AMOUNT].

6.2 The parties shall share equally and shall be jointly and severally liable for the mediator's fees and expenses and all the other mediation costs.

6.3 Unless otherwise specified in any settlement agreement, the parties shall bear their legal costs of preparation for, participation in, and representation at the mediation.

6.4 If the mediation does not result in an agreement to resolve the disputes, each party agrees that any court or tribunal, which has the power to assess costs, may treat the costs of the mediation, including the mediator's fee, the legal costs incurred by the parties, and other administrative costs of the mediation as costs in the case concerning any litigation or arbitration.

7. CONFIDENTIALITY
   7.1 The entire mediation process, including all communications before and during the mediation, will be kept confidential by the parties, their representatives, and the mediator.
   7.2 Information communicated to the mediator in private during the mediation shall not be repeated to the other party or parties without the party's consent.
   7.3 The requirement of confidentiality will not apply where:
      (a) the parties consent in writing to specific disclosure;
      (b) disclosure is necessary to implement or enforce this Agreement or any settlement agreement;
      (c) the parties are required by law to make disclosure or report to appropriate authority; or
      (d) disclosure is provided for under the terms of any settlement agreement.
8. EXCLUSION OF LIABILITY AND INDEMNIFICATION
   8.1 The parties agree not to call the mediator as a witness, expert, arbitrator, or consultant in any litigation, arbitration, or any other legal proceedings relating to this or any other dispute.
   8.2 If any of the parties acts in breach of clause 8.1, that party will fully indemnify the mediator regarding all costs incurred.
9. TERMINATING THE MEDIATION

   The parties or the mediator may, in their absolute discretion, terminate the mediation at any time without giving a reason. The mediation will terminate upon the occurrence of any of the following events:
   (a) the mediator, for any reason whatsoever, is unable to continue to assist the parties in the resolution of the dispute;
   (b) the parties advise the mediator that they have not been able to arrive at a settlement, and they do not want to participate further in mediation;
   (c) the mediator declares that the mediation is at an impasse;
   (d) the time limit for mediation to conclude in the parties' dispute resolution agreement has expired, and no extension has been agreed upon by the parties; or
   (e) a settlement agreement has been executed by the parties.

10. SETTLEMENT
    No agreement as to the terms of any settlement resulting from the mediation proceedings shall be binding on the parties unless and until it is memorialized in writing and signed by the parties or their representatives.

Signed by [NAME]
for and on behalf of [NAME OF Party 1]
....

Signed by [NAME]
for and behalf of [NAME OF Party 2]
....

Signed by [NAME Mediator]
....

APPENDIX 2: SAMPLE MEDIATION AGREEMENT 2

THIS AGREEMENT is effective this ___ day of _____, among the undersigned in consideration of their desire to resolve existing disputes or controversies between them through the process of mediation, with the assistance of __________, the mediator.

By participating in the mediation, each party agrees to make a good faith attempt to settle this dispute through mediation. During the session, each party will have opportunities to discuss its interests and concerns candidly and to suggest possible solutions it believes would be fair and equitable. The mediator will decide when to hold joint and separate meetings with the parties and their representatives and will not disclose to other parties the information provided to her in confidence without the permission of the party disclosing the information.

In order to promote communication and facilitate the settlement process, the undersigned agree that all statements made during the course of the mediation are confidential and privileged settlement discussions, are made without prejudice to any party's position, are inadmissible for any purpose in any legal or administrative proceeding, except as allowed by statute, and are not subject to discovery. If any complaint against the mediator should arise because of this mediation, confidentiality will be waived with respect to that information necessary to present or defend against such a complaint.

This agreement of confidentiality extends to all information disclosed during the course of this mediation, including but not limited to all statements made by the mediator, each party, their advocates and other representatives, and all other persons in attendance. The undersigned parties agree that they will not seek, nor will they encourage or permit another on their behalf, to compel the mediator to disclose any such confidential information in any legal or administrative proceeding, or in discovery, or otherwise. The parties further agree that they may not introduce in evidence, or use for any other purpose whatsoever, any statement made by them or the mediator in the course of mediation, except as provided in the preceding paragraph.

In entering into this mediation, the parties agree that efforts to reach an agreement will continue until: (a) a settlement is reached; (b) one of the parties withdraws from the process; or (c) the mediator concludes and informs the parties that further efforts would not be useful. The mediation conference may be continued from time to time at the discretion of the mediator.

The parties understand that the mediator is acting exclusively in a neutral capacity, does not provide legal advice, and is not acting as an advocate for any party to the mediation. The mediator facilitates the negotiations but may not force the parties to agree or impose her own views of what the agreement should be. A party who is not represented by an advocate may consult with advocate at any time during the mediation and are encouraged to do so. The parties acknowledge that the mediator has informed them that each party should have any draft agreement reviewed by an advocate or should waive that opportunity before an agreement is executed.

Notwithstanding the conduct of this mediation by the mediator, the mediator is not precluded from serving as an arbitrator or mediator or acting for or against any party in the future, nor is any other advocate from [the mediator's firm] precluded from acting for or against any party on other matters, provided in any event that the issues do not arise out of or relate in any way to this dispute or the project from which it arises.

The parties acknowledge that the mediator has consulted with them prior to the beginning of the mediation session about the nature of the mediation process, the limitations on the use of the mediator's evaluation, the mediator's approach, style and subject matter expertise, and the parties' expectations regarding the mediation process. The parties agree that the mediator may use evaluative techniques in this mediation if the mediator believes that such an evaluative method will be helpful and appropriate.

The parties agree that they will not rely upon the mediator for any legal advice related to this dispute and that the mediator and any program under which this mediation is administered will not be liable for any act or omission in connection with any mediation conducted under this agreement unless the act or omission is made or done in bad faith, with malicious intent or in a manner exhibiting a willful, wanton disregard of the rights, safety or property of another.

If an agreement is reached, the parties, with the assistance of the mediator if requested, will draft a written memorandum of agreement stating the terms of the settlement. Upon the parties' signing, the memorandum of agreement will be a binding and enforceable legal contract that affects the legal rights of the parties.

The parties hereby acknowledge that they have satisfied themselves as to the impartiality of the mediator.

Signed before the commencement of the mediation by the persons whose signatures appear below:

______________________________ ______________________________

Signature Printed Name/Affiliation

______________________________ ______________________________

Signature Printed Name/Affiliation

CHAPTER 17

Ready, Set, Mediate: *For the Advocate*

*Judith B. Ittig & Gracious Timothy Dunna**

No matter how much the cats fight, there always seem to be plenty of kittens.

—Abraham Lincoln

§17.01 INTRODUCTION

There is a wide disparity among parties and their advocates in their preparation for mediation. At a mediation, when the mediator asked what efforts had been made to settle the dispute, one of the advocates said, truthfully and quite bluntly: "Nothing. That is why we are here. We thought you were going to take care of that."

It is correct that the mediator's role is to resolve the dispute, but leaving it entirely up to the mediator can make for a lengthy, costly, and potentially ineffective mediation. Advocates must prepare themselves and their clients for the mediation. If they do not, the mediation session might have to be continued while the parties obtain pertinent information, consult with other decision-makers, or ponder aspects of proposals for settlement that could have been considered beforehand. Worse, the parties may fail to reach a resolution when they could have succeeded.

The advocate used to court trials or arbitration must recognize the radical change in his role in a mediation setting. His training and experience in argumentation and cross-examination are valuable skills useful in mediation, but the mediation advocate must also develop and use completely different skill sets.

These skill sets include informing the client about mediation, persuading the client to consider mediation and making the decision to mediate, carefully selecting the

* The authors thank the American Bar Association (ABA) for permission to use materials from a work entitled "An Inside View of Mediation: How To Advance Your Interests" for a presentation given by Judith B. Ittig to the Forum on Construction Law.

mediator, preparing the client for the mediation, assembling the pertinent facts and law, presenting the client's positions and interests persuasively, considered and tempered advice-giving, and effectively using negotiation skills with the opposing party, its counsel, and the mediator.

Advocates should plan for every stage of mediation. This chapter is a guide to mediation for advocates who want to take an active role in designing a mediation that fits their client's needs and increases the likelihood that the mediation will resolve the dispute.

§17.02 WHY AND WHEN TO INITIATE MEDIATION

[A] Save Relationships

This reason may be frequently touted as a good reason to mediate, but it is probably the least likely to occur. Disputes get resolved in mediation, but relationships take much more time and effort to heal. Most relationships that get dissolved by serious disputes are generally unrecoverable.

Perhaps the best way to rework this thought is that successful mediation puts an end to failed relationships and projects, bringing about a closure that the parties may never attain elsewhere by other means. Nevertheless, a resolution of the dispute in mediation may be the starting point to relationship building.

[B] Maintain Privacy

When confidentiality of the disputes and the details of the resolution are important, mediation is a very appropriate vehicle. Essentially, the mantra of "what goes on in here, stays in here" applies to mediation (much more than it applies to arbitration). Mediators are advised to destroy their notes, and most do. They know not to discuss disputes with others except in the most general and unidentifiable way. As many are lawyers by education, they are especially aware and respectful of the confidentiality rules that apply to mediation. Mediation agreements typically include provisions about confidentiality, and mediation law respects them.

[C] Power Differential Between the Parties

This factor favors early settlement. Power differentials usually result from uneven financial power. The one with the greater resources, or the less at stake, is the party with the power to dictate the terms of the resolution. Mediation cannot balance the parties, but the mediator's persuasive ability and impartiality may aid the weaker party.

[D] When There Is a Commitment from the Parties to Try to Resolve Their Dispute

Parties who are not interested in settlement, because their notion of principle binds them, and they have not recognized a need to put certain goals aside to end a dispute, put up barriers to a settlement that can be insurmountable.

How do you energize a party into committing to resolution? If it is your client, you have the freedom to work with them over a period of time. If it is the other side, the problem is immense. In that case, enlist the other party's counsel in working with the mediator, both at the mediation and beforehand, to find ways to educate the party about its options in mediation.

Consider contacting the other side's counsel in advance to make some progress before the mediation. For instance: "In furtherance to the agreement to mediate which our clients have recently executed, we think it would greatly help the mediation process to come to an understanding on certain aspects." Discuss mediator selection (if a mediator has not been appointed already). Exchange documents and respective position summaries and make any forward-looking/collaborative pitch about approaching the dispute.

[E] When the Advocates Have Committed to Resolving the Dispute by Settlement

If one participant in mediation can consistently make or break a mediation, it is the advocate. Often, settlements occur because the advocate did not stand in the way of the client's desires. Likewise, settlements have been derailed when the clients wanted them, but the advocates did not.

Are these motives selfish or ignorant? Perhaps. But as an advocate, you must recognize the influential role you and opposing counsel play in mediation.

Realize that your client is looking in multiple directions for guidance about whether to settle and on what terms. The client is surely affected by the views of the other persons on his team, be they employees, business partners, lenders, insurers, expert advisors and consultants, or spouses and other relatives. Everyone on the team is also looking to the mediator, assuming that trust has been established, to pass pertinent information to and from the other party, obtain the other party's answers to questions, and give fair and accurate readings of the issues in dispute and the progress being made toward resolution. However, as your client's legal counsel, you are the only one your client regards as having his interest in your singular objective.

Do not unknowingly be an obstacle to settlement, and let that be a conscious effort. But if you do have good reason to oppose the terms of a resolution, do not abandon the negotiation too hastily. Engage your client and the mediator in a productive discussion about the value of settlement at that time and explore new or different avenues that might lead to a resolution.

[F] The Parties' Expectations Must Be Addressed

Parties who are educated about how disputes are resolved, and the time and cost involved in each method, have a better frame of reference to judge the worth of a mediated settlement. Ask the mediator to assure himself that the parties have this knowledge.

Many clients believe that the mediator is an arbitrator of a sort and that eventually, the mediator will impose a settlement. Once they realize that mediation does not work that way and that compromise is an essential element, they can adjust to the mediation realm. You need to be sure that the parties understand that they are in the central position and have control over the outcome. This knowledge can lead them to shape a result they can adopt.

[G] Need to Resolve Conflict by a Definite Date

Mediators use time as a tactic, sometimes creating false deadlines in order to take advantage of it. Mediation is unlike any other form of dispute resolution, save for direct negotiation in that the timing of the solution is in the control of the parties. It is tailor-made for time-sensitive disputes.

[H] Need to Achieve Settlement for Other Reasons

Financing, surety obligations, and internal accounting needs are just a few of the types of commitments that press parties into mediation. Since there is no rule limiting the participants in mediation, if the parties agree, they can jointly invite other participants if necessary. Reaching a resolution that involves all aspects of a project, business venture, or other relationship is an important inducement to mediation and a unique aspect of mediation.

[I] Necessity of Apology or Perception of Victory

Sometimes the most combative disputants conclude a successful mediation on the most cordial terms with their former enemy. How can that be? Was the mediation a transformative experience?

It may have been the setting. Mediation is a place where movement happens quickly, and the results are often unexpected. But there may be another ingredient.

Even most corporate businesspeople have something personal on the line in a dispute. It may be that their reputation has been sullied, their company is financially at risk, or their job is at stake. No doubt, their personal feelings of worth and confidence in themselves and others have been jeopardized by the dispute. Ending the dispute is a huge relief.

Sometimes apologies can help. In other cases, a sense of having been victorious is necessary. Your respectful relationship with opposing counsel may mask the clients' underlying, unmet desires. Find out what the clients need personally and do what you can to see that those needs are also satisfied.

§17.03 SELECTING THE MEDIATOR

As the mediator is the person at the helm, the mediator's ability may be the most important single factor that the advocate can control that will affect the outcome of mediation. Of course, some disputes cannot be settled regardless of the talents of the mediator. But the settlement is more likely if the mediator's skills fit the demands of the dispute, which include not just the subject matter of the controversy but also the dynamics of the disputants.

On many occasions, a mediator is appointed by the court or a court-annexed institution. In other settings, the choice of mediator rests exclusively with the parties. When there is a choice, it is important to exercise that right and, in all cases, to bequeath confidence and trust in the appointed mediator.

In selecting a mediator, advocates may consider shortlisting potential mediators for the client. Advocates frequently circulate the names of potential mediators among their colleagues to obtain current information about mediators they are considering. Interviews with prospective mediators can also be employed, as can the request that the potential mediator answer written questions. Typically, these questions address the mediator's experience in mediation generally and specifically with the type of dispute at hand. You should also learn whether the mediator has had prior contacts with the parties, their attorneys, their experts, and other participants.

[A] Professional Background and Experience

The mediator's professional background and experience are important criteria. Must the mediator have legal training or even be a former judge? Attorneys are increasingly preferred as mediators by many parties, and some believe that former judges are preferable.

A mediator with several years of industry experience may be of particular advantage where the dispute concerns technical performance issues. An attorney might be more suited to handle the application of legal instruments. Some parties are most comfortable leaving the selection of the mediator to the other party. They reason that if the mediator is the other's party choice, the other party will likely have more confidence in the mediator's evaluation of the merits and suggestions of ways to resolve the dispute.

These approaches to mediator selection have a certain logic. Nevertheless, we urge you to consider the following additional factors that are important to consider and evaluate in mediator selection.

[B] Personality and Mediation Style

Mediation is an especially personal art. The personality and mediation style of the mediator infuses itself into the mediation process.

Much of a mediator's success is owed to his ability to "connect" with a party and its advocate, acquire their trust, and gain their confidence. A hard-edged and demanding mediator may be exactly the right person in one case, while a softer, more gentle persuader may have the qualities needed for another type of dispute. In selecting a mediator, consider the personalities on both sides of the controversy.

[C] Evaluative and Facilitative Styles

Most mediators find that their methods cannot be easily categorized. However, it is clear that some are more controlling than others and are more likely to express unconditional judgments. Those traits do not necessarily translate into evaluators, but they often do. If you are seeking a mediator who will "knock some sense" into the other side, be careful that the tables may be turned, and your client may be the recipient of the head-knocking. Your client may need that approach, but you should know in advance whether you want that.

A facilitative mediator assists the parties in identifying the issues, finding common interests, and helping the parties devise proposals to resolve the dispute. Unlike evaluative mediators, facilitators do not provide assessments or predictions. They also do not recommend the parties or give their advice or opinion about the merits of a position or probable outcome if the case were tried in arbitration or court.

Give serious thought to the type of mediator you want to employ for the case at hand. Our view is that a good mediator is a person who does not shy away from conflict. Call the approach what you will, but an effective mediator sees the dispute as a challenge to be overcome, not dispensed with. Some effective mediators would characterize themselves as only facilitators or evaluators, and some mediators use both sets of approaches to settle.

[D] Process Skills Versus Expertise

The act of mediating demands a great many skills. Effective negotiators, which is essentially what mediators are, can frequently resolve disputes in areas where they have no expertise. In those cases, though, they cannot function well as evaluators. A mediator untrained in the legal and business field of the dispute is not in a position to assess the merits of a claim or predict, with any degree of experience, the outcome at trial or arbitration if the dispute is not settled.

In selecting your mediator, ask yourself whether special expertise is a needed attribute. What are the elements of the dispute? They may not rest on an assessment of the law or technical knowledge of the field. An experienced facilitator familiar with general commercial law may be more valuable. Think about the dynamics of those involved in resolving the matter and choose the mediator with the needed abilities.

[E] Effect of Prior Association with a Party or Advocate

A mediator's prior association with one side or the other may be a factor in mediator selection. But in what way?

If the mediator is your colleague or friend, he may be distrusted by the other side. Or, to the contrary, he might be welcomed by the other side as just the person to convince your client to do something or accept a settlement that few others could persuade him was worthwhile.

Most arbitrators are generally of the view that unless the prior association was too close and personal, their decisions would not be affected by anything but the facts and the law. You may not believe that about arbitrators, and you may believe it even less about mediators. After all, the settlement is not their decision to justify, as would be true if they were the arbitrator. Because arbitrators usually explain the reasoning behind their findings in a written opinion, there is a degree of accountability. When arbitrators are part of a panel, accountability is heightened as they must justify their decisions to their fellow arbitrators.

Assess the nature and extent of the prior association with your knowledge of the dispute and disputants. Mediation is becoming a profession by itself and a full-time one for many mediators. With years of experience settling disputes and a track record of fairness and propriety, the professional mediator need not be a stranger to everyone involved to be effective.

Most mediation institutions today (like the International Mediation Institute (IMI)) have cataloged information about the past performance of mediators based on the feedback received from the participants (parties and advocates). Examining this information may prove useful in learning about a mediator's prior engagements.

§17.04 ADVOCACY APPROACHES THAT WORK

[A] Initial Preparations

An all-too-common perception is that mediation advocacy is easier and requires less skill than advocacy in arbitration or court. Effective mediation advocates know that these generalizations are not true. Although mediation advocacy skills may differ in some respects from the skills needed for adversarial proceedings in arbitration and court, they are no less demanding.

The preparatory work involved in mediation is significant. The advocate must acquire a thorough understanding of facts and law to make sound predictions about how the mediation can proceed to settlement.

The advocate needs to analyze his side's best and worst-case scenarios as well as the most likely alternatives to the parties' mutually agreed upon resolution. This analysis also involves taking into account factors such as the cost of not settling the dispute (which includes, among other costs, potential costs to arbitrate or litigate, the time value of money, lost revenue resulting from time devoted to arbitration or litigation rather than to the business) and how ongoing and future relationships between the parties will be affected if the dispute is not promptly resolved.

The IMI recommends using a Concise Case Analysis & Evaluation Tool that parties can use to analyze and assess a dispute to determine the best possible way forward, thereby potentially reducing risk, uncertainty, cost, and time. Advocates can employ this tool as starters or for framework purposes.

[B] Pre-mediation

Once the mediator has been retained, advocates need to concentrate on preparing the leading players. Many clients have never engaged in such a formal negotiation with a mediator as a leader in control of the discussions. Often, no real open-minded efforts at negotiation have occurred between the parties, and "amicable discussion" (as often found in disputes clauses) has only been in namesake. Without some preparation by counsel, the parties and their other advisors will feel uncertain about adjusting to the atmosphere of mediation.

They will wonder when they are free to express themselves? Why is the mediator meeting with the other side separately, and what are they talking about? Is the mediator going to decide the dispute, and if not, what is his purpose? Will the mediator give an opinion, and if so, what weight does it carry? Part of an advocate's preparation for mediation as an advocate includes working with the client on these points.

Another aspect of preparation should involve the mediator. Ensure that the mediator knows what is in dispute and how the dispute arose and why it has not been resolved. Position papers, also known as mediation statements, play a vital role in educating the mediator about your client's claims (and their grounds) against the other side. Often parties will supply the mediator with key documents, such as contracts, correspondence, and court pleadings to inform the mediator of the background of the dispute. Many mediators suggest that the parties supplement their mediation statements (often exchanged between the parties) with confidential notes to the mediator explaining prior negotiations, obstacles to settlement, and suggested settlement approaches.

[1] Objective: Control the Scene

[i] Mediation Agreement

Many mediators have developed their mediation agreement, which they distribute to parties and counsel in advance of the mediation. Common provisions address the confidentiality of the proceedings, the role of the mediator, and types of mediation approaches that may be used, as well as fees and billing.

The advocate should review this agreement to be sure that it is compatible with the client's needs and conforms to applicable law. In some jurisdictions, mediators must disclose in writing, in advance of the mediation, the type of mediation approach that they will use. However, even if not required, it is advisable that a mediator who intends to evaluate and facilitate discusses his intentions with the parties and obtain their approval in advance of the mediation.

In commercial disputes, it is difficult to conceive of a successful mediation where the mediator does not offer some evaluation of the merits of the claims. Although many commercial mediators consider themselves facilitators, in reality, they usually pass along to the parties their measurements of the strengths and weaknesses of individual claims as the mediation progresses. If the mediator does not have the parties' agreement on that approach, the settlement may be jeopardized.

If the mediation agreement is incomplete or needs revision, counsel should work with the mediator to amend it so that a proper document is in place to protect the parties and their ultimate settlement agreement. If no mediation agreement has been offered, counsel should consult with the mediator so that a satisfactory agreement is in place before the mediation proceeds.

[ii] Mediation Submissions

Mediators typically ask for written statements/position papers in advance of meeting with the parties. Arbitral institutions that administer mediation recommend that written statements be submitted to the mediator before the mediation.

Regardless of whether the mediator requests a mediation statement, it is wise to submit one. Mediation statements give the mediator a "heads up." Well-drafted ones identify the disputants, describe the disputed issues, and place dollar values on the claims. They really set the stage. They tell the mediator whether the parties have a relationship beyond the dispute, the efforts that have been made at the resolution, and why they failed, and they suggest ways in which the dispute might be resolved and any obstacles in the way of reaching that result.

Even with relatively limited disputes, the mediator must absorb a great deal of information very quickly. Not only is the mediator trying to figure out who will play what role in the mediation, and at the same time analyze their demeanor, but he is also sorting the disputes into categories large and small, attempting to decide which ones to tackle first and how best to conduct the discussions.

The advocate sharing as much of his thinking as he can with the mediator in this pre-mediation submission can put the mediator in an advantageous position for the client. On the one hand, the mediation is advanced by many hours, if not days, and on the other hand, the advocate has impressed the mediator with his knowledge of the situation and his willingness to work toward a settlement.

It is natural human behavior to gravitate to those who helpfully take command. One of the advocate's objectives throughout the mediation should be to garner the trust of the mediator and his appreciation of the reasonableness of the party's position. Through the mediation agreement and the position statement, the pre-mediation stage is the place to start to build that trust and appreciation.

[iii] Timing the Day

Does the advocate or his client have time restraints on the length of a mediation session? Find out and structure the mediation to suit that requirement.

The client may be elderly, disabled, have child or parent care responsibilities, or other aspects of life that make it difficult or impossible to engage in a marathon mediation. Perhaps beginning the mediation at an early hour will make it difficult or expensive for the client and his team members to travel to the session.

If there are any limitations, time the day accordingly. Courtesy to the client will enable him to focus on the dispute, not unrelated impediments to the mediation. And if the other side has special needs, finding ways to accommodate them sets a tone of conduct that helps both sides adjust the way they regard and act to one another.

[iv] Location

Location is often perceived as being about power and not about convenience. Insist on convenience. Schedule the mediation for a place where interruptions are limited, where a room has been set aside for private caucuses, and where there is a physical distance between the parties, but all parties are easily accessible to the mediator. Try not to repeat what happened at one mediation where the parties were in separate sections of a large building. Each caucus meant a trip to the lobby and the use of two different elevators.

If you plan to use PowerPoint slides, videos, or other technology, make sure that the location can meet those needs in advance. Know if there is internet access and, if not, that telephones are available with speaker capacity and that copy machines are accessible. If there will be a sizeable number of attendees in a large space, strategically placed microphones may be necessary. If secretarial assistance will be necessary, and it is often when drafting the settlement agreement, be sure that arrangements have been made for normal business hours and after-hours work.

[v] Plan to Continue Past Normal Office Hours

The advocate should prepare himself and his client for the likelihood that the mediation will not be concluded within a normal business day. Many cases do not settle until the later hours. Commit that you, your party, and others you rely on (such as experts) will stay as long as required. Having to leave early does not necessarily create a deadline for resolution; it often results in a deadlock.

Mediation may also occur virtually. Although remote mediation is a popular option for saving time and cost (particularly where there is multi-jurisdictional involvement), the advent of the COVID-19 pandemic has made it a necessity. Even after the effects of the pandemic have subsided, clients may still prefer remote mediation because of its convenience and cost savings.

A mediation need not be exclusively remote. For example, counsel may invite their parties and other participants to be online together in one location, or several participants may gather in one place with their counsel in another. The parties and the mediator may even decide on a mix of physical and online meetings. Effective mediations have been conducted where the mediator and the parties' attorneys met in person while the parties and other mediation attendees were present through a remote platform.

Discuss with the mediator a suitable protocol for virtual mediation. Arbitral institutions have developed guidance notes for remote mediation that contain helpful pointers.

[vi] Persons of Authority/Person with Knowledge

Those with knowledge of the business operations and those with authority to make decisions are needed for the mediation. In many companies, the person with authority is not the one in command of the facts, and there may be inconsistencies in their understanding.

Decision-makers (generally from the management level) often have only had the benefit of a briefing before the mediation, and they may not be aware of technical details. Discuss with your team a framework of roles so that all team members can be valuable participants.

Do not neglect to ensure that the other party will have the right people at the mediation. Check in advance of the mediation to find out who will be present and make sure decision-makers with full authority will attend. Ask the mediator to invite any others whose presence will contribute to resolution.

[2] Pre-mediation Contacts with the Mediator

[i] Should They Be Made?

Advocates know that ex parte contacts with judges and arbitrators are normally forbidden. Advocates new to mediation often believe, mistakenly, that the same rules apply to mediation. As a result, they are uncomfortable talking to the mediator before the mediation without the other client's counsel being present.

Mediation, however, is completely different. The mediator is not only free to have ex parte contacts with parties, advocates, and other participants at any time, but many mediators welcome and encourage them. Of course, ex parte contacts during the mediation session are the norm.

[ii] What Should Be Discussed?

These conferences are an excellent opportunity to make sure that the mediator understands the dispute. For example, if the dispute concerns construction, you could consider addressing what project documents would be helpful to the mediator and providing them in advance of the joint session for the mediator's review. If information or records are needed from the opposing party, enlist the mediator's help in obtaining them.

Identify who should be present at the joint sessions from your side as well as the opposing side. The mediator can assist in ensuring that the persons needed to resolve the dispute will attend. On the other hand, tell the mediator if someone's presence might be an obstacle to fruitful negotiation and work out how to deal with that potential problem.

The conference may also be used to address procedures. For example, many mediators employ joint sessions with everyone in attendance. However, if emotions are heightened and some attendees do not want to or should not meet directly with the other side, it is advisable to propose that separate caucuses be used instead of joint sessions. The pre-mediation conference is an opportunity to discuss whether the human dynamics of the dispute might be best approached by varying the mediator's normal approach.

[3] Versions of the Plot: Mediation Briefs

[i] Content

Craft a statement that reveals the salient facts of the dispute and pertinent law, but make it as pointed as possible. It is always the more difficult task to hone the written submission to the minimum. But the result is more likely to be read and absorbed by the mediator.

Include as attachments the relevant documents or their pertinent parts. Many mediators want to review contract documents, expert reports, and the parties' correspondence before the mediation session. Often these basic documents have prompted a mediator to consider approaches to a resolution not suggested by the counsel.

If you can, work with the other side to prepare an agreed bundle of documents to eliminate duplication in what the mediator receives. Consider including a timeline of significant events, with markings on events that you consider major. Having a factual framework arranged chronologically helps the mediator catalog the facts.

[ii] Exchanged Between Parties?

Should the mediation statements be confidential, for the mediator only, or should the parties share their statements with one another?

Confidential mediation statements for the mediator's eyes only protect sensitive information, the knowledge of which may be of great assistance to the mediator. However, each party has a real benefit to have access to the other's mediation statement. These competing concerns—protecting privileged information versus informing the other party of facts/law/positions they might not know—can be reconciled. If the parties exchange the mediation statements, consider appending to the mediator's copy a confidential section that addresses those matters that should not be disclosed in advance to the other side.

Mediators often grapple with confidentiality—they try to adhere to their promise to keep all confidences, but they know that not everything in a confidential statement qualifies for that protection. By separating the mediation statement into two parts—with the private section clearly distinguished—the mediator is made more aware of the confidences that should be maintained. If certain information is proprietary or must truly be kept secret, clearly identify it or communicate it verbally during a private pre-mediation session with the mediator.

[C] Joint Sessions

[1] Opening Presentation

Most mediators begin the mediation with the parties' opening presentations. Here is the opportunity, sometimes for the first time, when everyone present can actually listen to the other side's position in its entirety, and participants who may not have complete or firsthand knowledge can be educated about the dispute.

Knowing this, structure the presentation to accomplish several objectives. First, clearly lay out the facts and matters in dispute. Second, explain the reasons why your client's position should prevail. Third, anticipate the defenses and claims from the other side so that you can address them in the opening or as a rebuttal opening.

How much detail should be presented? That is your judgment, but use charts, PowerPoints, a claims book, an issues outline—tools that will aid in communicating your case to both the mediator and the other side.

An amazing aspect of mediation is the demands placed on the parties, counsel, and mediator to absorb a large quantity of information, analyze it, and then weigh it to arrive at a final resolution of the dispute in a matter of hours. Contrast that with arbitration or litigation where the same dispute might consume weeks of hearing time.

Do everything you can in your opening presentation to clarify the facts and issues so that most of the attention is paid to resolving the controversy, not deciphering the dispute.

A cautionary word: If you want to do a lengthy opening and the other party does not want you to do that, do not just immediately concede and forego your presentation. Think about what may be gained or lost by proceeding in your way; discuss it with the mediator in advance. If you decide to go ahead anyway, enlist the mediator to notify the other party and ask the mediator to express his approval of your approach.

[2] Content of the Presentation

The opening presentation should define the client's expectations for settlement. That does not necessarily mean that settlement terms should be proposed at this juncture. Rather, identify those issues which require the most attention and in what order. Doing so helps steer the discussions along the path that benefits your client. If your suggested approach is criticized or opposed by the other side, the opportunity is sooner presented to discuss which parts of the dispute have the most significance and the best order to take them up in discussion.

Sometimes attorneys use their opening to test their theory of the case on the mediator to see if the mediator seems convinced. In that instance, the presentation is not necessarily expected to convince the opposing party, who may have heard all of this before. Be careful, though, that this approach can backfire if the opposing party concludes that it would be a waste of time to negotiate with a party that is showing no interest in compromise. As it is a rare mediator who will endorse anyone's theory of the case at the joint opening session, it would be wiser to wait until you can have a private caucus with the mediator.

[3] Who Should Make the Presentation?

Normally, the attorneys make the opening presentation but consider varying that standard. Your client may want to interject with a few words about the dispute. Your client and his voice can be important aspects of your presentation. Do not attempt this approach with the client speaking unless you have rehearsed your client. You do not want an outburst that embarrasses your client, damages your case, or makes the mediator and other attendees uncomfortable. If you cannot trust your client to stay on script, then nix this idea.

Most parties enter mediation armed to battle their case. They have strong feelings about how they have been treated by the other side and/or its advocate. Voicing some passion about the dispute can be a real benefit to your client—he will probably feel better having had a say. It may also help the other side see and understand the emotional elements involved in the dispute.

One by-product, which deserves serious consideration, is the effect of energizing the mediator. When the mediator enters the first joint session, he may understand the facts and issues, but he has little, if any, knowledge of how the parties view them on a personal level. What may appear to the mediator to be a straightforward claim for money has layers of human interaction that brought it to an impasse. If you want the mediator's full commitment and willingness to get your story understood and adopted, there is value in showing the mediator why he should empathize with your position and objectives.

Mediators have been known to say that their "client" is the "deal," not any individual party. Regardless, mediators who see unfairness in the dispute often look, possibly subconsciously, for ways to bring about a result that makes sense and is reasonable.

[4] Rebuttal and Discussion

Some mediators use one technique to keep the parties in joint session until all productive discussion has been exhausted. Prepare your client for this possibility. Review what information you want to convey when the other party is present. Consider the timing of releasing certain information. Ensure that your client has a plan for his part of any dialogue and knows not to blurt out damaging comments that do not advance and may even harm the discussions.

[5] Skipping the Opening?

In one case, a mediator insisted on the parties giving opening presentations even though the dispute was three years old, one mediation had already been held with a different mediator, and the case had actually been tried before a judge and jury for five days, though it ended in a mistrial. Surely the parties and advocates knew what this dispute was about, and the mediator had been given confidential written statements before the session. Why, then, did the mediator ask for opening presentations? Was there anything to be gained by the repetition of each party's version of the dispute? Certainly, what was lost was valuable time and efforts that could have been used to fashion a resolution.

In another mediation, a party's attorney told the mediator he just wanted to do a short introduction and then move right into negotiations. Because the mediator knew that attendees to the mediation from the other party were less knowledgeable about the background of the dispute and the issues to be settled, the mediator advised him to prepare a comprehensive opening with slides and photos. The attorney followed that advice, and it affected the monetary outcome.

Skipping the opening can work, but why do so? This is your chance to put a human face to the dispute, personalize it, energize the participants, assure your client that his version of the dispute will be heard, and provide the road map for the joint and private sessions that will follow.

That said, there are situations where skipping the opening is the right approach. If the parties' relationship is so combative and hostile that they cannot reasonably communicate, it might be best to forego an opening presentation. Or, as in the above example, the parties may be so conversant with the dispute that there is no need for repetition of information they already know by heart.

An alternative to opening presentations from the parties is having the mediator summarize what he has learned about the dispute. This summary should be accompanied by the parties being permitted to clarify any points that the mediator may have overlooked or understood incorrectly. A summary by the mediator can be a helpful way to commence the mediation. It gives the mediator the opportunity to identify the issues objectively and relevant law/facts, and it relieves the attorneys and their parties from having to listen to recitations from each other that they have heard many times before.

[D] Caucuses/Private Sessions

Whether the first meeting is with the Claimant, or with the party whose position the mediator finds least understandable or persuasive, or with the party with the most money at stake, mediators eventually privately caucus with everyone, many times more than once. What the mediator learns and conveys in the caucuses is important, not the sequence of whom the mediator talks to first.

[1] *Build Trust with the Mediator*

Honesty is the trust-builder. Realistic expectations are critical. The mediator needs assurance that you are not wasting everyone's time with outrageous demands or histrionics.

Helping the mediator do his job is vital. Do not just reject an offer. Reject with a response the mediator can take to the other side. For example, you might say: "We can't agree to that because ..., but what can we offer that will satisfy the other side?" This response conveys two important points—the offer is not acceptable, and you are open to other approaches that should be explored. It shows that you are trying to make the mediation successful; it allows the mediator to trust that you mean what you say, but it gives him something to work with, and it may spur creative thinking that leads to a resolution.

An example: In a mediation between the employer and the contractor, the employer demanded liquidated damages under the contract for the contractor's failure to reach an interim milestone date. The contractor wanted a time extension for delays to that milestone caused by the employer. For the contractor, additional time was nonnegotiable. The mediator suggested that the completion certificate be artfully crafted to spare any particulars on the interim milestone's completion since the contractor was only seeking time concerning an interim milestone. The contractor agreed to pay the liquidated damages with that solution because there was nothing in the completion certificate that showed that the contractor had been inexcusably late in completing the interim milestone. The result was that the contractor's interest in showing timely completion of the project was satisfied, while the employer discreetly obtained liquidated damages for the interim delay. The contractor's holding firm on his position explaining why that was important to him enabled the mediator to craft a proposal that was acceptable to both the contractor and the employer.

[2] *Insist on Realistic Offers*

Empirical research has shown that realistic offers made too soon in mediation can negatively impact settlement.[1] Do not try too hard to rush to settlement.

Countering an unrealistic offer with an equally unrealistic one can stall or abort a mediation. Faced with a superficially large gap, the parties may want to give up. Rather, insist on receiving an offer you can consider.

One approach that has worked well in numerous mediations is to refrain from making offers until the parties have informally reached a range for potential settlements that may likely be bridged. Working together, the parties and the mediator,

1. *See* Russell Korobkin & Chris Guthrie, *Opening Offers and Out-of-Court Settlement: A Little Moderation May Not Go a Long Way*, 10(1) OHIO ST. J. DISP. RESOL. 1 (1994) (citing JEFFREY Z. RUBIN & BERT R. BROWN, THE SOCIAL PSYCHOLOGY OF BARGAINING AND NEGOTIATION 267 (1975) for surveying the experimental literature and "[t]he general conclusion reached in this research is that bargainers attain higher and more satisfactory outcomes when they begin their interaction with extreme rather than more moderate demands").

before concrete offers and counteroffers are made, spend a good deal of time determining the bracket of the settlement positions acceptable to each party.

For example, one party's original demand for USD 7.5 million and the other party's willingness to pay USD 400,000 is too great a disparity to resolve by offers and counteroffers without lengthy and frustrating negotiations. However, after serious, practical discussions with the parties about the merits of the controversy, the mediator discerned that the bracket for settlement could be reduced to within a couple of million dollars. Offers and counteroffers then were presented in a realm that made resolution possible.

The key to this approach is the mediator's facility to present a party's potential much lower or much higher position to the other party without committing either party to a formal offer or counteroffer. By figuring out what each party might be willing to do, the mediator, with the parties' cooperation, can delay official offers to the time when the bracketed differences between the parties appear manageable.

[3] Make Use of Downtime

The amount of time the mediator spends meeting with the other side is downtime for you and your client. Unless you accomplish something in those periods, they can be boring and demoralizing. Some suggestions on how to use downtime:

- Obtain information that buttresses your position or answers open questions (e.g., calling the home office to verify a damages calculation or flesh out a bidding number with the estimator's backup sheets).
- Analyze and strategize with your client over the status of the settlement talks to devise changes in approach or emphasis that move the discussions forward.
- Call others on your team who are not present at the mediation but are invested in the outcome and may have to ratify the settlement; bring them up-to-date on the negotiations and elicit their views about how to proceed.
- If settlement results in your client paying money to the other side, confer with the company's financial officer, banker, or insurer—they may help you formulate a payment plan that accommodates the company's financial status and may save on taxes and fees.
- Confirm with your client that all of the goals of the settlement are known. That may mean checking one more time with others at the home office who may not have told you before that the settlement will not be fully effective without a statement of dismissal for a separate legal proceeding or the sign-off by another claimant.

[4] Improve Your Arguments

Brainstorm potential options for settlement throughout the mediation. For example, in one mediation, the sale of the property to the contractor became the focus of the settlement (the theory being if he liked his workmanship so much, when the owner did not, the contractor should buy it). The owner had a recent appraisal, but the contractor distrusted it as it had been ordered by the owner, not by a lender. As the mediation progressed, the contractor contacted several realtors familiar with the property and obtained their proposed list prices. By improving his contention that the appraisal might be out of line, the contractor could secure the property at a lower figure.

[E] Managing the Cast of Characters

[1] Explain Roles and Expectations

Your client needs to know the script for the mediation: the likely order of the presentations, his role (during mediation, clients often ask if they can say something), how long the mediation may take, and most importantly, that the terms of a settlement are usually very different from those imposed by another, such as a judge or arbitrator.

Clients need to know the mediator's role: What is his job? How does that job differ from yours as an advocate or from the duties of a judge or arbitrator? Why is mediation a good idea for his case? What can you get in mediation that you could not obtain in arbitration or court?

The need for you to explain roles and expectations continues throughout the process. Advocates who help their clients understand the mediation environment and explain how the client should best behave to achieve an acceptable outcome are more likely to exit with a settlement and a satisfied client.

[2] Explore Even Unworkable Options

Do not regard the exploration of seemingly unworkable options as a waste of time. It is always possible that an unappealing approach to resolution can be reworked so that it is worthwhile. If not, the analysis of unworkable options teaches the client a lot about resolving the dispute. At first, clients who may have been reluctant to accept that settlement may just have to be about money usually feel more sanguine about the final dollar settlement number if they understand that nothing else would resolve the dispute. Problem-solving in many cases means eliminating all but the one clear choice.

An example: The Claimant purchased a condo to understand that the condominium association would pay all utilities. That understanding was problematic—the documents having to do with the sale were contradictory. The Claimant wanted the condo seller to reimburse him for his projected utility charges over a long future period. Unwilling to do that, the seller proposed that he buys back the condo, and the Claimant could use the proceeds (the condo was now worth more than he bought it for) to purchase another condo in the same neighborhood. Some time was spent in mediation discussing the buy-back price and other available condos for sale at that price point. When it became clear that the Claimant really liked his condo and did not want to move, that buy-back option hit a dead end. The only remaining remedy was to agree on how much money the Claimant could get in settlement. Having exhausted the discussion on an unworkable option, the parties were more amenable to finding an agreeable monetary amount to end their dispute, and they did so. As an aside, the mediator and the attorneys for the parties were fairly certain from the outset that the buy-back proposal would go nowhere. However, they were savvy enough to spend the time it took for the parties to figure that out for themselves and realize that a monetary settlement was the only way the dispute could settle.

[3] Practice Active Listening/Reflection

When you and your client extend beyond presenting your argument and actively listening to what the other side says, you can make your arguments more attractive. You are making them responsive. By reflecting on what is really being said, you may detect that issues you thought were in play are not a serious concern.

In one mediation, the contractor's advocate refrained from addressing the lien he had filed, knowing that he was willing to release it because it might be flawed but expecting that the owner saw it as an obstacle. As it turned out, the owner had no interest in the lien and had assumed that its release would just be wrapped into any settlement. The failure to mention the lien was a missed opportunity to show that something of value was being given up.

Help your client listen carefully. Ask: What did you hear the other advocate say? What did you not hear, and why? Is their emotion that needs to be handled before the dispute can be resolved on a strictly business level? Then, discuss the answers to these questions to see if the dispute needs to be realigned somehow.

[4] Be Flexible: Adapt to the Story as It Is "Being Told"

Do not expect that the dispute presented at the end of the day will be the same as when the mediation started. The exchange of ideas for settlement, including those from the mediator, can produce a new "story." Parties often raise new issues at the mediation that were never part of earlier discussions, and, surprisingly, they drop others. Prepare your client for that possibility and advise him to remain flexible.

[5] Deal with the Emotional/Human Issues in the Case

Some say that mediation works because clients, and sometimes their advisors and counselors, are given the opportunity to vent their emotions when they would not be able to do so in court or arbitration. There is a catharsis. Mediators know that one part of their job is to provide a safe place where emotion can be expressed without causing undue damage.

You might want to caution your client that the private caucus is the most desirable place to show their anger, disappointment, impatience, or sadness about the dispute and the other party. But do not try too hard to tamp down those feelings. Client satisfaction with mediation is often expressed when a client says it was the time when he was listened to and was able to tell what really happened. You do not want to take that away even as you and the mediator exercise the necessary control to get the dispute resolved.

[6] Identify Where the Dispute Is Morphing

Continually ask yourself: Where is this mediation headed? The other side's story may change "as it is being told," but are the discussions centered on resolution, or have they just repeated renditions of the wrongs that were done? It is difficult for clients to concentrate on "where we are today and where are we going" instead of how they got to this bad place and whose fault it is. The latter they know only too well; the future is uncertain territory. Keep everyone on track, and that means your client and the other side. If you work with the mediator to move forward, the movement will be in the direction of the settlement, one for which you are a part architect.

[7] Strategize on Less-Significant Issues

As the mediation reaches closer to settlement, minor, sometimes insignificant issues threaten to derail it. Consider dealing with those small matters early on and getting them resolved, so that they are not revisited. When you wait until the end of the mediation to handle them, they can become dangerous sticking points.

An example: Homeowners and their contractor have a dispute about renovation work that was performed. The contractor's goal is to get the final payment and be done with these homeowners. The homeowners want the contractor to correct some of its work, and if he does, the homeowners will pay in full. A mediation commences. What has not been mentioned are the warranties for the work. If the contractor waits too long before he asks that he not be held to any warranties, the homeowners may very possibly blow up the negotiations or refuse to sign the settlement that the parties have reached. Laying even small points of dispute on the table early on in the mediation helps avoid their impact at a later negotiation stage.

When to bring up lesser issues needs careful thought. Sometimes, waiting until everything of real importance has been agreed upon makes it easier to agree on a small but important issue that was not addressed earlier. The best advice is to strategize in advance of the mediation session about when and how to address each issue in dispute.

[8] Assess Risks and Expenses

Some mediators dislike having to review all of the costs of litigation or arbitration with the parties. The parties know what it has cost so far to be in dispute. As for future costs, the amount of projected attorney fees is a sensitive matter to both parties and their counsel. Allow the mediator to rely on you to convey this information privately to your client. It helps your client relations to do so, and it does not reveal information that the other side can learn and use aggressively.

Mediators are expected to engage in risk assessment, and it can be very helpful for you to permit the mediator to evaluate the risks openly with your client. As one advocate said to his client: "Listen to what the mediator has to say about your case. Even if we don't settle, we are paying for her time, and we should at least walk away from here with additional knowledge."

A word of caution: Know that there will be a risk assessment and prepare your client for the probability that it may be more negative than the advice you have given. Counsel your client to regard the mediator's assessment as valuable information and be prepared to view it on the merits.

[9] Art of Patience

About two hours after the mediation begins, or sometime around 11:30 a.m. if you began in the morning, one or both parties conclude that the process is never going to work. The parties think they are far apart in their demands; it would be best to recognize an impasse and depart.

Why so soon? Maybe it is because of the high expectations each side set for the winning argument they planned. Maybe they are just so tired of the whole dispute, having dragged on for so long that they cannot face thinking about it anymore. Or, maybe it is just nearing lunchtime?

Whatever the reason, be it good, bad, or no reason, this is the point at which patience must begin. Counsel your client in advance that even if they do not say or even think about abandoning the session, the other side will.

Successful mediators hang in there for as long as it takes. Make sure you and your client are prepared to do so, too.

[F] Reaching the Denouement: Offers and Counteroffers

[1] Who Opens?

Does it really matter who makes the first move if you are the better player? One way to avoid making a poor first offer is to delay talking money/figures until you have a good idea of the other side's thinking. The opening offer usually sets the stage for the acts that follow.

[2] When and How to Make Offers

It is not always wrong to "get down to brass tacks" with offers and counteroffers from the outset. Usually, though, the parties' initial positions are so far apart that it is important not to solicit offers until the parties have been brought into a range of settlements that likely can be bridged. That is when you need to consider how to make offers.

Big concessions early on are often better explained and understood than big moves at the end to reach an accord. If you make small moves in the early offers and then make a big move to settle, you send the message that there is more left in your position to give up. Consider making good, solid offers (still below your best offer) in the middle of the negotiations, with smaller increments of change in offers as the mediation nears completion. That sends the message that you and your client are really trying to settle, but your resources for changing your position are diminishing. That approach can help bring the mediation to completion with a settlement.

Think about what you expect the other party to do with your offer/counteroffer. You are not just stating settlement demand; you should be trying to get the other party to move enough in your direction that a settlement can be reached. If you do not see a benefit coming your way from your offer/counteroffer, rethink whether it is wise to have the mediator communicate it. Perhaps it would be better not to give a specific offer. Instead, have the mediator take back to the other party your concerns about the other party's last stated position. That message may open a dialogue that leads to a more receptive audience for the offer you eventually make.

[3] Timing/Sequencing of Partial Offers

If a dispute has several parts, analyze whether a global settlement offer makes sense or whether it is preferable to divide the issues into partial resolutions. With complex disputes, it is often helpful to have a series of mediation sessions, obtaining partial agreements from each one along the way.

For example, in construction mediation, that may mean handling subcontractor claims up front and getting them out of the way. Or deal with retainage or the amount of the contract balance that is undisputed. Agreement on those claims reduces the dispute to more manageable proportions. An acknowledgment that payment can be made of money owed to the contractor may make it more willing to forego other outstanding claims to settle up and close out the contract.

If the dispute does not settle by the end of the mediation session, do not give up. Think about whether any parts of the dispute have been resolved and, if so, whether those parts can be agreed to as a partial settlement at that time. With multiple parties in a dispute, maybe you can agree on settling with some of them. Or, maybe discrete issues can be separated from the entire controversy and settled without waiting for a complete resolution of the whole dispute.

Even if a partial settlement is unworkable, at least make whatever aspects of the dispute have been resolved the jumping-off point for the next round of negotiations. When the mediation is to be continued to another session, document and have everyone sign the next steps and the offer/counteroffer that will be the departure point when the parties return to mediation.

[4] Start High/Start Low?

Starting high (e.g., if you want to get paid) or low (e.g., if you will have to pay) can be a good thing. It is rare that a party recognizes the first offer as a good one, even when the offer was truly on the mark. Parties believe that they can better the first offer. The initiating party defines the strategy by making an opening offer that maintains a sizeable gap between the respective positions. Subsequent offers that narrow the gap appear as "concessions," which are a currency of real value in negotiation.

Making a low or high first offer is also helpful because it sends a message that you will not easily renounce your demand. But low or high first offers can be insulting to the other party, so much so that the party may feel that the mediation is useless and that it will be impossible to settle. To avoid insult, consider accompanying your offer with an explanation of the methodology you used to arrive at the offer. That explanation gives the mediator something to work with as he can focus the other party on the logic used by the offeror and more than likely return to you with an analysis that will keep the negotiations moving.

[5] Enhancing Your Offers

Tell the mediator if there are positive nonmonetary items that could make your settlement offer more appealing to the other side.

For example, if you represent a business that sold goods or provided services, you may be willing to continue your warranty obligations as part of the settlement. Or you may propose to couple your offer with a confidentiality/nondisparagement clause that promises that you will not talk about the dispute outside the mediation and that you will not say or publish harmful information about the other party. You might even go so far as to give the other party a written statement of what you would say if an inquiry were made about the other party and the dispute. With the widespread contribution to and reliance on reviews in social media, businesses value a promise that no negative comments will be forthcoming from their adversary in the dispute.

Similarly, if you are a designer, you may allow another party to use your designs and drawings if the employer wishes to continue the project with a different designer. This type of offer may be of real value to the other party and of little concern to you. Think creatively about things you can do for the other party that enhances your settlement offer but do not really cost you anything.

A word of caution: You may inform the mediator about these types of settlement options but think about when you want that information revealed to the other party. Do not just allow the mediator to make this timing decision. Rather, discuss it with the mediator and decide together when the other party would be most receptive to and value the enhancement you are offering.

[6] *Confidential Offers*

Use the mediator to assist you with figuring out what to offer. Discuss your thinking with him, but do not authorize him to convey an offer. Permit the mediator to investigate parameters. Then take another reading when the mediator returns from meeting with the other side.

If you follow this approach, be cautious. Although the mediator is entrusted not to convey your confidential offer to the other side, the mediator may feel free to inform the other side that they are in the "ballpark" if they do such and such or that he thinks that you will respond favorably to a certain proposal. Even if the mediator is more circumspect, he may still be more ready to carry back to you an offer he might otherwise have tried to improve but for his private knowledge of your position.

[G] Sealing the Deal

[1] *Mediator's Proposal*

This approach works as follows: The mediator, upon request or consent of the parties, offers his settlement proposal to each party separately.[2] Each party must then notify the mediator, usually by a deadline, whether it would accept the proposal if the other side accepted as well. If all parties agree, the dispute is settled on the terms of the proposal. Where there are multiple parties, the mediator can promise not to reveal whether the other parties were agreeable to it.

Before the proposal is put forward, you may be able to influence its terms by letting the mediator know what would likely be acceptable to your client. There is no harm in having such a private conference with the mediator, though you should be prepared for a proposal that may not include the terms you want.

You should ask the mediator how he will decide upon the mediator's proposal and explain it to the parties. Is the mediator planning to base the proposal on his view of the merits of the claims? Or, is the mediator going to recommend what he thinks would be a fair settlement? Or, will the mediator recommend a settlement that he thinks has a good chance of being accepted by the parties? Knowing what the mediator intends with his proposal will help you evaluate whether you want to agree to consider it.

Even if the parties do not accept the mediator's proposal, the negotiations may continue. At that point, though, the mediator's proposal may have accomplished the objective of guiding a party to reduce or better its offer to an agreeable settlement.

By its nature, a mediator's proposal is put forth as a last resort for settlement. It is usually used to break a logjam over a fairly small difference between the parties. Because it emanates from the mediator, it can carry greater weight than the same offer proposed by a party.

---

2. *See generally*, Arbitration and Conciliation Act, 1996, § 74 (a conciliator is required to propose a settlement if he sees element of settlement).

A variation on this theme is a binding mediator proposal. In this scenario, the parties agree in advance to appoint the mediator as "arbitrator" to resolve the dispute, with both parties agreeing to abide by the mediator's recommendation (actually, then, his decision).

Mediators who regard themselves as facilitators and not evaluators may be reluctant to participate in these approaches. Explore this proposal idea with the mediator, but you might want to discuss it with opposing counsel before doing so so that the decision is a joint one from the outset.

A word of caution: Many clients build up so much trust in the mediator that they are convinced that the settlement would be most favorable to them if the dispute were the mediator's to resolve. Make sure that your client knows that the other party may feel the exact opposite will be true. Do not agree to be bound by a mediator's proposal unless your client is willing to accept a worst-case result.

[2] Obtain an Evaluation from the Mediator

It is hard to conceive of a commercial mediation that does not involve evaluation by the mediator. Even when the mediator clarifies that he is not taking sides or conveying his own opinion of the case, the mediator is not just a water carrier. How he conveys positions and offers, his tone, his choice of words, even the decision to say or not say certain things inherently contain his opinions about the settlement.

If you ask for an evaluation, you may want to limit the persons who hear it firsthand from the mediator. Consider who would gain from an evaluation and the best time in the mediation to obtain such an evaluation. As counsel, you may want to pretest the evaluation by hearing it privately from the mediator before sharing it with your client.

[3] Draft a Full Settlement Agreement

Make sure all related issues are addressed and taken care of in the settlement agreement. Construction disputes, for example, may link to suretyship or insurance issues of property damage. Do not have your client sign the agreement until you are certain that all matters in controversy are covered.

[4] Using Arbitral Consent Agreements

Mediation can be converted into arbitration in order to resolve the matter. But there is another use of arbitration that is worthy. Because arbitration awards can be entered in court as a judgment, they are more readily enforceable than settlement agreements. If you doubt the other side's good faith or ability to pay the settlement, appoint the mediator as arbitrator (with the other party's consent, of course) and then have the mediator, now arbitrator, ratify the settlement as an arbitration award. For a discussion of various possibilities of combining mediation and arbitration, *see* Chapter on mixed-mode dispute resolution.

[H] Alternative Ending: Continuing the Mediation

Mediation need not end just because a settlement was not reached in the scheduled session. There may be pending proceedings elsewhere with other parties that, once decided, change the landscape of the case and make settlement more or less attractive. Business reorganizations, for example, may result in a new officer in charge who is more settlement-minded.

If the mediator does not offer to stay in contact, ask him to do so. Reengage him when circumstances change on either side. The mediator may have more success than an advocate in inducing the parties to return to negotiations.

[1] Memorandum of Positions/Commitments Reached

When a mediation session ends without a full agreement, there may still be commitments reached or procedures negotiated that can be made the basis for further discussion. Ask the mediator to work with the parties to document the items on which agreement has been reached. Even if those agreements are tentative or predicated on other items being resolved, it is helpful to have a memorandum of what was accomplished. If it would aid your client, ask the parties to sign off on the memorandum as a memorial of the mediation. The memorandum need not be an enforceable agreement, but it can be the basis for a further negotiation round.

[2] Committing to Another Mediation Session

If the mediation is definitely to be continued, get a commitment on scheduling and, if possible, a list of attendees for the next session. As negotiations continue, clients often reduce the number of representatives from their company or law firm. Consider also who should be present from the other side at the next session and request that they attend. You might ask the mediator to take charge of making these arrangements rather than risk a direct rejection from you by the opposing party.

[3] Homework

Breaks in mediation sessions can be especially worthwhile if information must be gathered and analyzed before the negotiations can progress. Again, ask the mediator (you can always do so privately) to review with the parties the steps they will take toward settlement in the period between mediation sessions. It may be advisable to commit these efforts to written directions, so that there is no misunderstanding about what has been agreed to be done.

[4] Keeping the Mediation Alive

Many mediators routinely call counsel at periodic intervals to check on the parties' desire to return to settlement discussions. There is no reason for you not to initiate these contacts.

Adjusting the mediator's objectives may prove to be especially valuable. Even if the mediator cannot deliver a full settlement, he may assist with other matters. For example, a mediator could help manage the discovery process or other such procedures as the parties prepare for arbitration. For a discussion about "Guided Choice" or "guiding mediator," *see* Chapter on mixed-mode dispute resolution. If the parties are not yet ready for an adversarial proceeding, the mediator could develop a protocol for the parties to analyze certain disputed claims, share those results and then satisfactorily deal with limited categories of claims.

Think of it this way: Both parties have invested a great deal of time and energy-expensive efforts—in educating the mediator about the dispute. There is no reason to let that resource go to waste because a complete settlement was not reached. Consider the next steps in the dispute resolution process and ask whether the mediator can work with the parties to make that process more efficient.

[I] Winding Up or Winding Down?

As a spinning top comes to the end of its spin, it is more disorganized than it was when it was spinning freely. This phenomenon, known as entropy, often happens to the mediator, the parties, and their counsel as the mediation winds down after a settlement in principle is attained.

At that point, often just minutes away from memorializing the settlement and fully completing the mediation, the parties and their counsel are ready to "leave the premises." They have agreed on the terms of the settlement, and their thinking is that they can manage the details of reducing the settlement to writing and getting the necessary signatures to the agreement in the next day or two.

More often than not, delaying the details endangers the settlement. Mediators often spend more of the mediation time helping the parties negotiate the fine points of their agreement than they spent reaching the agreement in the first place.

Why is that so? Perhaps some of the settlement details get submerged in the larger picture of the overall settlement deal. In some cases, remorse and obstinacy go hand in hand, and small and otherwise insignificant aspects of the settlement become major sticking points.

A certain momentum is created by the negotiation and resolution of a dispute. Senses are heightened; time is measured on a different scale than normal. The parties and their counsel are "in the moment," an acting term that translates well to the play of a mediation.

Momentum dissipates when the mediation session ends. The parties return to ordinary life and other worries and concerns. There is no longer the sense of urgency that caused them to reason to conclude a dispute that they regarded as significant and worthy of great attention (often over a long period of time). Their family, friends, and colleagues may cause them to question the decisions made in the mediation.

Do not permit yourself or your clients to succumb to tiredness or boredom at this important last stage. Get as much or all of the settlement done as is possible. Make sure every detail of the "deal" is taken care of unless it absolutely and unequivocally cannot or should not be done at that time. This last mediation session may be the only opportunity to write the document when everyone who agreed to the resolution is present, and the mediator is there to assist.

The way to accomplish the task of settlement drafting is to begin early. Bring a template of a settlement agreement to the mediation. It is something to work from and will help speed the drafting. When your side is waiting to caucus with the mediator at breaks in the mediation, begin outlining a settlement document. Arrange for someone at your office and/or at your client's business to be available during the mediation to send you information that may be needed to complete a settlement agreement.

Impress upon your client the desirability of finalizing the settlement before the mediation session ends. When both sides depart with a "done deal," it is a lot easier for them to close the door on that dispute and not revisit it.

A word of advice: Do not give in to entropy. Recognize that it is likely to occur, if not in you, then in others, including even the mediator. Keep the mediation going until the finish line has been crossed.

§17.05 MEDIATOR TACTICS AND HOW TO RESPOND TO THEM

Mediators have at their disposal several strategies that can be employed to move parties to a settlement. These tactics need not be viewed as intrinsically "bad" or "good." How you view them depends on the context in which they are offered and the motives of the mediator. What is most important is that you know what they are to recognize them and respond appropriately.

Trial balloon

The mediator offers a trial proposal along the lines of: "If the other side is willing to do 'X,' would you agree?"
An effective response: "Have they actually said that? What would be the consequences? How would that play out?"
Give your client the information he needs to evaluate that suggestion and meet privately with your client to flush out attendant problems.

The vise

Mediator: "You have to do better than that."
Response: "Why?" Or, "How much better?" Or, "What will it take?" Or possibly, "What will happen if I stay where I am?"

The wince

You know the look; imagine it on the mediator: part questioning, part annoyance, part frustration.
Response: "Translate it for us. What do you mean to say?"

False deadlines

With this approach, the mediator tries to get your side to move faster by setting a deadline that does not exist or can be avoided.
Mediator: "If you do not settle by 9 p.m. when the other side absolutely has to leave for the airport, all offers are off the table for good."
Response: Inquire about the deadline. Find out where it originates from and how it will affect the continuation of negotiation. One response might be: "We have an even earlier flight, so let's find a way to proceed with this discussion in a different way that will make the best use of the time that is left."

Put it in writing

Example: The mediator walks into your caucus room with a check written and signed for the offered amount along with a term sheet signed by the other side.
Response: Know that this can be a powerful approach. If your client is not satisfied with the offer, mark up the term sheet and have the mediator take it back (along with the check).
Another Response: Consider asking the mediator to get an agreement for a mediator's proposal.

Trade-offs

Mediator: "If they do that, what will you do?"
Response: Question the value of the trade-off. Amend the trade-off to suit, as in "We will do [X] if they do [Y]."

Party assesses opposing party's position

Mediators have been known to ask one party to assess the strengths and weaknesses of the other side's case to promote a more realistic appraisal of their position.
Response: You might want to have the mediator assist in identifying the issues that you should review more closely from the other side. It might be wisest to do your evaluation outside of the presence of the mediator. You can then decide what you want to share with him.

Take it or leave it offers

If your client does not want to take the supposedly nonnegotiable offer, then reply with questions. Find out what parts are firm and what is less solid. Propose alternatives to the more fluid parts. By breaking up the offer into as small pieces as possible, you may be able to isolate the one bargaining chip that will lead to settlement.

Spitting the difference

There is a certain symmetry in this approach that makes it seem fair and difficult to overcome.
Your Response: Redefine the difference. As in, "We already gave up this much (a higher or lower figure that widens the difference), so we can only move so much more to make the result fair to both sides."

"Executive" sessions or "advocates only"

Especially when the group is large, mediators want to whittle the decision-makers down to a select few. That can be fine, but be careful about who is being left out. Do not permit the mediator to exclude an essential person. For executive sessions without advocates, publicly proclaim to the mediator and the executive group that you reserve the opportunity to review with your client any proposal they arrive at before it is placed before the other side. It is a good idea to talk privately with your executive group about what may happen and how they should respond before they join an executive session. If these sessions involve representatives of both parties, caution your side to listen carefully, be wary of revealing too much, and consult with the group before committing to any decisions.

Splitting off a party or two

In a multiparty mediation, the suggestion may be made to split one or more of them in the mediation. For example, when the main contractor is sponsoring the subcontractor's claim, there may be value in keeping the contractor and sub together, or at an appropriate time splitting those two seemingly joined parties so that the sponsoring party is forced to become active in the negotiations.
Response: The party with the most at stake may likely be the least responsive to the split. Resist the split if it is in your client's interest.

Raising the stakes

This tactic revolves around concentrating on the consequences of not settling.
Mediator: "If you don't settle today, the value of this dispute will rise in favor of the other side because … ."
Response: Two can play this game. Raise the stakes from your end.

Breathing room: food and comfort

Mediation can be a "diet plan." Some mediators like to place the parties at their maximum discomfort level, depriving them of food, beverage, and comfort so they will settle at any cost just to be able to leave.
That approach can work, but do not let anyone do that to you and your client without good reason. Lunch or dinner, a walk around the block—these breaks can be enormously helpful to resolution. If you and your client are given a chance to think, ruminate, to relax for a few minutes, you may be more likely to make a more considered decision and possibly improve or approve of a settlement.

Buyer's remorse adversely affects the advocate. If your client feels as though he was pressured by time and circumstance to settle on less than perfect terms, the resulting anger/disappointment will be directed at you. Take charge and insist on the quiet time and sustenance you and your client need.

Playing to the weak link

This is one of the reasons behind "executive sessions." The mediator's goal is to exclude the stronger members of the team and negotiate with the weaker links.
Response: Do not allow this to happen. Insulate your weak link by surrounding him with a strong partner. Or, isolate him yourself by removing him from the smaller group, perhaps by giving him a task that will take him out of service.

Disarming the leader

If your leader is being disarmed, and it may even be you, insist on keeping the leader in the fray. Whether the disarming is being accomplished by charm or bullying, stay close to the leader and do not leave him alone with the mediator or representatives from the other side. A private talk with the leader may be in order to tactfully discuss this strategy.

Gaining momentum with minor concessions

Not an intrinsically bad approach, but dangerous in that the minor concessions may be too generous in light of the overall disputed amount.
Response: Consider putting some or all of these "concessions" under a different title. Call them "Suggested Resolutions" or "Contingent Remedies," or another heading that conveys that they are not final but tentative approaches worthy of more consideration down the line when larger issues are taking positive turns.

Using the big issue to sweep away other problems

This tactic is the reverse of the prior one. The idea is that the mediator says, in essence: "This offer is a global one. Take care of this issue, and the deal is done. The remaining problems are minor, so the offer is a package deal."
Response: Tempting though it may be to package the dispute, this is the time to answer the general with the specific. Reply with your analysis of the minor points and demand that they be considered before a package is assembled.
As in the case of minor concessions, consider putting your major issues under a special bracket. Call it "Priority Claims" (or something similar) while keeping the minor issues alive.

Expanding the territory

The mediator lets on that the dispute will get more complicated if not settled because of the addition of new parties, other claims, and other remedies.
Response: This information is probably not new. Respond to it as the threat that it is.

Sweetening the pot

The other side conveys through the mediator that there are added incentives to a settlement that have not been considered. For example, where the employer has multiple similar projects in his pipeline, the employer conveys that a settlement of the current dispute would benefit the contractor in obtaining additional future work.
Response: Be wary of sweeteners, as they can turn out to be elusive. They may sound good, but in reality, they may not be meaningful or valuable. Say you may consider them, but keep the attention focused on resolving the present dispute.

Exaggerations and bluffs

Mediator: "You can't know how hard I have been working on your behalf with the other side. Blood has been spilled."
Response: Know that the mediator has probably said the same thing in so many words to the other party. This is a personal appeal. It is a signal that the mediator believes he is coming to the very end of the negotiations, and settlement must be reached soon, or it will elude him.
Bolster his spirits, but do not buy into this ploy. If you must, say: "Do they know what we are going through in here?" Then tell him about all the sacrifices your client has made and how his job, bonus, marriage, children, etc., are all on the line. The purpose is to shunt the mediator off this track and get back to what it will take to resolve matters.

§17.06 POST-MEDIATION

Post-mediation efforts matter. After the mediation is concluded, make sure you understand how the negotiations evolved, how the client viewed the experience and what you have learned that will be useful in future mediations with this client and others.

Consider conducting a review with your client about the mediator and the mediation. Evaluate whether your client believes his concerns/views were heard and acted upon? Was the mediator clear and effective in the way he managed the process? How likely is your client to use mediation again for another dispute, and if not, why not? Was your client content with the costs of the mediation? Was your client satisfied with the mediation process and its conclusion, and if not, what could have been done differently to make the mediation more productive? This kind of information gives the advocate a greater perception about mediation for this client, the effectiveness of this mediator, and your negotiation skills in this mediation.

Coupling your client's views with your analysis of the mediation aids in your becoming more skilled as an advocate in mediation. Post-mediation analysis can help you understand the skills the other advocate(s) used and how effective they were in this case, the advocacy you used that worked well, and the skills you need to enhance. It should also enable you to become more conscious of the qualities you want in a mediator and how to tell if a mediator possesses them.

Growing your practice as an advocate in mediation involves spotting potential opportunities for mediation by proposing mediation to your clients when a dispute arises and by including mediation provisions in your clients' agreements. As the time and cost are so high for adversarial dispute resolution in arbitration and courts, your proficiency as an advocate in mediation can be of real service to your clients.

§17.07 CONCLUSION

Ethos, logos, and pathos were primary to Aristotle's theories of persuasion. Ethos refers to a speaker's credibility, logos refers to the reasoning or logic of an argument, and pathos refers to emotional appeals. The mediation advocate should emphasize all three: use his stature as an advocate and legal representative, employ logic to his submissions, and play to the bias of the audience (the other party, as well as the mediator). The key is preparation because opportunity serves itself on a platter before those who are well prepared. "By failing to prepare, you are preparing to fail."[3]

3. A quote by Benjamin Franklin.

GLOBAL TRENDS IN DISPUTE RESOLUTION

1. Nadja Alexander (ed.), *Global Trends in Mediation,* Second Edition, 2006 (ISBN 978-90-411-2571-2).
2. Giuseppe De Palo and Mary B. Trevor (eds), *Arbitration and Mediation in the Southern Mediterranean Countries*, 2007 (ISBN 978-90-411-2684-9).
3. Lars Kirchhoff, *Constructive Interventions – Paradigms, Process and Practice of International Mediation*, 2008 (ISBN 978-90-411-2685-6).
4. Nadja Alexander, *International and Comparative Mediation: Legal Perspectives*, 2009 (ISBN 978-90-411-2684-9).
5. Ewald A. Filler, *Commercial Mediation in Europe: An Empirical Study of the User Experience*, 2012 (ISBN 978-90-411-3116-4).
6. Ian Macduff (ed.), *Essays on Mediation: Dealing with Disputes in the 21st Century*, 2016 (ISBN 978-90-411-8366-8).
7. Nadja Alexander, Sabine Walsh and Martin Svatos (eds), *EU Mediation Law Handbook: Regulatory Robustness Ratings for Mediation Regimes*, 2017 (ISBN 978-90-411-5859-8).
8. Nadja Alexander and Shouyu Chong, *The Singapore Convention on Mediation: A Commentary*, 2019 (ISBN 978-94-035-1481-9).
9. Anna Howard, *EU Cross-Border Commercial Mediation: Listening to Disputants – Changing the Frame; Framing the Changes*, 2021 (ISBN 978-94-035-1753-7).
10. Lenka Holá, Martina Urbanová, Miloš Večeřa, David Fiedor & Jan Holas, *Mediation in the Reflection of Law and Society: European Perspectives*, 2022 (ISBN 978-94-035-4214-0).
11. Gracious Timothy Dunna (ed.), *Conciliation and Mediation in India*, 2022 (ISBN 978-94-035-2015-5).

www.ingramcontent.com/pod-product-compliance
Lightning Source LLC
LaVergne TN
LVHW020647300926
849161LV00004B/853

* 9 7 8 9 4 0 3 5 2 0 1 5 5 *